NEW PRODUCTS MANAGEMENT

THE IRWIN/MCGRAW-HILL SERIES IN MARKETING

Alreck & Settle
The Survey Research Handbook, 2/E

Anderson, Hair & Bush
Professional Sales Management, 2/E

Arens
Contemporary Advertising, 7/E

Bearden, Ingram, & LaForge
Marketing: Principles & Perspectives, 2/E

Belch & Belch
Introduction to Advertising and Promotion: An Integrated Marketing Communications Appreciate, 4/E

Bernhardt & Kinnear
Cases in Marketing Management, 7/E

Berkowitz, Kerin, Hartley, & Rudelius
Marketing, 6/E

Bowersox & Closs
Logistical Management, 1/E

Bowersox & Cooper
Strategic Marketing Channel Management, 1/E

Boyd, Walker, & Larreche
Marketing Management & Strategic Approach with a Global Orientation, 3/E

Cateora & Graham
International Marketing, 10/E

Churchill, Ford, & Walker
Sales Force Management, 6/E

Churchill & Peter
Marketing, 2/E

Cole & Mishler
Consumer and Business Credit Management, 11/E

Cravens
Strategic Marketing, 6/E

Cravens, Lamb, & Crittenden
Strategic Marketing Management Cases, 6/E

Crawford & Di Benedetto
New Products Management, 6/E

Dillon, Madden, & Firtle
Essentials of Marketing Research, 5/E

Dillon, Madden, & Firtle
Marketing Research in a Marketing Environment, 3/E

Douglas & Craig
Global Marketing Strategy, 1/E

Dwyer & Tanner
Business Marketing, 11/E

Etzel, Walker, & Stanton
Marketing, 11/E

Futrell
ABC's of Relationship Selling, 5/E

Futrell
Fundamentals of Selling, 6/E

Gretz, Drozdeck, & Weisenhutter
Professional Selling: A Consultative Approach, 1/E

Guiltinan & Paul
Cases in Marketing Management, 1/E

Guiltinan, Paul, & Madden
Marketing Management Strategies and Programs, 6/E

Hasty & Reardon
Retail Management, 1/E

Hawkins, Best, & Coney
Consumer Behavior, 7/E

Hayes, Jenster & Aaby
Business to Business Marketing, 1/E

Johansson
Global Marketing, 1/E

Johnson, Kurtz, & Scheuing
Sales Management: Concepts, Practices & Cases, 2/E

Kinnear & Taylor
Market Research: An Applied Approach, 5/E

Lambert & Stock
Strategic Logistics Management, 3/E

Lambert, Stock, & Ellram
Fundamentals of Logistics Management, 1/E

Lehmann & Winer
Analysis for Marketing Planning, 4/E

Lehmann & Winer
Product Management, 2/E

Levy & Weitz
Retailing Management, 3/E

Levy & Weitz
Essentials of Retailing, 1/E

Loudon & Della Bitta
Consumer Behavior: Concepts & Applications, 4/E

Mason & Perreault
The Marketing Game!, 2/E

McDonald
Direct Marketing: An Integrated Approach, 1/E

Meloan & Graham
International and Global Marketing Concepts and Cases, 2/E

Monroe
Pricing, 2/E

Moore & Pessemier
Product Planning and Management: Designing and Delivering Value, 1/E

Oliver
Satisfaction: A Behavioral Perspective on the Consumer, 1/E

Patton
Sales Force: A Sales Management Simulation Game, 1/E

Pelton, Strutton, & Lumpkin
Marketing Channels: A Relationship Management Approach, 1/E

Perreault & McCarthy
Basic Marketing: A Global Managerial Approach, 13/E

Perreault & McCarthy
Essentials of Marketing: A Global Managerial Approach, 7/E

Peter & Donnelly
A Preface to Marketing Management, 8/E

Peter & Donnelly
Marketing Management: Knowledge and Skills, 5/E

Peter & Olson
Consumer Behavior and Marketing Strategy, 5/E

Peter & Olson
Understanding Consumer Behavior, 1/E

Quelch
Cases in Product Management, 1/E

Quelch, Dolan, & Kosnik
Marketing Management: Text & Cases, 1/E

Quelch & Farris
Cases in Advertising and Promotion Management, 4/E

Quelch, Kashani, & Vandermerwe
European Cases in Marketing Management, 1/E

Rangan
Business Marketing Strategy: Cases, Concepts & Applications, 1/E

Rangan, Shapiro, & Moriarty
Business Marketing Strategy: Concepts & Applications, 1/E

Rossiter & Percy
Advertising Communications and Promotion Management, 2/E

Stanton, Spiro, & Buskirk
Management of a Sales Force, 10/E

Sudman & Blair
Marketing Research: A Problem-Solving Approach, 1/E

Thompson & Stappenbeck
The Marketing Strategy Game, 1/E

Ulrich & Eppinger
Product Design and Development, 2/E

Walker, Boyd, & Larreche
Marketing Strategy: Planning and Implementation, 3/E

Weitz, Castleberry & Tanner
Selling: Building Partnership, 3/E

Zeithaml & Bitner
Services Marketing, 2/E

NEW PRODUCTS MANAGEMENT

SIXTH EDITION

C. Merle Crawford
The University of Michigan

C. Anthony Di Benedetto
Temple University

Boston Burr Ridge, IL Dubuque, IA Madison, WI New York San Francisco St. Louis
Bangkok Bogotá Caracas Lisbon London Madrid
Mexico City Milan New Delhi Seoul Singapore Sydney Taipei Toronto

McGraw-Hill Higher Education

*A Division of The **McGraw-Hill** Companies*

NEW PRODUCTS MANAGEMENT

This book is printed on acid-free paper.

domestic 3 4 5 6 7 8 9 0 FGR/FGR 0 9 8 7 6 5 4 3 2 1
international 7 8 9 0 FGR/FGR 0 9 8 7 6 5 4 3 2 1

ISBN 0-07-027552-1

Vice president/Editor-in-chief: *Michael W. Junior*
Publisher: *David Kendric Brake*
Senior developmental editor: *Nancy Barbour*
Senior marketing manager: *Colleen J. Suljic*
Project manager: *Susan Trentacosti*
Production supervisor: *Kari Geltemeyer*
Designer: *Kiera Cunningham*
Cover illustration: *©Bob Commander*
Supplement coordinator: *Craig S. Leonard*
Compositor: *ElectraGraphics Inc.*
Typeface: *10.5/12 Times Roman*
Printer: *Quebecor Printing Book Group/Fairfield*

Library of Congress Cataloging-in-Publication Data

Crawford, C. Merle (Charles Merle), (date)
New products management / C. Merle Crawford, C. Anthony Di Benedetto. — 6th ed.
p. cm. — (Irwin/McGraw-Hill series in marketing)
Includes index.
ISBN 0–07–027552–1
1. New products—Management. I. Di Benedetto, C. Anthony. II. Title. III. Series.
HF5415.153.C72 2000
658.5'75—dc21 99–34882

INTERNATIONAL EDITION ISBN 0-07-117516-4

http://www.mhhe.com

PREFACE

The first thing professors will notice in this book is that there is a new co-author. Merle Crawford wrote the first edition and made the four revisions. But times change, and the market has recently said they want additional materials for classroom use, even though adoptions have increased steadily. This move is best put under the direction of a different person, and that person for the 6th edition, is Anthony Di Benedetto. The changes made to this new edition will be described in a moment, but first, the field's history is relevant.

New products have always been of interest to both academics and practitioners, and organized, college-level instruction on the subject of new products management traces back to the 1950s. By the 1990s a new products management discipline had evolved. The Product Development & Management Association has flowered to over 2,000 members in some 30 countries around the world; over 300 colleges have courses on the subject of new products; and the field's journal, the *Journal of Product Innovation Management,* is now successfully into its 15th year of publication. The job title new products manager or director is becoming much more common and is offering much earlier entry than 10 years ago; we also see the emergence of higher level positions for careers to build to. The Association is currently developing a practitioner certification; it has a strong international operation; and has been able to do what those in many fields have not, that is, merge the thinking and activity of professors and practitioners.

How This Book Views the Field of New Products Management

Such exploding growth means that we still take a variety of approaches to the teaching of the new products subject—marketing, technical, creative, design, and so on. This book provides the management approach, with a marketing perspective. In every organization (industry, retailing, government, churches, etc.) there is a person or group of persons who, knowingly or unknowingly, are charged with getting new goods and services (both are products) onto the "market." More and more today those people are new products managers, project managers, or team leaders. They lead a multifunctional group of people, with the perspective of a general manager, operating as a company within a company. They must deal with the *total task*—strategy, organization, concept generation, evaluation, technical development, marketing, and so on. They are not finished with their work until the new product has achieved the goals assigned to the team—this usually means some form of sales or profit, and certainly means the task is not finished when the new product is put onto the shipping dock.

We try to avoid a functional myopia, and it is rare today to hear that "marketing tells everyone what to do" or "R&D runs our new products activity." When a functional specialist is assigned leadership of a new products team, that person must learn the general manager viewpoint, but one usually has to succeed as a functional member of new product teams before getting a shot at being a team leader. Marketing people, working as team members or as team leaders, need the types of information in this book.

Some Basic Beliefs that Guided the Writing

People who have used the first five editions of this book know its unique viewpoints on the subject. But for newcomers, and of course all students are newcomers, here are some of them.

1. Product innovation is one single operation in an organization. It has parts (strategy, teams, plans, etc.), but they are all just parts. Any operation that runs as separate pieces misses the strength of the whole.

2. The field is still new enough that it lacks a systematic language. This makes it very difficult for students, who are accustomed to studying subjects where a term means something, and only that something. We wish this were so in new products. What should we do—slip and slide around over the many terms and their variations? We believe we should not. So terms are used consistently throughout the book, and we urge students to use them. Naturally, new terms come and go; some survive and some don't.

Because of the terminology problem in a rapidly growing field, the Index has been expanded considerably. Every term that might require definition has been made bold the first time it is used, and the Index directs the reader to that section. We agree with the past users who recommended this approach when they argued that a definition of a term should be presented in the context of its actual use in the text, not separately in a glossary.

3. Ideas learned without application are only temporary residents in your mind. To become yours, a concept must be applied, in little ways or in big ones. Thus the book is peppered with applications, short cases, and other opportunities for using the concepts studied. Projects are encouraged in the *Instructor's Manual.* There are many examples from the business world, and up-to-date references on all important topics.

4. As much as we would like them, and have diligently tried to find them, we believe there is no standard set of procedures for product innovators, nor particular sets for makers of consumer packaged goods, consumer durables, industrial goods, services, and so forth. There are no recipes. Like a marketing plan, there is a best plan for any particular situation. A manager must look at a situation, and then compile a set of tools and other operations appropriate to that situation. All large firms use scores of different approaches, not one.

5. Next, there is the *halo* effect, which hurts the field of new products more than anything else—more than competition, more than government, more than tight budgets. The halo effect shows in the statement "It must be a good thing for us to do—3M does it, or GE does it, or Hewlett-Packard does it." Those are excellent companies, but one reason they're good is they spend lots of time and money studying, learning from others. They have huge training programs in product innovation, and bring in every expert who appears on the scene with what looks like a good new products management idea. They assume everything they do is wrong, and can be improved. You should too. This book does. Citations of their actions are given as examples, not recommendations. These well-known firms have many divisions, and hundreds of new products under development at any one time. Managers there can't know what each other is doing, nor do they care, in the prescriptive sense. Each group aims to optimize its situation, so managers look around, see what others in comparable situations are doing (inside and outside their firm), and pick and choose to fit them. You will find some generalizations; these will stand out as you work your way through the course. But what strategy to choose, and exactly how one should determine it, is situational.

6. An example of this lies in rejection of the belief that new products strategy should rest on the base of either technology or market. The choice has been argued for years. But the argument is usually specious, moot. Most firms seek to optimize in both areas, using a sort of dual-drive strategy. Of course, true to the previous point, firms will build more on one or the other if the situation seems to fit—for instance, DuPont's platform program to find applications for the superstrength fabric, Kevlar, or auto components firms' reliance on process development engineering to better meet the needs of original equipment manufacturers. And yet, DuPont works to advance that technology via marketing, and the components firms are evolving their own research and development operations!

7. We believe that students should be challenged to think about concepts they have been introduced to. This book contains lists of things from time to time, which are useful catalysts for thinking. The belief that the best new products approach is situational is based on the need to analyze, consider, discuss, apply. The great variety of approaches used by businesspeople is a testament to their intelligence. On a majority of the issues facing us today, intelligent people can arrive at any number of different views.

Decisions are not necessarily right or wrong, at the time they are made. Instead, the manager who makes a decision then has to *work hard to make that decision turn out right.* The quality of the work is more important than the quality of the decision. We feel sad when a manager says, "We're looking for the really great idea." Managers of product innovation *make* ideas great—they don't come that way.

8. Lastly, we have tried to implement more clearly the view that *two* things are being developed—the product and the marketing plan. Two development processes are going on in tandem. Marketing strategy begins at the very start and runs alongside the technical work and beyond it.

Changes in the Sixth Edition

Past adopters of *New Products Management* will notice substantial changes in this edition. Most obviously, we have added much more analytical rigor. Chapter 7 from the 5th edition (Analytical Attribute Approaches) has been split into two chapters for this edition. The new Chapter 6 goes deeply into perceptual gap analysis and shows how perceptual maps are derived using both attribute rating and overall similarity techniques. The new Chapter 7 provides an illustrative application of conjoint analysis and also presents several qualitative analytical attribute approaches. In addition to the expanded treatment of these topics, the instructor will note more analytical depth in several other chapters. For example, joint space analysis and preference regression are presented in the context of concept testing, and the discussions of screening, forecasting, quality function deployment, and A-T-A-R models are richer.

Furthermore, we use the analytical models to integrate the stages of the new products process. Perceptual mapping, for example, may well be used early in new product development, during concept generation. The output from perceptual mapping may guide selection of attributes in a conjoint analysis task, and may later be used in benefit segmentation and product positioning. Conjoint analysis results may be used in concept generation or evaluation, and may provide a set of desired customer attributes for house-of-quality development. Qualitative concept generation techniques can provide perspectives that complement those derived using quantitative approaches. We have tried, through text discussion, the use of running examples, and the sequence of three Magicphone end-of-chapter cases, to illustrate wherever possible how the analytical models bind the new products process together. As in the previous edition, many other concepts—product innovation charter, A-T-A-R models, evaluation techniques, the multifunctional nature of new products management—are also used to integrate topics horizontally throughout the text.

Besides the upgrading of analytical rigor, the reader will note other changes. Chapter 2 from the 5th edition, which was an overview of key concepts in new product development, has been deleted. After a single introductory chapter, we "hit the ground running" with a standard New Products Process early in the new Chapter 2 (Figure 2–1). This process serves as an outline for the whole text (and, essentially, dictates the organization of chapters into the five parts). The instructor will note some reorganization and refinement of this process from the previous edition.

Also, Parts IV and V have been extensively rearranged and rewritten. Part IV is now enlarged from Technical Development to simply Development (which includes both technical and marketing tasks). Product design and team management issues have been organized into two chapters (Chapters 13 and 14 respectively), and the new Chapter 15 expands on the role of marketing throughout the development stage. Product use testing (Chapter 16) remains in Part IV, as a part of the development activity. That's where business does it, and it "learns" best that way. In Part V, Chapters 17 and 18 from the 5th edition (Strategic Launch Planning and Strategic Action Dimensions) have been streamlined to a single Chapter 17. Part V is now devoted to launch: launch plan development, launch management, and public policy issues. Part V also includes market testing, following launch plan development, because that is where it occurs in real life.

Up-to-date examples and applications—such as computer-assisted creativity techniques and virtual reality in concept testing—have been added throughout. Several end-of-chapter cases are totally new or greatly rewritten, and others have been "tweaked." For the first time, we are including more than one case at the end of a few chapters, to provide an analytical challenge or just a different perspective. The changes and reorganizations have resulted in a net loss of one chapter. Expanding the Index (as discussed above) also allowed us to eliminate the Glossary from the text (though it is still available as part of the Instructor's Manual).

As always, effort has been aimed at making the book increasingly relevant to its users. We consider a text revision to be a "new product," and thus an opportunity for us to become even more customer-oriented. Academic colleagues have made many thoughtful suggestions based on their experiences with previous editions, and have provided much of the driving force behind the changes you see in this edition. While we have received helpful suggestions from many of our colleagues, we would particularly like to recognize Alan Flaschner, University of Toledo; Geoff Lantos, Stonehill College; and

Indrajit Sinha, Temple University, for their contributions. Thanks also to the thoughtful and constructive reviewers recruited by Irwin/McGraw-Hill:

Goutam Chakraborty, *Oklahoma State University*
Douglas J. Ayers, *Northern Illinois University*
Terrence L. Holmes, *University of Southwest Louisiana*
Eunsang Yoon, *University of Massachusetts, Lowell*
Richard Spiller, *California State University, Long Beach*
Paul L. Sauer, *Canisius College*
Minakshi Trivedi, *SUNY at Buffalo*
K. N. Rajendran, *University of Northern Iowa*
John Crawford, *University of North Texas*

This was a major revision, and we sincerely hope it meets your needs. A new Instructor's Manual, reflecting the changes in this edition, is available through your Irwin/McGraw-Hill representative.

To the Practitioner

Because this book takes a managerial focus and is updated extensively, it is useful to the practicing new product manager. It has been used in many executive education programs. Great pains have been taken to present the best practices of industry and offer footnote references to business literature.

The Applications

From the first edition, the ends of chapters do not have a list of questions. Rather, we have culled mainly from many conversations with students the questions and comments they received from business managers on their flybacks. These comments are built into a conversation with the president of a conglomerate corporation. Explanation of how to use them is given at the end of Chapter 1. As has been the practice since the 2nd edition, several of these have been newly written to reflect new material or to update illustrations. We have also brought back a few of the favorite applications from previous editions, due to requests from adopters.

Merle
Tony

ACKNOWLEDGMENTS

After acknowledging students, faculty, practitioners, and family as key inputs of ideas and encouragement in the preparation of the first five editions, I want to give thanks to all of the people who grew the Product Development & Management Association into the international leadership position it has today. I can't cite all of the individuals whose contributions made that possible, but I must thank Professor Thomas Hustad of Indiana University. He was the greatest single force for growth in that association, and the whole world is the innovation beneficiary.

The other person I want to acknowledge is the book's new co-author: Anthony Di Benedetto. Most of you academics know Tony, and your students soon will too. Under his leadership, we have made a major turn in the life of this book, recognizing certain suggestions users have made from the beginning. The freshness and vigor of his writing contribution will certainly be evident. No single author ever had a more pleasant relationship with a new partner, even as he showed me many ways we could be more helpful to our customers. Any suggestions you have for further improvements should now go direct to Tony, as he will carry the total load of future revisions.

C.M.C

At the risk of sounding repetitious, I would also like to acknowledge the leadership of the Product Development & Management Association (PDMA). The efforts of Merle Crawford and Thomas Hustad resulted in the creation of this organization, completely dedicated to the discipline of new products management, and the establishment of the *Journal of Product Innovation Management.* Many capable individuals have helped the PDMA grow and thrive, from its origins in the mid-1970s to its prominent position today.

With the publication of the first edition of *New Products Management,* Merle set out to create a unique textbook for this discipline, and he has nurtured it through four succeeding editions as our discipline matured. In my contributions, I have tried to stay close to his original vision and intentions. It is truly an honor to be a part of this book.

My work on this edition is dedicated to Kim and Alessandra.

C.A.D.B.

Contents in Brief

Part I

Overview and Opportunity Identification/Selection

Part II

Concept Generation

Part III

Concept/Project Evaluation

PART IV

Development

PART V

Launch

CONTENTS

PART I

OVERVIEW AND OPPORTUNITY IDENTIFICATION/SELECTION

PART III

CONCEPT/PROJECT EVALUATION

NEW PRODUCTS MANAGEMENT

FIGURE I–1

Opportunity identification and selection

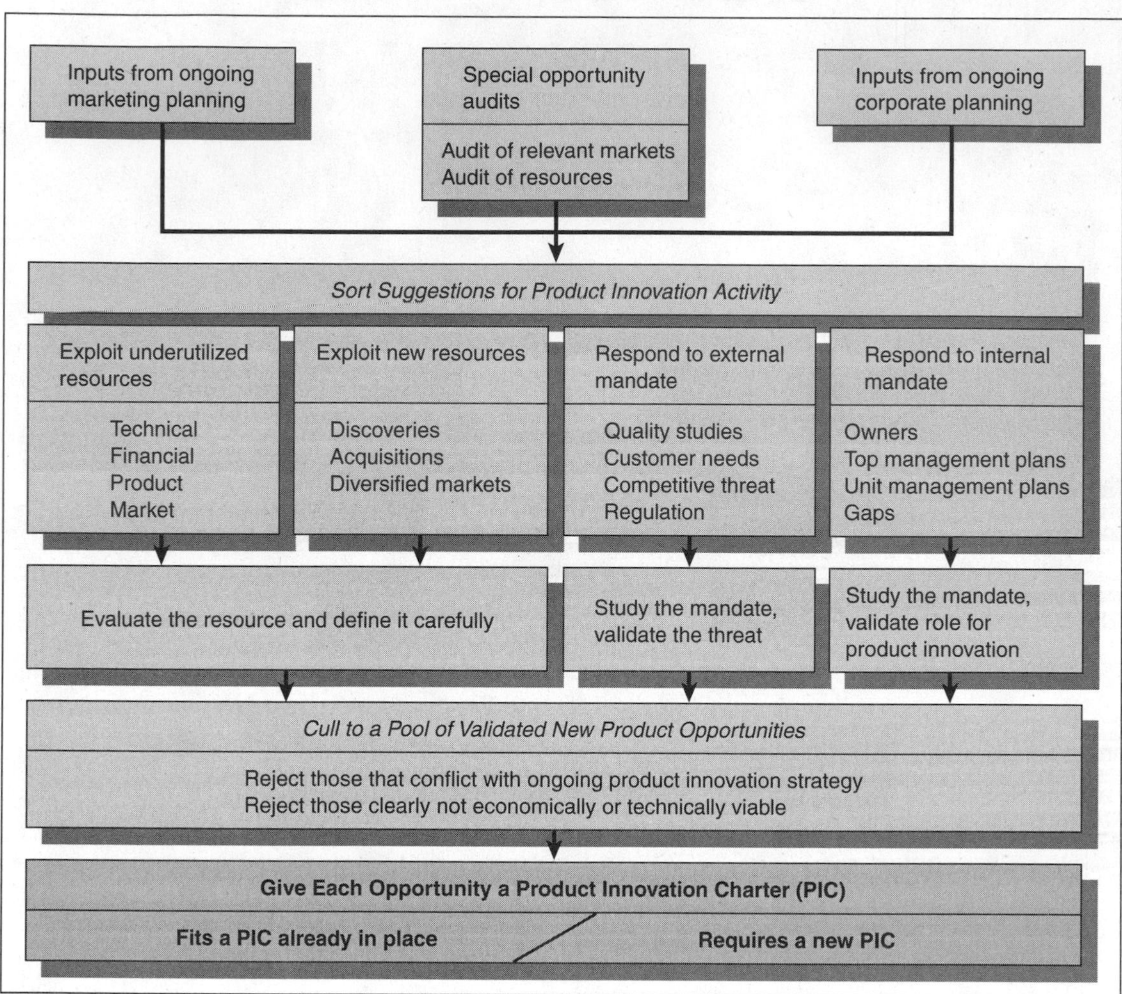

PART

I

OVERVIEW AND OPPORTUNITY IDENTIFICATION/ SELECTION

This book is divided into five parts. They are (I) Overview and Opportunity Identification/Selection, (II) Concept Generation, (III) Concept/Project Evaluation, (IV) Development, and (V) Launch. They follow the general flow of the new products process, though we will see later that the stages are not sequential, compartmentalized steps or phases. They are almost fluid, and overlap each other.

Before getting to opportunity identification and selection, we begin Part I with two introductory chapters. The first chapter is the customary introduction. It attempts to answer the questions most often asked about such a course. The second chapter covers the new products process as a whole and sets up what is to come throughout the rest of the book.

Chapter 3 treats opportunity identification and selection, which deals with the strategic planning that lies at the very base of new products work. Strategic planning guides a new products group or team, just as corporate or SBU strategy guides the unit as a whole.

Figure I–1 provides a flow model that describes the processes of opportunity identification and their development into the Product Innovation Charter (PIC). Innovative ideas that can be converted into high-potential new product opportunities can come from many sources—from new or underutilized resources possessed or acquired by the firm, or in response to internal or external mandates. However the opportunity is arrived at, its fit with the firm's product innovation strategies and with its economic and technical viability, need to be assessed. If the opportunity passes this first cut, a formal Product Innovation Charter should be developed. Chapter 3 gives ample detail on the development of a PIC, which can be thought of as a statement of strategy that will guide the new product development team: the arena in which they will operate, their goals and objectives, and other considerations.

CHAPTER

1

THE MENU

Mention new products and people think about technology—virtual realities, fiber optics, Intel chips, cloning, and the like. But most new products are far simpler—caffeine-free colas, new movies, new musical groups, fast foods, and new flavors of frozen yogurt. New products run the gamut from the cutting edge of technology to the nth version of the ball point pen.

You have chosen to study how new products are developed, so it would be convenient to say they come from an orderly process, managed by experienced persons well-versed in product innovation. But some do and some don't. Years ago, Art Fry became famous for an idea that became Post-it notes, when his hymnal page-marking slips kept falling out. He had a rough time persuading others at 3M that the idea was worth marketing, even though it soon became the second largest volume supply item in the office supply industry!

Thus the uncertainty you meet in this book may confuse you. If so, welcome to the land of creative exploration. In this field, we strive to create new products, not knowing just what they will be, what they will cost, who will want them, how we will distribute and sell them, or how government regulators will react to them. We know how new products *should* be developed, but the ideal conditions discussed in a textbook are rarely matched in practice.[1] Managers must face the world as it is, not as they would like it to be, and deal with problems posed by downsizing, regulatory actions, competitive moves,

[1]Things can go wrong even in firms recognized for their new product successes. See Abbie Griffin, "PDMA Research on New Product Development Practices: Updating Trends and Benchmarking Best Practices," *Journal of Product Innovation Management,* November, 1997, pp. 429–58. The study found little standard practice, and one-third of firms still do not use a formal process for managing new product activity.

new Internet technologies, and even personal problems such as illnesses, all of which can impact the new products process.

Some people call the creation of new products **product innovation management,** some call it **product planning,** and some (from a very biased perspective) call it **research & development (R&D)** or **marketing.** In this book, we use the most descriptive term we have: **new products management,** but our viewpoint is that of the marketing manager, and we ask, What is the specific role for marketing in the overall task?

This opening chapter is entitled "The Menu" because it is built around a series of questions students often ask.

Why Is This an Important Field of Study?

First of all, it is *big business.* Over a hundred billion dollars are spent yearly on the technical phase alone. In addition, untold thousands of new products are marketed every year, perhaps millions if we call each new web site a new product. One web site itself may be marketing hundreds of products. Moreover, hundreds of thousands of people make their living producing and marketing new products.

But, let's go behind those numbers—the real reason for this course is that *new products hold the answer to most organization's biggest problems.* Competitors do the most damage when (1) there is so little product differentiation that price cutting takes away everyone's margins or (2) when they have a desirable new item that we don't. Profits fall when we cannot ask for, and get, a good margin over our costs; when total sales fall because customers no longer prefer our product over the products of others; when new competition enters our markets with lower prices or superior features; when regulators pressure us not to market a proposed new product or alter one already out there; when customer service has to carry all the load instead of acting as a strong partner to the product itself; when our best technical employees drift away to competition; when there are not enough monies to permit manufacturing innovations that enhance product quality; and when our product development programs take forever to come up with something that excites customers.

In short, *a successful new product does more good for an organization than anything else that can happen.* The very reason for an organization's existence is the benefit or value its operations provide to others, and for which they pay. In a competitive world this means that what we offer must be better than what someone else offers, at least part of the time. This is true in all organizations, including hospitals, churches, colleges, and even political parties. Look at the winners in those arenas and ask yourself which ones are popular and growing. In the article "How to Escape a Price War,"[2] *Fortune* gave

[2]Andrew E. Serwer, "How To Escape A Price War," *Fortune,* June 13, 1994, pp. 82–88.

FIGURE 1–1
New product failure rates

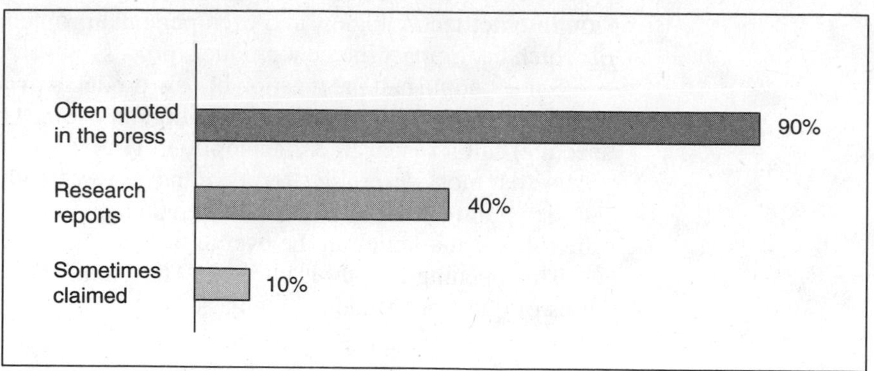

product innovation as the primary answer, and who doesn't want to escape a price war?

A cartoon once showed two obviously unsuccessful street musicians, and the tambourine player complained: "You say it's a market research problem . . . I say you're a lousy fiddle player."

Business firms expect, and get, a *high percentage of their sales and profits from new products.* For example, in a study by the Product Development & Management Association, business managers said that, on average, "33.2 percent of this year's sales will come from internally developed products introduced within the past five years."[3] Five years out, they were expecting 45.6 percent from new products.

Another reason for studying about new products is that *the new products process is exceedingly difficult.* Hundreds of individuals are involved in the creation of a single product, representing many separate departments (sales, engineering, manufacturing, etc.), each of which may have its own agenda. In addition, new products fail, but at roughly a 40 percent rate, as opposed to the 80–90 percent rate you often hear.[4] (See Figure 1–1.) But even 40 percent is too high, and some well-managed firms now shoot for a maximum of 10 percent failure. Others, like large food firms, may be happy to hold failure to 60 percent. The failure rate in Japan is lower than that in the UK.

The 40 percent failure rate is surprising in view of repeated research findings that demonstrate another key concept: The number one reason for

---

[3]Albert L. Page, "Assessing New Product Development Practices and Performance: Establishing Crucial Norms," *Journal of Product Innovation and Management,* September 1993, pp. 273–90.

[4]Griffin, "PDMA Research on New Product Development Practices." Success rate hangs steady at 59 percent of products marketed. There is evidence that this figure holds in the Netherlands and the United Kingdom as well. See Erik Jan Hultink, Susan Hart, Henry S. J. Robben, and Abbie Griffin, "Launching New Products in Consumer and Industrial Markets: A Multi-Country Empirical International Comparison," Proceedings of the Product Development and Management Association International Research Conference, Monterey, CA, 1997, pp. 93–126.

FIGURE 1–2

The excitement of recent winners

Apple's eMate	Sony's Crash Bandicoot	Direct TV
Crunchy cereals	NetPlay	Ski blades
John Grisham's latest	Dilbert	Turbo Tax software
Gillette's MACH3	BeOS	Kimberly-Clark breathable diaper
Lego's Mindstorms	Windows 98	GM's EV2
The web site	Plymouth Spyder	Sippy cup
Star Wars Episode I	Clipfone 6300	John Deere's Gator
Titanic	Kodak digital camera	Giant shredders
Cisco Systems	Audible mobile player	Vans shoes
Amazon.com	VW's new Beetle	Electronic tags
Beanie Babies	Senso CIC hearing aid	Lincoln minivan
Great Harvest Bread		

success is a *unique, superior product.* This finding ties in with studies on the causes of failure—they show that the number one cause of failure is "no need for the product," and the number two is "there was a need, but the new product did not meet that need." In other words, it was not unique and superior. It did not offer the user sufficient **value added** relative to the costs of purchase and use. Value added is a key concept to keep in mind as you travel the new product highway.

Finally, *it's a great life.* Perhaps the best reason for studying this field is that *it is fun and exciting:* so many new products (see Figure 1–2), competitors trying to outguess each other, battlefield promotions when things are going well, huge successes where small clusters of people can honestly claim they made hundreds of millions of dollars for their firms. It is rewarding and stimulating to see an object come into being for the first time; to see a critical consumer or industrial need squarely met; to see a new service performed for the first time; to be invited to a corporate dinner where the CEO shakes the hands of persons awarded patents during the past year; to have distributors fighting for shipments of your new product; to see your brand make its television debut. New products managers cannot be rewarded commensurate with their dollar contributions (except in entertainment fields) for various reasons, but winners get promoted. They often have a personal imprint on bigger pieces of the corporate charter and the rewards of general managers, not to mention the pride of meaningful accomplishment.

Of course, there is risk—personal risk and corporate risk in the process. But we are not uncomfortable with that. In fact, we spend a lot of time seeking out opportunities where we gladly assume risk in order to achieve the very qualities a new product manager's life is honored for. Nothing ventured, nothing gained.

Are There Special Slants We As Students Should Be Aware of?

For starters, all members of a new products team (often including the leader) live in a functional area of the firm. Marketing people need to help the entire team succeed, so we have to soften any narrow, functional slants. We have to learn to work with scientists, engineers, lawyers, production managers, and so on. We may come from marketing, and we will often return there when the project is finished, but for now we are all *new products people,* working with all functions, biased to none. And biased against none, too. A marketer may not appreciate the thoroughness of a research scientist. The research scientist may not appreciate the marketer's enthusiasm, which sometimes leads to what the scientist thinks are rash and unwarranted conclusions. However, now is a good time to begin thinking like a general manager and develop a wider perspective than we would normally have.

Secondly, this course of study calls for a *strong creative contribution.* We do more than simply create new product concepts; in many firms, that's easy. The tough part is *how best to develop and market them*—devising a concept-testing method that works, screening a totally new idea the firm has never faced, figuring out how to integrate engineers into a trade show booth effectively, how to position a product that creates its own new category, how to produce it on present equipment, how to name it in a way that communicates yet doesn't confuse, and on and on. No answers are found in the back of this book. We never will know whether any one decision was right, just whether the total package of decisions worked out.

Being creative means we *travel on unmarked roads.* Most of our decisions are made on grossly inadequate facts. Not that we don't know what facts we need or how to get good estimates of them—we usually do. But there's never enough time or money to gather them. Worst of all, *what seems to be a fact in January may not be a fact come June, when we actually introduce the new item.*

So, we do several things that make lots of people nervous. One, we use **heuristics**—little rules of thumb that firms have found work for them: "On items such as this, about 30 percent of the people who hear of a new brand, try it," or "When the product engineer from R&D disagrees with the process engineer from manufacturing, it's better to go with manufacturing." Heuristics sometimes leave us holding an empty bag, but without them projects won't move forward fast enough.

Another technique we use is *simple intuition*—hunch, gut feel. This explains why most managers want new products people to have spent time in ongoing operations before moving on to new products work.

Another way to handle the problem is to *select people to rely on,* a reverse twist on the usual adage, "Look to how a recommendation is defended, not to who is making it." We build close team relationships similar to those often found in sports, politics, or a surgery—other areas where tough decisions have to be made under impossible conditions.

FIGURE 1–3

Not all new products are planned—but their managers knew them when they saw them

A Raytheon engineer working on experimental radar noticed that a chocolate bar in his shirt pocket melted. He then "cooked" some popcorn. The firm developed the first commercial microwave oven.

A chemist at G. D. Searle licked his finger to turn a page of a book and got a sweet taste. Remembering that he had spilled some experimental fluid, he checked it out and produced aspartame (NutraSweet).

A 3M researcher dropped a beaker of industrial compound and later noticed that where her sneakers had been splashed, they stayed clean. ScotchGard fabric protector resulted.

A DuPont chemist was bothered by an experimental refrigerant that didn't dissolve in conventional solvents or react to extreme temperatures. So the firm took the time to identify what later became Teflon.

Another scientist couldn't get plastic to mix evenly when cast into automobile parts. Disgusted, he threw a steel wool scouring pad into one batch as he quit for the night. Later, he noticed that the steel fibers conducted the heat out of the liquid quickly, letting it cool more evenly and stay mixed better. Bendix made many things from the new material, including brake linings.

Others? Gore-Tex, dynamite, puffed wheat, Dextro-Maltose, LSD, penicillin, Dramamine, X rays, pulsars, and many more. In each case, a prepared mind.

Sources: DuPont and Bendix cases, *The Innovators* (New York: Dow Jones, 1968); Raytheon, Searle, and 3M cases, Kenneth Labrich, "The Innovators," *Fortune,* June 6, 1988, p. 56.

This suggests another key difference between this course and many others. We are *dealing with people under intense pressure.* Take, for example, the group of about 15 people sent by IBM from Armonk to Boca Raton during the dawn of the personal computer era, 1980. They were given one year to create and market a new product, which eventually became known as the IBM PC. Literally billions of dollars were at stake—the difference between becoming a major player in a new market or missing the boat completely. Virtually every day, someone on that team had to make a decision that could close the show. When studying how strategy guides teams throughout a project, or how firms telescope their market testing into simultaneous regional rollouts, remember that pressure.[5]

You may also take a course that deals with innovation in manufacturing (often called operations in service firms), and you may wonder how *process* innovation differs from *product* innovation. The term *process innovation* usually applies to functions, especially the manufacturing or distribution process, and every new product benefits from this type of innovation. The term *product innovation* applies to the total operation by which a new product is created and marketed, and it includes innovation in all of the functional processes.

The last difference worth noting here is in *application.* Sometimes the new product process is almost accidental; we call it **serendipity,** which means accidents happening to the prepared mind, as shown in Figure 1–3. But such

[5]Two books tell the story of pressure: Tracy Kidder, *The Soul of a New Machine* (New York: Avon, 1981), the story of a new minicomputer at Data General, and G. Pascal Zachary, *Show Stopper* (New York, Free Press, 1994), the story of Windows NT operating system.

events are not really accidents. At least 28 scientists had observed mold killing off their bacteria colonies before Alexander Fleming pursued the phenomenon in the discovery of penicillin.[6] So, you must practice. You cannot learn how to develop a new product concept by *reading* about attribute analysis or gap analysis. You must *do* them. The same goes for product use testing, positioning, contingency planning, and many more. Application opportunities appear at the end of every chapter, along with small cases that give you a chance to think about the chapter's material in a market setting.

OK, So What Is a New Product?

Figure 1–4 lists the types of items included in the definition of **new product.** This list is from the developer's view, and may include things you would exclude. For example, can we have a new item just by **repositioning** an old one (telling customers it is something else)? Arm & Hammer did, several times, by coming up with a new refrigerator deodorant, a new carpet freshener, a new drain deodorant, and more, all in the same package of baking soda with even the same brand name. These may be considered just new uses, but the firm's process of discovery and development are the same. And a new use (particularly in industrial firms) may occur in a completely separate division. DuPont, for example, uses basic fibers in many different ways, from technical to consumer. Financial firms use their common data bases for different markets. Similarly, brand names have long been used as platforms for launching line extensions. The familiarity of leading brands, such as those shown in Figure 1–5, indicates how easy this is.

The **new category** listing in Figure 1–4 raises the issue of the imitation product, a strictly "me-too." If a firm introduces a brand of light beer that is new to them but identical to those already on the market, is it a new product? Yes, it is new to the firm, and it requires the new products process. It is a new product, managerially.

People often get the idea that to imitate is bad and to innovate is good. This idea is incorrect. The best strategy for any situation is the one that maximizes attainment of company goals, in that situation. Imitators may get rich while far-out inventors go to bankruptcy court. Though it has been presumed that the first firm into a new market gets a solid head start, recent research shows that true innovators actually don't do very well—smart followers tend to take over.[7]

That the other types of new products (**new-to-the-world,** *additions to the line,* and *improvements*) are included in Figure 1–4 is no surprise. Generally speaking, the farther down the list, the less expensive and difficult they are to

[6]For a timeless summary on serendipity, see Martin F. Rosenman, "Serendipity and Scientific Discovery," *Journal of Creative Behavior,* Second Quarter 1988, pp. 132–38.

[7]See Peter N. Golder and Gerald J. Tellis, "Pioneer Advantage: Marketing Logic or Marketing Legend?" *Journal of Marketing Research,* May 1993, pp. 158–70.

FIGURE 1–4

What is a new product?

Commonly accepted categories:

1. *New-to-the-world products:* Products that are inventions; e.g., Polaroid camera, the first car, rayon, the laser printer, in-line skates.
2. *New category entries:* Products that take a firm into a category new to it. Products are not new to the world; e.g., P&G's first shampoo, Hallmark gift items, AT&T's Universal Card.
3. *Additions to product lines:* Products that are line extensions, flankers, etc., in the firm's current markets; e.g., Tide Liquid detergent, Bud Light, Apple's Mac IIsi.
4. *Product improvements:* Current products made better; virtually every product on the market today has been improved, often many times.
5. *Repositionings:* Products that are retargeted for a new use or application; the classic case is Arm & Hammer baking soda, which was repositioned several times as drain deodorant, refrigerator deodorant, etc.

Variations not commonly accepted as new products: New to a country, new channel of distribution, packaging improvements, and different resource or method of manufacture.

FIGURE 1–5

Classic brand names

Long-time brands, many dating to the 1800s:

Budweiser	Bell	Grape Nuts	Sears
Ivory	Wrigley	Post	Colgate
Coca-Cola	Kleenex	Domino	Hershey
Maxwell House	L.L. Bean	Lipton	Goodrich
Kodak	Ford	JCPenney	Gillette
General Electric	Fruit of the Loom	Brooks Bros.	Ticonderoga
Steinway	John Deere	Standard Oil	Waterford
Titleist	Maytag	Jeep	Schwinn

Which of these have the most value today as launch pads for new products?

make. In Chapter 3 we will look at the strategic dimension of these different new product options.

Does This Book Cover Such Things As New Services, New Business Products, and New International Products?

Professionals in all fields often use terms differently than the public uses them. We do, too, and a clear example is the term *product.* The public often talks about products and services. But many new products professionals (not all, by any means) talk about **goods** and **services,** both of which are products. The reason is simple: Almost anything marketed today has a tangible component and an intangible component. Fax machines are tangible, but they yield a service, which is intangible. Automobiles must be serviced, both before and after the sale. Does one get an intangible hair cut or a tangible head of cut hair? Insurance companies provide a carefully written policy as a tangible component to their intangible service. In fact, some service marketers believe it is important to force a tangible component, something for the user to see and hold.

Some people go further and say there are *only* services. Everything we buy does something for us (whether food, machine, or sermon), and if we keep this in mind we can see the importance of involving the end user in the development process. So the simplest approach is to talk about new products, whatever the ratio of goods and services in them. Banks, for example, commonly organize their marketing and service innovation around "product" managers.

Some people say services are different because their creation involves the user; but many industrial goods are developed in partnerships with users. Others point out that services cannot be inventoried and thus do not have a distribution system. But the means of creating those services can be inventoried and must be distributed (for example, window-washing franchises or motel beds).[8]

The distinction between **business-to-business products** and **consumer products** is equally vague. A spectrum from, say, a nuclear power installation on one end to a package of chewing gum on the other end has no middle dividing point. Individuals, whether insurance agents or parents interested in helping their children, may buy computers for use in their homes. Is the computer, then, a business product or a consumer product? Businesses buy printer paper, as do homemakers, and often from the same store. How about a retirement plan offered by a bank? Or a protest sign designed and produced by a local printing firm? Does it really matter?

Sometimes the distinction is based on who buys the product: business products by *groups of people* and consumer products *by individuals.* But billions of dollars' worth of industrial goods are bought by individuals, often by computerized purchase-order systems based on inventory-level trigger points. And most consumers buy houses, cars, $10,000 trips, and college educations as family groups.[9]

Regarding **global** new product development, it doesn't really matter whether a new product is developed for customers nearby or around the world.[10] The farther away the end users are and the more they differ in cus-

---

[8]Most studies show little difference in methods of product innovation between goods and services. A good recent example is Stephan A. W. Drew, "Accelerating Innovation in Financial Services," *Long Range Planning,* August 1995, pp. 11–21.

[9]In general, the process does not differ between the two types of firms. See Nessim Hanna, Douglas J. Ayers, Rick E. Ridnaur, and Geoffrey L. Gordon, "New Product Development Practices in Consumer versus Business Organizations," *Journal of Product and Brand Management,* Number 1, 1995, pp. 33–55.

[10]See A. Coskun Samli, *International Consumer Behavior: Its Impact on Marketing Strategy Development,* (Westport, CT: Quorums, 1995.) For more on this, see Chapter 15.

toms and preferences, the more difficult the innovation task will be. But struggles in Yugoslavia and in Ireland remind us that there is little homogeneity even *within* nations.

Thus the key lies in doing what is appropriate for the situation, much as a carpenter's choice of materials and tools depends on the job. A particular saw or piece of sandpaper has no merit in itself but may be perfect for a particular piece of work, whether a church door, factory door, or a doll house door. The same applies to the new products process, in which we package different programs from an assortment of "tools." The point is that the methods used for different types of product innovation differ. The manager's task is to decide that unique *set* of methods appropriate to a case at hand. Much as we would like them, there are no generic packages called "tool kit for business product innovators" or "tool kit for service developers."

Incidentally, the same thinking applies to so-called high-tech products and to nonprofit organizations as well. Many religious, art, musical, and social service organizations send people to the same executive new product programs attended by managers from Kimberly-Clark and 3Com.

On What Basic Ideas or Concepts Is This Field of Activity Built?

The *complexity of operations and decisions* is the most dramatic hallmark of product innovation. New products managers must be orchestrators. There has never been a simple new products operation. Scores, or even hundreds, of individuals are involved; for many of them, a new product simply means more work. One new products manager said, "We've got fine people working at this company, so my job is to see that no ball hits the ground." He meant it is easy for slip-ups to occur, even when capable people are doing the work.

Another hallmark of this field is the regrettable fact that *product innovation (like all innovation) must be pushed.* Innovation is an unnatural human event. As individuals and as organizations, we build roadblocks against it. Thus, new products managers have to spend a major share of their energy just opening doors to change. By the way, fear of change, and thus resistance to it, is called **kainotophobia,** a word as complicated as the phenomenon it describes. Chrysler once marketed a new fold-down child's seat so popular the firm couldn't make enough of the cars containing it. But new product manager Ron Zarowitz had to spend two years getting management interested in that seat, and four more years overcoming internal resistance.

Yet another hallmark of product innovation is *the conflicting set of management demands that product innovators must meet.* This dilemma is shown in Figure 1–6. We must serve up products that have valuable attributes (i.e., meet the end user's needs), but also are high in manufacturing and design quality, low in (competitive) cost, and get to market quickly. These mandates can sometimes work in tandem (e.g., some firms have found they

FIGURE 1–6
The conflicting masters of new products management

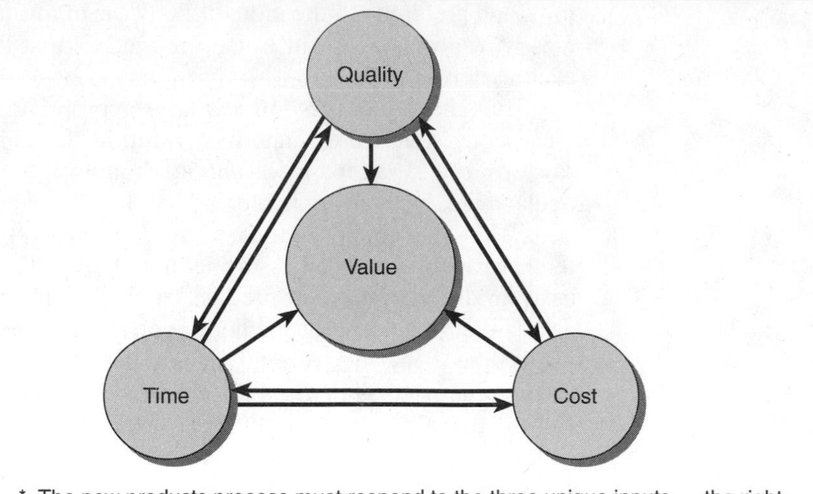

* The new products process must respond to the three unique inputs — the right quality product, at the right time, and at the right cost.

* The three inputs tend to conflict with each other, though there are synergies too.

* The three inputs contribute to the value of new products, but in different ways and in different amounts from project to project.

Problem: How to optimize the set of relationships in each new product situation?

can make things better when they make them fast, and others claim by increasing the design quality they can lower the real, net cost of production), but the demands can also conflict. Marketing activities contribute to all three of the requirements—for example, market studies tell the team the nature and urgency of customer needs, product testing studies point out where design and manufacturing can be altered, and several marketing research techniques help us understand the tradeoffs between price (cost) and product features.

Where Do Real Innovations Come From?

Breakthrough innovation (see Figure 1–7 for examples) is difficult and usually disappointing; it is comparable to wildcatting for oil. Investors must be willing to take great risks, as small firm owners are. But owners of larger firms often are not, so we find the ballpoint pen was not invented by a pen firm, paperback books did not come from the leading publishers, overnight package delivery did not come from transportation firms, and the jet engine

FIGURE 1–7

Breakthrough innovations that changed our lives

1. Personal computer	2. Microwave oven	3. Photocopier
4. Pocket calculator	5. Fax machine	6. Birth control pill
7. Home VCR	8. Communication satellite	9. Bar coding
10. Integrated circuit	11. Automatic teller	12. Answering machine
13. Velcro fastener	14. Touch-Tone telephone	15. Laser surgery
16. Apollo lunar spacecraft	17. Computer disk drive	18. Organ transplanting
19. Fiber-optic systems	20. Disposable diaper	21. MS-DOS
22. Magnetic resonance imaging	23. Gene-splicing technique	24. Microsurgery
25. Camcorder	26. Space shuttle	27. Home smoke alarm
28. CAT scan	29. Liquid crystal display	30. CAD/CAM

Source: A survey of technology people by *R&D Magazine,* reported by Carl Vogel, "Thirty Products That Changed Our Lives," *R&D Magazine,* September 28, 1992, pp. 42–46.

did not come from any of the motor industries. Some big firms support technical research, from which come many new-to-the-world products—Merck, DuPont, and Corning come to mind. Technology is a key player today, in all sizes and types of organizations.

Is New Products Management an Art or a Science?

We believe very strongly that new products management is a combination of art and science. Managers use art when they base their decision on intuition, hunch, or gut feel: when they lack the experience or information required to make a reasoned decision. Executives may say that a particular project was "something never done before, so there's no book on this one."

Yet managers should also avail themselves of the chance to use analytical techniques that can make better products. Three tests, for example, are critical in product innovation: the *concept test* (to determine if the intended user really needs the proposed item), the *product use test* (to see if the item developed actually meets that need), and the *market test* (to see if we have an effective marketing plan).

In addition, these tools of marketing science (e.g., conjoint analysis and mathematical models used for sales forecasting), developed by marketing academics, are operational in some of the best firms in the world, yet they are not used nearly as much as they should be. At many points in this book you will see applications of them.

This book offers no criticism of art—the intuitive greats in this field are cited for their success. But analytical methods are important, too, for those with the time, money, and ability to use them.

Can Innovation Really Be Taught?

Yes it can. We know this both from experience in running executive seminars and college courses, and from field research. Every project set up to produce new products can benefit from the proven methods of new products management.[11]

Does This Field of Activity Have a Unique Vocabulary?

Yes, it does, for two reasons. One, it is an *expanding field,* taking on new tasks and performing them in new ways. Second, it is a *melting pot field,* bringing in the language of scientists, lawyers, advertisers, accountants, marketing planners, corporate strategists, organizational behaviorists, and many others. Because many of these people talk about the same event but describe it differently, communication problems abound. The solution is to forge a common acceptance of terms and to urge acceptance of one term for each new concept or activity as it arises. We are rapidly doing this, and this book has been consistently supportive of the cause.

But your study of new products management will be complicated by unresolved problems. For example, there is continuing confusion over the terms **invention** and **innovation.** To managers invention refers to the dimension of uniqueness—the form, formulation, and function of something. It is usually patentable. Innovation refers to the overall process whereby an invention is transformed into a commercial product that can be sold profitably. The invention may take but a few moments, while the innovation may take months or years. We have far more inventions than we do innovations.[12]

The problem becomes much worse from a global perspective. Take, for example, the term **design.** In U.S. new product work, design means essentially industrial design or engineering (premanufacturing) design; in Europe, however, design means the entire technical creation function from initial specs to the shipping dock. To some design people, the term means the entire product innovation function.

The new products field has no definitional authority, as the accounting and legal professions have. The American Marketing Association recently issued the second edition of a definitions book, and many of the new product terms came from one of the authors of the book you are reading. But we have a long way to go, and for now we just have to slog along, the best we can.

---

[11]See Jan A. Buijs, "Innovation Can Be Taught," *Research Policy,* 1987, pp. 303–14. In this Netherlands research study, consultants taught managers in 155 small- and medium-sized industrial firms.

[12]For a discussion of these terms, plus many more that cause us problems, see Tudor Rickards, "Innovation and Creativity: Woods, Trees, and Pathways," *R&D Management,* April, 1991, pp. 97–108.

Does the Field of New Products Offer Careers?

It does indeed, though not many are entry positions for people right out of college. Generally, managements want new products people to know the industry involved (for the required understanding of customers mentioned earlier) and the firm's various operations (the multidimensional, orchestration task also mentioned). So most new products managers get assigned to new products work from a position in a functional department. For example, a scientist finds working with marketing and manufacturing people interesting, a market researcher specializes in benefit segmentation, or a salesperson earns a reputation for good new product concepts. Each of these people is a candidate for full-time work on new products.

The specific jobs in this field are three. First is the **functional representative** on a team, sometimes full time, more often part time. An example is a marketing researcher or a production planner. These people may be representatives on several teams or just one. The second job is the **project manager** or **team leader,** who leads a team of people representing the functions that will be required. The third position, the **new products *process* manager,** is responsible for helping project managers develop and use good new product processes.

Some of the career tips we hear are:

1. Be multifunctional, not functionally parochial. Have experience in more than one function (marketing, manufacturing, and so on). The broader your experience, the better.
2. Be risk takers, willing to do whatever is necessary to bring a product to market, including facing the wrath of co-workers.
3. Think like a general manager. Scientists and sales managers can lead new products teams, but they must cease being solely scientists and sales managers.
4. Be a combination of optimist and realist, aggressor and team player, leader and follower.
5. Develop your creative skills, both for new product concepts and for new ways of doing things.
6. Be comfortable in chaos and confusion. Learn to work with depressives, euphorics, and those with no emotion at all.

Fortunately, managers with such exemplary traits do exist—and in increasing numbers. We hope you become one of them.

Given All of This, What Will We Be Doing in This Book?

Chapter 2 shows the road map—the entire product innovation process. It begins in the organization's strategic planning; for example, Intel wants leadership in chips, Microsoft wants to dominate the information/communications market, and the Bell companies want customers to buy time on their wires and glass fibers. These goals help shape the new products program.

The end point of a new product project is reached when the new product achieves its objectives. Many students think the program is complete when the new product is marketed; so do many businesspeople, and they talk about turning a new product over to the "regular" people when it goes to market. But the project is complete *only* when the new product has sold enough, made enough profit, established a strong toehold in a new market, effectively thwarted a particular competitor . . . whatever the goal was at the time the new product project was initiated. And, in a new view gaining popularity, no one who worked on that new product should be permitted to "finish early." They shouldn't sign off until the goal has been reached.

A mile relay race run as a new product project would be a four-person mile, not four people running quarter miles. When a customer buys a new item and says it arrived in bad shape, someone from manufacturing and/or distribution had better be on hand to take care of that problem. In firms that still think of product innovation as a linear process (a relay race), the salesperson has to deal with customer problems alone. The support people are busy on other projects.

After the overview of the process in Chapter 2, we will take up the task step-by-step. First, we deal with **strategy:** identifying opportunities and giving the best ones a preliminary strategic statement to guide further work. Second, we look at **concept generation,** how we arrive at new concepts. Third, we move into the **concept/project evaluation** stage. We try to decide just how good those concepts are, both now and later as they evolve through stages where they are fleshed out. Fourth, we discuss **development,** including the big pair of semisimultaneous activities: marketing and technical development. During this stage, cost estimates become budgets, manufacturing processes become factories, and sales plans become sales calls. Though the activities in this stage go on side-by-side in true cross-functional format, we will look at design, team management, and other organizational issues first, then proceed to product use testing. We then move to **launch**—implementing and managing the commercialization of the plans and prototypes we have developed.

Then, knowing the entire process, we can look at **public policy** issues—how we handle the products that some members of society think we shouldn't have, from internal combustion engine cars to 60 sizes of potato chips in nonbiodegradable packaging.

At the end of each chapter are four applications. These are either questions asked or statements made by the president of a firm where you are interviewing for a job. (Many of them actually came from job interviews students had after taking a new product course.) They are conversational questions asked by a top manager who wants answers, not evasions. If you have no idea what the president is talking about, glance back through the chapter for clues.

Finally, if your course is built around some form of practice (individual or team projects and other such assignments), each chapter may offer a practical challenge. If not, try to come up with your own new product concept during your study of Chapters 4 through 7, and then work that idea down through the course. You can do your own concept testing, your own strategic market planning, and so on.

Does All This Actually Work?

The Product Development & Management Association sponsors a Corporate Innovator of the Year award. This award is not for a great new product, but rather for a sustained program of new product success, over at least five years. At the Association's annual conference, award winners must tell attendees "how they did it." In most cases, one could take their systems right from this book. Winners range from Merck to New Pig, from American Cardiovascular Systems to Nabisco, from Keithley Instruments to NordicTrack, and from Marriott to Bausch & Lomb to Chrysler. Frank Svet, speaking for winner Harris Broadcasting, said the firm had actually done so well on new products that their Japanese competitor withdrew from the market. The Nabisco story is given in the case for Chapter 2.

The opportunity for people who do the job right must be huge, given such flops as LaChoy's Fresh and Lite line of egg rolls (what was it, a deodorant or a beer?) and BIC's perfume bottled in a lighter-fluid-shaped container. But we can't be too confident—do you remember one author's first book, a small, thin volume selling for around $15 (violating all the rules) titled *The Bridges of Madison County,* which appeared for over four years on the *New York Times* Best Seller List? Wonders like this do happen, particularly in the worlds of art, entertainment, and taste.

Summary

This chapter has introduced you to the general field of new products management. You learned how the activity is (or should be) found in all organizations, not just business. You discovered how this course of study relates to others, what a new product actually is, and that services and business products are covered in the definition, not just cake mixes, videos, and cars. You also found out about the field today, the hallmarks of our activity, our problems with vocabulary, and possible careers.

Applications

At the end of each chapter are four questions that arose (or could have) during a job interview. The candidate was a student who took a course in new products management, and the interviewer was a high-ranking person in the firm (here portrayed as the president). The questions came up naturally during discussion, and they are tough. Often, the executive didn't intend them to be answered so much as talked about. Occasionally, the executive simply made a comment and then paused for the applicant's reaction. Each question or comment relates to something in the chapter.

Imagine you are the person being interviewed. You do not have the option of ducking the question or saying "I really don't know." If, in fact, you really don't know, then glance back over the reading to see what you missed. It's also a good idea to exchange answers with another student taking the course, given that most of the applications involve opinions or interpretations, not recitation of facts.

1. "I'm a great believer in serendipity. We've gotten several big winners that way. I've always wondered, though, how to manage an operation to get more of it. Any ideas?"
2. "When you were talking a while ago about taking risks, I wondered just whose money you were talking about. A fellow I know out in California insists that all new product team members invest their own money (with his) in their projects. Fifty thousand dollars is not unusual. Under that system I'll bet you would be seeking to *avoid* risks, not trying to *find* them."
3. "Funny thing, though, it sure does frustrate me when I hear a division general manager's strategy is to imitate other firms. I know some firms might reasonably use imitation, but none of my divisions should. Should they?"
4. "I'd like to be sure as many of our people as possible support innovation, but I know some people in the firm just can't react positively to proposed innovation, no matter how much we need it. Tell me, how should I go about spotting the worst offenders, and what should I do with them when I find out who they are?"

CHAPTER

2 The New Products Process

Setting

Chapter 1 introduced the field of new products management. Now we will discuss *the overall process—the combination of steps/activities/decisions/goals, and so forth, that, if performed well, churns out the new products the organization needs.* It involves the who, what, when, and how of new products management.

First, we need a word about our special viewpoint in this chapter, after which there will be a short story (saga) to help show the overall picture and identify several key activities. This will lead into the full process and its managerial aspects.

"It Doesn't Work That Way"

Businesspeople often look at designs of the overall new product process and say, "It doesn't work that way in our firm." As you read in Chapter 1, a carpenter doesn't use all the tools in the toolbox when building any particular door. Similarly, a manager using the generic system outlined in this chapter must cut and fit it to the situation at hand. If the competitive situation is very tight, it may not be feasible to do concept testing. If the firm is cash short, it may be necessary to roll out a new product faster than they would otherwise prefer.

The Highlighter Saga

The following story introduces the new products process.

Betty Wall had been covering a sales territory in Omni Manufacturing Company's college market for three years, selling, among other office supplies, a line of highlighting products. They were the usual collection of colors, widths, sizes, and shapes. This was an important market for Betty's firm, and Omni shared the lead with Trion, Inc. Betty knew the market was mature, the life cycle far past the dynamic growth stage with no real excitement for several years. Moreover, she had heard from the purchasing agent at Kinsville College that Trion was developing a new concept in highlighters. Apparently, it involved a clear liquid that reacted with ink to give each letter a broader, deeper, and more shiny appearance. Trion was having trouble with the concept, but Betty was worried about her commissions from the Omni line.

Betty called David Raymond, the newly appointed product manager for office supplies, and told him her story and her fears. David asked the market research department to make a quick scan of the highlighter situation—sales, shares, profits, rumors of innovation, and so on. Sure enough, the market was very mature; competitors and customers were complacent. Market research also uncovered the Trion test product, which sounded impressive.

David then discussed the situation with the vice president of marketing, who agreed there was a significant threat to the cash flow from office supplies. When Omni's president confirmed that highlighters were important to the firm's future, David was asked to come up with a solution to the combined problem of maturity and competitive innovation.

Fortunately, brainstorming within the product management group, combined with astute thinking on the part of two technical people, led to the concept of a *solid* highlighter. No one was sure it would work (pulling liquid from the air), but the basic idea seemed sound. Several focus group sessions with office workers and students were positive, technical people reaffirmed its feasibility, a scan of its fit with the rest of the firm (safety, production facilities, and so on) scored highly, and preliminary financial analysis gave it an OK.

David, as product manager, was given leadership on the project. He decided to put together a team of four people to run the operation, ordered more market research, wrote out what the work to date indicated should be the benefits of the new item to the consumer, and laid out a time schedule that would get this new product to the market before Trion got there with theirs. Technical people went to work on the solid material concept, and David began thinking about the best marketing strategy for the product. On one of his visits to the lab, Phyllis Chaterji, the technical member of the team, showed him the first prototype, finished just the evening before. David arranged to show it to some potential customers. They liked the idea very much. Thus Phyllis continued her work, final specifications were written, some semifinished product was produced for David to place in offices and dorms to see if it worked in practice, and manufacturing went on to plan the facilities change and a new production process.

With this information, David put together a financial analysis, with preliminary product cost estimates and a marketing budget. Management approved, and the product was headed for market. Further field testing was undertaken to get users' full reactions, the product's formulation was fine-tuned, manufacturing locked in on a process and bought the equipment, and marketing fleshed out the marketing plans with an advertising agency and help from the sales department.

When everything looked good, David got approval to start production on the final product and introduce it to markets along the Middle Atlantic coast (Trion's strongest area) and in the province of Quebec. He and a market research analyst practically lived in those areas for almost a month. They knew customers might misunderstand how the product was to be used, so they were ready to run off some expensive in-store displays that gave better instructions. As it turned out, the displays were needed, the problem was overcome, sales took off, and the product was rolled out to the rest of the U.S., Canadian, and selected European markets. Fortunately the process went smoothly for Omni because Trion was ready with its product at about the same time. Suddenly, a very mature market was exciting again.

What Happened in That Saga?

We just read a whole year's activity in a few minutes. The story, of course, was fabricated, but the situation was typical. The story began with an ongoing operation that faced a problem. The problem was studied, and the solution was checked against ongoing new product strategy and then approved for action. Various developmental and evaluative steps followed, along with gradual development of the marketing plan. Launch was on a limited basis, and the manager anticipated a problem that he was able to handle quickly and successfully. By the time you finish this book, however, you may have some criticisms of David Raymond's decisions and actions.

This situation is typical in that the new products process does not usually begin with a new product idea. It is folklore that someone, somewhere, wakes up in the middle of the night with a great insight. It can happen, but successful new product programs are not built on such slender hopes. If an idea walks in through the door, fine, but the process usually begins with what amounts to strategy—the mature market and the competitive activity were threats to Omni. With management's concurrence, action got under way.

Note, too, that development does not take place behind the closed doors of a research lab—there are many interim tests of fit and progress. And marketing doesn't start when the product is finished—it often starts before ideation, as it did here.

Last, the process is not over when the new product is launched. It ends when the new product is *successful,* usually after some in-flight corrections (such as with the special in-store display piece).

Let's now look at the full process, including many steps and options that didn't appear in the highlighter story. Incidentally, the new product concept in that story may have seemed crazy, or dumb, or impossible. Most great ideas look pretty bad when they first appear, but we have good methods for sorting them out.

The Basic New Products Process

Figure 2–1 shows, in an abbreviated fashion, the way the new products process is usually presented and talked about. There are five sequential phases, when one is finished another begins, and so on to launch. If you think about the highlighter saga above, you can identify those phases. Study Figure 2–1 carefully—read what is in each of the phases.

However, the neat, linear sequencing of phases or stages shown in the process chart is just not typical. Figure 2–2 offers a more realistic view. That figure shows the same five phases as in Figure 2–1, but there is a huge difference. The activity is not *sequential,* but *overlapping.* For example, in the very beginning of a project most attention should be on the strategic aspect—how would this project jibe with our mission statement, do we have the basic interests and capabilities for the work being considered, what would we expect to gain from it, and so on. But technical people are already beginning to think about the technical issues. Marketers are already sensing how the proposed activity might aid other products in the line.

Having neat sequential stages, with clear checkpoints, has other drawbacks. For one, it tempts one firm to adopt the process of another firm, only to find that it doesn't fit. Second, staging causes queues, where projects pile up in line waiting for big review meetings. One chief engineer, following such a review meeting, released 500 drawings for one product in a single day. The glut resembled a rodent going down the throat of a snake.

The model illustrated in Figure 2–2 is significant for another reason. The titles of the five phases do not refer to functions or departments. Technical people *lead* the technical portion of the development, but others participate, some very actively, including marketing research and sales people. Launch sounds like a marketing activity, but much of the marketing is done during earlier phases, *and* during launch the manufacturing people are busy setting up production capability. Legal people are clearing brand names, lab people are running tests on early production output, and so on. Emphatically, this is no hand-off-a-baton relay race.

Even if a firm were to use the process as described here, keep in mind that they may group the activities differently. Ken Munch of Herman Miller, accepting the Product Innovator of the Year award from the Product Development & Management Association, said his firm uses three steps—Opportunity (collapsing the first three of the five steps below), Development, and Launch. Some other firms treat launch as part of development, figuring that one is not through developing until the launch is successful. So it is important to look for the bigger picture of a large, evolving, general purpose

FIGURE 2–1

Basic new products process

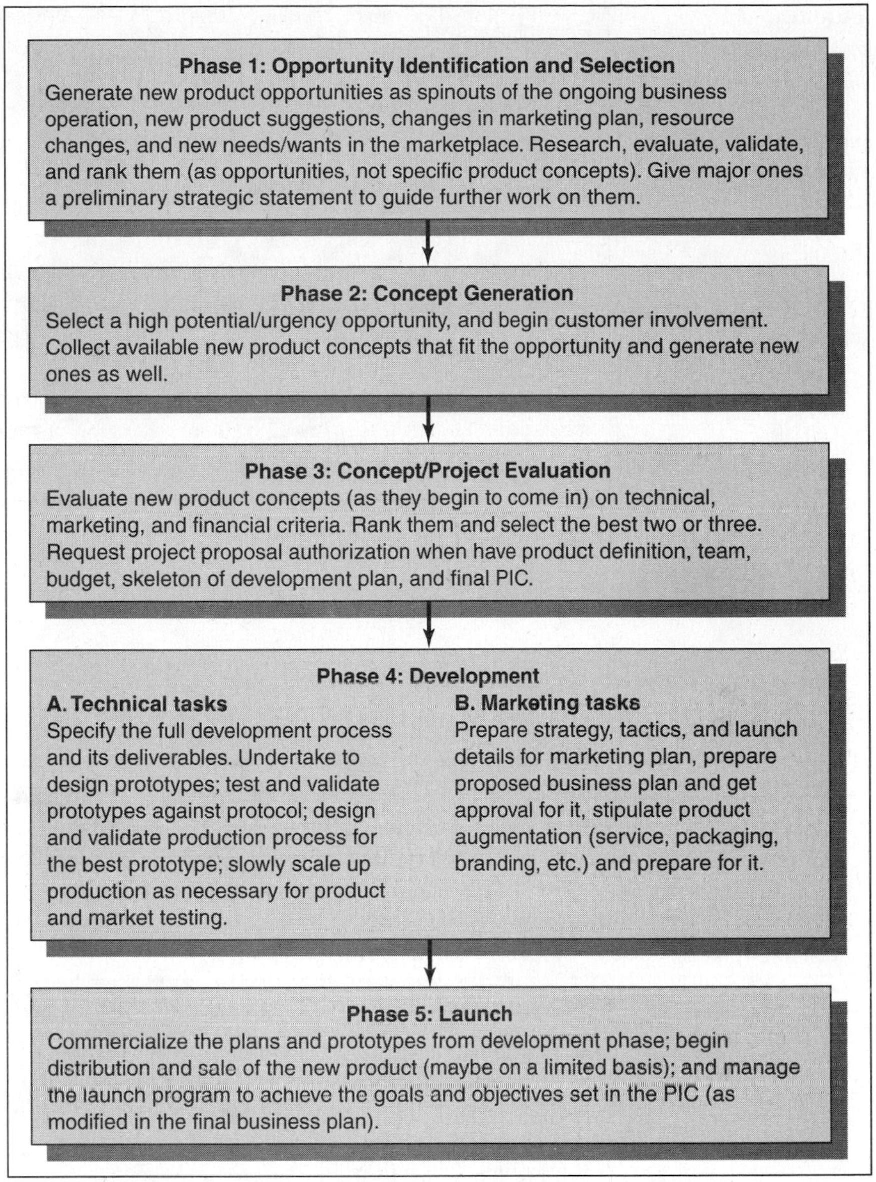

Phase 1: Opportunity Identification and Selection

Generate new product opportunities as spinouts of the ongoing business operation, new product suggestions, changes in marketing plan, resource changes, and new needs/wants in the marketplace. Research, evaluate, validate, and rank them (as opportunities, not specific product concepts). Give major ones a preliminary strategic statement to guide further work on them.

↓

Phase 2: Concept Generation

Select a high potential/urgency opportunity, and begin customer involvement. Collect available new product concepts that fit the opportunity and generate new ones as well.

↓

Phase 3: Concept/Project Evaluation

Evaluate new product concepts (as they begin to come in) on technical, marketing, and financial criteria. Rank them and select the best two or three. Request project proposal authorization when have product definition, team, budget, skeleton of development plan, and final PIC.

↓

Phase 4: Development

A. Technical tasks

Specify the full development process and its deliverables. Undertake to design prototypes; test and validate prototypes against protocol; design and validate production process for the best prototype; slowly scale up production as necessary for product and market testing.

B. Marketing tasks

Prepare strategy, tactics, and launch details for marketing plan, prepare proposed business plan and get approval for it, stipulate product augmentation (service, packaging, branding, etc.) and prepare for it.

↓

Phase 5: Launch

Commercialize the plans and prototypes from development phase; begin distribution and sale of the new product (maybe on a limited basis); and manage the launch program to achieve the goals and objectives set in the PIC (as modified in the final business plan).

FIGURE 2–2

The product innovation process, in actual practice: the impact of simultaneous operations for speed

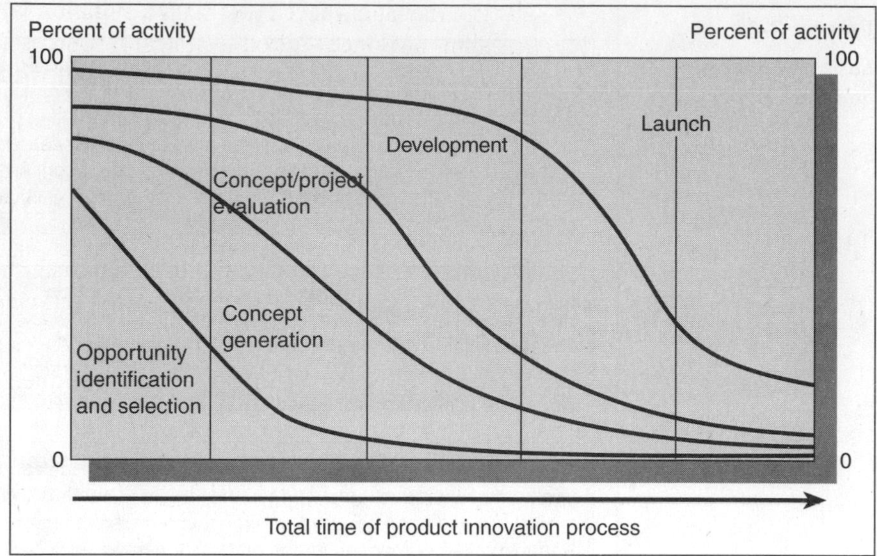

process, broken into steps partly for our benefit in presenting the story about new product activities.

All of which makes it tough for us to label the work being done. Department labels imply territory, or turf, and those are rejected today. Activity labels, such as those in Figure 2–2, mislead, but they do make one point: Today's product development is a **multifunctional program,** where all functions work together to accomplish the required tasks.

Now let's take a longer look at each of the five general phases of the new products process.

Phase 1: Opportunity Identification and Selection

The first phase is strategic is nature and is the most difficult to describe or define. The best approach probably is to tell you what businesses actually do, and then show how this yields strategic guidance to the firm.

At least three main streams of activity feed strategic planning for new products. They are (with an example for each):

- **Ongoing marketing planning.** The annual marketing plan for a CD-ROM line calls for a line extension to meet encroachment of a new competitor selling primarily on price.
- **Ongoing corporate planning.** Top management adopts a strategy that says either "own" a market (meaning get either a first or second place share) or get out of it. This requires new product activity in all desirable markets where the firm holds a minor position. General

Electric managers faced just such a situation when Jack Welch took the helm. 3M once shifted technical resources from basic research toward "nitty-gritty" product development, with profound impact on most new product processes.[1]

- **Special opportunity analysis.** One or more persons (in the firm or a consulting firm) are assigned to inventory the firm's resources (people, facilities, reputations, whatever). Example: A firm in the auto parts business calls for an audit of its manufacturing operation. It turns out that manufacturing process engineering has been overlooked or just not appreciated—that skill could serve as the base for a new products program.

From these activities, the opportunities identified sort naturally into four categories, again with examples:

- **An underutilized resource.** A bottling operation, a strong franchise with dealers, or the previously mentioned manufacturing process engineering department.
- **A new resource.** Du Pont's discovery of Kevlar, a material with hundreds of potential uses.
- **An external mandate.** The stagnant market combined with a competitive threat, as in the highlighter story.
- **An internal mandate.** Long-range planning often establishes a five-year-out dollar sales target, and new products people often must fill part of the gap between current sales and the target. The gap is referred to as the **product innovation** (and/or *acquisition*) **gap.** Other common internal mandates are simply upper management desires.

The process of creatively recognizing such opportunities is called **opportunity identification.** The opportunities are carefully and thoroughly described, then analyzed to confirm that a sales potential does, indeed, exist. Recall that one of the first things David Raymond did was order a scan of the highlighter market.

Of course, no firm wants to exploit *all* opportunities; some are better than others. Some may not fit with company skills, some are too risky, some require more money than the firm has. Thus most firms have **ongoing strategies** covering product innovation. For example, Waterford had a strategy that no new product would jeopardize the firm's great image. Cincinnati Milicron's strategy demanded that any new product be highly innovative, not a me-too.

Once an opportunity is approved, managers turn to various techniques to guide new product people in exploiting it. This we will call the **Product Innovation Charter,** and it will be explained in Chapter 3.

---

[1]Kevin Kelly, "The Drought Is Over at 3M," *Business Week,* November 7, 1994, pp. 140–41.

Phase 2: Concept Generation

In some cases, merely identifying an opportunity determines what is wanted (for example, an opportunity to add a small size of deodorant for travelers). Most of the time, however, it's not so clear, so an immense set of ideation tools has evolved. Creating new product ideas, usually called **product concepts** by new products people, is not as simple as it might appear.

The most fruitful ideation involves identifying problems people or businesses have and suggesting solutions to them. For example, if the opportunity focused on "people moving their families over long distances," the first ideation step is to study those people and find out what problems they have. This problem-finding-and-solving activity has become quite sophisticated; it is no longer the caricature of a group sitting around a table, pouring out ideas. Chapter 5 discusses problem-based ideation in detail.

While the systematic problem-based ideation is going on, unsolicited ideas are pouring in via phone, mail, and Internet from customers, erstwhile customers, employees (especially sales, technical, and operations), and every other source imaginable. These ideas are reviewed briefly by whomever receives them to see if they are relevant to the firm and its strategies. They are then put into the pool with the ideas that came from problem-solving activities.

Concept generation is covered in detail in Chapters 4 through 7.

Phase 3: Concept/Project Evaluation

Before development work can begin on new ideas, they need to be evaluated, screened, and sorted out. This activity, sometimes called **screening** or **pretechnical evaluation,** varies tremendously. But most firms more or less follow a sequence from quick looks to complete discounted cash flows and net present value. The quick look is necessary because the flow of new product concepts is huge—into the thousands in many firms. You no doubt gave the highlighter idea such an immediate "screen," liking it or disliking it.

But what happens next is the first formal type of evaluation. Depending on the idea, this may be end-user or technical screening, or both. The work may be extensive and difficult, or it may take no more than a few telephone calls. In the highlighter saga, technical people actually proposed a solution to the competitive problem, and then there was a **concept test** to see what potential consumers thought about it. Ultimately, these views all come together in what is often called THE screen, or the **full screen.** It uses a scoring model of some type and results in a decision to either undertake development or quit.

If the decision is to go ahead, the evaluation turns into **project evaluation,** where we no longer evaluate the idea but rather the plan we propose for capitalizing on that idea. This involves preparing a statement of what is wanted from the new product. Firms using **Quality Function Deployment** (a method of project management and control) see this as the first list of customer needs. A more common generic term is **product description** or **product definition.** In this book it will be called **product protocol.** Protocol means agreement, and it is important that there be agreement between the various groups *before* extensive technical work gets under way. The protocol should, to the extent possible, be *benefits* the new item is to yield, not the features the new item is to have.

The lack of good hard information complicates all pretechnical evaluation. In fact, the first three stages (strategic planning, concept generation, and, especially, concept/project evaluation comprise what is popularly called the **fuzzy front end** (of the new product process). This doesn't mean our *minds* are fuzzy; the *product concept* is. By the end of the project, most fuzz will have been removed, but for now we move with more daring than the data allow.[2] The various pretechnical evaluation actions are covered in Chapters 8–12.

Phase 4: Development

This is the phase during which the item acquires finite form—a tangible good or a specific sequence of resources and activities that will perform an intangible service. It is also the stage during which the **marketing plan** is sketched and gradually fleshed out. Business practice varies widely, but we often find the following pieces.

Resource Preparation. Often overlooked by new products managers is a step called **resource preparation.** For product improvements and some line extensions, this is OK because a firm is already up and going in a mode that fits products that are close to home. The culture is right, market data are more reliable, and ongoing managers are ready to do the work. But a particular innovation charter may leave familiar territory, forcing problems of fit. If a firm wants **discontinuous products** (that is, products quite different than those now available), then the team may need special training, new reward systems, revisions in the firm's usual project review system, and special permissions. Without adequate preparation of the ball field, a firm doesn't get much home advantage.

The Major Body of Effort. Next comes what all of the previous steps have been leading up to—the actual development of, not one thing, but three—the item or service itself, the marketing plan for it, and a business (or financial) plan that final approval will require. The product (or better, the concept) stream involves industrial design and bench work (goods) or systems design

---

[2]The fuzzy front end has been the subject of much research the past five years. A good example is a study of how eleven companies handle it: Anil Khurana and Stephan Rosenthal, "Integrating the Fuzzy Front End of New Product Development," *Sloan Management Review,* Winter 1997, pp. 103–20.

(services), **prototypes,** product specifications, and so on. It culminates in a product that the developers hope is finished—produced, tested, and costed out.

While the technical developers are at work, marketing planners are busy making periodic market scans (to keep up with changes out there) and marketing decisions as early as they can be made—first strategic ones and then tactical. Marketing decisions are completely interlaced with technical ones and involve package design, brand name selection, and tentative marketing budgets. A technical disappointment down the line may junk the early package design, name, or whatever. But we have to pay that price; we can't wait for each step to be concluded before going to the next one.

Along the way, concept evaluation continues; we've already evaluated the concept well enough to permit development work (discussed earlier), but we have to keep evaluating technical and marketing planning *results.* We evaluate prototypes primarily, checking to be sure each generation of prototype meets the needs and desires of the customer. By the time this stage winds down, we want to be assured that the new product actually does solve those problems we began with.

Comprehensive Business Analysis. If the product is real and customers like it, some firms make a comprehensive **business analysis** before moving into launch. The financial analysis is still not firm, but it is good enough to assure management that this project will be worthwhile. The financials will gradually be tightened during the launch phase, and where the actual Go/NoGo point is reached varies with the nature of the industry. Approval for a new food product can be held until just before signing TV advertising contracts, but a new chemical that requires a new manufacturing facility has to Go much earlier, and the pharmaceutical industry really makes the Go decision when it undertakes a 10-year, $50 million, R&D effort. The development phase is covered in Chapters 13–16.

Phase 5: Launch

Traditionally, the term **launch,** or *commercialization,* has described the time when or decision where the firm decides to market a product (the Go of Go/NoGo). We associate this decision with building factories or authorizing agencies to proceed with multimillion-dollar advertising campaigns.

However, it's a bit more subtle than that now. The launch decision is more attitude than anything else. A firm can always pull out, even during a test market, so some people say most projects actually don't have a Go/NoGo decision. Regardless, the last few weeks or months just before and after announcing the new product is really a launch *phase.* New products teams are enjoying life in the fast lane (or, unfortunately, in a pressure cooker). Everything is rush; everything is critical. Manufacturing is now doing a gradual scale-up of output. Marketing planners, who got a good glimpse of their ultimate target market as early as the opportunity arose, are now deep into the hundreds of tactical details required for launch. The critical step—if a company takes it—is the **market test,** the first time the marketing program and the product dance together. This step is pure dress rehearsal, and managers hope any problems discovered are fixable between dress rehearsal and opening night. If they aren't, the opening has to be delayed; General Foods and Procter & Gamble have in a few cases kept products in market test for years.

Sooner or later (hopefully) these preparation activities lead to a public announcement of the new product—advertising, sales calls, and so forth. The announcement is often called launch, meaning that launch takes place on one day, or even at one hour. Dramatic, yes, but practically speaking most firms today are gradually moving the new item into commerce over a period of at least several weeks—there are suppliers to bring on line, sales forces to be trained, distributors to be stocked and trained, and a large set of market support people to be educated (columnists, scientists, government people, and thousands more). These things cannot happen in one day, nor can the secret be kept—details yes, but the emergence of a new item, no.

One thing that is often overlooked at this point is the activity of planning for **launch management.** Everyone knows that when space shuttles leave the launch pad in Florida, a plan of tracking has been carefully prepared. Mission Control runs it, seeking to spot every glitch that comes up during launch and hoping it was anticipated so that a solution is on board, ready to use. New products managers often do the same thing, sometimes formally but often *very* informally.

The launch phase is covered in Chapters 17 through 22.

The Concept Life Cycle

You may have noticed by now that the new products process essentially turns an opportunity (the real start) into a profit flow (the real finish). It begins with something that is not a product (the opportunity) and ends up with something else that is not a product (the profit). The product arises from a situation and moves toward an end.

What we have then is an **evolving product,** or better, an evolving concept that, at the end, if successful, becomes a product. Even a new product announcement simply tells the world about a concept, hopefully a winner, but actually one just in temporary form. Even now, forces are standing by to see what revisions need to be made, if it is off track.

We call this process the **concept life cycle.** (See Figure 2–3.) Here are the stages of the cycle, using a new skim milk product as an example:

Opportunity concept—a company skill or resource, or a customer problem. (Assume that skim milk drinkers tell us they don't like the watered look of their favorite beverage.)

FIGURE 2–3

The life cycle of a concept

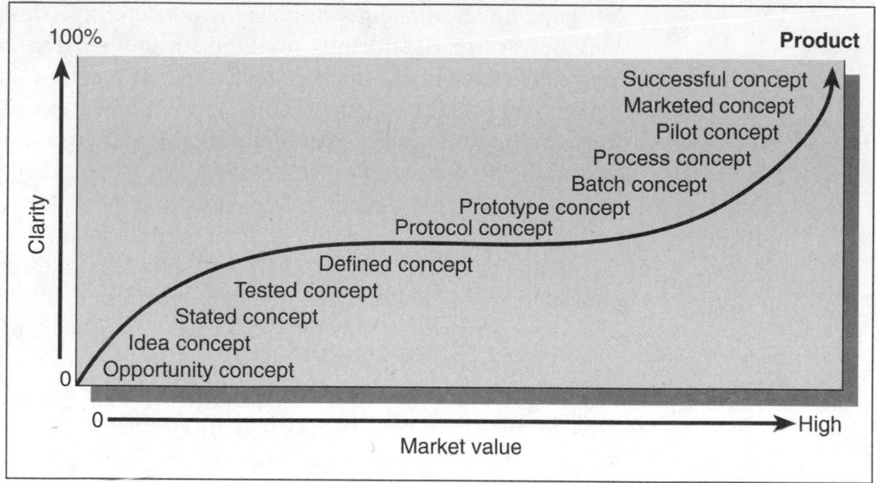

Idea concept—the first appearance of an idea. (Maybe we could change the color.)

Stated concept—a form or a technology, plus a clear statement of benefit. (See Chapter 3.) (Our firm's patented method of breaking down protein globules might make the liquid more cloudy; emphasis on *might,* at this time.)

Tested concept—it has passed an end-user concept test; need is confirmed. (Consumers say they would very much like to have such a milk product, and the method of producing it sounds workable.)

Defined concept—it passes the test of fit with the company's situation.

Protocol concept—a product definition that includes the intended market user, the problem perceived, the benefits that a less watery skim milk would have to have, plus any mandatory features. (Our new product must taste as good or better than current skim milk, and it must yield exactly the same nutritional values.)

Prototype concept—a tentative physical product or system procedure, including features and benefits. (A small supply of a "full-bodied" skim milk, ready to consume, though not yet produced in quantity.)

Batch concept—first full test-of-fit with manufacturing; it can be made. Specifications are written as to exactly what the product is to be, including features, characteristics, and standards. (Skim milk ingredients: Vitamin D source, fat, fiber, and so on.)

Process concept— the full manufacturing process is complete.

Pilot concept—a supply of the new product, produced in quantity from a pilot production line, enough for field testing with end-users.

Marketed concept—output of the scale-up process from pilot. (Milk product that is actually marketed, either for a market test or for full scale launch.)

Successful concept (new product)—it meets the goals set for it at the start of the project. (New, Full Body Skim has achieved 24 percent of the market, is very profitable, and already competitors are negotiating licenses on our technology.)

The idea that a new product suddenly "emerges" from R&D—like a chicken from an egg—is simply incorrect. In fact, throughout this book we will examine how analytical techniques are applied throughout the new product process, from early idea generation and concept evaluation, through screening, and on to positioning, market testing, and launch management.

Closing Thoughts about the Basic New Products Process

All Firms Are Different

The Anheuser-Busch (A-B), Strohs, and Coors brewing companies seem to have quite different new product strategies. Strohs, being smaller, for a long time had a more defensive strategy (and thus a very fast, lower-risk development process), while A-B, the leader in technology, spent far more time early in the process making sure that required product qualities were not lost. (A few, such as Schlitz, failed to do this.) Coors quickly changed its "beer only" product strategy when nonalcoholic beers came along. Some large firms, with strong product lines, will quickly develop a me-too product just to keep distributors happy.[3]

If a concept fails its screening test with intended consumers, it heads back to the ideation stage or even farther back to the opportunity identification stage. And if a competitor makes a surprise entry, the project may take a risky skip of several stages and move right into production. Believe it or not, a key task of a new products manager is to keep other team players up to date on just where the project is.

Processes also vary in complexity, perhaps the grandparent of all being the "new health care plan" that floundered after so many months of strategy, ideation, technical developments, and so on, early in the Clinton administration. The steps that any new product management group uses will be a

[3]Two studies that address the matter of which steps are taken and which are skipped are Robert G. Cooper, "New Products: The Factors that Drive Success," *International Marketing Review,* Number 1, 1994, pp. 60–76 (where comparisons are made between industrial products in general and chemical products in particular) and Larry Dwyer and Robert Mellor, "New Product Process Activities and Project Outcomes," *R&D Management,* January 1991, pp. 31–41.

FIGURE 2–4

Rates of use of selected new product process steps

	Percent of Firms Using			
Step	*PDMA Members**	*Canada†*	*Australia, England, and Belgium‡*	*PDMA Members Plus Others***
1. Detailed market study	Not reported	25%	57%	NR
2. Concept searching	90%	NR	NR	57%
3. Concept screening	76	92	96	55
4. Concept testing	80	NR	NR	NR
5. Business analysis	89	63	76	59
6. Product development (technical)	99	89	93	64
7. Customer field (use) testing	NR	66	78	61
8. Market testing	NR	23	34	NR
9. Use testing or market testing	87	NR	NR	NR
10. Trial production setup	NR	49	70	NR
11. Separate marketing plan	NR	68	NR	

*Product Development & Management Association, in Albert L. Page, "Assessing New Product Development Practices and Performance: Establishing Crucial Norms," *Journal of Product Innovation Management,* September 1993, pp. 273–90.

†Robert G. Cooper and Elko J. Kleinschmidt, "An Investigation into the New Product Process: Steps, Deficiencies, Impact," *Journal of Product Innovation Management,* June 1986, pp. 71–85.

‡Larry Dwyer and Robert Mellor, "New Product Process Activities and Project Outcomes," *R&D Management,* January 1991, pp. 31–41.

**In Abbie Griffin, "PDMA Research on New Product Development Practices: Updating Trends and Benchmarking Best Practices," *Journal of Product Innovation Management,* November 1997, pp. 429–59.

function of pressures like these, as well as resources of the moment, education and experience, and much more. By no means have we achieved full adoption of the best methods. (See Figure 2–4.) Some of the best techniques are widely used by the most successful new product firms, but many still are used only by a minority; innovation strategy is the most discriminant variable.[4]

Some activities occur at certain points in the basic new product process (e.g., a financial screen) but others go on at several points (or almost continuously). For example, competitive analysis can never end—we must know what competition has and is doing at all times, through to well after announcement. The same goes for what some call the **Voice of the Customer**—today we partner up near the beginning and get customer reactions and suggestions at many if not most of the points in the concept life cycle. Only our customers (and our accountants) can tell us when the concept evolves into a new product.

---

[4]Abbie Griffin, "PDMA Research on New Product Development Practices: Updating Trends and Benchmarking Best Practices," *Journal of Product Innovation Management,* November 1997, pp. 429–58.

Keeping an eye on the competition and the customer throughout the process is not the only way we recognize concept life cycle continuing until success. Formerly when a product was marketed, the team disbanded. Today many firms keep key team members active until success is reached, especially those in manufacturing and engineering/R&D.

In fact, more managers are coming out in protest at the recent tendency to make that process tight and rigid. They say that we do not need precise dates and stage "toll" gates. The most recent study of industry practice of this issue shows the most success with what the research described as third-generation stage gate processes—those with "fuzzy and flexible" gates.[5] One of the authors recently heard a manager from a highly regarded firm describe how they go out one year after announcement and assess the success of a new item. Upon being asked why one year, he answered, "That's what the system calls for, one year, regardless of the product." This is not what is recommended by Sheldon Buckley, widely recognized for his work at Polaroid.[6] Nor by the 24 innovator firms studied by Thomas.[7] Nor by Toyota, which violates several of the most popular development techniques of today. For example, they do not integrate their suppliers, they try to jump to final designs as soon as possible, and they use only those stage gates that are absolutely mandatory.[8]

It certainly is good to have *some* process in managing new products—the famous **skunkworks** (where a few brilliant people work by themselves and open the door when they are finished) has not been successful. One consultant recently said thinking about process can take the manager's eye off of nurturing; helping people become more excited and committed makes for productivity of the best kind, in any process.[9]

On the lighter side, Figure 2–5 shows what one veteran new products writer once claimed made for success, and he wasn't entirely tongue in cheek. Keep in mind that every process is hard to define in practice, although new product **benchmarking** has proven successful to some firms.[10]

---

[5]Ibid., p. 440.

[6]Karn Anne Zien and Sheldon A. Buckley, "Dreams to Market. Crafting a Culture of Innovation," *Journal of Product Innovation Management,* July 1997, pp. 274–87.

[7]Robert J. Thomas, *New Product Development* (New York: John Wiley and Sons, 1995).

[8]Allen Ward, Jeffrey K. Liker, John J. Cristiano, and Durward K. Sobek II, "The Second Toyota Paradox: How Delaying Decisions Can Make Cars Faster," *Sloan Management Review,* Spring 1995, pp. 43–61.

[9]Ronald J. Jonash, vice president at Arthur D. Little, in a speech at the 1997 International Conference of the Product Development & Management Association, Monterrey, October 21, 1997.

[10]Certain firms are well-known for processes that others feel warrant benchmarking: Beckman Instruments, Calcomp, Cincinnati Milacron, DEC, Hewlett-Packard, 3M, Motorola, and NCR are leaders. Otis Port, "Beg, Borrow—and Benchmark," *Business Week,* November 30, 1992, pp. 74–75. A good basic reference on benchmarking is Robert G. Cooper and Elko J. Kleinschmidt, "Benchmarking The Firm's Critical Success Factors in New Product Development, *Journal of Product Innovation Management,* November 1995, pp. 374–91.

FIGURE 2–5

20 Clues to New Product Success

1. Has the product been in development for a year?
2. Does your company now make a similar product?
3. Does your company now sell to a related customer market?
4. Is research and development at least one-third of the product budget?
5. Will the product be test marketed for at least six months?
6. Does the person in charge have a private secretary?
7. Will the ad budget be at least 5% of anticipated sales?
8. Will a recognized brand name be on the product?
9. Would the company take a loss on it for the first year?
10. Does the company "need" the product more than it "wants" it?
11. Have three samples of advertising copy been prepared?
12. Is the product really new, as opposed to improved?
13. Can the decision to buy it be made by only one person?
14. Is the product to be made in fewer than five versions?
15. Will the product not need service and repair?
16. Does the development team have a working code name?
17. Will the company president (or division general manager) see the project leader without an appointment?
18. Did the project leader make a go of the last two projects?
19. Will the product be on the market for more than 10 years?
20. Would the project leader quit and take the item along if the company said it wouldn't back it?

Note: According to the developer of this list (New Product Development, a newsletter firm in Point Pleasant, New Jersey), 11 to 14 yes answers indicates probable success, 8 to 10 yes answers indicates a coin toss, and below 8 says to forget it.

Source: Reprinted by permission of *The Wall Street Journal,* © Dow Jones & Company, Inc., September 24, 1981.

Visitors who ask to see a firm's new products process won't see much. The process is so intertwined with the firm's ongoing operation that new product dimensions are vague. In small firms, for example, where much innovation originates, the ongoing and the new are essentially the same. In addition, all players on one team are players on the other. Even in large firms, where many people specialize full time on new products, most of the players do not.

Moments of Truth

When the first Saturn automobiles were introduced, the management team laid plans to deal with what they called **moments of truth.** For example, their market research had shown that potential car buyers were especially affected by *what they encountered the first time they went to a dealership to look at a new car.* Their impressions at that point were burned into their minds, and influenced everything they later saw or heard. So Saturn arranged a special reception for visitors who came to the showrooms—host sales people who were salaried, refreshment counters with hot coffee, products clearly on display and open to full examination, and information sheets that answered common questions.

One technology-based firm developed a waste-water treatment system that could be hooked up to toilets in rural service stations located on land that perked poorly (that could not support field tile systems). The device returned water approved for drinking. But the firm failed to note that professional sanitary engineers must evaluate all such systems before local public health bodies will approve them for installation. A moment of truth was missed, and marketing was put on hold for over a year.

In every new product process there are several such moments of truth or, as some people prefer to call them (in reverse), potholes. Any place where the project can be torpedoed should be marked with stars and italics. All stages are not alike, with regard to where these potholes may occur.

Summary

In this chapter, we studied essentially one thing: the system of phases and activities used in the process of developing and marketing new products. We looked at a simplistic version of this process in a hypothetical situation with highlighter pens. We then went through the basic process phase by phase, talking about each one. In that explanation, we noted actions taken or not taken by people in the office supplies firm. Last, you saw that what "should" be is often not, and often for very good reason. Don't think this or any new product process is etched in stone. It is a guide and an integrator, not a straitjacket.

We now turn to Chapter 3, and the first of the five major stages in the process—Opportunity Identification and Selection. This chapter will include the various strategies used to guide the evaluation of available opportunities. In turn, it will prepare us to begin the study of concept generation.

Applications

More questions from the interview with a company president:

1. "I've got to make a speech down in Dallas next month. It's part of a conference SMU is having on opportunity identification (OI). They want me to explain why OI is sometimes more important than brainstorming and other techniques of concept generation. Seems to me it isn't. What do you think?"
2. "You were telling me a moment ago about a three-pronged development process for new products (technical, marketing, and evaluation). Well, I disagree. We develop a new product first; we

have to. When we know what the product will be, *then* we can estimate its costs, prepare advertising for it, and so on. We simply couldn't do all of these things at one time."

3. "Several years ago I was general manager of our high-technology metals division in Italy. We were developing some fabulous applications of space-age technologies in products throughout Europe and parts of Asia—both in government labs and with private firms. Some of our metals were half glass, and no one really knew all they could do. I tell you this because you said your book argued against tight controls by upper managements at the stage-ending points. No way. On some projects I would let them go a long way, but on others I wanted approval rights frequently! I never had time to figure it out, but I often wondered why I let some of the projects go and kept tight rein on others. Suppose it related to government restrictions? Or maybe I just trusted some people more than others."
4. "One of the scientists working in our German office furniture subsidiary told me the other day that he actually has to be involved in developing at least six different products for every one we market. He said they were "precursors," of the final product. He even said he didn't know what product we would ultimately end up marketing. What in the world did he mean by all that?"

Case: Nabisco SnackWell's[11]

In 1993 Nabisco put intense emphasis on new products and had 30 percent of sales from them. In the previous five years they had had five $100 million products. They stressed that the story of SnackWell's (first year sales of almost $200 million) was typical of their firm, but the process might not work for other firms because all innovators are not alike. Nabisco's methods were the result of an overhaul, made when they realized they were suffering the "silo" problem and others. People were not talking to each other. In their new process, they sought new segments, not confined to foods, and not confined to traditional food channels. For example, one new product effort involved selling individual-size packages of snacks in video stores and movie theaters.

Nabisco's new process had three key requirements: (1) The item had to fill a real gap, (2) the item had to be on a key trend, and (3) the whole project had to be executed flawlessly. Satisfying less than these three requirements did not suffice in the food business. Gaps were discovered in two ways. First, Nabisco used a sophisticated gap analysis

---

[11]In 1993, the Product Development & Management Association gave Nabisco their Outstanding Innovator Award for having a sustained program of new product creation and marketing. Two members of that firm told this Nabisco story to the annual International Conference of that association in San Diego.

method of studying markets, probably built around the methodologies in Chapters 6–7. Second, they used a method of attribute analysis that sought ways a cookie could be created especially for a user, for an occasion, or just made physically different. For SnackWell's, the gap was a user gap—cookies for *adults.* Kids had theirs, but adults did not have cookies with the attributes *they* wanted—namely "great taste, fat-free, better for you."

The second requirement, on a key trend, was satisfied easily—there was very strong growth in adult population, and adults clearly desired wellness.

The third key, flawless execution, was achieved as follows. Nabisco believed in ideation and creativity. Ideas came from employees generally, from gap analysis (above), and from their special environment in the technical development departments. Nabisco encouraged blue sky ideation, provided a "skunkworks" environment by allowing time off to further personal concepts, allowed staffers to present ideas to management at annual May Fairs, and ran brainstorming sessions where development people were joined by marketing, finance, operations, and R&D.

A new product concept that looked good (as SnackWell's did) was given a feasibility check (could they retool for it, did it interfere with production, etc.). Then it went into quantitative testing—first screened against the firm's market research database to see if the numbers generally looked OK (the trend issue), and then into simulated test marketing (STM) with volumetric financial scenarios. The STMs sought consumers' reactions to the concept and used sales waves of actual product so that they could get consumers' reactions to the taste and measure reuse. At this point, if consumers liked it, they were ready to reconfirm the company's ability to produce and market such a product.

Next came the marketing and technical development phases. Marketing tasks included branding. Nabisco wanted a direct, memorable name that communicated something positive about the product. In this case, the apostrophe in SnackWell's communicated a homemade sound—like grandma's. Television commercials were developed for social settings where the key points were stressed—here were cookies that had no fat (or very low fat) but tasted great and were "better for you." The settings were also full of fun. Later a different campaign was built around the shortage of product (with factory people running to hide from customers), showing how what happens *after* launch can change plans. In this case, a problem became a sales booster.

Next came a major public relations effort: press kit, recipe suggestions, a nutrition booklet and other items. Then Sunday coupons, inserts, cash register coupons, samples, and other material.

In the meantime the development work was under way on a cross-functional basis, with teams representing all of the key player groups. They tested various technologies, checked production sites, and insisted on cost feasibility.

The commercialization phase (which followed evaluation and technical feasibilities) called for several things. First, advertising and packaging graphics were developed (the green package color associated with health), product formula was settled on, final product specifications were written, an acceptance run was made in production, cost feasibility was checked again, and finally they were ready for the implementation phase. Implementation involved actual production, shipment of samples to the sales force, shipment of product to the trade, and running of commercials.

Senior management was involved early in this project, as soon as the product concept was shaped, and again at select points down the line. At Nabisco they tried hard to get top management's contributions early, not near the end when most of the plan has been implemented.

The presenters insisted that there was no one thing that made them successful, but three keys: a gap, an on-trend product to fill that gap, and a technical and marketing development process that provided flawless execution.

How does this process compare with what you read earlier in Chapter 2? In spite of their obvious success, would you question anything they did?

CHAPTER

3

Opportunity Identification and Selection

Strategic Planning for New Products

Setting

Chapter 2 discussed the process of creating and marketing new products, from opportunity identification to launch. Chapter 3 examines the first step in that process. Strategy is the foundation for new products management and serves as a loose harness for the integration of all the people and resources used in generating new products. We will look first at what a team needs in its strategy statement and then at where its inputs originate—that is, in corporate strategy, in platform strategy, and in influences from many other sources. We will then take a more complete look at team strategy, what we will call a product innovation charter—its drivers, its goals and objectives, and its "rules of the road."

Why Have Strategic Planning?

Let's look in on a team of people developing a small, portable computer printer. One member is thinking of using a new battery-based technology, while another is concentrating on potential customers who happen to work in environments where wall plugs are available! Marketing research people plan to pretest the product extensively, while manufacturing engineers assume time is critical and are designing finished production capability from the beginning! A vendor picked to supply the tractor mechanism has to check with the team leader almost every day because the team has not decided exactly what functions the printer will serve or who will be the target user! In addition, the team is being guided by requests from the sales department, which is currently calling on smaller firms when, in fact, the biggest potential is thought to lie in large firms and governments! This team has not developed strategy.

Team guidance, just as corporate or strategic business units (SBUs) guidance, comes partly in the form of strategy. Its purpose is *to focus and integrate team effort and to permit delegation.* Bausch & Lomb almost lost its market position when its managers concentrated for too long on improving old products and thus almost missed new products like extended-wear contact lenses. Forced to review their strategy, they found many more opportunities and went on to capitalize on them (e.g., disposable contact lenses).

But note: not all product innovation is done by teams. Much innovation is done by very small firms, and larger competitors envy small company managers their focus, their ease of communication and cooperation, and their clear dependence on the strengths necessary for the firm's success. Small firms are working units that larger firms imitate using teams.

What Form Does a New Product Team's Strategy Take?

The group of people who lead the development of a new product function as *a company within a company.* They may be loosely tied together in a committee, or they may be fully dedicated (full-time) managers sent off somewhere in a skunkworks, to address a difficult assignment. Regardless of the precise form, the group represents all of the necessary functions. They are led by a group leader, a team manager, or a project manager. For these people, a new products strategy does several things. It charts the group's direction—where it must go and where it must *not* go. It also tells the group its goals and objectives and provides some rules of the road.

For this, we will use the name **product innovation charter (PIC)** because it is for products, not processes and other activities; it is for innovation; and it is a charter (defined as a document that gives the conditions under which an organization will operate). It allows delegation, permits financing, and calls for personnel assignments, all within an agreed upon scope of activity. For new product teams plowing off into unknown waters, such a charter is invaluable.[1]

An example of one PIC (written for a firm in the computer business) is shown Figure 3–1. Before we look further at PIC specifics, let's look at the various sources of information that help managers make strategic decisions: upper levels of management and a mix of other sources.

---

[1]New product strategy has been receiving empirical support, though firms vary in specific format. See Robert G. Cooper and Elko J. Kleinschmidt, "Winning Businesses in Product Development: The Critical Success Factors," *Research Technology Management,* July-August, 1996, pp. 18–29. An example at Kodak is given in Diana Laitner, "Deep Needs and the Fuzzy Front End," *Visions,* July 1997, pp. 6–9. In fact, some firms claim they have no strategy and then go on to describe methods of project management that are clearly strategic. See Albert L. Page, "Product Strategy for Product Development," *Visions,* July 1997, pp. 15–16.

FIGURE 3–1

Contents of a product innovation charter, and its application to a firm in the computer industry

Product Innovation Charter

Background: Key ideas from the situation analysis; special forces such as managerial dicta; reasons for preparing a new PIC at this time.

Focus: At least one clear technology dimension and one clear market dimension. They match and have good potential.

Goals-Objectives: What the project will accomplish, either short-term as objectives or longer term as goals. Evaluation measurements.

Guidelines: Any "rules of the road," requirements imposed by the situation or by upper management. Innovativeness, order of market entry, time/quality/cost, miscellaneous.

A sample PIC for an intangible, in the business-to-business world, written from inquiry. It combines the background in with the market portion of the focus.

Focus	A major growth opportunity for a new field service is the smaller office that over the past three years has bought one of the new computer systems designed for such offices. Because they are found in every conceivable location and because they purchase computer equipment with the intention that it last a long time, they offer a unique service problem. This opportunity will be addressed using (1) our systems analysis skills and (2) our field service capabilities.
Goals-Objectives	The goals of this activity are (1) to overcome all reasonable objections about service levels by this group and (2) to increase our net operating revenues from the sale of these new services by at least $18 million per year.
Guidelines	These goals will be achieved by creating unique service approaches that are based on current field service resources, hopefully protected from quick competitive emulation, without extensive development expenditures either inside the firm or outside, and with an absolute minimum of development time.

Some Inputs Come from Corporate Strategy

Corporate leaders make many strategy statements. Figure 3–2, a list of such statements, demonstrates how important they would be to a new products team. Top-level statements like these guide a whole firm and are parts of what are sometimes called **mission statements.** Back in the 1980s when Kellogg's president kept insisting that his firm was in the cereal business and only in the cereal business, every new products team had to put such a restriction into any team mission statement they wrote.[2]

Figure 3–3 gives a picture of the flow from top corporate strategic thinking down to where a PIC can be written. Note that there are at least three levels of strategy—the corporate level, a platform level, and a new product project level (where the charters are). They differ only in the breadth of their application, since they all concern focus, goals, and activities.

Corporate strategies apply to platforms and also directly to projects that are not a part of platforms (note the heavy line going directly from corporate level to a PIC); platform strategies apply to those projects created under them (some so directly that they in effect bypass the thinking of the

[2]Some CEOs use corporate strategies more aggressively than do others, as told in Rita Koselka, "It's My Favorite Statistic," *Forbes,* September 12, 1994, pp. 162–76.

FIGURE 3–2

Corporate strengths

These are examples of actual corporate strengths that managements have asked be used to differentiate the firm's new products. Many others are discussed in this chapter. These terms can be used to complete the following sentence: *New products in this firm will:*

Technologies

Herman Miller: Utilize our fine furniture designers
Braun: Utilize innovative design in every product
Otis Elevator: Build in new levels of service as key benefit
Coca Cola: Gain value by being bottled in our bottling system
White Consolidated: Be made on our assembly lines

Markets

Gerber: Be for babies and only babies
Nike: Be for all sports and not just shoes
IBM: Be for all people in computers, not just techie types
Budd: Be specially created to meet the needs of Ford engineers

Guidelines

Rubbermaid: Proliferate our lines
Lexus: Offer genuine value
Polaroid: Be almost impossible to create
Cooper: Never be first to market
Ford Tractor: Not upset the regulators
Bausch & Lomb: Use only internal R&D
Ty Warner: Be offered to the market hard-to-get (Beanie Babies)
Colgate: Not threaten P&G
Kodak: Have high value to us and to the customer
Toro: Solve outdoor environmental problems
Sealed Air: Offer more protection with less material
Argo: Copy Deere, at lower price

project team.) Thus, a new products team receives some strategies from corporate, some from platforms and other parts of the firm, and develops some itself.

At the team level, any PIC would also have to contain corporate mandates. In Figure 3–3 an example is the top management's demand that all operations put *value* into their planning. (Any group wanting to form a unit to develop new products that were original Parisian designs would have to ask for an exception.)

And at the team level, any PIC would also have to meet the demands of intermediate strategy from what we call **platforms.** Note, in the example, that the team on Project 2 had to develop products that were innovative, while the Project 4 team had to develop evening gowns that were durable.

Within those four PIC boxes the white space is for the thinking of the team, additional focus, goal, or guideline items they want for their particular project—in this case, perhaps, a requirement that new clothing would use the unique color technologies in a recent acquisition or a requirement that the output be a line of clothing designed specifically for sale through the Ital website.

Platforms require some explanation. There are several types, all of them for situations where several projects are close together and share some strategic needs. In the automobile business, Chrysler has its LH **car platform,** from which the Concorde and Intrepid models came. (Though long used in the auto industry, the term platform gained widespread usage shortly after Chrysler's success with the LH.) A platform of interest to sneaker wearers is Nike's focus on ground/melted sneaker soles—after several years trying to find product/

FIGURE 3–3
The flow that produces PICs—special emphasis on role of corporate and platforms

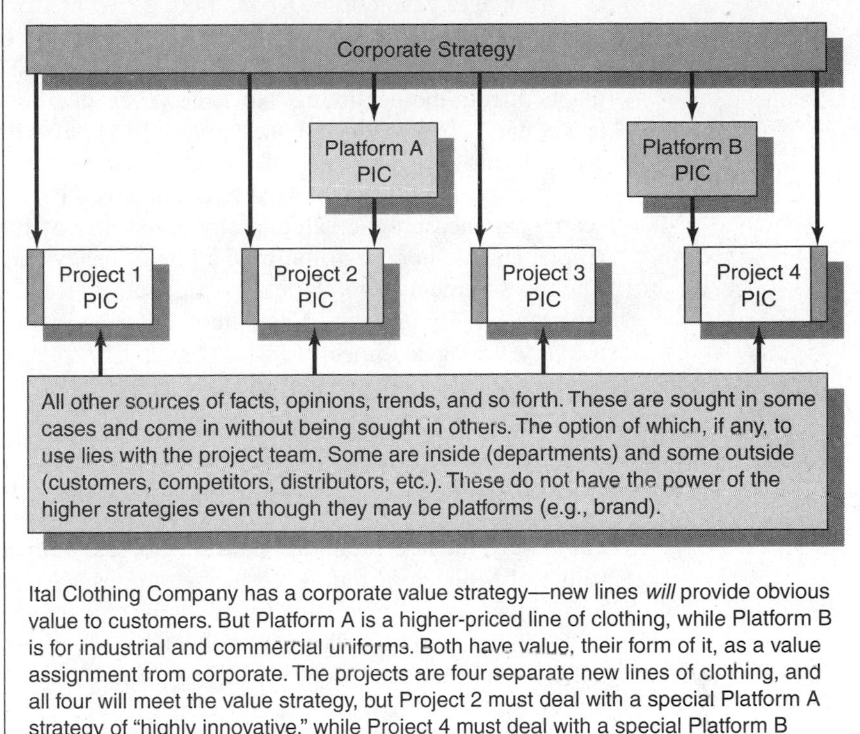

Ital Clothing Company has a corporate value strategy—new lines *will* provide obvious value to customers. But Platform A is a higher-priced line of clothing, while Platform B is for industrial and commercial uniforms. Both have value, their form of it, as a value assignment from corporate. The projects are four separate new lines of clothing, and all four will meet the value strategy, but Project 2 must deal with a special Platform A strategy of "highly innovative," while Project 4 must deal with a special Platform B strategy of "attractive styling but durable."

markets (dog beds, medicine balls) they have found success in basketball courts, and are cutting their annual $300,000 landfill costs for this waste material. These are all platforms where a particular technology was the common element.

Perhaps the most used platforms, however, are **brand platforms.** Brands may be billion dollar assets, so many brand platforms are personally driven by CEOs. For example, when Robert Siegel took over management of Stride Rite, he identified Top Siders and Keds as brands he would build the firm around. He changed the firm from a *product* maker to a *brand* maker, and said, "They want mules, we'll sell mules."[3] Brands can serve as launching pads for scores of products, all having in common the brand and any strategies applying to that brand. Chrysler recently saw value in its Plymouth nameplate, and rescued it as the platform for a stream of new products aimed

[3]Zina Moukheiber, "They Want Mules, We'll Sell Mules," *Forbes,* September 12, 1994, pp. 42–44.

at the younger generations. Kodak built a new platform when it marketed the Fun Saver, from which came what some call **derivatives:** Weekender, a flash format, Funsaver II, Portrait, Weekender II, and other versions, all perhaps planned from the beginning. Note, however, that any team using a platform brand must conform to the strategy of that brand; in the case of Waterford glass, all products had to be of top quality, with no exceptions.[4]

The *value* of an established brand is called its **brand equity.** Market research can measure the value of any brand for any particular market (for example, Duracell brand, if put onto a line of heavyweight industrial batteries). The measurements actually tell the amount of "free" promotion and integrity the brand equity brings to a new item that uses it. Estimates of this value can be very wrong at times, as when Time Life licensed its name to an entrepreneur who marketed a medical-video series.[5] A strong brand usually cannot carry a poor product concept.

Pierre Cardin once said, "I have the most important name in the world. I give my name only to the best products."[6] He knew that brand-franchise strategy is not without its dangers. A bad product can damage a good name. Or conversely, the new product can be so successful it takes over the main brand (think of Miller Lite and the formerly famous Miller High Life). We will return to the issue of managing brand equity in Chapter 17.

Another common platform is the **category,** which applies to either product type or customer. Most marketing effort today is conducted at category group levels—one overall plan for cake mixes, for do-it-yourself tools, or for finance courses in a college. For example, DuPont has special finishes platforms for doing business with the automobile industry, the marine industry, and the furniture industry, among others. Any strategic change in one of those areas influences all new products developed under that umbrella. Oddly, though Intel has its chips (e.g., Pentium) as *corporate* strategic platforms (remember "Intel inside"?), they are not *new product* platforms because each is a product, not a group of products. Customers such as Gateway will have the latest Intel chip as a platform for a line of products using it.

A firm may have a corporate strategy that is global, then a regional platform (South America), a country platform (Chile), and then new product projects within the Chilean operation.

---

[4]Guidance on using brand platforms for product innovation can be found in Dennis A. Pitts and Lea Prevel Katsanis, "Understanding Brand Equity for Successful Brand Extension," *Journal of Consumer Marketing,* Number 4, 1995, pp. 51–64. These authors warn of brand equity dilution (unsuccessful extensions) and equity wear-out (too many different extensions). For an excellent discussion of benefits and issues in platform planning and a detailed example in the car industry, see David Robertson and Karl Ulrich, "Planning for Product Platforms," *Sloan Management Review,* Summer 1998, pp. 19–32.

[5]Ellen Joan Pollock, "How One Media Deal Became Hazardous to Investors' Health," *The Wall Street Journal,* February 13, 1997, p. A1.

[6]Richard C. Morais, "What Is Perfume but Water and a Bit of Essence?" *Forbes,* May 2, 1988, pp. 90–95.

A **strategic business unit** is a platform (e.g., the industrial diamonds division of General Electric). So is a **trade channel** grouping (e.g., Kraft's institutional foods operation). And then there are variations within almost every firm. Marriott, for example, has, among other things, a very serious corporate-wide strategy of *customer satisfaction,* a platform strategy of *value* for its Courtyard, and a prestige platform for its *giant new resorts* (each one big enough to have its own new products team). A resort built and operated under the Courtyard platform would be different from a resort built and operated by the prestige platform, and different from a new, experimental resort being developed for application on the moon. (If there were one, it would certainly be so important it would be directly under corporate control, and not inhibited by restrictions common to any one of the platforms.)

In short, any new products team that sets out to develop its own product innovation charter for management's approval had better take into consideration all the baggage that comes from corporate and platform strategies. Most teams would hope to be as lucky as the teams at Calvin Klein Cosmetics, where the CEO has a rule there will be "no rules"—he thinks his approach permitted the first (and very successful) unisex scents to emerge.

New Product Strategy Inputs from Other Sources

Opportunity Identification

Many firms have persons working full time looking for new opportunities. They essentially audit the firm and any environment relevant to it.[7] Throughout the firm people in the course of doing their jobs discover new opportunities—a salesperson learns that a customer is moving into a new market, a scientist finds unexpected activity in a compound, a finance VP notes a fall in the prime rate, a director urges that we look more carefully at what the Environmental Protection Agency is doing. These findings tend to fall into four categories.

Underutilized Resource. It may be that the organization has not sufficiently exploited past technological breakthroughs. Perhaps R&D leadership decides its people have not built the ideal strategic alliances with particular customer groups.

New Resource. Managers in Division A have been encouraged to develop products that utilize the strong market position (or, say, telecommunications resources) of newly acquired Division B.

[7]Hopefully, managements find customers' and other stakeholders' advice useful in this work, but a Burlington Northern manager said, "We all have our fans out there, but just like football coaches, we don't consult the fans on our strategies." Daniel Machalaba, "New Paint Job Stokes Controversy Over a Warbonnet's True Colors," *The Wall Street Journal,* September 18, 1995, p. B1.

External Mandate. Regulators impose new restrictions on use of petroleum-based synthetics, and the CEO wants all divisions to seek new products that capitalize, actively, on these regulations.

Internal Mandate. New corporate leadership orders a companywide design program to clean up a hodgepodge of packages and brands. Toshiba said they wanted to be king of the MS-DOS laptop market, and thus automatically rejected all suggestions about developing a laptop for other operating systems.

Truly, there is no end to these opportunities, every one of which may reveal additional opportunities for new products. Unfortunately, each opportunity takes time and money to investigate, so we don't exploit nearly as many as we would like.

Noncorporate Strategic Planning

Although the major thrust of strategic planning comes from the top down (see discussion of corporate and platform strategies earlier), much of it also comes from the heads of the functions (**silos** or chimneys) in the firm—marketing, technical, manufacturing, and finance—and from the planning of suppliers, customers, and others. Such groups frequently have the power to affect new product work. For example, paper manufacturing is done on huge, expensive machines; such firms often have strategies with a statement: All new items, if paper-related, must be manufacturable on our current lines. Financial conditions may warrant restrictions such as "no new products that require more than $3,000,000 capital investments." Suppliers of materials (e.g., chemicals or metals) often require (usually smaller) firms to buy and use what they make. But the greatest functional inputs come from marketing, where ongoing planning utilizes a range of techniques designed to give sharper market focus and new positionings. For example, look at Figure 3–4. It shows a variation on the traditional **product-market matrix.** The cells show variations in *innovativeness risk* as a firm brings in new product types or technologies or markets products that require change in how people buy or use them. A simple flavor change (product improvement) would probably involve low or no risk, but substituting a computer line for face-to-face dealings in the field of medicine (**diversification** for a computer services firm) would involve dangerous risk to the producer of the service ("great" change on both technology and use mode). Marketing managements want to have balanced risk portfolios, yet want to take advantage of new technologies and new markets; their decisions are major inputs to new product strategy.

A second analytical device is the traditional **"dogs and cows" matrix,** where the various "pieces" of a business are plotted in a matrix with dimensions on current share of market and on market growth. Requests for new product work often take such form as:

FIGURE 3–4

Degree of innovativeness as a matter of strategic risk

Risk		Change in operations or marketing mode		
		None	*Some*	*Great*
Change in use/ user mode	*None*	None	Low	Medium
	Some	Low	Medium	High
	Great	Medium	High	Dangerous

Application: This matrix has gone by several names: Product/Market, Technology/Application, and Market-Newness/Firm-Newness. In all cases, the issue is the risk of innovativeness. Risk on the user side is just as much a concern to us as risk within the firm. Every new product can be positioned on this chart somewhere, and that position is important if it is accepted as a project. Selecting one section to be preferred over the others is a matter of strategy.

- We need continuing, modest improvements in Product X to lengthen the time it can be kept as a cash cow.
- We need immediate, major improvements in Product Y if we are to keep its position at the top of its rapidly growing market.

Miscellaneous Sources

In contrast to the corporate-platform downward pressure approach and the horizontal functional pressure approach, some inputs can start at the lower level of activity and influence upwards, as when a new product is so successful it drives corporate strategy to change. For example, an ethical pharmaceutical firm once "unintentionally" marketed a very successful new proprietary food product, with the result that a new division was created (to isolate the consumer advertising activity from the rest of the firm), and new strategies were created to optimize its opportunity.

Sometimes, a slow and gradual restructuring of business practice can influence new product strategies almost without anyone realizing it. For example, the 1980s and 1990s have seen a gradual movement in service products to add **tangibility** and for tangible products (goods) to add (or emphasize) services. McDonald's features its arches, Prudential has long had its rock, and Federal Express gains tangibility from its employees and the computers they hold in their hands.[8]

A Closer Look at the PIC

Strategy statements take almost as many forms as there are firms preparing them, but they tend to build around the structure given in Figure 3–1. They can be made for an *entire firm* (if very small or very narrowly conceived), a *standing platform* of activity within a larger firm (e.g., Black & Decker brand of tools), or a *specific project* (e.g., Hewlett-Packard's 6L laser printer). A PIC generally speaks to an opportunity (the focus), not to the specific product or products the group is yet to create. Oscar Mayer embarked on the development of the "big wiener" only to find later they needed Big & Juicy in six different flavors for various U.S. regions. Of course, when products are very complex (the Saturn automobile, an air express service for the Asian market, or a nation's new health plan), one product is all a team can handle.

The PIC should be in writing and given to all participants, but for various reasons it often is not. This is unfortunate because a secret strategy that exists only in the minds of a few will not do much for a team of 30 people.

Background Section of the PIC

This section answers the question: "Why did we develop this strategy, anyway?" To the extent necessary, it recaps the analysis behind it.

Focus, or Arena, Section of the PIC

In today's competitive marketplaces, it takes focus to unlock the power of innovation. Just as a laser can take a harmless light and convert it into a deadly ray, so can a commitment to, say, the delivered-pizza business or to the web site construction process convert limited resources into a strong competitive thrust. As one developer said, "We like to play on fields that tilt in our direction." This is why it is so critical for the PIC's focus to be specified early on, and for firms to be thinking about the playing field, or arena, in which its people will operate.

In recent years we have heard a great deal about **core competencies.** They are an excellent place to start the search for charter arena definitions.

[8]Allan C. Reddy, Bruce D. Buskirk, and Ajit Kaicker, "Tangibilizing the Intangibles: Some Strategies for Services Marketing," *Journal of Services Marketing,* Number 3, 1993, pp. 13–17.

Marketers narrow their focus by targeting and segmentation. However, technical people, all too often fenced in by time, limited facilities, and money, don't relish yet another focus mechanism.

But the idea of an arena is growing—managed, of course, in a way that is constructive, not harmful. Focus is achieved almost entirely by use of four types of strengths or leverage capabilities: *technology* (AT&T's satellite technology or Kimberly Clark's paper processing technology), *product experience* (Strohs chose to focus on the "beer business"), *customer franchise* (Stanley Tool's hold on the woodworker), and *end-use experience* (Chase Manhattan's international division). We used to have lots of these "one-legged" strategies, but today competition makes them risky. Edwin Land relied totally on the polarization technology for many years, until he tripped on something his salespeople could not sell—Polavision, instant movies.[9]

Similarly, market-oriented firms (especially consumer packaged goods firms in food, drug, and toiletry categories) used to survey consumers, find they wanted green widgets rather than yellow ones, and tell the lab people to create them. This also worked pretty well, as long as there were significant unmet needs and competitors who reacted slowly.

Today, either approach is too big a gamble. One recent report told how two PC makers differed on drivers. One, Fujitsu, bet on technology and lost, while NEC bet on customer needs, and won.[10] Gambles like this are too expensive today; thus consumer giants Frito-Lay and P&G have major laboratory research facilities, and technology-driven Hewlett-Packard has announced that it wants a strong market commitment behind every new product program. Whereas we used to talk about a **technology-driven** firm or a **market-driven** firm, we now talk about **dual-driven** firms. The balanced strategy of dual drive is clearly the winner (see Figure 3–5).

Technology Drivers. The most common technological strengths are in the *laboratories.* Corning used to say it would develop those products—and only those products—that exploited the firm's fabulous glass technology. Today's global competition makes it tougher for Corning (and others) to hold a superior position in a technology defined so broadly.

Many times, a firm finds it has a valuable *non*laboratory technology. Avon has an efficient small-order-handling technology. Other operations technologies include soft-drink distributed bottling systems and White Consolidated's efficient appliance production lines. Deloitte & Touche

---

[9]For an interesting story about what can happen to product innovation strategies built solely on technology, see Lawrence Ingrassia, "How Polaroid Went from Highest Flier to Takeover Target," *The Wall Street Journal,* August 12, 1988, p. 1.

[10]David T. Menthé, Ryoko Toyama, and Junichiro Miyabe, "Product Development Strategy and Organizational Learning, *Journal of Product Innovation Management,* September 1997, pp. 323–36.

FIGURE 3–5
Power/potential dual-drive matrix

Power Matrix

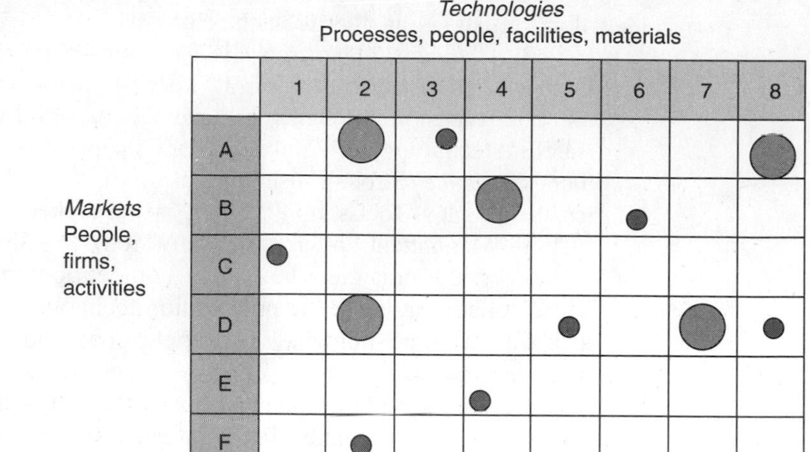

Potential Matrix

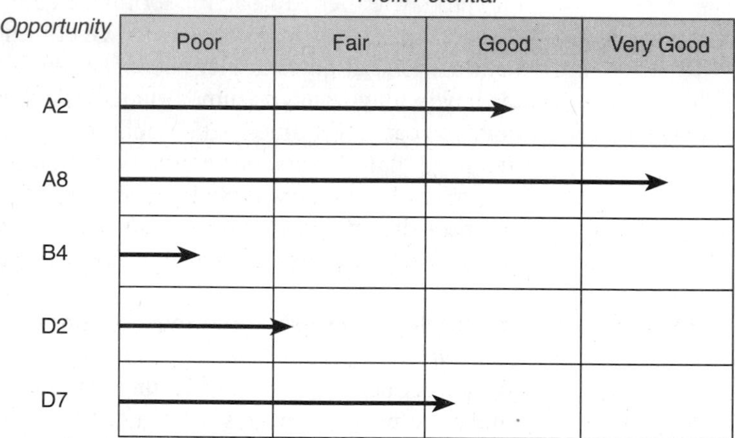

Explanation: The bubble chart at top displays 5 key strength fits. Each one, e.g., A2 is then scored for profit potential. Opportunity A8 would seem to be the best of the bunch.

consulting division built new services around its capabilities of analysis and interpretation of financial information.

Even harder to see are the technologies in marketing. For example, some packaged goods firms view their product management departments as technologies. (If their product manager system is especially good, they seek market opportunities where such an organization is appropriate.) Other examples include physical distribution systems, customer technical service, or creative advertising departments.

A rapidly growing Korean manufacturer said, "I want to be the Toyota of furniture." whatever the material or wherever the global location.[11]

Market Drivers. The other half of the dual-drive strategy comes from two market sources: *customer group* and *end-use.* Many of the best new product ideas are based on customer problems, which serve as the heart of the concept generation process described in Chapter 4.

The Hoover Company once had a strategy of developing new vacuums for "people who already had one"—the two-vacuum home concept. (Today they may be working on the five-vacuum home!) Other firms have relied on demographic dimensions for focus, for example, Toro's "young couples," and Olivetti's "banks and law offices." As examples of more abstract dimensions, Hallmark concentrates on "people who care enough," and Helena Rubenstein once targeted "real women." Welch-Allen, maker of high-tech medical devices that are used in doctors' offices and hospitals, says, not jokingly, if you have a cavity we want to see it, and if you don't have a cavity but need one we will make it. The latter part of that strategic focus brought about their device for aiding in noninvasive gall bladder removal.

Firms producing services find customer-focus comfortable, since many of their operations involve the customer as an actual **coproducer** of the service. The logic of this arrangement has led many service firms, in all industries, to involve the customer as an integrated partner in the new product development process.

Occasionally, a firm can concentrate on one single customer; for example, an auto-parts firm may build new items for Ford or General Motors. But when Cullinet focused successfully on its customer base and made lots of money, IBM focused on its *non*customers and ended up blindsiding Cullinet with a new language (SQL). A variation on the single-customer focus is **mass customization**—where we offer all customers a product of their individual choice. Marriott's Courtyard has made this successful in the motel business, but a recent example (that did not fly) was *Dow Jones' Personal Journal.* The customer selected favorite columns, news topics, the stocks and mutual funds to follow, and so forth, and the personal paper was

[11]Wee Sang-sik, as quoted in an article by that name in *Forbes,* May 16, 1988, p. 92.

delivered *continuously* via computer.[12] We will see more of mass customization in Chapter 17.

The second way of focusing on the market side is on a particular *end-use,* such as sports, or skiing. General Instrument Corporation's new products program concentrated exclusively on wagering. User and end-use focus may sound alike, but they are not. For example, focusing on skiers or skiing would both provide new equipment, but skiing would also lead to new lodges, new slopes, new travel packages, and services for lodge owners (who may not even be skiers). Industrial firms also make great use of end-use. You may wonder how we know when to use which focus? The answer lies in the opportunity analysis that took place earlier—you studied markets, people in them, and activities they engage in. You selected a given opportunity because you thought its needs fit the firm's capabilities.

A variation on market drivers is the *distributor*—when a producer develops new products to meet the needs of, or capitalize on the franchise of, resellers. Hallmark's line of small gift items was originally developed to help their card shop franchisees make more money. Anheuser-Busch's Eagle snacks was developed to "capture distributor share of mind" (read, attention and interest).[13]

Combinations: Dual-Drive. Putting one technical driver together with a market driver yields a clear and precise arena focus. University Microfilms International (UMI) used the *technology of microfilming* and the *market activity of education* as their original mainstay, but later added *photocopiers* for schools and microfilm readers for *law offices.*

Penn Racquet Sports switched species of markets, putting their *tennis ball technology* to work making a line of ball toys for *dogs.*[14] Toro also has been having success recently with a series of dual drives, one of which is *global-satellite technology* and *golf course superintendents.*[15]

The Signode Corporation set up a series of seven new product venture operations and asked each group to select one company technology and one market opportunity that matched that company strength. The first team chose *plastics extrusion* (from Signode's primary business of strapping materials) and *food manufacturing.* This team's first new products were plastic trays for packaged foods headed into microwave ovens.

---

[12]For more on mass customization, see B. Joseph Pine II, Don Peppers, and Martha Rogers, "Do You Want To Keep Your Customers Forever?," *Harvard Business Review,* March–April 1995, pp. 103–14.

[13]Some feel distribution is in a state of disintermediation—splitting apart. They argue that scores of opportunities as market drivers now exist, for example, kiosk shopping. See Edith Weiner and Arnold Brown, "The New Marketplace," *The Futurist,* May-June 1995, pp. 12–16.

[14]Dennis Berman, "Now, Tennis Balls Are Chasing the Dogs," *Business Week,* July 13, 1998, p. 138.

[15]Richard Gibson, "Toro Charges into Greener Fields with New Products," *The Wall Street Journal,* June 22, 1997, p. B4. This article gives many details on a very sophisticated use of the dual-drive system of defining an arena.

Gap has been extremely successful with a dual drive of European styles and American women. Both drives are a bit general, but to date they have produced the nation's most successful apparel retailer.

Goals and Objectives Section of the PIC

Anyone working on product innovation ought to know the purpose because work can change in so many ways if the purpose changes. The PIC uses the standard definition that **goals** are longer-range, general directions of movement, whereas **objectives** are short-term, specific measures of accomplishment. Thus, a PIC may aim for market dominance (as a goal) and 25 percent market share the first year (as an objective).

Both goals and objectives are of three types: (1) *profit,* stated in one or more of the many ways profit can be stated; (2) *growth,* usually controlled, though occasionally a charter is used defensively to help the firm hold or retard a declining trend; and (3) *market status,* usually increased market share. Many top managements insist that new product teams entering new markets plan to dominate them. But the American Regitel Corporation, for example, marketers of point-of-sale machines, aimed to be number three in its markets, even though the parent firm wanted to be number one as a general policy. There has been much criticism of market share as a new product goal, but a recent analysis of available data shows it is still a popular objective.[16]

There are also miscellaneous goals that have been used. They are not trivial to the firms using them. For example, Kimberly-Clark may or may not achieve its goal of getting Kleenex into every room in the home. A computer components firm that tried to "avoid acquisition," didn't. And Hewlett-Packard may or may not turn its gear into the "home digital darkroom" of the future.[17]

Special Guidelines Section of the PIC

To this point, we have filled out three sections of the PIC form. We know the team's arena or focus, and we know what they are supposed to accomplish there. But research shows that almost every new product strategy has a fourth section—some guidelines or "rules of the road." They may be managerially imposed or consensus thinking of team members, and they are certainly strategic. We have no research that shows what such guidelines *should* be, but we do have lots of research showing what firms put into this section, right or wrong.

---

[16]Mark J. Chussil, "Does Market Share Really Matter?" *Planning Review,* September-October 1991, pp. 31–37. For more on goals and objectives used by business, see Abbie Griffin and Albert L. Page, "PDMA Success Measurements Project-Recommended Measures for Product Development Success and Failure," *Journal of Product Innovation Management,* November 1996, pp. 169–95.

[17]"HP Pictures the Future," *Business Week,* July 7, 1997, pp. 100–109.

Degree of Innovativeness. How **innovative** does a management want a particular group to be? The options range from first-to-market (whether a nylon or a Frisbee) to strict imitation.

First-to-market is a risky strategy. It goes by several other names, including pioneering. There are three ways to get it, the first of which is by *state-of-the art breakthrough.* Pharmaceutical firms use that route most of the time. Other products that came from such programs include bubble memory, the pacemaker, compact discs, and television. But most first-to-market products do not extend the state of the art. They tweak technology in a new way, sometimes called **leveraged creativity,** and constitute the most common first-to-market category. The third way to be first is via **applications engineering,** where the technology may not be changed at all, but the use is totally new. Loctite, for example, has done this scores of times by using glue to replace metal fasteners in electronics and automotive products.

Far more common than pioneering is the strategy of developing an **adaptive product.** Being adaptive means taking one's own or a competitive product and improving it in some way. The improvement may be technical (a CD drive for the PC) or nontechnical (the 17-inch PC screen). It may be useful or trivial. Adaptation is especially popular where the firm needs cash, fast.

Some adapters seek almost any change that can be used in advertising. Others follow what is called "second but best"; the improvement is major, and the follower intends to take over the market, if possible. Maytag followed this strategy for many years prior to Leonard Hadley's leadership in 1998. Harris Corporation, on the other hand, entered markets where others had pioneered and used its great technical know-how to create a niche with a slightly improved product. The firm's chairman said Harris tried to be strong in technology and to enter a product in a timely manner.

Adaptation, alone, is risky. The pioneer often obtains a permanent advantage; if other things are equal, the first product in a new market gains an average market share of around 30 percent. But the second firm can take over the market and win the category if its adaptation is clearly superior.[18] There is a tendency for a firm to discover a first-to-market, and then follow with increasingly less innovative adaptive extensions, even straight imitations to hold against competitors.

Michael Porter helped clarify the type of adaptation needed in successful competitive strategy when he listed the three key criteria: (1) The firm must be capable of delivering the adaptation, (2) it must be difficult for a competitor to copy, and (3) it must be one for which the customer is willing to pay a sufficient premium in the price.[19]

---

[18]Peter N. Golder and Gerard J. Tellis, "Pioneering Advantage: Marketing Logic or Marketing Legend," *Journal of Marketing Research,* May, 1993, pp. 158–70. Information on 28 later entrants who overtook pioneers can be found in Steven P. Schnaars, *Managing Imitation Strategies* (New York: The Free Press, 1994).

[19]As interpreted by Byron Sharp in "Competitive Marketing Strategy: Porter Revisited," *Marketing Intelligence and Planning,* No. 1, 1991, pp. 4–30.

The third level of innovativeness is **imitation,** or **emulation.** In a now classic event late in 1979, *Advertising Age* quoted S. W. Lapham, the new products director of Sterling Drug's subsidiary Lehn & Fink, saying "Replicate, don't innovate." Imitation was a surefire way to succeed.[20] Lapham cited several products that had been successfully copied—Jell-O Pudding followed My-T-Fine; Country Time lemonade mix followed Wyler's; and Stayfree feminine napkins followed Kotex. After recommending that any imitator be careful to sufficiently research the right entry to copy, Lapham described how his firm copied Airwick's Carpet Fresh. Love My Carpet was "developed" and marketed in less than six months. He said, "Trying to innovate as the only way to success is one of the greatest myths of new products ever invented. I have to believe it was created by a marketing research company." A few weeks later, another *Advertising Age* article announced that Lehn & Fink was being sued by Airwick for infringing on the Carpet Fresh patents.[21] Imitation has its risks, too!

Cooper Tire & Rubber (on tires) and White Consolidated (on white appliances) are well-known for deliberately waiting to see winners emerge from among the pioneers and early adaptors.

Timing. This category of guidelines variation has four options: first, quick second, slower, and late. The decision to be *first* is pioneering, just discussed. A *quick second* tries to capture a good second-share position, perhaps making no significant improvement, or just enough to promote. The strategy is very demanding, because such a firm has to make the decision to enter the market *before the innovator is successful or has even come to market.* This turns the quick second into a forecaster—how successful will the innovator be? Waiting risks letting the second spot go to aggressive competitors. Striving for a *slower* entry is safer in the sense that a firm knows the outcome of the pioneer's efforts and has time to make a more meaningful adaptation. But the good market opportunities already may be taken by quick seconds. The last timing alternative, *late* entry, is usually a price entry keyed to manufacturing skills.

Miscellaneous Guidelines. Innumerable specialized guidelines can be found in product innovation charters. Some are surprising. Hewlett-Packard was trying to decide what to do with its new digital photography for use in printers and scanners. But it took hard selling for the technical people to persuade HP's printer division it should try to compete with Kodak. An unwritten guideline had banned such competition for many years.[22]

Some firms recognize weaknesses. For example, a large mining machinery firm told its product innovators to come up with products that *did not* require strong marketing; the firm didn't have it and didn't want to invest in

[20]"Different Strokes," *Advertising Age,* December 17, 1979, p. 4.

[21]"Lehn & Fink Philosophy Draws Suit by Airwick," *Advertising Age,* February 11, 1980, p. 71.

[22]Eric Nee, "What Have You Invented for Me Lately?" *Forbes,* July 28, 1997, pp. 76–82.

getting it. A pharmaceutical firm said, "It must be patentable." A small computer firm said, "All new products must be parts of systems," while an even smaller computer firm said, "Nothing that must be part of a system"! A food firm said, "Don't put anything in a can that Frito-Lay can put in a bag." And so on.

Another executive with an inviolable guideline was Rupert Murdoch who said (of his Twentieth Century Fox), "We're not making huge, expensive bets on movies," and for 1993 budgeted only one film over $30 million.[23]

Another miscellaneous guideline is **product integrity,** meaning that all aspects of the product are internally consistent. An example: Honda was very successful using the new four-wheel steering system because it put the innovation into a two-door coupe with a sporty image, whereas Mazda failed when putting it into a five-door hatchback that was positioned for safety and durability.

A Word on How to Prepare a Product Innovation Charter

The process for developing a PIC lies in its contents. *First,* we are always looking for opportunities, inside or outside the firm. Each strategy can be traced to a strength of the company involved. No one firm can be strong in everything. *Second,* we have to evaluate, rate, and rank the opportunities. *Third,* we simply begin filling out the PIC form—focus, goals, and guidelines. Usually there is no shortage of suggestions for all of the sections, as with any marketing situation analysis.

Potentially fruitful options in technologies or market places may seem hard to find, but we are surrounded by them. Figure 3–6 shows a partial list. Every one has been the basis for a team's new product assignment, at least once.

The second step, evaluating and ranking the opportunities is extremely difficult. In fact, one of the most valuable creative skills in product innovation is the ability to look at a building, an operation, a person, or a department, and visualize how it could be used in a new way. This skill can be developed—and should be practiced. Not only is there no ready quantitative tool for measuring, say, the strength of the pharmaceutical chemistry department of a small drug manufacturer, there is also politics, because people are involved. And, unfortunately, it is much easier to see the potential in some technology or market *after the fact.* Take Amazon.com, for example. Thousands of people have said that the idea of selling books on the Internet was an obvious one, but where were they when Amazon.com stock was selling for $10 a share?

Many firms use one key question to get them through these disputes. DuPont asks, will our technology be a *necessity* in the application being

---

[23]Nancy J. Perry, "The Future Is Glued to the Tube," *Fortune,* September 21, 1992, pp. 99–100.

FIGURE 3–6
Market and technology opportunities

Market Opportunities	*Technology Opportunities*
User (category)	Product type
User (for our product)	Specific product
Customer (buyer)	Primary packaging
Influencer	Secondary packaging
Potential user	Design process
Nonuser	Production process
Demographic set	Distribution process
Psychographic set	Packaging process
Geographic set	Patent
Retailer	Science
Wholesaler	Material
Agent	Individual
Use	Management system
Application	Information system
Activity	Analytical skill
Franchise	Expert system
Location	Project control
Competitor	Quality attainment
Regulator	Project design

discussed? Dow asks, can we *own* that market? Other firms ensure the presence of someone high enough in the firm to help the technology weather annual budget revisions.[24] A form that sometimes helps is given in Figure 3–7. Most of these evaluations are based directly on intense market research input, and the data files prepared are useful to the new products team throughout the project.

This chapter ends with the story of the marketing of Microsoft's Windows 95, an adaptive improvement on Windows 3.1. The case assignment involves writing out what the PIC *might have been for that product.* The exercise will demonstrate some of the difficulties we have been talking about, because you will have to replicate Microsoft's knowledge and process.

Issues That Arise in the Process of Creating Charters

Are there *standard* PICs to choose from? No, there are not. The PIC should reflect the situation for which it is written. But there are useful concepts to employ; for example, one set is: Prospectors (new business), Analyzers (new

[24]These and other special views are discussed in W. David Gibson, "A Maze for Management: Choosing the Right Technology," *Chemical Week,* May 7, 1986, pp. 74–78. A variation on the evaluation of technologies is to evaluate the technologists (place your bets on people and technical teams). For this, see Nicholas Kandel, Jean-Pierre Remy, Christian Stein, and Thomas Durand, "Who's Who in Technology: Identifying Technological Competence Within the Firm," *R&D Management,* July 1991, pp. 215–28.

Figure 3–7

Evaluation forms for market and technology opportunities

Factors for Judging a Market Opportunity	*Score 1–5 Points*		*Factors for Judging a Technology Opportunity*
How large is the demand in this area? Is it, for us, a major source of new business or a minor one?	______	______	How unique is this technology? Are we the only ones who have it?
What is the current degree of felt need or unrest in this area? Do potential customers agree?	______	______	What is the value of things it does or permits us to do?
How well will our new product solve the customer's problem?	______	______	In what stage of the technology life cycle is this technology? (The earlier the better.)
How unique, relative to competition, will our product be?	______	______	How controllable is it? Do we have it tied up with a patent, with licensing, as a trade secret?
How easy will it be for us to explain and demonstrate our new products?	______	______	Can we extend the technology by further work?
What is the life-cycle stage of the marketplace activity involved with this opportunity?	______	______	Is it going to be inexpensive for us to use, or will it take major investments?
Is there a ready technology that would match this opportunity?	______	______	Is it going to take a long time to use?
Is this market free of any entrenched competitors?	______	______	Will it take us into new, risky ball games?
Do we have a trade channel that fits this opportunity?	______	______	Are products of this technology marketable by us alone?
Is this opportunity easy for us to study?	______	______	Are products of this technology manufacturable by us alone?
Will this market opportunity stir controversy within the firm?	______	______	Will this technology receive the support of company people who must support it?
Total Score	______	______	(Over 35 in each column = Good.)

ways of doing current business), Defenders (moving early to protect a business), and Reactors (move after competitors do). But these concepts are more aids to situation analysis than replacements for it.[25]

Now that a new products manager has written a PIC, *is that it?* Hardly. Upper managements must approve them. Moreover, projects must fit together as a product innovation portfolio, in the usual financial sense. When Nabisco won an Outstanding Corporate Innovator Award from the Product Development & Management Association in 1993, the company said good

[25]R. E. Miles and C. C. Snow, *Organizational Strategy, Structure and Process* (New York: McGraw Hill, 1978). Comments on this and similar analytical devices can be found in Michael H. Morris and Leyland F. Pitt, "The Contemporary Use of Strategy, Strategic Planning, and Planning Tools By Marketers: A Cross-National Comparison," *European Journal of Marketing,* 1993 No. 9, pp. 36–57.

management execution made their strategies successful (see the Chapter 2 case).

Are there differences in PIC creation when the firm has a *global perspective?* Only in amount, not kind. The more countries in which a firm operates, the more options and opportunities it has. Many product developers today assume new products are (or soon will be) headed for world markets, so they call them global products.[26]

How does the idea of *strategic window* come into this process? Being first or second (hit the window) has large rewards. Yet being too early has also cost many firms dearly, so a window's fleeting existence should not dominate common sense.

Where does **licensing** or **acquisition** fit in? Acquirable technologies or market strengths are certainly fair game for inclusion in strategies. In mid-1997 *Star Wars* creator George Lucas opened bids from toy makers for licenses on *Episode 1.* Some of them approached $1 billion.[27]

We haven't mentioned *fads,* yet millions of dollars are made this way. They seem to happen every day, and there are firms whose major strategy is capitalizing on fads. But it is risky, and action must be taken too fast to use most of the techniques in this book.

Do these new product strategic techniques apply to *nonprofit organizations?* Indeed. A study of the best-run nonprofits contained comments about unified sense of direction, fewer high-risk projects when resources are limited, acquisition versus internal development, orienting to the customer, and building coalitions.[28]

Is strategic new product planning all good, or are there legitimate *criticisms* of the approach discussed in this chapter? A cartoon often shown around this field has a senior executive standing beside a person sitting at a drawing board. The executive says, "Panelli, we've completed our market analysis. Design something domestic and electrical."[29] This of course would be a reasonable (though very broad) dual-drive focus, but technical people often object. They sometimes ask whether Thomas Edison could have worked for GE, the firm he founded. The answer is to have planned—as well as unplanned—innovation. Many firms now have programs specifically designed to aid the bootlegger or moonlighter. One 3M scientist received an Oscar from the Hollywood film industry for his method of increasing the reflectiveness of movie screens, but he had to develop the process at night and on weekends because his (strategically driven) superior had to deny him time for it.[30]

---

[26]In the late 1980s, a Gillette scent expert was told to find his first "intentionally global" fragrance. Barbara Carton, "Thank Carl Klumpp for the Swell Smell of Right Guard," *The Wall Street Journal,* May 11, 1995, p. A1.

[27]Lisa Bannon and Joseph Pereira, "Toy Makers Offer the Moon for New 'Star Wars' Licenses," *The Wall Street Journal,* August 19, 1997, p. B1.

[28]John A. Byrne, "Profiting from the Non-Profits," *Business Week,* March 26, 1990, pp. 66–78.

[29]This cartoon is by "Nelson," but its origin is undocumented.

[30]The fabulously successful new product system used at 3M has been described many times, but a good presentation is in "Masters of Innovation," *Business Week,* April 10, 1989, pp. 58–63.

Summary

Chapter 3 has dealt with the most important and difficult step in the entire new products process—developing a sound strategy to guide the subset of people and resources charged with getting new products. Strategy turns such a group into a miniature firm, a microcosm of the whole.

We first looked at what such strategic guidance might be—a format here called a product innovation charter. We then studied the opportunities and mandates that yield charter and how charters can vary. The chapter ended by looking at some important issues that often arise when discussing new product strategy.

We can now begin the study of concept generation—the subject of four chapters in Part II.

Applications

More questions from the interview with the president:

1. "I'm afraid I don't follow your reasoning very well when it comes to this matter of innovativeness—being a pioneer, an adapter, quick second, and so on. Seems you've always got to come up with something new, or it simply won't sell. I believe we agreed on that earlier when we discussed the concept that winners market unique, superior products. Further, if you've got something new, why in the world would you ever want to be less than first to market with it? You'll lose your uniqueness that way. Sounds like you've taken a simple practice and made it complex."
2. "On the other hand, I must admit to being rather 'antiproclamations' when it comes to strategy and policy. Some things are just as well left unstated—that gives a manager more leeway to change a position, without embarrassment, if it turns out wrong, and more opportunity to exploit situations that come up. No, I guess I really don't agree that new products strategy should be written down, and it certainly shouldn't be shown around where it might get to a competitor."
3. "Somewhere along the line, R&D gets the short end of the stick. I know about the arguments for strategy, but I really feel that R&D deserves a better shake than to simply be told to do this or that. Some of our top people are in R&D—our electronics division has a couple of the world's best fax technicians. If I were doing it, I think I would have R&D prepare the first draft of a PIC, at least their areas of a PIC, and then have other areas like manufacturing add to it. When all of the interior departments have their sights properly set, I would ask marketing to reconcile the PIC with the marketplace.

Otherwise, we'd have the tail wagging the dog when it comes to the new products function."

4. "I saw the other day where film makers (large as well as small) are finding profits in low-budget films. It seems they aim for narrow, but very reachable market segments (e.g., young kids), and they use standard film-making technologies but use only what they call "emerging" actors and directors (meaning "cheap now"). They try hard to capture the interests of their core target group, and they mean it when they say low-budget. I also read where several of them are trying to move out rapidly from the core when they have a winner—little kids, bigger kids, and so forth. They think this approach yields the best return on investment even though it causes them to miss out on the occasional block-buster. You may not even remember hearing of some of these low-budget specials, but they had names like *The Waterboy, There's Something About Mary, Rush Hour,* and *The Wedding Singer.* That last one focused on boys and men, but they added a love story line with Drew Barrymore that brought women in, too. Now, can you fit all that into what might be the PIC of these films? What are the negatives of this approach?"[31]

CASE: MICROSOFT WINDOWS 95[32]

On Thursday, August 24, 1995, the greatest marketing event ever (or so observers thought at the time) took place. Not in the United States, but around the world. Thousands of articles had been written about Windows 95, but on that day over 500 reporters descended on Redmond, Washington, to hear the world's richest man announce it, though over 2,000 beta test sites had been using it for up to two years. A PR extravaganza of the first order, the events of the day included perhaps a hundred million dollars of advertising, high balloons, the Empire State Building swathed by color spotlights, dancers and music groups from Broadway to New Zealand, and long lines of people waiting at 11:59 PM on the 23rd to get an early package—including many who didn't particularly need the product at that time but wanted to be in one of the truly all-time great hypes.

In the meantime, back at the ranch, industry observers were thinking along other lines. They saw the announcements, but they speculated on what lay behind them. Microsoft (and Gates) had done a lot of things the past few years, and word had leaked out about several more initiatives coming over the next couple years. Windows 95, almost certain to be a dominant new industry standard, was part of a huge wave of activity in the general area of computer-based communications. Internal data processing and spreadsheets were important on PCs, but industry profits were thought to ride on networking, communicating *between* PCs and *between* PCs and computers in other items such as printers and telephones.

---

[31]This application is taken from Bruce Orwall, "Hollywood's Champs: Cheap Little Flicks," *The Wall Street Journal,* November 11, 1998, p. B1.

[32]This case is prepared from many public information sources.

Many observers said Microsoft was not actually marketing an operating system (95), but another link in a system that would ultimately serve a market composed of managers of server computers and networks that run corporations. For example, in 1985 Merrill Lynch was buying 25,000 PCs and 600 servers to network their entire system of 600 regional offices and 12,000 brokers. Union Carbide announced plans to replace a mélange of servers and networked desktops (including 15 different e-mail systems) with 70 servers and Windows 95 on every desktop.

These corporate users needed communication of all types. Microsoft was already marketing its Windows NT networking system. Another new product, combining Windows NT, Windows 95, and other tools, was scheduled for entry in 1996. An additional item would involve team computing (where IBM held sway at the time with Lotus Notes). Gates also had admitted talking with Ted Turner and the people at NBC relative to news services. To some, Microsoft seemed to be trying to serve the needs of all nontechnical people who wanted to use the information superhighway. Ease of use was a common phrase.

One observer voiced the opinion that Windows 95 would turn out to be Bill Gates' Trojan horse, particularly with its built-in Microsoft Network (MSN). Punch one button and be on the Internet. No need to rely on traditional access firms such as CompuServe or the hundreds of smaller firms around the world. No need to use the products of what threatened to be the toughest competitor Gates ever faced, Netscape Communications. Netscape was trying to develop any and all software used on the Internet, especially that used to stroll down the Web. Microsoft was said to be about ready to market Blackbird, software for "enriching" the Web sites.

Gates' actions made almost everyone in the industry an enemy. The Windows 95 launch had focused on managers at America Online and associates, Novell networking, IBM (again), Oracle, and on and on. Still, Microsoft had failed. They had been years behind schedule on some products, and had failed outright on Microsoft at Work and others. Perhaps even more dangerous, industry has always feared being dependent on one supplier—already there was concern that Microsoft should not be allowed to push competition out. The Justice department had protested the marketing of Windows 95 because of the Internet access program (MSN) it contained, but did not move to stop the launch.

Question: Given what you know about the computer world plus the information above, try to write out what the Windows 95 product innovation charter might have said. Follow the format of Figure 3–1. Include in the background section of that charter what higher level strategic plans may have been in place to help guide it.

FIGURE II–1

Concept generation

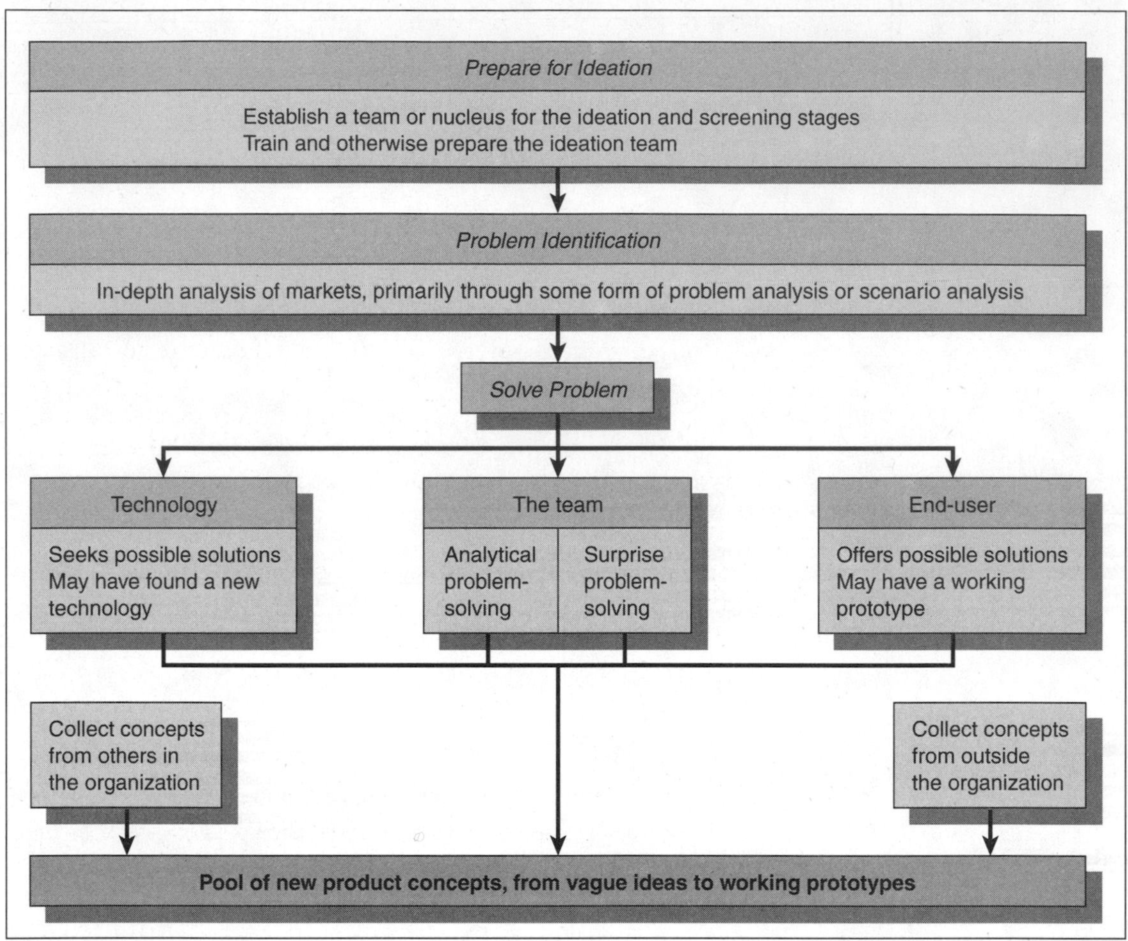

PART

II CONCEPT GENERATION

Chapter 2 showed the overall new products process, which provides for strategic planning first. The rationale is that one should seek new products that are best for the particular firm.

Ideation goes on constantly. Many employees of every organization come up with new product possibilities, but the act of creativity will never be constrained into a diagram. That's part of the fun of it! However, there are common patterns, and we manage to those.

Look at Figure II–1. Starting at the top, we see Prepare for Ideation. People inside, and outside, the firm don't hold up ideating until we "prepare," of course, but managed creativity is much more successful if we assign much of the task to people with strong creative capabilities. Then, early on, we want to focus on problems and needs. So by one means or another, we try to identify and clarify one or more specific problems that creativity can be focused on. Most of what follows does just that, but there still is a lot of freelance ideation going on.

Activity takes place in five areas, shown on the figure. On the left, most firms have a technology operation (R&D, engineering, whatever) in which completely new technologies (e.g., Kevlar, OCR) are being sought. Technical people are also on hand to help solve problems identified earlier. On the right side, end-users (indeed, all stakeholders in the marketplace) also do freelance ideation, and some of them actually design their own products, produce prototypes, and put them to work. For example, a dentist or an X-ray technician may well conjure up some device this way. They, too, stand ready to help us solve problems we identify.

In the meantime, in the middle of the diagram, the in-house team or group of people working on this project do their own problem-solving. And, they engage in other activities (Chapters 5 through 7) which produce "surprise" products. These, of course, are not problem-driven, so the team must find out if someone has a problem that fits the "solution." While all of this is going on, people everywhere are telling us about their ideas—employees throughout the organization, their families, complete strangers . . . everybody, it seems. They come in on the left and right sides of the figure, lower down. The consequence is a pool of ideas—we will call them concepts—and filling this pool is the subject of Chapters 4–7.

One caveat: Ideation is a huge topic, involving hundreds of methods. The best are discussed here, and a set of others often used is available in Appendix B. What works on a pizza would not work on a fiber-optic sensor. And nothing in the world of creativity lends itself very well to research, so what most firms do is what satisfies themselves, in particular.

CHAPTER

4

Preparation and Alternatives

Setting

This chapter takes us through several topics. First, to managers, comes the task of preparing the firm for ideation. This means getting the right people and putting them in the correct environment. Second, a creative person needs to know what is being searched for—that is, what is a concept and how it is typically found and identified? Third, you will explore a specific system of active (not reactive) concept generation, including approaches that seem to work. Fourth, one part of that system—using employees and nonemployees in a search for ready-made ideas—will be discussed in this chapter, and the other parts will follow in Chapters 5, 6 and 7.

Preparation

Many people think of product innovation beginning with a new product idea. But Chapter 3 showed it's far better to select a playing field and some rules (have a strategy) before starting the game.

The Product Innovation Charter

Think about these items from a hypothetical charter (Chapter 3) in a firm making bathtubs:

- Our new product concepts should be useful to older people, and others with physical handicaps.
- New products coming from these concepts must make use of the firm's strong design capabilities, as well as copper metal.

Assuming the PIC work was well done, any person trying to come up with new bathtub ideas for this firm had better know the game plan, or many ideas created will simply be wrong. Strategy helps.

Finding the Right People

Organizations known for their innovative product programs are also known for their highly creative people. Deciding which people will be creative ones is not easy. Research has shown that cognitive abilities are essential, and one summary of the data cited intelligence, knowledge, and thinking style.[1] The intelligence is essentially IQ, especially for scientific fields, but non-IQ street smarts are felt to be equally important outside the highly technical areas. Creative people, to us, are those who get ideas with a high degree of usefulness. "Unconventional individuals"—those with diverse experiences, great enthusiasm for innovation, and more foreign experience, for example—are better bets to come up with successful innovations than are "run-of-the-mill" technical personnel.[2]

Research reports suggest two different types of creative people: those with artistic creativity and those with scientific creativity. But new product creatives (inventors, really) need both, as depicted in Figure 4–1. Engineers without the touch of the artist and artists without scientific strength are probably less successful in new products ideation.

The field of industrial design is so clearly a merger of art and engineering that controversy exists over which school in a university should house it. The inventor is not inconsistent if sensitive *and* analytical, intuitive *and* observant, impulse-sensitive *and* persevering.

Some great creative talent has been labeled eccentric. One historical review showed the following:

> Schiller kept rotten apples in his desk; Shelley and Rousseau remained bareheaded in the sunshine; Bossuet worked in a cold room with his head wrapped in furs; Milton, Descartes, Leibniz, and Rossini lay stretched out; Tycho Brahe and Leibniz secluded themselves for very long periods; Thoreau built his hermitage, Proust worked in a cork-lined room, Carlyle in a noise-proof chamber, and Balzac wore a monkish working garb; Grety and Schiller immersed their feet in ice-cold water; Guido Reni could paint and de Musset could write poetry only when dressed in magnificent style; Mozart, following exercise; Lamennais, in a room of shadowy darkness; and D'Annunzio, Farnol, and Frost, only at night.[3]

---

[1]Firdaus E. Udwadia, "Creativity and Innovation in Organizations," *Technological Forecasting and Social Change,* 1990, pp. 65–80.

[2]Carol J. Steiner, "A Philosophy of Innovation: The Role of Unconventional Individuals in Innovation Success," *Journal of Product Innovation Management* 12, no. 5 (November 1995), pp. 431–40.

[3]H. B. Levey, "A Theory Concerning Free Creation in the Inventive Arts," *Psychiatry,* no. 3, 1940, pp. 280–91.

FIGURE 4–1
The three forms of human creativity

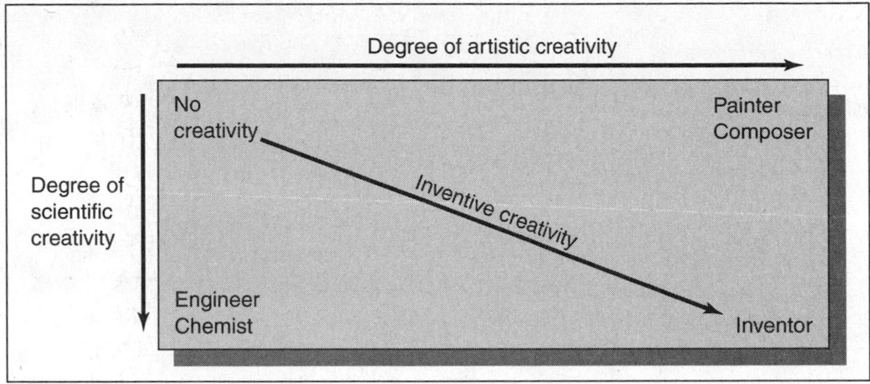

Most creative persons are not eccentric, but they do announce themselves by leaving a lifetime trail of creative accomplishments. They are creative as children and never become uncreative. This is the "bottom line" for us, since people under consideration for new product team assignments can be evaluated on their past. People without a lifetime trail usually blame unfamiliar environments, overpowering bosses, limited opportunities, and the like.

Management's Role in Making Creative People Productive

Creative people can benefit from training, though their personal capabilities serve as barriers to making them Einsteins. Figure 4–2 shows that we can enhance creativity, to a point. One study showed that 32 percent of firms did creativity training, using particularly (1) in-house courses, (2) the Center for Creative Leadership in Greensboro, North Carolina, and (3) the Center for Studies in Creativity at State University of New York at Buffalo. Many smaller companies have good reputations as suppliers of this training. As an executive at DuPont said, "We are in a race with a lot of competitors, here and abroad. If we are going to outperform them, we will have to think and act more creatively than they do."[4]

Such training programs run the gamut from introductory classes in traditional brainstorming to elaborate sessions that include games and horseplay. Some of the busiest creativity trainers use some of the wildest techniques, including variously colored hats and "guided fantasies." Obvious, but often overlooked, is training in the company's products, its markets, competition, technologies used, and so forth.

Newly born ideas are extremely fragile, quite the opposite of the strong and almost unstoppable concepts that are 80 percent of the way through the

[4]Ray Wise, "The Boom in Creativity Training," *Across the Board,* June 1991, pp. 38–42.

FIGURE 4–2

Creative performance as a two-factor consequence

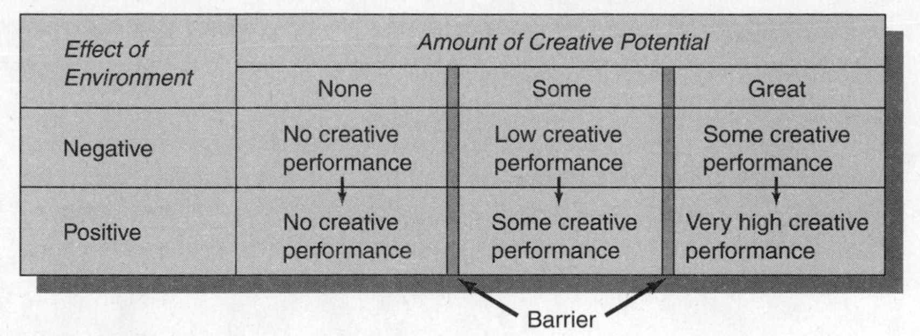

Effect of Environment	*Amount of Creative Potential*		
	None	Some	Great
Negative	No creative performance	Low creative performance	Some creative performance
Positive	No creative performance	Some creative performance	Very high creative performance

Comment: The environment (including management) can markedly increase an individual's creative performance, but only within the limits of the individual's basic creative potential.

process. By then, many ideas have picked up one or more powerful "owners." So, if we give creative people a hard time, show no appreciation for their ideas, offer no particular encouragement, they simply let the ideas slide by, vowing to "not waste my 'genius babies' on those clods." Or they don't seem to find the time to work them into more useful and acceptable shape. John Cleese, formerly of Monty Python, became a training consultant. He joked, "No more mistakes and you're through!" This sparks a sense of excitement in creative people, and there's nothing like excitement to get the innovative juices going.

Managements therefore have two packages of activity, one designed to encourage the creative function, and the other to remove roadblocks that thwart it.

Activities to Encourage Creativity

Today's managers recognize that innovators are apt to be different and need special treatment. "Accommodative" is the word. Innovators can't be allowed to violate rules at will, but it's good to recognize individuality, tolerate some aberrations, and be supportive under stress. Former Apple CEO John Sculley said, "I would worry if there weren't always a little bit of anarchy in the organization. It's like arsenic: A little is medicinal, but a lot can kill you."[5]

In addition, managements should allow innovators freedom to associate with others in similar positions. This freedom extends to all functional areas

[5]"Sculley's Lessons from Inside Apple," *Fortune,* September 14, 1987, p. 117. This article speaks directly to the matter of managing creative people productively.

and to outside the firm as well—no locked cells. Management should also permit innovators to help select projects for development, though this is often difficult. Job assignments should be challenging. Creative people don't lack confidence and, in fact, often consider their present assignments a waste of time. This means *they* will determine whether an assignment is worthy—no one can tell them.

Some firms deliberately create competitive teams and have them race to a deadline. Bell & Howell's management once faked the news of an impending competitive breakthrough to urge a scientific group to speed up. Another technique is "free time." It runs as high as 20 percent in some firms. The 3M Company is a major follower of this technique (with Post-it notes being one beneficiary). Flextime is a similar tool, but for creative types it means letting employees take work home or stay in their work places and work all night if they want.

Surprisingly perhaps, transferring creative personnel also helps. Creative people have a "need for novelty" and want to change situations occasionally.

Then, of course, we see a wide range of unique techniques developed by individual firms, especially those known for their creative achievements. Texas Instruments, for example had a program called IDEA (identify, develop, expose, and action). Sixty IDEA representatives throughout TI could dole out funds (without higher approval) for projects proposed by personnel who did not have enough influence to get funds through normal channels. Speak & Spell and Magic Wand were two notable results of such funds. 3M also awards "genesis grants" of up to $30,000 to fund innovative new projects that don't fit the business structure. Polaroid's SX-70 system began this way too: the project was actually "special experiment number 70," developed outside the normal structure at Polaroid. Sony and Toshiba will give teams a six-month project budget to take a new product concept all the way through development and out to market, on a small scale. This investment not only gives the team development resources, but also allows the firm to establish a technology standard and identify the early adopters in the market.[6]

The 3M Company has a long history of innovation, so it is not surprising that a chairman once said: "We do expect mistakes as a normal part of running a business, but we expect our mistakes to have originality."[7] Here is a characteristic 3M story.

> Another young lab worker was experimenting with tiny glass beads, more a novelty than a product. He was told to get back to his regular work. And he did. But, fortunately, because he was a bachelor, he could return to his lab and his pet bead project after normal working hours. This he did, and many nights he burned the midnight

---

[6]Karen Anne Zien and Sheldon A. Buckler, "From Experience: Dreams to Market: Crafting a Culture of Innovation," *Journal of Product Innovation Management* 14, no. 4 (1997), pp. 274–87.

[7]L. W. Lehr, "The Role of Top Management," *Research Management,* November 1979, pp. 23–25.

candle. Today those tiny beads are on reflective road bridges and bridge safety signs all over the world. And, no longer a bachelor, he eventually took his wife to an Academy Awards presentation where he received an Oscar for a bead-based front screen projection system for moviemakers.[8]

One very creative product design firm, IDEO of Palo Alto, California, takes several specific steps to create a culture of creativity and innovation. They seek out individuals who "love product design," set up offices in cities like Chicago, San Francisco, Boston, and Tokyo that attract creative types, and encourage employees to swap positions and locations frequently. Creative firms have more ideas than they know what to do with. Oce, a computer peripheral manufacturer, uses a computerized database to collect and document ideas, even those that are not used at first. They call this their "refrigerator" of ideas.[9] In general, creative operations should be in areas conducive to exchange of ideas, office arrangements should make people comfortable, and distractions should be held to a minimum.[10]

A good summary of practice in some firms with reputations for creativity used these terms: Accommodate, stimulate, recognize and reward, but also direct, protect, and be creative yourself.[11] The conclusion of that article was: "The chief rewards for most creatives remain exactly as H. L. Mencken described them more than 60 years ago: 'Freedom, opportunity, and the incomparable delights of self-expression.' "

Special Rewards

There is no question about the value of recognizing creative achievement. But creative people are usually unimpressed by *group* rewards. They believe group contributions are never equal, especially if the group is company employees, for many of whom creatives have great disdain. This is unfair; large portions of successful creativity are now set in groups, and we know more now about how to make group judgments work. But creatives do like personal accolades—preferably immediately. The famous Thomas Watson of IBM commonly carried spare cash in his pockets so he could reward persons with good ideas when he heard them.

Campbell Soup has Presidential Awards for Excellence. Many firms have annual dinners to recognize employees who obtained patents during

---

[8]Ibid., p. 24.

[9]Tekla S. Perry, "Designing a Culture for Creativity," *Research-Technology Management,* March-April 1995, pp. 14–17, and Zien and Buckler, "From Experience."

[10]Many firms today achieve a good environment in California research centers. In one of them, IBMer Ted Selker had an idea: It took about one second for the hand to move from a keyboard to a mouse, and one second to return; the human thumb and forefinger have the greatest sensory and motor control. Ten years later, IBM marketed the ThinkPad, with Selker's fingertip device on it. Selker shows an amazing fit with the stereotype of inventor scientist. Laurie Hays, "Abstractionist Practically Reinvents the Keyboard," *The Wall Street Journal,* March 6, 1995, p. B1.

[11]Alan Farnham, "How to Nurture Creative Sparks," *Fortune,* January 10, 1993, pp. 94–100.

the year. At IDEO, there are no organization charts or job titles: parties and trophies, rather than job promotions, are the rewards for a job well done. In one of the most dramatic reward systems, Toyota and Honda have their champions follow the new product out the door and take over its ongoing management.[12]

The Removal of Roadblocks

Figure 4–3 shows a compilation of "killer phrases" that can do so much to stop creativity. They are easy to use, and occur regularly in conversation. They are often well-intentioned, and they may be accurate statements of status quo. But they are extremely discouraging to fragile ideas, and only conscious effort by managers can help scare them away.

Some organizations use a technique called **itemized response.** All client trainees must practice it personally. When an idea comes up, listeners must first cite all of its advantages. Then they can address the negatives, but only in a positive mode. The recommended language for bringing up a negative is "OK. Now—let's see what would be the best way to overcome such-and-such a problem." Note that this constructive comment assumes the problem can be overcome, and the listener offers to help. To encourage creativity, some firms deliberately encourage conflict by putting certain employees together on the same team—for example, a "blue skyer" creative person and a practical type. This technique is sometimes called *creative abrasion.*[13]

FIGURE 4–3

Killer phrases: roadblocks to creativity in the generation of new product concepts

"It simply won't work."
"Are you sure of that?"
"You can't be serious."
"It's against our policy."
"Let's shelve it for the time being."
"That won't work in our market."
"Let's think about that some more."
"I agree, but . . ."
"We've done it the other way for a long time."
"Where are you going to get the money for that?"
"We just can't do that."
"Who thought of that?"
"It's probably too big for us."
"I believe we tried that once before."
"We don't usually do things that way."
"It seems like a gimmick to me."
"It's good, but impractical."
"That sounds awfully complicated."
"Production won't accept that."
"People will think we're crazy."
"Engineering can't do that."
"You could never sell that downstairs."
"But who is going to drive that idea?"
"OK, but let's slow down a bit."
"I'm afraid there's precedent in this."
"We have too many projects now."
"We'll need more background on that."

---

[12]These ideas, and many more, are discussed in Tekla Perry, "Designing a Culture for Creativity," and Russell Mitchell, "Masters of Innovation," *Business Week,* April 10, 1989, pp. 58–62.

[13]James Krohe, Jr., "Managing Creativity," *Across the Board,* September 1996, pp. 16–22.

A classic review of history, *Failure of Success,* had a section presenting the most famous rejections of all time, one of which was by a journal editor to rocket pioneer Robert Goddard: "The speculation . . . is interesting, but the impossibility of ever doing it is so certain that it is not practically useful."[14] This shouldn't surprise us, given the conviction of many people that "managing creatives" is an oxymoron.

The Concept

Given creative and exciting people, just what is it we want them to produce? What is this thing called concept? How does it differ from a new product? When does it come about?

Let's start with the end point, the successful marketing of a new product, and back up. A new product only really comes into being when it is *successful*—that is, when it meets the goals/objectives assigned to the project in the PIC.

When launched, it is still in tentative form because changes are usually necessary to make it successful. Therefore we say it is still a concept, an idea that is not fulfilled.

Back before technical work was finished, the product was even more of a concept. To understand this, and see how it relates to the ideation process, we have to look at the three inputs required by the creation process.

- **Form:** This is the physical thing created, or in the case of a service, it is the sequence of steps by which the service will be created. Thus with a new steel alloy, form is the actual bar or rod of material. On a new mobile phone service it includes the hardware, software, people, procedures, and so forth, by which calls are made and received.
- **Technology:** This is the source by which the form was attained. Thus for the steel alloy it included, among others, the steel and other chemicals used for the alloy, the science of metallurgy, product forming machines, cutting machines, and more. Technology is defined in product innovation as the power to do work, as you will recall from Chapter 3. In most cases there is one clear technology that is at the base of the innovation, the one that served as the technical dimension of the focus-arena. Sometimes there are two.
- **Benefit:** The product has value only as it provides some benefit to the customer that the customer sees a need or desire for.

We put these dimensions together this way: *Technology permits us to develop a form that provides the benefit.* If any of the three is missing, there cannot be product innovation, unless one buys a product ready-made and resells

[14]Tomas E. Frank, "Rejection," in Alfred J. Marrow, ed., *The Failure of Success* (New York: AMACOM, 1972), Chapter 5, pp. 76–93. This reading offers many examples.

it without change. Even then, there would be some change in the service dimension—where it is sold, how it is serviced, and so forth. Even clone makers add value, if nothing more than price; we even hear computer buffs say something like: "XYZ makes better clones than PDQ does!"

Oddly, the innovation process can start with any one of the three dimensions, and can vary in what happens second (see Figure 4–4). Here are the primary ways:

> Customer has a NEED, which a firm finds out about. It calls on its TECHNOLOGY to produce a FORM that is then sold to the customer.
>
> A firm has a TECHNOLOGY that it matches with a given market group, and then finds out a NEED that group has, which is then met by a particular FORM of product.
>
> A firm envisions a FORM of product, which is then created by use of a TECHNOLOGY and then given to customers to see if it has any BENEFIT.

Any of the three can start the process, and in each case either of the other two can come second. Now, you may say, so what is the difference? The difference is too often that between success and failure. Putting benefit last is very risky, since it comprises a solution trying to find a problem. DuPont for example spent several years finding applications where Kevlar could yield a profitable benefit.

Apple's experience with the Newton Message Pad personal digital assistant shows the risk firms take when they put benefits last. Technology developed by Apple's R&D department allowed a user to enter handwritten inputs, eliminating the keyboard. From this technology, a form was conceived: a pen-based, digitized notepad designed to capture and process ideas and data. Apple didn't check with customers, however, to see if this form actually satisfied customer needs or addressed customer problems. Customers were apparently satisfied with the tried-and-true ways of capturing ideas and data: pen and paper, sticky notes, calendars, and electronic address books. The fact that it retailed at about $800, and that handwriting recognition did not work flawlessly, did not help Newton's case either. The Newton never sold well.[15]

Therefore we like to put benefit first. Incidentally, even technology-driven scientists actually put benefit first in most cases because they have some idea of need that is leading them in their efforts. For example, a pharmaceutical chemist seeking a new compound for lowering blood pressure knows how widespread that problem is. Given benefit, preferences vary. Some people like to visualize what type of finished product could meet the

---

[15] Abbie Griffin, "Obtaining Customer Needs for Product Development," in *The PDMA Handbook of New Product Development,* M. Rosenau, A. Griffin, G. Castellion, and N. Anscheutz, eds. (New York: Wiley, 1996), pp. 153–66.

FIGURE 4–4

The new product concept

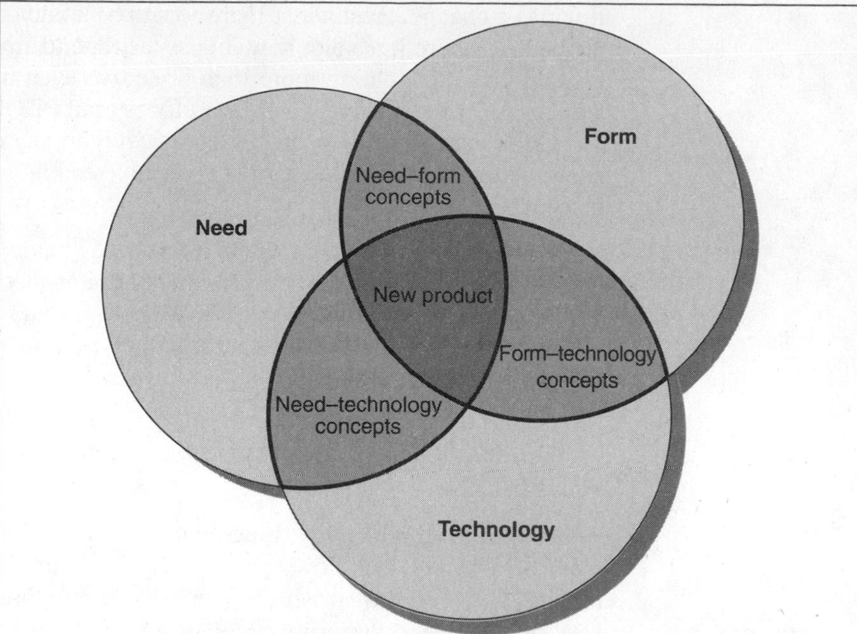

Concept: "A far better way of meeting the learning needs of computer users is to utilize modem-based online systems to let them see training videos on the leading software packages." (This has a well-known need/benefit and stipulates the several technologies that will be used; but exactly how this service will function is still to be worked out.)

Another way of stating this concept would be: "XYZ Corporation has a national telecommunications network in place, and also owns a chain of video rental stores. Surely there is some way we can use these capabilities to help meet the training needs of home-based computer users." Again, this offers the market need and the technologies; it still lacks method/process, which is the service product's equivalent of form. (Note how close a new product concept can come to sounding like the focus/arena of a product innovation charter.)

Here are two statements that may *sound* like new product concepts, but clearly aren't:

"Let's create a new way of solving the in-home training/educational needs of personal computer users." (Need, but no form and no technology. Just a wish, like a cure for cancer.)

"I think we ought to develop a line of instructional videos." No specific market need/benefit, and no form—just a technology.

need, and then design that form. Others like to give technical people the basic benefit(s) and let them use their available technologies without restraint on form. This book follows the latter. Granting that in practice, all versions exist, and no one would throw out a good idea just because it came up in the "wrong" way, the fact remains that we are speaking about management. If one wants to design the best way to go about product innovation, then, in general, the best way is to have first the benefit, then the technology, and then the finished form.

Thus, for example, the whole of Chapter 5 will deal with how we go to customers and find out what their problems are. In Chapter 12 we will talk about a form of product description (called a protocol) that is written out prior to undertaking technical development; the description is primarily benefits. Features (form) are put into it only if they seem absolutely essential (e.g., required by law).

Let's put this all into a simple case, and maybe the issues will become clearer.

The Soft Bubble Gum Example

Many years ago, bubble gum was sold in small chunks, rolls, or sheets. The material was quite hard and difficult to soften to the point where bubbles could be blown. Let's imagine we worked at a bubble gum company in those years. Imagine also three different people walked into the new product office one week, at different times, each with an "idea" for a new product. Each was unaware the others were coming in.

One person said, "Our most recent customer satisfaction report disclosed that consumers would like a bubble gum that doesn't take five minutes to soften up. No bubble gum offers this *benefit*." The second person was a product manager who said, "I was thinking last week about the features of bubble gums and noted that all of them are hard; maybe ours could be made softer, and flexible" *(form)*. The third person was a scientist who had just returned from a technical forum and said, "I heard discussion of a new chemical mixing process that keeps foods from drying out; maybe it would be useful in our business" *(technology)*.

Each of these people had a germ of an idea, but as a concept each suggestion wasn't really very useful. The first person had something on a par with a cancer cure—benefit, but no way to supply it. The product manager had no idea whether consumers would like flexible gum or how it might be made. The scientist didn't know what the technology would do to traditional bubble gum or whether consumers wanted a change.

A new product concept would result if the first person met up with either the second or the third. If the second, they would ask the lab for a technology that would produce the sought form and benefit. If the third, they would undertake lab work to find the exact form of the new technology (for example, how soft).

What might best sum up the point that a concept is evolving from its creation until it metamorphoses into a new product is the saying of one manager: "Don't waste your time trying to find a *great* new product idea; it's our job to take a rather ordinary idea and *make it* into a successful new product."

The Concept Statement

Ideas, concepts, new products, and so forth, are all words in common use. But, as in all disciplines, we have to clarify them for understanding. Medical books draw sharp distinction between common cold, sinusitis, upper respiratory infection, and so forth, even though as patients, we don't care.

Figure 4–4 showed that any two of the three (form, benefit, technology) can come together to make a concept, a potential product. All three together produce a new product that may or may not be successful. Often, there is little difference. For example, inventors frequently call on companies with a prototype in hand. This is a concept that is virtually finished—it has form, based on a technology, and you can be sure the inventor knows a benefit it provides. Of course, firms know from experience that the inventor usually overstates the benefit, the technology will have drawbacks that make it impractical to use in a plant, and the form is very tentative based primarily on tools and space in a crude workshop.

At the other extreme the very first thought about a new product may be so incomplete that nothing can be done with it as is. For example, the scientist returning from the technical forum had only capability—nothing that had value to anyone in the bubble gum firm.

Once a concept appears with two of the three dimensions (technology, form, benefit), we have to screen it before undertaking development. That part of the process comes in Chapter 9, and it requires what we call a **product concept statement.** Technical people and intended customers must tell us the concept is worthy of development. Their review of the concept statement allows this, *if* the concept tells them what they need to know to make that judgment. A concept statement will usually do this if it has two of the three basic essentials (technology, form, benefit).

If you were asked "How would you like zero calorie ice cream?" you could not really answer. You probably already find yourself thinking, what will it taste like, what is it made of, what's the catch? To do concept testing, we need a concept statement that meets these information needs. It would be a waste of time to ask taxi company owners whether they would like a cab with a 10-cents-per-mile operating cost. They might say sure, but that answer would change quickly if told we planned to use Caterpillar tractor technology.

Sometimes the technology will tell us something useful about the concept: a flashlight that burns 10 times as bright because it uses arc-welding technology. Or a light based on fiber optics technology that comes wound on a wooden spool of the size used for thread. Or a flashlight that uses a pyramidal reflector rather than a conical one. Each of these statements offers more or less information, and permits you to get better or worse reactions.

A concept then is *a verbal and/or prototype expression that tells what is going to be changed and how the customer stands to gain (and lose).* Early on, the information is quite incomplete, but when marketed the concept is (hopefully) complete. Anything that doesn't communicate gain and loss to the intended buyer is still just an idea that needs work.

An interesting demonstration of the three-facet concept source came when Eddy Goldfarb, a famous toy inventor, was asked how he did it. He replied, "Notice what things your child plays with, and try to spot what's lacking." He also said he likes to look for new processes and materials and "for holes—you know, a lack of a certain item on the market." These statements cite benefit, technology, and form, in that order.[16]

The importance of these three dimensions varies by industry. In most industries, one of the three often needs no attention because of general knowledge within the industry. Pharmaceutical new products people do not have to check out the desirability of stopping body fluid buildup, or of eliminating cancer. Furthermore, pharmaceutical expertise is available to manufacture virtually any new drug, so technology is the only unknown and thus the focus of attention. On the other hand, the leading food companies presume the kitchens and factory can put together anything the customer wants, so benefit (ascertained through taste tests, for example) becomes the prime variable. In the automobile industry, car manufacturers so dominate the new products process that components suppliers are told what benefit is wanted and then work with either technology or form for its innovation.

In these three different industry situations, discussion with new products people quickly indicates the critical avenue of innovation for *their* firm or industry. And the distinctions are not moot—they provide the direction for the idea stimulation process. Still, it takes all three. If a project aborts, it may be the fault of the department with the "easy" task. For example, a television manufacturer's marketing research may show that consumers want a television set that will increase in volume as room noise picks up and decrease in volume as room noise subsides. This research engenders the idea for the new product, so the process would be demand-induced. But, in reality, the technical side of the business has the toughest task.

The reverse of this came when a small Michigan firm attempted to find markets for a new development in reticulated vitreous carbon. The situation was clearly one where technology provided the breakthrough; but, again ironically, the pressure was on marketing to find applications to yield adequate volume for a profit. It couldn't, and the firm folded.

Two Basic Approaches

Now, given some agreement on language, we can go back to the original question: How should we go about generating new product concepts? The diagram given in the figure at the start of Part II showed five routes—technology, end-user, team, other insiders, and other outsiders. Two of these

[16]Fran Carpentier, "Can You Invent a Toy?" *Parade,* December 1981, pp. 14–15.

involve receiving product ideas created by others, and three involve a managed process run by the team. This distinction is the one that makes managerial difference, and it is the one we will use in this book. Like getting a new garment, we can buy one ready-made or make it ourselves. Here we will discuss the ready-made source, and in Chapters 5 through 7 doing it ourselves.

Of course, most firms use both ready-made and tailored sources. But in each industry it is common knowledge as to which has a better batting average. For example, food manufacturers usually will not even read new product suggestions sent in by consumers. They have more than enough concepts of their own, consumer suggestions are very repetitive or old ideas, and even just glancing at hundreds of thousands of ideas every year would be almost impossible.

Yet, in some other industries (e.g. toys and tools) inventors thrive. There are even inventors' fairs, where inventors are invited to display their creations. And some manufacturers have employee and customer idea contests. Even in the food industry, one firm (Pillsbury) has found it profitable to run an annual Bake-Off Contest to capture thousands of new recipes for their possible use. NordicTrack had outstanding success (for a while) relying almost entirely on ideas from inventors; they had no internal R&D. Some inventors become famous, such as Andrew Toti, now almost 80, a classic eccentric with *hundreds* of patents, and still active.[17]

One thing we know for sure, concept generation should be an active not reactive process. This is no time for the Maytag repairman posture.

Gathering Concepts Already Created

Experience in the field of product innovation has it that 40 to 50 percent of new product ideas are ready-made, coming at least partially from employees, suppliers, end-users and other stakeholders, and published information. (See Figure 4–5.)

Many organizations have evolved ways (seminars, visits to customers' plants, and so on) to more systematically involve user groups because these groups have been so productive. ARCO actually ran full-page *Wall Street Journal* ads that reproduced good suggestions sent in by the public and encouraged more.

Appendix A lists and discusses the most common sources of ideas already created. They are many, diverse, and of varying quality. However, one of those sources deserves special attention—the customer, consumer, user. People who use a product often have ideas for improving it, but unfortunately

[17]Michael Ryan, "Don't Throw Out That Good Idea," *Parade,* June 11, 1995, pp. 12–13.

FIGURE 4–5

Sources of ready-made new product concepts; the best sources have bold box lines

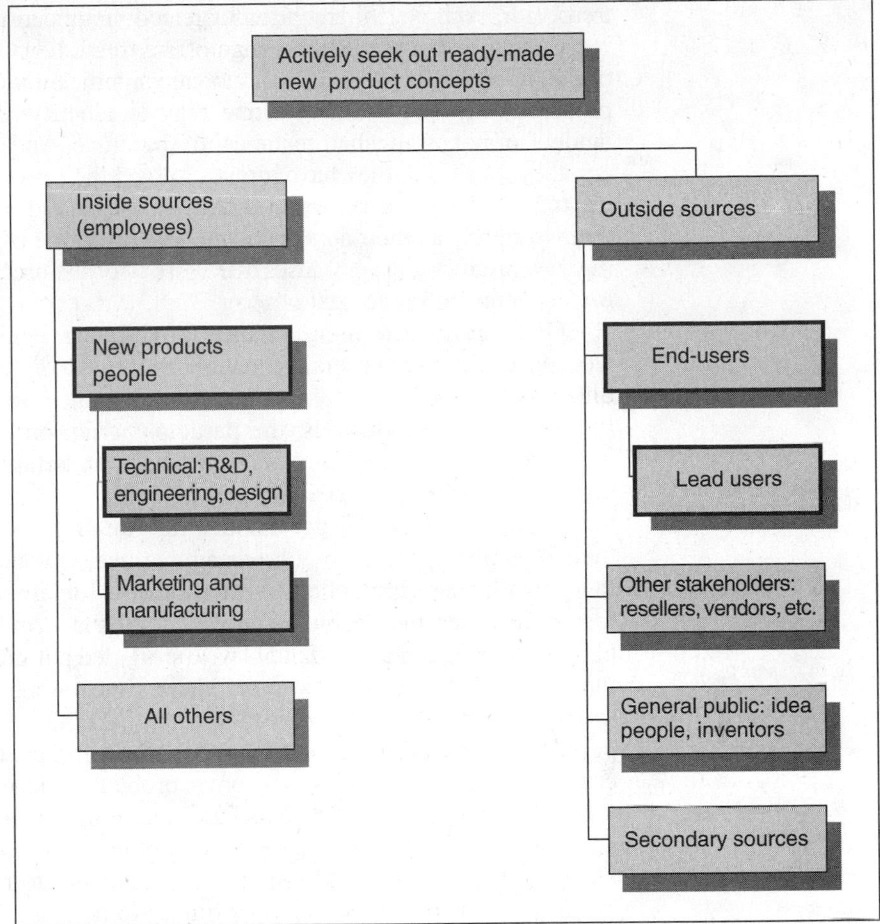

their ideas are usually rather obvious. Black & Decker reportedly received over a thousand suggestions for a new product that would be a Dust-Buster type bug catcher.

Even if new, most consumer users' concepts are for product improvements, not significant line extensions or new-to-the-world products. But, in some industries, the end-user plays quite a different role. For example, manufacturers of scientific instruments and plant process equipment report the *majority* of their successful new products came originally from customers. (In contrast, manufacturers of engineering polymers and of chemical additives for plastics report no projects coming from customers.)

The most useful development in user-oriented ideation involves identifying the **lead** (meaning out-in-front) **users** associated with a significant current trend (for example, fiber optics in telecommunications).[18] These firms (or individuals) are at the leading edge of the trend, have the best understanding of the problems faced, and expect to gain significantly from solutions to those problems. Although usually fairly easy to identify, they may also be outlanders, or not established members of that trade. And, if they are really leaders, they may think they have already solved their problems. But in an *evolving* trend, their solutions will not hold up; product developers can work with them to anticipate their next problem. Lead users are especially helpful in giving new product ideas because their work is of the problem-find-solve type, a method stressed in the next chapter.

One way to determine whether a particular industry can benefit from working directly with users to gather concepts is to ask whether customers are tinkerers. For example, dentists are; so are medical technicians and farmers. In some of these industries, the participants not only have good ideas, but have prototypes as well, and may even have undertaken a form of manufacturing by making prototypes for their friends.

Reportedly, Chrysler got the idea for building 32-ounce cup holders into their Ram pickup trucks by observing that many pickup drivers had installed their own large-size cup holders themselves. Sometimes, observing the customer identifies the problem, leaving it to the firm to find a solution. A Chrysler engineer noticed that his wife struggled putting a child's car seat into their minivan. He came up with the idea of integrating car seats into the van's seating system; Chrysler added this feature which turned out to be extremely popular. Being a customer, of your competitors' products as well as your own, can also provide insights on customer problems and needs. A company that makes checkout scanner systems has its employees work as checkout clerks a few days a year to get a sense of the product in use, and the kind of problems that can crop up. GM requires its employees to rent GM cars when on business—thus passing up an opportunity to compare its cars with the competition in a real use situation.[19]

In time, we will probably see less emphasis placed on going to end-users for new product ideas because we are now involving end-users so effectively on our new product teams (see Chapter 14). This brings their needs and problems directly onto the table.[20] But there will always be firms where they

---

[18]The best summary of findings and recommendations in this area can be found in writings of the person who essentially invented the approach: Eric von Hippel, *The Sources of Innovation* (New York: Oxford University Press, 1988).

[19]The examples from this paragraph are from A. Griffin, "Obtaining Customer Needs for Product Development."

[20]The "lead user" method was recently studied in an application that was not based on advanced technology: German construction materials. The method worked well, but was managed essentially as an application of what is called Problem Analysis in Chapter 5. See Cornelius Herstatt and Eric von Hippel, "From Experience: Developing New Product Concepts Via the Lead User Method: A Case Study in a 'Low-Tech' Field," *Journal of Product Innovation Management,* September 1992, pp. 213–21.

don't wait to be asked—they go right ahead and prototype up their ideas. A new example of this today is the information technology field, especially computers and telecommunications, where end-users have become quite sophisticated.

The use of the public at large, rather than end-users, came out lately when Nordic-Track won the Outstanding Innovator Award from the Product Development & Management Association. In the company presentation to the conference, the new products manager gave complete credit to its complement of freelance inventors; the firm does no systematic ideation itself because it gets such a good flow of good ideas from inventors, which, incidentally, it cultivates much as the internal creatives are cultivated as shown earlier.

Not as dramatic, but as a demonstration that good ideas can come from almost anywhere, is the case of Nicholas Graham, founder of the Joe Boxer Corporation. His rock singer career failed to "pay the rent," so he turned to bold-patterned neckties. These sold well, and a Macy buyer suggested the patterns might look great on boxer shorts. He made them, they sold well too (both male and female, apparently), and he quickly became a millionaire.[21]

New products managers also do not forget employees outside the mainstream of technical or marketing new product work. In fact, collecting these ideas is thought to be so desirable that a new method has been developed for it, and case studies are now beginning to appear.[22]

Summary

Chapter 4 has introduced concept generation for new products. First we noted that management has the task of preparing an organization for concept generation. This includes applying the strategic guidance of a product innovation charter, finding and training creative people, and then creating an environment for them to work in where they can be motivated to produce.

Next came a look at the concept itself, what it is, what it isn't, and how it comes into existence. The concept is built around ideas of technology, form, and benefit, and is tested by whether it can communicate to an intended buyer what the proposed product is all about and whether it appears useful.

After noting that there are two broad categories of approaches to getting good new concepts, we explored the one that involves looking for ready-

[21]Randall Lane, "The Boxer Rebellion," *Forbes,* September 12, 1994, pp. 74–78.

[22]The method, called Organization Sweep, is discussed in Chris Miller, "Panning for Gold," *Visions,* published by the Product Development & Management Association, July 1994, pp. 6–9. The case history is Jeff D. Felberg and David A. DeMarco, "From Experience: New Idea Enhancement at Amoco Chemical: An Early Report from a New System," *Journal of Product Innovation Management,* December 1992, pp. 278–86.

made concepts. Many firms use this approach heavily, and all should make at least some use of it. There are legal problems here, of course, and the chapter concluded by outlining the steps to follow in handling ideas that come from nonemployees.

This prepares us to look at the most difficult, but by far the best, method for creating new product concepts: problem-based ideation. This is the subject of Chapter 5.

Applications

More questions from that interview with a company president.

1. "You mentioned this guy Nicholas Graham, the one who introduced those boxer shorts with loud and colorful designs. I didn't know what was going on at the time, but I was flying Virgin Air to London one night and a couple people from that firm stood up, and began passing out yellow boxer shorts decorated with eyes and smiles. They invited everyone to put them on and then parade up and down the aisle singing songs. Believe it or not, many did. Now, I found out later that the Britisher who owns Virgin also owns Joe Boxer. So when you told me about that great idea coming from a Macy buyer, I had to laugh. Seems to me that the admittedly great boxer shorts were more a promotional success than a creative one. With marketing people like those at Joe Boxer, who needs great new product concepts?"
2. "Lots of our people try to get good new product ideas from outsiders, but they are careful to keep it legal. I wonder though about something I ran into on a trip to Australia last fall. I met what our company people there called a professional espionage agent. He employs a network of stewards and air hostesses to gather tidbits of information overheard in the first-class compartments of international flights. Sells this information for over a million dollars a year! I wonder what suggestions I should put in a memo for employees to minimize the chances that our key new product information will be stolen by competitors."
3. "In-house inventors are tough to deal with. Right now we have this Ph.D. in physics, a really great person, bright as they come, and terribly creative. Has had no less than 11 ideas go to market since she joined the firm four years ago. But she feels we don't reward her properly, even though she is on a good salary, shares an annual bonus with all the other persons in research, and even got a special bonus of $5,000 last year. Frankly, I think she will leave us if I don't find some way to let her have an equity position in some of her ideas. What do you think of her argument, and how might I arrange something if I wanted to?"

4. "We have a small operation in Spain, running a computer repair, resale, and rental operation, for businesses, not residential. They are supposedly trying to be creative and innovative, but so far as I can tell they haven't had a good new service idea for four years. I've got my eye on a good consultant to go in there and review their environment, their motivating systems, and so on, but first I want to know if they have creative people. How could I find that out?"

Case: Concept Generation in the Toy Industry[23]

The toy industry has seen its ups and downs in recent years. Industry analysts often say that it is one of the most difficult to predict. Some years, a given toy like Teenage Mutant Ninja Turtles or Tickle Me Elmo comes out of nowhere to become the year's blockbuster. In the early 1980s, Speak & Spell was huge, largely because it was featured in the movie E.T. Other years, there are no "blockbusters" anywhere on the horizon, and competitors just slog along through the peak holiday season. Making matters worse is that many toy products are popular for a very short window: while some building toys (like Lincoln Logs) and board games (like Monopoly) seem to have been around forever; many others are quickly viewed by children as passé.

During the 1980s, the educational toy market heated up. Manufacturers (established as well as new startups) were quickly designing electronic toys and flash cards to sell to parents eager to give their kids a head start on learning, and new retailers like Enchanted Village, specializing in educational toys, were springing up. By the early 1990s, many analysts were saying that this market was behaving like a typical mature market hitting its peak. A stock market analyst said calling a toy "educational" was the kiss of death. The term "edutainment" was dead. Enthusiastic parents who liked to flash cards in front of crib children had apparently slacked off, or gone to other devices. Enchanted Village, and other specialty retailers, closed up shop.

Some of the reasons were thought to be known: some educators had been less than enthusiastic, the developers had sometimes created confusion about what exactly their products were, and child development experts sometimes told parents to just let their children play. Worst of all, perhaps, the basic idea—parents should use toys to con their children into more school when they thought they were playing—hadn't worked. The kids caught on fast. And, of course, many of these edutainment toys were not entertaining.

Not all educational toy producers were willing to throw in the towel. Some were focusing their attention on preschoolers, while others were tying toys that actually were more fun to educational characters like Big Bird and Cookie Monster. Many competitors felt the real problem was that they hit a really good idea only rarely. When they did, sales were fine—in a typical year, educational toys account for about 5 percent of all toy sales, yielding a sales volume of around $750 million. The big issue, then, seemed to be generating high quantities of good new product concepts.

---

[23]Source: Based partly on Joseph Pereira, "Educational Toys Receive a Failing Grade As Kids Wise Up to Their Parents' Game," *The Wall Street Journal,* April 11, 1989, p. B1.

There is no end of inventors in garages and basements around the world; hundreds of ideas for educational toys are submitted to toy makers by these sources in a given year. Maybe these ideas should have been studied more carefully. In addition, the big manufacturers had their own staffs with literally thousands of ideas, generated from spending their time making and selling the current lines. In fact, some of the bigger competitors actually refused all ideas coming "off the street" from inventors. They felt that the garage tinkerer often overestimated the play value of his or her invention, and that their own inside toy designers had a better understanding of the entertainment and educational value a given idea would offer. Still, these approaches had always been available, and as one manufacturer said, "Look where we are!"

One toy developer said she wanted to get into a new dimension of creativity—something that would produce toys that were genuinely fun, so much fun that kids would want to play with them as such. Yet these toys would be almost secretly educational. But how to do that, she didn't know. She did know that she couldn't survey kids and ask them what problems they had. And she had great faith in her own creative skills, if she could just think of a new way to give them a new boost of power. Supposedly, creative people could come up with new things, including methods of creativity.

You have been called in as a creativity consultant to assist this toy developer. How could new product concepts that would satisfy this developer's wishes be generated?

CHAPTER

5 PROBLEM-BASED IDEATION

Setting

Chapter 5 will be devoted to what is the most productive concept generating system that we know—the problem-based approach of finding and solving customers' problems.[1] It seems obvious, and easy: Ask customers what their problems are and have a scientist put together the solution! But it's not that simple.

Just getting customers involved is often difficult. Learning their toughest problems is more difficult, partly because they often don't know their problems very well. Many departments of a firm may be involved, not just the technical ones. You might want to glance back at the diagram on the page starting Part II, which shows how problem-based ideation fits in with other gathering of new product concepts.

The Overall System of Internal Concept Generation

Every ideation situation is different and varies by the urgency, the skills of the firm and its customers, the product, the resources available, and so on. But one general approach, that of problem-based ideation, works best, and can be modified to fit virtually every situation. The steps are diagrammed in Figure 5–1.

The flow essentially is from study of the situation, to use of various techniques of problem identification, to screening of the resulting problems, and

[1]Regardless of today's popular emphasis on creativity, Doug Carlston, CEO of Brøderbund, insists he does best building software (even for children) squarely on needs. Andrew Kupfer, "Identify a Need, Turn a Profit," *Fortune,* November 30, 1992, pp. 78–79.

FIGURE 5–1

Problem-based concept generation

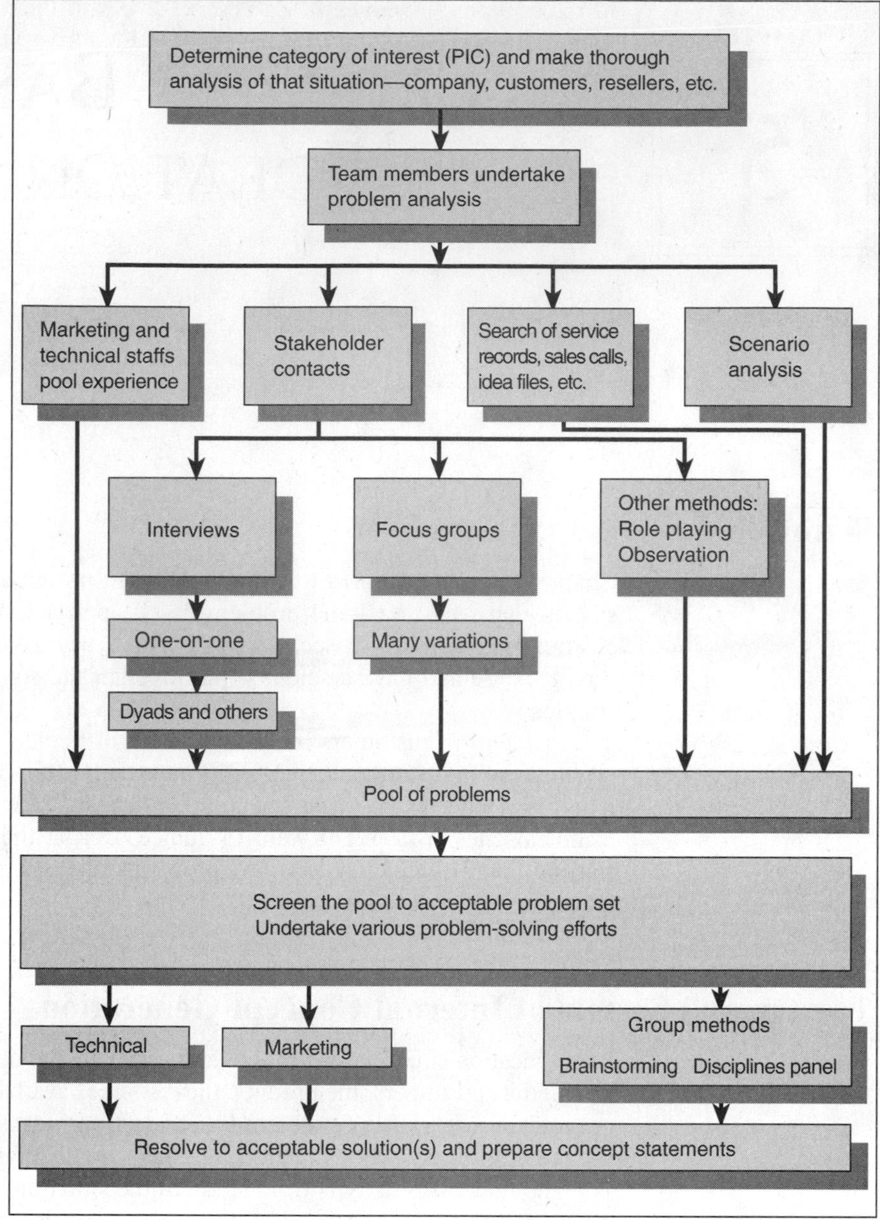

to development of **concept statements** that will then go into the evaluation phase. The whole system is based on close involvement with parties who have information to help us, primarily stakeholders, the biggest part of which are end-users.[2]

Recall from Chapter 2 that the leading cause of new product failure is the absence of a perceived need by the intended end-user. If our development process begins with a problem/need the end-user has and agrees is important, then we have answered the toughest question. Fortunately, organizations today are getting close to their stakeholders. But stakeholder integration is especially tough on high-security *new product* matters. So we figure out how to do it, just as customer satisfaction managers have. New ways appear almost daily. For example, Martin-Marietta has what the Japanese call an "antenna shop" in Reston, Virginia, where 33 high-power workstations sit in readiness for customers to visit, try out the firm's latest software developments, talk with company people about their problems on software, and actually take short steps toward developing new software there in the facility.

Gathering the Problems

Figure 5–1 showed four sources for needs and problems of stakeholders. Two of these involve direct access within the firm, a third calls for **problem analysis,** and the fourth for scenario analysis.

Internal Records

The most common source of needs and problems comes from an organization's routine contacts with customers and others in the marketplace. Daily or weekly sales call reports, findings from customer or technical service departments, and tips from resellers are examples. Sales files are peppered with customer (and reseller) suggestions and criticisms. Warranty files will show where problems are. Customer satisfaction studies are useful, as are the files of the groups working on total quality management.

Industrial and household consumers sometimes misunderstand products and erroneously project into their use of products what they are *seeking.* A complaint file thus becomes a psychological projective technique. One approach to handling user complaints is the hot line or toll-free number. It helps defuse criticism and can lead to new products. And at least one firm's R&D

[2]Stakeholders include the full set of end-users and all persons who influence the behavior of the end-user—advisors, financiers, consultants, architects, physicians, even many resellers. In some markets, such as that for medical equipment, the nonusers may be more influential than users are. See Wim G. Biemans, "User and Third-Party Involvement in Developing Medical Equipment Innovations," *Technovation,* April 1991, pp. 163–81.

employees actually work at customer sites to hear their problems firsthand. Hallmark and American Greetings have carried market contacts to a new level by mall-installations of kiosks where consumers can actually create their own new cards. American calls it Createacard and learns from what the customers create. Unfortunately, long-standing problems can become "part of the wallpaper" and thus forgotten. The routine market contacts should be heavily supplemented with the technique of problem analysis.

Direct Inputs from Technical and Marketing Departments

Understanding about end-users and other stakeholders also lies in the minds of marketing and technical people. Most of them have spent time with customers and end-users, sometimes many years of it. Team representatives from these two functions should canvass their colleagues, seeking out every piece of evidence on problems. They have to take the initiative on this, because most of these people are busy; it's strictly "you call me."

It's good to remember too that technical people may be found anywhere in the business, not just in R&D or engineering—especially in manufacturing, technical service, and regulatory affairs. Salespeople may not be considered in marketing, and thus are sometimes overlooked.

The only real problems with using in-house people to report on customer problems are (1) each suggestion is usually someone's *perception* of what the customer problem is and (2) there is usually a solution given with each suggestion. In fact, sometimes we have to ask what new product customers are asking for and then ask why; the why is what we want to know at this time.

These problems, including the time and difficulty of actually gathering memories, lead us to depend more on *active* search for stakeholder problems. That is, making direct contact with all relevant stakeholders, asking *them* what their problems and needs are. And, although all of the above market contacts and searches around the firm help us compile useful problems, the methods of direct user contact are what we usually mean when we say problem analysis.

Problem Analysis

It seems that every history of an industry, a business firm, or a famous businessperson cites some key time when a new good or service capitalized on a problem that others didn't sense or appreciate. But problem analysis is much more than a simple *compilation* of user problems. Although the term problem *inventory* is sometimes used to describe this category of techniques, taking the inventory is only the beginning—analysis is the key.

As an advertising agency executive once said: If you ask people what they want in a new house and also ask them what are their problems with their current house, you will get distinctly different subject matter on each list. If you then observe their subsequent behavior, it becomes clear their problem

FIGURE 5–2

Problem analysis applied to the telephone

Here are 22 telephone problems that came up in a consumer study. See if you can generalize to a smaller number of problems. Then select the one big problem that sounds most productive for telephone new products people.

Keeping the unit clean.
It keeps falling on the floor.
Getting entangled with the cord.
Finding it in the dark.
Getting privacy in the house.
Who "out there" can hear me?
Staying away from message phones.
Getting past message phones.
Difficulty in looking up numbers.
Dealing with the busy signal.
Hard to hold, if arthritic.
Can't just move the phone from room to room, building to building.
Peddlers and pollsters.
My arm and ear get tired.
Bell ringing conflict: too loud but sometimes I can't hear it.
It is a very disruptive instrument.
I can't see facial and body language.
Getting flustered making emergency calls.
People who call wrong number in the middle of the night.
Fear of what a ringing may be for.
"If you want Sales, punch 1," etc.
Knowing when to call people, the best time.

---

list is a far better predictor than the want list. Users verbalize their wants in terms of current products, whereas problems are not product specific. Thus, if you ask what a person needs or wants from a shampoo, the answers will be clean hair, manageable hair, and so on—replies reflecting recent promotions of product benefits. But if you ask, "What problems do you have with your hair?" the answers may range into areas (for example, style or color) unrelated to shampoo. See Figure 5–2 for an example of what we are looking for in problem analysis.

Several recent award-winning product designs have resulted from the application of problem analysis. In one case, homeowners reported several problems with smoke and carbon monoxide detectors: ugly designs, too hard to shut off (without climbing up on a chair), nuisance alarms, poor instructions on what to do in case of emergency. Coleman developed its line of Safe Keep Monitors to be aesthetically pleasing in appearance, and added a "broom button" for easy reach. The carbon monoxide monitor comes with a door that opens to reveal instructions when activated (thus eliminating the need to hunt for a manual during an emergency). When developing the Aptiva S computer line, IBM sent researchers out to get pictures of home PCs. They found that space is at a premium for home computer users, as home desks tend to be smaller than office desks. The research also suggested that IBM was not a favored brand for home PCs. The Aptiva S was given a sleek design in which only the CD-ROM, diskette drive, and power switch are located in a console sitting on the desk—the rest of the computer is hidden under the desk. Speakers are built into the monitor to avoid taking up more space, and the keyboard can be stored on the console under the monitor when not in use. By being designed to solve real customer problems, both the Safe Keep line and the Aptiva S line have done well in terms of sales.[3]

The General Procedure

There are several variations in problem analysis. But the general approach is the following:

Step One. Determine the appropriate *product or activity category* for exploration. This has already been done if the product innovation charter has a use, user, or product category dimension in the focus statement.

Step Two. Identify a group of *heavy product users* or activity participants within that category. Heavy users are apt to have a better understanding of the problems, and they represent the bulk of the sales potential in most markets. A variation is to study *non*users to see if a solvable problem is keeping them out of the market.

Step Three. Gather from these heavy users or participants a set of *problems* associated with the category. Study the entire system of product use or activity. This is the inventory phase mentioned earlier, but far more is involved than just asking respondents to list their problems. A good method of doing this is where respondents are asked to rate (1) the benefits they *want* from a set of products and (2) the benefits they are *getting.* The differences indicate problems. Complaints are common, and often taken as requests for new products. But they are apt to be just the result of *omniscient proximity,* meaning that users face a minor problem frequently, so it is the first one mentioned. Some firms have had success *observing* consumers or business firms actually use products in a given category; for example, observing skiers as they shoot down a hill, or office workers handing a mailing operation. More on this in a minute.

Step Four. *Sort and rank* the problems according to their severity or importance. Various methods can be used for this, but a common one is shown in Figure 5–3. It uses (1) the extent of the problem and (2) the frequency of its occurrence. This "bothersomeness" index is then adjusted by users' awareness

---

[3]Examples are from Bruce Nussbaum and contributing writers, "Winners: The Best Product Designs of the Year," *BusinessWeek,* June 2, 1997, pp. 94–111.

FIGURE 5–3

The Bothersomeness technique of scoring problems

The following is an abbreviated list of pet owners' problems found by manufacturers of pet products.

	A *Problem Occurs Frequently*	*B* *Problem Is Bothersome*	*C* *A × B*
Need constant feeding	98%	21%	.21
Get fleas	78	53	.41
Shed hairs	70	46	.32
Make noise	66	25	.17
Have unwanted babies	44	48	.21

Source: Burton H. Marcus and Edward M. Tauber, *Marketing Analysis and Decision Making* (Boston: Little, Brown, 1979), p. 225.

of currently available solutions to the problem. This step identifies problems that are important to the user and for which the user sees no current solutions.

Georgena Terry made a special study of women's bicycle needs and came up with a line of bikes that have shorter tubes to permit easier reaching of handlebars, smaller brake levers and toe clips, and wider seats. An interesting feature of her bikes is a smaller front wheel, which gives better stability.[4]

Another unmet need that had existed for years was the noisy candy wrapper in the theater. Gene Shalit, of NBC's "Today Show," complained one morning about crackling candy bar wrappers. An expressway-commuting executive from Hercules, Inc., overheard his comment and asked the laboratory for a "silent candy wrapper." Polypropylene provided the answer, though not without tricky effort on heating, waterproofing, and airproofing.

A problem that had been obvious for years was only recently solved—making scissors that have *vertical* squeezing action and *horizontal* blade action. The leverage makes weak hands effective working units. Still another problem was found where people would have bet there were none—in the consumption of yogurt. When asked, people said they always wished for something to chew on! General Mills answer: *Yoplait Crunch 'N Yogurt*—over $50 million the first year, just sitting out there waiting for someone to ask users about their use!

A classic example occurred when Nike let Reebok storm past them in the women's market for athletic shoes. Reebok simply went out and talked to women about their athletics—and found them with leg and knee injuries sustained while doing aerobics. Out came a special line of shoes. Subsequently, Nike started pouncing on every consumer need—by 1994 they had 799 shoe models!

[4]Mary Guterson, "A Bicycle Built for Women," *Venture,* April 1987, p. 15.

Methodologies to Use

The generalized structure of problem analysis still contains the question of how to gather the list of consumer problems. Many methods have been used, but the task is difficult. The consumer/user often does not perceive problems well enough to verbalize them. And, if the problems are known, the user may not *agree* to verbalize them (for many reasons, including being embarrassed). Much of the sophistication in newer technologies was developed specifically to deal with these problems, and will be discussed in Chapter 6.

Experts. We have already mentioned going to the experts—using them as surrogates for end-users, based on their experience in the category under study. Such experts can be found in the sales force, among retail and wholesale distribution personnel, and in professionals who support an industry—architects, doctors, accountants, and the staffs of government bureaus and trade associations. Zoo experts first publicized the problem of elephant keepers being killed when trying to cut the big animals' toenails. Today an Elephant Hugger grabs an elephant, rolls it over on its side and holds it there, while the keeper cuts away. The inventor is now working on a giraffe-restraining device.[5]

Published Sources. Also as mentioned earlier, published sources are frequently useful—industry studies, the firm's own past studies on allied subjects, government reports, investigations by social critics, scientific studies in universities, and so on.

Stakeholder Contacts. The third, and most productive way, is to ask household or business/industry consumers directly. The most common method of doing this, by far, is direct, one-on-one interviewing. Sometimes this is a full scale, very formal and scientific survey. Other times the discussion is with lead users, an idea generating method discussed in Chapter 4; lead users often are the first to sense a problem, and some go on to respond to it themselves. Still other times, it may be no more than conversations with some key customer friends at a trade show, because a problem statement may come from only one person and yet be very significant for us. Because many end-users don't think all that much about the products they use, and often just accept them as parts of living, even very informal discussions with individuals can reopen thinking and bring to mind things forgotten.

A second technique for stakeholder inquiry, and a popular one, is the **focus group.** The focus group is designed to yield the exploratory and depth-probing type of discussion required, and it *can be* easy and inexpensive to set up and use. If done wrong, it only *appears* that way. Granted, in this case we are not seeking facts or conclusions, just genuine problems, and the focus

---

[5]Laura E. Keeton, "Marketers Debate the Best Way to Trim an Elephant's Toenails," *The Wall Street Journal,* February 25, 1995, p. B1.

group method works well by stimulating people to speak out about things they are reluctant to when in one-on-one interview situations. It's much easier to talk about one's problems when others in the group have already admitted they have problems, too.

But even in a single focus group, the costs are deceptive. Such sessions can cost from $3,000 to $10,000 in normal usage. Even at $3,000, a two-hour meeting of 10 people will yield about 10 minutes of talk per participant. Since the cost is $300 per participant, that's talk at the rate of $30 per minute, or $1,800 an hour! It had better be very good indeed.

Although the focus group technique is common, the outcome is not always, or even usually, successful. The focus group is a **qualitative research** technique. Unlike the traditional survey, it depends on in-depth discussions rather than the power of numbers. A problem analysis focus group should be asked:

What is the real problem here—that is, what if the product category did not exist?

What are the current attitudes and behaviors of the focus group members toward the product category?

What product attributes and benefits do the members of the focus group want?

What are their dissatisfactions, problems, and unfilled needs?

What changes occurring in their lifestyles are relevant to the product category?[6]

Other suggestions for helping guarantee the usefulness of focus group findings are to invite scientists and top executives to the sessions, and to avoid what some people call *prayer groups:* managers sit behind the mirror and pray for the comments wanted rather than really listening to what users are saying. Be sure the focus groups are large enough for the interactions and synergy that make them successful, and don't expect focus group members to like your products, or care about the activity being studied, or be consistent, or hold back from hurting your feelings.[7] Focus group moderators know not to begin the session "cold," but instead to let people get comfortable and introduce themselves—a rule of thumb is to treat participants as one would treat strangers at a party. The best moderators genuinely like people, and generate openness and trust by asking ice-breaker questions and by contributing personal experiences and practices.[8]

---

[6]"When Using Qualitative Research to Generate New Product Ideas, Ask These Five Questions," *Marketing News,* May 14, 1982, p. 15.

[7]Judith Langer, "Personal Encounters with Buyers the Key to Successful New Products," *New Product Development* (newsletter), February 1988, p. 5.

[8]Joseph Rydholm, "Respondent Collages Help Agency Develop Ads for New Pontiac," *Quick's Marketing Research Review,* March 1995, p. 7; and Tim Huberty, "Sharing Inside Information," *Quick's Marketing Research Review,* March 1995, p. 10.

Observation is another method of gathering problems directly from stakeholders. As an example, one firm studied the maintenance and cleaning of hospital floors by setting up a special motion study laboratory: Hospital personnel were brought in to clean floors under observation by company personnel. Observation may also be quite simple—as when Ziba Design noticed people holding to the crosspiece of a window washing squeegee, rather than to the handle. So the firm designed a new squeegee without a handle, just a round holder for the rubber strip.[9]

Another stakeholder contact method is **role playing.** Though role playing has long been used in psychology to enhance **creativity,** there is little evidence of its successful use in generating ideas for new products. Presumably, it would be valuable in instances where product users are unable to visualize or verbalize their reactions. It should also be valuable where consumers are emotionally unable or unwilling to express their views—for example, in areas of personal hygiene.

Unfortunately, though users are the best place to begin the ideation, and problem analysis is widely used in one form or another, most firms still do not have organized systems to exploit this source. Considering that Levi Strauss got the idea for steel-riveted jeans from a Nevada user in 1873, one must wonder why not.[10]

Scenario Analysis

So far, we have talked about going to technical and marketing people within the firm for ideas on customer problems, about searching the many files and record-keeping places where customer concerns can be found, and about problem analysis. The fourth general method shown in Figure 5–1—**scenario analysis**—comes into play because the ideal problem for us to find is one that customers or end-users don't know they have at this time. As hockey star Wayne Gretzky said, "I don't skate to where the puck is. I skate to where it's going to be." Similarly, we have to stay one step ahead of the customers by anticipating their problems.[11]

A future problem is a good problem because most problems we find in interviews and focus groups have already been told to competitors and anyone else who will listen. Providers of the goods and services have been

---

[9]Industrial designers are increasingly involving the end-user. Three case histories (two of them services) are discussed in Susan Ciccantelli and Jason Magidson, "From Experience: Customer Idealized Design: Involving Customers in the Product Development Process," *Journal of Product Innovation Management* 10, no. 4 (September 1993), pp. 341–47.

[10]Two general sources that are helpful on the matter of working with customers are P. Ranganath Nayak, Albert C. Chen, and James F. Reider, "Listening to Customers," *Prism,* Second Quarter 1993, pp. 43–57; and Karl T. Ulrich and Steven D. Eppinger, *Product Design and Development* (New York: McGraw-Hill, 1995).

[11]Mark Henry Sebell, "Staying Ahead of Customers," *U.S. Banker,* October 1997, p. 88.

working on them for many years, for example, flimsy music stands and steam on bathroom mirrors. We have time to solve a *future* problem and have that solution ready to market when the time comes.

Unfortunately, end-users usually don't know what their future problems will be. And they often don't really care, at least not right now. So they are not much help in interviews. This is where scenario analysis becomes valuable. Here's how it works.

If we were to describe apartment life 20 years from now, we would probably see lots of windows and sunlight coming in. If a furniture manufacturer were doing this scenario analysis, an analyst could immediately see problems, such as those apartment dwellers will need (1) new types of upholstery that are more resistant to the sun and (2) new types of chairs that will let them continue such activities as conversing and eating but also let them gain exposure to all that sunlight.

The Whirlpool Corporation has had a continuing task force painting a picture of what life will be like in the kitchen and laundry room when the United States hits a predicted water shortage crisis. This tells them what problems we *will be* having, and they will be ready with a line of appliances that will wash with very little (or actually no new) water.

The scenario analysis procedure is evident: first, paint a scenario; second, study it for problems and needs; third, evaluate those problems and begin trying to solve the most important ones. Painting a scenario does not yield a new product concept directly; it is only a source of problems, which still must be solved.

Scenarios take several different forms. First, we distinguish between (1) *extending* the present to see what it will look like in the future and (2) *leaping* into the future to pick a period that is then described. Both use current trends to some extent, of course, but the leap method is not constrained by these trends. For example, (hypothetically) an extend study might be: Currently, homeowners are converting from individual housing to condominium housing at an annual rate of 0.9 percent. If this keeps up for 20 years, there will be 7 million condominium units in use, which will present a need for 250,000 "visitors" motel units in major condominium areas to house visitors who cannot stay in the smaller units with their hosts. The thinking of the "utopian" school is sometimes used.

By contrast, a leap study might be: Describe life in the year 2010 in a major urban area of Germany contrasted with life in a similar setting in France.

Leap studies can be *static* or *dynamic.* In dynamic leap studies, the focus is on what changes must be made between now and then if the leap scenario is to come about—the interim time period is the meaningful focus. In static leaps, there is no concern about how we get there. Figure 5–4 shows a dynamic leap period in which the auto dealer service problem no longer exists. The time between now and then is broken down to yield the technical breakthroughs needed soon to reach that ideal condition. The leap scenario needn't be high probability; it can be just a goal or anywhere in between. For

FIGURE 5–4

The relevance tree form of dynamic leap scenario

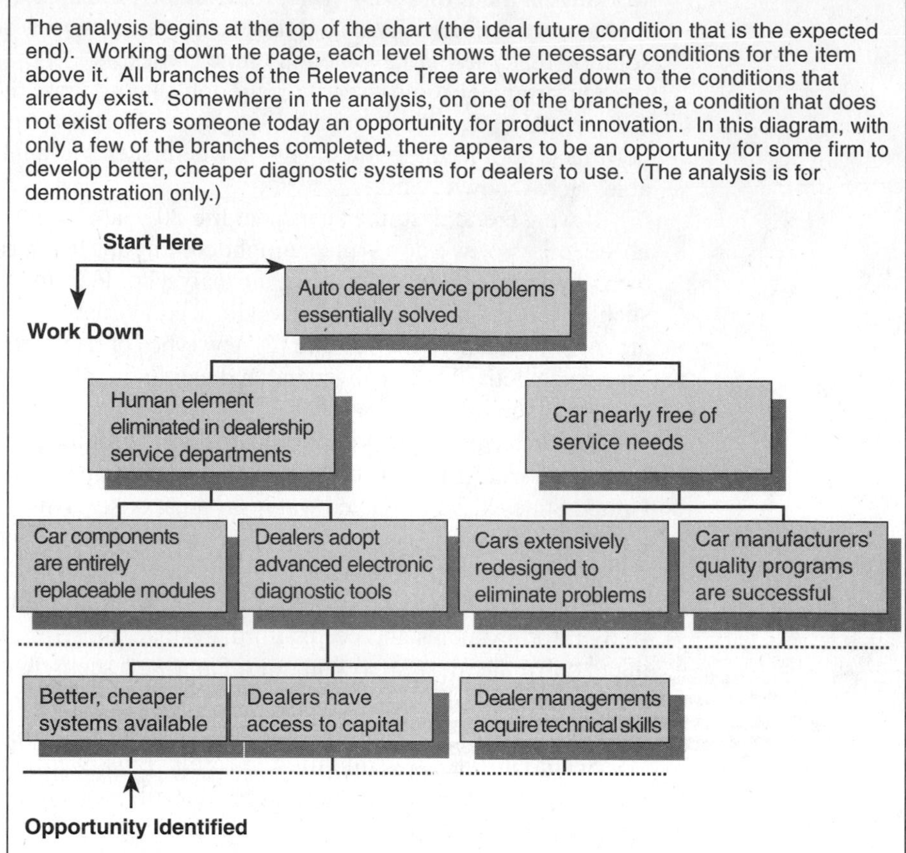

example, a bicycle manufacturer might imagine a city built entirely on pillars, steel-mesh roadways, people wearing virtually no clothing at all in air-conditioned hothouse environments, and so on. What implications would these conditions have for new bicycles?[12]

Scenario analyses lead to great learning and insights, but are hard to do well. Several guidelines have been suggested for conducting a good scenario analysis:

1. *Know the now.* The participants must have a good understanding of the current situation and its dynamics, otherwise the future they envision will not be realistic or useful for idea generation.

[12]For more on using scenarios, especially how to separate temporary fads from meaningful trends, see Harold S. Becker, "Developing and Using Scenarios—Assisting Business Decisions," *The Journal of Business and Industrial Marketing,* Winter/Spring 1989, pp. 61–69.

2. *Keep it simple.* Participants will likely have difficulty understanding really complex scenarios.
3. *Be careful with selecting group members.* A group of about six, with contrasting or complementary viewpoints and prior experiences, works best.
4. *Do an 8- to 10-year projection.* Too far out, and the participants are guessing. Not far enough out, and the respondents will just extend whatever is going on now.
5. *Periodically summarize progress.* This keeps the group on track and avoids contradictions.
6. *Combine the factors causing changes.* Scenarios should not be determined by just one factor.
7. *Check "fit"* or consistency at the end.
8. Once you have done the scenario analysis, *plan to use it several times.* These can be expensive.
9. *Reuse the group.* The more scenario analyses they do, the more they enjoy the task and the better they get at it.[13]

Solving the Problems

Once an important user problem has been identified, we can begin solving it. Most problem solving is probably done by members of the new products group that have been leading the concept generation work so far. They do it instinctively, from the moment they hear of a problem. There is no way we can quantify or describe the methods they use, since most of it is intuitive.

Many problems, however, are sent into the technical areas for more systematic attempts at solution. Here science and intuition rule, side by side. Some firms have it as strategy that problem solutions must come from R&D or engineering, with the solution itself being found in the application of some specific technology. A bus line wants travel problems solved by buses, and a bank probably wants problems solved by borrowing money. Besides technical people, the creative talents of marketing people are often used as well.

Note that the problem has to be carefully specified in order that a good, creative solution is found. P&G product developers reportedly spent months trying to solve the problem "How can we make a green striped soap that will draw sales from Irish Spring?" It was only when they focused their attention

[13]These points are from David Mercer, "Scenarios Made Easy," *Long Range Planning,* August 1995, pp. 81–86; and Audrey Schreifer, "Getting the Most out of Scenarios," *Planning Review,* September-October 1995, pp. 33–35.

on a new problem, "How can we make a soap that connotes freshness in its appearance, shape, and color better than Irish Spring?" that Coast (a soap with blue and white swirl patterns and a more oval shape) was developed and was ultimately successful.[14]

Group Creativity

New products people use individual problem solving effort, but many think that *group* effort can do more. The secret of **group creativity** is that two heads are better than one. Some scientists protest loudly that this is not true, that the synergism of groups is way overplayed. Generally, individuals can handle really *new* ideas and find *radical* solutions to problems better than groups can. Some feel that one reason small firms are more innovative than large firms is that they do not often use group creativity.

Students understand the values of individual and group thinking; you know pretty well when it is better to work on an assignment alone, and when with a group. You also know the problems of managing a group discussion.

The essence of today's group efforts to solve problems first appeared in 1938. Advertising executive Alex Osborn wrote a book about a technique he called **brainstorming.** All of the group ideation techniques developed since that time are spin-offs of his process and embody one idea: One person presents a thought, another person reacts to it, another person reacts to the reaction, and so on. This presenting/reacting sequence gives group creativity its meaning, and the various techniques developed simply alter how ideas are presented or how reactions take place.

Brainstorming

Osborn's approach, still taught and used today, includes two basic principles and four rules of conduct. Because the term has worked its way so deep into our language, it is widely abused. It is good for new products people to recognize bad brainstorming when they see it because bad brainstorming just won't work. The two basic principles are:

Deferral of Judgment. This requires participants to be free to express any idea that comes to mind without having to worry about criticism from others in the group. The judicial mind weighs evidence, but it discourages the free flowing of ideas.

Quantity Breeds Quality. Psychologists say that our most dominant thoughts are the habitual thoughts with which we are most comfortable. To

---

[14]Peter Wilson, "Simplex Creative Problem Solving," *Creativity and Innovation Management* 6, no. 3 (September 1997), pp. 161–67.

have really new ideas we must break through these conventional thoughts and ideas, and Osborn felt that achieving a large number of ideas requires breaking from the habitual.[15]

These two principles led to the following four rules for conducting a brainstorming session:

- All criticism is ruled out; even chuckles and raised eyebrows are banned.
- Freewheeling is welcomed—the wilder the better, with no inhibitions whatsoever. Divergent or **lateral thinking** should be forced by the leader.
- Quantity is wanted, so nothing is permitted to slow the session down (such as taking time to record an idea clearly or completely).
- Combination and improvement are achieved when each person's suggestion is carried to another stage of development or application by the next person.

These rules, in their pure form, are impossible to follow. Leaders often interrupt the process itself by trying to follow them. In addition, since brainstorming was invented as a method of problem-solving, participants should have experience in the general field with which the problem is concerned—product experience, in our case. They should be told the precise problem being attacked. They should be a diverse group but able to communicate (they can be co-workers or strangers).

The biggest change in the practice of problem solving over the past 20 years is to use brainstorming combined with other tools of creativity. We still try to avoid the *bazooka effect* (state an idea only to have someone shoot it down), but also to avoid the scores of easel sheets with hundreds of "ideas" scribbled on them. As one group creative says, the easel sheets are "full of spaghetti—a lot of bright ideas that are full of flaws . . . brainstorming is, too often, just permission to dump everything that has been in your head."[16] Instead, the group deliberations are exploratory, evaluative in a constructive way, hours long (versus the 20 minute brainstorming session), and built toward a few specific solutions that appear operational.

There have been many attempts to stick with the basic idea of brainstorming, but to tweak it in some way to overcome the problems. Some of the more common techniques, such as the Phillips 66 Groups and reverse brainstorming, are described in Appendix B.

[15]Alex Osborn, *Applied Imagination,* 3rd ed. (New York: Charles Scribner's Sons, 1963).

[16]Personal quote from Mark Sebell, co-founder of Creative Realities, a creativity training firm in Boston.

Electronic Brainstorming and Computer-Assisted Creativity Techniques

Despite its popularity, brainstorming has several drawbacks. Only one person can talk at a time, and "social loafing" may occur (average work intensity may be lower in a group setting). Further, some individuals may still fear being criticized for having unpopular ideas. **Electronic brainstorming,** a form of brainstorming assisted by **group support systems (or GSS) software,** are said to overcome these limitations of traditional brainstorming, as they allow participants to "all answer at once," and also to answer anonymously.

A GSS-assisted brainstorming session may take place in a room set up with a network of computer terminals. Participants sit at the terminals and respond to questions provided by the moderator, who runs the GSS software. The GSS software gathers the participants' responses, and projects them onto a large screen at the front of the room, or on the participants' monitors. Seeing the responses stimulates even more ideas and encourages follow-up discussion. The GSS also automatically takes electronic notes of all the proceedings, so nothing is lost or erroneously transcribed![17]

One is not restricted to a single location, either. GSSs can facilitate activity at many sites simultaneously (through computer linkups or videoconferencing), and handle group sizes into the hundreds.

GSSs are becoming much more popular in facilitating meetings, and there is increasing evidence that electronic brainstorming outperforms traditional brainstorming in terms of productivity and output of unique ideas.[18]

An increasing number of firms are using computer programs such as Mindlink, Mindfisher, and NamePro to assist their creative efforts in idea generation, and also to help out in other creative tasks such as brand name generation and selection. While they come in many forms, many of these work by drawing from large databases of words, phrases, or even pictures, encouraging the user to *think laterally* (gather unrelated thoughts, then try to associate them to the problem at hand). Most are straightforward and stimulating to use.[19] Also, many are adaptable to use in a GSS setting.

---

[17]A recent assessment of GSSs is found in Robert O. Briggs and Gert-Jan De Vreede, "Meetings of the Future: Enhancing Group Collaboration with Group Support Systems," *Creativity and Innovation Management* 6, no. 3 (June 1997), pp. 106–16.

[18]Keng L. Siau, "Group Creativity and Technology," *Journal of Creative Behavior,* Third Quarter 1995, pp. 201–17.

[19]Tony Proctor, "New Developments in Computer Assisted Creative Problem Solving," *Creativity and Innovation Management* 6, no. 2 (June 1997), pp. 94–98. For a critique of several of these computer programs, see Arvind Rangaswamy and Gary L. Lilien, "Software Tools for New Product Development," *Journal of Marketing Research* 34, February 1997, pp. 177–84.

FIGURE 5–5

The disciplines panel for group ideation

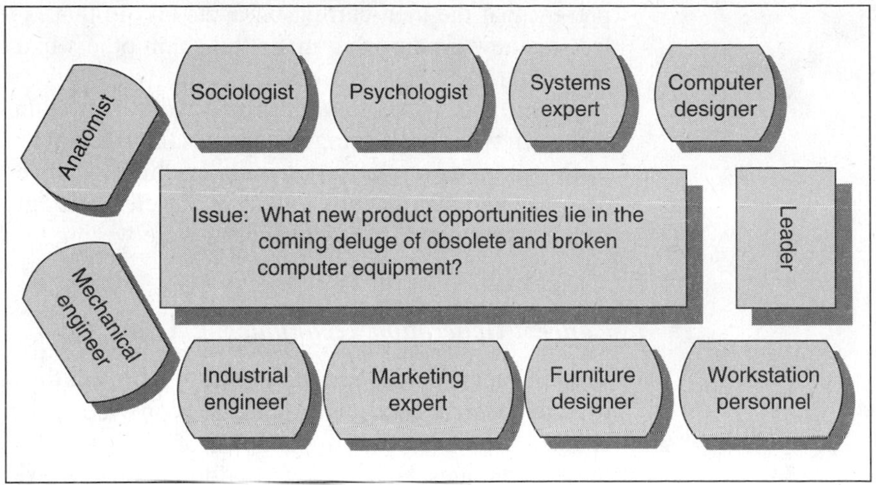

Disciplines Panel

Several of today's leading new products consulting firms believe creativity groups should actually work on a problem, not just talk about it, particularly in situations calling for significant innovation, not line extensions.[20] Their approach is to assemble experts from all relevant disciplines and have them discuss the problem as a **disciplines panel.** There may be just one meeting of the panel, but usually there are several lengthy meetings (see Figure 5–5).

A panel on new methods of packaging fresh vegetables might include representatives from home economics, physics, nutrition, medicine, ecology, canning technology, marketing, plastics, chemistry, biology, industrial engineering, agriculture, botany, and agronomy. Sometimes the panel consists of both company personnel and outside expert personnel. An example of a combined effort was when executives from Atlas Copco Roc Tec, a mining-equipment firm, met with a group of experts to solve this problem: How to dig ore and feed it onto a conveyor belt in one operation. Among the people on the panel was an entomologist who described how a praying mantis functions, from which came a large tractor with shovels on each side that dug the ore and shoveled it onto a belt that ran down the middle of the machine. Another example came from the shampoo industry, where a consumer need (to use hair conditioner that actually sought out split ends and went to work there) was expressed, only to be met by a statement from an R&D person

[20]The disciplines panel is part of the approach used by a leading creativity consultant, Innotech, Inc. For a good description of its operation, see Robert A. Mamis, "The Gang That Doesn't Think Straight," *INC,* October 1985, pp. 108–11.

present that the then-current products all did that! That surprising comment led to a new product that made the claim others had overlooked, and which turned out to be very successful.

Whirlpool had always heard that different countries in Europe wanted their own types of washing machines. Disagreeing, the firm used a disciplines panel, set up a few platforms, made machines with very little differences, and designed and manufactured them very well. Such "global" thinking led them into market dominance—consumers were willing to change when they were given a good alternative!

Concept Generation Techniques in Action

This chapter provided several **creativity-stimulating techniques** that can be used to generate concepts; Appendix B provides many more. Throughout the chapter, we have offered examples of firms that have successfully applied these techniques. Here are a few additional recent examples that illustrate the successful use of some other, perhaps less common, techniques.

1. *Using Props.* Life Savers Company wanted to develop new flavors. They hired a consultant who filled a room with samples of fruits, varieties of perfumes, and lists of dozens of ice cream flavors. Life Savers' "Fruit Juicers" line came out of the session. P&G's Duncan Hines Pantastic party cakes came from an idea stimulation session where greeting cards were among the props used.
2. *Role Playing.* Bausch and Lomb's Polymer Technologies Division came up with the idea of cushioning material bonded to the lens surface by getting pairs of executives to play the roles of eyeball and contact lens. The "actors" had to think of ways the lens could stop hurting the eyeball while role playing.
3. *Imitating Nature.* Goats eat waste and emit it in the form of small pellets. This idea inspired Whirlpool in its development of the Trash Smasher compactor.[21]

Summary

Chapter 5 began our study of the many specific techniques developed by concept creators to aid them in their work. The most common approach is based on the paradigm of "find problem, solve problem," requiring participation by many people in the firm, plus stakeholders and others outside the firm. Then we looked at the many techniques developed to spot problems. These included (1) inputs from technical and marketing departments, (2) search of

[21]Bryan Mattimore, "Eureka: How to Invent a New Product," *The Futurist,* March–April 1995, pp. 34–38.

internal records from sales calls, product complaints, customer satisfaction studies, and more, (3) problem analysis as a way of involving end-users and other stakeholders, and (4) scenario analysis as a way of learning about future problems. Once problems are discovered, efforts at solution can begin; most efforts involve individual thinking and analysis, whether in the office or in the lab. One major group of techniques uses the label of group creativity; it includes a great variety of approaches, but most are variations of brainstorming.

Next we will turn to some methods called analytical attributes, created over the years to aid marketing managers in seeking improvements while they are waiting for the approach of problem-find-solve to bear fruit. This is the approach where we start with form, then see if there is a need, and if so, then develop the necessary technology.

Applications

More questions from that interview with the company president.

1. "I recently met the president of a Florida university who had previously researched the new products operation in Silicon Valley firms. He wasn't impressed. Said that sales reps told him over and over about getting suggestions and tips from their customers and sending them in on call reports, but nothing ever happened. Apparently, upper level sales and marketing executives only rarely have customer contact, yet don't capitalize on the contacts of sales people. You have any ideas on how I might go about being sure this condition doesn't exist in our various divisions?
2. "I personally love to watch for a trend and predict some new product from it. For example, just to see how good you are at creative thinking, here are some trends I noted recently in the press. Can you think of two possible products suggested by each?
   a. Lofty goals are giving way to very personal wants; there is less social globalism; the focus is inward; support for many social programs such as environmentalism is clearly on the wane.
   b. There has been great growth in bulk foods, items in barrels that we dish up ourselves, while at the same time an overwhelming trend to eating out (cutting in-home meal preparation).
   c. AT&T tells us that the very idea of long-distance calling will soon disappear. All calls will be charged by distance and time, even within a city. They will be even cheaper than now, and in fact many of them will go via computer networking in digital form.
   d. Life is more and more focused around celebrities—sports, TV, politics, etc. Population has grown so big that people can only relate to famous faces and names. Every thing they do is interesting and attracts intense involvement by *many* millions of people."

3. "I believe in problem analysis—that's at the heart of things. But I sure don't like those focus groups. I sat in on a couple last year, and all the people did was chat. And the chatting never seemed to lead to anything. After the second one was over, I quizzed the moderator, and she agreed that there had been a lot of rambling. She kept talking about the gems of knowledge we found—common threads, I believe she said. Now, honestly, isn't that pure bunk? However, she did say she thought focus groups would be especially useful in Eastern Europe, where businesses have so many needs, and we have to be sure to cull down to the most critical ones. I wonder, suppose our Swiss trucking division could use focus groups to help them develop new services for Eastern European businesses?"
4. "You know a lot about rental of formal wear, like tuxedos and formal gowns, I imagine. Can you take me through a problem analysis, using the formal wear rental market as an example? Several of our divisions are involved in retail business, and I'm curious to see what problems you come up with that we haven't solved yet."

Case: Campbell's IQ Meals[22]

In 1990, Campbell Soup was the undisputed leader among U.S. soup manufacturers, with a market share of over 75 percent. Soup consumption, however, was leveling off, and top management was looking for opportunities for growth in related markets. Competitors such as ConAgra (Healthy Choice brand) and H. J. Heinz (Weight Watchers brand) were making sizeable sales and profit gains in their frozen foods lines, stressing their dietary benefits, and this seemed like a good place for Campbell to begin generating new product ideas.

At the time, the U.S. public was becoming more interested in the relationship between diet and disease prevention. It seemed that every day health benefits were turning up in one food or another, causing fads such as oat bran to sweep the country. Campbell's R&D department soon turned to investigating the diet-disease relationship, focusing on foods that could be used to prevent illnesses such as diabetes or cardiovascular disease (including high blood pressure). Given that 58 million Americans have some form of cardiovascular disease, and another 16 million have diabetes, this focus seemed very reasonable. Soon enough, the rough idea had been generated: a line of foods with medical benefits. The rough idea now needed to be further developed.

The challenge was to develop a food line that not only played a role in the prevention of these diseases, but also would be accepted and adopted by the U.S. population. Dr. R. David C. Macnair, Campbell's chief technical officer, built an advisory board consisting of leading nutrition, heart disease, and diabetes specialists, who would scientifically analyze the new products. Campbell's CEO at the time, David W. Johnson, was 100 percent behind

[22]This case is largely based on Vanessa O'Connell, "Food for Thought: How Campbell Saw a Breakthrough Menu Turn into Leftovers," *The Wall Street Journal,* October 6, 1998, pp. A1, A12.

the food-with-medical-benefits idea, saying that it had "explosive potential." Soon he was attending the advisory board meetings as well. Mr. Johnson said, "Wouldn't you be dumbfounded by the opportunity to take a quantum leap and develop a product that could help improve the health and nutrition of the world?"

With the backing of the Campbell CEO, the project was underway, with a clear goal: to make the concept of healthy, vitamin-and-mineral-rich meals a reality. The Campbell food technologists found this a challenging task—one of the early prototype fiber-enriched rolls "could have been marketed as a hockey puck," according to Macnair. By fall 1994, however, about 24 meals that passed early taste tests were ready for clinical trials to determine health benefits. Over 500 subjects ate the meals for ten weeks, and most reported improvements in cholesterol, blood pressure, and blood sugar levels. None experienced side effects, and many reported they liked the taste. Meanwhile, Mr. Johnson created Campbell's "Center for Nutrition and Wellness," based in the Camden, New Jersey, head office and employing 30 nutrition scientists and dietitians.

Next came the market test. Campbell marketing staff selected the name "Intelligent Quisine" (or IQ Meals), and a blue box or can for packaging. The plan was for UPS drivers to deliver 21 meals (mostly frozen, a few in cans) each week to test subjects' doors. By January 1997, the product was being test marketed in Ohio, backed up with a print ad campaign and a ten-minute infomercial designed to stimulate toll-free calls to Campbell's information line. Campbell also hired part-time pharmaceutical sales reps to pitch IQ Meals to doctors, and contacted leading hospitals such as the Cleveland Clinic to distribute IQ Meals and promotional material. Things were looking up!

The first sign of trouble was at the phone bank. Callers found out that the one-week "sample pack" cost $80, and the recommended plan (10 weeks) cost $700, and promptly hung up. Fixed-income households found the price especially steep. At the American Heart Association's Columbus office, Campbell sponsored a lunch to promote IQ Meals' benefits, but failed to impress many of the dietitians present. Further, Wall Street analysts had their doubts as well: one of them wrote a report titled, "UPS T.V. Dinners Drive Top Line?"

Soon Campbell executives were doubting the IQ Meals as well. Consultants were called in to assess the project's viability, and Dale Morrison, head of international and specialty foods, cut IQ's budget drastically. By May 1997, sales in the Ohio market test were dismal, and another problem was arising. Those that had stuck with the program since January were showing health benefits, but now many of them were reporting that they were getting tired of the same nine meals over and over again.

The fate of IQ Meals was sealed in a corporate shakeup at Campbell in July 1997. Mr. Johnson, its biggest supporter, gave up his CEO position (and became Campbell's chairman). Mr. Morrison rose to president and CEO, with a plan to expand international sales and to focus on key brands. Swanson, Vlasic, and other Campbell brands were spun off—and the marketing and promotion for IQ was terminated (though clinical trials were continued). The Center for Nutrition and Wellness researchers were reassigned. By fall 1997, Campbell announced plans to sell IQ Meals.

IQ Meals seemed to be a classic case history. The idea that was generated seemed foolproof with respect to the marketplace opportunity and the associated demographic trends. Campbell would appear to be the perfect company to pull it off, given its core competencies and its willingness to expand into growth areas. The line even did well in both clinical trials and early consumer tests. But, somehow, something got lost in the translation. And clearly, this is not an isolated incident. What went wrong? And what might Campbell product developers or executives have done differently? Or was this one just doomed from the start?

CASE: EARNING ORGANIZATIONAL RESPECT

In this case, you and your classmates play the role of the marketing department in a firm involved in new product development (NPD). Your firm is struggling with instituting team-based NPD, and over the last several months several of the marketing staff have been placed on product teams with personnel from engineering, design, and manufacturing. The experience so far has not been positive for you and your marketing colleagues. You feel that marketing is routinely left out of key team decisions, and that top management seems more sympathetic to the engineers when conflicts arise within the team. You suspect that part of the reason is that most top management personnel in your firm come from an engineering background and just understand the perspectives and the decision-making style of the engineers better. You also feel that marketing has a lot to contribute to NPD. There is an excellent marketing research department that can provide quick feedback on customer behavior using state-of-the-art equipment, and the sales force is second to none in the industry and routinely gathers key market information and intelligence. There are several very good creative people on staff responsible for generating high-potential ideas, which your firm has developed into many successful new product launches.

One of your creative colleagues in product development suggests using a problem-based ideation approach, commonly used to generate new product ideas, to try to find a way to get top management to respect the marketing department more. Ideally, you would like them to recognize their skills, training, and experience, and to appreciate and use the unique information they can bring to the NPD process. You succinctly state your problem as follows:

> "How can we communicate the value and potential contributions of the marketing department effectively to top management, so that they will respect us more?"

Using the ideation techniques given in Appendix B (or any others you prefer), develop creative solutions to this problem. First, generate at least half a dozen ideas individually. Keep a basic rule in mind: there are no bad ideas—the more, the merrier. Then, with your instructor working as a group facilitator, boil these down to the four or five best ideas, and, as a group, discuss and refine these. Your goal is to arrive collectively at one or more clear, well-thought-out programs that you could realistically begin implementing soon. One other rule: use your imagination! This is an exercise where you can really "stretch." Though you can try any of the techniques given in Appendix B, some you might find particularly useful are the following:

Scenario Analysis: Identify a set of trends (fashions, hot places to live/work, celebrities, exciting new products, etc.). Think about what might be suggested by or associated with any of these.

Creative Stimuli: Look at the set of stimulus words provided in Appendix B, and select a few of these at random. Ask yourself how each of your words suggests something that helps you solve your problem. Be creative.

Forced Relationships: Forget about your problem altogether for a little while. Select a magazine. Turn randomly to a page, and look at the picture on that page. (If none, leaf through the magazine until you get to one.) What does the picture suggest to you? Jot down at least half a dozen thoughts. Now, return to your problem, and use the thoughts you came up with to help you think creatively about possible solutions. For a variation, use a dictionary, encyclopedia, or Yellow Pages instead, and find a random word on a random page.

Use of the Ridiculous: Think of the most ridiculous idea you can. Then ask yourself if it suggests to you a not-so-ridiculous new idea.

CHAPTER

6 ANALYTICAL ATTRIBUTE APPROACHES

Introduction and Perceptual Mapping

Setting

In Chapter 5, we studied an approach to concept generation that involves identifying users' problems and finding solutions to them. The problem-based approach is the best because product concepts found by the problem/solution route are most likely to have value for the user.

As part of the problem-solving phase and also independently from the problem approach, however, techniques from another approach are also used. Everyone involved with the creation and sale of goods and services can make use of these techniques, including some who don't even know they are doing formal concept generation. What these techniques do is create views of a product different from the usual ones—they can seem almost magic, but are quite deliberate. They can appear to be strictly fortuitous, or lucky, when they work, and they have indeed worked—many times, as with adding a third stocking to a package, quick-drying inks, and VCRs combined with TVs. But actually they are quite deliberate and purposeful, allowing discovery—serendipitous findings that come to people who know what they are looking for.

What Are Analytical Attribute Techniques?

We have found many methods for getting different views of current products. As an example of how "far out" these methods can appear: Light a candle, sit close to it, and hold near the flame the product you are studying, stare directly at and through both the flame and the product, describe what you "see" in that vision. Although they may seem odd, actually, most of these techniques are quite reasonable, with clear logic to them.

Analytical attribute techniques capitalize on the concept that any future change in a product must involve one or more of its current attributes. Therefore, if we were to study those attributes, changing each one in all the ways it could be changed, we would eventually discover every change that could ever come about in that product. Other techniques capitalize on relating one attribute to another (or to something else in the environment—forcing these relationships whether normal and logical or strange and unanticipated. They all can work, as you will see. And they have been used in all product categories from polymer processing technologies at Kodak to the newest car lines at Chrysler to eyeglasses and cereal.

Analytical attribute techniques are felt to be more useful in Western culture than in Eastern. Western (particularly European and North American) thought goes heavily toward rearranging things, while Eastern (Asian) thought tends to start work anew.[1] Commodity-type products are a major focus of these techniques because slight rearrangements can differentiate one item from its competitors, thus allowing it to carry a higher price. What is a **product attribute?** Figure 6–1 shows the set of them. A product is really nothing but attributes, and any product (good or service) can be described by citing its attributes.[2]

Attributes are of three types: **features, functions,** and **benefits;** benefits can be broken down in an almost endless variety—uses, users, used with, used where, and so forth. Due to the creative nature of concept generation, great liberty has been taken with the definitions and use of these terms in the past. The classification system used in this book is an attempt, and no more than that, to arrange them for study.

One way to look at attributes is with an example. A spoon is a small shallow bowl (*feature*) with a handle (another *feature*) on it. The bowl enables the spoon to *function* as a holder and carrier of liquids. The *benefits* include economy and neatness of consuming liquid materials. Of course, the spoon has many other features (including shape, material, reflection, and pattern). And many other functions (it can pry, poke, project, and so on, as school cafeteria managers know all too well). And many other benefits (such as pride of ownership, status, or table orderliness).

Theoretically, the three basic types of attributes occur in sequence. A feature permits a certain function, which in turn leads to a benefit. A shampoo may contain certain proteins (feature) that coat the hair during shampooing (function), which leads to more shine on the hair (benefit).

---

[1]Jacquelyn Wonder and Jeffrey Blake, "Creativity East and West: Intuition versus Logic," *Journal of Creative Behavior,* Third Quarter 1992, pp. 172–85.

[2]Attribute measurement and assessment is not the exact science its techniques suggest. For a rather distressing but enlightening report, see James Jaccard, David Brinberg, and Lee J. Ackerman, "Assessing Attribute Importance: A Comparison of Six Methods," *Journal of Consumer Research,* March 1986, pp. 463–68.

FIGURE 6–1

A typology of attributes

A. Product attributes (for our purposes) are of three types:

Features Functions Benefits

Features can be many things:

Dimensions	Esthetic characteristics	Components
Source ingredients	Manufacturing process	Materials
Services	Performance	Price
Structures	Trademarks	And many more

Benefits can be many things:

Uses	Sensory enjoyments	Economic gains
Savings (time, effort)	Nonmaterial well-being	And many more

Benefits are either direct (e.g., clean teeth) or indirect (e.g., romance following from clean teeth).

Functions are how products work (e.g., a pen that *sprays* ink onto the paper). They are unlimited in variety, but are not used nearly as often as benefits and features.

B. Analytical attribute approaches use different attributes:

Dimensional analysis uses features
Checklists use all attributes
Trade-off analysis also uses determinant attributes
Several methods in Appendix B use functions and benefits

There are a variety of quantitative and qualitative **attribute analysis** techniques available. In this chapter, we explore one common quantitative technique: **perceptual gap analysis.** After an introduction to determinant gap maps, we will show how perceptual mapping techniques such as factor analysis and multidimensional scaling (MDS) can be used to generate perceptual gap maps. These techniques are frequently used in concept generation, and indeed, throughout new product development, during launch, and even beyond. We shall be returning to them from time to time as we proceed through the new products process. Chapter 7 examines a second common quantitative technique, conjoint analysis, and several qualitative techniques such as dimensional analysis, checklists, relationships analysis, and analogy. Many more techniques are also given in Appendix B.

Gap Analysis

Gap analysis is a statistical technique with immense power under certain circumstances. Its *maps of the market* are used to determine how various products are perceived by how they are positioned on the market map. On a geographical map, New York City is much closer to Pittsburgh than it is to Los Angeles. But on a *nearness-to-the-sea* map, New York City would be right next to Los Angeles. On any map the items plotted tend to cluster here and there, with open space between them. These open spaces are gaps, and a map that shows gaps is, not surprisingly, called a **gap map.**

Several levels of sophistication will be cited because many firms prefer to use the technique in a simple form, while others have achieved their greatest success with the more complex versions. Gap maps are made in three ways: (1) *managerial expertise and judgment* is used to plot products on a map and make a **determinant gap map;** (2) a manager uses customer *attribute ratings* to get data from users for an **AR perceptual gap map;** and (3) a manager uses *overall similarities* to get data from users for an **OS perceptual gap map.** Thus, determinant maps use *our* factors and *our* scores, AR perceptual maps use *our* attributes and *customers'* scores, and OS perceptual maps use *customers'* attributes and *customers'* scores.

Determinant Gap Maps

Figure 6–2 shows a map of snacks prepared by a new products manager seeking to enter the snack market. The map consisted of two dimensions (he personally thought crunchiness and nutritional value were important on snacks). Scales ran from low to high on both factors. Each brand then in the market was scored by the manager on each of the two factors.

This may appear rather arbitrary and dangerous. But remember, concept generation takes place *after* strategy (the PIC) has targeted a market or user group on which to focus. Either the firm had experience in this market (a

FIGURE 6–2

Gap map for snack products

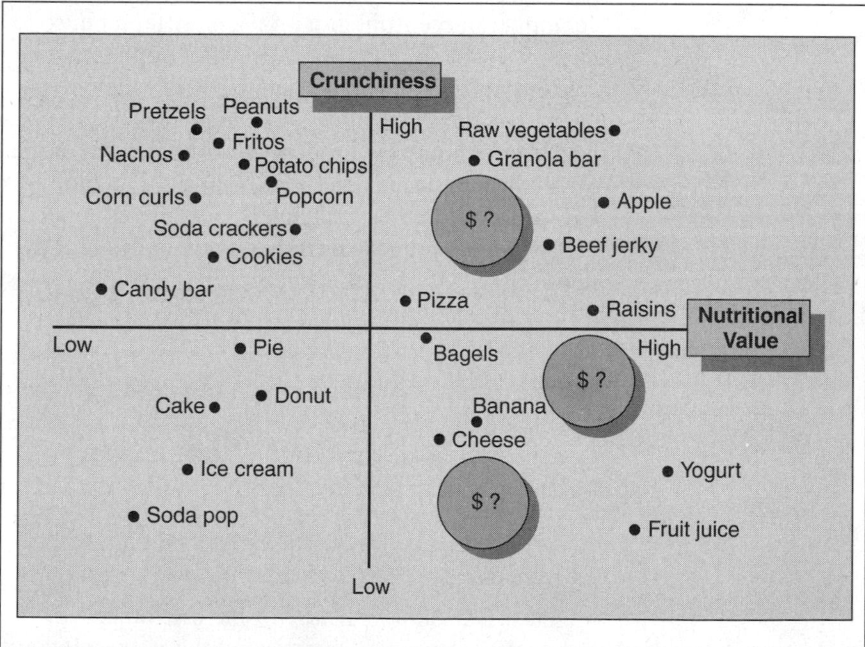

Note: This map is purely for demonstration, not research-based.

strength) or the market was researched. Each snack type was then entered on the diagram (Figure 6–2) according to its scores. The result was a map of the snacks, each in relationship to all others, on these two factors. Many maps could have been prepared, each with a different pair of attributes. They can also be three-dimensional.

Attributes used in gap analysis should normally be *differentiating* and *important.* Consumers differentiate snacks on their crunchiness, and on their nutritional value. And these attributes are important in buying snacks. Snacks also have different shape esthetics, but these are not often used to differentiate one from another. Even if they were, most people would probably not think them important.

Attributes that both differentiate and are important are called **determinant attributes** because they help determine what snacks are bought. In an industrial study of vinyl siding, some of the determinant attributes identified were appearance/status, maintenance/weathering, application/economy, and dent resistance.[3] The reason we use determinant attributes in making the maps is that our purpose is to find a spot on the map where a gap offers potential for a new item, one that people might find "different" and interesting.

For example, on the snacks map in Figure 6–2 the circles marked "$?" are gaps, and thus offer new product possibilities. Note that the large number of snacks makes our gaps few and small—for example, the gap of semihigh crunchy and semihigh nutritional is close to the granola bar, the apple, beef jerky, and soda crackers.

Determinant gap maps are speedy and cost efficient, but are driven only by managerial judgment. The manager may learn that customer perceptions are quite different. Techniques that gather customer perceptions and use them to develop gap maps can provide important (and perhaps surprising) insights to the manager. We now explore two commonly used types of perceptual gap maps.

AR Perceptual Gap Maps

Unlike the determinant gap map method, attribute ratings (AR) perceptual gap mapping asks market participants (buyers and users of the product) to tell what attributes they believe products have. For example, product users may think candy bars are high in nutrition—doubtful, but if this were so, then any map putting candy bars low in nutrition is incorrect for seeing perceptual gaps. Determinant maps are based on reality as viewed by the new products manager (or, perhaps, by the firm's R&D personnel). Perceptual maps, as the name implies, are based on marketplace perceptions of reality, which may or

---

[3]Steven A. Sinclair and Edward C. Stalling, "Perceptual Mapping: A Tool for Industrial Marketing: A Case Study," *Journal of Business and Industrial Marketing,* Winter/Spring 1990, pp. 55–66.

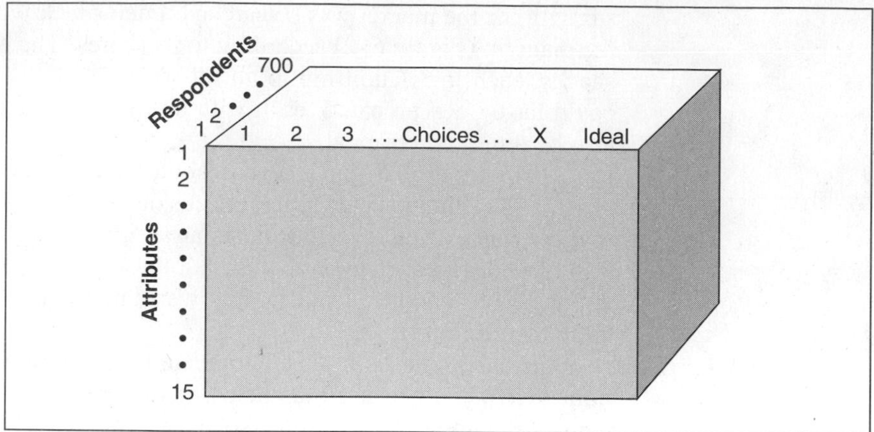

FIGURE 6–3
A data cube

may not be accurate. They can complement each other, and both have a place in our work.

In AR perceptual gap mapping, we begin with a set of attributes (again, these can be features, benefits, or functions) that describe the product category being considered. We gather customers' perceptions of the available choices (e.g., brands) on each of these attributes. Typically, this is done using 1-to-5 or 1-to-7 scales, where the endpoints are "strongly disagree" and "strongly agree" with each attribute statement provided. We also ask customers which attributes are important in their purchases of products in this category. This procedure results in a formidable **data cube** (Figure 6–3), which while perhaps impressive in size, is not very helpful to managers. In Figure 6–3, the perceptions of the available choices on each attribute would appear under Choices 1 through X, while the importances of the attributes would be given in the "Ideal" column.

The challenge is then to reduce the data cube into something more manageable—namely, a perceptual map. **Factor analysis,** a statistical technique available in computer packages, is typically used to reduce the attributes to a small number of underlying dimensions (also called factors), that can then serve as the axes of the perceptual map. **Cluster analysis** (to be presented in a later chapter) can then be used to group individual respondents together into benefit segments based on their preferences.

Suppose, for example, that you are a product manager at a firm that makes women's swimsuits. Based on your industry experience and your knowledge of the market, you have developed a set of attributes that customers use in evaluating and comparing swimsuits. You have commissioned a research study in which female respondents were asked to identify all the brands of swimsuits they are familiar with, and to rate them on each of the attributes on 1-to-5 Likert-type scales (see Figure 6–4). They are also asked to state how important each of these attributes is when deciding which brand of

FIGURE 6–4

Attribute perceptions questionnaire

Rate each brand you are familiar with on each of the following:

	Disagree Agree
1. Attractive design	1. . 2 . . 3 . . 4 . . 5
2. Stylish	1. . 2 . . 3 . . 4 . . 5
3. Comfortable to wear	1. . 2 . . 3 . . 4 . . 5
4. Fashionable	1. . 2 . . 3 . . 4 . . 5
5. I feel good when I wear it	1. . 2 . . 3 . . 4 . . 5
6. Is ideal for swimming	1. . 2 . . 3 . . 4 . . 5
7. Looks like a designer label	1. . 2 . . 3 . . 4 . . 5
8. Easy to swim in	1. . 2 . . 3 . . 4 . . 5
9. In style	1. . 2 . . 3 . . 4 . . 5
10. Great appearance	1. . 2 . . 3 . . 4 . . 5
11. Comfortable to swim in	1. . 2 . . 3 . . 4 . . 5
12. This is a desirable label	1. . 2 . . 3 . . 4 . . 5
13. Gives me the look I like	1. . 2 . . 3 . . 4 . . 5
14. I like the colors it comes in	1. . 2 . . 3 . . 4 . . 5
15. Is functional for swimming	1. . 2 . . 3 . . 4 . . 5

swimsuit to buy, again using 1-to-5 Likert-type scales. The average ratings of each brand on each attribute are presented in the snake plot of Figure 6–5.

The **snake plot** (the name refers to the snake-like shape of the lines that join the points) reveals some useful information. For example, respondents tend to think that Aqualine is more comfortable to wear and easier to swim in than Sunflare (attributes 3 and 8), while Sunflare has a more attractive design and is more stylish than Aqualine (attributes 1 and 2). But there is just too much in Figure 6–5 for it to be of much help in identifying a lucrative perceptual gap, and we still seem to be far away from a simple pictorial representation as seen in Figure 6–2.

Closer inspection of Figure 6–5 suggests that there may be underlying patterns in the data. We notice, for example, that brands that are rated high on "attractive design" tend also to be perceived as "fashionable," "designer label," and so on. We might say that these attributes seem to "hang together." Similarly, other attributes ("comfortable to wear," "easy to swim in," and "comfortable to swim in") also seem to "hang together." There may be a small number of such underlying dimensions or factors that explain most of the variation in perceptions presented in Figure 6–5. If we could identify these factors, then we would no longer need all the attributes: we could present most of what we know about customer perceptions using just the factors. We apply a factor analysis computer program to the customer perception data to identify these factors.

The first challenge we face is to determine how many underlying factors to retain in the model, as this is seldom clearcut. One rule of thumb is to plot

FIGURE 6–5

Snake plot of brand ratings

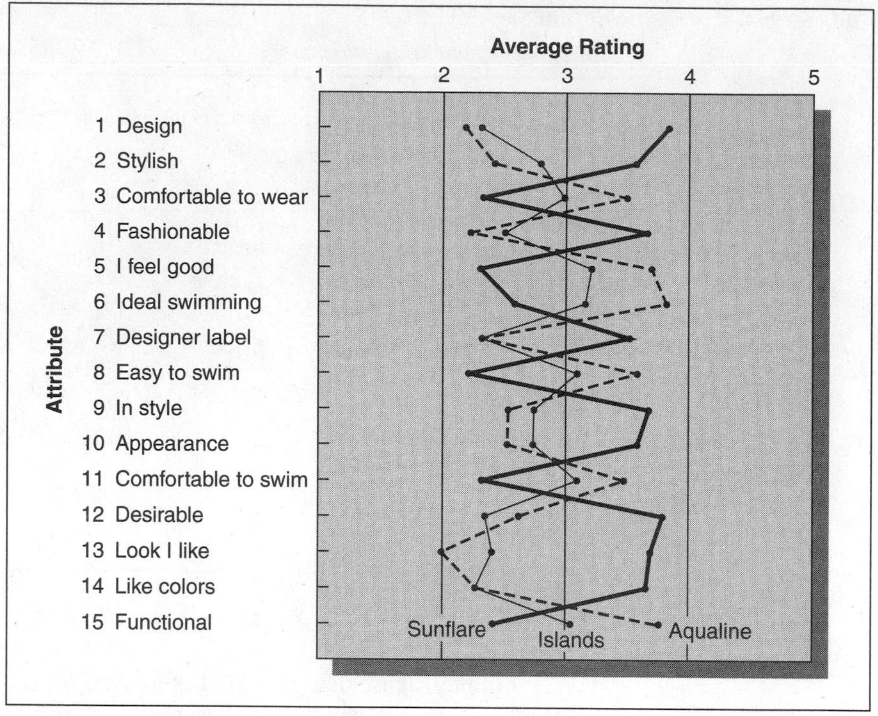

incremental percent variance explained as shown in Figure 6–6. As this figure shows, Factors 1 and 2 both explain a lot of variance, but going from two to three factors does not add very much to the model. This provides some evidence that two factors should be retained. This procedure is called the "scree test." (A "scree" is a pile of rocks at the foot of a mountain. Figure 6–6 resembles the side of a mountain, and the cutoff is made at the "scree.") The factor analysis procedure also provides an "eigenvalue" for each factor, which is mathematically related to the amount of variance explained. A second rule of thumb is to keep only those factors whose eigenvalues are greater than 1. Figure 6–6 shows that the first two eigenvalues pass this hurdle (they are 6.04 and 3.34 respectively). Thus, both the scree test and the eigenvalue rule suggest that the two-factor solution is satisfactory.

The factor analysis program then calculates a factor loading (or factor pattern) matrix, showing the correlation of the original set of attributes to their underlying factors. Figure 6–7 shows the rotated factor loading matrix obtained for the swimsuit data.[4] Attribute 1 ("attractive design") clearly loads on

[4]The factor loading matrix of Figure 6–7 has been varimax rotated. This procedure rotates the axes to aid in interpretation of the resulting factors by forcing the column entries to be close to 0 or 1. For details, see Gilbert A. Churchill, Jr., *Marketing Research: Methodological Foundations,* 6th ed. (Fort Worth, TX: Dryden, 1995).

FIGURE 6–6

Scree plot and eigenvalue test

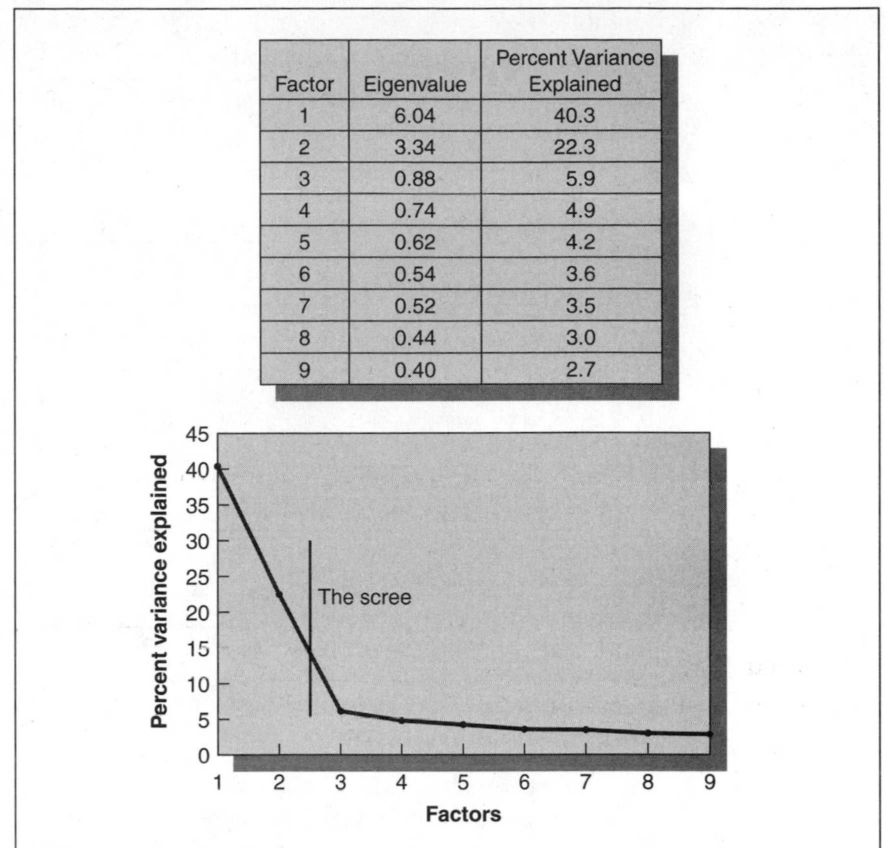

Factor	Eigenvalue	Percent Variance Explained
1	6.04	40.3
2	3.34	22.3
3	0.88	5.9
4	0.74	4.9
5	0.62	4.2
6	0.54	3.6
7	0.52	3.5
8	0.44	3.0
9	0.40	2.7

the first factor much more than on the second factor (the loadings are 0.796 and 0.061 respectively; in Figure 6–7, the "large" loadings are underlined and bolded for clarity). As the table shows, Attributes 2, 4, 7, and five others also load on the first factor. Similarly, a different set of attributes (3, 5, 6, and so on) load on the second factor.

So what should we call the two factors? Again, there is no right answer; this is part of the "analyst's art." But glancing at the attributes that loaded onto Factor 1 ("attractive design," "stylish," "fashionable," "looks like a designer label," "in style," and so on), we see a common thread. We might call this factor "fashion." The second factor might be called "comfort" as its attributes all seem to have to do with comfort or ease of wear. Figure 6–7 shows the factor names at the top of each column. Incidentally, the fact that these two factors are easily interpretable is further proof that the two-factor solution is good. Several apparently unrelated attributes can sometimes get "forced" together onto a single factor: this may be a sign that too few factors were chosen.

The program also calculates the matrix of factor-score coefficients (see Figure 6–8). These are regression weights that relate the attribute scales to the

FIGURE 6–7

Factor loading matrix for swimsuit data

Attribute	*Factor 1 "Fashion"*	*Factor 2 "Comfort'*
1. Attractive design	**.796**	.061
2. Stylish	**.791**	.029
3. Comfortable to wear	.108	**.782**
4. Fashionable	**.803**	.077
5. I feel good when I wear it	.039	**.729**
6. Is ideal for swimming	.102	**.833**
7. Looks like a designer label	**.754**	.059
8. Easy to swim in	.093	**.793**
9. In style	**.762**	.123
10. Great appearance	**.758**	.208
11. Comfortable to swim in	.043	**.756**
12. This is a desirable label	**.807**	.082
13. Gives me the look I like	**.810**	.055
14. I like the colors it comes in	**.800**	.061
15. Is functional for swimming	.106	**.798**

factor scores. Thus, since we know how each brand is rated on each individual attribute (this information is in the snake plot), we can use the factor-score coefficient matrix to estimate how they would have been rated relative to the underlying factors. These estimates, called factor scores, can be used to draw the perceptual map, which appears in Figure 6–9.

The perceptual map shows that Aqualine is perceived as the most comfortable brand but is low in fashion (its scores on the two factors are 2.48 and 4.36, respectively). Sunflare is the most fashionable brand but is also perceived to be the most uncomfortable. Splash is rated quite low on both factors, and the other two brands occupy intermediate positions in perceptual space. Recall that this is information on how *customers* perceive the products; it may be quite unlike what management had previously believed.

So we have gone from the messy snake plot of Figure 6–5 to the perceptual map of Figure 6–9. Granted, the perceptual map does not have *all* the information contained in the snake plot. But we have retained the two most important factors (in terms of variance explained) underlying customer perceptions. Thus we have a simple visual representation that is easily used and understood by managers, and that contains *most* of the information we started with.

The perceptual map we just built resembles the snack map of Figure 6–2, and the search for gaps can proceed as before. Since the perceptual map was

FIGURE 6–8

Factor score coefficient matrix

Attribute	*Factor 1 "Fashion"*	*Factor 2 "Comfort'*
1. Attractive design	0.145	–0.022
2. Stylish	0.146	–0.030
3. Comfortable to wear	–0.018	0.213
4. Fashionable	0.146	–0.017
5. I feel good when I wear it	–0.028	0.201
6. Is ideal for swimming	–0.021	0.227
7. Looks like a designer label	0.138	–0.020
8. Easy to swim in	0.131	0.216
9. In style	–0.021	–0.003
10. Great appearance	0.146	0.021
11. Comfortable to swim in	–0.029	0.208
12. This is a desirable label	0.146	–0.016
13. Gives me the look I like	0.148	–0.024
14. I like the colors it comes in	0.146	–0.022
15. Is functional for swimming	–0.019	0.217

Sample calculation of factor scores: From the snake plot, the mean ratings of Aqualine on attributes 1 through 15 are 2.15, 2.40, 3.48, . . . , 3.77. Multiply each of these mean ratings by the corresponding coefficient in the factor score coefficient matrix to get Aqualine's factor scores. For example, on Factor 1, Aqualine's score $(2.15 \times 0.145) + (2.40 \times 0.146) + (3.48 \times -0.018) + \ldots + (3.77 \times -0.019) = 2.48$. Similarly, its score on Factor 2 can be calculated as 4.36. All other brands' factor scores are calculated the same way.

built using actual customer perceptions, any gaps found are more likely to interest the potential users.[5] For example, the perceptual map suggests that customers perceive some swimsuits to be comfortable, and others to be fashionable, but none offers both high comfort and high fashion (Gap 1 in Figure 6–9). Congratulations—you've just uncovered a gap!

OS Perceptual Gap Maps

AR perceptual maps early on suffered a criticism that led to a variation preferred by some product innovators. The problem was that users sometimes make purchase decisions using attributes they can not identify. These "phantom" attributes don't show up on the lists, are not included as map

[5]For more information on the use of factor analysis in new products, see Uwe Hentschel, "On the Search for New Products," *European Journal of Marketing* 5, 1976, pp. 203–17.

FIGURE 6–9
AR perceptual map of swimsuit brands

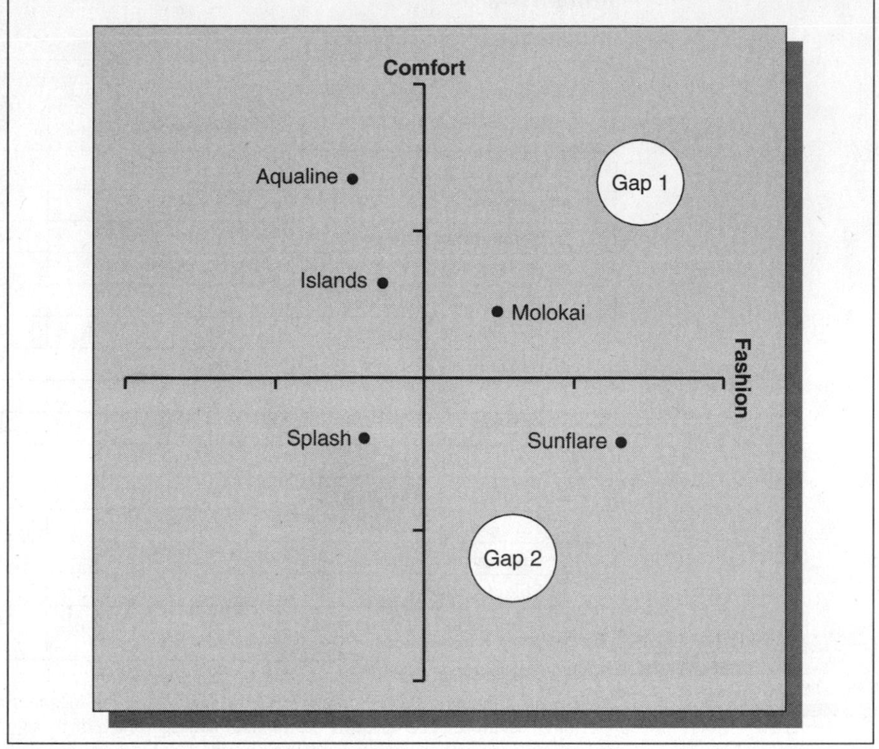

dimensions, and by their absence distort the analysis. Also, some users have difficulty scoring attributes, even when they are aware of them, because of various aspects of focus group settings, privacy, and so on. AR methods essentially view products as bundles of attributes. For AR to be effective, then, the attribute set needs to be complete. (If we had forgotten to include comfort-related attributes in the above analysis, our results would have been very different, and very misleading!) Also, customers should, by and large, make their purchase decisions according to these attributes. In a product category like cologne, for example, the customer's decision may be driven more by brand image, aesthetics, or other attributes that are notoriously difficult for them to verbalize.

DuPont offered an early example of the phantom problem. The company sold filler material for pillows and wanted to find the best type and form of filler to enhance its sales to pillow manufacturers. But DuPont market analysts found that consumers could not clearly describe the attributes of pillows and could not communicate the attributes they wanted in pillows. So the firm created many different types of pillows and then gave them to consumers three at a time, along with the question "Which two are most similar, or which one is least like the other two?" DuPont's research was much more complex than this question implies, but, in essence, the firm was now able to use a

FIGURE 6–10

Dissimilarity matrix

	Aqualine	*Islands*	*Sunflare*	*Molokai*	*Splash*
Aqualine	X	3	9	5	7
Islands		X	8	3	4
Sunflare			X	5	7
Molokai				X	6
Splash					X

computer algorithm to convert the "similarities" data into a map showing closeness of products, *without knowing a priori which attributes created that closeness.*

OS techniques do not require customers to rate choices on individual attributes. Rather, these techniques run on perceptions of overall similarities between pairs of choices. If there are five choices (as in the swimsuit example), there are ten possible pairs. There are a couple of ways the data can be collected. Respondents could rank the pairs from most similar to most dissimilar, or rate pairs on, say, a 1-to-9 Likert-type scale where 1 is "very similar" and 9 is "very dissimilar." If we had gathered similarities data on swimsuits using Likert-type similarity scales, we might have ended up with average similarity ratings as shown in Figure 6–10. This figure shows that customers tend to see Sunflare and Molokai as relatively similar (recall that lower ratings mean greater similarity), and Aqualine and Sunflare as very dissimilar.

The next step is to convert the similarity ratings into a perceptual map. In a very simple example, if you think Coke and Pepsi are very similar, and both are very different from Dr Pepper, you could easily draw a map of your perceptions on a single line: put Coke and Pepsi on the left and put Dr Pepper on the right. In the same way, we could "eyeball" the ratings in Figure 6–10, though the task would admittedly be difficult. Alternatively, we could use a computer program such as **multidimensional scaling (MDS)** to develop a perceptual map from the similarities data.

MDS attempts to plot the brands on a map such that the similarities are best preserved (i.e., brands that should be together are together). Figure 6–11 shows the perceptual map obtained from the similarity ratings.

The MDS-based perceptual map seems very similar to Figure 6–9, which was derived from factor analysis. In fact, the relative positions of the brands are not that different. There is one important difference, however: the axes are not defined! MDS provides the relative positions only; follow-up analysis must be done to define the axes (there may be more than two) and determine what the relative positions mean. A manager knowledgeable about the industry might be able to infer the meanings by examining the brands. For example, since Aqualine is known to be the most comfortable brand, and Splash and

FIGURE 6–11

OS perceptual map of swimsuit brands

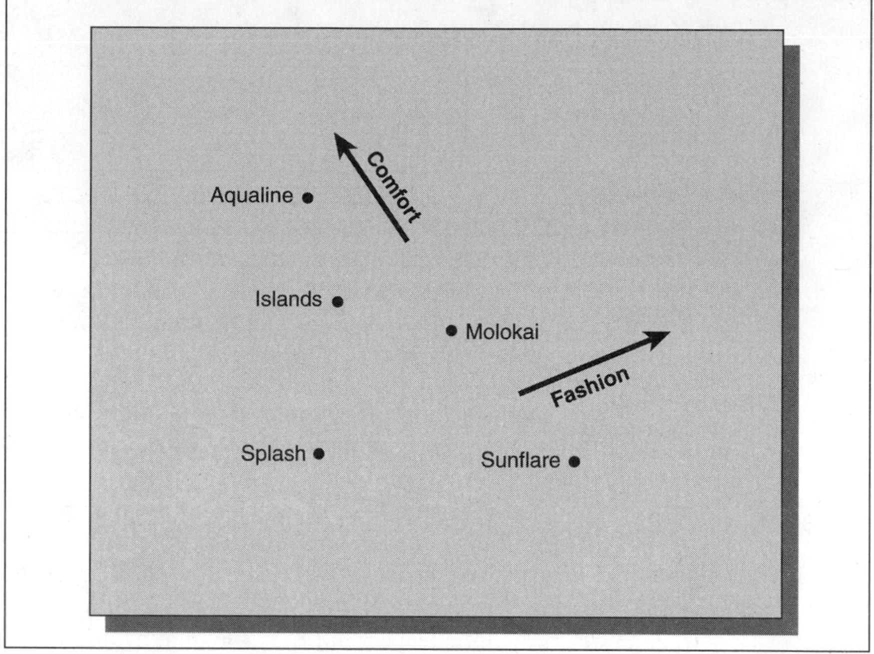

Sunflare are generally viewed as less comfortable, the north-south direction might represent comfort (north being more comfortable). In the same way, the more fashionable brands seem to be towards the right, suggesting that the east-west direction represents fashion.

Alternatively, computer programs can be used to assist in naming the axes if measures on specific attributes had been obtained from the respondents. One of the most common of these is PROFIT (for PROperty FITting), which fits vectors to the map that best correspond to the brands' positions. If, for example, customers were asked to rate each brand on comfort and fashion, PROFIT might have fit vectors corresponding to these attributes as shown in Figure 6–11. The most fashionable brands tend to be in the direction of the fashion vector.

Figure 6–12 compares the advantages and disadvantages of AR and OS perceptual mapping methods. Both methods are readily available as parts of easy-to-use commercial software packages, and can generate detailed results at quite low cost.

Comments on Gap Analysis

All gap mapping is controversial, but perceptual maps especially so. The input data come entirely from responses to questions about how choices differ. Nuances and shadings are necessarily ignored, as are interrelationships and

FIGURE 6–12

Comparing AR to OS perceptual mapping

AR Methods	*OS Methods*
Input Required	
Ratings on specific attributes	Overall similarity ratings
Attributes must be prespecified	Respondent uses own judgment of similarity
Analytic Procedures Commonly Used	
Factor analysis; multiple discriminant analysis	Multidimensional scaling (MDS)
Graphical Output	
Shows product positions on axes	Shows product positions relative to each other
Axes interpretable as underlying dimensions (factors)	Axes obtained through follow-up analysis or must be interpreted by the researcher
Where Used	
Situations where attributes are easily articulated or visualized	Situations where it may be difficult for the respondent to articulate or visualize attributes

Source: Adapted from Robert J. Dolan, *Managing the New Product Development Process: Cases and Notes* (Reading, MA: Addison-Wesley, 1993), p. 102.

synergies. Creations requiring a conceptual leap are missed. In the early 1800s, for example, gap analysis might have led to breeding faster horses or to wagons with larger wheels, but it probably would not have suggested the automobile.

The most troublesome aspect is that gap analysis discovers gaps, not demand. Gaps often exist for good reasons (e.g., fish-aroma air freshener or aspirin-flavored ice cream). New products people still have to go to the marketplace to see if the gaps they discovered represent things people want.

Returning to Gap 1 in Figure 6–9, we do not know yet whether the market wants a very comfortable, very fashionable swimsuit. Inspection of Figure 6–9 also suggests there is a gap at medium fashion, low comfort (Gap 2). Maybe this is a better bet for a new concept. To answer this question, we need to turn to the importance data, which, as you will recall, we collected at the same time as we gathered the perceptual data. We will continue this example in Chapter 9 when we analyze customer preferences and identify benefit segments.

And, as in all of ideation, new products people must avoid being bound by what is now "impossible." For example, for years gap maps on analgesics showed a big hole where strength was paired with gentleness. The strong/gentle part of the map was always empty, and everyone knew why—an over-the-counter analgesic could not be made that was potent yet didn't irritate the stomach. Of course, Extra-Strength Tylenol proved everyone wrong. As a more recent example, most popular brands of soap were positioned as either deodorants (like Dial) or moisturizers (like Dove), and a perceptual gap (a brand that offered both attributes) existed. In 1991, Lever 2000 soap very successfully filled that gap, having been launched as a combination deodorant/moisturizing bar and supported by a first-year advertising campaign of $25 million—which was increased to $40 million in the second year![6]

Summary

In this chapter, we have examined the use of gap maps in identifying potential product concepts. As we have noted above, this technique will come in handy in later stages of the new products process, when we begin working with customer preferences and positioning (and repositioning) our products. We have looked in depth at both attribute-based and overall-similarity-based perceptual mapping, each technique having its own advantages and disadvantages.

Other attribute-based approaches are also available to us at the concept generation stage. Chapter 7 will introduce us to conjoint (trade-off) analysis, and also several other less-quantitative approaches, which can also be useful in generating potentially lucrative product concepts.

Applications

More questions from that interview with the company president.

1. "One method you say you studied is of great interest to me, for reasons I'll not go into. It's gap analysis, especially the idea of maps. Several of our best divisions produce and sell services. Is the gap map method applicable to services? Could you please take, say, the college education "market" and draw up a product map for it? I understand it can be done by a manager at a desk, although, of course, it wouldn't be nearly as accurate as if we had all the technical data, and so on. But could you try?"
2. "You describe a very fancy way to arrive at positioning maps using an array of statistical techniques. I'm not convinced, however, that the maps you generate are any better or more useful than the ones I and a couple of my senior colleagues can draw from scratch. After all, we do know the industry pretty well!"

---

[6]See Robert M. McMath and Thom Forbes, *What Were They Thinking?* (New York: Times Business Books, 1998), pp. 184–85.

3. "OK, you've identified a gap in the swimsuit market in your little example. Some customers like fashionable swimsuits, some like comfortable ones. We already know that. So isn't it obvious you should design a swimsuit that's both fashionable and comfortable? What insights did you get from the gap analysis that you couldn't have figured out on your own?"
4. "A few years ago, most peanut butters were sold on the basis of their perceived quality (well known brands vs. store brands), and crunchiness. There wasn't a lot of difference among the competitors. Then Skippy (the CPC competitor) hits the market, claiming to be healthier than other brands because it uses less salt. They didn't even position themselves on the "traditional" attributes in their market. How does your gap map account for that?"

CASE: AT&T MAGICPHONE PHONE-FAX-COPIER (A)[7]

In early 1992, AT&T had two business communications systems available to the small-to-medium-size business owner. The Merlin system was designed for users with modest communications needs (it supported an office network with as many as eight lines and twenty telephones), and the System 25 was targeted to larger users (up to 150 telephones). Both the Merlin and the System 25 could be used as a stand-alone office network. At that time, AT&T was about to announce the launch of the Magicphone Phone-Fax-Copier (PFC). This product was to be the first fully integrated phone system with a built-in fax and copier, and could be added to either the Merlin or the System 25 network as part of an office automation network. The Magicphone PFC offered business users several desirable features: conferencing capabilities, call pickup, speakerphone, exclusive hold, and simultaneous phone-fax usage. The Magicphone PFC was projected to hit the market at a price to customers of $1,175.

AT&T management believed that several categories of businesses would be interested in the Magicphone PFC: project managers, information managers (such as banks and stockbrokers), hotels/motels, care providers, and so on. AT&T had a very "pro-marketing" approach to new product development: customer surveys were frequently undertaken, in order to determine likes and dislikes with existing systems and to identify potential product improvements.

Due to its innovativeness and anticipated quality, AT&T believed that it would be difficult for competitors to duplicate the performance capabilities of the Magicphone PFC. No directly competitive products were on the market at the time, but AT&T anticipated that similar PFC-type products would be eventually launched by ROLM, TIE, and Executone.

---

[7]This case is based on "AT&T Magicphone PFC," a case in Roger J. Calantone and C. Anthony Di Benedetto, *The Product Manager's Toolbox* (New York: McGraw-Hill, 1993). Used with permission. The material on product features and competitive information presented in this case was compiled from numerous published sources, and the name of the product is disguised. The positioning data are for illustrative purposes only.

In addition to these direct competitors, other companies (including many smaller ones) offered in-home fax machines that offered a copier feature as well as a built-in phone. Although not directly competitive to the Magicphone PFC, such products were thought of as substitutes and therefore indirect competition.

Based on early test market results, competitive intelligence, and managerial judgment, AT&T management developed a positioning map for the Magicphone PFC and its most relevant competitors, using the two salient attributes of Convenience and Productivity. The positions of each brand (on scales of 1 to 5) are as follows:

	Convenience	*Productivity*
AT&T Magicphone	4.25	3.25
ROLM	2.50	3.00
TIE	3.75	1.75
Executone	2.00	3.50

Construct the positioning map for this industry, using the information presented in the case. Discuss the relative positions of AT&T Magicphone and its major competitors on the two key attributes. Do you think AT&T is well positioned with respect to its competitors? Which competitor(s) should AT&T be the most concerned about? Why? What additional information might you want to have about the competitors and/or about the marketplace at this point? How might a seemingly "weaker" competitor (i.e., outpositioned by AT&T on both key attributes) like ROLM make a dent in AT&T's market share, given that by the time they enter, AT&T will have been on the market for at least several months?

CHAPTER

7 ANALYTICAL ATTRIBUTE APPROACHES

Trade-Off Analysis and Qualitative Techniques

Setting

The previous chapter presented market research techniques that are very frequently used to analyze customer perceptions and tradeoffs and to generate promising product concepts. We begin this chapter with another useful and common quantitative technique: trade-off (or conjoint) analysis. These techniques will be encountered in subsequent stages of the new product development process and, in a way, serve to provide continuity and guidance to the process (i.e., customer perceptual and preference data generated here can be used as inputs into protocol specification).

We will then encounter several analytical attribute approaches that are more qualitative in nature. While less numbers-oriented, they are very helpful in getting customers and managers to think in creative ways to generate new product concepts. These and the quantitative approaches complement each other well in concept generation and development. For example, dimensional or relationships analysis could be used to help identify determinant attributes for subsequent use in an AR gap analysis, or any of the qualitative approaches could aid in interpreting a perceptual map produced by AR or OS methods.

Trade-Off Analysis

Trade-off analysis (often called **conjoint analysis**) is a technique that is more commonly used in concept evaluation, so we will meet it again in Chapter 9. But it can be used in generating high-potential concepts for future evaluation, so it is introduced here. You will likely encounter both terms, though they are not interchangeable. Trade-off analysis refers to the analysis of the process by which customers compare and evaluate brands based on their attributes or features. Conjoint analysis is the name of one of the most common analytical tools used to assess tradeoffs (much like factor analysis is a tool that is used to develop perceptual maps). Trade-off analysis is thus the "broader" term. In this text, we will use "conjoint analysis" when we are specifically referring to that technique for assessing tradeoffs.[1]

Recall that after finding the determinant attributes (important attributes on which the available products differ), gap analysis plots them on maps. In using conjoint analysis, we assume we can represent a product as a set or bundle of attributes. Conjoint analysis puts all of the determinant attributes together in new sets, and identifies which sets of attributes would be most liked or preferred by customers. In fact, AR gap analysis output can be used to select the attributes used in conjoint analysis.

Using Trade-Off Analysis to Generate Concepts

Presume coffee has three determinant attributes: flavor, strength, and intensity of aroma. As Figure 7–1 shows, there are several different levels available for each of these attributes. If somehow we could get customer preferences (or **utilities**) for each attribute separately, we could combine the "best" level of each attribute into an overall favorite product. As shown in Figure 7–1, customers prefer medium strength, no (added) flavor, and regular aroma. Unless this particular combination was already on the market, we would have our new product concept. Other high-potential concepts are also suggested in the figure: for example, a strong hazelnut coffee might not be a bad idea.

Trade-off analysis was used by the Sunbeam Corporation when it wanted to expand its kitchen mixing appliances sales in various countries around the world. The company identified three types of attributes—silhouette, features, and benefits. The determinant attributes for each appliance were identified, and the range for each selected. For instance, silhouettes had about 10 combinations—low versus high, strong versus stylized, and so on.

Cards representing new products that combined specific silhouettes, features, and benefits were prepared. Consumers in the various countries were asked to sort the cards by preference from top to bottom. If a person wanted a low, strong silhouette, a large number of variable speeds, a very quiet motor, and the ability to use on semiliquids, one card may have had the right silhouette, speed, and noise but couldn't be used on liquids. Another could be used on liquids and had the right silhouette and noise but had only three speeds. To choose one, the consumer would have to trade off speed variety

---

[1]Another trade-off method that can be used as an alternative to conjoint is presented in Peter D. Morton and Crispian Tarrant, "A New Dimension to Financial Product Innovation Research," *Marketing and Research Today,* August 1994, pp. 173–79.

FIGURE 7–1

Factor utility scores—coffee example

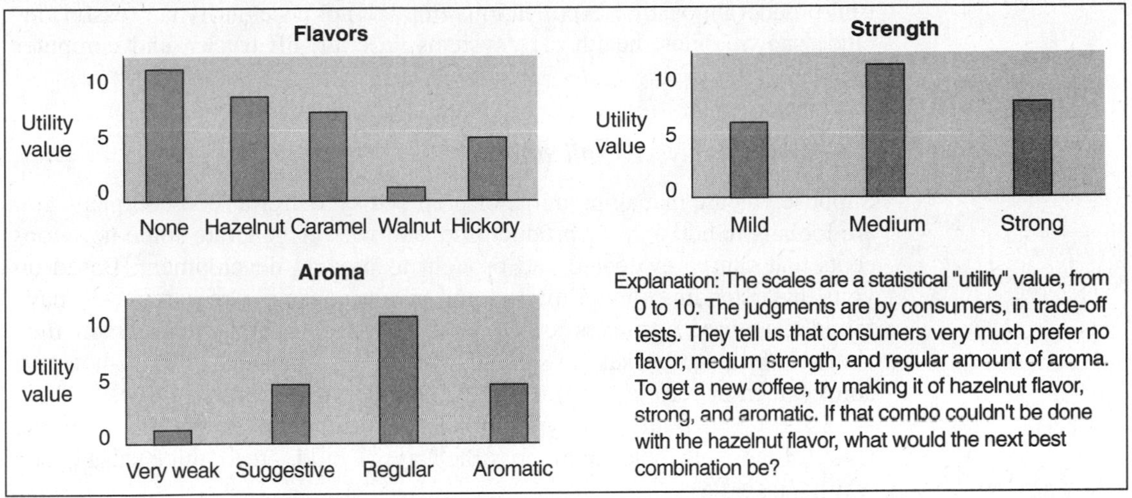

against use on liquids. With hundreds of consumers doing this, a good picture for each attribute can be obtained and the optimization process begun.[2]

Another example concerned not a consumer good, but an industrial service—information retrieval for sale to financial institutions.[3] Twelve attributes were considered important, and each was given a range for the test. Here are three of the twelve:

Nature of output	**Speed of delivery**	**Output format**
Citation only	Within hours	Photocopy
With documentation	Within days	Microform
With interpretation		

The research procedure was the same one that Sunbeam used. The research firm put together a set of cards representing many different versions of the proposed service and covering all characteristics of the 12 attributes. Financial firms were approached, rankings of the cards were made, utility functions were determined, and the ideal service was calculated and returned to the financial institutions for evaluation.

---

[2]The Sunbeam example is described in Albert L. Page and Harold F. Rosenbaum, "Redesigning Product Lines with Conjoint Analysis: How Sunbeam Does It," *Journal of Product Innovation Management,* June 1987, pp. 120–37.

[3]The financial information example is discussed in detail in Yoram Wind, John F. Grashof, and Joel D. Goldhar, "Market-Based Guidelines for Design of Industrial Products," *Journal of Marketing,* July 1978, pp. 27–37.

Because business buyers tend to make a more rational analysis of product features, trade-off analysis is becoming increasingly valuable for industrial product innovation. Applications (though not necessarily successful) include snowmobiles, health care systems, aircraft, lift trucks, and computer software.[4]

A Conjoint Analysis Application

Suppose you are managing a line of prepared salsas for a food company. You are looking to add to your product line, and need to generate some new concepts that can be evaluated and brought to product development. Based on your understanding of the market and recent consumer research, you have found that three attributes are uppermost in customers' minds when they choose a brand of salsa: (1) spiciness (mild, medium-hot, or extra-hot), (2) color (green or red), and (3) thickness (regular, thick, or extra-thick). There are $3 \times 2 \times 3 = 18$ different types of salsa that can be made by combining the levels of these attributes in all possible ways (a mild, green, thick salsa is one way).

We begin by designing 18 cards, each with a picture and/or verbal description of one of the combinations. Each respondent customer is then asked to rank the cards from 1 to 18, where 1 is "like most" and 18 is "like least."[5] As this task may be challenging, we can suggest that the respondent make three piles of cards ("like," "neutral" and "don't like"). The six or so cards within each pile can more easily be sorted, then the piles can be combined and final adjustments to rank order can be made. The rankings provided by one respondent are given in Figure 7–2. (Figure 7–2 also shows rankings as estimated by the model, which can be ignored for now.)

Suppose a given customer likes extra-hot salsa. There are several cards in the stack (six, to be exact) that depict extra-hot salsa, in combination with other attributes. He or she would tend to rank these cards favorably (that is, give them a low rank number—the lower the rank number, the more the concept is liked). If he or she *really* likes extra-hot, we might expect almost all of the extra-hot cards to be assigned low rank numbers—that is, a pattern would be evident in the rank orderings. If the customer couldn't care less about

---

[4]For details on usage of the trade-off technique, see Dick R. Wittink and Philippe Cattin, "Commercial Use of Conjoint Analysis: An Update," *Journal of Marketing,* July 1989, pp. 91–96; and Dick R. Wittink, Marco Vriens, and Wm Burhenne, "Commercial Use of Conjoint Analysis in Europe: Results and Critical Reflections," *International Journal of Research in Marketing,* January 1994, pp. 41–52.

[5]In addition to ranking, other types of responses can also be gathered. For example, respondents can be presented with pairs of cards and asked to state which they prefer. The different techniques lead to similar results. See Gilbert A. Churchill, Jr., *Marketing Research: Methodological Foundations,* 6th ed., (Fort Worth TX: Dryden, 1995).

FIGURE 7–2

Preference rankings of one respondent

Thickness	*Spiciness*	*Color*	*Actual Ranking**	*Ranking as Estimated by Model*
Regular	Mild	Red	4	4
Regular	Mild	Green	3	3
Regular	Medium-Hot	Red	10	10
Regular	Medium-Hot	Green	6	8
Regular	Extra-Hot	Red	15	16
Regular	Extra-Hot	Green	16	15
Thick	Mild	Red	2	2
Thick	Mild	Green	1	1
Thick	Medium-Hot	Red	8	6
Thick	Medium-Hot	Green	5	5
Thick	Extra-Hot	Red	13	13
Thick	Extra-Hot	Green	11	11
Extra-Thick	Mild	Red	7	7
Extra-Thick	Mild	Green	9	9
Extra-Thick	Medium-Hot	Red	14	14
Extra-Thick	Medium-Hot	Green	12	12
Extra-Thick	Extra-Hot	Red	17	18
Extra-Thick	Extra-Hot	Green	18	17

*1 = Most preferred, 18 = Least preferred.

whether the salsa was green or red, we would expect the rank numbers assigned to red salsa to be not that different from those assigned to green—no patterns would emerge.

Conjoint analysis uses monotone analysis of variance **(MONANOVA),** a data analysis technique, to find these patterns within the rank order data. That is to say, we identify the customer's underlying value system: which attributes are important and which levels of the important attributes are favored. To do this, we use the rank orderings to estimate the utilities (sometimes called *part-worths*) of each level of each attribute for each customer. The graphical conjoint analysis output for the data of Figure 7–2 is given in Figure 7–3(a).

The graphs in Figure 7–3(a) provide a visual representation of the relative importances of the attributes. The largest range in utilities is found for spiciness—the utilities assigned to mild and extra-hot are +1.667 and –1.774, for a range of 3.441—thus, spiciness is this individual's most important attribute influencing likes and dislikes in salsa (using the same logic, color is the least important). The graphical output also indicates which levels of each attribute are preferred. As shown, mild salsa is favored over medium-hot or extra-hot, other things being equal. This particular customer also prefers medium-thick salsa to both regular and extra-thick, and likes green salsa slightly more than red salsa.

FIGURE 7–3

Conjoint analysis output—salsa data

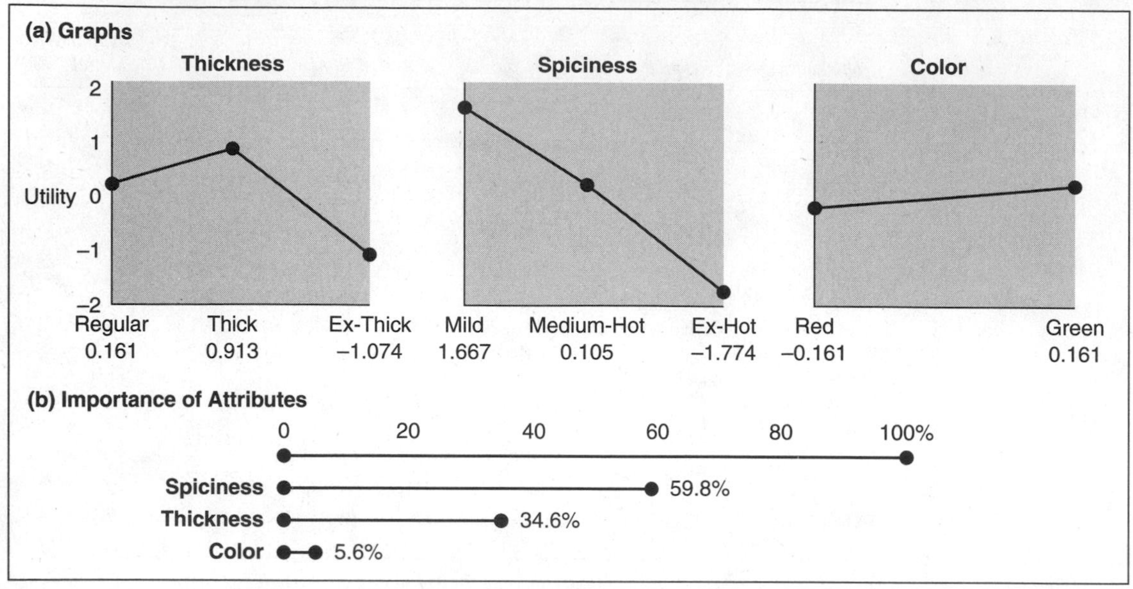

Figure 7–3(b) expresses the relative importances of the three attributes as percentages.[6] As can be seen, the relative importance of spiciness to this individual is almost 60 percent. Thickness is also relatively important (about 34.5 percent), while this respondent seemed almost indifferent to color. One should keep in mind that these results are very dependent on the levels actually selected for the conjoint task. The customer might not have been indifferent to color if the options were red, green, and paisley.

How well does our model predict this customer's choice patterns? We can check predictive accuracy by adding the utilities comprising each of the 18 choices to get estimates of overall preference. For example, the estimate we would obtain for the extra-thick, mild, red salsa would be –1.074 + 1.667 – 0.161 = +0.432. We can then rank order these preferences as predicted by the model and compare these to the rankings actually made by the respondent. As shown in the last column of Figure 7–2, the estimates predict the actual preference order almost perfectly for this customer, and identified the most-favored and least-favored combinations with ease.

[6]These are estimated by looking at the ranges of utilities of the three attributes (that is, the gap between the highest and lowest utilities). As seen, the range for spiciness is 3.441. The ranges for thickness and color can be calculated as 1.987 and 0.322. Summing the three ranges yields a total of 5.750, and each range is divided by this amount to get its relative importance. For spiciness, 3.441/5.750 = 59.84 percent.

Usually, the next analytical step is to combine the responses of all respondents by taking the averages of the utilities of each attribute level. This allows the manager to identify which attributes are the most important overall, and also which levels of these attributes are the most popular. If, in this example, this individual customer were typical of the target market, we might concentrate on developing a medium-thick, green, mild salsa. (Note that these are the levels of each attribute with the highest utilities in Figure 7–3(a).)

Clearly, there may be segments within the market. It may be that about half the market likes mild salsa and about half likes extra-hot. If we only examined the average, we might conclude that medium-hot is best, though in reality nobody may like it! Thus, the next analytical step is to identify benefit segments based on the utilities. This will be discussed later, in Chapter 9.

The ranking task was relatively easy in this simple case, as there were only 18 cards to rank order. What if you had to consider many more attributes and/or levels? For example, in addition to the three attributes given above, you might need to consider type of container (glass jar vs. plastic bucket), size of container (10 ounce vs. 16 ounce), type of ingredients (organic vs. not organic), and three different potential brand names. That's $3 \times 2 \times 3 \times 2 \times 2 \times 2 \times 3 = 432$ different cards—equivalent to eight decks of playing cards stacked together, including jokers! No respondent, however well intentioned, will have the patience for this task.

Fortunately, the full set of cards need not be rank ordered. By using a fractional factorial design, we can still estimate the relative preferences of all possible products using only a small subset of the cards.[7] With a reduced set of cards, most respondents won't be able to find the exact combination they want. So they must choose the combination that most closely meets their desires by trading off attributes wanted more against those wanted less. We all do this when our favorite brand of something is not in the store, and we have to find a close substitute.

A set of practical guidelines for the use of conjoint analysis would include the following:

1. One should specify the product as a bundle of attributes. As seen in our discussion of factor analysis in Chapter 6, this is not always easily done, especially in the case of image products such as perfumes, where attributes may be more difficult for the respondent to articulate.
2. We need to know what the determinant attributes are before we do the conjoint analysis. As mentioned above, AR gap mapping, or one of the qualitative techniques, can be helpful in this regard.

---

[7]See discussion in David R. Rink, "An Improved Preference Data Collection Method: Balanced Incomplete Block Designs," *Journal of the Academy of Marketing Science* 15, Spring 1987, pp. 54–61; also Joel H. Steckel, Wayne S. DeSarbo, and Vijay Mahajan, "On the Creation of Acceptable Conjoint Analysis Experimental Designs," *Decision Sciences* 22, Spring 1991, pp. 435–42.

3. Respondents should be familiar enough with the product category and the attributes to provide meaningful data on preference or purchase likelihood. Thus, conjoint may be less useful in the case of completely new-to-the-world products.
4. The firm should act on the results—in other words, actually develop a product that delivers the combinations of attributes preferred in the conjoint analysis.[8]

Finally, we should reiterate that trade-off (conjoint) analysis is most commonly used in concept evaluation, and we will pick up the discussion of this technique in Chapter 9.

Recent Modifications in Conjoint Analysis

Other techniques are sometimes used to handle large numbers of determinant attributes and levels. In a property insurance example, analysts had to restructure a traditional form of conjoint measurement called **SIMALTO** by adding *cost* and *savings* to each of the attribute trade-off utilities. They then gave consumers "budgets" to spend on their choices, and thus captured a lot of variables in a *willingness to pay.* They kept the power of the original set of trade-off attributes without having to use the data-losing method of conjoint calculations.[9]

Another method of dealing with the complexities of many product situations is use of what is called **discrete choices.**[10] Yet another method of reducing complexity is to mail respondents floppy disks on which are product feature attributes. The trick is to sort down quickly to only the very important features. This reduces the number of choice combinations. The whole procedure, including making up the choice sets (like the cards) and taking votes on them, is done in the disk and is mailed back in the same form.

Recent work has examined some of the practical difficulties and concerns encountered in concept testing. Since concept testing is done so early in the NPD process, often before a prototype is available for customer trial, can the respondent conceptualize the product, and its uses, well enough? If not, does the method still produce valid results? A recent study of a simple product line extension (a baking-soda toothpaste) suggested that conjoint results obtained when customers were only exposed to the product concept were very similar to those obtained if customers were actually allowed to try

---

[8]Adapted from Robert J. Dolan, *Managing the New Product Development Process: Cases and Notes* (Reading, MA: Addison-Wesley, 1993), p. 125.

[9]Peter D. Morton and Crispian Tarrant, "A New Dimension to Financial Product Innovation Research," *Marketing and Research Today,* August 1994, pp. 173–79.

[10]Steven Struhl, "Discrete Choice Modeling: Understanding a 'Better Conjoint than Conjoint,'" *Quirk's Marketing Research Review,* June/July, 1994, pp. 12–15.

the product.[11] Thus, conjoint results are a valid early indicator of ultimate product success, at least for product line extensions. Of course, conjoint analysis and perceptual mapping, as well as product trial, will be rich sources of customer information later in the NPD process.

In the case of major innovations (such as a new computer or telecommunications technology), customers without a high level of expertise in the product category may be unable to assess the innovation's benefits, and concept test results may not validly predict how well the actual product will be received. Some have advocated using only customers with at least moderate levels of expertise, even for minor innovations.[12] Furthermore, as respondents learn more about the unfamiliar innovation's attributes or design during the concept test, their preferences may change. An alternative technique, called the Interactive Concept Test (ICT), investigates how customers form preferences. This test seems to be a promising complement to common conjoint testing.[13]

Virtual Reality in Concept Testing

Improvements in **virtual reality** computer and video technology are providing marketers with many exciting new ways to test concepts with customers. One new measurement method, called **information acceleration** (IA), has recently been developed, and was first applied by General Motors in testing new electric car concepts.[14] The unique feature of IA is that respondents are brought into a virtual buying environment that simulates the information typically available in a realistic purchase situation. Through the use of a video monitor and laser videodisk player, the respondent can see ads, read car magazines, and hear statements from salespeople and word-of-mouth comments from customers. Using surrogate travel technology, customers could "walk

---

[11]John R. Dickinson and Carolyn P. Willey, "Concept Testing With and Without Product Trial," *Journal of Product Innovation Management* 14, no. 2, 1997, pp. 117–25.

[12]Jan P. L. Schoormans, Roland J. Ortt, and Cees J. P. M. de Bont, "Enhancing Concept Test Validity by Using Expert Consumers," *Journal of Product Innovation Management* 12, no. 2, 1995, pp. 153–62.

[13]Gerard H. Loosschilder, Mia J. W. Stokmans, and Dick R. Wittink, "Convergent Validity of Preference Estimates of the Interactive Concept Test and Conjoint Analysis," in *Maximizing the Return on Product Development,* L. W. Murray (Ed.), Proceedings of the Research Conference of the PDMA, Monterey, CA, October 1997. For another approach, see Steven H. Cohen, "Perfect Union," *Marketing Research,* Spring 1997, pp. 12–17, for a discussion of choice-based conjoint analysis.

[14]For detailed information on information acceleration, see Glen L. Urban, Bruce D. Weinberg, and John R. Hauser, "Premarket Forecasting of Really New Products," *Journal of Marketing,* January 1996, pp. 47–60. See also Phillip J. Rosenberger III and Leslie de Chernatony, "Virtual Reality Techniques in NPD Research," *Journal of the Market Research Society,* October 1995, pp. 345–55.

around" a dealer showroom and look at virtual, computer-generated car prototypes.

While expensive (an application might cost $100,000 to $300,000), IA is a potentially valuable complement to existing concept testing methods. Simple concept pictures or descriptions may not provide enough information to customers to enable them to make a realistic purchase decision, especially in the case of a very complex product like a new electric automobile. IA also allows testing of many virtual variations of the same basic concept, so that preferences can be observed. As video technology improves, IA will become less expensive, and further extensions to it will be made (for example, the respondent may be able to "virtually drive" the car).[15]

Qualitative Techniques

We have seen several quantitative techniques that can be used to incorporate customer input into concept generation. As seen at the beginning of this chapter, however, these techniques have natural complements: namely, a collection of qualitative techniques, which we will now explore.

It is tempting to be "dazzled" by the fancy outputs generated by MDS or factor analysis, especially if one is not that familiar with them. Managers, however, should resist this temptation and not take the results at face value. The qualitative techniques presented below are useful ways to challenge the assumptions (for example, about what attributes are really determinant) that underlie the sophisticated approaches, and can very frequently bring the manager perspectives that may go overlooked otherwise. Although our discussion of these is briefer, they are by no means less important or useful in concept generation.

Dimensional Analysis

Dimensional analysis uses any and all features, not just measurements of dimensions (such as spatial—length, width, and so on). The task involves listing *all* of the features of a product type. Product concept creativity is triggered by the mere listing of every such feature because we instinctively think about how that feature could be changed. Rarely is anything worthwhile found in dimensional analysis until the list is long. It takes a lot of work to push beyond the ordinary and to "see" dimensions that others don't see.

[15]Reportedly, Caterpillar lets its customers virtually test drive tractors under different driving conditions using a similar virtual reality technique. See Brian Silverman, "Get 'Em While They're Hot," *Sales and Marketing Management,* February 1997, pp. 47–52.

FIGURE 7–4

Dimensional attributes of a flashlight

Using dimensional analysis, here are 80 dimensions. There were almost 200 in the analyst's original list. A change in any one of them may make a new flashlight.

Overall unit:
Weight
Rust resistance
Balance
Gripability
Shock reistance
Shear force
Heat tolerance
Insulation material
Automatic flasher
Manual flasher
Distance visible
Length
Hangability
Stain resistance
Cold tolerance
Flexibility
Insulation color
Translucence
Focus of beam
Closure type
Lining material
Buoyancy
Flammability
Malleability
Compressibility
Reflectiveness
Surface area/color
Closure security
Material of case
Color
Number body seams
Water resistance
Diameter
Washability
Weight of metal
Explosiveness
Smell of unit
Number of tags
Snagability
Sealant material

Lens:
Material
Opacity
Color
Strength
Texture

Springs:
Number
Material
Length
Strength
Style

Switches:
Number
Pressure
Noise
Type
Location

Bulb:
Number
Shape
Size
Gas type
Thread strength
Length of stem
Filament shape
Thread size
Filament material
Shatter point
Thread depth
Amperage

Batteries:
Number
Size
Terminal type
Direction
Rechargeability

Reflector:
Depth
Diameter
Shape
Durability
Surface
Color
Temperature limit

Some of the most interesting features are those that a product doesn't *seem* to have. For example, the spoon previously discussed also has aroma, sound, resilience, "bendability," and so on. Granted, the aroma may be hard to detect, the sound (at the moment) may be zero, and the resilience may be only when pushed by a vice. But each feature offers something to change. How about spoons that play musical notes as children move them to the mouth? How about spoon handles that can be squeezed to play notes? How about spoons that smell like roses?

Listing hundreds of features is not uncommon. Figure 7–4 shows a shorter list, but perhaps it suggests what must be done. Successful users claim that just citing a unique dimension sparks ideation, and that the technique has to be used to be believed.

FIGURE 7–5

Checklist of idea stimulators for industrial products

Can we change the physical, thermal, electrical, chemical, and mechanical properties of this material?
Are there new electrical, electronic, optical, hydraulic, mechanical, or magnetic ways of doing this?
Find new analogs for parallel problems.
Is this function really necessary?
Can we construct a new model of this?
Can we change the form of power to make it work better?
Can standard components be substituted?
What if the order of the process were changed?
How might it be made more compact?
What if it were heat-treated, hardened, alloyed, cured, frozen, plated?
Who else could use this operation or its output?
Has every step been computerized as much as possible?

Checklists

From early forms of dimensional analysis evolved one of today's most widely used idea-generating techniques—the **checklist.** The most widely publicized checklist was given by the originator of brainstorming:

Can it be adapted?	Can something be substituted?
Can it be modified?	Can it be magnified?
Can it be reversed?	Can it be minified?
Can it be combined with anything?	Can it be rearranged in some way?

These eight questions are powerful; they do lead to useful ideation. If you want more, Appendix C has the ultimate in checklists; it contains 112 questions, in many categories, with *examples for each.*

Business and industrial goods analysts use such features as source of energy, materials, ease of operation, subassemblies, and substitutable components. (See Figure 7–5 for an abbreviated list of such industrial checklist questions.)

Checklists produce a multitude of potential new product concepts, most of them worthless. Much time and effort can be spent culling the list. The technique is frequently used as an aid in *problem-solving.* Some people make up a matrix, putting product types or brands down the left side, and the checklist factors across the top. This helps find individual product deficiencies that can be capitalized on for particular market segments.

Relationships Analysis

Several of the concept-generating methods we have been looking at *compare* things: perceptual maps compare attributes, and group creativity is stimulated by reasoning from a known to an unknown, for example. But the comparisons are incidental to a larger issue in those methods. We will now look at two analytical attribute techniques that go right to the point—forcing things together for examination. These two techniques are the **two-dimensional matrix** and the **morphological matrix.** Both are examples of types of **relationships analysis,** so named because they require the respondent to find relationships among dimensions to generate new product concepts.

About the Dimensions Used in Relationships Analysis

Recall that Figure 6–1 said attributes are *features* (such as length), *functions* (such as coating hair with protein), and *benefits* (such as economy and health). But other aspects of products are not always included as attributes in definitions—for example, different places of use, occupations of users, or other items the product is used with. Relationships analysis techniques use them, too. We seek any and all dimensions that help, and there is no fixed set of these. It is hoped that the examples shown in this chapter will suggest the view you should take in creating the matrixes.

Two-Dimensional Matrix

The simplest format for studying relationships is seen in Figure 7–6, which shows two attribute sets for insurance. Only partial lists of two dimensions (event insured against and person/animal insured) are used, but just these two provide 50 cells to consider. Notice that only by forcing relationships could we *expect* to come up with a special policy that protects new parents if they happen to misplace their new child, or that protects newlyweds from the costs

FIGURE 7–6

Two-dimensional matrix used for new insurance products

	Person/Animal Insured									
Event Insured Against	*New-borns*	*Geniuses*	*Troubled Kids*	*Rich Uncles*	*Dogs/ Cats*	*Tropical Birds*	*Salt Water Fish*	*New Job-holders*	*Newly-weds*	*New Parents*
Injury from fire	1	2	3	4	5	6	7	8	9	10
Getting lost	11	12	13	14	15	16	17	18	19	20
Normal death	21	22	23	24	25	26	27	28	29	30
Being insulted	31	32	33	34	35	36	37	38	39	40
Being kidnapped	41	42	43	44	45	46	47	48	49	50

Examples of new product concepts: An insurance policy that protects new parents if they get lost (20), or that protects newlyweds from the risks of being kidnapped while on their honeymoon (49), or that protects geniuses from the damage of being insulted (32). Fortuitous scan methods mostly produce nonsense, but like the others, the two-dimensional matrix often produces a surprise that, upon careful thought, makes sense.

of over-celebrating their honeymoon. In the case of the insurance example, to analyze the results one would start with #1, think about it, then move to #2, and so on.

In contrast to most of the methods studied to this point, relationships analysis goes directly to a new product idea, for example, aerosol ice cream. The number of two-dimensional matrices that can be prepared is almost unlimited. Keep looking at different ones until satisfied with the list of new possibilities found, or convinced that the technique "just isn't for me."

Morphological or Multidimensional Matrix

The next method, morphological matrix, simultaneously combines more than two dimensions. The matrix can include many dimensions, and the technique originated many years ago when a scientist was trying to further development on what became the jet engine.[16]

A classic example, shown in Figure 7–7, covers household cleaning products. Consumers were surveyed and asked to provide the following information about their recent use of such items:

1. The cleaning instruments used.
2. The basic ingredients in the cleaners used.
3. The objects cleaned.
4. The type of package or container the products came in.
5. The substances removed with the cleaners.
6. The textures or forms of the cleaners.

Figure 7–7 shows the six categories and the items reported within each category. The new product manager's task was to link up combinations of those items. One common technique is to have a computer print out all possible combinations, which are then scanned for interesting sets.

Other analysts just use a simple mechanical method of reading the rows across; the top row says, how about a cream substance, in an aerosol package, to be applied to a broom, whereby the alcohol in the cream would clean blood from screens? The second row asks about a bag of ammonia crystals to be applied with a brush so body odors can be removed from shoes! After going through the rows, the analyst systematically alters one item in each row with one from another, and so on. All analytical attribute techniques produce noise from which good ideas must be picked, but what at first appears to be noise

---

[16]The scientist used 11 parameters (dimensions), each of which had between two and four alternatives; that set yielded 36,864 combinations (possible engines). Incidentally, that matrix also yielded two combinations that became the German V-1 and V-2 rockets in World War II. See Fritz Zwicky, *Discovery, Invention, Research: Through the Morphological Approach* (New York: Macmillan, 1969).

FIGURE 7–7

Relationships analysis: morphological technique—dimensions relevant to a household cleaner

Dimension 1: Cleaning Instrument	*Dimension 2: Ingredients*	*Dimension 3: Objects to Be Cleaned*			*Dimension 4: Package*	*Dimension 5: Substance to Be Removed*	*Dimension 6: Texture*
Broom	Alcohol	A/C filters	Fences	Pool	Aerosol	Blood	Cream
Brush	Ammonia	Air	Floors	Refrigerators	Bag	Body odors	Crystals
Damp mop	Deodorizing agents	Aluminum	Glass	Screens	Bottle	Bugs	Gaseous
Dry cleaning	Disinfectant	Boats	Glasses (eye)	Shoes	Box	Burns	Gel
Dry mop	Pine oil	Brooms	Grill	Skis	Can	Dirt	Liquid
Hose	Scenting agents	Brushes/combs	Jewels/jewelry	Stainless steel	Easy-carry	Dust	Powder
None		Cabinets	Leather	Stoves	Easy-pour	Food	Solid
Rag		Carpet	Linoleum	Synthetics	Jar	Germs	Wax
Sponge		Cars	Mops	Tiles	Spray	Glue	
Steel wool		Cement	Motorcycles	Toilets	See-through	Grass stains	
Vacuum		China/crystal	Ovens	Tools	Tube	Grease	
Wet mop		Clothes	Paint brushes	Toothbrushes	Unbreakable	Mildew	
		Corfam	Pans	Toys	Unspillable	Mud	
		Curtains/draperies	Pets	Upholstery		Odors	
		Diapers/pails	Pictures/paintings	Vinyl		Oil	
		Dog houses	Pillows/mattresses	Walls		Paint	
			Plastic	Water		Rust	
				Windows		Spots	
				Wood		Streaks	
				Wool			

Interpretation: Using only the top item from each of the six dimensions, we could get a cream substance packaged in an aerosol package, to be applied to a broom, whereby the alcohol in the cream would clean blood from screens. This is only one of many thousands of combinations the morphological approach would generate from the above lists.

Source: Charles L. Alvord and Joseph Barry Mason, "Generating New Product Ideas," *Journal of Advertising Research,* December 1975, p. 29.

may simply be a great new idea no one would have thought of easily without the matrix.

In any event, the structure shown in Figure 7–7 should be followed. Creation of the columns was discussed at the beginning of this section of the chapter. The number of items in each column is either (1) the entire set, as in the survey above, or (2) a selection representing the full array. For example, a study of play wagons might have a column headed number of wheels, and the rows would be two, three, four, five, and six; but the height column might just have rows of 6 inches, 8 inches, and 12 inches (low, medium, and high).[17]

[17]For a recent report of several applications of this technique, see Simon Majaro, "Morphological Analysis," *Marketing Intelligence and Planning* 2, 1988, pp. 4–11.

Analogy

We can often get a better idea of something by looking at it through something else—an **analogy.** Analogy is so powerful and popular that it is used heavily as part of the problem-solving step in problem-based methods (Chapter 5).

A good example of analogy was the study of airplane feeding systems by a manufacturer of kitchen furniture and other devices. Preparing, serving, and consuming meals in a plane is clearly analogous to doing so in the home, and the firm created several good ideas for new processes (and furniture) in the home kitchen.

An analogy for bicycles might be driving a car—both incorporate steering, moving, slowing, curving, and so on. But the auto carries more passengers, has four wheels for stability, variable power, built-in communications, on-board service diagnosis and remedial action, and the like. Each difference suggests another new type of bicycle; some of these types are already available. The bicycle could also be compared to the airplane, to skating, to the submarine, to swimming, and at the extreme (for illustration) to a mouse in a maze.

The secret, of course, is finding a usable analogous situation, which is often difficult. The analogy should meet four criteria:

1. The analogy should be vivid and have a definite life of its own.
2. It should be full of concrete images.
3. It should be a happening—a process of change or activity.
4. It should be a well-known activity and easy to visualize and describe.

Airplane feeding systems and driving a car qualify easily. And, perhaps to their surprise, an analogy of the machine gun ammunition belt helped seed company developers think of a roll of biodegradable tape studded with carefully placed seeds to be laid along a furrow.

Analogy is used in several of the specialized techniques in Appendix B.

Summary

In this and the preceding chapter, we have presented a review of several analytical attribute techniques. Qualitative techniques included the very simple yet challenging dimensional analysis, and more advanced methods such as the morphological matrix. Quantitative approaches included gap analysis and trade-off analysis. These can be used in complementary fashion: as seen above, the qualitative methods can be used prior to the more numbers-oriented models (to specify or double-check the attributes included in the analysis) or after the fact (to help interpret results).

The essence of attribute analysis, in every case, is to force us to look at products differently—to bring out new perspectives. We normally have fixed ways of perceiving products, based on our sometimes long-term use of them, so forcing us out of those ruts is difficult. Anyone reading this in preparation for a specific ideation activity is encouraged to scan the list of over 40 other techniques in Appendix B.

We are now finished with concept generation, and hopefully have several good concepts ready for serious review and evaluation before undertaking costly technical development. We meet evaluation in Part III, Chapters 8–11, entitled Concept/Project Evaluation. We will also find that several of the analytical techniques we encountered in these chapters will be of assistance to us in assessing customer preferences, specifying product design characteristics, and even beyond in the new product development process.

Applications

More questions from that interview with the company president.

1. "I guess I really like checklists best—they're easy for me to understand and use. I've never seen this one by Small that you mentioned—wow, four pages of ways. Is all that really necessary? Couldn't just as good a job be done with, say, one page? And incidentally, I must confess I'm slightly confused by the terminology. Tell me, what is the difference again between the checklists I like and what you call dimensional analysis?"
2. "As you can probably tell by now, I am an engineer by training and have always enjoyed playing around with one form of attribute analysis. We call it attribute extension, where we forecast the future changes in any important attribute of a product. You know, like the amount of Random Access Memory in a PC. I recently asked our cable TV division to take five dimensions of a cable TV service and extend each out as far as they can see it going and tell me what ideas they get from it. I mentioned number of channels and types of payment as examples. Could you do something like this for me now . . . that is, take five dimensions of cable TV service and extend them? It would help me get ready for their presentation Thursday."
3. "I find your conjoint analysis example very interesting and relevant in my line of work. Will you go over again how you calculated those rankings as estimated by the model, that you showed in Figure 7–2? Also, it's clear that the medium-thick, mild salsas came out number 1 and 2 for this individual. But what are we to make of the intermediate ranks? Medium-thick, medium-hot, red came in eighth, while extra-thick, mild, green ranked ninth. Should I care about this? Does that help me in product planning?"

4. "Several of our divisions work in the women's clothing markets. As you know, they are all specialized these days, this segment or that segment. Getting hard to come up with a new segment, one that has some size and would be responsive. So when you were talking about morphological matrix, which I liked, I thought about women's attire. One way to innovate would be to come up with new settings, or occasions, situations where we could devise a whole outfit. Sort of like wedding, or racetrack, or picnic, though we know of them and have clothing for them, of course. Sort of a *package* of apparel and accessories. But there must be many we don't think of now. Would that morphological matrix method work on that?"

Case: Rubbermaid Inc.[18]

Rubbermaid has consistently received awards as a well-managed company. It made the *Fortune Magazine* list for three consecutive years in the early 90s. It posts growth rates of 15 percent, even in tough times, with important contributions from new products. About 200 new items are introduced each year. Some are line extensions, and others enter, or even create, entirely new markets.

The firm's success is based partly on creating and producing high quality, functional, plastic products for the housewares, the office, the industrial, and the farm markets in addition to specialty products such as toys, educational and recreational products, and furniture. In recent years items have ranged from a spatula to a cooler used on a golf course and from a child's 15 pound mini-car to lawn furniture. Category brands include Little Tikes, Gott, Blue-Ice, Sunshine, and others.

The firm makes almost a half-million different items, boasts a 90 percent success rate on new products, and obtains at least 30 percent of its sales each year from products less than five years old.

The firm's new product strategy is to meet the needs of the consumer. The new product rate is high, and diversification is desired. The firm is market-driven, not technology-driven, although in recent years it has identified such technologies as recycling new plastic parts from old tires for which it is seeking market opportunities. This practice of seeking opportunities for specific technologies will increase as a fall-out of the firm's current use of simultaneous product development.

For idea generation, Rubbermaid depends on finding customer problems that can be built into the strategic planning process. Problems are sought in several ways, the principal one of which is focus groups. It also uses comments and complaints from customers, an example of which came when then-CEO Stanley C. Gault heard a Manhattan doorman complaining as he swept dirt into a Rubbermaid dustpan. Inquiry determined that the doorman wanted a thinner lip on the pan, so less dirt would remain on the walk. He got it.

Each complaint is documented by marketing people, and executives are encouraged to read the complaints. One complaint by customers in small households who found the

[18]This case was prepared from many public information sources.

traditional rack-and-mat too bulky to store, led to a compact, one-piece dish drainer. The Little Tikes toy division actually molds a toll-free number into each toy to encourage complaints and comments. They have to watch the legal ramifications, of course, and may require idea submitters to sign a waiver giving up their rights to their ideas. The firm generally finds its problems by using problem analysis in focus groups and solves them internally. They occasionally use scenario analysis to spot a problem. But scenario analysis is much less useful than problem analysis because the lead times are so short; their new product cycles make them concentrate mainly on already existing problems. The organization is kept conducive to newly created ideas by promoting cross-functional association between workers. Problem-find-solve is encouraged at all levels.

Some other new items have been:

- Bouncer drinkware was created for people who fear using glassware around their swimming pools.
- A lazy susan condiment tray and other patio furniture products came from studies of life-style changes.
- People working at home told of problems that led to a line of home office accessories, including an "auto-office," a portable device that straps onto a car seat and holds pens and other office articles.

The firm also runs a daycare program, where researchers observe children having problems with toys and test their new toys.

Generally speaking, Rubbermaid does not make much use of attribute listing and other fortuitous scan methods of ideation, including the various mapping approaches. It does find that product life-cycle models can be useful, and it closely tracks competitive new product introductions.

Rubbermaid is, however, always looking for new ways by which it can come up with good new product concepts. They know from experience, for example, that they will find new ways for using problem-find-solve techniques. And perhaps the fortuitous scan methods can be of greater use than what is now perceived.

FIGURE III–1

Concept/project evaluation

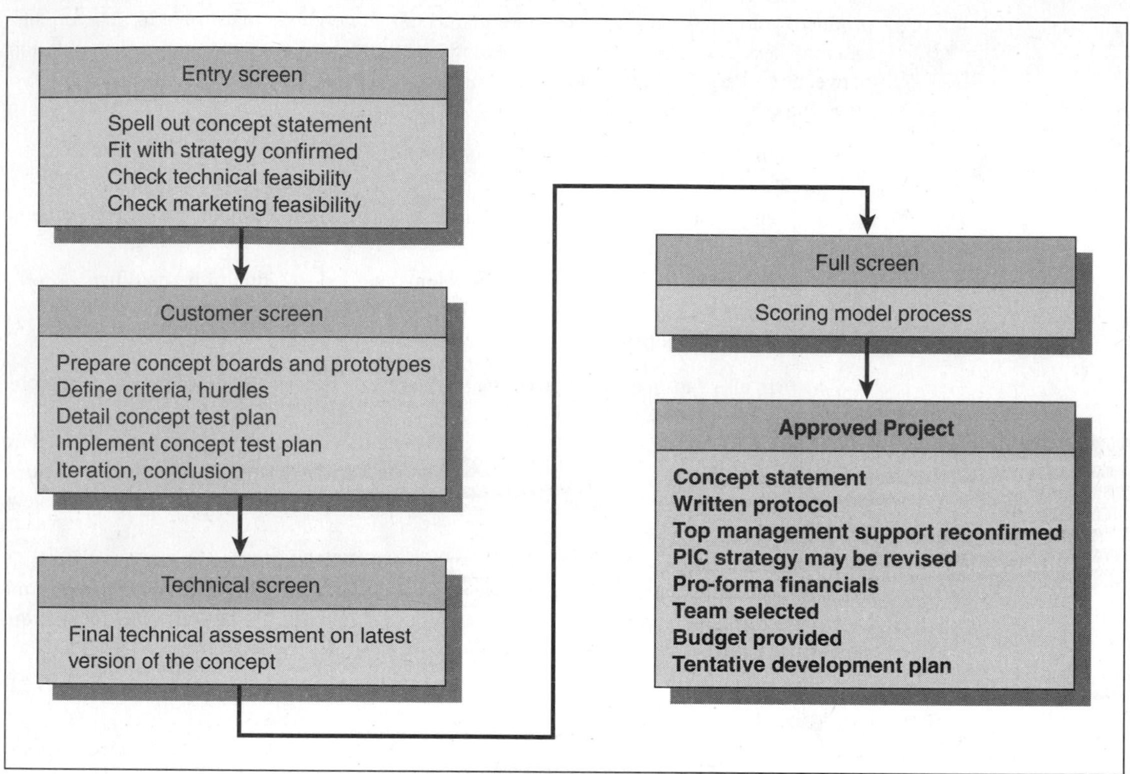

PART

III

CONCEPT/PROJECT EVALUATION

Part II completed our study of the various methods of generating new product concepts. The next task is to undertake evaluation of these concepts. Evaluation takes place at many different times and in different ways, by different people, and for different reasons. Therefore, a *system* of evaluations is needed, an idea that will be explained in Chapter 8.

Then, beginning in Chapter 9, we will look at the different phases in that system. (See Figure III–1.) Concept testing, the first major tool, will be discussed there. Chapter 10 covers the activity generally called a *full screen,* a step where the concept is judged by how well it fits the company and its marketing strengths. Chapter 10 also covers some work needed before the concept can be moved into development, a subject that we will face in Part IV.

The evaluation tools discussed in Chapters 9 and 10 are those that precede development. Once prototypes or service configurations begin to appear, evaluation begins again, first in the form of product use testing and later in market testing, and more. These are covered in later chapters. All efforts at evaluation are themselves major topics, so our discussions must be selective. Unfortunately, industry uses many of the tools in different ways, so they tend to blend together at the edges. When, for example, does a prototype concept test become a product use test?

Likewise, industry often combines two or even three of the tools. For example, in some industries it is very easy to prepare prototypes, so some firms do an early customer survey that is partly market analysis, partly concept test, and partly prototype test, particularly when the idea first emerged in prototype form.

Finally, industry developers have been all too willing to invent terminology. Therefore, we have had to standardize terms, and some of the decisions won't be acceptable to all people.

CHAPTER

8

THE CONCEPT EVALUATION SYSTEM

Setting

Before looking into the various specific techniques used to evaluate new product concepts, we need an overview of the techniques available. Throughout the new product development process, we do evaluations, using techniques appropriate to each phase of the process. However, none of these techniques is used all the time or in all cases. Chapter 8 offers this overview, presenting key models such as the cumulative expenditures curve and the A-T-A-R model to help us decide which evaluation techniques to use in any particular situation. We will also cover potholes and surrogates, among other ideas. In Chapters 9 and 10, we will look more closely at concept evaluation and full screen techniques that are specifically appropriate to Phase III (concept/project evaluation), while Chapters 11 and 12 round out the discussion with a look at sales forecasting, financial analysis, and product protocol specification.

You will recall from Chapter 2 that new products fail because (1) there was no basic need for the item, as seen by intended users, (2) the new product did not meet its need, net, considering all disadvantages, and (3) the new product idea was not properly communicated (marketed) to the intended user. In sum, they didn't need it, it didn't work, they didn't get the message. Keep these in mind as you see how an evaluation system is constructed.

What's Going On in the New Products Process?

New products actually build up the way rivers do. Great rivers are systems with tributaries that have tributaries. Goods that appear complex are just collections of metal shapes, packaging material, fluids, prices, and so on. A good analogy for this complexity is the production of automobiles, with a main assembly line supported by scores of subsidiary assembly lines scattered around the world, each of which makes a part that goes into another part that ultimately goes onto a car in that final assembly line.

If you can imagine the quality control people in auto parts plants evaluating each part before releasing it to the next step, you have the idea of a new product **evaluation system.** The new product appears first as an idea, a concept in words or pictures, and we evaluate that concept first. As workers turn the concept into a formed piece of metal, or software, or a new factory site preparation service, that good or service is then evaluated. When a market planner puts together a marketing plan, its parts are evaluated separately (just as minor car parts are) and then evaluated again in total, after it is added to the product.

The fact that we evaluate the product and its marketing plan as separate and divisible pieces is what lets us telescope the development process into shorter periods of time. There was an era when we went through a new product's development step by step, nothing "ahead of its time." But today we may be working on a package before we actually have finished the product, we may be filming part of a commercial before the trademark has been approved and finalized, or we may be preparing the trailer to promote an upcoming movie long before the final edits are completed.[1]

This sometimes causes some backtracking, but the cost of that is less than the costs of a delayed introduction. It does require, however, that we have thought through carefully the item's overall development needs—and which of those needs are crucial, and which not crucial. Any evaluation system *must* cover the crucial ones.

The Evaluation System for the Basic New Product Process

Although the overall purpose of evaluation is to guide us to profitable new products, each individual evaluation step has a specific purpose, keyed primarily to what happens next. For example, the very first evaluation *precedes* the product concept—in fact, it takes place in Phase I, when an opportunity is identified and assessed. (Refer back to Figure 2–2, which shows graphically where evaluation takes place relative to other activities.) Someone decided the firm had a strong technology, or an excellent market opportunity, or a serious competitive threat—whatever. As discussed in Chapter 3 on strategy, a judgment was made that if the firm tried to develop a new product in a given area, it would probably succeed.

This early evaluation step (direction) is shown at the top of Figure 8–1. Where should we look, what should we try to exploit, what should we fight

[1]There is a (perhaps apocryphal) story about an Alberto Culver shampoo. Television commercials were finished and at the networks ready for showing before the chemist could find an appropriate formulation!

FIGURE 8–1
The evaluation system

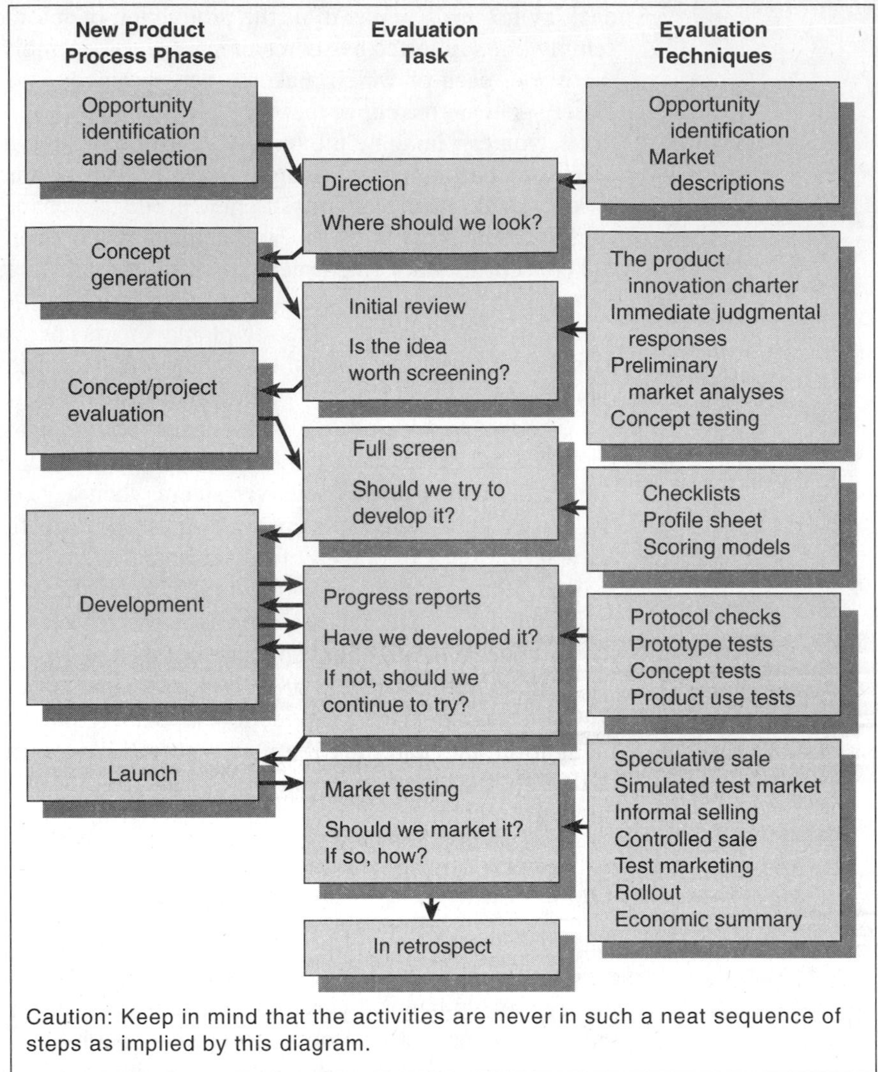

against? The tool is opportunity identification and evaluation, also discussed in Chapter 3. This tool keeps us out of developments where we stand a poor chance of winning; in other words, it makes sure we play the game on our home field. This direction is provided in the product innovation charter.

Now continue down Figure 8–1 to see how the evaluation tasks change as we progress through the basic new product process. In Phase II, concept generation, ideas begin to appear, and the purpose of evaluation changes: now the goal is to avoid the big loser or the sure loser. We want to cull them out and spend no added time and money on them. We're sometimes wrong, of course, but usually we're right, and this step is essential if we are to focus limited resources on the worthwhile concepts.

The initial review segment of activities also tries to spot the potential big winners. Most good concepts are just that—good. A few are great, and we want to recognize them as soon as possible. These get added effort, usually in the form of a very complete concept testing and development program.

That activity leads us to Phase III, concept/project evaluation, and the decision on whether to send the concept into full-scale development. This decision, if the amounts to be spent make it an important decision, will benefit from a very thorough scoring model application that answers the questions: Should we try to develop it?

The decision to enter Phase IV, development, introduces the part of the process where the parallel or simultaneous technical and marketing activities are done (as seen in Figure 2–1). All through this phase we are continually asking, Have we got what we want? Is this part ready? Is that system subset cleared for use? Does the software not only work, but produce what the customer needs? A protocol check tells whether we are ready to develop a product for serious field testing.

Development is naturally iterative: One new discovery leads to another; directions are changed; specific attempts fail, and we have to back up. At Hollingsworth & Vose, an industrial specialty paper company, gaskets are tested five times in this stage—in-house lab test, customer lab test, customer engine test, car manufacturer engine test, and fleet test.

Sooner or later the technical efforts yield a product that evaluators say meets the customers' request. We then enter Phase V, and attention turns to launching the item. The evaluation issue now is whether the firm has proven itself able to make, and market, the item on a commercial scale. This is usually resolved by some form of market testing.

Later on, of course, the developers (and others in the firm too, unfortunately) will be asking the "in retrospect" question, should we have done all this? The purpose is not to find a guilty party for a product that bombed but, rather, to study the evaluation process to prevent a repetition.[2]

The Balanced Product Innovation Portfolio

The evaluation system keeps the new product operation efficient; we will talk more about this in a minute. Keep in mind, however, that any one product being evaluated is not alone. Most organizations have several products under development simultaneously, sometimes scores or even hundreds of them. Managements would like to think that every project will yield a big profit.

[2]For a thorough discussion of new product evaluation techniques and their use at different phases in the new products process, see Muammer Ozer, "A Survey of New Product Evaluation Models," *Journal of Product Innovation Management* 16, no. 1 (January 1999), pp. 77–94.

They won't, so managements think in terms of a **portfolio** of new product projects.

Different firms put together different portfolios of new product projects. The stable, healthy firm usually has a mix of projects from low-risk, short-term ones to high-risk, longer-term ones. The portfolio of a conservative firm avoids high-risk projects. A firm in trouble seeks only higher-risk projects of a short-term nature. Of course, a firm that hasn't heard of product innovation portfolio strategy will have no focus and will accept anything that comes along and looks good.

An evaluation system can be developed for each of those project types. For example, the firm that needs new product help fast will tend to skip early checkpoints and narrow down to just one or two alternative formats during development. They will tend to put in one major check late in the process, not to warn it to stop (that risk has already been accepted) but rather to make sure the marketing plan communicates and that the distribution system is in place.

Unfortunately, some firms take pride in one evaluation system, and force it to fit all evaluation situations. Overevaluation and underevaluation usually result.

The Cumulative Expenditures Curve

As we have seen, the new product evaluation system flows with the development of the product. What evaluation occurs at any one point (how serious, how costly) depends greatly on what happens next. Figure 8–2 shows a key input to the design of any evaluation system: In the middle of that figure, a gradually upward-sloping curve represents the accumulation of costs or expenditures on a typical new product project from its beginning to its full launch.

This generalized curve, taken from various studies over the years, is just an average. It need not reflect any one firm, but it is typical of many durable consumer goods, nontechnical business-to-business products, and many services. Shown with the average curve are two others. The early expenditures curve is representative of product development in technical fields, such as pharmaceuticals, optics, and computers. R&D is the big part of the cost package here, and marketing costs are relatively small. The lower curve in the figure shows the opposite type of firm, say, a consumer packaged goods company. Here the technical expenditures may be small, but a huge TV advertising program is needed at introduction.

These are generalizations, and individual exceptions do occur, such as when Procter & Gamble spends years developing a fat substitute called Olestra or Upjohn markets a line of generic drugs. The point is, whoever develops a concept evaluation system needs to know what situation it is for. No evaluation decision is independent of considerations on what will be done next, how much will be spent, or what points of no return are passing. An old

FIGURE 8–2

Cumulative expenditures—all-industry average compared to occasional patterns

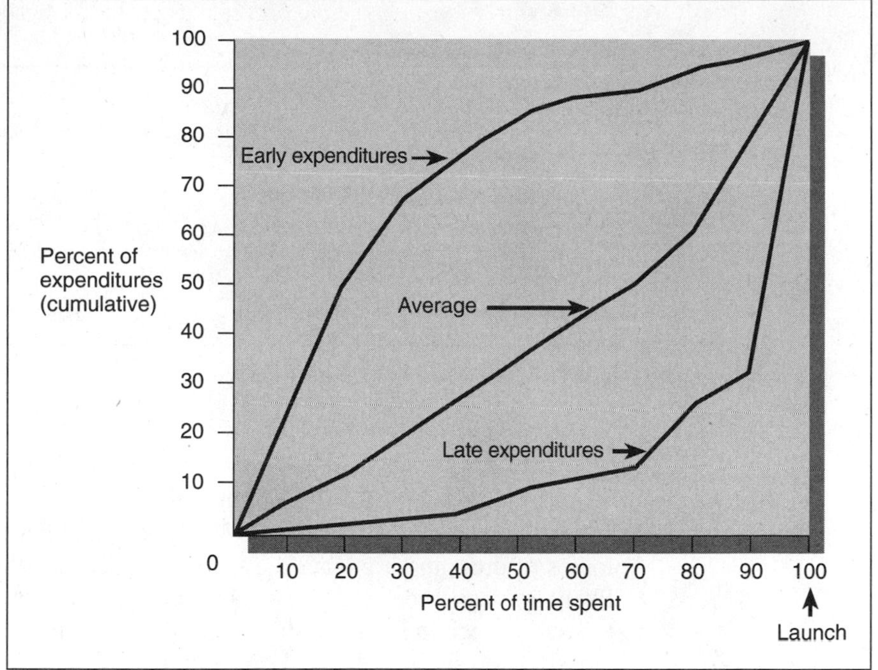

Chinese proverb says, "Spend your energy sharpening the edge of the knife, not polishing the blade."

The Risk/Payoff Matrix

Figure 8–3 applies the ideas in a **risk/payoff matrix.** At any single evaluation point in the new product process, the new products manager faces the four situations shown. Given that the product concept being evaluated has two broad ultimate outcomes (success or failure) and that there are two decision options at the time (move on or kill the project), there are four cells in the matrix.

The AA cell and the BB cell are fine; we drop a concept that would ultimately fail, or we continue with a concept that would ultimately succeed. The managerial problem arises in the other two cells. AB is an error: a winner is discarded. But BA is also an error: a loser is continued to the next evaluation point.

Which error does the manager most want to avoid? The answer depends on the dollars. First, throwing out a winner is very costly because the ultimate profits from a winning product are bound to be much greater than all of the development costs combined, let alone those in just the next step. So error AB is much worse than BA.

FIGURE 8–3

Matrix of risk/payoff at each evaluation

Decision is to: → / ↓ If the product were marketed	A Stop the project now	B Continue to next evaluation
A. It would fail	AA	BA
B. It would succeed	AB	BB

Comment: Cells AA and BB are "correct" decisions. Cells BA and AB are errors, but they have different cost and probability dimensions.

The exception, of course, is the opportunity cost. What other project is standing by waiting for funding? When good candidates wait in the wings, the losses of dropping a winner are much less because the money diverted will likely go to another winner. The point is, a manager must think of these matters when deciding what evaluation to do. If the net costs of the next step in any situation are low, then a decision will probably be made to go ahead, perhaps with very little information. For example, when IBM had just one year to develop and market the original PC computer, it felt the losses from delay greatly exceeded the gains from concept tests, lengthy field use tests, market tests, and so on. The company didn't do any. On the other hand, General Foods kept Brim coffee in market test for several years because it wanted to make sure the market plans were correct before undertaking the very expensive national launch.

A good example of the risk matrix in action occurred when Pillsbury announced that it had, in one year:

1. Failed with Appleeasy because it had, at the last minute, cut the amount of apples in reaction to increasing apple prices.
2. Failed with vegetable yogurt because people simply didn't like the idea.
3. Failed with presweetened baked beans because people liked to sweeten their own.
4. Succeeded with Totino's Crisp Crust Frozen Pizza.

Sales of the frozen pizza were over $60 million the first year, while none of the losers cost the company as much as $1 million. There were some morale problems in this case because no developers like to have a new product fail. And the R&D people were very much aware that the losers were internal developments whereas the frozen pizza came mainly from an acquisition. But no one can fault the overall financial outcome from this "package" of four decisions.

FIGURE 8–4

Mortality of new product ideas—the decay curve

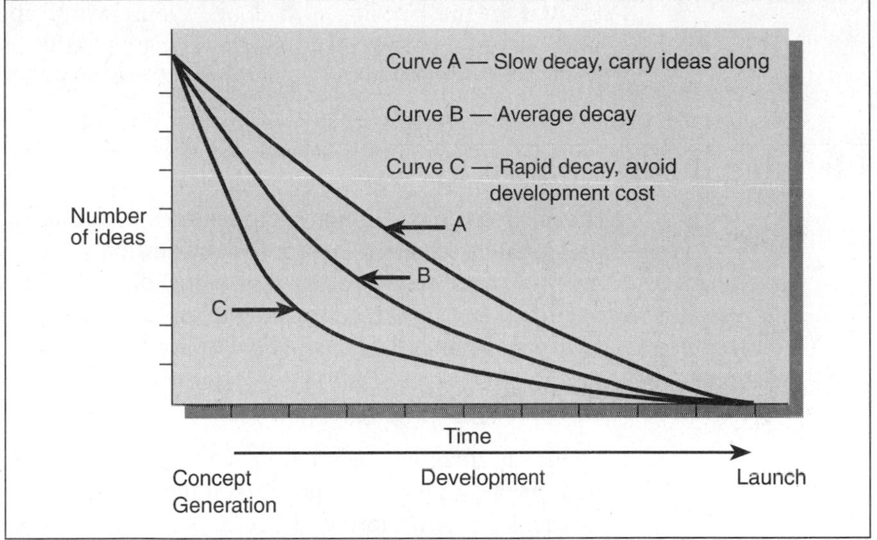

Source: Hypothetical representation based on empirical data in various sources, including *New Products Management for the 1980s* (Chicago: Booz Allen & Hamilton, 1982), p. 14.

The Decay Curve

The risk matrix decisions lead to the idea of a **decay curve,** as shown in Figure 8–4. That figure depicts the percentage of any firm's new product concepts that survive through the development period, from the 100 percent starting out before concept testing to the 2 percent (estimated from various studies) going to market. The discarded 98 percent dropped off at various times during the process, and when they drop off is primarily determined by the analysis of the risk matrix.

Decay curve C is roughly the shape of one decay curve from a leading company in the paper industry that wanted to kill off all possible losers early and spend time developing only those proposals worthy of marketing. This was their strategy, and their evaluation system implemented it faithfully. Decay curve A represents one for a service firm that had very low development costs and wanted to drop a project only when there was solid evidence against it. The paper company spent time making careful financial analyses even before technical work began; the service firm started up a project and just let it keep going until contrary evidence built up.

Thus, the decay curve is partly a plan and partly a result. The two should be synchronized. Its value as a managerial concept lies in helping the manager see the need for thinking through the stream of development costs and the risk/payoff matrix (above) for each new product concept as it starts its journey through development. When it is working, you will hear statements such as, "On that chip, let's make sure the customer will want it if we can make it; no sense in spending all that money only to find there's no buyer for it." And, in the building next door, "Don't worry about Ed's doubts at this time; we can reposition the fertilizer spreader at the last minute if we have to, even change several of the key attributes if we want. Let's just get going, now!"

Planning the Evaluation System

The previous considerations help set the tone for management decisions on an appropriate evaluation system for any particular new product concept. There are four other relevant, but less demanding, concepts that help us decide whether to concept test, how long to run a field use test, whether to roll out or go national immediately, and how thorough a financial analysis to demand.

Everything Is Tentative

It's easy to imagine that building a new product is like building a house—first the foundation, then the frame, then the first floor, and so on. Unfortunately, product aspects are rarely locked in that way. Occasionally they are, as when a technical process dominates development, or when a semifinished product is acquired from someone else, or when legal or industry requirements exist.

We usually assume, however, that everything is tentative, even up through marketing. Form can usually be changed, and so can costs, packaging, positioning, and service contracts. So can the marketing date and the reactions of government regulators. So can customer attitudes, as companies with long development times have discovered.

This means two long-held beliefs in new product work are actually untrue. One is that everything should be keyed to a single Go/No Go decision. Granted, one decision can be critical—at times, for example, when a firm must invest millions of dollars in one large facility or when a firm acquires a license that commits it to major financial outlays. But many firms are finding ways to avoid such commitments, for example, by having another supplier produce the product for a while before a facilities commitment, or by negotiating a tentative license, or by asking probable customers to join a consortium to ensure the volume needed to build the facility.

The other "untrue truism" is that financial analysis should be done as early as possible to avoid wasting money on poor projects. This philosophy leads firms to make complex financial analyses shortly after early concept testing, although the numbers at that time are inadequate. The paper products firm whose decay rate was presented in Figure 8–4 (curve C) rejected hundreds of ideas before realizing that early financial analysis was killing off ideas that would have looked great after further development. The financial analysis is best built up piece by piece, just like the product itself. We will see later how this works.

Still another tentative matter is the marketing date. Marketing actually begins very early in the development process (for example, when purchasing agents are asked in a concept test whether they think their firm would be interested in a new item). Rollouts (launching a product to a limited market or geographical region and gradually expanding to others, further discussed in Chapter 20) are now so common it is hard to tell when all-out marketing begins. General Electric once invested in a small, $20 million facility for a new heat-resistant plastic for circuit boards. After IBM and some other customers approved the product, GE announced it would build a full-scale, $50 million plant. Dr. Roland W. Schmitt, chief of research in the lab where the product was invented, put it this way: "Marketing people are wrong as often as technical people. It is important to approach markets as well as science in an experimental fashion."[3]

Often no one pulls a switch and marketing instantly begins. But we more frequently "sneak up" on it, which clearly affects the evaluation system.

What results in some cases is a sort of "rolling" evaluation. The project is assessed continuously, figures are penciled in, premature closure is avoided, and participants avoid mindsets of good and bad.

Potholes

One critical skill of product developers is the ability to anticipate major difficulties: the potholes of product innovation. In automobile travel, potholes are always a problem, but they only become costly when we fail to see them coming in time to slow down or steer around them. The same thinking applies to new products: we should carefully scan for the really damaging problems (the "deep holes") and keep them in mind when we decide what evaluating we will do.

For example, when Campbell Soup Company undertakes the development of a new canned soup, odds are in its favor. But experience has shown two points in the process when it may fail, and if it does, the product won't sell. The first is manufacturing cost—not quality, that's one of the company's key strengths. But there is always a question of whether the chosen ingredients can be put together to meet market-driven cost targets. The second is whether consumers think it tastes good. So the company's evaluation system is set never to overlook these two points.

A flour miller once said his biggest pothole was a quick entry by a price-cutter because that industry had virtually no patent protection or other barriers to competitive entry. He planned on it in every case, and didn't go ahead without knowledge on that specific issue. A software developer said his biggest pothole was customer unwillingness to take the time to learn to use complex new products. He had several worthwhile products in the graveyard to prove it.

In fact, if a manager thinks through the matter of potholes carefully (scans the "road" ahead) there are more benefits than just to the evaluation system.

---

[3]Stratford P. Sherman, "Eight Big Masters of Innovation," *Fortune,* October 15, 1984, p. 80.

The People Dimension

Product developers also have to remember they are dealing with people, and people cause problems. For example, although R&D workers are quite enthusiastic early in the life of a new product, the idea may have little support outside of R&D; it is fragile and easy to kill. Late in the development cycle, more people have "bought in" on the concept and are supportive because they have played a role in getting it to where it is. Consequently, the now-strong proposal is tough to stop.

This means that an evaluation system should contain early testing that is supportive. In fact, concept *testing* is sometimes called concept *development,* to reinforce the idea of helping the item, not just killing it off. Later in the cycle, hurdles should usually be tough and demanding, not easily waved aside. One firm designated its market research director as a "manager of screens." His task was to impose absolute screens, such as "New food products, in home placement testing, must achieve a 70 percent preference against their respective category leaders." If less than 70 percent of the testers preferred the new item, it was stopped, period. This sounds severe and arbitrary, but it shows how difficult it sometimes is to kill off marginal products late in development. Another people problem relates to personal risk. All new product work has a strong element of risk—risk to jobs, promotions, bonuses, and so on. Consequently, some people shy away from new product assignments. We're always under the gun from someone—an ambitious boss, a dedicated regulator, an aggressive competitor, a power-hungry distributor, an early critic who was overruled within the company, and more. A good evaluation system, built on a thorough understanding of the road the new item will follow as it winds its way through development, protects developers from these pressures. The system should be supportive of people, and offer the reassurance (if warranted) that players need.

Surrogates

The timing of factual information does not often match our need for it. For example, we want to know customer reactions early on, even before we develop the product, if possible. But we can't really know their reactions until we make some of the product and give it to them to try out. So we look for **surrogate questions** to give us pieces of information that can substitute for what we want to learn but can't. Here are four questions to which we badly need answers and four other questions that can be answered earlier (thus giving *clues* to the real answer):

Real Question	Surrogate (Substitute) Question
Will they prefer it?	Did they keep the prototype product we gave?
Will cost be competitive?	Does it match our manufacturing skills?
Will competition leap in?	What did they do last time?
Will it sell?	Did it do well in field testing?

Note that each response has little value except to help answer a critical question that cannot be answered directly.

Surrogates often change at different times in the evaluation process. For example, let's go back to one of the questions above: Will cost be competitive? At different times during the project, the surrogate used might be:

Time 1: Does it match our skills?

Time 2: Are the skills obtainable?

Time 3: What troubles are we having in making a prototype?

Time 4: How does the prototype look?

Time 5: Does the manufacturing process look efficient?

Time 6: How did the early production costs turn out?

Time 7: Do we now see any ways we can cut the cost?

Time 8: What is the cost?

Time 9: What is the competitive cost?

Only when we know our final cost and the competition's cost can we answer the original question. But the surrogates helped tell us whether we were headed for trouble.

The A-T-A-R Model

The last tool that we use for designing an evaluation system for each new project as it comes along is based on how we forecast sales and profit on a new item. The calculation is much like a pro forma income statement, an *array* of figures allowing us to see what the profits will look like based on where we are at any one time in the development.

The basic formula, shown in Figure 8–5, is based on what is known in the marketing field as the **A-T-A-R concept** (awareness-trial-availability-repeat). This is taken from what is called **diffusion of innovation,** explained this way: for a person or a firm to become a regular buyer/user of an innovation, there must first be awareness that it exists, then there must be a decision to try that innovation, then the person must find the item available to them, and finally there must be the type of happiness with it that leads to adoption, or repeat usage.[4]

We want to use the formula to calculate all the way to profit, so we expand it to include target market size (potential adopters), units purchased by each adopter, and the economics of the operation. But at the heart of the calculation is A-T-A-R.

---

[4]The basic A-T-A-R sequence has been broken down further into many microsteps. One example of this extension is John H. Antil, "New Product or Service Adoption: When Does It Happen?" *Journal of Consumer Marketing,* Spring 1988, pp. 5–16. Also, some people use this model in abbreviated form, stopping at unit sales. They calculate market share and make conclusions on that.

FIGURE 8–5

The A-T-A-R model

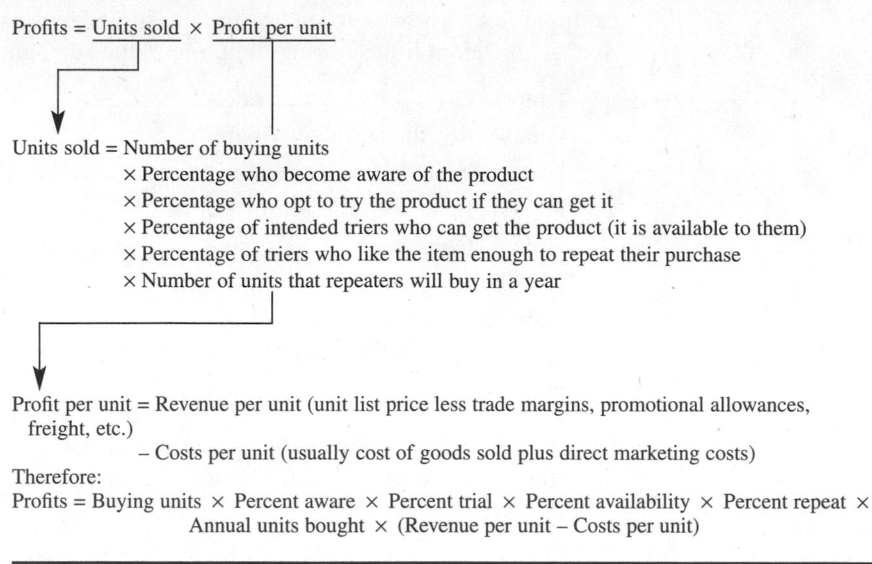

Let's take a simple example to explain how it works. Assume we have developed a new device to replace the security bars owners attach to steering wheels in expensive sports cars. It is built on an electronic principle of metal adherence. To use the paradigm for a final sales forecast, we need the following (hypothetical) data:

- Number of owners of such sports cars: 3 million.
- Percentage of target owners who we think we can make aware of our new device the first year on the market: 40 percent.
- Percentage of "aware" owners who will decide to try the device during the first year and set out to find it: 20 percent.
- Percentage of customary auto parts and mass retailers whom we can convince to stock the new device during the market introduction period: (To keep it simple for this demonstration, assume that potential buyers are busy and probably will not seek beyond one store if they cannot find it there.) 40 percent.
- Percentage of the actual triers who will like the product and buy one for a second car: 50 percent.
- Number of devices a typical user will buy in the first year of ownership: $1^1/_2$.

- Dollar revenue at the factory, per device, after trade margins and promotion discounts: $25.
- Unit cost of a device, at the intended volume: $12.50.

The profit contribution forecast, based on the A-T-A-R model, would be 3 million × 0.40 × 0.20 × 0.40 × 0.50 × 1.5 × ($25 – $12.50) = $1,800,000.

What we did was prepare a mathematical formula and run it through one set of data. Since the development was about finished when the calculation was made, the forecast was fairly solid. But the formula could have been used at the very beginning as well. Only a few figures (e.g., number of potential adopters) are known at the start, but estimates can be "plugged" into the other spots, and the whole thing set up for use down the line.

As with the other parts of this chapter, the A-T-A-R model gives us guidance on evaluation system design. You can immediately see the importance of awareness, trial, and so on. That means tests will have to be run where customers are checked out for their interest in trying, their reactions after trying (how likely would they be to try again?), and whatever else contributes to the formula.

There is nothing magic in the formula; it simply states the critical factors and shows their relationship to each other and to the sales and profit forecasts.

Two points are important about this model's sales and profit forecasts for the security device:

1. *Each factor is subject to estimation,* and in every development phase we try to sharpen our ability to make the estimates. For example, we may try to check the introductory promotion's awareness-building capability. Or just how much price discounting we must do to motivate a first purchase of the device. Or how much trust the buyer places in the unit after it is installed. We may be worried about how we're going to get enough distribution to make the product available when car owners seek it.
2. *An inadequate profit forecast can be improved only by changing one of the factors.* For example, if the forecast of $1,800,000 profit contribution is insufficient, we look at each factor in the model and see which ones might be changed and at what cost. Perhaps we could increase the retail margin by 5 percent and get another 20 percent of stores to stock it. On the other hand, perhaps an increase in advertising would produce more awareness.

Qualitative changes (such as a new advertising theme) can be made in addition to the quantitative. The proposed changes are then run through the formula again, which yields another set of results, some more changes, and so on. Sometimes the issue raised is so fundamental that it is more efficient to cycle back to an earlier phase in the development. The fact that the model is set up in spreadsheet format makes for easy simulations and "what if" tests.

FIGURE 8–6

Definitions used in A-T-A-R model

Buying unit means purchase point; may be each person or department who participates in the decision.

Aware means someone in the buying unit hears about the existence of a new product with some characteristic that differentiates it; subject to variation between industries and even between developers.

Available means the percentage chance that if a buyer wants to try the product, the effort to find it will be successful; often "percent of stores that stock it." Direct sellers have 100 percent availability.

Trial is variously defined; may be use of a sample in an industrial setting where such use has a cost associated with it; in most situations, means an actual purchase and at least some consumption.

Repeat is also varied; on packaged goods, means to buy at least one (or two or three) more times; on durables, may mean be happy and/or make at least one recommendation to others.

A-T-A-R is a term that came from consumer products marketing. Industry has traditionally used slightly different language, so a natural question is "Does the model apply to all types of new products, including industrial ones, and services too?" The answer is absolutely, though each term may be defined slightly differently in different settings.

See Figure 8–6 for the definitions of terms that vary. A **consumer buying unit** may be a person or a home. For office furniture, it will perhaps be a facility manager; for industrial products, it will generally be a purchasing or engineering person (part of a team); and for a consumer bank loan, it will once again be a person or a family. Product developers know what these definitions should be; the target users were selected partly because we know them well.

Without a precise definition there can be no worthwhile measurement. In each case, something about the term tells you how to define it. For **awareness,** we want to know if the buying unit has been sufficiently informed to stimulate further investigation and consideration of trial. If it has only heard the product's name, it probably won't. For **trial,** you may already be wondering how a potential buyer could "try" the security device that must be installed in a car, that is, try it in risk situations, waiting for a thief to challenge it. The answer is that we get as close to the perfect answer as we can, and that sometimes calls for ingenuity. Otis Elevator Company, for example, is not selling cake mixes—they simply take prospective buyers to a site where the elevator under consideration is already installed. The trial is not perfect, but it is close enough for real customer learning. Sometimes firms use **vicarious trial** where a person or firm who *did* try something shares results with someone who can't try it. But trial there should be, and Chrysler once wanted a new item tried so badly that they paid people $50 if they would take a demonstration ride (and later show proof of purchase of a new car within a month or so.) It can be done.

In a trial, we want two things to happen:

1. The buying unit went to some "expense" to get the trial supply—if there was no cost, then we can't be sure there was evaluation of the product message and interest created. Anyone can taste some sausage in a supermarket, but that doesn't mean the taste was a true trial.
2. The buying unit used the new item enough to have a basis for deciding whether it is any good.

For **availability,** we want to know whether the buyer can easily get the new product if a decision is made to try it. This factor is more standard, and for consumer products is usually the percent of those outlets where our target buyers shop where the firm has stocking of the new item. If the firm sells direct, there is always availability (unless the factory has extended back orders). Business-to-business often uses distributors of some type, usually under some franchise or semifranchise agreement, again pretty much assuring availability. But many small firms cannot be sure of availability, and spend much of their marketing money on trying to get it.

Repeat is easy for consumer packaged goods (usually, a repeat purchase), but it really means the trial was successful—the buying unit was pleased. For one-time purchases (industrial or consumer), we have to decide what statistic will tell us that. Some people use the direct one: "Were you satisfied?" Sometimes, an indirect one—such as "Have you had occasion to recommend the product to others?"—is better. In the case of the car security device, buying one for another car would be a good measurement. In any case, a firm should arrive at some acceptable definition and stick with it, thus building up experience to measure against.

Where Do We Get the Figures for the A-T-A-R Model?

Figure 8–7 shows where we customarily get the data for the A-T-A-R model and, thus, how the model ties the entire evaluation process together. You are not yet acquainted with the various tests, but they will be tied into the A-T-A-R model as they come up. Though various evaluation events can help on several of the key factors, we are usually most interested in the one event that makes the biggest contribution—noted as "best" in the figure. And we should know which these are prior to starting the evaluation. That way, we spend our limited funds first on the best steps and then on others if funds are available. Also, if we have to skip a step (for example, the concept test), we immediately know we are leaving open the question of whether users are likely to try the item when it becomes available. If we are going to do product use testing, then it should be set up in a way that lets us go through a concept test in the process of getting people to sign up for the use testing. It's later than we wanted, but better now than not at all.

FIGURE 8–7

Items in the A-T-A-R model have multiple sources: a rolling evaluation

	Various Sources of Estimates for It				
A-T-A-R Item	*Basic Market Research*	*Concept Test*	*Product Use Test*	*Component Testing*	*Market Test*
Market units	Best	Helpful	Helpful		Helpful
Awareness*		Helpful	Helpful	Best	Helpful
Trial		Best	Helpful		Helpful
Availability†	Helpful				Best
Repeat (adoption)			Best		Helpful
Consumption	Helpful	Helpful	Helpful		Best
Prices per unit	Helpful	Helpful	Helpful	Helpful	Best
Cost per unit‡				Helpful	Best

Key: Best = The best source for that item.
Helpful = Some knowledge gained.

*Awareness is often gauged by the agency that develops the advertising.

†Availability is usually estimated by sales management, and doubts about the figure are key to selection among market testing methods.

‡The cost component in profit contribution is internally estimated, usually prior to actual start-up. But valid figures can come only after some significant production.

Regarding Sales Forecasting in General

What we have been doing, of course, is making sales forecasts—predicting just how many of an item or new service we will sell. We need forecasts so badly that they are a basic input into every stage of the evaluation process—from opportunity to retrospect. (After the whole thing is over, some critics will be making their "forecasts" of what might have been!) Forecast importance has led to many techniques and devices, far more than can be covered here. Many of them are not relevant to new products, and many of them are just elaborate techniques of guessing. As one wit said, "Forecasting is difficult, especially of the future." And no business situation has more unknowns than a new product.

Most sales forecasting techniques have a paradigm of some kind—a model of the situation. For example, one of the most common is analogy—forecasting a new item compared to a prior new item. Another is to use market share—forecasting the percentage of customers who will switch and multiplying that percentage times total market sales. But A-T-A-R brings the paradigm right down to a specific new product—it calls for numbers that usually can be researched, and it uses them in a managerial way.

A-T-A-R is a concept that we will return to occasionally in this book. In Chapter 11, we will use it as the basis of a sales forecasting model. It is implicit throughout the discussion of market launch planning (Chapters 17 and 18): what else could be more important for the marketing effort to do than achieve awareness, trial, availability, and repeat use?[5] Finally, in Chapter 21, we revisit it again, this time as a tool to assess the launch, identify where the problem areas are, and steer it back on course.

Summary

This chapter looked at the factors that aid in designing an evaluation system for the basic new product process, that will provide information that guides the project on its journey to the market. First came the cumulative expenditures curve, the risk/payoff matrix, and the decay curve. Then we looked at several descriptors of most situations, the primary one being that almost everything about a process situation is tentative. The product itself is still evolving, at least until it sells successfully; the actual date of marketing is increasingly unclear as firms adopt limited marketing approaches; evaluation actually begins with the innovation charter well before ideation, and a product is an assemblage of many parts, each requiring its own evaluation.

Lastly, we introduced the A-T-A-R model, which tells us some of the critical steps in new product evaluation, and how our information about them can be used to forecast sales and profits and to design an evaluation system accordingly.

What are the specific tools, what can each do, and what are their weaknesses? The ones we use in Phase III of the basic process, prior to entering the development phase, are covered in the next two chapters. Others come later.

Applications

More questions from that interview with the company president.

1. "During a recent management meeting, two of my division managers (both in the UK incidentally) got into quite a tussle over the programs they use to evaluate new product ideas. One of them said he felt evaluation was very important; he wanted to do it quite completely, and he certainly didn't want anyone working to further the development of an item unless the prospects for it looked highly promising. The other manager objected to this, saying she wanted products to move rapidly down the pike and save the serious evaluation for the time when she had the data to make it meaningful.

[5]One of our top sales forecasting experts recently addressed the new product situation, particularly the issues surrounding the many techniques. Robert J. Thomas, "Issues in New Product Forecasting," *Journal of Product Innovation Management,* September 1994, pp. 347–53.

Both persons seemed to have a point, so I just let it ride. What do you think I should have said?"

2. "Recently I was reading an article about Xerox, and its president was saying how he wanted to drive new product costs down earlier, freeze the specs earlier, eliminate duplication of effort, and get new products into customer hands earlier in order to learn more about performance and costs. Using the idea of an evaluation system, can you tell me what you would say to that president about what he wants to do?"
3. "I don't know what your profs would say, but it often seems to me that we might be just as well off if we didn't do any evaluation on new products. Just produce the ones we're convinced will sell the best and really support those. Let's face it—we never have reliable data anyway, and everyone is always changing minds or opinions. Never knew so many people could say I told you so."
4. "Tell you another funny thing about evaluation—seems as though the folks involved in it never use the facts or data that they should and instead use some sort of surrogate data. I don't see why you have to beat around the bush. Why not just gather the real facts in the first place and not use those substitutes?"

Case: Concept Development Corporation (Revised)[6]

Late in 1990, three bridge-playing friends in a southern college town decided to start their own firm. One, Bob Stark, worked for General Motors as a planning manager in a local assembly operation. The second, Betsy Morningside, was a speech and theater professor at the college. The third, Myron Hite, was a CPA who worked for one of the Big Eight accounting firms.

All three were exceptionally creative and especially enjoyed their bridge sessions because they had a chance to brag about their new creations and to hear about the creations of the others. It was all for fun until one evening it struck them that it was time to stop the fun and start making some money from their many ideas. So they quit their jobs, pooled their savings, rented a small, three-room office, hired a couple of people, coined the name Concept Development Corporation, and started serious work.

A professor from the college was asked to "make a contribution to local entrepreneurship" by setting up a system to evaluate their ideas. They fully realized they were better at thinking up things than evaluating them. They also were aware of their deficiencies: little staff, little money, little experience in making what they created, and little time before their meager savings disappeared completely.

They began with two product areas. One was toys, broadly defined as things children played with, especially educational activities. The other area was writing services,

[6]This is a real situation, slightly camouflaged.

something they had not intended to work on but which arose as temporary spin-offs from the abilities of one of the two people they hired. These services primarily involved designing and writing instruction sheets for area firms (training manuals, copy for package inserts, instruction signs—anywhere words were used to instruct people in doing things). The individual had some background in instructions, and was experienced in writing and layout work. So they decided to develop new items along that line as well.

Their strategy was to develop unique toys that required little up-front expenditures (for example, dies and packaging equipment). They were all three too creative to settle for imitation. Most toys would have some game or competitive aspect, be educational, and involve paper, color, numbers, and the like. They figured "most of the stuff would be for children under 12." And, of course, they needed products that would catch on fast and sell well.

The writing services would be partly reactive in that they would do whatever clients asked them to do. But, being creative, they also planned to create innovative services—new ways of meeting industry and business needs. For example, they wanted to offer a special test/training service, whereby after developing a training manual or instruction sheet they would have some employees for whom the piece was developed come to a special room where they would read the material, apply it in some fashion, be tested on it, and so on. What they delivered to the client would be proven to work. They had many such ideas.

The professor went back to the college and decided to let a new products class assist in the assignment. The students were asked to think about the new firm's situation, the general evaluation system in Figure 8–1, and the various purposes and special circumstances discussed in Chapter 8, and then come up with one general guideline statement of evaluation policy for the toy ideas and another for the new services. The students hadn't yet studied specific techniques (such as concept testing), but they could clearly indicate which of the six major stages in Figure 8–1 were the most critical, where the toughest decisions would be, and so on. The professor was especially interested in the differences between goods and services. He wanted the students to state, as specifically as possible, what they felt were the major differences between the evaluation of tangible goods (like toys) and services, why these differences existed, and what the consequences are with respect to evaluation techniques and methods.

CHAPTER

9

CONCEPT TESTING

Setting

This chapter is the first of two spelling out the various tools for evaluating new products (goods and services) *prior* to undertaking technical development. Chapter 9 will cover the product innovation charter and market analysis activities, which occur before the idea appears, and the initial reaction and the concept testing, which occur immediately after the idea appears.

Recall that, at the end of Chapter 6, we had left unresolved the issue of whether customers would actually buy products corresponding to the gaps we had identified. We need to be able to relate customer needs and preferences to these gaps, to insure that we don't develop the "wrong" product. In this chapter, we will use perceptual mapping and conjoint analysis to analyze market needs and preferences, to segment the market according to benefits sought, and to test how well our concept will be accepted by the market.

The Importance of Up-Front Evaluations

In recent years there has been a big increase in activity at this pretechnical stage of the process. There still is not nearly enough, but the practice is spreading, for four reasons. Three come from a key concept discussed in Chapter 1—the triad of quality, time, and cost, and the fourth comes from marketing.

The biggest cause of new product failure is that the intended buyer did not see a need for the item—no purpose, no value. It is in concept testing, a key part of this chapter, where we get our first confirmation that this will be a *quality* product that will address a market need. We save *time* by gathering information and making decisions that help assure the product will move through development fast, with a minimum of looping back to correct problems. Spending time here saves time overall.[1] We lower cost in several ways, one when we avoid the rising cumulative expenditures curve you met in Chapter 8—with the cost curve ever rising, the best time to drop a loser is at the bottom of the curve. Another cost cutter is the elimination of the many losers naturally picked up in an aggressive concept generation program. It's difficult to cut at this point, but we have to, so we want to do it in the correct way. Last, on cost, information gathered helps us make cost forecasts—just how close are we going to be to competition on the proposed item, and how draconian must our efficiencies be.

Quality, time, and cost—there is no better reason for taking action at this point. But this is also the stage where we set the basic marketing strategy on firm ground. We confirm the target market (the user whose needs we are trying to find and solve) and settle on a product positioning statement (just how the new item will be better than others already out there). The positioning statement guides all the rest of the marketing activities.

So, we will look at what happens here, what firms are doing, and how one sets about doing what seems to be the very best approach—concept testing.

The Product Innovation Charter

The first evaluation that a firm makes is *of itself and its situation.* That evaluation yields a priori conclusions about new product proposals. The firm reaches these conclusions while making basic strategic decisions, as discussed in Chapter 3 on the product innovation charter. These decisions decree what types of new products fit best. For example,

Smith & Wesson wanted items to sell to law enforcement agencies.

Remington sought new uses for powdered metal technology.

Nabisco sought technological breakthroughs in snack foods.

The PIC is intended to eliminate most new product ideas. In advance, and without knowing the concepts, the firm decides to reject ideas that violate PIC guidelines. Hence, ideas of the following types will be excluded:

[1]Several studies show this, a recent one being Albert L. Page and John S. Stovall, "Importance of the Early Stages in the New Product Process," *Bridging the Gap from Concept to Commercialization* (Indianapolis, IN: Product Development & Management Association, 1994). Others are Robert G. Cooper and Elko J. Kleinschmidt, "Determinants of Timeliness in Product Development," *Journal of Product Innovation Management,* November 1994, pp. 381–95, and Mitzi M. Montoya-Weiss and Roger Calantone, "Determinants of New Product Performance: A Review and Meta-Analysis," *Journal of Product Innovation Management,* November 1994, pp. 397–417.

- Ideas that require technologies the firm does not have.
- Ideas to be sold to customers about whom the firm has no close knowledge.
- Ideas that offer the wrong degree of innovativeness (too much or too little!).
- Ideas wrong on other dimensions: not low cost, too close to certain competitors, and so forth.

The charter given to new products management thus eliminates more product ideas than all the other evaluations combined. By coming at the beginning of the new products system, it precludes the unfortunate practice of having unwanted proposals eat up valuable development funds. Firms that use the PIC include Hallmark (whose management negatively evaluated all low-quality gift items several years ago), and Rucker (who pre-reject all items not related to oil wells).

Market Analysis

The second evaluation that precedes appearance of the concept is an in-depth study of the market area that the product innovation charter has selected for focus. The study takes place immediately after the PIC is approved, and the depth of the study depends on how well the firm already knows the market selected. Ongoing ideation in support of present product lines takes place within a standing type of PIC, and no special study is necessary (assuming current product managers do their jobs correctly).

In the Rucker Company example above, new products people knew the oil industry well, but they didn't know everything about it. Moreover, their new products would probably be developed for specific new uses within that industry, about which the firm perhaps knew very little. But, in most cases, the PIC-designated market is not thoroughly understood, and the market analysis is helpful.

Initial Reaction

Concept generation follows the market analysis just discussed. Concepts begin flowing in, usually very fast, and opinions on them are formed instantly. Most firms have evolved a special technique to handle this deluge systematically, which we will call **initial reaction.**

At Oster, each idea that came from the marketing or administration departments went to the sales vice president first, and each idea from the technical departments or production went to the engineering vice president first. If one of these vice presidents approved the idea, it was sent to the other. If both approved, the idea went to a committee, and the system became more formal. The two people making the initial reaction primarily based their decision on their experience of many years in the small-appliance industry.

Quick and inexpensive initial reactions must resist the "bazooka effect" (where suggestions are quickly disapproved or "blasted out"), so several provisos apply:

1. *The idea source does not usually participate in the initial reaction.* A person who has an idea may want to explain it and argue for it, but this person should probably not have a vote in the decision to advance the idea or drop it.
2. *Two or more persons are involved in any rejection decision,* based on the "fragility of new ideas" concept discussed in Chapter 8. The rejection percentage is much higher here than at any other stage, but involving two or more persons dilutes the biases of a single person. The Oster system did not have this safeguard because either vice president could kill the suggestion.
3. *The initial reaction, though quick, is based on more than a pure intuitive sense.* The evaluators are trained and experienced, records are kept and reviewed, and objective aids are sought.

One of several techniques used in this initial reaction is the product innovation charter. Knowing whether a firm wants to be first or last, high risk or low risk, internally or externally developing, and stay in shoes or add handbags leads to quick and decisive action.

Most firms also make use of heuristics (rules of thumb) for this rough screening. For example, managers look at the scale required (is it in our league?), the competitor they would have to face, state of the art the idea would require, and the fit with their manufacturing and marketing operations. One suggested way for firms to do a rough early screen is to evaluate the new product on three factors:

- *Market worth:* What is the attractiveness of the new product to the targeted customer population?
- *Firm worth:* Is the new product project viewed positively by management? Does this project enhance the firm's competencies?
- *Competitive insulation:* Can the product's advantage be maintained against competitive retaliation?[2]

Some managers prefer to use a small-scale informal survey at this initial reaction point, particularly when some aspect of the proposal extends beyond the evaluator's experience. But such surveys should be held to the level of telephone checks with professional colleagues.

[2]Rita Gunther McGrath, "Advantage from Adversity: Learning from Disappointment in Internal Corporate Ventures," *Journal of Business Venturing,* 1995, pp. 121–42.

Concept Testing and Development

Years ago, when Alan Ladd, Jr. reigned as top judge of new movie scripts at Twentieth Century-Fox Film Corporation, he revealed that his product proposal evaluation system ended about as soon as it began. He would simply read a script and decide whether or not to make the movie. He and his small staff knew their markets well, had a guiding product innovation charter, and combined their knowledge and the charter with personal judgment to reach decisions. They did not use concept testing, full screening, or product use testing. Ladd said, "It's based on my intuition and experience. There's no way to put it on a chart or graph or formulate it."[3]

Perhaps. Some agree with Mr. Ladd, but most do not. Most major firms make frequent use of **concept testing.** It is a mandatory part of the process for makers of consumer packaged goods. And its use is growing in industrial firms, which actually invented it. Business-to-business firms have always spent much time talking with users about their needs and problems, what suggestions they have, what they think about various ideas, and so on. They just never called it concept testing.

But first, let's deal with some concerns about this activity—there are times when it doesn't help. When the prime benefit is to a *personal sense,* such as the aroma of a perfume or the taste of a new food, concept testing usually fails. The concept cannot be communicated short of actually having some product there to demonstrate. A type of kids' gum popular in the early 90s (sour gums called Cry Baby and Warhead) tasted so bad that even product use testing showed they hated it. But, when available, they became masochistic to the tune of almost $100 million a year.

Second, concepts embodying new *art and entertainment* are tough to test. Whistler could not have concept-tested his idea for a painting of his mother; nor could the inventor of the Ferris wheel have surveyed people to ask what they thought of it. The thrill simply had to be experienced personally. And the same idea applies to Arnold Schwarzenegger's movie *Junior.* It tested poorly, and sold well.

Third, when the concept embodies some *new technology* that users cannot visualize, concept testing is again a weak tool. Kodak realized this when it tried to concept test its new disc camera. So did Alberto-Culver when it first tested the concept of hair mousse. Women accustomed to sprays could not imagine putting "stuff like that" on their hair. Only after the company developed the product and set up training classes in salons did women agree to try

[3]Earl C. Gottschalk, "How Fox's Movie Boss Decides That a Script Is a Powerful Winner," *The Wall Street Journal,* May 17, 1979, p. 1. Many years later, he was still doing the fast reaction, and had some major successes—e.g., winners *Star Wars, Nine to Five,* and *Thelma & Louise.* But he had also worked at several different studios, and had marketed some misses—*The Right Stuff, Quigley Down Under,* and *Not Without My Daughter.* Ronald Grover, "Can Alan Ladd Jr. Make Leo the Lion Roar?" *BusinessWeek,* August 12, 1991, pp. 65–66.

the mousse. Another example was when physicians rejected the concept of a heart pump—they could not know the full attributes (and thus the risks) of such a product before work on it was completed. Ditto on pump baseball gloves, which kids thought would be great until they put them on and found a snugger fit.

Fourth, there are times when firms mismanage concept testing and then blame the tool for misleading them. Coca-Cola asked their customers to taste-test New Coke and got favorable replies. But they then took that taste testing to mean customers would buy the product when it got a new name. This is actually the same problem as the heart pump—customers were asked to predict their behavior without knowing all the facts. They can't, but will if asked, and will unintentionally deceive developers who aren't careful. Another mismanaged test was when several fast food chains asked customers if they wanted diet burgers. Not only was it an unknown taste situation (above), but people are notoriously inclined to predict "worthy" behavior and then do something else.

Fifth, consumers sometimes simply do not know what problems they have. We discussed this in the chapter on problem-based ideation. Steelcase, for example, found they could not use concept testing on special furniture for use by teams. The team members had no feeling for what they didn't have, so Steelcase observed them in action and came up with a winner: furniture that lets them do some of their work collaboratively and some privately. The microwave oven was another similar example—consumers didn't know what to do with it even after it hit the market, and certainly could not have responded helpfully to researchers asking us what we thought about the concept.[4]

Oddly, in spite of evidence to the contrary, some new products people have doubts about concept testing on business and industrial products and on services. Regarding industrial products, if the customer has the ability to make judgments, those judgments are worth gathering; but major technological breakthroughs often don't qualify for that, and we just have to take the risk. On services, there is no question as to whether or not people can tell us what they see is useful if they can see it (but watch for the intangibles above). They can. But because there is usually little technical development, there is less *need* to do concept testing. If it is simple to go from concept to full service description (a form of prototype), then the services firm can proceed to what is called **prototype concept testing.** Such testing is, of course, much more reliable, with a physical prototype to talk around.

Despite the concerns noted above, concept testing is useful in most cases, and right now the burden of argument lies with the person who wants to skip it. We will hear for a long time about such firms as Suga Test Instruments Company of Tokyo, which marketed a \$1.3 million artificial snow machine.

[4]Some of these examples are discussed in Justin Martin, "Ignore Your Customer," *Fortune,* May 1, 1995, pp. 121–28.

Designed for utilities, car manufacturers, battery makers, outdoor clothing makers, and others, the snow machine met with almost zero adoption. True, it made more and better snow than any other machine, and it did the work inside a five-story building. But every target market already had methods for product testing and did not need the new machine. No one had bothered to ask them.[5]

A similar case came up when CalFare Corporation (without concept testing) developed shopping carts with a "special fifth wheel" that locked into place if the cart was taken from the premises (and run over a rough surface). The cart would then only go in circles. But most stores said no thanks. They feared negative publicity, and customers being scared away. A competitor said that often the cart went awry and started circling around the dairy departments. The unknowing developers were caught off guard by the very negative reactions they got.[6]

What Is a New Product Concept?

Webster's says a concept is an idea or an abstract notion. Businesspeople use the term *concept* for the product promise, the customer proposition, and the real reason why people should buy. It is a stated relationship between product features (form or technology) and consumer benefits—a claim of proposed satisfactions.

This promise is open to four interpretations:

1. The *producer's* perception of the *features* of the new product.
2. The *consumer's* perception of the *features* of the new product.
3. The *producer's* estimate of the *benefits* delivered by that set of features.
4. The *consumer's* estimate of the *benefits* delivered by that set of features.

These interpretations are only forecasts, or guesses, at this time—not reality, even with a prototype in hand. They rest on expectations.

Thus a complete new **product concept** is a statement about anticipated product features that will yield selected benefits relative to other products or problem solutions already available. An example is "A new electric razor whose screen is so thin it can cut closer than any other electric razor on the market."

Sometimes a part of the concept can be assumed; for example, saying "a copier that has twice the speed of current models" assumes the benefits of speed can go without saying.

---

[5]Marc Beauchamp, "Cold Shoulder," *Business Week,* October 6, 1986, p. 168.

[6]David Jefferson, "Building a Better Mousetrap Doesn't Ensure Success," *The Wall Street Journal,* November 18, 1991, p. B2.

The Purposes of Concept Testing

Recall that concept testing is part of the **prescreening** process, preparing a management team to do the full screening of the idea just before beginning serious technical work. We look for information to help the screeners use scoring models and write out product protocols, in Chapter 10.

Therefore, the *first* purpose of a concept test is to identify the very poor concept so it can be eliminated. If music lovers, for example, cannot conceive of a compact disk that will last forever and thus reject it out of hand, the concept is probably a poor one.

If the concept passes the first hurdle, a *second* purpose is to estimate (even crudely) the sales or trial rate that the product would enjoy—a sense of market share or a general range of revenue dollars. Some people believe this buying prediction is worthless. Others claim a clear, positive correlation between intention and purchase. One longtime practicing market researcher claimed to have confidential data showing correlations of 0.60 and well above.[7]

The buying intention question appears in almost every concept test. The most common format for purchase intentions is the classic five-point question: How likely would you be to buy a product like this, if we made it?

1. Definitely would buy.
2. Probably would buy.
3. Might or might not buy.
4. Probably would not buy.
5. Definitely would not buy.

The number of people who definitely would buy or probably would buy are usually combined and used as an indicator of group reaction. This is called the **top-two-boxes** score, as it is the total number of times one of the top two boxes on the questionnaire ("definitely" or "probably") were checked. Incidentally, Nabisco says "try" (not "buy") because buyers really are still quite tentative at this point.

Whether this many people actually purchase the item is not important. Researchers have usually calibrated their figures, so they know, for example, that if the top two boxes total 60 percent, the real figure will be, say, 25 percent. They do this from past experience, discounting what people tend to say in interview situations. Direct marketers can do the best calibration because they will later be selling the tested item to market groups they surveyed; they can tell exactly how actual behavior matches stated intentions. The data banks of the Bases Group, the largest supplier of concept tests, literally let a client company calibrate all of its concept test questions, by product type.

[7]Personal communication with Anthony Bushman, now professor of marketing, San Francisco State University.

For a price, Bases translates a client's raw intentions data into probable intentions.[8]

Incidentally, sometimes experience calibrates the probable intention *higher* than the respondents say now. On complex products, people often use caution at concept testing time but end up buying the product when they have a chance to see the final item and hear all about it. (Recall the heart pump.)

Obviously, the concept's sales potential will be closely related to how well it satisfies customer needs or offers desired benefits to the customer. Later sections of the chapter show more advanced analytical procedures that identify customer segments based on benefits sought. Knowing the benefit segments that exist in the marketplace, the firm can identify concepts that would be particularly desirable to specific segments or niches.

The *third* purpose of concept testing is to help develop the idea, not just test it. Concepts rarely emerge from a test the way they went in. Moreover, a concept statement is not enough to guide R&D. Scientists need to know what attributes (especially benefits) will permit the new product to fulfill the concept statement. Because the attributes frequently oppose or conflict with each other, many trade-offs must be made. When better to make them than when talking with people for whom the product is being developed? Near the end of this chapter, we will see how conjoint (trade-off) analysis, a technique we discussed in Chapter 7, is frequently used for this task.

Considerations in Concept Testing Research

Prepare the Concept Statement

A concept statement states a difference and how that difference benefits the customer or end-user: "This new refrigerator is built with modular parts; consequently, the consumer can arrange the parts to best fit a given kitchen location, and then, rearrange them to fit another location." If you think this sounds somewhat like a positioning statement, you are correct. And if the interviews are with a logical target group of potential buyers, the principal parts of a marketing strategy are in place—target market and product positioning. This is consistent with the basic new products process, where we say that the product and its marketing plan are developed simultaneously.

Format. Practitioners urge that any concept statement should make the new item's difference absolutely clear, claim determinant attributes (those that make a difference in buying decisions), offer a chord of familiarity by

[8]Other concept testing suppliers listed recently in a publication from the Leo Burnett Advertising Agency were: Conway/Milliken, Custom Research, Elrick & Lavidge, FRC Research, Information Resources, Longman-Moran Analytics, Market Decisions, Moskowitz Jacobs, NFO Research, Total Research, and The Vanderveer Group. Most of these have international operations.

FIGURE 9–1

Mail concept test format—plain verbal description of the product (good or service) and its major benefits

A major soft-drink manufacturer would like to get your reaction to an idea for a new diet soft drink. Please read the description below before answering the questions.

New Diet Soft Drink

Here is a tasty, sparkling beverage that quenches thirst, refreshes, and makes the mouth tingle with a delightful flavor blend of orange, mint, and lime.

It helps adults (and kids too) control weight by reducing the craving for sweets and between-meal snacks. And, best of all, it contains absolutely no calories.

Comes in 12-ounce cans or bottles and costs 60¢ each.

1. How different, if at all, do you think this diet soft drink would be from other available products now on the market that might be compared with it?

   ☐ Very different
   ☐ Somewhat different
   ☐ Slightly different
   ☐ Not at all different

2. Assuming you tried the product described above and like it, about how often do you think you would buy it?

	Check one
More than once a week	☐
About once a week	☐
About twice a month	☐
About once a month	☐
Less often	☐
Would never buy it	☐

Source: NFO Research, Inc., Toledo, Ohio.

relating in some way to things familiar to the customer, and be completely credible and realistic. And short, as short as possible, although there have been concept statements of three to five pages that worked very well in complex technical situations.[9]

The concept statement is usually presented to potential buyers in one of several formats: a narrative (verbal) format, a drawing or diagram, a model or prototype, or in virtual reality. All the concept testing techniques we discuss

[9]Robert E. Davis calls these "testable concepts" in "From Experience: The Role of Market Research in the Development of New Consumer Products," *Journal of Product Innovation Management,* September 1993, pp. 309–17. Regarding clarity, Anheuser-Busch said consumers had difficulty understanding Bud Dry, even when it was marketed. Perhaps the reason lies in what an executive said it was: "A cold-filtered draft beer—not pasteurized—with no aftertaste, basically a full-alcohol, light beer, a cleaner beer."

FIGURE 9–2

Mail concept test—sketch

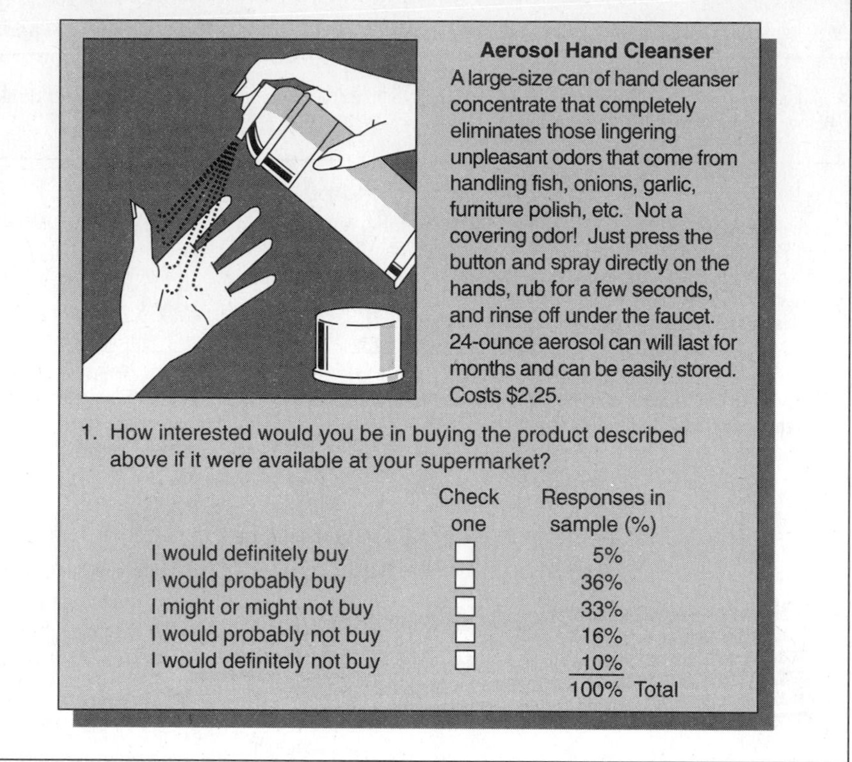

Note: These hypothetical response percentages are for illustrative purposes only.
Source: NFO Research, Inc., Toledo, Ohio.

here are commonly used for business products, though in those cases it is especially important to provide sketches, models, and/or other renditions of the concept such that meaningful, objective reactions can be obtained.[10]

Figure 9–1 shows an example of the narrative format. Some people prefer a very brief presentation, giving only the minimum of attributes and letting the respondent offer additional ones. Others prefer a full description, approaching what a diagram or prototype would provide. In the pure narrative, the concept is totally intangible, though there are ways to provide some measurement when doing concept tests of services.[11]

---

[10]Ronald L. Paul, "Evaluating Ideas and Concepts for New Business-to-Business Products," in M. Rosenau, A. Griffin, G. Castellion and N. Anscheutz, eds., *The PDMA Handbook of New Product Development* (New York: Wiley, 1996), pp. 207–16.

[11]An example of how services can be somewhat quantified is shown in a study of retail service by A. Parasuraman, Valarie Ziethaml, and Leonard L. Berry, *Servqual: A Multiple-Item Scale for Measuring Customer Perceptions of Service Quality* (Cambridge, MA.: Marketing Science Institute, 1986).

Drawings, diagrams, and sketches comprise a second way to present concepts to respondents. Figure 9–2 demonstrates the use of a drawing. Drawings and the like usually must be supplemented by a narrative statement of the concept. Figure 9–2 also shows what the results might look like. As shown, 5 percent of respondents said they would "definitely" buy the product, and 36 percent said they would "probably" buy it, so the top-two-boxes score is 5 + 36 = 41 percent.

Prototypes, or models, are a third, more expensive form of concept statement, because many decisions have to be made about the new product to get it into a prototype. Whoever builds an early prototype makes lots of decisions about the item that probably should be kept open at this early date. Prototypes are useful only in special situations, as, for example, with simple-to-prepare food products or, at the other extreme, with concepts so complex that the buyer cannot react without more knowledge than a simple narrative would give. A firm in Canada tried to get reactions to the concept of a traveling medical examining unit that would be driven to various corporation offices where examinations would be given. The answer was to build a small model of the unit, showing layout, equipment, and so on.[12]

The fourth type of concept format, virtual reality, captures the advantages of the prototype without most of the disadvantages. Steelcase, the office supply firm, has a software system that allows them to "build" three-dimensional images of office concepts. The interviewee can actually walk around rooms, seeing things from any angle. This virtual reality approach permitted them to win a big contract for the Olympic Village at the Atlanta Olympics—the Games management could literally see, and even modify on the spot, every room in the layout.[13]

The real question is "What does it take to communicate to the buyer what we have in mind?" From that point on, it is a question of the cost of better displays versus the need for information in making forecasts of buying intentions. For office furniture, most buyers want lots of details, but for turnip-flavored yogurt, one sentence would probably work.[14]

Commercialized Concept Statements. A special variation, regardless of format, concerns whether to make the statement as a **commercialized concept statement,** which means to present it in promotional style. Compare these two concept statements:

---

[12]Robert G. Cooper, *Winning at New Products* (Reading, MA: Addison-Wesley Publishing, 1986), p. 59.

[13]Information from William Miller, director of research and business development, at a Product Development & Management Association conference in Southfield, Michigan, January 1995. Further information on use of personal computers in concept testing can be found in William M. Bulkeley in "More Market Researchers Swear by PCs," *The Wall Street Journal,* March 15, 1993, p. B1.

[14]Don't laugh. Green Giant Vegetable Yogurt in four "flavors" (cucumber, beet, tomato, and garden salad) scored well on concept tests (87% top-two boxes). But the firm couldn't deliver what the concept seemed to promise to consumers (should it be crunchy?). This one failed in the marketplace.

> Light Peanut Butter, a low-calorie version of natural peanut butter that can provide a tasty addition to most diets.
>
> A marvelous new way to chase the blahs from your diet has been discovered by General Mills scientists—a low-calorie version of ever-popular peanut butter. As tasty as ever and produced by a natural process, our new Light Peanut Butter will fit most weight-control diets in use today.

These statements show little *substantial* difference, yet they will draw different reactions. Commercialized formats produce "more realistic" evaluations (that is, greater acceptance), but they risk the bias of good or poor advertising copy writing. Proponents say noncommercialized statements won't provoke typical market reactions in this commercial world. Critics answer, why evaluate the advertising when all we want at this time is reaction to the concept?

Neither form is *better* than the other, and many managers simply go for a compromise—a gentle sell that puts advantages in language stakeholders are used to. Some practitioners say that it is most important to keep the idea simple, and to be clear and realistic—don't "oversell" the concept. Also, if you are testing several concepts, remember to use the same format for all of them so they can be directly compared![15]

Offering of Competitive Information. Customers of all types know much less about their current products and other options than we would like. A new concept may well offer a benefit that the customer doesn't realize is new. One solution is to provide a full data sheet about each competitive product. The issue was researched (on dog food), and results showed no significant difference, though most of the data did bend slightly in favor of the new product when there was full information.[16] And many new product managers don't like to overload the concept statement; it diffuses the message and confuses the customer.

Price. Another issue turns on whether to put a price in the concept statement. The examples in Figures 9–1 and 9–2 both mention price. The Bases Group insists on price in its concept tests. Some people object, saying reaction to the concept is wanted, not to its price. Yet price is part of the product (actually, a product attribute in the customer's eyes), and buyers can't be expected to tell purchase intentions without knowing price. An exception occurs for those complex concepts (for example, the medical examinations van, above) requiring many decisions before the cost is known.

---

[15]Ned F. Anscheutz, "Evaluating Ideas and Concepts for New Consumer Products," in M. Rosenau, A. Griffin, G. Castellion and N. Anscheutz, eds., *The PDMA Handbook of New Product Development* (New York: Wiley, 1996), pp. 195–206.

[16]James B. Miller, Norman T. Bruvold, and Jerome B. Kernan, "Does Competitive-Set Information Affect the Results of Concept Tests?" *Journal of Advertising Research,* April/May 1987, pp. 16–24.

Define the Respondent Group

We would like to interview any and all persons who will play a role in deciding whether the product will be bought and how it might be improved. When the New Zealand Wool Testing Authority came up with a new wool testing service, it had to test the concept with three levels in its channel—brokers who sell the raw wool, scourers who scour the wool and prepare it for shipment, and exporters who sell the wool to manufacturers.[17] A cement company, which created a new concept in cement for use in construction, had to seek advice from brick makers, siding makers, architects, builders, designers, and regulators, among others, in addition to the people who would be buying the buildings. Some industrial products may involve five to ten different people at each buying point; durable consumer goods usually involve more than one person. Yet that peanut butter mentioned above could probably be tested with just one person in a family setting—the homemaker who does the buying—or could it?

That's why we think about **stakeholders**—any person or organization who has a stake in the proposed product. Our new product wastebaskets are filled with products that made sense to the end-user but could not get to them—for example, when professional sanitary engineers refused to endorse a new system of water treatment.

Reaching this full set of influencers sounds simple, but is complex and expensive. Some people try to seek out a small number of lead users (see Chapter 4), or influencers, or large users. This approach saves some money and gets more expert advice but often fails to reflect key differences (and misunderstandings) in the marketplace. It would seem to be a technique for situations where there is a "right" understanding or perception or preference.[18] Of course, we should always watch out for critics, people who have a reason for opposing the concept. A developer came up with a device that "read" electrocardiograms and needed the reactions of cardiologists, but the obvious conflict of interest made the interviewing tricky.

Some new products people, aware that they will first have to interest the innovators and early adopters in a market, concentrate their concept testing solely on them. If this group is interested, it's a good bet others will be also.

Select the Response Situation

There are two issues in the response situation: (1) the mode of reaching the respondent and (2) if personal, whether to approach individually or in a group.

---

[17]Arch G. Woodside, R. Hedley Sanderson, and Roderick J. Brodie, "Testing Acceptance of a New Industrial Service," *Industrial Marketing Management,* 1988, pp. 65–71.

[18]This is discussed (and tested) in Jan P. L. Schoormans, Roland J. Ortt, and Cees J. P. M. de Bont, "Enhancing Concept Test Validity by Using Expert Consumers," *Journal of Product Innovation Management,* March 1995, pp. 153–62.

Most concept testing takes place through personal contact—direct interviewing. Survey samples typically run about from 100 to 400 people, though industrial samples are usually much smaller. Personal contact allows the interviewer to answer questions and to probe areas where the respondent is expressing a new idea or is not clear.

Some research suppliers offer a service of interviewing in which the client can submit product concepts on a shared-cost basis. In the Omnibus program at Moskowitz Jacobs, a fully equipped central testing facility conducts periodic waves of interviewing which yield 100 interviews at a cost per concept of around $3,000. Other research firms use pseudo stores in vacant locations at shopping malls.

The high costs of personal contact have led developers to try other methods, especially the mail and the telephone, though both media offer problems today. NBC used cable TV. Viewers from 20 cable systems were conscripted; they viewed pilots in their homes and were interviewed by telephone for their responses. Of course, creative people in the television industry were aghast that programming people would use concept testing, in any form![19]

The second issue concerns individual versus group. Both are widely used. Groups (usually just called focus groups) are excellent when we want respondents to hear and react to the comments of others and to talk about how it would be used.

Prepare the Interviewing Sequence

Simple interviewing situations state the new product concept and ask about believability, buying intentions, and any other information wanted. The whole interview may take only two or three minutes per product concept, if the item is a new packaged good and all we really want is a buying intention answer.

Usually we want more than that. In such cases, we first *explore the respondent's current practice* in the area concerned, asking how people currently try to solve their problems, what competing products they use, and what they think about those products. How willing would they be to change? What specific benefits do they want? What are they spending? Is the product used as part of a system?

This background information helps us understand and interpret *comments about the new concept,* which are asked for next. The immediate and critical question is, "Does the respondent understand the concept?" Given understanding, we then seek other reactions:

---

[19]Louis Weisberg, "Audience Reaction Steers TV Program Pilots," *Advertising Age,* February 28, 1985, p. 26.

Uniqueness of the concept.	Does it solve a problem?
Believability of the concept.	How much they like the concept.
Importance of the problem.	How likely would they buy.
Their interest in the concept.	Their reaction to the price.
Is it realistic, practical, useful?	Problems they see in use.

We are especially interested in what changes they would make in the concept, exactly what it would be used for and why, what products or processes would be replaced, and who else would be involved in using the item.

You can see that services present a problem here. A service offers an image, or a feeling, or a hard-to-measure convenience. This makes it difficult for the respondent to give useful information along the lines just listed.

In all this interviewing, remember we are not taking a poll but, rather, *exploring what people are doing and thinking.* Only a few questions will be in standard form, for tabulation. Each new concept addresses a very specific problem (or at least it should), and we need to know what people think about that problem in the context of the new concept. It doesn't pay to get too formal in the questioning, unless you are conducting many concept tests where there is a database for comparison.

Variations

There are variations to all the above procedures. Avon markets 50 new products every 60 days, with a three-month development cycle. Every two weeks they meet with some of their test bank of 150 sales reps. Many ideas are shown to them for their quick reaction, by computer-driven projectors. Their "appeal rating" correlates very well with sales, in some cases more accurately then field consumer concept testing predicted. A garment must be cut to fit a body, and bodies vary greatly.

Customer Preferences and Benefit Segments

A great number of firms will rely on a simple top-two boxes score (or top two-boxes plus 30 percent, based on industry experience) in doing concept testing. Occasionally, more information is needed. We cannot assume all customers will have the same needs or look for the same benefits when making a purchase. In fact, through **benefit segmentation** a firm may identify unsatisfied market segments and concentrate its efforts on developing concepts ideally suited to the needs of these segments. We now turn our attention to ways in which we can identify benefit segments in our desired market, and develop products that will be most preferred by key benefit segments.[20]

[20]Note that, in our typology, benefits are one type of attribute (the others being features and functions). The terms "benefit segmentation" and "benefit segments" are commonly used for the procedure described in this section, and should not imply that only benefit-type attributes can be considered.

Identifying Benefit Segments

Let's return to the swimsuit example of Chapter 6. Recall that, when we were collecting respondents' perceptions of the existing swimsuit brands, we also got them to rate how important each attribute was in determining their preference among brands. These **importance ratings** can be used to model existing brand preferences and predict likely preferences for new concepts.

Suppose there were only two attributes to consider: comfort and fashion. It might be very simple to identify benefit segments on an importance map as in Figure 9–3. Each customer is indicated by a dot in this figure, according to the importance she attaches to each of the two attributes. In this simple case, three obvious benefit segments emerge of approximately equal size: customers that think comfort alone is important, those that think fashion alone is important, and those that think both are important.

Rarely are the benefit segments so easily visualized, however. In this case, like most others, many more than two attributes were important to customers in forming their preferences. Thus we need to turn to one of the many computer programs that can do **cluster analysis,** which puts observations (in this case, individuals) together into relatively homogeneous groups. Like factor analysis, cluster analysis is also a data reduction method. In Chapter 6 we learned that factor analysis reduces the data cube by grouping many attributes together into a small number of underlying factors; cluster analysis groups together many individuals into a small number of benefit segments.

Different criteria and rules of thumb can be used to select the best number of clusters (benefit segments) that exist in the market, since there is no one

FIGURE 9–3

Importance map showing benefit segments

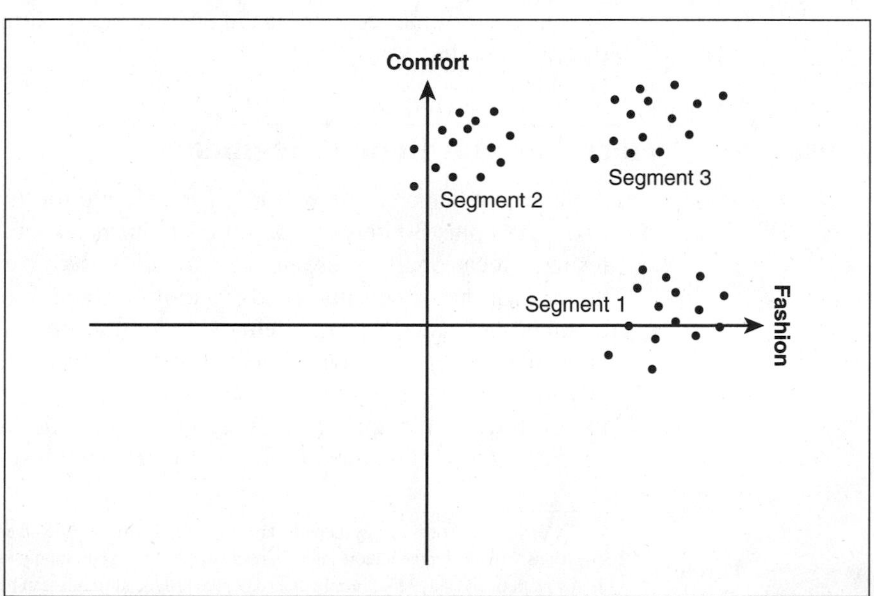

correct answer. Generally, practical judgment or experience will play an important role. For example, in this case we may feel it is unlikely that more than five or six benefit segments exist. When cluster analysis was run on the swimsuit importances data, a satisfactory solution with three benefit segments was obtained. Conceptually, it is not too different from Figure 9–3, even though we considered many more attributes: the three clusters we obtained more or less correspond to those depicted in the figure.

Joint Space Maps

We can now overlay the benefit segments onto our perceptual map (previously built in Chapter 6). The result is called a **joint space map,** and it allows us to assess the preferences of each benefit segment for different product concepts. Joint space maps can be developed using ideal brand ratings or preference regression.

Ideal Brands. The most direct way is to get customers to rate their **ideal brand** on each attribute. Using the factor score coefficient matrix (which we obtained in Chapter 6 from the perceptions of existing brands), we convert the ideal brand ratings to factor scores, and plot the ideal brand positions directly on the perceptual map. Clusters of individuals may be detected visually from this map—each cluster represents a segment with its own ideal brand positioned at the center of the cluster. Figure 9–4 shows what a joint space might look like if three segments existed as shown in Figure 9–3.

FIGURE 9–4
Joint space map showing ideal points

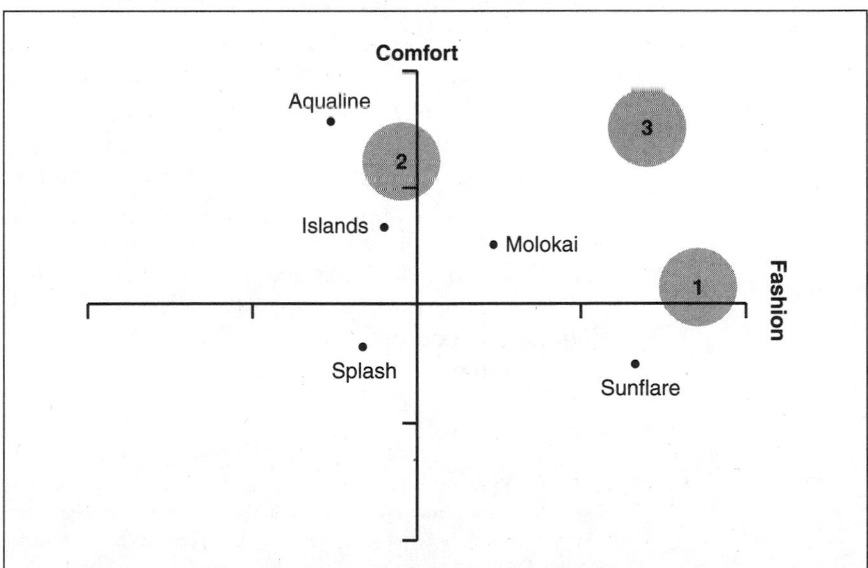

The preferences of each segment can be obtained from Figure 9–4. We expect that the brand that is located the closest to a segment's ideal brand will be preferred by that segment. Market share estimation models often assume that the market shares obtained by the various brands are inversely proportional to the square of the distance of that brand from the ideal point: This technique makes brands very close to the ideal highly preferable.

In Figure 9–4, Segment 1 is likely to prefer Sunflare, while Segment 2 seems to be satisfied with either Aqualine or Islands. The brand nearest to Segment 3's ideal point is Molokai, but none of the brands is really that close. Thus, a new brand high in both fashion and comfort has a chance to draw substantial market share from competitors.

Preference Regression. **Preference regression** is another method that can be used to identify the optimum combination of attributes desired by the market. This method relies on a different kind of numerical input—often, rankings of brands are obtained (paired comparisons can also be used). In preference regression, we do a regression analysis to relate the factor scores of each brand to the rankings of brands. The relative sizes of the regression coefficients we obtain give us an indication of the relative importance of each factor. Preference regression can also be done on attribute ratings instead of factor scores.

Instead of the importance ratings we discussed above, assume that customers were asked to provide rank orderings of the five existing brands, where 1 = most favored and 5 = least favored. First, we reverse scale the rank orderings such that higher numbers represent more favored brands. Then, we can solve the regression equation:

$$\text{(Reversed) Preference rank} = b_0 + (b_1 \times \text{Fashion score}) + (b_2 \times \text{Comfort score}) + e.$$

If we ignore benefit segments and put all the respondents together, we find the values of b_1 and b_2 are 0.28 and 0.21. Thus, the relative importance of fashion to customers is 0.28 / (0.28 + 0.21), or 57 percent, and the relative importance of comfort is 43 percent. Hence, while fashion comes out as the more important factor, we cannot ignore the fact that customers also place a lot of importance on comfort when we are assessing product concepts. We can also plot the overall regression line on the perceptual map as shown in Figure 9–5.[21] This line is referred to as the **ideal vector,** as it visually represents the optimum proportion of attributes desired by this market. A product concept lying near the regression line, at Point X on the map, is in a desirable position for this market.

---

[21]Though we actually do estimate b_0 in the regression equation, we ignore it when drawing Figure 9–5, as we are most interested in the relative importance of the revealed weights b_1 and b_2. The b_0 term simply defines the scale. Thus, in Figure 9–5, the regression line is shown passing through the origin.

FIGURE 9–5
Joint space map showing ideal vectors

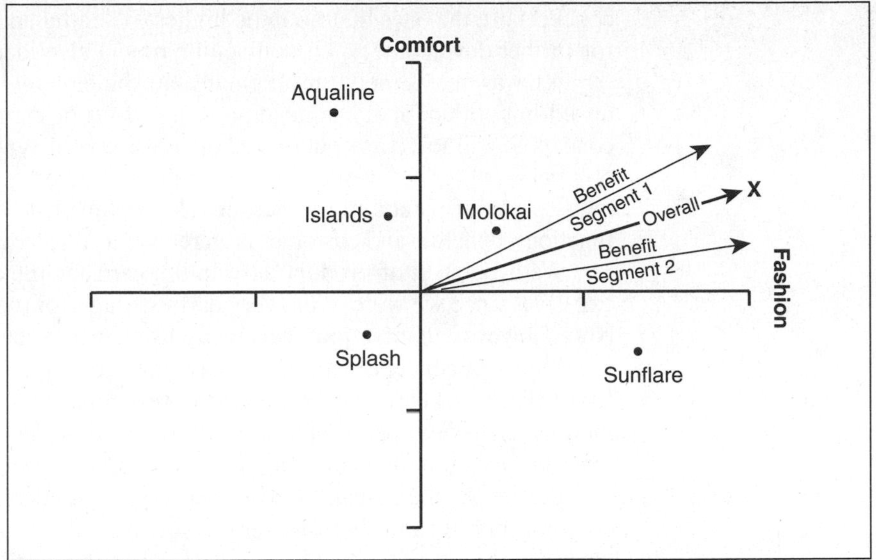

We can also cluster analyze the rank orderings to get benefit segments. In this case, two benefit segments were found to exist in this market, represented by the two other lines in Figure 9–5. One of these appears to consider only fashion (the relative importance of this factor is 94 percent), while the other considers a blend of fashion and comfort (the relative importances are 30 and 70 percent respectively). Product concepts aimed at one or the other of these segments may do better than the concept represented by Point X, which in fact may not directly appeal to either segment.

Conjoint Analysis in Concept Testing

We were first introduced to conjoint analysis in the context of concept generation. In actuality, conjoint analytic techniques are extremely useful in concept testing as well, and are frequently used in this stage.

In the conjoint analysis of Chapter 7, you assumed the role of product manager for a line of salsas. We selected three key attributes of salsa and two or three levels for each attribute, and used conjoint analysis to identify high-potential gaps: combinations of attributes that (*a*) customers like and (*b*) are not on the market yet.

Without going through the quantitative analysis again, it should be clear how conjoint analysis can be used at concept testing. The model identified the levels of the key attributes that are preferred by customers, and rank ordered the possible combinations from most to least preferred. Each of these combinations could be thought of as a concept, and the top-ranking concept or concepts are the ones that hold the highest potential and should be considered for further development. Of course, the model also identified the real losers!

As was mentioned earlier, many attributes and levels can feasibly be tested in conjoint analysis, using a reduced set of cards. The most preferred concept(s) will still come out ranked on top, even if they were not included in the original set of cards. Overall, conjoint analysis is extremely useful in concept testing because of its ability to uncover relationships between attributes (features, functions, benefits) and customer preferences, as illustrated in the salsa example.

We used a set of product description cards as the stimuli in our original example, since we were at the very earliest stages of the new product process. Note, however, that conjoint can easily use concept statements in other forms as stimuli. At concept testing, we may have concept statements in any of the forms discussed earlier in this chapter (verbal narratives, drawings, sketches, models or prototypes, even virtual-reality representations). The analysis would proceed in the same way regardless of the stimuli used.

Benefit segments can also be identified in conjoint analysis. Recall that conjoint identifies each customer's value system, that is, the relative importances of the attributes to each customer and the preferred levels of each attribute. We took a shortcut in Chapter 7 by assuming that all customers had about the same value system, so we identified the medium-hot green salsa as the best combination.

As we have seen earlier in this chapter, however, there may be underlying benefit segments. We noted in Chapter 7 that aggregating all customers may disguise the fact that half of the market might like extra-hot salsa and half might like mild. We can apply cluster analysis techniques to the importances and preferences generated by conjoint analysis to identify benefit segments of customers who have similar value systems. For example, in the industrial service example of Chapter 7, price came out as the most important variable (with a relative importance of about 27 percent) when all the respondents were aggregated. Follow-up cluster analysis revealed as many as five benefit segments, which varied widely with respect to the importance ascribed to price. In one segment, more concerned with performance quality, price's relative importance was under 9 percent, while in a second, price-driven segment, the comparable figure was about 35 percent![22]

Conclusions

The advantages of concept testing and development prior to full screening are many. It can be done quickly, and easily gives the screeners invaluable information for sorting out less valuable concepts. Proven market research

[22]Y. Wind, J. Grashof and J. Goldhar, "Market-Based Guidelines for Design of Industrial Products," *Journal of Marketing,* July 1978, pp. 27–37.

technology exists, it is reasonably confidential, we learn a lot about buyer thinking, and segments and positionings can be developed in tandem with the concept. Unfortunately, some developers (especially industrial designers) still refuse to do concept testing. Herman Miller, for example, was unable to market successfully a Hygiene System that incorporated a toilet, sink, and tub. It had not been concept tested, and after it failed, the designer claimed that industry people still did not understand it.

Nevertheless, concept testing is a bit treacherous—mistakes are easily made and can be costly. It is not a tool for amateurs. There have been classic flops, most of which passed concept tests—dry soups, white whiskey, clear soda, and so on. The original chewable antacid tablet floundered because the concept test missed the idea that people then wanted water with antacids. One firm studied executions of a single new product idea by three copywriters and found that the most important determinant of high scores in the concept test was the skill of the copywriter.

In addition, people find reacting to entirely new concepts difficult without a learning period, the stimulus of a concept statement is very brief, many situation variables will change by the time the product is marketed, and certain attributes cannot be measured in a concept test—for example, rug texture, shower nozzle impact, and what color will be "in" next season. Perhaps most troublesome, the technique has just enough slippage in it that persistent product champions often argue successfully against its findings.

Summary

This was the first chapter covering the tools used to evaluate new product proposals. Because evaluation actually begins prior to ideation (that is, deciding where to seek ideas), we first looked at the product innovation charter. By focusing the creative activity in certain directions, the charter automatically excludes all other directions and thus, in effect, evaluates them negatively.

Once the strategic direction is clear, most firms undertake a market analysis of the opportunity described by it. The customer should be a major input to any product innovation program, and immediately after strategic decisions have been made is an excellent time to seek this input. Then, as the ideas begin to roll in, an initial response is made—highly judgmental, quick, and designed primarily to clean out worthless ideas. Once an idea passes that test, more serious evaluation begins. The tool at this point is concept testing, or concept development, which now has a lengthy history of successful use. The chapter gave the overall procedure for concept testing, including its purposes, options in concept format, respondent selection, and the interviewing procedure. An immediate benefit of concept testing is that it gives management the information needed to make the judgments required by the scoring models used in the following step: the full screen of the concept, which is the subject of Chapter 10.

Applications

More questions from that interview with the company president.

1. "You know, most of our new products people do a great deal of marketing research—concept testing, attitude surveys, and the like. But let me read something that one automobile designer thought about marketing research." (She then read from a yellowed clipping on her desk.)

   > Market research is probably the greatest single deterrent to excellence in modern business. It's a crutch for managers with no vision and no conviction. On the surface, it sounds sensible enough: Find out exactly what the buyers want before you come to a design. But in practice, it's impossible. The public doesn't know what it wants without being shown the choices, and even then, preference is apt to veer off in the direction of K mart. Market research gives you Malibus with Mercedes grilles, refrigerators in avocado hues, and Big Macs with everything. You do not, however, produce greatness with this technique.[23]

   "Perhaps you would comment on that statement."
2. "Last year, a firm in New York called Telesession Corporation claimed that it had perfected a system of conference calling where telephones could be used for a focus group. Telesession claims to have used it on specialized groups as well as homemakers—for example, hospital lab directors and electrical engineers. It even has a deal whereby packages are mailed to the persons to be interviewed (after they agree to participate) with instructions not to open the package until told to do so during the conference call session. I'm thinking of three divisions—orthopedic equipment (crutches, suspension systems, etc.), advanced electronic systems for use in assembly line controls, and commercial fax machines. Could they use this system of concept testing effectively?"
3. "A cosmetics competitor is trying to speed up its new product work on lipsticks by a system that uses (1) brainstorming to create ideas (392 in a recent session); (2) evaluation of those ideas by the same group of people, down to only the best 50 ideas; and then (3) focus group sessions for concept testing those ideas down to the few that should be developed rapidly. Do you see anything wrong with this system?"
4. "I would be curious to test your personal judgment on some new ideas from one of our recent idea sessions. They were all accepted in

[23]"The Best Car in the World," *Car and Driver,* November 1979, p. 92.

later concept tests with consumers, and that concerns me. Are we safe to go ahead?

a. A gasoline-powered pogo stick.
b. A combination valet stand and electric pants presser.
c. Transistorized golf balls and an electric finder.
d. An Indian arm wrestling device so you can arm wrestle with yourself.
e. An electrically heated bath mat.
f. Chocolate candy in an edible chocolate box."

CASE: WOLVERINE CAR WASH[24]

In 1968, Jerry Waldrop opened his first car wash, called the Wolverine Car Wash, in Columbus, Ohio. He had never worked for car washes but had run various small businesses as he worked his way through Ohio State University. He was convinced that better ways of running car washes rested primarily on money, which he was fortunate enough to have access to. Given ideas, money, and small-business talent, he was sure he could succeed.

And he did. By 1992, he had four establishments, was one of the leading car wash independents in the Midwest, and was still seeking better ways to do things. In 1984, he had put in a car detailing service ($110 for total cleaning of a car, inside and out, motor, under fenders, everywhere), and it was selling well.

About this time, he participated in a college concept-generating program that the son of his office manager was running in a course he was taking at another university. The subject was "The car wash—how can it be improved?" The experience was interesting—and fun to a guy like Jerry—but now he was giving hard thought to one idea from that session—a portable car wash that offered home or office delivery service. The idea itself wasn't new, of course, but several aspects of this particular proposal were. The idea was this: Many people would get their cars washed more often (and probably waxed, too) if they didn't have to take the time to drive to the wash facility and chance having to wait in line. The answer to these people was a portable car wash. Somehow, a self-contained car wash unit would be built that could be pulled around town, taken to a home or to a company parking lot on order, hooked up to a source of water (it would do its own immediate heating of the water), and have the vehicle(s) driven through it. Granted the washing would be less thorough than at the central units, but some individuals may prefer the greater personal attention. And the service would be of maximum convenience, for which selected individuals would probably pay a good price.

But Jerry really wondered what to do next. He knew the car wash business and the people who bought the service. He had thought favorably about the idea, impossible as it seemed at first, but now figured he had better do something other than rely on gut feelings.

He had heard of concept testing at a recent Chamber of Commerce meeting and thought this might be the time to try it. So he called the university marketing department, was referred to the placement office, and ended up with two marketing majors (of whom you are one). He asked each of them to prepare a concept testing proposal. The proposal was to

---

[24]This is a realistic, but hypothetical, case situation.

contain a statement of the specific concept, the research format(s) of that concept, and the general research methodology.

He told them that if the idea passed the concept test, he planned to have a unit built and put into service on a limited basis in Columbus. He could start it with businesses, or with homes, or in shopping centers, so he hoped the concept test would help on that decision, too. And what would he have to tell people about the new service? That is, what questions and problems would they have? And . . . but then he thought he had better let the students get started.

Case: AT&T Magicphone Phone-Fax-Copier (B)[25]

Refer back to the AT&T Magicphone case (A) at the end of Chapter 6. In addition to the competitive information made available there, AT&T management believed there were two key market segments for the Magicphone PFC: new system customers and the aftermarket (replacement purchasers), who comprised about 60 and 40 percent of anticipated business respectively. Preliminary market research revealed that new system customers were primarily interested in system productivity. Aftermarket customers expressed some dissatisfaction with available fax-copier products in terms of their convenience in use, and therefore placed more importance on that attribute. Using this market research, AT&T management placed the ideal points of the two segments as follows:

	Convenience	*Productivity*
Aftermarket	3.50	2.00
New customers	1.75	3.75

Add these ideal points to the positioning map you drew for the case in Chapter 6. Which are Magicphone's most serious competitors in the new customer segment? In the aftermarket segment? What are the competitive implications for the Magicphone?

[25]This case is based on "AT&T Magicphone PFC," a case in Roger J. Calantone and C. Anthony Di Benedetto, *The Product Manager's Toolbox,* New York: Mc Graw-Hill, 1993. Used with permission. The material on product features and competitive information presented in this case was compiled from numerous published sources, and the name of the product is disguised. The positioning and ideal brand data are for illustrative purposes only.

CHAPTER

10

THE FULL SCREEN

Setting

As we saw in Chapter 9, business approaches to the prescreening tasks vary considerably. The full screening step also varies because businesses differ so much in how they follow the screening. Some firms need very little technical work to come up with a suitable product. For them, the screen is a minor exercise on the way to a much more important step—field testing of the finished item, i.e., product use testing.

For other firms, the technological breakthrough is the whole ball game; their R&D may require millions of dollars and many years. The full screen is the last low-risk evaluation, and managers want it done well.

Consequently, this chapter cannot present what any particular firm should do. That's up to the new products manager. But we can present the range of alternatives and a middle ground that actually fits most firms. If needed, it can easily be modified. See Figure 10–1 for how screening relates to concept testing and the protocol step that follows from it.

Unfortunately, the step is not glamorous. It isn't discussed weekly in the business press, and, in fact, you may never have heard of a full screen step until you read about it in this book. But business has heard of it, and has been using it for many years. Research on it continues, as we will see later, even in large firms known for their ability to generate successful new products.[1]

[1]Procter & Gamble is one, as reported in Robert E. Davis, "The Role of Market Research in the Development of New Consumer Products," *Journal of Product Innovation Management,* September 1993, pp. 309–17.

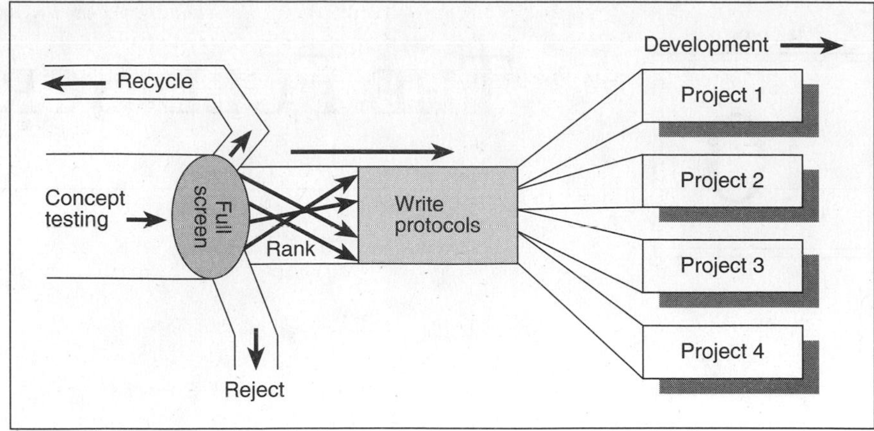

FIGURE 10–1
Flow of new product concepts through the screening/protocol process

Purposes of the Full Screen

Recall where we are in the product innovation process. After the original idea emerged, we put it into concept format and then gave it a brief initial exposure for reaction by key players. Concept testing then enabled us to add the thoughts of potential users to the set of market and other data collected since the time of the product innovation charter. Along the way, we have been compiling the inputs of key functional people in the firm—technical, marketing, financial, operational, and the like.

This work (which is situation dependent, and may take from a couple days up to several months) culminates in a step called the full screen. It is full in the sense that we now have as much information as we're going to get before undertaking technical work on the product. The following material deals with how that step can be made most worthwhile, and the first issue is, why do we do it? There are several good reasons.

First, we need a screen that helps us decide whether technical resources (R&D, systems design for services, engineering, etc.) should be devoted to the project and, if so, how vigorously. This decision rests on whether we *can* do the job and whether we *want* to do it. "Can do" means feasibility—is technology up to the task, do we have it, can we afford it? "Want to" means will we get out of the project the profits, market share, or whatever it is we are doing product innovation for? Sometimes these issues are called *feasibility of technical accomplishment* and *feasibility of commercial accomplishment.*

Second, the screening step helps manage the process—by (1) cycling unacceptable but potentially worthwhile concepts back into concept development where more work may make them acceptable, (2) rank-ordering the good concepts such that we have some options on standby when an ongoing project stalls or is canceled, and (3) recording the appraisals on rejected concepts to prevent "reinventing the wheel" when a similar concept comes up again later. The latter may seem almost trivial to you, but to managers who screen hundreds or even thousands of new product concepts a year it is not trivial. It's a good "corporate memory" too, to help settle arguments later. For example, business people know that a winning new product finds scores of "parents" who proposed it, whereas a losing new product is always an orphan. In firms that like to reward creativity, it helps to know who suggested what, and when.

Third, the screening process encourages cross-functional communication. Scoring sessions are peppered with outbursts like: "Why in the world did you score that ratchet idea so low on such-and-such a factor?" The screening process is a learning process, particularly in making managers more sensitive to how other functions think. And it flushes out all basic disagreements about a project (including the ever-present politics) and sets them up for discussion. These disagreements put the spotlight on "potholes" or hurdles that the concept will face during development, and show where new people may be needed.

Screening Alternatives

There are three schools of thought on how the full screening should be done. Some firms, especially smaller ones and those not doing much new product work, prefer what really is an opinion poll, where one or more people make a judgment on some informal checklist.[2] In some of these cases participants may have a printed list of evaluation points as memory joggers, taken from the more formal lists that follow.

Second, there are some packaged goods firms whose development process is really nontechnical—me-too products and simple variations on what is already on the market. Knowing they can easily make the item and market it reasonably well, the only issue is whether consumers will like it. Thus they do a more complete concept test (Chapter 9) and what they call **premarket testing** sales forecasting models, which we will meet in Chapter 12. They don't have to forecast technical and commercial feasibility. When there are major technical issues (and there more often are, today, as the Procter & Gamble footnote showed), even the packaged goods firms won't depend on concept testing.

So the third approach is what we will study here. It involves the use of a **scoring model,** which is nothing more than a mechanical arrangement of checklist factors with weights (importance) on them. A scoring model serves

---

[2]Even some very capable firms feel they can't answer the issues in the more complete scoring models shown later. Instead, one unit of AT&T uses: Do customers care, Do we care, Can we do it, and Can we stay ahead if we do?

the purposes listed above; the other methods do not. This means that without a reasonably formal scoring model system (with inputs from all functions), technical people must do their own screening. Someone has to decide which concepts will get technical development effort, and R&D departments have historically used what they call **portfolio models** to do the same thing scoring models do.

The Scoring Model

Scoring models are simple but powerful things. Let's look at them through the eyes of a student who has a decision to make.

Introductory Concept

Assume a student is trying to decide what social activity to undertake this weekend. The student has several options, and more options may appear between now and then. The student could list criteria on several decisions that are personally important, specifically:

1. It must be fun.
2. It must involve more than just two people.
3. It must be affordable.
4. It must be something I am capable of doing.

These four criteria (commonly called *factors,* but don't confuse these with the factors we discussed in factor analysis) are shown in Figure 10–2. Of course, 20 or 30 factors might be involved in this student's weekend social

FIGURE 10–2

Scoring model for student activity decision

	Values			
Factors	*4 Points*	*3 Points*	*2 Points*	*1 Point*
Degree of fun	Much	Some	Little	None
Number of people	Over 5	4 to 5	2 to 3	Under 2
Affordability	Easily	Probably	Maybe	No
Student's capability	Very	Good	Some	Little

Student's scorings:	*Skiing*	*Boating*	*Hiking*
Fun	4	3	4
People	4	4	2
Affordability	2	4	4
Capability	1	4	3
Totals	11	15	13

Answer: Go boating.

decisions, but let's stick with the 4. These factors are not absolutes; they can all be scaled—some fun, lots of fun, and so on. Figure 10–2 shows a four-point scale for each factor.

Next, each scale point needs a number so we can rank the options. With that done, the student can proceed to evaluate each option (as indicated in Figure 10–2) and total the score for each. The final answer is to go boating—even though it isn't quite as much fun—primarily because it can involve lots of people, it is cheap, and the student is a capable rower.

But suppose the student protests at this point and says, "There's more to it than that. If I go hiking, I'll get more exercise, but if I go skiing, a certain person is apt to be there." Or the student may argue that affordability is more important than the other factors because without enough money, there is no need to score the other points. Or the student may say, "Having fun is really more important than skill, so let's double the points for fun." And then there are objections that "skiing really is not all that much fun, boating is more expensive than you think," and so on.

A scoring process is what we actually use in making decisions like this, whether we realize it or not. The student's objections contain the basic problems of new product scoring models, and we will see how the criticisms can be handled to fashion a system that works pretty well.

The Procedure

It takes a while to develop a system, but once it is running, the fine-tuning does not require much effort.[3]

What Is Being Evaluated. In the case of the above student, we chose to base the model on four arbitrarily selected factors. Selecting factors in real life is not that easy, and how we pick them is no accident. *First, if we could, we would use only one factor.* There is one factor that covers both technical and commercial accomplishment, a financial term called *net present value of the discounted stream of earnings from the product concept,* and it considers all direct and indirect costs and benefits. That mouthful is simply the finance way of saying "the bottom line on an income statement for the product, where we have included all costs (technical, marketing, etc.) and then discounted back the profits into what their value is today." That factor is shown on Level One in the abbreviated graphic of Figure 10–3. If we can make a pretty good estimate of that net present value, no other factors would be

[3]Though quite easy when done in the mode of the scoring model example given later in this chapter, we should note that an immense body of theory lies behind all scoring decisions. For example, our scoring model is technically a linear compensatory model. That model, plus the conjunctive, disjunctive, and lexicographic models, is discussed (and compared in a new product screening exercise) in Kenneth G. Baker and Gerald S. Albaum, "Modeling New Product Screening Decisions," *Journal of Product Innovation Management,* March 1986, pp. 32–39.

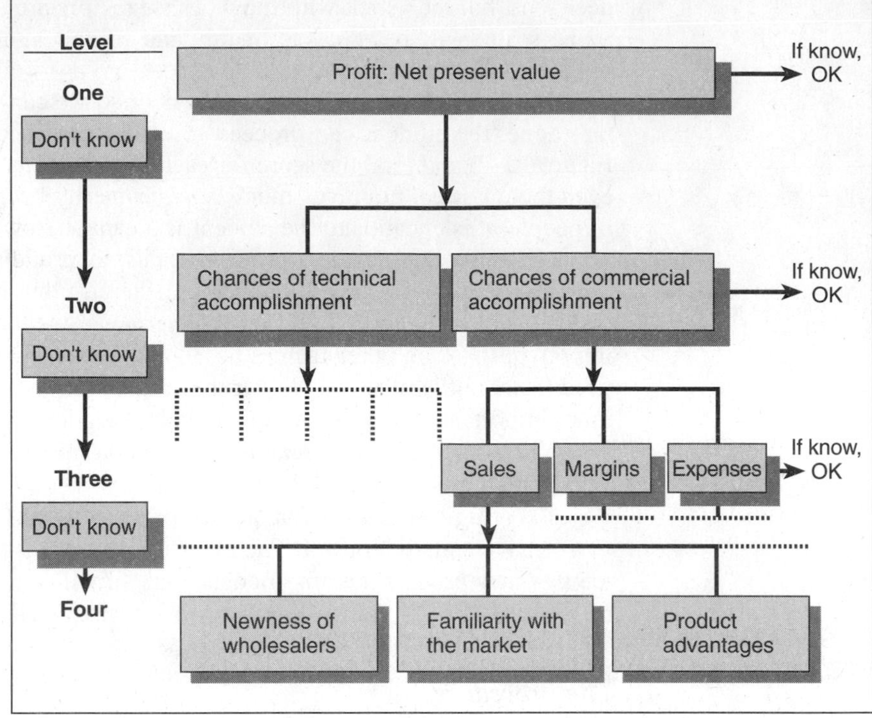

FIGURE 10–3

Source of scoring model factors

needed. But we almost never can; at this early stage all financial estimates are quite shaky.

So, instead, we use *surrogates* (or substitutes) for it. Level Two in Figure 10–3 shows the obvious two: the likelihood of technical accomplishment (meaning, whether we can create something that will do what customers want) and the likelihood of commercial accomplishment (meaning, whether we can sell it profitably). There is again nothing left to do. These two convictions would predict financial success of Level One, and we are finished.

Unfortunately, experience shows we usually can't make these two estimates either. So we reach for more surrogates, this time at Level Three. To save space, Figure 10–3 shows only the three that produce commercial accomplishment; if we know our sales, our margins on those sales, and our marketing and administrative expenses, we have the commercial half of the answer.

Alas, again we fall short; we don't have a very good fix on those figures either, at this early point. Note, however, that the packaged goods firms developing marginally different new products, discussed above, *can* make these estimates, and do so, in their forecasting models. Most firms have to seek surrogates for the Level Three factors, too. This leads us to Level Four, which is where the action is. Level-Four factors have answers, or at least answers we can estimate better than the factors at higher levels. Figure 10–3 lists only three of the many factors at this level.

The reasoning goes like this: If you tell me the new product will enter a market with which we already have great familiarity, chances are we will be able to communicate with buyers in that market. This raises the chances for good sales (up to Level Three), and greater sales make for more likely commercial fulfillment (up to Level Two), which, in turn, leads to profit (Level One, and we're home). So the trick in all this is to spot those Level Four factors that contribute to the technical and commercial operations in this firm on this particular product concept. Level Four factors comprise the scoring model shown in Figure 10–4. Some firms include profit, sales, and so on, as factors even though their surrogates should be there already.

In general, a firm should start with the list of factors in Figure 10–4, scratch out any obviously not applicable, insert any obviously omitted, and then use it for a few times to see how the scores set with the people involved. Over time the list should be reduced as much as possible, and always kept fluid. Nothing about this system should be set in stone; after all, it is just an *aid* to decision.[4] The Wilson Sporting Goods Case, at the end of this chapter, will show how each situation is somewhat different.

The Scoring. Given a scoring form such as that shown in Figure 10–4, the team members who will be doing the scoring first undergo a period during which they get acquainted with each proposal (market, concept, concept test results). Then each scorer starts with the first factor (in this case, the difficulty of the technical task) and rates each one by selecting the most appropriate point on the semantic differential scales given in the third column. These scorings are multiplied by the assigned importance weights, and the factor totals are extended. The scorings continue for the other factors, and the ratings are then totaled to get the overall rating for that concept by each individual.

Various methods are used to combine the individual team member's ratings, an average (mean) being the most common. Some firms use the Olympic method of dropping the highest and lowest ratings before averaging. Some firms have an open discussion after the averages are shown, so individuals can make a case for any view that is at odds with the group. Many firms have found that **groupware** (e.g., Lotus Notes) aids the process greatly.[5]

---

[4]For further information, especially from a more corporate management view, see Thomas D. Kuczmarski, *Managing New Products: The Power of Innovation* (Englewood Cliffs, NJ: Prentice Hall, 1992), pp. 135–57. From the consumer products view, see Larry A. Constantineau, "The 20 Toughest Questions for New Product Proposals," *Journal of Product and Brand Management,* no. 1 (1993), pp. 51–54.

[5]For another matrix scoring model, see Bob Gill, Beebe Nelson, and Steve Spring, "Seven Steps to Strategic New Product Development," *The PDMA Handbook of New Product Development* (New York: Wiley, 1996), pp. 19–34.

FIGURE 10–4 *Scoring model for full screen of new product concepts*

Category	*Factor*	*Scale* 1	2	3	4	5	*Score*	*Weight*	*Weighted score*
Technical accomplishment	Technical task difficulty	Very difficult				Easy	4	4	16
	Research skills required	Have none required				Perfect fit	5	3	15
	Development skills required	Have none required				Perfect fit	2	5	10
	Technical equipment/processes	Have none required				Have them			
	Rate of technological change	High/erratic				Stable			
	Design superiority assurance	None				Very high			
	Security of design (patent)	None				Have patent			
	Technical service required	Have none required				Have it all			
	Manufacturing equipment/processes	Have none required				Have them now			
	Vendor cooperation available	None in sight				Current relationship			
	Likelihood of competitive cost	Well above competition				Over 20% less			
	Likelihood of quality product	Below current levels				Leadership			
	Likelihood of speed to market	Two years or more				Under six months			
	Team people available	None right now				All key ones			
	Dollar investments required	Over 20 million				Under 1 million			
	Legal issues	Major ones				None in sight			
									Total 210
Commercial accomplishment	Market volatility	High/erratic				Very stable	2	3	6
	Probable market share	Fourth at best				Number one	5	5	25
	Probable product life	Less than a year				Over 10 years			
	Similarity to product life	No relationship				Very close			
	Sales force requirements	Have no experience				Very familiar			
	Promotion requirements	Have no experience				Very familiar			
	Target customer	Perfect stranger				Close/current			
	Distributors	No relationship				Current/strong			
	Retailers/dealers	Trivial				Critical			
	Importance of task to user	No relationship				Current/strong			
	Degree of unmet need	None/satisfied				Totally unmet			
	Likelihood of filling need	Very low				Very high			
	Competition to be faced	Tough/aggressive				Weak			
	Field service requirements	No current capability				Ready now			
	Environmental effects	Only negative ones				Only positive ones			
	Global applications	No use outside national				Fits global			
	Market diffusions	No other uses				Many other areas			
	Customer integration	Very unlikely				Customer seeks it			
	Probable profit	Break even at best				ROI>40%			
									Total 240
	Concept: ______ Date of screen: ______ Action: ______								Grand Total 450

Unusual Factors. On some factors, a bad score constitutes a veto. For example, in the case of the student seeking to decide what entertainment to pursue this weekend, a money shortage may block anything costing more than $30. This problem should be faced in the beginning so no time is wasted drumming up options costing more than $30. Industry is the same, and a key role for the product innovation charter is to point out those exclusions. Some call these **culling factors.**[6]

Another problem occurs when the factor being scored has all-or-nothing, yes-or-no answers; for example, "Will this concept require the establishment of a separate sales force?" This type of factor is handled by using the end points on the semantic differential scale, with no gradations. If possible, such factors should be scaled as, for example, "How much additional cost is involved in setting up sales coverage for this concept?" Columns might be None; Under $100,000; $100,000 to $300,000; and so on.

The Scorers or Judges. Selecting the members of a scoring team is like selecting the members of a new products team. The four major functions (marketing, technical, operations, and finance) are involved, as are new products managers and staff specialists from information technology, distribution, procurement, public relations, human resources, and so on, depending on the firm's procedure for developing new products.

Top business unit managers (presidents, general managers) should stay out of the act, except, of course, in small firms. Such people inhibit the frank discussions needed when assessing the firm's capabilities (for example, in marketing or manufacturing). Some CEOs are intuitively so good at this task they can't be excluded.[7]

Screening experience is certainly valuable. So is experience in the firm and in the person's specialty. Technical people generally feel more optimistic about probable technical success, and marketers are more pessimistic.

Problems with individuals are more specific. Research indicates that (1) some people are always optimistic, (2) some are sometimes optimistic and sometimes pessimistic, (3) some are "neutrals" who score to the middle of scales, (4) some are far more reliable and accurate than others, (5) some are easily swayed by the group, and (6) some are capable but erratic. Scoring teams need a manager to deal with such problems. Some firms actually weight each evaluator's scores by past accuracy (defined as conformity with

---

[6]See Rodger L. DeRose, "New Products—Sifting through the Haystack," *The Journal of Consumer Marketing,* Summer 1986, pp. 81–84. This article shows some direct connections between product strategy at Johnson Wax and the firm's new product screening; for example, its screening factors include "only safe products," "use existing capabilities," and "reflect the company's position and style."

[7]One leading packaged goods firm's CEO was so expert at selecting among product manager job applicants that other evaluations were considered unnecessary.

the team's scores). Dow Brands uses a computerized groupware approach primarily because they like the scorings to be anonymous.

Weighting. The most serious criticism of scoring models is their use of weights, because the weightings are necessarily judgmental (an exception from new research will be discussed in a moment). Let's go back to the student seeking a weekend activity. To a money-cautious student, affordability deserves more weight than the other factors. But how much more? Should it be weighted at two and the other factors at one? Because of weighting's importance, some firms measure its effect using **sensitivity testing.** Scoring models are actually just mathematical models or equations, so an analyst can alter the scorings or the weightings to see what difference the alterations make in the final score. Spreadsheet programs handle this easily, and so does most groupware.

Profile Sheet

Figure 10–5 presents an alternative preferred by some firms for its graphic capability. The **profile sheet** graphically arranges the five-point scorings on the different factors. If a team of judges is used, the profile employs average scores. The approach does indeed draw attention to such patterns as the high scores given near the bottom of the profile (in Figure 10–5) compared to those near the top.

The NewProd Screening Model

A scoring model based on a large database of actual product successes and failures is known as the NewProd model.[8] Some 100 Canadian industrial firms cooperated in the study, which required product managers to identify a recent product success and a recent failure. Respondents then cited a total of 80 descriptive characteristics when asked why each product succeeded (or failed). From these, 48 characteristics that would have been known at the time of the screening (pre-R&D) were selected to build the screening model. For example, a failure is sometimes caused by unexpected competitive entry, but no one could have known this at screening time. Thus, the screening model was designed to correlate success and failure with the characteristics of the new product project at the time it would have been screened.

Using factor analysis, the 48 characteristics were reduced to 13 underlying factors that captured the essence of the original 48. Next, regression coefficients were calculated that showed the extent of the relationship between each factor's score and the success or failure of the project. Eight of the 13 factors were found to be significant, and the regression coefficients serve as the weights for the eight factors in the model. Figure 10–6 shows these

[8]Robert G. Cooper, "Selecting Winning New Product Projects: Using the NewProd System," *Journal of Product Innovation Management,* March 1985, 34–44.

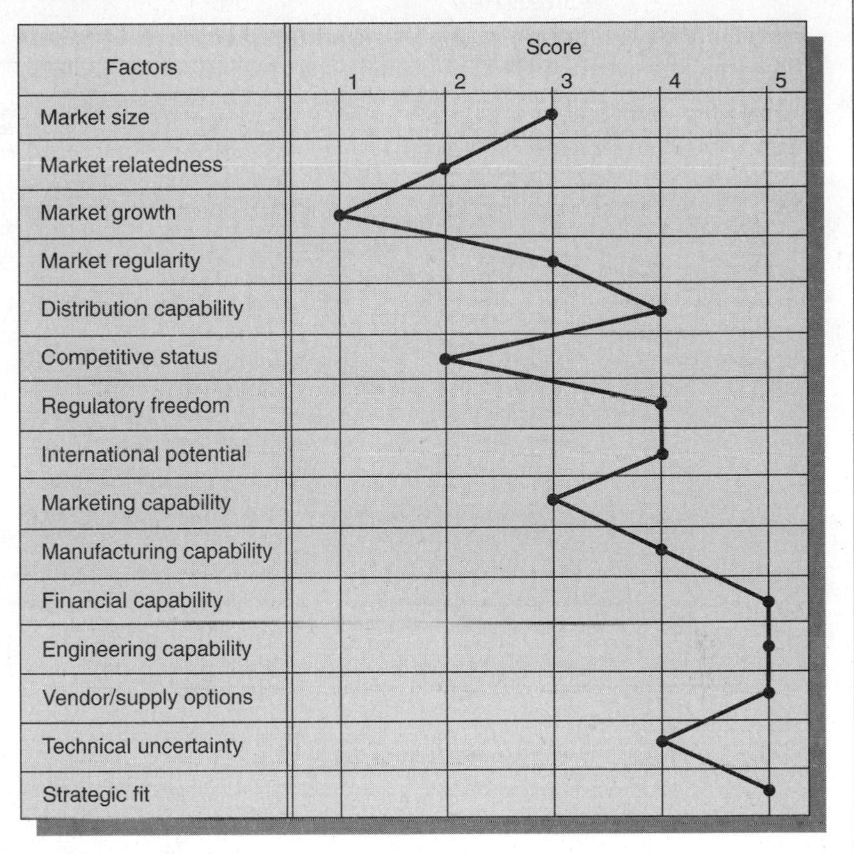

FIGURE 10–5
The profile of a new product proposal

eight factors, as well as the characteristics that loaded on the first factor for illustrative purposes. The regression coefficients are also shown, as they are indicative of the relative importance of each factor.

The first factor, "product superiority, quality, uniqueness," has the highest regression coefficient (1.744), indicating it is a very important determinant of product success. Two of the factors had negative regression coefficients (market competitiveness and newness to the firm). This indicates that low scores on these two factors tend to be related to greater product success. All told, the typical industrial firm should use all eight factors in its scoring model, with the weights indicated.

Figure 10–7 shows a typical application of the NewProd scoring model. Early in the process (pre-R&D), the new product concept was assessed on each of the eight factors: these scores appear in the top half of Figure 10–7. The bottom half of the figure interprets these scores. The concept clearly scored well on product superiority/quality, market need, growth and size, and market competitiveness (remember, a low score on this last factor is a

FIGURE 10–6

The eight factors of the NewProd model

The Eight Significant Factors	*Weight from the Regression Coefficients*
Product superiority, quality, uniqueness	1.744
Product is superior.	
Product has unique feature.	
Product is higher quality.	
Product does unique task.	
Product cuts user's costs.	
Product is first of kind.	
(See source for the other 42 variables.)	
Overall product firm/resource compatibility	1.138
Market need, growth, and size	0.801
Economic advantage of product to end user	0.722
Technological resource compatibility	0.342
Product scope (mass rather than narrow specialty)	0.225
Market competitiveness	–0.301
Newness to the firm	–0.354

Note: This table reads as follows: The most important factor in screening industrial products is the degree of product superiority, quality, or uniqueness. This superiority factor is derived from six specific scorings, the first of which is how superior the proposed product is to its probable competitors. If a score for all six variables is determined and then put into a score for the factor as a whole (see source for method), that factor is then given a weight of 1.744. After all eight factors have been scored, the total is determined and compared with other product proposals.

Source: Robert G. Cooper, "Selecting Winning New Product Projects: Using the NewProd System," *Journal of Product Innovation Management,* March 1985, pp. 34–44.

FIGURE 10–7

An application of the NewProd model

Factor	*Mean Evaluation*	*Impact*
Project superiority	1.19	POSITIVE
Economic advantage	–0.49	negative
Company-project fit	–0.16	marginal (–)
Tech. compatibility	–0.19	marginal (–)
Newness to firm	–0.24	marginal (+)
Market need/growth/size	0.88	POSITIVE
Market competitiveness	–1.82	positive
Product scope	0.90	marginal (+)

Note: The capitalized "POSITIVES" in the Impact column signify large positive impacts. Note that there are apparently no large negative impacts!

Source: Robert G. Cooper, "Selecting Winning New Product Projects: Using the NewProd System," *Journal of Product Innovation Management* 2, no. 1 (March 1985), pp. 34–44.

good sign). It scored marginally (near zero) on most of the other factors. The only real weak point identified was economic value to the user. This suggests that the concept has some potential, and the firm should concentrate its R&D efforts on building in more economic value for the customer. The scores obtained for this concept could be compared to those obtained for other product concepts and the best option(s) can be selected for further development.

Even better, of course, if the firm has lots of new product experience, is to go back and develop data on *their own successes and failures,* as was done is this study; then the statistical analysis would yield factors and weights most appropriate for that firm. The service is being sold commercially.[9] There are some concerns that the judgments managers make *now* are influenced by the known outcomes of the concepts being scored.

The Analytic Hierarchy Process

Another technique for product project screening and evaluation is the **Analytic Hierarchy Process (AHP).**[10] It uses managerial judgment to identify the key criteria in the screening decision, obtain scores for each project under consideration relative to these criteria, and rank the projects in order of desirability. Commercially available software such as Expert Choice makes AHP very easy to use.[11]

The product manager begins by building a hierarchical decision tree. The tree will show the manager's ultimate goal (in this case, choosing the best new product project) at the top. The next level below will include all the *primary criteria* the manager considers important in reaching the goal. There may be several levels of criteria (secondary, tertiary, etc.) under the primary criteria in the tree. Lastly, the choices (new product projects under consideration) are placed at the bottom of the tree.

Next, the manager provides pairwise comparison data for each element in the tree, with respect to the next higher level. That is to say, the criteria are compared in terms of their importance in reaching the goal, and the choices are compared in terms of their ratings on each criterion. The AHP software takes over from this point. It converts the comparison data into a set of relative weights, which are then aggregated to obtain composite priorities of each

---

[9]By The Adept Group, in Jacksonville, Florida. Research on this method continues, but the applications are almost always confidential. An exception is in Robert E. Davis, "The Role of Market Research." A slightly different approach to factor selection and weighting can be found in Ulrike de Brentani and Cornelia Droge, "Determinants of the New Product Screening Decision: A Structural Model Analysis," *International Journal of Research in Marketing,* no. 2 (1988), pp. 91–106.

[10]For a full treatment of AHP, see Thomas L. Saaty, *The Analytic Hierarchy Process* (New York: McGraw-Hill, 1980).

[11]Expert Choice is presented in Arvind Rangaswamy and Gary L. Lilien, "Software Tools for New Product Development," *Journal of Marketing Research* 34 (February 1997), pp. 177–84.

FIGURE 10–8

An application of the analytic hierarchy process (AHP)

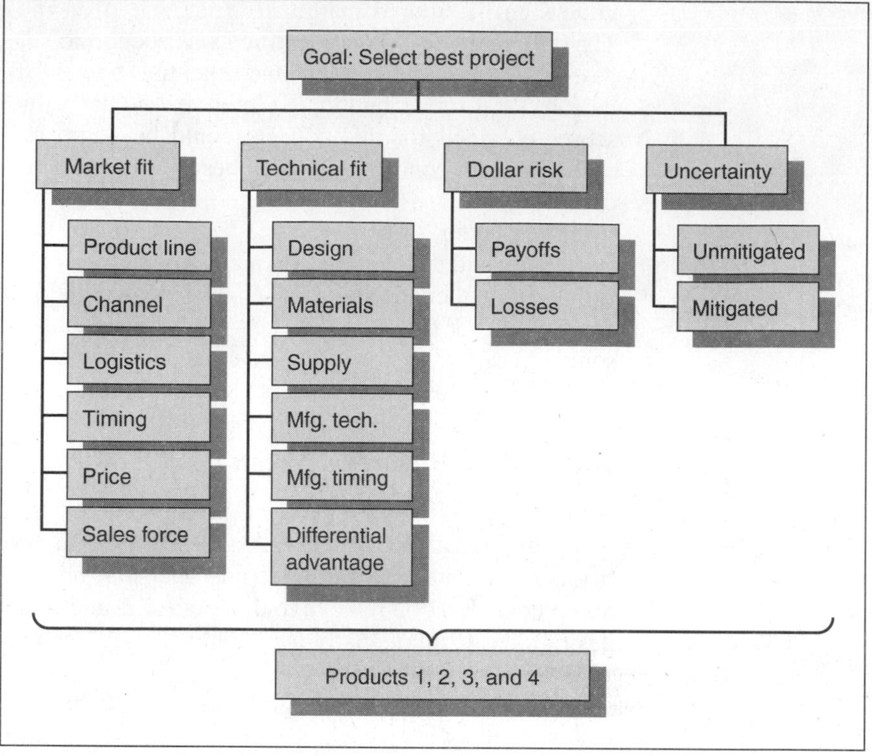

element at each level. Ultimately, the available choices (new product projects) are rank ordered in terms of their preferability to the manager.

A sample application of AHP in a project screening setting is provided in Figure 10–8.[12] In this case, the product manager screens projects with respect to four primary criteria: fit with core marketing competencies, fit with core technical competencies, total dollar risk profile of the project, and managerial uncertainty about the project's outcomes. As shown in the figure, each of these primary criteria can be assessed in terms of several secondary criteria. Finally, there are four projects under consideration (P1 through P4); these are placed at the bottom of the decision tree.

After the decision tree is built, the paired comparisons are obtained. Usually, this is done by asking the manager to rate the relative importance or preference of each pair of items on a scale of 1 through 9. Figure 10–9 shows the manager's ratings of the primary criteria in terms of their importance in selecting projects. For example, the 1.5 in parentheses under "Dollar Risk" indicates that the dollar risk criterion is 1.5 times more important than the

[12]R. J. Calantone, C. A. Di Benedetto, and J. B. Schmidt, "Knowledge Acquisition in New Product Project Screening with the Analytic Hierarchy Process," *Journal of Product Innovation Management* 16, no. 1 (January 1999), pp. 65–76.

FIGURE 10–9

Some AHP inputs in pairwise comparison form

Compare Relative Importances with Respect to Goal			
	Dollar Risk	*Technical Fit*	*Market Fit*
Uncertainty	(1.5)	(1.6)	(1.3)
Dollar risk		1.6	1.0
Tech. fit			(1.4)

Legend: Row element is *X* times more important than column element unless enclosed in parentheses. *X* can range from 1 to 9.

Examples: DOLLAR RISK is 1.5 times more important than UNCERTAINTY; DOLLAR RISK is 1.6 times more important than TECHNICAL FIT.

uncertainty criterion, according to this manager. Once this table is completed, more tables are filled in showing the relative importance of the secondary criteria. Finally, pairwise comparisons of the projects with respect to each of the secondary criteria are made.

Using these data, the AHP software calculates overall global weights for each project. These weights can be interpreted as the relative contribution of each alternative to the overall goal. The computer output, shown at the bottom of Figure 10–10, clearly shows P1 to be the preferred project, having the highest overall global weight (0.381). P2 is second best at 0.275, while P3 and P4 are also-rans.

While all the AHP results cannot be shown here, Figure 10–10 summarizes some of the key findings and provides some insights on how P1 came to be the top choice. The Level 1 weights indicate the relative importance of the primary criteria. This manager views dollar risk to be the most important criterion, followed by market fit, technical fit, and uncertainty. Similarly, the Level 2 weights indicate how important each of the secondary criteria are to this manager. For example, under market fit, timing and price are rated more important than sales force or product line fit. The last column shows the project that was ranked highest on each secondary criterion. P1 was ranked highest on most of the secondary criteria, and almost all of the really important ones (as judged by the Level 2 weights). P2 tended to do a little better on several of the technical fit criteria, but technical fit is less important to this manager than dollar risk or market fit. So it is perhaps not surprising that P1 comes out ranked first, with P2 in second place.

Special Aspects

A few other aspects round out our discussion of scoring models. One concerns the product champion (discussed fully in Chapter 14). Champions are sometimes needed to push past normal resistance to change and to see that the concept gets a fair hearing at all turns. They try to give the scorers all

FIGURE 10–10

AHP results and overall project selection

	Level 1 Weights	*Level 2 Weights*	*Highest Ranked Project*
Dollar Risk	0.307		
Payoffs		0.153	P1
Losses		0.153	P1
Market Fit	0.285		
Timing		0.094	P1
Price		0.064	P2
Logistics		0.063	P1
Channel		0.036	P2
Product line		0.014	P1
Sales force		0.014	P2
Technical Fit	0.227		
Differential advantage		0.088	P1
Manufacturing timing		0.047	P2
Design		0.032	P2
Materials		0.027	P2
Manufacturing technology		0.023	P2
Supply		0.010	P1
Uncertainty	0.182		
Unmitigated		0.104	P1
Mitigated		0.078	P1

Ranking of Alternatives:

Project	*Overall Weight*	
P1	0.381	xxxxxxxxxxxxxxxxxxxxxxxxxxxxxxxxxxxxxx
P2	0.275	xxxxxxxxxxxxxxxxxxxxxxxxxxxx
P3	0.175	xxxxxxxxxxxxxxxxxx
P4	0.170	xxxxxxxxxxxxxxxxx

favorable information and may argue that standard forms don't fit their special situations.

Some developers try to use computer technology with **expert systems** (often called knowledge-based systems). Such systems are essentially scoring models, with the factors developed on the basis of expert experience.[13]

[13]For more on this, in an application to financial services using an algorithm called INNOVATOR, see Sundaresan Ram and Sudha Ram, "Expert Systems: An Emerging Technology for Selecting New Product Winners," *Journal of Product Innovation Management,* June 1989, pp. 89–98. For a recent look at expert system performance, see Sundaresan Ram and Sudha Ram, "Validation of Expert Systems for Innovation Management: Issues, Methodology, and Empirical Assessment," *Journal of Product Innovation Management* 13, no. 1 (1996), pp. 53–68.

Last, experience shows that management sometimes misuses scoring models. One consumer products manufacturer threw out a scoring model system because it:

1. Rejected products that would help round out the line.
2. Rejected products that would help forestall competitive entry into the market.
3. Rejected too many products, according to the sales department.

The first two problems arose from either faulty factor selection or faulty factor weighting and were easily solved. The third arose because the cutoff score was set too high. Scoring models require competent management.

Summary

If an idea progresses through early concept testing and development to the point where it is a full-blown concept ready for technical workup, it must then be screened. Screening is commonly done with scoring models, whereby the firm's ability to bring off the required development and marketing is estimated. If the concept scores well by whatever criteria the firm uses, it is sent into technical development.

Just prior to that, however, some firms try to spell out a protocol—an agreed upon set of benefits and other requirements that the technical development and marketing phases must deliver. Once the team feels the product parts of the protocol have been achieved, the concept is in prototype form. It then can be taken to the field for further concept testing. The concept test is much more productive when the concept is in prototype form, though it may be more expensive because substantial technical expenditures have already been made. The matters of protocol and prototype testing will comprise Chapter 11.

Applications

More questions from that interview with the company president.

1. "Our small electrical engines division recently threw out a screening system that was based on a fairly complete scoring model, as they called it. Seems the model kept rejecting too many of their product ideas, some of which looked like sure winners to them—and to me, incidentally. Under their new system, a top-management committee reviews these ideas personally, without all that paperwork, and it looks like things will be better. Do you have any reaction to that?"

2. "We experimented with a numerical scoring model some years back—it just didn't work. Brought in all the senior people, sales managers, product managers, you name it. We selected several dimensions of technical and commercial viability, not too different from the scoring model you presented. Rated everything on scales of 1 to 5. Guess what? All the projects that were the "pet projects" of senior management came out as 5's. The ones they all could care less about came out as 1's. And all the ones we really lacked good information on came out as 3's. A lot of help that was!"
3. "Yet, another new service that tries to give consumers information on TV shows and movies is rather widely criticized. A firm named ASI Market Research, Inc., has a service called Preview House. The service hooks up movie theater audiences (which it gets from telephone lists with promises of free movies) with an instantaneous response machine that has dials for recording likes and dislikes. The firm can test upcoming shows, entire movies (for example, if they had tested *Heaven's Gate,* a bundle might have been saved), records, and so on. Granted, audiences go especially big for sex, puppies, little children, and so on, but if that's what they like, that's what they want. Mr. Magoo goes especially well. What do you think of a service like this?"
4. "If it happens that one of our divisions absolutely must use a scoring model, as you call it, I strongly prefer the one you said that division of AT&T uses. You know, just get answers to the four questions: Do customers care, Do we care, Can we do it, and Can we stay ahead if we do? What more is relevant? That list covers technical feasibility and commercial feasibility both, doesn't it?"

CASE: WILSON SPORTING GOODS (A)[14]

In the late 1980s, the Wilson Sporting Goods Division of PepsiCo, Inc., began trying to bring engineering and other technology to the sporting goods business, and continued the effort well into the 90s. Materials-based technologies had already produced easy-to-hit tennis balls and a more responsive softball (which produced games with scores of 50 to 48).

Other firms were also active. Puma produced a running shoe with an electronic device that measured time, distance, and calories expended. AMF had a chemical compound to reduce the shock for tennis rackets.

[14]The original thrust for this case came from Hal Lancaster, "For the Poor Athletes Who Blame Their Tools, New Ones Are Coming," *The Wall Street Journal,* May 14, 1985, p. 37. Later additions came from several sources, with the pump glove details from Justin Martin, "What Fits Better than a Glove?" *Across the Board,* September 1992, pp. 41–46.

The reason for Wilson's interest in technology was its conviction that technology could be used to lure consumers back into the market. Tennis and golf had fallen off rather badly, for example, and many participative sports were suffering in varying degrees. There had been successes, however: better running shoes showed that technology could advance a sport, shoulder pads benefited from space-age technology, and baseball centers were now sometimes polyurethane. Computers had already helped tennis rackets, golf ball designs, and more. Of course, there were also failures.

But the present need was for some way to screen through the many ideas that came naturally out of such a campaign. Wilson had the engineers, and the firm knew sports. It had a broad product line, an excellent distribution system, and was one of the leading firms in the athletic goods industry. But money in the industry was short, especially for higher-risk R&D. So, Wilson needed a scoring model to help select the new product ideas most likely to contribute to company profits. They have asked you to develop one.

The firm's considerable experience in new product work enabled it to shoot for a full scoring model (not just a few factors), and it wanted a good weighting system built in. Wilson executives did not indicate whether the firm routinely used concept testing as a prescreening step, but it probably did.

Unfortunately, the sporting equipment market had hit a rough period in the recession of 1991–92, sales showing annual gains of only 4–5 percent, greater push by consumers to find lower cost equipment, and some shifting of activity to lower cost sports such as camping, soccer, and volleyball. More money was being spent on the clothing worn during sports, and less on equipment.

There had also been some efforts by firms in the industry that had been less than successful with new-technology equipment, and perhaps their troubles might suggest key factors for your scoring model. Spaulding Sports Worldwide, for example, decided that baseball gloves had remained unchanged for 70 years, and choose to develop an improved product. They knew from their many research studies and focus groups that ballplayers always wanted custom fit, custom fit, and custom fit. So they retained Design Continuum, Inc., a Boston design firm that had developed the Pump sneaker for Reebok International.

A project team was formed, and the work begun. Spaulding chose to shoot for a new glove that would still look, behave, and feel like a ball glove. They went to work on the stretch points (on the back of the glove) and the flex points (in the pocket of the glove). These permitted a tip-to-tip closure around the ball. Material chosen for the stretch points was neophrene-lycra blend (like wet suits), and the flex material was to be nylon.

After searching for all possible ways to help close the glove, designers went back to the same pump idea they had for the sneakers. An air bladder was sewn into the back of the glove, and prototypes built. Tests were conducted on company people and on baseball players in winter leagues. Some 40 prototypes later, they had what they wanted. The ball players said they liked it.

But then Spaulding found that they would have to use five different manufacturers to make the specialized parts of the glove. Leading glove manufacturers all rejected the opportunity of assembling the final item, so the operation was performed in the Philippines. Production product suffered for a while (the first batch squeaked), but eventually good product came off the line. Dubbed AirFlex, it was introduced at a national sporting goods show, where Reebok people saw it and promptly sued to stop its display there. Though later negotiations permitted Spaulding to continue marketing Air-Flex, Reebok soon paired up with Rawlings (the leading glove manufacturer) to produce and sell another version of pump glove.

Also at the meeting, Spaulding people were surprised to find that a Japanese firm had been marketing a type of pump glove called AirFit. It wasn't close enough to cause a legal problem, but there soon were three suppliers. At that time, it still wasn't clear what would happen because some managers felt that when children have a chance to use the item, grow to like it, and then continue its use as they move up to college and professional baseball, "Everybody will want one." In the meantime, retailers' comments were quite critical: "A serious baseball player couldn't care less whether a glove has custom fit," and "I don't remember selling one."

You don't have the information to compose an entirely new scoring model for use on the new product concepts discussed in this case, but you can put together the five most important factors under each of the technical and commercial halves of the model in Figure 10–4. Give them weights. Then apply your model to a new product concept they had recently been toying with—a new set of bowling pins that would exploit technology, enliven the game, and attract new attention to it. Beyond the task of *developing* a scoring model for Wilson, give some thought to the problems of *implementing* the scoring model system in this firm. Which of the functional groups (departments) would be the biggest problem, that is, the least likely to live with the results of a scoring session?

CHAPTER

11

SALES FORECASTING AND FINANCIAL ANALYSIS

Setting

Now that we have finished the full screen, we know the product concept meets our technical capabilities (present or acquirable) and our manufacturing, financing, and marketing capabilities as well. Also, we know it offers no major legal problems. So we are ready to charge ahead.

Or are we? Most managers don't think so—they are very interested in the financial side of the proposition. In fact, they have been interested in money from the very start—think back to the product innovation charter where we talked about the size of potential markets and objectives on market shares and profits. And they will still be interested in money when they look back and total up whether the whole project was worthwhile.

Now seems to be a good time to take a closer look at the *managerial* side of financial analysis—how should we manage a new product project such that it achieves reasonable financial goals?[1]

The Real Problems of Financial Analysis

Sales forecasts and financial analysis systems are no problem as such. Experts often do a remarkably good job of predicting how advancing technologies will result in new products, even 30 years or more into the future, provided

[1]This book cannot go into the details of financial analysis, but it can give references to readers who wish to go deeper. Any general financial management book will give step-by-step methods for doing a net present value method of capital budgeting. Several excellent articles are cited for mathematical models and sales forecasting.

FIGURE 11–1

What the future looked like in 1967

In 1967, noted authorities in science, computers, and politics made a series of long-term forecasts about the coming 30 years. Many of these turned out to be highly accurate:

- We would have artificial plastic and electronic replacements for human organs by 1982, and human organ transplants by 1987.
- Credit cards would virtually eliminate money by 1986.
- Lasers would be in common use by 1986.
- Many of us would be working at home by the 1980s, using remote computer terminals to link us to our offices.
- By 1970 man would have walked on the moon.
- By 1986 there would be explosive growth in expenditures on recreation and entertainment.

While about two-thirds of the forecasts were remarkably accurate, about a third were just plain wrong. Samples:

- Manned planetary landings by 1980, and a permanent moon base by 1987.
- Private cars banned from city centers by 1986.
- 3D television globally available soon.
- Primitive life created in the laboratory by 1986.

What can we learn from the correct, and from the incorrect, forecasts? Firstly, forecasts do not have to be absolutely perfect to be used for planning. Recall that old-time ship captains used maps that contained inaccuracies, but still got where they wanted to go. Secondly, incorrect forecasts seemed to fit into two categories: underlying factors driving the projections changed or the forecaster was overly optimistic in the speed of development. Space funding was substantially cut back after the 1969 moon landing, throwing off forecasts about future space exploration. 3D television may indeed be big a couple of decades from now—of course we were saying that about video phones back in the 1960s.

Source: Edward Cornish, "The Futurist Forecasts 30 Years Later," *The Futurist,* January-February 1997, pp. 45–58. For more on good and bad forecasts, see also Steven Schnaars, Swee L. Chia, and Cesar M. Maloles III, "Five Modern Lessons from a 55-Year-Old Technological Forecast," *Journal of Product Innovation Management* 10, no. 1 (1993), pp. 66–74.

they keep a "level head." (See Figure 11–1 for some forecasts—good and bad—about today's society and products, made by a panel of futurists about 30 years ago.) We have an immense arsenal of forecasting methodologies, most based on many years of experience. We know, for example, what makes for sales (recall the A-T-A-R model in Chapter 8). This model does an excellent job and serves as the basis for some very advanced mathematical systems used by sophisticated new product marketers. And every firm has people who can make an income-statement-based net present value calculation (using discounted cash flow methods). The usual approach, step by step, is given in the Bay City case at the end of the chapter, with data for a new product.

The only drawback is that those systems require information. A-T-A-R requires a solid estimate of how many people/firms will become aware of our new item, how many of those will opt to try some of the item in one way or another, and so on. Each of these figures, however, is very difficult to estimate. For example:

Nabisco did not *know* we would storm the dealers for its SnackWell's.

Ty Inc. did not *know* we would buy millions of Beanie Babies as collector's items.

Amazon.com did not *know* we would buy millions of books over the Internet.

Also, the financial model requires product cost, prices, the current value of money, probable taxes on the future income, the amount of further capital investments that will be required between now and when we close the books on the product, and much more.

These will never be certain, even after living out the product's life cycle. Sales will be known, but we might have had a better marketing strategy. Costs are always just estimates. We will never know the true extent to which a new item cannibalized sales from another product. If we had not marketed the new item a competitor probably would have. And on and on.

The fact is, we rely on estimates. Management's task is to make the estimates as solid as we can, and then manage around the areas of uncertainty in a way that we don't get hurt too badly.

On minor product improvements we do this pretty well—a new Troy-Bilt lawn mower with a pepped-up engine is not a wild guessing game. On near line extensions, we also do well, but with more misses. Totally new products, using technologies never so applied before, are pure guessing games. For over 30 years business schools used a Polaroid pricing case in which Edwin Land was trying to decide whether people would pay $15, or maybe $25, or (dream on) $50 for his first instant camera! They paid the top price, in huge numbers, making Land a very rich "financial and technical genius."

Recent Experiences

Some more recent managers have done the same. A 1995 *Fortune* article was actually entitled "Ignore Your Customer."[2] Chrysler didn't believe car buyers when they said they saw no value in a minivan. Compaq rejected rejections of the PC network server and made many millions of dollars. Barry Diller of Fox Television didn't believe people who said we didn't need a fourth TV network. An air-based system of package movement? VCRs? Fax machines that just sent pieces of paper a bit faster than the mails did? A heart pump? Winners all, and very big ones.

How about when customers themselves tell us to market something new—surely we can trust them. They liked the taste of the New Coke and said they would buy it. They liked the idea of (lower fat) burgers that McDonalds called McLean and the upscale Arch Deluxe burgers. They said they liked the

[2]Justin Martin, "Ignore Your Customer," *Fortune,* May 1, 1995, pp. 121–26.

idea of a movie about "Godzilla." And so on. Business closets are full of things customers demanded or said they would buy.

Fortune's conclusion was that smart companies are using nontraditional methods to get sales and profit estimates. Steelcase didn't *ask* business managers what they would like as a special office for teams—they went out and observed teams in actions, and returned to the labs to design what *they thought* would be better. Called Personal Harbor, it was. Urban Outfitters does not use focus groups and surveys—they go to stores and hangouts and watch customers in action—what they are wearing and how they wear it. Urban Outfitter's founder said, "We're not after people's statements, we're after their actions."

The ultimate perhaps in showing how managers do their best to forecast the future, but still hedge a bit, came in 1993. A fire destroyed the Japanese plant of Sumitomo Chemical Company, makers of resins for encapsulating computer chips. It turned out that most of their customers were not the JIT (just-in-time) purists they claimed to be. Turned out they had JIC (just-in-case) supplies stashed away in various warehouses![3]

Summary of the Problems

What makes forecasting so difficult? For one thing, target users don't always know what the new product will actually be, what it will do for them, what it will cost, and what its drawbacks will be, nor will they have had a chance to use it. And if they do know, they may want to keep some information from us or offer outright falsehoods. Complicating this problem is that market research on these potential users is often poorly done—for example, horror stories about focus groups abound.

At the same time, competitors don't sit still. In fact, they try very hard to ruin our data, just as we do theirs. Resellers, regulators, and market advisers are in a constant flux.

Information about marketing support—what kind of service will be available in the firm, for example—may be lacking. No sales manager can make promises a year ahead about sales time and support. Internal attitudes can be biased, and politics are always present. Many new products managers won't be ready to show just how good the new item is for some time, so they try to delay official forecasting.

In their excitement to get to market, new products managers sometimes get themselves into trouble by rushing their products out, without stopping to field-test the new item. Steelcase management, responding to some disappointments, now demands that new office furniture systems be *thoroughly* tested in *end-user offices.*

---

[3]The March 1995 issue of *The PA Perspective,* a newsletter published by Princeton Associates consulting firm, in Buckingham, PA.

It is difficult to tell how long it will take people to change to a new technology. A classic case concerns Kodak's frustrations in trying to estimate whether and when CD technology would replace film in the photographic market.[4]

Finally, most common forecasting methods are extrapolations, and work well on established products. New products don't have a history. Even forecasting methods that seem free of history (use of leading indicators and causal models) use *relationships* established in the past.[5]

Actions by Managers to Handle These Problems

Given that we badly need financial analyses and that good analyses are difficult to make, what is a manager to do?

Improve the New Product Process Currently in Use

Most of the horror stories given earlier from the trade press are embarrassing to their managers. In most of them a key step was skipped. In an effort to hurry, or to capitalize on the conviction of someone working in or around the project, a bad assumption was made. For example, New Coke was heavily taste-tested, but was not *market*-tested—that is, no one was actually asked to buy the product with that new name. Same for the low-fat burger. Chrysler was wiser—it knew that consumers were negative toward the minivan because they couldn't see the value in it until they actually drove it for a while. So they made sure they drove it. Top new product professionals today know good new product process, but many others don't. They lack information and don't realize it. All the standard forms will not make up for omissions of key data pieces.

Use the Life Cycle Concept of Financial Analysis

Firms sometimes err by focusing their financial analysis at one particular point—perhaps a stage in a stage-gate system. That point is often right where we are in this book, at full screen. Another popular time is later, near where some major financial commitment must be made—for example, building a plant or releasing an expensive marketing introductory program. Managers talk about a point of no return. It is indeed a stage-gate, a hurdle, and new product managers may spend weeks getting ready for the meeting.

---

[4]See Joan E. Rigdon, "Kodak Tries to Prepare for Filmless Era Without Inviting Demise of Core Business," *The Wall Street Journal,* April 18, 1991, p. B1.

[5]An interesting view on forecasting methods is in Joseph P. Martino, "Technological Forecasting," *The Futurist,* July-August 1993, pp. 13–16. He gives a classification like the one just mentioned, but also talks about genius forecasting, pushing the panic button, window-blind forecasting and others, down to no forecast!

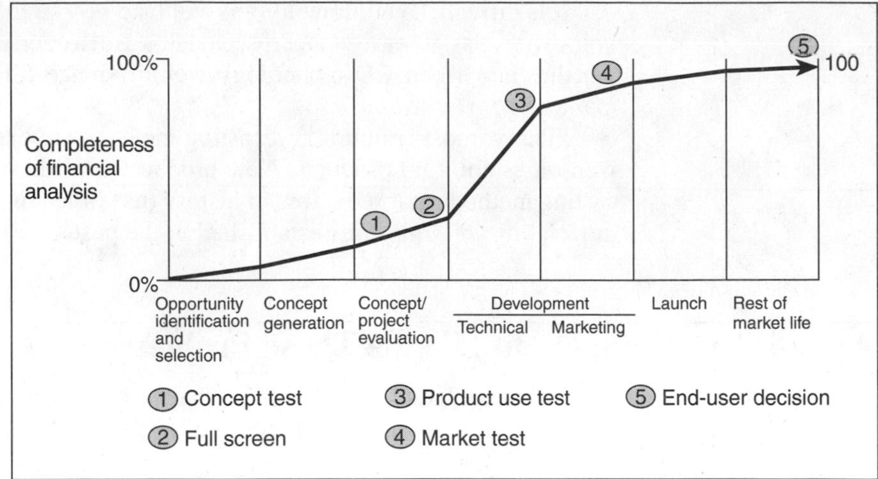

FIGURE 11–2

Financial analysis as a living thing: the life cycle of assessment

But both instances are exaggerated. Technical work can begin without committing the firm to a huge technical expenditure. Building a plant can often be avoided by contracting out early production, or by building a large pilot system for trial marketing in a restricted rollout.

It is far better for managers to see their project as a living thing—a bottom line that is created gradually, over the life of the project, never being completely accurate, even well after the item is launched (See Figure 11–2). A product innovation charter is accepted only because the management believes the combined technologies and market opportunities fit well with each other and with the firm. A PIC describes a home field where we can't ever be sure of the final score but where we should be able to win. A concept test result doesn't assure financial success either, but it can say we are one step further along—the intended user agrees there is a need for something like our concept and wants some to try out. An early field use test with a prototype also won't assure success, but it can say intended users like what they see. An advertising agency or a sales manager cannot guarantee success either, but they can assess whether the new item will be brought to the attention of potential end users and that it will be tried. If it delivers, it will sell, and if manufacturing was able to do what it felt it could, there will be profit in the item. And so on. The best we can do at any point is to ask whether progress to date is consistent with a successful life cycle.

It is the same with financial analysis—where are we today, is what we know at this time consistent with profit goals, is there reason to change our past projections? Some financial analysts now prefer to set up with full financial sheets at the beginning, and then compare progress against those spreadsheets. Many boxes are blank in the beginning, but will be filled in when we know them. But the profit figures at the bottom of the page are not current *forecasts,* just current *goals.* As long as current progress is consistent with those goals, we proceed. A successful cola taste-test is not a reliable indicator of consumers' ultimate trial. If we get trial, the taste test says the chances are we will get repeat business.

The life cycle concept of financial analysis enables us to avoid setting up systems where make-or-break decisions rest on one sales forecast or one cost forecast.

Reduce Dependence on Poor Forecasts

If it is difficult to make sales and profit forecasts, are there ways of avoiding having to make them? Yes, several, and many firms use them, though with caution.

Forecast What You Know. This is actually an attitude towards forecasting. Why try to forecast what people in the marketplace will do, if there is no reasonable way we can do so? A blank in a spreadsheet can be filled in with a range of estimates to see where the failure point is. If failure is very unlikely, then go ahead.

Approve Situations, Not Numbers. This is a variation on what was mentioned earlier. Analyze to find what the success factors are, and then look to see if the situation offers them. If so, go ahead, knowing that success should come about even though we don't know just how much. An extreme example of this occurred once when a marketing vice president was asked to predict what he would do if he could get a license to use the Coca-Cola trademark on a line of new products. His answer was, right now I don't know, but with that trademark it's only a matter of how much, not whether.

One way of betting on a situation has a parallel in horse racing; some betters bet on the jockey not the horse (about whom they may be able to learn very little). Many firms "bet" on a top-notch scientist, sales force, trademark, or reputation.

Another situation variable is *leadership.* Some firms encourage the *champion system.* They expect champions to force their way past a restrictive financial system. This makes for a strange but very workable practice of evaluating teams and their leaders, rather than the ideas they come up with. These firms don't seek "great" new products; they seek concepts that they can *manage* into great new products. You may recall reading in Chapter 3 about the movie producer who builds a staff of outstanding creative people and depends on them to work miracles with ordinary scripts. A competitor invests in top scripts instead. But both were avoiding the necessity of relying on complex forecasts and financial analyses.

People who love to fish do this all the time; they spend lots of money to find and reach top trout streams. One manager recently said, "If there is a good trout stream with lots of trout in it and a good angler with good equipment, we don't need an accountant to tell us how many fish we will catch. Whatever happens will be good." This strategy is not as folksy as it may sound. A firm must know what the success factors are in any situation. One of those two movie producers may be wrong. Notice how the manager included the trout stream, the angler, *and* the good equipment.

Recall from Chapter 8 the two "potholes" to success identified by Campbell Soup: the taste of the soup and the manufacturing cost. Their name and skills could overcome any other limitation. Precise forecasting wasn't necessary under this strategy, but being sure on taste and cost was.

Commit to a Strategy of Low Cost Development and Marketing. There are times when a company can do the type of product innovation that some call temporary products. They develop a stream of new items that differ very little from those now on the market, insert them into the market without great fanfare, and watch which ones end-users rebuy. They drop those that don't find favor. Japanese makers of electronics goods do this regularly, with Honda introducing several hundred new items in a year; there even are cities in Japan where firms introduce their flood, and since consumers know this, marketing costs can be kept low.

Go Ahead with Sound Forecasts but Prepare to Handle the Risks. This strategy especially appeals to managers who feel business is suffering from "paralysis by analysis." There are lots of ways to put risk back into product innovation while managing it well. One approach is to isolate or neutralize the in-house critics (a strong reason for setting up project matrices and spin-outs).

Another approach defers financial analysis until later in the development process. One firm realized it was consistently killing off good new product ideas by demanding precise financial analyses at the time of screening. It didn't have the data. Another strategy is to use market testing rollouts (see Chapter 20). If a financial analysis looks weak, but the idea seems sound, try it out on a limited scale to see where the solution might lie. This thinking may violate several popular management theories (e.g., empowered teams), but it may be necessary at times.

Managing risk is a major field in itself today, since we know business needs risk as a source of profits. Figure 11–3 shows the risk situation new product managers face in their evaluations—they know their product will bring more risk than the average risk of the firm, but how much? It seems that firms do not know what their current level of risk really is (the first vertical line), so the **risk premium** is not very useful in quantitative evaluations. And the **required rate of return** line moving upward across the figure is itself just a conception, not a measurement. It may have many different slopes, giving the product innovation premium many different roles.

Figure 11–3 compounds this problem by showing that the risk of a new product, if put into one figure as demanded in Figure 11–3, is itself just some

FIGURE 11–3

Calculating the new product's required rate of return

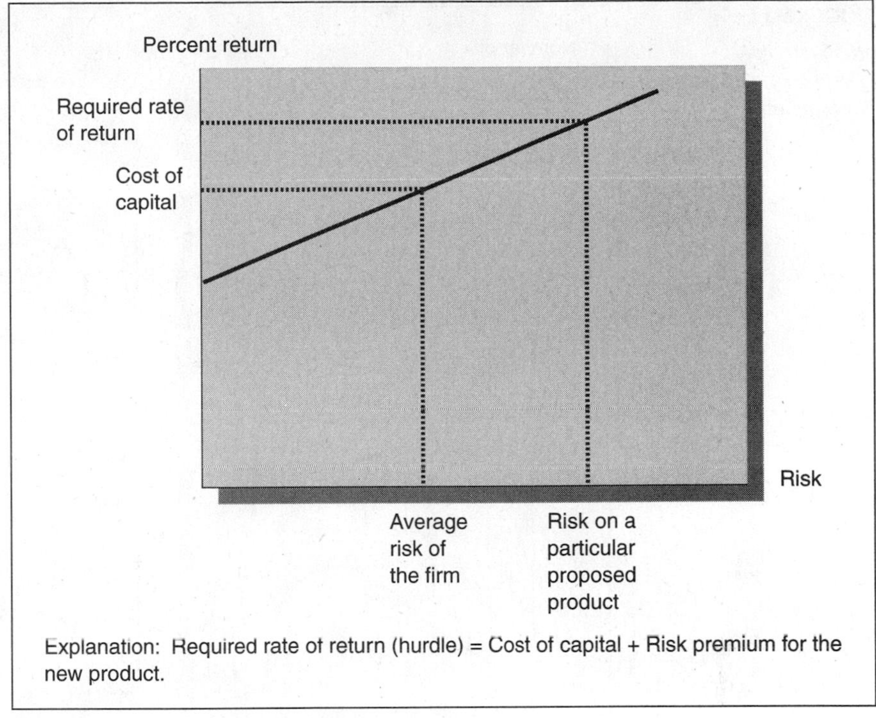

Explanation: Required rate of return (hurdle) = Cost of capital + Risk premium for the new product.

kind of average. The mean profits expected from the four new products in Figure 11–4 are the same, but the distributions of their possible outcomes vary widely. B and C in particular hide some major risks.

Use Different Methods of Financial Analysis on New Products, Depending on the Situation. In most product innovation (in terms of sheer numbers of items) we hit singles—product improvements and close line extensions—not home runs. This innovation is managed deep within the ongoing operation, neither using empowered teams, nor huge technical breakthroughs. The item is often demanded by a key customer or key channel, and the decision to develop it is not based on item profitability at all. The risks are relatively small; sometimes the development is in a partnership with a customer who will provide profitable volume.

But home runs are something else entirely. They are a big gamble—big risks for potential big gains. They need lots of attention and cannot be handled easily with methods such as those in the previous section. So the best approach is to have *two* systems of financial analysis, one for singles and one for home runs. Alternatively, some firms have no standard system at all, just develop a *financial analysis for each project,* keying the information to those issues where the risks really lie and unknowns prevail.

FIGURE 11–4

Risk curves—frequency distributions of outcomes

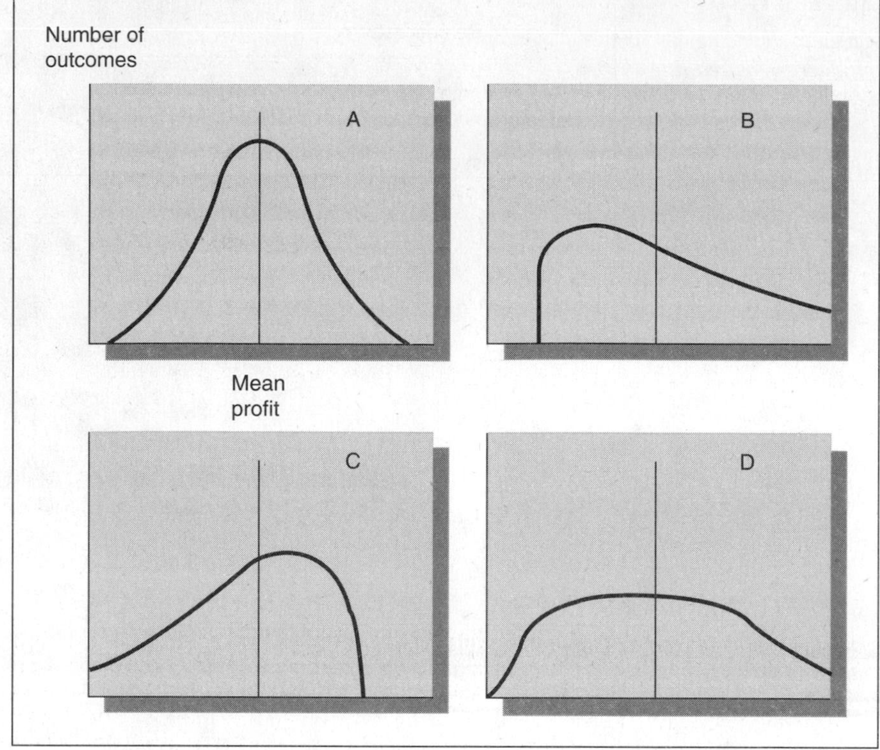

Improve Current Financial Forecasting Methods. Marketing people, for example, sometimes make use of mathematical sales forecasting models (more in a moment). These models were developed for use on consumer packaged goods firms over 30 years ago, but improvements continue to this time. Efforts also continue to make them work better on durable goods.[6]

Some firms are beginning to analyze their own past efforts too. More progress will come when firms systematically study their most recent 50 (or 25 or whatever they have) new products to summarize what financial methods were used and how well they forecast the actual outcomes. This is what we now call success/failure analysis, and leads to best practices. It is rather common in other phases of new product work—for example, recall the

[6]See Glen L. Urban, John S. Hulland, and Bruce D. Weinberg, "Premarket Forecasting for New Consumer Durable Goods: Modeling Categorization, Elimination, and Consideration Phenomena," *Journal of Marketing,* April, 1993, pp. 47–63.

FIGURE 11–5

Hurdle rates on return and other measures

		Hurdle Rates		
Product	*Strategic Role or Purpose*	*Sales*	*Return on Investment*	*Market Share Increase*
A	Combat competitive entry	$3,000,000	10%	0 Points
B	Establish foothold in new market	$2,000,000	17%	15 Points
C	Capitalize on existing markets	$1,000,000	12%	1 Point

Explanation: This array shows that hurdles should reflect a product's purpose, or assignment. For example, combating a competitive entry will require more sales than would establishing a toehold in a new market. Also, we might accept a very low share increase for an item that simply capitalized on our existing market position.

screening model work by Cooper in Chapter 10. There have also been some recent improvements in accounting methods, and probably will be more.[7] Lastly, some new products managers make a general plea that all financial analysis should be advisory—not fixed hurdles and mandates but flags that warn of potential problems. Of course, hurdle rates can be *managed* in the sense of being situational (See Figure 11–5).

Sales Forecasting

Given this background of general problems and issues in new product forecasting, we should now look at how a new product's sales can be forecasted. We must keep in mind several considerations when developing this **sales forecast.** First, a product's *potential* may be extremely high, but sales may not materialize due to insufficient marketing effort. Advertising may not adequately create awareness, or inadequate distribution may make the product unavailable to much of the market. The A-T-A-R model we discussed in Chapter 8 will help us adjust sales forecasts based on awareness and availability. Second, sales will grow through time if we successfully get customers to try the product and convert many of these customers into repeat purchasers; if they pass along favorable word of mouth to their friends; if greater demand

[7]See, for example, Carliss Y. Baldwin, "How Capital Budgeting Deters Innovation—And What To Do About It," *Research-Technology Management,* December 1991, pp. 39–45; Timothy M. Devinney, "New Products and Financial Risk Changes," *Journal of Product Innovation Management,* September 1992, pp. 222–31; George T. Haley and Stephan M. Goldberg, "Net Present Value Techniques and Their Effects on New Product Research," *Industrial Marketing Management,* 1995, pp. 177–90.

encourages more dealers to stock the product; and so on. After this growth period, sales will eventually stabilize. Thus, we will be interested in developing projections of long-run sales or market shares. Third, we should recognize that our product's sales will depend on our competitors' strategies and programs as well as our own.

There are several general approaches that can be taken to forecast a new product's sales at this early stage in the NPD process. We will review a few of the more frequently used ones here.

Forecasting Sales Using Purchase Intentions

Think back to concept testing (Chapter 9). Among other things, we gathered purchase intentions from respondents. When presented with a concept, they were asked (typically using a five-point scale) to state their likelihood of purchasing that product if it were made available. As mentioned at that time, it is common to look at the top-two-boxes totals (the number of customers who stated they would either definitely or probably buy the product). This measure can be refined and calibrated through experience.

For instance, recall that in our example of a concept test for an aerosol hand cleanser (Figure 9–2), we found that 5 percent of the respondents would definitely buy it, and 36 percent would probably buy it. Based on averages from data collected on similar products launched in the past, about 80 percent of those people who say they would "definitely" buy actually buy the product, and 33 percent of those who say they would "probably" buy actually buy. From this information, our first estimate of the percentage of potential purchasers would be $(0.05)(0.80) + (0.36)(0.33) = 16\%$. This estimate assumes 100 percent awareness and availability, and so would have to be adjusted downward. If we expect that 60 percent of the market will be aware of the product *and* have it available to them at a nearby retail outlet, our predicted percentage of actual purchasers would be $(0.16)(0.6) = 9.6$ percent. As a refinement to this method, we could also vary the concept and get separate purchase intentions for each variation. For example, we might have asked respondents to state their purchase intentions for an aerosol hand cleaner that disinfects as well as cleans, using the same five-point scale.

Forecasting Using the A-T-A-R Model

In Chapter 8 we worked through a simple example of the A-T-A-R model in action, and briefly mentioned where some of the data could be obtained. This simple model can be used to construct a sales or profit forecast, and market researchers long ago developed the early, simple models into far more powerful forecasting devices. These advanced research models are used largely on consumer packaged goods, where firms have lots of new product experience on which to develop model parameters and to calibrate the raw percentages they get from consumers.

The A-T-A-R model is the basis of many of the simulated test markets we will encounter in Chapter 19. This is one of the pseudo sale market testing methods used later in the new product process, typically when the physical product is available for the consumer to take home and try. Post-trial data are then collected from the consumer and used as input to the A-T-A-R model. At this early stage in the new product process, before product design and prototype manufacture, the A-T-A-R model can still be applied using data from other sources and even assumptions. Trial and repeat rates that need to be achieved to reach sales or profit projections can be estimated early on and adjusted as the product goes through later stages and more information becomes available.

First-time product trial might be estimated using the purchase intention method described above. For frequently-purchased consumer packaged goods, it is critical to get a good estimate of repeat purchase as well as trial, since long-run market share can be expressed as

$$MS = T \times R \times AW \times AV$$

where T = Ultimate long-run trial rate (the percentage of all buyers who ultimately try the product at least once),

R = Ultimate long-run repeat purchase rate (share of purchases of the product among those who tried the product),

AW = Percent awareness,

AV = Percent availability.

Repeat purchase rate, R, can be obtained by analogy to similar products for which such data are available. It can also be calculated using a switching model.[8] We can define R_s as the proportion of customers who will switch to the new product when it becomes available, and R_r as the proportion of customers who repeat-purchase the product. The switching model estimates long-run repeat purchase rate, R, as $R_s/(1 + R_s - R_r)$. If R_s and R_r are estimated as 0.7 and 0.6 respectively, repeat purchase is estimated as (0.7/1 + 0.7 – 0.6) = 0.636. If awareness and availability are 90 percent and 67 percent respectively, and 16 percent of the market that is aware of the product and has it available to purchase tries it at least once, long-run market share is calculated as

$$\begin{aligned} MS &= 0.16 \times 0.636 \times 0.90 \times 0.67 \\ &= 6.14\%. \end{aligned}$$

Furthermore, if the total number of purchases in this product category is known, this market share can be converted into long-run sales. If total number of purchases is 1,000,000 units, the firm's long-run sales are estimated

[8]This switching model is an application of a Markov model (a form of model used to determine equilibrium states), in which the long-run repeat purchase rate is the equilibrium state. Details on the switching model are given in Glen Urban, "PERCEPTOR: A Model for Product Positioning," *Management Science* 21, no. 8 (1975), pp. 858–71.

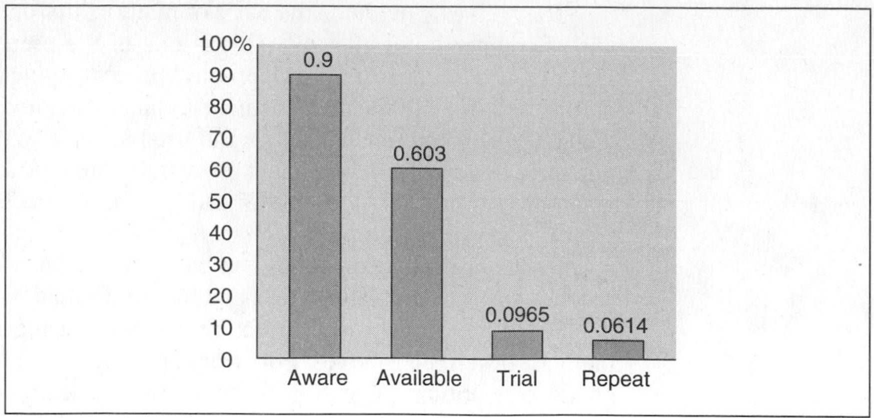

FIGURE 11–6
A-T-A-R model—results in bar chart format

to be 1,000,000 × 6.14% = 61,400 units. The process of calculating market share is illustrated in the bar chart in Figure 11–6. The *y*-axis represents the total market (100%). The figure shows that 90 percent of the market is aware of the product, 67 percent of the "aware" market (67% × 90% = 60.3%) also has the product available to them, 16 percent of the "aware" market that has the product available tries it at least once, and 63.6 percent of the latter become repeat purchasers.

We shall return to A-T-A-R models of this type when we have a product prototype we are ready to test with customers, a little later in the new product process.

Forecasting Product Diffusion

Diffusion of innovation refers to the process by which an innovation is spread within a market, over time, and over categories of adopters. The adopter categories, which we will look at more closely in Chapter 17, are often called innovators, early adopters, early and late majority, and laggards. In theory, individuals in the earlier adopter categories influence the purchase behaviors of later ones, through word of mouth and other influence processes. The rate of diffusion of a product can be difficult to assess, especially at this early stage, since it is unknown how influential the earlier adopter categories will ultimately be.

To get a handle on the growth potential of an innovative product, we can use an analogous, existing product as a guideline. If we are assessing the market potential of a new kind of automobile tire (that could, say, run safely for 100 miles after being punctured), we could reasonably use common radial tires as an analogy. They are sold to the same populations (car manufacturers and service centers) and provide basically the same benefit. Thus, as a rough estimate, long-run market potential for our new tire is probably similar to the sales level achieved by radial tires. Managerial judgment regarding our new product might suggest that actual market potential be somewhat higher or lower than this initial estimate.

Quantitative innovation diffusion models can also be used in predicting future product category sales based on historical product sales levels. A diffusion model commonly used for durable goods is the **Bass model,**[9] which estimates the sales of the product class at some future time t, $s(t)$, as:

$$s(t) = pm + [q - p]\ Y(t) - (q/m)\ [Y(t)]^2$$

where p = Initial trial probability
q = Diffusion rate parameter
m = Total number of potential buyers
$Y(t)$ = Total number of purchases by time t

The Bass diffusion model is based on the diffusion curve of new products through a population. The initial diffusion rate (growth in total number of purchases) is based on adoption by innovators. Following these early purchases, the growth rate accelerates as word-of-mouth helps promote the product and more of the market adopts the product. Eventually, however, we reach the point where there are not that many potential purchasers left that have not yet tried the product, and growth rate slows.

Managerial judgment, or standard procedures for market potential estimation, can be used to estimate m, the number of potential buyers. If the product category has been around for a while and several periods of data exist, one could use past sales to estimate the size of p and q. To set these values for a recent innovation, one might look at similar (analogous) products for which these values are known, or rely on judgment or previous experience with this kind of model. Previous studies suggest that p is usually in the range of about 0.04, and q is typically close to 0.3, though these values will vary depending on the situation.[10]

A desirable feature of this growth model is that, once p and q are estimated, the time required to reach the sales peak (t^*) can be predicted, as can the peak level of sales at that time (s^*). These are given as:

$$t^* = (1/(p + q))\ \ln\ (q/p)$$
$$s^* = (m)(p + q)^2/4q$$

[9]The model was originally published by Frank Bass in "A New Product Growth Model of Consumer Durables," *Management Science* 15 (January 1969), pp. 215–27, and has since been extended in dozens of research articles. This stream of literature is reviewed in Vijay Mahajan, Eitan Muller and Frank M. Bass, "New Product Diffusion Models in Marketing: A Review and Directions for Research," *Journal of Marketing* 54 (January 1990), pp. 1–26.

[10]Parameter estimation issues are discussed in Vijay Mahajan and Subhash Sharma, "Simple Algebraic Estimation Procedure for Innovation Diffusion Models of New Product Acceptance," *Technological Forecasting and Social Change* 30 (December 1986), pp. 331–46, and Fareena Sultan, John U. Farley, and Donald R. Lehmann, "A Meta-Analysis of Applications of Diffusion Models," *Journal of Marketing Research* 27 (February 1990), pp. 70–78.

FIGURE 11–7

Bass model forecast of product diffusion

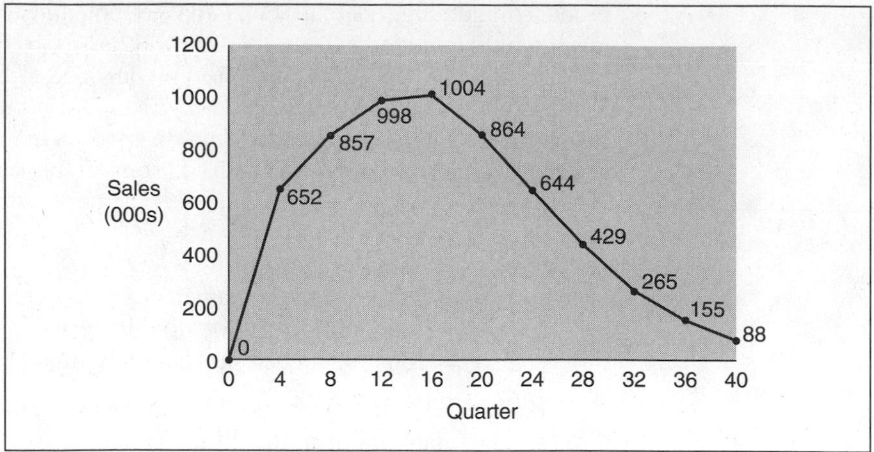

Let's say you work for a company that is assessing the viability of a new product category: a combination cappuccino maker-miniature convection oven. You believe the long-run potential for this product is in the area of 25,000,000 households. For similar small household appliances your company has sold in the past, innovation and imitation rates have tended to be in the area of 2 percent and 12 percent. Figure 11–7 presents a sales forecast derived for this new product category, based on applying the Bass model to these estimates. This preliminary forecast suggests that peak sales will occur about 14 quarters from now, and that total product category sales during that quarter will be about 1 million units. Of course, if these sales projections are combined with price, cost, and market share projections, the product's potential projected contribution to profit can be assessed. The Bay City Electronics case at the end of this chapter shows a set of sales projections for a new product (derived using Bass or some similar model), and takes you through these steps.

Bass showed that, despite its simplicity, his model did a good job at predicting the time and magnitude of the sales peak for many durable consumer goods, including clothes dryers, televisions, coffee makers, irons, and others. Later extensions of the Bass model have shown how it can be applied to nondurable goods where repeat sales need to be considered.[11]

Observations on Forecasting Models

Model makers are rapidly accumulating experience and sharpening their models. They are now readily available to consumer packaged goods innovators,

[11]See Vijay Mahajan, Yoram Wind, and Subhash Sharma, "An Approach to Repeat Purchase Diffusion Models," in *AMA Proceedings,* Series 49 (Chicago: American Marketing Association, 1983), pp. 442–46.

quite inexpensively compared to test markets and roll-outs, and allow diagnostic output as well as sensitivity testing.

Unfortunately, they also require massive amounts of data to work well, are built heavily on assumptions, and are so complex that many managers are wary of them. Having developed initially in the 1950s and 1960s, they often incorporate assumptions no longer valid—for example, reliance on mass advertising and easy-to-get distribution. But they are now a mature industry, a large and profitable one.

It is interesting that the most successful firm by far uses the simplest methodology and requires the least data. In BASES II, Burke staffers combine a concept test and a product use test, calibrate the trial and repeat percentages from their massive files of past studies, and use a set of experience-honed heuristics (rules of thumb) to translate those percentages into market shares.

But product innovators outside of consumer packaged goods still most often use the simple version of the A-T-A-R model shown in Chapter 8, if they use any forecasting model at all. Research continues toward improving all of the sales forecasting models.[12]

Summary

This chapter has dealt with the matter of how to make judgments on the financial merits of new products. There are good basic methods for doing financial analysis (net present value calculations using discounted cash flow), and there are excellent methods for doing sales forecasting. Most firms use them daily. However, new products managers know they often do not have the data these sophisticated methods require. So they may also need to use "risk-reducers"—actions that give them nonquantitative guides to probable financial success.

The method of making financial analyses is given in the Bay City case, which comes after the Applications section. The case offers data for a new electronics product and gives the opportunity as well to look at some nondata issues involved in financial analysis.

At this point in the new product process, we are ready to begin Phase IV: development.

[12]For a summary of where we stand on these sales forecasting models, see Vijay Mahajan and Jerry Wind, "New Product Models: Practice, Shortcomings and Desired Improvements," *Journal of Product Innovation Management,* June 1992, pp. 128–39.

Applications

More questions from that interview with the company president.

1. "You're still a student, but when you tell me about all the problems new product managers have putting together financial worksheets you sound like the people we have around here. They complain that all finance numbers are unreliable, estimates, guesses, and so forth. What they really want is no financial appraisal at all—just leave them alone and they'll eventually bring back the bacon—big slabs of it. That's simply not true—our financial evaluations have a weak figure or two, sure, but how else can we keep reasonable managerial control over the use of sometimes very great corporate resources?"
2. "One thing I know for certain—I don't want any sales managers or technical research people making new product forecasts. I've never seen such lousy forecasting as we get from these people. Sales managers either love a new item so much they think it will outsell everyone, or they think it is a dud and underforecast just as badly. Absolutely no objectivity in them. And the technical people, well, they become so enamored of their inventions that they lose all objectivity, too. What I like is forecasting done by independent people—project managers or new products managers in separate departments. Have you run into any good ways of keeping sales managers and technical researchers out of forecasting? You agree that they should be excluded, don't you?"
3. "I was talking just the other day about our most recent acquisition—a chain of four large general hospitals on the West Coast. These are private hospitals, and we fully intend them to be profitable, but it is a service, I guess, and there are some *public* service overtones in the deal, whether we want them there or not. My concern, as we talk about evaluating new products, is how would this new division go about making financial evaluations on new service proposals? The same as our divisions making goods?"
4. "Actually, I agree with one thing you said a while ago, and that related to the desirability of making financial analyses on a threshold basis. I realize how many unknowns there are in the new products business. As a president, I realize too that most of the financial projections I read are just air. If a new products group can convince me that they can sell *at least X* volume, and at that volume their costs will be *Y, or lower,* then I am inclined to go along with them. But, deep in my heart, I don't like it—those thresholds are just as much subject to manipulation as are the more structured NPV projections. You agree?"

CASE: BAY CITY ELECTRONICS[13]

Financial analysis of new products at Bay City Electronics had always been rather informal. Bill Roberts, who founded the firm in 1970, knew residential electronics because he had worked for almost seven years for another firm specializing in home security systems. But he had never been trained in financial analysis. In fact, all he knew was what the bank had asked for every time he went to discuss his line of credit. Bay City had about 45 full-time employees (plus a seasonal factory work force) and did in the neighborhood of $18 million in sales. Bill's products all related to home security and were sold by his sales manager, who worked with a group of manufacturers' reps, who in turn called on wholesalers, hardware and department store chains, and other large retailers. He did some consumer advertising, but not much.

Bill was inventive, however, and had built the business primarily by coming up with new techniques. His latest device was a remote-controlled electronic closure for any door in the home. The closure was effected by a special ringing of the telephone: for example, if a user wanted to leave a back door open until 9:00 P.M. it was simple to call the house at 9:00 and wait for 10 rings, after which the electronic device would switch the door to a locked position. A similar call would reopen the door.

The bank liked the idea but wanted Bill to do a better job of financial analysis, so the loan officer asked him to use the forms shown below in the Bay City Appendix as Figure 11–8 and Figure 11–9. After some effort, Bill was able to fill out the key data form, Figure 11–8, and his work is reproduced here. To date, Bay City had spent $85,000 in expense money for supplies and labor developing the closure and had invested $15,000 in a machine (asset). If the company decided to go ahead, it would have to invest $50,000 more in a new facility, continue R&D to validate and improve the product, and—if things went according to expectations—invest another $45,000 in year 3 to expand production capability.

He also had to fill out the financial worksheet, Figure 11–9; for this he used a friend of the family who had studied financial analysis in college. The friend had relied on a summary of how to do this, and this summary is attached. He also warned Bill that there were lots of judgment calls in that calculation, "so don't get into an argument with the people at the bank about details."

While waiting for his appointment at the bank, Bill spent some time just thinking about his situation. Did the numbers look good? Where were the shaky parts that the banker might give him trouble on? Most of all, he was curious about whether a friend of his at the La-Z-Boy chair firm in Monroe had to do the same thing, and would 3M require the same type of form from his daughter who now worked for them? Frankly, he didn't feel he personally had learned much about his situation from the exercise and was already wondering whether there weren't better ways for him to go about reassuring the bank that their loan was a good proposition.

---

[13]This is a realistic, but hypothetical, situation.

FIGURE 11–8

Key data form for financial analysis, part A

Financial Analysis Proposal: *Bay City Electronics Closure**
Date of this analysis: ________ Previous analysis: ________

1. Economic conditions, if relevant:
   Corporate scenario OK

2. The market (category):
   Stable—5% growth

3. Product life *5* years

4. List price: *$90*
   Distributor discounts: *$36*
   Net to factory: *$54*
   Other discounts:
   Promotion: *$1*
   Quantity: *$1*
   Average dollars per unit sold: *$52*

5. Production costs:
   Explanation of any unique costing procedures being used:
   None. Experience curve effect.
   Applicable rate for indirect manufacturing costs: ________
   20% of direct costs

6. Future expenditures, other capital investments, or extraordinary expenditures:
   Build production facilities: $50,000
   Ongoing R&D: $15,000; $10,000; $15,000; $10,000 for first four years after intro
   Special UL test during the 2nd year will cost $5,000
   Expand facilities in 3rd year for $45,000

7. Working capital: *35* % of sales
   10% inventory; recover 80% in period 5
   15% receivables; all recovered in period 5
   10% cash, all recovered

8. Applicable overheads:
   Corp.: *10* % of sales
   Division: *–* % of sales

9. Net loss on cannibalized sales, if any, expressed as a percent of the new product's sales: *10* %

10. Future costs/revenues of project abandonment, if that were done instead of marketing: *Abort now would net $3,000 from sale of machine.*

11. Tax credits, if any, on new assets or expenditures: *1% of taxes due to state and federal, based on positive environmental effect.*

12. Applicable depreciation rate(s) on depreciable assets: *25% on orig. plant and machines; 33 1/3% on expansion facilities*

13. Federal and state income tax rate applicable: *34* %
    Comments:

14. Applicable cost of capital: *16* %
    ± Premiums or penalties: *high-risk project* *8* %
    ________ _ %
    Any change in cost of capital anticipated over life of product? *No*

*This key data form is filled in with demonstration data for the Bay City Electronics case.

FIGURE 11–8 (CONCLUDED)

Key data form for financial analysis, part B

15. Basic overall risk curve applicable to the NPV: Standard OK ✓

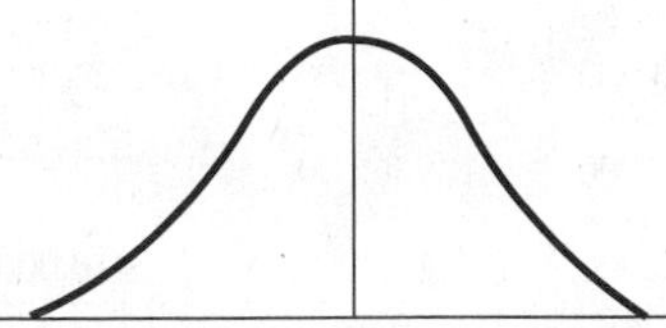

16. Key elements to be given sensitivity testing (e.g., sales, price cuts) *(see below)*

17. Sunk costs:
Expenses to date: *Ignore*
Capital invested to date: *$15,000*

18. Elements of new product strategy that are especially relevant on this proposal: (e.g., diversification mandate or cash risk):
Strategy calls for us to strengthen company in diversified markets, which this product will do.

19. Basic sales and cost

Year	Unit sales	Direct production cost per unit	Marketing expenses
1	4,000	$16	$100,000
2	10,000	12	80,000
3	18,000	11	50,000
4	24,000	9	60,000
5	5,000	14	10,000

20. Hurdle rates:
Must have 40% gross margin after production costs.

21. Any mandatory contingencies: *None*

22. Other special assumptions or guidelines:
(1) The total $110,000 of facilities and machines will salvage for $10,000 when production is finished.
(2) The firm has other income to absorb any tax loss on this project.
(3) Ignore investment tax credit.

Sensitivity testing (Calculate the effect on NPV of the following):
(1) We may have to cut the price to $34 net at start of third year.
(2) Our direct manufacturing cost estimate may be overly optimistic. What if we never get the cost below the original $16?
(3) Competition may force much higher marketing costs—what if starting in year 2 the level we have to spend at is just twice what we forecasted above?
(4) How about a worst-case outcome, in which all of the above three contingencies are tested at one time?

FIGURE 11–9

Financial worksheet, Bay City Electronics

Product Proposal: Electronics Closure Date:

			Years on the Market			
	0	1	2	3	4	5
Unit sales	0	4,000	10,000	18,000	24,000	5,000
Revenue per unit	0	52	52	52	52	52
Dollar sales	0	208,000	520,000	936,000	1,248,000	260,000
Production costs:						
Direct	0	64,000	120,000	198,000	216,000	70,000
Indirect	0	12,800	24,000	39,600	43,200	14,000
Total	0	76,800	144,000	237,600	259,200	84,000
Gross profit	0	131,200	376,000	648,400	988,800	176,000
Direct marketing costs	0	100,000	80,000	50,000	60,000	10,000
Profit contribution	0	31,200	296,000	648,400	928,800	166,000
Overheads (excluding R&D):						
Division	0	0	0	0	0	0
Corporate	0	20,800	52,000	93,600	124,800	26,000
Total	0	20,800	52,000	93,600	124,800	26,000
Other expenses:						
Depreciation	16,250	16,250	16,250	31,250	15,000	15,000
Cannibalization	0	20,800	52,000	93,600	124,800	26,000
R&D to be incurred	0	15,000	10,000	15,000	10,000	0
Extraordinary expense	0	0	5,000	0	0	0
Project abandonment	3,000	0	0	0	0	0
Total	19,250	52,050	83,250	139,850	149,800	41,000
Overheads and expenses	19,250	72,850	135,250	233,450	274,600	67,000
Income before taxes	(19,250)	(41,650)	160,750	414,950	654,200	99,000
Tax effect:						
Taxes on income	(6,545)	(14,161)	54,655	141,083	222,428	33,660
Tax credits	(65)	(142)	547	1,411	2,224	337
Total effect	(6,480)	(14,019)	54,108	139,672	220,204	33,323
Cash flow:						
Income after taxes	(12,770)	(27,631)	106,642	275,278	433,996	65,677
Depreciation	16,250	16,250	16,250	31,250	15,000	15,000
Production facilities	50,000	0	0	45,000	0	0
Working capital: Cash	0	20,800	31,200	41,600	31,200	(124,800)
Working capital: Inventories	0	20,800	31,200	41,600	31,200	(99,840)
Working capital: Acc. Rec.	0	31,200	46,800	62,400	46,800	(187,200)
Net cash flows	(46,520)	(84,181)	13,692	115,928	339,596	492,517
Discounted flows	(46,250)	(67,888)	8,904	60,803	143,725	168,001
Net present value	$267,025					
Internal rate of return	73.7					
Payback	Nov., Year 3					

Test 1: NPV = $88,885
Test 2: NPV = $149,453
Test 3: NPV = $196,013
All 3: NPV = ($99,699)

Worst case is very undesirable, even here where indirect effects, sunk costs, and salvage were omitted.

Bay City Appendix: Financial Analysis For New Products

New products financial analysis requires two separate activities: (1) gathering the full set of data and other "givens" in the situation and (2) using them in calculations to derive whatever final figure is sought. These two tasks are shown in Figure 11–8 (the key data form) and 11–9 (the financial worksheet).

Compiling the Key Data

Economic conditions. Most firms have ongoing economic forecasts, but sometimes a team wishes to differ. If so, the difference should be noted here.

The market or category. The market for the new product is defined carefully, and the growth rate assumption is noted. Also, the current total market unit and dollar volumes are recorded.

Product life. The number of years used in the economic analysis of new products is usually set by company policy, but any particular project may be an exception.

Pricing. Start with the end-user list price, work back through the various trade discounts to get a factory net, then deduct any planned special discounts and allowances. The average dollars per unit sold is the price used in worksheet calculations.

Production costs. Is anything unusual being done on this project? Actual anticipated cost goes directly onto the financial worksheet. Cite factory burden percent rate.[14]

Future special expenditures. These typically include factory facilities, licensing rights, the one-time introductory marketing cost, up-front payments to suppliers, further R&D on improvements and line extensions, and plant expansions as volume grows. These are all *investment outflows.*

Working capital. This estimates cash, inventories, and receivables needed to support the sales volumes. How are they to be recovered?

Applicable overheads. Some firms assign only direct overheads—those caused by the new product (such as an expanded sales force or a new quality function). Other firms believe overheads tend to grow as functions of volume and should be included.

Net loss on cannibalized sales. These are dollar sales lost as the new product steals sales from current products. This is to be deducted from revenue. Some experts believe if we don't do this a competitor will, so they omit it.

Future costs/revenues of project abandonment. Along the way, the project may have accumulated facilities, people, patent rights, inventories, and so on. If abandoned now, disposal of these will produce revenue, money that is actually a *cost of abandoning the project.* But disposing of radioactive chemicals may be expensive, thus a *revenue* of going ahead.

---

[14]New thinking proposes that factory overheads be assigned using an Activity Based Costing (ABC) system. If adopted, new items have a greater chance of realistic allocations. See Bernard C. Reimann, "Challenging Conventional Wisdom: Corporate Strategies that Work," *Planning Review,* November/December 1991, pp. 36–39.

Tax credits. Federal or state incentives for activity in the public interest.

Applicable depreciation rate. Policy question, set by management.

Federal and state income tax rate. Company figure, provided.

Required rate of return. This one tells us the cash flow discount rate to be used, and can be complex and political. Theoretically, the figure to use is the *weighted average cost of capital,* including the three sources of capital—debt, preferred stock, and retained earnings. Often is simply the *firm's current borrowing rate.*[15] It may be the *rate of earnings from current operations.* New product managers want it low; conservative financial people may want it high. The actual rate to be used is often an arbitrary decision. Whatever the rate, the next step is to decide how the riskiness of this project compares with the rest of the firm's activities. Look at Figure 11–3, which shows that a relationship between risk and rate of return exists for every business, as discussed in the chapter.

Given the current average cost of capital and the level and slope of the line, the manager can mark off the risk of the particular new product, go up to the risk/return line, and then read off the required rate of return. Except in unusual circumstances, that required level will represent a premium over the current cost of capital. The premium is entered in section 14 of the key data form.

Risk curve. Figure 11–4 shows the typical **risk curve** of possible profit outcomes from a given new product project, as discussed in the chapter. In the B pattern, for example, chances are the project will have a lower payout, but a very high payout is also possible. Imitative competition is expected, but if it doesn't come the profit will be high. This risk pattern information is good to keep in mind when making the financial analysis, though few firms undertake the probability-adjusted risk analysis it permits.

Sensitivity testing. After an analysis has been completed using original data, the analyst goes back and recalculates the profit using other figures for especially sensitive factors.

Elements of strategy. When evaluating new product proposals, it is important to remember the strategy that prompted them. Less-profitable products may well be warranted under certain strategies.

Basic sales and cost forecasts. This section gives the primary data inputs. The number of units to be sold, the direct production cost per unit, and the total marketing expenditures.

Hurdle rates. A company sometimes has hurdle rates on variables other than rate of return.

Mandatory contingencies. A firm may want one or more contingencies worked into the analysis every time, not left optional.

Other special assumptions or guidelines. This is the typical miscellaneous section, totally situational.

---

[15]A variation on this is to use the current market risk-free cost of capital (interest rate on treasuries, for example). We then add a premium reflecting the general level of risk in the industry at hand. For this, and views on some of the other matters in this chapter, see Philip J. Eynon, "Avoid the Seven Deadly Sins of Strategic Risk Analysis," *The Journal of Business Strategy,* November/December 1988, pp. 18–22.

Beyond the key data form: sunk costs. Sunk costs should not enter into this analysis. Sunk money is just that—sunk. It stays sunk whether we go ahead at this time or abandon the project. **Salvage:** NPV forms sometimes call for the dollars obtained at the end of the product's life from sale of salvaged equipment. The amounts are usually small, and are best omitted. **Portfolio:** If the new item is playing a special role as part of an overall portfolio of projects the value of that role should be mentioned. The new project may be a high risk but still worthwhile to balance a large number of low-risk projects. Or the reverse.

CHAPTER

12 PRODUCT PROTOCOL

Setting

When a new products group finishes the full screen and the financial analysis coincident with it, they have reached what many feel is the most critical single step in the new product's life—more critical than the market introduction and more critical than the building of manufacturing capacity. This is the point where very important things *all around the firm* begin to happen.

Review

Granted, some managements still use a relay race system, where one department does its work, passes the product concept to the next department which does its work, . . . and so on. The leading product innovators do not—they use some type of **concurrent system,** one in which all of the players begin working from the onset, doing as much as they can at any time as the project rolls along. When technical work begins, process engineers do not sit around waiting for the final prototype to be tossed to them. When process engineers lay out the manufacturing system, procurement people do not wait to hear when certain components will be built. And as the technical/operations work continues, marketing people do not sit around waiting for a hand-off that will trigger their thoughts about advertising and customer technical service.

No, they all begin work at the same time. In fact, many have been watching the concept testing and screening to see how positive the early word is. If a concept looks like a winner, even if financial screening won't take place for a couple of months, these down-the-line people are already starting to do what they will *eventually* have to do. Some workers actually may be a year ahead of need, especially if there is some built-in delay in what they do.

For example, while process engineers wait for product specs so they can begin their work, packaging people think about the concept. Many products require packaging—durable, value-producing packaging or impressive shelf-talking promotion packaging. Packages, in turn, require product names. So purchasing cannot order new packages until brands are settled, and brands cannot be settled until product content is known and marketing strategy is settled. Marketing strategy involves price decisions, which must await costs, which must await final manufacturing systems and component costs, which is where this paragraph started.

What do we do? We do it all, side by side, doing what we can, when we can, making minor commitments at some risk, holding off on costly commitments.

Occasionally we do what one firm actually did—produced a product (brand, packaging, advertising, pricing, everything) while still waiting for a chemist to settle on the item's actual formulation. All of these efforts are risky and will never work well without *something that keeps the team together,* something that allows them to make reasonable speculations.

That something currently has no standard form, no accepted name, and no established practice. But most firms do part of the task, a few all of it, waiting for it to gel.[1] In this book we will call the activity *protocol preparation,* and the output is a **product protocol.** Other names the protocol goes by are *product requirements, product definition,* and *deliverables.* All terms mean the same thing—what is the final package of output from the development system—what benefits or performance will the product deliver to the customer, and what changes will the marketing program bring in the market place.

Use of the term *protocol* follows from its dictionary definition: A signed document containing a record of the points on which agreement has been reached by negotiating parties (*Webster's New World Dictionary*). The negotiating parties are the functions—marketing, technical, operations, and others. Signed agreement is a bit formal, perhaps, but the financial analysis which triggered this phase depended on certain assumptions—product qualities and costs, certain support facilities, certain patents, and certain marketplace accomplishments. If they are not delivered, all bets with management are off. Since most projects today involve some form of multifunctional team, the

---

[1]At the 1994 International Conference of the Product Development & Management Association, the following firms, among others, expressed activity in this area: Apple Computer, IBM, Quaker Oats, Compaq Computer, Hewlett-Packard, and PRTM Consulting. In a study on speeding up the new product process, the number one reason for product delays was poor definition of product requirements. See Ashok K. Gupta and David L. Wilemon, "Accelerating the Development of Technology-Based New Products," *California Management Review,* Winter 1990, pp. 24–44.

whole group is responsible for writing a protocol. Although new products do indeed require tradeoffs, they are negotiated in a very positive use of the term.

A word on the matter of negotiations. Negotiations here are not the adversarial activities stereotyped from labor-management struggles. But there are often technical limitations that may make quick agreement difficult. For example, customers may want a product that "removes all grease in 10 seconds." But technical people say no solvent can do this in a kitchen setting. So should they begin basic research? Management answers no, but asks what time frame is possible? Technical responds that they can't know for sure, but 15 seconds seems to be tops, given today's state of the art. Marketing asks if technical knows how they will achieve this? No, they respond, but it seems to be an achievable goal. This type of discussion may go on for days, as various customer requirements are dealt with.

Negotiations may sometimes occur between two desirable parts of a protocol. For example, a market situation may be so competitive that real innovativeness is necessary at this time, yet the firm's overall strategy may be to make more incremental advances. It's better to settle this conflict immediately. A review of minivan development at Chrysler showed how often Lee Iacocca and others had to fight traditional thinking in the automobile industry to really meet customer needs and desires.[2]

Protocol preparation is the subject of this chapter. In prior chapters you saw the new product process from an overall perspective—how the process moves from strategy to market success; how strategy gives the process focus; how concepts are first created and gathered, then tested and evaluated; and how the evaluation process comes to a temporary conclusion with the full screen and financial analysis.

Purposes of the Protocol

Figure 12–1 shows the role of protocol. In the lower half of the figure, a series of concentric rings represent the **augmented product concept.** The figure shows that the core of a product is end-user benefit, the real purpose for which the product was created. This benefit can vary from market segment to market segment, and from time to time. What the customer actually buys, however, consists of not only one or more core benefits, but also a formal product presentation (physical form or service sequence), *and* further augmentation that can range from presale technical service to a money-back guarantee. The point here is that customers and end users buy fully augmented products, and their core benefits may partly come from the augmentations. Thus new products managers cannot focus only on the formal product. All three of the concentric rings must be designed and executed, and two

[2]Alex Taylor III, "Iacocca's Minivan," *Fortune,* May 30, 1994, pp. 56–66.

FIGURE 12–1

The integrating and focusing role of protocol

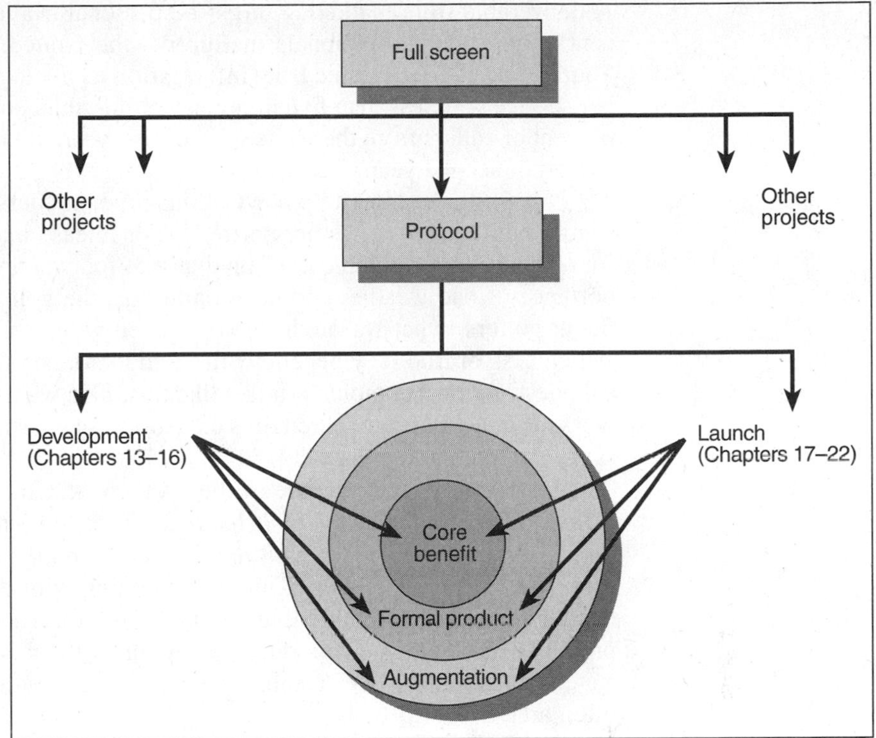

functional groups, marketing and technical, play a role in all of them, as shown by the arrows leading into the augmented circles.

Figure 12–1 also shows that the technical departments (with help from manufacturing, quality, procurement, and others) work pretty much as a unit, and marketing (with help from its allies in sales, market research, promotion, channel management, and others) does the same on the right side of the diagram. In addition, both groups keep in close touch with each other.

The first general purpose of the protocol is to answer the question: W*hat do these two groups need to do their work?* The answer differs by firm, industry, and situation, but nevertheless should be consolidated into a protocol statement. The protocol is, in fact, one step in the life cycle of a concept, as you saw in Figure 2–3 of Chapter 2. It is more than the simple statement approved in the screening and less than what will exist when the first prototype appears. But it is what we need now, what all departments need to begin their work.

This idea of how others use the protocol is what gave it the name *product deliverables*—what each department will deliver to the final product that the customer buys. For a new type of golf footwear, a deliverable from technical might be "can be used in all types of weather and on all turf conditions."

A deliverable from marketing might be personal trial use by at least 80 percent of the golf professionals in Europe, the United States, Australia, and South Africa. A deliverable from information technology might be "800 number service with less than five minutes waiting time, covering the needs of 80 percent of callers from the United States this year and from the other markets by end of second year."

Not all deliverables are known at this time, of course, but the critical ones should be. Otherwise, we are not ready for release into a system of parallel (or concurrent) development. If, on that golf footwear, we don't know the importance of bad weather and turf conditions, the golf pro's influence on affluent golfers (what we produce we can see will have to be expensive), the criticalness of trial (key benefits will be hidden), and the certainty of technical questions on a complex product like this, then we haven't done our homework. The fact is, protocol requires us to do what we should be doing anyway, such as good market research!

A second general purpose of the protocol statement is that *it communicates essentials to all players, helps lead them into integrated actions, helps direct outcomes consistent with the full screen and financials, and gives all players targets to shoot for.* This is in keeping with the product innovation charter you read about in Chapter 3, that clearly directs and integrates the new product team. Some new products people think the mere call for the protocol statement leads to early customer contacts that should always be made, but often aren't.

A third purpose of the protocol relates to length of the process, or cycle time. The Coleman Company recently told how they had used a better product definition process to help cut development time on a new home lantern from two years to one. On prior developments, they said, "We were always changing our minds and not getting anywhere." So the better definition "set clear boundaries."[3]

Fourth, if done right, the protocol makes requirements in words the results of which can usually be measured. It permits a development process to be *managed.* It tells what needs to be done, when and why, how (if required by some power beyond our control), by whom, and perhaps most important, whether. Thus, we know at any time whether requirements have been met. If there are still any unsatisfied protocol requirements, we are warned that we are not yet ready to market the item. Many of the techniques we have learned in preceding chapters (perceptual gap analysis, preference mapping, conjoint analysis) provide us with information that can be used as inputs to various requirements of the protocol.

In classic lay language, if you don't know where you're going, any road will get you there. Without protocol and its call for measurements, you've no idea where (or when) you will end up.

---

[3]Brian Dumaine, "Earning More Money by Moving Faster," *Fortune,* October 7, 1991, pp. 89–94.

Protocol's Specific Contents

You have just read what a protocol includes, in general terms. The details can vary greatly, and probably always will. We do know, however, that there is a scale of demand or commitment. Not everything we call for *must* be delivered. Some firms use the terms Must and Wants—that is, some requirements we must have, and some are simply what we *would like* to have if feasible and practical within technology, cost, and time frames.

Others have used such terms as *central utility factors* (CUFs), and denote the difference between must and want by hard and soft CUFs.[4] But each firm has its own language for these things. Some have put the musts in a protocol and the wants or hoped-fors in an attachment (or literally, in one case, on the *backs* of pages!).[5] The following sections list items often found in protocols, and an abbreviated version of a simple protocol is given in Figure 12–2.

Target Market

Most firms *manage* most of their new product projects using new product techniques we have been presenting: PICs, concept testing, screening models, protocols, and so on. Other projects involve *wildcatting*—betting on a technology that hasn't yet been shown to work, betting on a new application where an end-user will partner with us to see what works, or betting on a scientist with a good track record for coming up with saleable new products. None of these approaches is appropriate for a protocol; we just don't have the knowledge to write one, and if we tried to its only effect would be to bother the developers, who, actually, would ignore it completely.

In most cases, however, we know the target market very well—first through finding their problems to solve, later through asking if our new product concept meets their need and seems reasonable to them, and still later through screening factors (e.g., do we have a sales force that can reach them or will we have to build a new one?) Perceptual and preference mapping techniques we discussed in earlier chapters can be very helpful in developing this part of the protocol, as benefit segments will have been identified and their specific needs will be understood.

The target market needs to be spelled out here—specifically. Some firms like to have a primary target market, one or more secondary (smaller) target markets to move to after successful introduction, and at least one fall-back target market if the primary becomes infeasible or unattractive due to technical failure, regulation, competition, or whatever, during our development.

---

[4]Shad Dowlatshahi, "A Novel Approach to Product Design and Development in a Concurrent Engineering Environment," *Technovation,* no. 3 (1993), pp. 161–176.

[5]Puritan-Bennett uses one category of protocol benefits called "excitement needs," those that, if filled, would happily surprise the end-user. John H. Hauser, "How Puritan-Bennett Used the House of Quality," *Sloan Management Review,* Spring 1993, pp. 61–70.

FIGURE 12–2

Abbreviated sample protocol for a trash disposal/recycling system for use in the home

1. **Target market:**
   Ultimate: Top 30% of income group, in cities of over 100,000, with upscale lifestyle.
   Intermediate: Stakeholders in building industry for homes over $300,000, especially developers, architects, builders, bankers, and regulators.
2. **Product positioning:**
   A convenient, mess-free method for recycling items in the home.
3. **Product attributes (benefits if possible):**
   - The system must automate trash disposal in a home environment with recycling (separating trash, compacting, placing bags outside, and rebagging the empty bins and notifying user when the bag supply is running out) at a factory cost not to exceed $800.
   - The system must be clean, ventilated, and odor-free. The user will want an easy-to-clean appliance. Rodents, pets, and angry neighbors could become a problem if odors exist.
   - Installation must be simple. Distributors and other installation personnel must have favorable experience in installations.
   - The system must be safe enough for operation by children of school age.
   - The entire working unit must not be larger in cubic feet than twice a 22 cubic foot refrigerator.
4. **Competitive comparison:**
   None: First of a kind.
5. **Augmentation dimensions:**
   Financing arrangeable with us, if necessary. Generous warranty. Competent installation service, and fast/competent post-installation service. Education about recycling and about the product will be difficult and essential.
6. **Timing:**
   Being right overrides getting to market fast. But the window will not be open more than two years.
7. **Marketing requirements:**
   - Marketing announcement must be made at national builders shows and environment/ecology shows.
   - A new channel structure will be needed for the intermediate target market, but it will eventually be collapsed into our regular channel.
   - We will need a small, select sales force for this introduction.
   - To capitalize on announcement value, we need 50 installations during the first four months.
8. **Financial requirements:**
   - Development and intro period losses will not exceed $20,000,000. Break-even is expected by end of second full year on the market.
   - Ultimately, this project must achieve a five-year net present value of zero, based on 35% cost of capital.
9. **Production requirements:**
   - Once we announce, there must be no interruption of supply.
   - Quality standards simply must be met, without exception.
10. **Regulatory requirements:**
    Regulations are from many sources and vary by states and localities. There are various substakeholders here; we need to know them well. A surprise, significant holdup (after launch) cannot be allowed on this development.
11. **Corporate strategy requirements:**
    Corporate strategy is driving this project, and has personal leadership at the corporate general management level. We seek diversification of markets, enhanced reputation for innovativeness, and sustainable margins higher than those in our major markets today.
12. **Potholes:**
    This project has massive pothole potentials, because of its newness. The most worrisome ones are (1) regulatory approval of health issues, (2) accomplishing the $800 cost constraint, and (3) getting fast market approvals for early installations.

Positioning

This one is trickier, and is still difficult to use in some firms. **Product positioning** is a concept that came out of the advertising world about thirty years ago. Essentially, it says, "Product X is better for your use than other products because . . ." It announces the item as new and gives the end-user a real reason for trying it. In the process, positioning shows the end-user what problem the product attacks, and what about the product makes it better than whatever they are using now. This concept will be developed more completely when we get to Chapter 17, but for now it is enough to state the target market and complete that sentence above. Fortunately, this should be easy, because joint space mapping and other concept testing activities will have provided key information on desirable positioning options for our product. In effect, the concept test assures us stakeholders will be interested in trying an item and a positioning claim.

Technical people are often not told how a new item will be positioned. It's almost as though we say, develop a new item and do it in a way the customer will like. That's not management; that's abdication. Even in large packaged goods firms today, with their excellent staffs, products a bit off the beaten track often get neglected; many of these firms' R&D staffs have had to build market research departments to do concept testing on items they are originating. Misunderstandings on positioning have probably been the cause of more technical/marketing fights than anything else.

Product Attributes

As discussed earlier, product attributes define the product. They are of three types—features, functions, and benefits. Protocols can list any of these, and do. "The new bulk laxative will dissolve completely in a four-ounce glass of water in 10 seconds" (Merrill Dow). This is function—how the item will work, not what it is (feature) or what the benefit is of fast dissolving. Note that by being asked for speed, technical people were allowed to select any chemical they wished (and did, it is now second only to Metamucil in this market.) Stride Rite called for a new version of Topsiders by requesting that it "must not slip on polished wood at 30-degree pitch."[6] The protocol could have asked for a "safer" shoe (benefit), but they knew that slipping on a slanting deck was a big safety problem and the specifics helped technical. Benefits are the most desirable form for a protocol to use—better than functions or features. Information gleaned from conjoint (trade-off) analysis and other concept testing techniques can be extremely useful in determining what combinations of features, functions, and specifications ought to be built into the product.

[6]"Setting the Pace in Shoe Design," *The Wall Street Journal,* August 13, 1987, p. 21.

Functions. Function attributes sometimes cause confusion. Marketers tend to use them a lot, and they are often called performance specs, or performance parameters, or design parameters. One everyone knows is: "The car must accelerate from 0 to 60 miles per hour in 8 seconds." This requirement does not tell us what features will yield that performance. What it *does* do is answer the question of how the customer achieves the benefits of exciting (or safe) startups.

Some people feel a performance parameter (a function) may come to be expressed as a design parameter. For example, on the matter of the car pickup above, the statement might be "Use the new German 11-Z4 engine." Such a new engine would be a technology but clearly might be a *solution* to a need, not a *description* of it; there are probably many other ways rapid pickup could be achieved. Car platforms are heavily laced with such statements.

Protocols for services are especially likely to be stated in performance terms, since the production of a service is a performance, not a good. But protocols are also much less necessary on services because of the smaller investment in technical development. These producers can, in many cases, get to prototype very quickly, so that prototype concept testing or even product use testing can easily gain confirmation of customer need fulfillment.

Features. Features are also a problem. Technical people often come up with features first, based on technologies they have. A scientist at a firm such as PPG might figure out a way to make a boat deck out of finely ground glass left over from a production operation. The scientist may pursue the thought for several months only to have it knocked out by a shipbuilders' need for reduced weight. A full protocol statement might have avoided that waste of time. In another case, a scientist did in fact figure out a solution to a certain worm infestation in children, only to be told that this infestation occurs only on scattered Pacific islands and could never constitute a viable market for a pharmaceutical firm. That's why firms ask scientists to keep others informed and to seek input about markets being worked on.

The bigger problem with features is that they deprive the firm's most creative and inventive people of the freedom to use their skills. A large computer firm 30 years ago was known for having a strong technical research staff. They originated some useful technology. But the firm never achieved much success in reacting to changing needs in the marketplace. Some insiders said it was the result of a system that had a central engineering group take each situation and spell out the features and characteristics their research staff were to produce. One such spec sheet ran for 13 pages, and the scientist getting it said he felt like a beginning law clerk. He left the firm as soon as he could.

An extreme version of a protocol was reported by a pharmaceutical firm in which a new products manager sent a comprehensive advertising layout to his technical counterpart in R&D with an attached note, "Please prepare an item that will back up this ad." The first reaction was negative, until technical realized they were given carte blanche to do whatever they wanted, so long as the result met the listed claims.[7]

Occasionally, a firm knows from long-time market contact what features are associated with what functions (performance) and benefits. They occasionally will put through a work request that calls for "a new pump with electronic valves that give faster reaction to down-line stoppages and thus prevent blowouts." If the valves are standards, this protocol statement gives feature, function, and benefit.

Detailed Specifications. On occasions, customers make such decisions, calling for products with specific features. This can be dangerous. However, if the customers are qualified and have reason to know better than we do what features will do for them, we are wise to listen. In Chapter 4 we talked about getting finished product concepts from lead users (sometimes even a finished prototype).

Another case where features may be needed is where a firm is benchmarking competitive products. Their strategy is to have the "Best of the Best." Take the best features in the market, all products combined, and assemble them in the new product. This sounds great, but it means product design is being led by competitors, not end-users.[8]

Still other situations where features will appear in protocols are (1) where regulations stipulate a particular feature (e.g., prescription containers), (2) where end-users own major items of equipment that impose limitations (e.g., under-dash space limitations for CB radios), (3) where established practice in a customer industry is too strong for one supplier to change (e.g., for many years software makers had no choice but to use MS-DOS as a feature requirement," and regrettably (4) where upper managements have personal preferences.

In general, as a conclusion to this section on attributes, the best policy is still to write protocols in benefits, using performance if that helps explain and doesn't inhibit too much.

Competitive Comparisons and Augmentation Dimensions

Benchmarking has been mentioned, but there are many other competitive standards that can be put into a protocol—matching an important policy, the degree of differentiation to meet, and many aspects of the marketing plan

---

[7]One retired scientist creates laughter during his speeches when he refers to such "unalterable laws" as MS = MD. This translates into Monkey See = Monkey Do. "Marketing generally cannot relate to a product or product category that does not already exist." See *Marketing, a Bimonthly Briefing from the Conference Board,* December 1987, p. 4. The scientist, Raymond C. Odioso, presented the total set of "laws" in a Conference Board Research Management Report, according to the cited source.

[8]This is explained very well by Milton D. Rosenau, Jr., in "Avoiding Marketing's Best-of-the-Best Specification Trap," *Journal of Product Innovation Management* 9, no. 4 (December 1992), pp. 300–302.

(e.g., size of sales force, price, distribution availability, and more). Information on competitive comparison can be derived from perceptual maps, and the gaps appearing on the perceptual map can provide guidance on selecting an appropriate competitive position.

Just as the product itself was described in attributes above, the augmentation ring of the product can also be cited. Sometimes the product itself may be me-too, but still is a legitimate competitive offering as it may give the customer a new level of service, a better warranty, or better distributor support. Recall that there are three rings in the fully augmented product—ring one (core benefit) is covered in the positioning statement, ring two (the formal product) is covered in the attribute requirements, and ring three (augmentations) is covered here.

Marketing Requirements

Only in recent years have marketing requirements been seen as a part of protocol, so no widespread agreement exists on what should be in this section. One of the earliest public mentions of marketing requirements came from Apple Computer, around the time the firm was receiving the Outstanding Innovation Award from the Product Development & Management Association. These days, we hear about virtually every aspect of a marketing plan and its objectives. Here are some of them:

Trade show schedule.	Trial use to be obtained.
Trade channel, new form.	Availability level.
Trade channel, service output.	Repeat use, satisfaction.
Sales force, size, training.	Advertising break date.
Positioning awareness level.	Brand awareness.

In what is apparently the only research report covering marketing requirements, the authors found target markets, channels, and price.[9]

Other Components of the Product Protocol

There are several other components of product protocol that we will handle here very briefly. These are probably best illustrated through example, such as in Figure 12–2.

Timing. Most new products today must come out fast, but not all do. Some involve major technical breakthroughs that cannot be put on the clock. This

[9]Glenn Bacon, Sara Beckman, David Mowery, and Edith Wilson, "Managing Product Definition in High-Technology Industries: A Pilot Study," *California Management Review,* Spring 1994, pp. 32–56. The six firms studied so far were General Electric, General Motors, Hewlett-Packard, IBM, Motorola, and Xerox.

distinction needs to be clear to all. And if there is a date to meet, it should be specified here.

Financials. Typically, the protocol includes price level, discounts, sales volume, sales dollars, market share, profits, net present value, and many of the other financial data introduced in the previous chapter.

Production. These requirements are much like those of marketing, some focusing on what the function will prepare to do, and what that will accomplish—thus, plants to be built, volumes and quality to be achieved.

Regulatory Requirements. These are highly varied, but managements today understand the need to have advanced understanding of them.

Corporate Strategy Requirements. This area is growing, but most of the key ideas (e.g., core competencies) have already been captured in the product innovation charter, if the firm uses one. Development startup is too late for most strategic items. One angle that does come in at this time, however, and one important enough to list as a requirement, is upper management support assurance. It's easy to assume the team will have such support. And a new products team doesn't in any way "bring management to the mat." But managements should get a clear picture of just what is expected of them, as seen by the project people.

Key Potholes. This is not a fancy management term. It means just what it means when you're driving down the boulevard on a rainy night. There are potholes in product innovation—things can happen (though they shouldn't) that will bring a new product down. A management that doesn't take a good look ahead deserves to hit one. We don't usually drive into *known* potholes, so listing them here helps.

An Example of Requirements

The 10 items in Hewlett Packard's product definition were recently given as:[10]

- Understanding user needs.
- Strategic alignment, charter consistency.
- Competitive analysis.
- Product positioning.
- Technical task assessment.
- Priority criteria.
- Regulation compliance.
- Product channel issues.
- Product endorsement by upper managements.
- Total organizational support.

[10]As reported by Shiela Mello, at the 1994 International Conference of the Product Development & Management Association, Boston, MA.

Several of these items use company terminology, but the list indicates at least one firm that views the protocol as comprehensive.

Protocol and Quality Function Deployment (QFD)

Quality Function Deployment (QFD) was invented in the Japanese automobile industry years ago as a tool of project control in an industry with horribly complicated projects. It can lead to reduced design time and costs, and more efficient communication between project team members from functional areas.[11] In fact, QFD has been credited with a major contribution to the U.S. automobile industry's comeback against Japanese competition. We present it here, as it is one way in which many firms have fostered the kind of cross-functional interaction mandated by the product protocol.

In theory, QFD is designed to ensure that customer needs are focused on all through the new product project: product engineering, parts deployment, process planning, and production. In practice, the first step of QFD has received the most attention and has been useful to the largest number of firms, and that is the so-called **house of quality (HOQ).** The value of the HOQ to firms is in the way it summarizes multiple product aspects simultaneously and in relationship to each other. Figure 12–3 shows a sample HOQ for the development of a new computer printer.

The HOQ requires inputs from marketing and technical personnel and encourages communication and cooperation across these functional areas. Down the left-hand side of the figure appear the customer attributes (CAs), variously called needs, whats, or requirements. This is a critical marketing input into the HOQ. Compatibility, print quality, ease of use, and productivity were identified in this case as the most important CAs for a printer. CAs are identified through market research: focus groups, interviews, and the like. This section of the HOQ corresponds to the part of protocol relating to what the end user will get from the product. It is usually filled with benefits, though occasionally (as above), features are so mandatory that they are put there. The CAs in this example seem to be primary attributes; in a more complex application there may be secondary or even tertiary attributes under each. For example, ease of use might include "easy to learn how to operate," "easy to connect," "easy to replace the paper" and so on. CAs are also frequently weighted in terms of importance.

[11]John R. Hauser and Don Clausing, "The House of Quality," *Harvard Business Review* 66, no. 3 (1988), pp. 63–73; Abbie Griffin and John R. Hauser, "Patterns of Communication among Marketing, Engineering and Manufacturing: A Comparison Between Two Product Teams," *Management Science* 38, no. 3 (March 1992), pp. 360–73; and Abbie Griffin, "Evaluating QFD's Use in U.S. Firms as a Process for Developing Products," *Journal of Product Innovation Management* 9, no. 3 (1992), pp. 171–87.

FIGURE 12–3
QFD and its house of quality

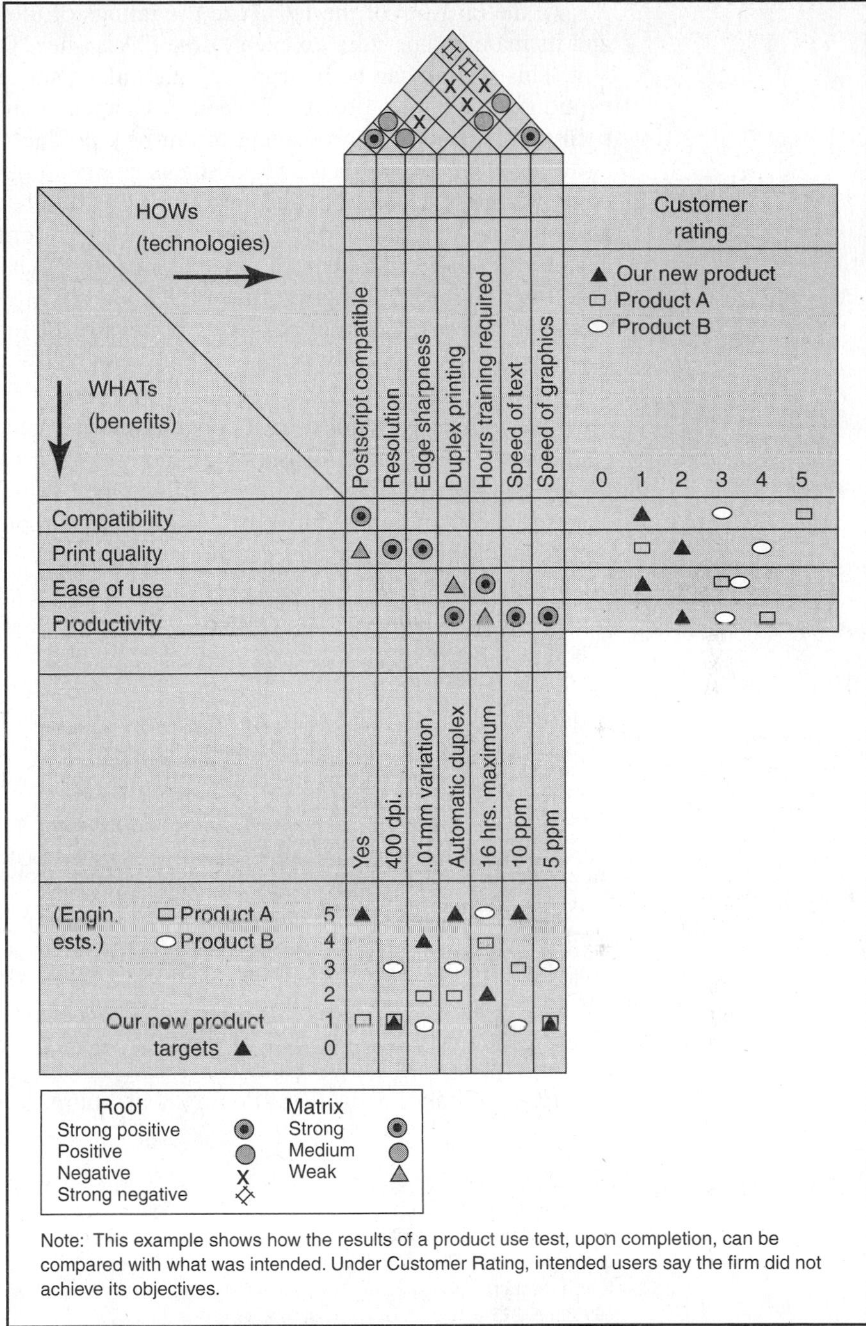

Note: This example shows how the results of a product use test, upon completion, can be compared with what was intended. Under Customer Rating, intended users say the firm did not achieve its objectives.

Source: This modified diagram is from Milton D. Rosenau Jr. and John J. Moran, *Managing the Development of New Products* (New York: Van Nostrand Reinhold, 1993), p. 231. Rosenau wrote an earlier book called *Faster New Product Development,* but the new coauthored book includes the acceleration materials.

At the far right of the HOQ are the ratings of the proposed new product and its main competitors on each of the CAs, where 0 = poor and 5 = excellent. This section can be interpreted much like a snake plot of customer perceptions, as we have previously seen in Chapter 6, and identifies the strong points and areas for improvement of our new product.

The upper section of the HOQ shows engineering characteristics or ECs: edge sharpness, resolution, and so forth. ECs are often technologies, but can also be stated in terms of performance or design parameters. This is where the customer's needs are translated into technical specifications. The project team goes through the central grid of the HOQ, identifying those ECs that will affect one or more CAs either positively or negatively. In this case, "hours training required" is positively related to both ease of use (strongly) and productivity (less strongly); "Speed of text" is strongly related to productivity. Obviously, this step requires real cooperation between marketing and technical personnel. Objective measures are then set for each EC (usually by engineers), and the team can now begin setting target values for the ECs based on customer need and competitive offerings. For example, speed of text can be objectively measured in pages per minute (ppm); and in this case, 10 ppm was set as the objective.

In the automobile example earlier of fast pickup speed, one CA might be "teenage pride among peers." Related ECs might be a new engine (a technology), the 0–60 time (a performance parameter), or a weight switch putting more load at the point of drive-wheel contact (a design parameter). Practice varies such that we can't give instruction here, but there are other sources.[12]

Finally, the top part of the house (the peaked "roof") shows the tradeoffs between ECs that technical personnel must consider. Each diamond in the roof represents the interaction between a pair of ECs, and the technical staff must identify each significant interaction. The strong negative sign at the crossing of "resolution" and "speed of graphics," for example, indicates that if the printer's resolution quality is boosted, it is likely to slow down speed of graphics printing. However, some of these interactions are positive: a single design change may boost both speed of text printing and of graphics printing.[13]

As noted above, the HOQ is really only the first part of the full QFD procedure. Figure 12–4 shows what comes next. The HOQ, which translates CAs into ECs, is linked to a parts deployment house, which takes the ECs as

---

[12]See Hauser and Clausing, "The House of Quality," for a general introduction. For applications, see John R. Hauser, "Puritan-Bennett, The Renaissance Spirometry System: Listening to the Voice of the Customer," *Sloan Management Review* 34 (1993), pp. 61–70; and Milton D. Rosenau and John J. Moran, *Managing the Development of New Products* (New York: Van Nostrand Reinhold, 1993), pp. 225–37.

[13]In a real-life application (iron ore products), increasing a metal's hardness reduces its malleability. See Magnus Tottie and Thomas Lager, "QFD: Linking the Customer to the Product Development Process as a Part of the TQM Concept," *Research-Technology Management,* July 1995, pp. 257–67.

FIGURE 12–4
Later stages of QFD

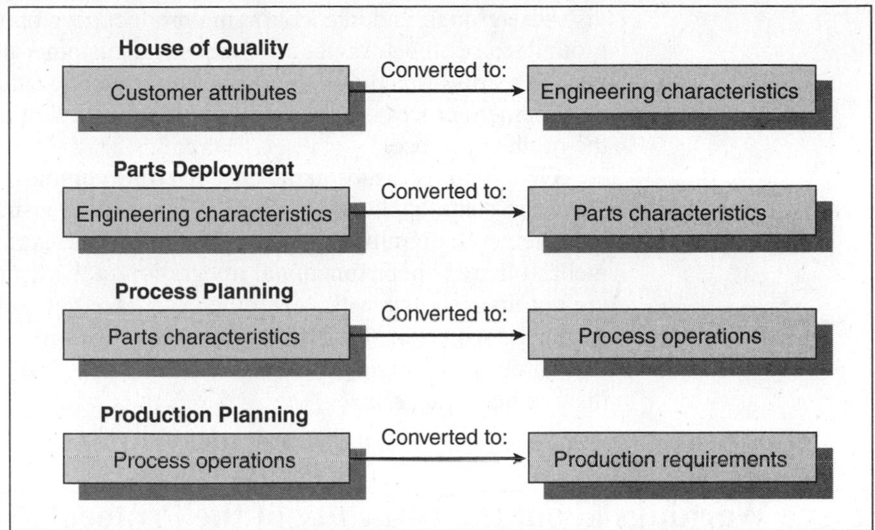

Source: Adapted from John R. Hauser and Don Clausing, "The House of Quality," *Harvard Business Review*, May–June, 1988.

inputs and converts them into parts characteristics. Subsequent houses specify the key process operations and production requirements.

In a very simple illustrative example, suppose we had decided on the concept of extra-hot green salsa on the basis of our conjoint analysis in Chapter 7. The CA of "extra-hot" might be translated to an EC such as hotness on a 10-point "chili" scale (where habaneros, the hottest peppers, are rated 10). We might aim at no more than 7 on this scale (as only the most daring would want salsa to be hotter!). Customers might have specified other CAs, such as thickness. The EC in turn suggest which parts—or, in this case, ingredients—to use: which types of hot chilis, how much tomato and garlic, and so on. Process requirements might specify what kind of food processing (chopping, boiling, etc.) will be involved. Related production requirements would be the settings of the food processing equipment that give the desired consistency and appearance. A setting of puree on the chopper might make the salsa too runny.

There are several benefits, then, of QFD. For one thing, everything—from product engineering to designing the production process—is driven by customer needs (or, more specifically, by the stated customer attributes). The likelihood that the product to be developed is one of those "better mousetraps" without a market is minimized. Furthermore, to get benefits out of QFD, the various functional areas really have to work together. This is especially an issue in the development of some industrial products. While consumer-good firms may routinely collect market data used in the HOQ, industrial product developers often question why they need to assess customer needs (or even talk to the folks in marketing)—after all, they "know the market!" QFD has been useful in such firms in promoting dialogue between disparate groups, and in encouraging product developers with technical backgrounds to see the advantages of assessing customer needs. In sum, QFD encourages cross-functional dialogue and interaction throughout the technical development process—which is precisely the kind of agreement called for by the product protocol.

QFD requires a substantial cost and time commitment, and has had mixed results in some applications. It is likely to be less successful if there is low management commitment, if it is viewed as an expense and not an investment, if there is poor functional integration in the firm, and if team members are not that familiar with each other and have not worked together before.[14] As can be seen from this discussion, its application can also be very complex, and on occasion, highly-trained technology personnel are not able to resolve the conflicts that arise.[15]

Some Warnings about the Difficulty of the Protocol Process

If the matter of protocol sounds simple, you have been done a disservice. It is very difficult indeed. For one thing, it is fraught with politics. The departments compete for power and budget. Key individuals are as different as night and day, being scientist, marketer, accountant, and factory manager. The situation itself is fluid and changing, seemingly never nailed down. Management senses the importance of the various projects and puts heavy pressure on them. A big winner on the product frontier can make a career, exonerate a general manager's other disappointments, award very large bonuses; and of course, a major failure can make a mess of everything close to it.

This means that people have their own agendas for incorporating (or not incorporating) into a protocol. Most want others nailed down to specific accomplishment requirements (with dollar signs and dates clearly attached) but with no similar requirements made of themselves.

Given that a protocol is needed early on, just prior to the start of broadscale work, many people are not yet on the scene. They have more pressing, near-term problems, so they delay the process, or weaken it by their absence.

But beyond the politics and pressures, we also see a hardening of the requirements in a protocol. People think they are all wise when developing the document, and presume the contents are set in concrete. But it shouldn't be seen that way. A protocol is an *aid to management,* not a *substitute for thinking.* All protocols have to change, some of them many times. The burden of proof rests on those who want to make the change.

---

[14]See Abbie Griffin, "Evaluating QFD's Use in U.S. Firms as a Process for Developing Products."

[15]See Magnus Tottie and Thomas Lager, "QFD: Linking the Customer to the Product Development Process as a Part of the TQM Concept."

FIGURE 12–5
Protocol Accomplishment

Requirement	*Company Call*	*Customer Call*
1. Reduce setup time	OK	OK
2. Lower initial cost	OK	Not needed
3. Easier replacement during manufacturing process	OK	OK
4. Safety in customer's plan	Doubtful	Later
5. Easier federal approval on finished item	?	Not needed
6. Lower cost disposal of trim	Vendor	Later
Date:		

Explanation: A form such as this, listing all protocol requirements, can serve as a good exercise for the team: How are we going to measure each of the requirements? Must we go outside? When do we do all this? Is a judgment call enough or do we need data?

Ironically, in some situations the protocol is ignored, so a smart new products team manager will prepare something like the protocol accomplishment form shown in Figure 12–5. It is especially needed for product requirements (benefits, etc.), and there should be agreement in advance about who is going to make the call on each. Some calls can be made by the team but others must be made by the person the product is being made for.

Along the way, bureaucracy sneaks in. One leading computer firm recently made a presentation on product requirements that must have contained at least 25 acronyms; the "sound" of that presentation was right out of government.

Last, most of these problems go away if preparation of a protocol is assigned to a multifunctional new products team. Technical by itself doesn't write one, and neither does marketing. Most assuredly, top management does not write one.

Summary

This chapter has dealt with a powerful concept—protocol. As an agreement among the functions about the required output or deliverables of a specific new product program, protocol sets the standards. Its purpose is to communicate the required outputs as product benefits and other dimensions, integrate the team, make clear the timing importance, and make it easier to manage the process against specific targets.

You saw a simplified version of a typical protocol. At this time we are ready to blow the whistle and charge into the development activity. Action will flow along three lines) the triple process talked about in earlier chapters—product, marketing program, and evaluation. Each line of activity has its own requirements, and they should be reasonably precise if they are to do their job.

Applications

More questions from that interview with the company president.

1. " Let's cut right to the quick on this one. I understand the theory of having benefits rather than features, but to me it is just that, theory. I knew one of the top people at that computer company your book talked about—the one where a corporate new product engineering group spelled out the specifications of each new product before technical work was funded. I heard the same criticism your author did, so I called this woman and asked her about it. She said the facts were right, but the implication was wrong—corporate staff did indeed spell out most of the features, but only to get the project moving. She said if they just gave their research people the benefits or needs of the customer, those dreamers would never reach a prototype. Every item would be a Taj Mahal. You know, I think she had a point. What do you think?"
2. "I really don't think you understand what parallel or concurrent new product development is all about. You said you had studied in your course that all of the functions get involved. No, concurrent development means just that—*technical development phases*—design engineering, and so forth. They are all doing work very much alike, they work with each other, they can feel how things are going and when they can take a chance and make a premature commitment. Marketing people can't do that. Even production people (process engineering) have trouble on this score."
3. "I've never liked that term *requirements.* It seems negative, like something imposed on a manager or department. Same as *deliverables.* Yet I sure agree that we should have targets for everyone in the new product operation. Maybe that term *targets* would be better. Do you have a better term in mind?"
4. "Seems one of our senior R&D people went to a new products management conference a while back, and he returned steamed. Called me for a talk right away. Now, you know what a protocol is, and so do I. But he didn't. At the conference a speaker said it was a device whereby the head of a new products team communicated to R&D exactly what was wanted from the technical group. R&D even had to "sign on the dotted line" swearing that they thought it could

be done. He said top management could give directions like that, but no new product team manager could. Said he used to serve on those teams and the managers were just facilitators, not really managers. They didn't have any authority. And he threatened to quit if I made him *promise* to deliver anything in particular. He used terms like stifling. I wish you had been in here that day. What would you have said to that senior scientist?"

CASE: WILSON SPORTING GOODS (B)

Glance back at the Wilson case, given at the end of Chapter 10. Assume that a new products group has proposed applying some new technology to bowling pins. Apparently they think that some space-age metals simulate wood very well and would give the pins much more "bounce to the ounce." That is, they would keep the basic weights and shapes, but permit more responsiveness, or action. Granted, the bowling game might never be the same again, but it would be a lot more interesting to hit the new pins than the current pins.

First, think about whether the protocol idea would fit the situation of these bowling pins. Then, write up five lines of benefits that consumers would probably stress if they were interviewed. Decide how you would actually measure whether the benefits were being achieved when the new pins were used in play.

Second, refer to the list of contents in a protocol and see if there are any other points that could be added to the benefits you just wrote out. There won't be many in a simple situation like this, but there will probably be some. Look especially at the marketing requirements.

FIGURE IV–1

Development

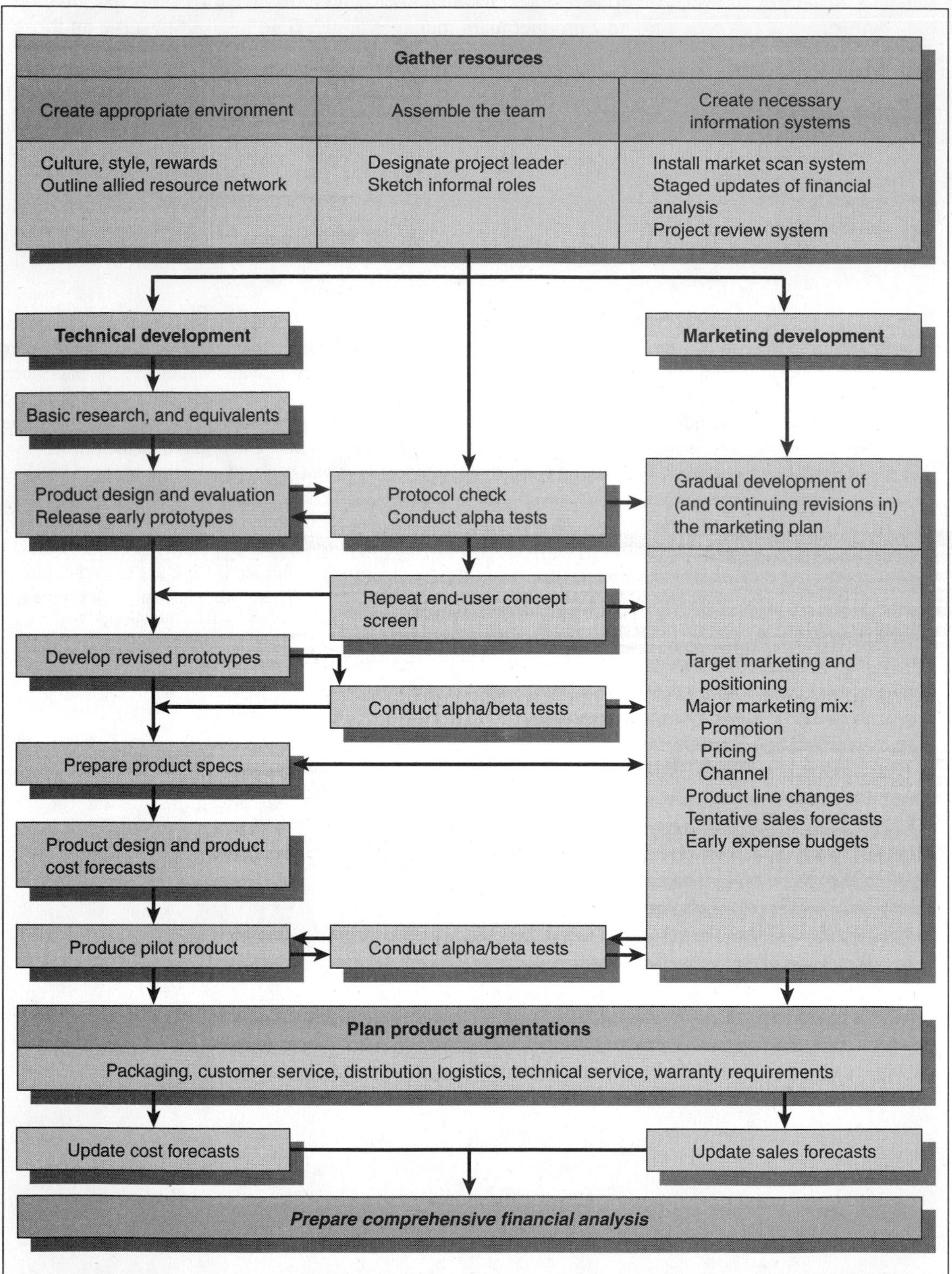

PART

IV

DEVELOPMENT

Somewhere during the process of creation and early evaluation, a decision was made to develop the concept under consideration. The decision may have come quickly (a key customer wanted the item and was ready to help develop it) or slowly, after concept testing and extensive review of required capital and operational expenditures. A product protocol was written, and an early financial plan released funds for the development.

The question now is how to fulfill that protocol. There may be extensive technical search (e.g., for a new pharmaceutical) or (as on service products) none. The key problem may be in industrial design or in the very technical characteristics of a 686 or 786 chip. Fulfillment may consist of nothing more than confirming a recipe that was used to produce new cookies for the concept testing. Or, as in the case of Frito Lay's O'Gradys, two years of technical development may be necessary.

This is the key creative stage, and there is usually a major art component, even when dealing in scientific areas. Progress in this stage has the attention of managers in all functions. No longer is technical work isolated between protocol and prototype, as when everyone waited for the classic slot in the R&D door to open and disgorge the finished prototype.

Development today includes creation of everything needed to *market* the product, including funding, distribution, promotion, and technical service. Look at Figure IV–1. The technical work (including design, engineering, and manufacturing) is displayed down the left side of the stream. Testing, marketing, and legal, among others, are displayed on the right. Both continue through the launch.

Several aspects of that figure may surprise you.

- First, note that what we commonly think is the technical creation task is just one box on a page with 15 boxes in the technical (left-hand) stream. That one box, in practice, is broken down into literally thousands of other boxes. Many firms use a project control system called Program Evaluation Review Technique (PERT) that was developed for the first nuclear submarine. In the automobile industry, a PERT diagram for just one assembly (e.g., the dash board) is so complicated that it cannot even be printed out on paper.

- Note, too, the large box at the top of the diagram. Getting ready to do technical development sometimes takes months—finding the people, acquiring the rights to certain materials, creating a particular culture, training the team, and, so important today, creating the information system to support the complex of activities.
- Typically there is not just one prototype. Sometimes there will be scores or even hundreds, depending on how lucky the team is. Granted, a new Frisbee with an edge shaped to grab a dog's teeth may be real progress for competitors in that sport, but hardly an afternoon's work for the designer. Edison was said to have tried hundreds of materials for the filament in the first electric light bulb.
- Developers must stop frequently to have their work checked—note terms like *evaluation, check, screen, test,* and *clearance.* Generally this is good, because to advance a design with a flaw is wasteful, yet to stop at every possible turn grinds things to a halt, including morale.
- The technical side is a *rolling evolution.* Even when an early prototype looks good, it must evolve into a tested prototype, then into a process, then into a pilot product, then into a production scale up product, then into a marketed product. This follows the same route as the life cycle of a concept that was diagrammed and explained in Chapter 2 on Process. We don't really *develop* a thing so much as we *evolve* one. There are fewer eureka's than people think. It's hard work, step by step.
- Note, too, how items on the right-hand stream associate with items on the left-hand. Thus producing a prototype may start design on a package, producing a scale-up product stimulates start on a technical customer service activity, producing a marketable product means a distribution network must be in place.

But rather than try to discuss both streams simultaneously, we cover marketing's role in the technical work here in Part IV and marketing's role in the other stream in Part V. Actually, we have been working on the marketing stream from Chapter 3 on—for example, target market is usually known at PIC time and new product positioning statements are used in concept testing.

Thus Chapter 13 talks about the players involved, the essence of design, and productivity in the development process. Chapter 14 covers the creation and management of today's cross-functional teams, and Chapter 15 covers the topic of speeded-up development and several other important aspects of the development phase. Chapter 16 tells how the team finds whether the latest prototype is indeed ready to launch.

Before we get into all that, however, let's be sure we know just what marketing's role is in the work that takes place on the technical side. There are nine important dimensions.

1. *To make absolutely clear to everyone what the protocol calls for.* What is the end point? How can technical groups know when they are finished?
2. *To make sure that this protocol task is technically feasible and doable within the time and dollars imposed by the development budget.* That is, do all technical people agree?
3. *To provide an open window for industrial and systems designers to all influential forces in the marketplace.* Marketing should not be a gate keeper, but rather an enthusiastic tour guide. It is truly in their best interests, and in the firm's as well, that all development effort (technical and marketing) be based on market knowledge.
4. *To provide a continuous interim of opportunity to pretest various versions of the new product.* This means to cooperate in early in-house testing and in later customer use testing.
5. *To be available to technical people at all reasonable times.* Some marketing people seem to forget that technical work is going on. A common joke in the labs is the scientist who left for lunch with the request to an aide: "If my product manager calls, get the name."
6. *To stay informed about technical progress, via team meetings, lab visits, social contacts, and so forth.* This is not spying. It is seeking an opportunity to pass along some market information technical people didn't know about. Well-led teams today soften this problem, but marketers have to learn how to be good team members.
7. *To involve technical people in the decision-making on the marketing side of the development stream*—especially any changes in the givens at the start of development, such as choice of target market. Again, teams help, but just as marketers can get distracted so can technical people. We have to show them why we need their input to matters they may not feel as important as the technical ones they are busy on.
8. *To stay continuously alert to the project's progress and to creatively find ways to help.* For example, in Chapter 15 you will see that marketing has many ways to speed up a new product's development. Saving a day in marketing may be as good as saving a day in technical.
9. *To flag the various ways that work in nonmarketing departments impacts directly on marketing plans.* This action, often called internal marketing, involves technical departments (for example,

technical information for sales brochures); manufacturing (for example, cost reductions and stand-by production capability), packaging (for example, promotion claims made on front panel), and human resources (for example, selection of new personnel needed in the launch effort).

It is the purpose of the material in Part IV to help you perform those roles, but be aware—the technical side of the development stream is immensely more complicated than most outsiders realize. Don't take the roles lightly.

CHAPTER

13

DESIGN

Setting

In the 1990s it was evident that product innovation in America and Europe took too long, far too long. There was also a concern about product quality. The result of these concerns is already history—redesigned work, customer involvements, high-performance teams, smashed bureaucracies, and a general new enthusiasm across the board. *Fortune* noted the change in a "Search for the Organization of Tomorrow."[1]

Some firms seem to have always done well. 3M was virtually born to free-form innovation. Merck learned how to manage its technical function in ways that unlocked innovativeness. And Rubbermaid, in the ho-hum market of housewares, showed what could be done when top management made a genuine commitment to the needs of its customers and to the design and manufacture of products that worked. Despite these successes, firms like these also experienced change. Market information began to reach all who needed it, technical groups created parallel and concurrent operations that devastated the historical linear movement of projects. One proponent called the new system a "seamless enterprise."[2]

[1]Thomas A. Stewart, *Fortune,* May 12, 1992, pp. 92–97.

[2]Dan Dimancescu, *The Seamless Enterprise: Making Cross Functional Management Work* (New York: Harper Business, 1992).

Variations in Development Semantics

The technical phase of a new product project involves an array of people, departments, and actions that absolutely defy definition. There is no reason to think that it will ever be otherwise, so we do the best we can.

First, rather fundamental creative technical work is done in different departments depending on the industry involved. Chemical and pharmaceutical industries use the term *Research and Development.* Research is the stage where a new chemotherapeutic agent is found. The activity may take a few weeks or 10–15 years. Development is the stage where the new chemical moves through necessary changes to meet market needs such as strength, form, delivery system, and so forth, and then is tested. This stage may also last many years; it ends with a complete set of specifications for which a manufacturing process will be created. But manufacturing people also do "development," with a little "d," that ends when the product is on the shipping dock ready for sale.

Second, there are industries where industrial design is the key ingredient—for example, in office furniture. Here there are usually no R&D departments and no basic research for new chemicals or materials. Instead, the creation of the new occurs in the minds of designers, and the end point for that work is again a set of specifications for production. However, the manufacturing departments still need to create their new processes, and the item again ends up on the shipping dock ready for sale.

In addition, development in one industry may be called something else in another industry. Arthur D. Little, a leading consulting firm specializing in the technical side of product innovation, provided the list of steps or product forms given in Figure IV–1 (in the introduction to Part IV). The steps are as widely useful as any, but keep in mind that the very next situation we talk about may use different terms, and no reader wants to stop for definitions at each situation.

The services industry is particularly frustrated (and frustrating) in this semantics minefield. Most of today's commercial terminology emerged in the era of physical things, so managers talked about prototype, working model, and so forth. Much of this doesn't fit service firms at all, although they tend to use established terminology anyway.

The leading term in all this confusion is simply **design,** including industrial, chemical, engineering, and service. Design will be defined and explained in the following sections.

What Is Design?

There is no doubt that top management sees the importance of design in boosting competitiveness. In half of the companies surveyed in a recent study, the CEO had primary responsibility for design decisions![3] But what is

[3]Peter Dickson, Wendy Schneier, Peter Lawrence, and Renee Hytry, "Managing Design in Small High-Growth Companies," *Journal of Product Innovation Management* 12, no. 5 (1995), pp. 406–14.

design? One writer defines it as "the synthesis of technology and human needs into manufacturable products."[4] In practice, however, *design* as a term has many meanings. To a car company, it means the styling department. To a container company, it means the customer's packaging people. To a manufacturing department, it most likely means the engineers who set final product specifications.

Design can be the basis for a total company strategy, or an afterthought where industrial designers are asked to "pretty up" a product that is about ready to be manufactured. Look at the long-term strategies of these two firms (in recent years they have begun to move toward each other):

Herman Miller. From its very beginning their strategy had been to invest in furniture designers who would, in their own ways, create new pieces of furniture for use in offices. Their new products program was totally driven by this commitment; there was little effort to study a product on the market and improve it. Their designers worked in the proverbial closed room, where the door opened every few years so a designer could hand to production a new item ready for sale. Top management stated market research was not the basis for new products. This rejection of marketing research as a conduit for customer input to development still lingers today.[5]

Steelcase. A much older and larger office furniture manufacturer about 40 miles up the road from Herman Miller, Steelcase was quite different. They were "metal benders"; that is, their strategy was based on their ability to manufacture office furniture that worked, needed almost no repairs, and lasted forever. They followed creative inventions of others. When Herman Miller came out with the office panel system (the Open Office) in 1968, and jumped out to huge sales volumes, Steelcase watched and waited. Eventually they entered the market with high quality product, lower costs, and better dealer organization, and captured first place in the market, outselling Herman Miller by almost two to one.

At first glance one might say Herman Miller was design-driven, and Steelcase was manufacturing driven. In today's language this would be wrong. Industrial designers do lead Herman Miller, but there are other designers—design engineers—who help make Steelcase successful. We'll see in a moment that the terminology is not very helpful to textbook writers and to students.[6]

---

[4]See Michael Evamy, "Call Yourself a Designer?" *Design,* March 1994, pp. 14–16. This article was part of a series in this publication, all on the matter of design definition. Useful also is Karl T. Ulrich and Steven D. Eppinger, *Product Design and Development* (New York: McGraw-Hill, 1995).

[5]For the argument that design people should provide the user focus, see the statements by one of those Herman Miller designers, Bill Stumpf, "Six Enemies of Empowering Design," *Innovation,* Spring 1992, pp. 29–31.

[6]See Michael Evamy, "Call Yourself a Designer?"

The Impact of Design

In a trend that is growing dramatically, design has widespread impact. For example:

- *On manufacturing,* where it saves time and cost, and enhances quality. No amount of factory automation can make up for poor design. On average, up to 80 percent of a product's cost is determined by the time it is designed.
- *On product use.* Well-designed products are easy to use and explain. No lengthy instruction books are necessary. No magnifying glass is needed to read labels on the product.
- *On service.* Properly designed, products are easy to install, maintain, and repair. Modular construction is more common than people realize, and sure to grow more.
- *On product disposal.* Products are now being designed with disposal in mind; for example, there is a technique called design for disassembly that permits products to be taken apart for separate recycling of metal, glass, and plastic parts.
- *On living,* well beyond what we think of as designed products—scenes, roads, parks. Most of our surroundings today are simply much more attractive than they used to be, and functional too.

In fact, Figure 13–1 shows the variety of design dimensions, using only the two criteria of "purpose of design" and "item being designed." Design is not simply a field in which artists draw pictures of new microwaves. It blends form and function, quality and style, art and engineering. In short, a good design is aesthetically pleasing, easy to make and use, reliable, economical to operate and service, and fits recycling standards. An excellent design can play a big role in determining how well a new product will meet the needs of

FIGURE 13–1

Range of leading design applications

Purpose of Design	*Item Being Designed*
Aesthetics	Goods
Ergonomics	Services
Function	Architecture
Manufacturability	Graphic arts
Servicing	Offices
Disassembly	Packages

Comment: Design is a big term, covering many areas of human activity, especially new products. The new products field contributes to two classes of items, and to all six classes of purpose. Some people hold that even the other four classes of items are really products to the organizations producing them.

FIGURE 13–2

The best product designs of 1997

- **Ford Ka:** Straight lines and angular appearance represent a bold move away from the "jellybean" car design typified by the Taurus. Cycle time (concept to commercialization) was only 24 months! Design, small size, and small price tag ($12,000) have made it a hit in Europe and plans for the North American launch are underway.
- **Apple eMate:** Dark green case and space-age look appeals to kids, from kindergarten to high school. Runs on Newton software which eliminates need for heavy disk drives and preserves sleek look. Designed for rough handling by kids. Price of $800 retail about half the price of a typical classroom computer.
- **Rubbermaid's Clear Classics Intellivent food storage containers:** A steam vent in the lid allows the user to transfer food from freezer to microwave without removing the cover.
- **Bissell's Little Green portable vacuum:** Not only designed to be easy to carry and use, but also to *look* easy to carry and use when seen in a retail store. This is an example of "Wal-Mart Design": keeping the needs of the powerful retail distributor in mind as well as the consumer.

Other winners: IBM Aptiva S Series and Coleman Safe Keep Monitors (both discussed in Chapter 5), Haworth Inc. (Office Explorations furniture), John Deere and Henry Dreyfuss Associates (Gator off-road utility vehicles), Samsung (Junior TV and Weeble telephone), Lexmark (Jetprinter).

Judges: Industrial Designers Society of America.

Source: Bruce Nussbaum and contributing writers, "Winners: The Best Product Designs of the Year," *BusinessWeek,* June 2, 1997, pp. 94–111.

customers, as well as retailers and other stakeholders, and therefore is an important determinant of success. Look at what Black & Decker did with the Snake Light. Another innovatively designed product is the Cross Action toothbrush by Gillette's Oral-B division. Researchers videotaped people using toothbrushes to determine actual brushing patterns, then built a robot arm to simulate brushing action. High-speed video cameras and computer imaging were used to test several different prototypes, and to arrive at the bristle configuration that was most effective in cleaning teeth.[7] For other examples of recent award-winning designs, see Figure 13–2.

The problem for new product managers is simply that design is too important to be left to designers. Historically, in the era of powerful functional chimneys and slow, linear, stage-based development, industrial designers dominated the action in most firms making tangible products. Today, they have to share this traditional role with several other functions, an example being where NCR Corporation hired packaging engineers and cognitive engineers (psychologically trained) to help design products that complement the way people think and act.

[7]Mark Maremont, "New Toothbrush is Big-Ticket Item," *The Wall Street Journal,* October 27, 1998, p. B-1.

The net result was recently expressed:

> Large multinational companies have begun to "unchain" product designers capable of bridging and building upon the expertise of both marketing and engineering. Working at last as equal members of multidisciplinary teams, under the new kings and queens of the product development process—"project," "product," or "program managers."[8]

Ironically, by "joining the team" and seeming to lose power, design stands on the verge of winning its ultimate position of influence. But it is the new product manager's task to bring this about.

The Players and Their Relationship

Confining ourselves now to the field under study (the development of new goods and services), let's look at the set of people who participate in the product design task.

Direct Participants	**Supportive Participants**
Research & development	Design consultants
Industrial designers and stylists	Marketing personnel
Engineering designers/product designers	Resellers
Manufacturing engineers and system designers	Vendors/suppliers
Manufacturing operations	Governments
	Customers
	Company attorneys
	Technical service

One model of how these people participate is shown in Figure 13–3. The representation there is somewhat linear, but with substantial overlapping or parallel effort.

It is easy to see how this model of operations gives people problems, particularly the designers. Industrial designers, trained to develop aesthetics (styling), structural integrity, and function (how the product works), directly overlap with the design engineers, who are technical people who convert styling into product dimensions or specifications. Technical people are not devoid of ideas on styling, and stylists are not devoid of thoughts on how the mechanics can work. This is especially true on common products (like shoes or dinnerware) where all parties have experience.

Another dimension of complexity is added by some of the supportive participants in the preceding list. Suppliers usually know their materials better than their customers do. That's why Black & Decker picked its supplier for the Snake Light before its design was finished. Large firms, for example,

---

[8]Christopher Lorenz, "Harnessing Design as a Strategic Resource," *Long Range Planning,* October 1994, pp. 73–83. The author goes on to make it very clear that he considers the industrial designer as the greatest among equals.

FIGURE 13–3

Model of the product design process

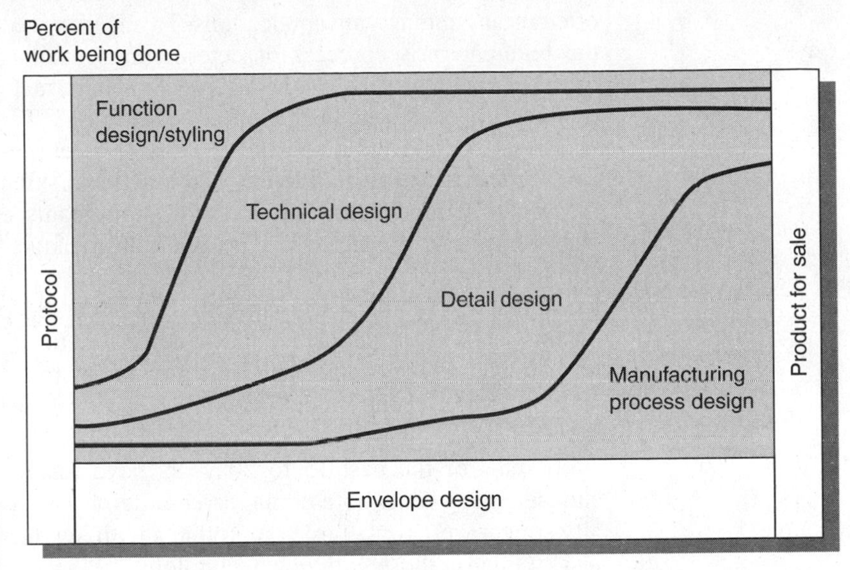

Development time scale

The members of a core team all participate in all four stages, but leadership in the first stage is often given to industrial designers, the middle two to engineering design, and the last to process design or manufacturing design. Terms in use vary widely. In chemical and pharmaceutical industries the design and engineering functions are replaced by research and development. And in some firms the term *product engineering* replaces engineering design; they want to contrast product engineer and process engineer.

For services, the same steps apply, but instead of a "thing" we are developing a service sequence and technical capability. Think of an investment service developed in a financial institution, or a cable TV system, or office design service.

Simultaneous with development (on goods *and* services) is the development of the augmented aspects of the product—pre- and postsale service, warranty, image, and so on. This activity, most often led by marketing people, is called *envelope design*, running across the bottom of the figure.

Philips, have the funds to establish large central styling centers where styling skills exceed those of the typical plant stylist. Customers almost always have overriding ideas to contribute. Consequently, the styling function is a synthesis of many views beyond those of the direct participants. If we add all of the other company people listed as supportive, we get back to the list of functions usually represented on the teams discussed in Chapter 14.

The result of all this can be chaos, and in general the problems are thought to be at the heart of why some countries' producers are so often beaten out by new products from Japan and Germany. In Japan, for example, product design means more than how a product looks and feels to the user; it often means engineering applications. To one observer, design in Japan "means the total-enterprise process of determining customer needs and converting them to concepts, detailed designs, process plans, factory design, and delivered products, together with their supporting services."[9] This merges a holistic view of end-user needs and a holistic structure to meet those needs. Design is seen as a vertical means of fulfillment, and individual skills are not central.

In the United States and Europe, participants end up playing musical chairs from one project to the next, as roles change. The most critical problem in the model of Figure 13–3 is faced by the design engineer, and we will get to that in a moment. But most discussion centers on the industrial designers (stylists). These people are particularly able to see things, both as they really are and as they might be. They also have strong problem-solving skills and are expert in the media (sketching, drawing, modeling) through which they communicate their ideas.

Events of the past 15 to 20 years have forced industrial designers to choose among four professional career alternatives: (1) stick to the traditionally sought we-do-it-all role on products with low technology, but back off to just styling on those with new technology; (2) study the necessary new technologies and continue the "full" design role, (3) convert totally to a stylist role (increasingly common among young designers), pairing up with engineering and systems designers; (4) permit themselves to be integrated into company teams.

A good example of the second choice is the designer who picked up computer and anatomical technologies and developed the first fully-simulated human hand, via computer-aided design.[10] The Chrysler development of its LH line is an example of the fourth alternative. It probably will be the role in common use, once the dust settles, though many design purists and traditionalists will fight a strong retreat action. Design and marketing operate in drastically different cultures, and cultural gaps are hard to erase.[11]

In some cases, designers take on an expanded role, as a liaison from end user to top management. Greater integration with end users can lead to better information about what design changes are desired. Designers can also serve as a conduit of information from industry, for example, making recommendations to the product development team on new materials to use.[12]

Both the design engineer and the stylist have been accused of continually trying to make a product just a little better, and refusing to release it for production. There used to be a statement around the auto industry that

---

[9]Daniel E. Whitney, "Integrated Design and Manufacturing in Japan," *Prism,* Second Quarter, 1993, pp. 75–95.

[10]Mike Jones, "Gripping Stuff," *Design,* July 1989, p. 487–88.

[11]Matthew K. Haggerty and Brian L. Vogel, *Innovation,* Winter 1992, pp. 8–13.

[12]See Michael Evamy, "Call Yourself a Designer?" and Jeneanne Marshall Rae, "Setting the Tone for Design Excellence," *Innovation,* Fall 1994, pp. 7–9.

engineering never released anything; the new car managers had to go in and take it away. Another derogatory way of putting it was, "There comes a time in the life of every new product when it is necessary to shoot the engineer and go into production." Otherwise, products have too many engineering characteristics or gimmicks, and are late onto the market. The quadraphonic sound system and the Xerox 8200 copier are products that failed to live up to expectations, partly because of their complexity. 1980s-era PCs could also fit in this category—Apple's initial success was based on its ease of use.[13]

The hard feelings sometimes run deep, and lead to cross-functional animosity. The Japanese showed the world how to handle this when they began freezing the specifications at an early date in the technical cycle, forcing later ideas to be put into the schedule for the next model.

Current Situation Is in a State of Flux

Most of the problems surrounding design concern concurrency—overlapping the steps in technical development. Designers of award-winning products have summed up what excellence requires of design:[14]

- Design from the outside in, customer's use being central.
- Partner deeply—with all relevant units of the firm.
- Partner widely—with all stakeholders involved.
- Define product up front—protocol and firm prototype, prior to ordering tooling and manufacturing.
- Get physical fast—prototype as fast as you can.
- Design for **manufacturability**—it's as important as ergonomics and aesthetics.
- Surprise the user—build something in that the user doesn't expect, deliver more than promised.

Produceability Engineer. But if there is no easy solution, firms cast about for other alternatives. One being tried today is the produceability engineer. This is an independent, third party who understands both design and production, and who can work in the design studios to see that production requirements are met by design decisions. Because the person is a third-party, turf is partially avoided. But it is not a satisfactory solution—today we know that adding another person rarely is. Effort continues.[15]

---

[13]Paul A. Herbig and Hugh Kramer, "The Effect of Information Overload on the Innovation Choice Process," *Journal of Consumer Marketing,* no. 2 (1994), pp. 45–54.

[14]According to a writer who studied winners of the 1993 Annual Industrial Design Excellence Awards: Bruce Nussbaum, *BusinessWeek,* June 7, 1993, pp. 54–57; see also Paul A. Herbig and Hugh Kramer, "The Effect of Information Overload."

[15]See Gerda Smets and Kees Overbeeke, "Industrial Design Engineering and the Theory of Direct Perception," *Design Studies,* April 1994, pp. 175–84, for ideas on how users deal with the expressiveness of products, and the impact of that on industrial design activities.

Benchmarking. Another trend is to use benchmarking. This practice of identifying the practices of successful firms has proven very successful but may not be good news to the designers. The benchmarks are sometimes laid down as product requirements, thus again restricting design freedom.

Market Integration. We also see many cases where the players in the design system do not get good participation by the marketing/sales/customer/reseller view.[16] Even when a good protocol is written, the designers sometimes ignore it in favor of their own criteria. As we have seen in Chapter 12, Quality Function Deployment has helped, because it begins with a set of needs (benefits) of the intended customer, and then integrates the technologies that will yield a solution to those needs in a way superior to competition. The customer's needs (counterpart of protocol) comprise an inherent part of the system and cannot be overlooked.

Vendor Integration. Another part of the model that is in flux is that of the vendor/supplier. Partnering upstream is not uncommon today—firms were first introduced to it in the early days of the Consumer Product Safety Commission, when they had to get vendors in line. They got another dose when such cooperation was mandated by the quest for product quality and Baldrige Awards. So the idea of cooperating with vendors in the development of new products was a comfortable one.[17]

Of course, there are security risks, patent uncertainties, cooperation that cannot be mandated in an emergency, and the like. But most companies tell us they are doing it, using the following tools in a style called integrated: reverse marketing, technology searches, demanding that suppliers value engineer their product, getting source guarantees, putting supplier people on the new product teams, cost-input analyses, contingency planning, employee rotations, and demanding that suppliers make a profit even if they have to tell them how to do it. Chrysler, as an example, has recently cut its supplier base, establishing longer-term relationships with its suppliers, and insisted on high supplier quality, in order to increase global competitiveness.[18] It is in any vendor's best interest to offer something an end-user genuinely needs, so both parties gain from integrated activities.[19]

---

[16]A strong plea for market information and how designers can get it can be found in Antonio J. Bailetti and Paul F. Litva, "Integrating Customer Requirements into Product Design," *Journal of Product Innovation Management,* January 1995, pp. 3–15.

[17]See David Asmus and John Griffin, "Harnessing the Power of Your Suppliers," *The McKinsey Quarterly,* no. 3 (1993), pp. 63–78; or Sang-Lin Han, David T. Wilson, and Shirish P. Dant, "Buyer-Supplier Relationships Today," *Industrial Marketing Management,* 1993, pp. 331–38.

[18]Jeffrey H. Dyer, "How Chrysler Created an American Keiretsu," *Harvard Business Review,* July–August 1996, pp. 42–60.

[19]The good and the bad of this partnership are shown in Fred R. Beckley, "Some Companies Let Suppliers Work On Site and Even Place Orders," *The Wall Street Journal,* January 13, 1995, p. A1.

Communication. The technical phase has long been a communications snake pit. When the different groups are not in regular contact and cooperating, there is a tendency for information to be lost (or hidden). This causes wasted work and slows the whole operation down. Further, research long ago showed that communication goes down with the square of the distance between two people,[20] so the problems intensify in large firms with their research centers hundreds of miles from the offices of marketers and the production lines of manufacturing people. Therefore, a key criterion for new operating systems is that there be open and frequent communication, which happens to be the greatest strength of the multifunctional teams we have been talking about in the last couple of chapters.

Many firms have tried **co-location** (i.e., putting the various individuals or functional areas in close proximity) to shorten communication lines and increase team cohesion. Motorola, for example, co-located its development team when developing the Bandit pager, completing the project in 18 months (less than half the normal development time), and Ford sped up time to market with the 1996 Taurus/Sable using co-location. Many other firms such as Honda, AT&T and John Deere have used co-location successfully.[21]

Co-location helps integrate departments and improve information flow, and also allows team members to identify and resolve product development problems quicker. It must, however, be carefully planned and handled. It is probably not a good idea to break up a center of technological excellence in order to co-locate its members. Too distant co-location (i.e., employees have to get in their cars and drive to another building rather than walk down the hall) might lead to team members "batching up" their problems rather than resolving them immediately. There may be an unintentional "home court advantage" (if the meetings are at the marketing facility, marketing team members may be perceived to be more powerful). And team members must be willing to tear down the functional walls and change their attitudes about working with individuals from other functions—otherwise, co-location facilitates social exchange but doesn't really achieve cross-functional integration.[22] In many firms, the effects of co-location are achieved without actual physical proximity of team members, using the resources of communications

---

[20]First reported by Jack Andrew Morton, *Organizing for Innovation: A Systems Approach to Technical Management* (New York: McGraw-Hill, 1971). Confirmed by T. J. Allen, *Managing the Flow of Technology* (Cambridge, MA: MIT Press, 1977).

[21]Anthony Lee Pratt and James Patrick Gilbert, "Collocating New Product Development Teams: Why, When, Where, and How?", *Business Horizons,* November–December 1997, pp. 59–64; and Kenneth B. Kahn and Edward F. McDonough III, "An Empirical Study of the Relationships among Co-Location, Integration, Performance, and Satisfaction," *Journal of Product Innovation Management* 14, no. 3 (May 1997), pp. 161–78.

[22]See Pratt and Gilbert, "Co-locating New Product Development Teams"; and Farshad Rafii, "How Important Is Physical Collocation on Product Development Success?", *Business Horizons,* January–February 1995, pp. 78–84.

technology such as Lotus Notes provides. This is sometimes known as **digital co-location**. As a final note, there is a recent increase in the use of **global teams** (that is, teams comprising individuals from at least two different countries). Improved information technologies such as videoconferencing, teleconferencing, e-mail, and company databases combine with phone calls and regular mail to make global teams an increasingly feasible option. Some believe that global teams will be more frequently used than co-location in the near future.[23]

Computer-Based Design Technology. Another development is helping to bring people together and at the same time show the importance of all players. That is the technology of the acronyms: CAD (computer-aided design), CAM (computer-aided manufacturing), CAE (computer-aided engineering), DFM (design-for-manufacturing, sometimes called DFA, design-for-assembly), and variations.

These technologies offer lots of advantages—people have to work together to understand and use them, they force the integration of all needs into one analytical set, they are fast, and they do more than the human can do alone even if there were ample time. They also help improve the images of team players who may lack status. For example, manufacturing used to have to take a back seat to design and marketing. It was uncommon in many firms for the factory people even to be invited to meetings; they were expected to take what came from design and make it, somehow. In most firms that time is gone, and it should be in all firms.

CAM can be used to check the feasibility of a product design and to make design changes easily where necessary. Boeing, for example, used CAM in its design of the 777. They simulated climbing into the newly-designed aircraft for maintenance using a computer-generated "human"—and found that one of the navigation lights would have been hard for a real serviceperson to reach. There was no need to build an expensive prototype to find this flaw, and the fixup was easily made.[24]

One innovation in this area is getting the most attention. It is DFA, a complex and expensive program that takes whatever the designer has designed and tells how it fits with the manufacturing facility. There are now several versions, but the first one came from Boothroyd & Dewhurst, a Rhode Island software firm. By programming in the manufacturing conditions and information about the particular assembly operation (whether furniture, cars on an assembly line, or whatever), the DFA program can react to any design proposal with information about its time and cost result. It also points out the

---

[23]Edward F. McDonough III, Kenneth B. Kahn, and Gloria Barczak, "Effectively Managing Global New Product Development Teams," *Proceedings,* 1998 Research Conference, Product Development & Management Association, pp. 176–88.

[24]Marco Iansiti and Alan MacCormack, "Developing Products on Internet Time," *Harvard Business Review,* September–October 1997, pp. 108–17.

major design elements contributing to slow time or high cost, so the designer can work directly on them.

Unfortunately, the designer does not have comparable software that would be called DFM (design-for-marketing). Unless the protocol is very clear and accepted, or unless marketing or customer people are present during the design process, developers may be acting favorably to factory time/cost but unfavorably to customer value and usefulness.

Other examples of current progress are (1) stereolithography and (2) MCAE (mechanical computer-aided engineering). Stereolithography is software that in just one to three days can convert a container of liquid into a hard plastic prototype. The process, which used to take a modeler several weeks, sends "hardening" beams of electrons into the container causing the liquid to solidify in tiny bits at a time, yielding very precise models.

MCAE permits engineers to test before they build, with all criteria being considered. It's a type of simulation that plays "what if" games with a design.[25]

Productivity

Before going into the matter of teams (Chapter 14) let's look at something that new products people are thinking especially hard about today. It is vital to marketing people, as well as to technical.

Everyone seems to agree that we must destroy oppressive bureaucracy in the new products operation. Of course, any organization, even on a kids' baseball diamond, needs some bureaucracy, and even venture teams that have been spun out from their firms need a little. It is a glue, and its policies reduce the time spent on routine decisions.

But consider John A. Young. As CEO of Hewlett-Packard, he managed one of the world's most successful innovation factories. But things had started to slow down; customers commented on how long proposals took. Young discovered that a new product required contacts with no fewer than 38 committees. Just for a *new name* on the firm's NewWave Computing software the project manager had to work with nearly 100 people on nine committees. That is oppressive bureaucracy. H-P's "penchant for egalitarianism and mutual respect had led them into a quagmire of consensus."[26] Today an H-P new products manager may be able to get by with only three committees to worry about.

A consulting firm analyzed H-P's problem and found these causes: unwritten rules of the game, awkward engineering organization, ineffective

[25]See Otis Port, "A Smarter Way To Manufacture," *BusinessWeek,* April 30, 1990, pp. 110–17 and R. Van Dierdonck, "The Manufacturing/Design Interface," *R&D Management,* no. 3 (1990), pp. 203–9.

[26]Barbara Buell, "Hewlett-Packard Rethinks Itself," *BusinessWeek,* April 1, 1991, pp. 76–79.

program management, lack of discipline in work schedules, excessive hand-offs, and general lack of sharp performance in every single aspect of the technical development operation.[27] Most participants are now convinced that they need to measure things better—how long does something take, what does doing that particular step cost? These measurements are called **metrics,** and new products management is using them increasingly. A complex development system, along the lines of the diagram in the Part IV introduction, can create the need for thousands of metrics. And then, to judge how well you are doing leads to gathering similar numbers from successful firms. This is the heart of the benchmarking systems we have heard so much about.

Interestingly, managements are not reaching out for more formality, more system, more standard methods of doing things. Quite the opposite. For example, one new product management system widely hailed the past 10 years has been that of **stage-gate,** with **phased reviews** where set deliverables are checked by top management. The creator of the term has been studying managements again, and now sees a much looser, fluid, more adaptive, and less procedural process being used.[28] This is reflected in the chapters in Part IV, but actually throughout this book as well.

Summary

This chapter has dealt with the design process, the people and the activities. Design is many-faceted, so is different from one industry to another. Marketing people have found it important to be flexible here, helping to shape a role for design that fits each situation and corporate policy. But in most firms, design joins manufacturing and other functions to form a working, multifunctional group (usually a team), and in Chapter 14 we will look at its structure and management.

Applications

More questions from that interview with the company president.

1. "One of our divisions makes an electric scooter. Classic case of where a designer, looking for new modes of ultralight transportation, came across the scooter and electrified it. Boy, people said he was crazy. Kids begged their parents not to ride one (shame), and a cop said, 'It's not a moped. It's not a motorcycle. It's not anything, and I don't ride

---

[27]Michael S. Rosenberg and Bruce McK. Thompson, "Rooting Out the Causes of Inefficient Product Creation," *Prism* (Arthur D. Little external house organ), Second Quarter, 1993, pp. 97–111.

[28]Robert G. Cooper, "Third Generation New Product Processes," *Journal of Product Innovation Management,* January 1994, pp. 3–14.

anything when I'm not sure what it is.'[29] Best example I know of why designers have to be free to do their thing, without having market researchers be responsible for picking up on market trends."

2. "Most of our divisions believe in customer integration—involving the user in the new product process. I am a fanatic on it. But some people want us to carry this right into the technical design phase. This would be dangerous. A lot of what we do must be secret—we can't patent most of our ideas, and timing is everything. That's why we put so much emphasis on speed of development. But I still get pushed to do more. Help me. Tell me all the things we might do to get integrated customers but at the same time minimize the risks of losing our secrets."
3. "About this matter of design, I am stumped. I agree design is critical today, and I always support it. But, you've got to admit that industrial designers sometimes get into arguments with the engineers who are trying to make products as functional as possible. For example, I once saw a beautifully styled computer mouse that had lost its ergonomic value. As a general executive matter, how do you suggest we evaluate these trade-offs? How can we find where to stop styling and let the engineers rule?"
4. "You said a moment ago that you read about the role of marketing people relative to the technical development stage. This could be very useful to me, if it makes any sense. Take two of our divisions. One makes tough shredders especially for use in business—here's a list of items one shredder was recently used for: mismanufactured Oscar statutes, police uniforms, denture molds, Big Bird dolls, crack vials, discontinued postage stamps, you name it. The other division makes sippy cups—you know, those plastic cups with spill-proof lids and a drinking spout? But their cups are specially designed for special situations: hiking, hospitals, flying, bus rides, football games, and so forth. They're all a bit different, somewhat in function but mainly in styling. Would the role of marketing people (during the technical development stage) be the same in these two divisions?"

Case: Gillette MACH3[30]

For decades, The Gillette Company has followed a simple strategy for success: replace excellent blade technology with an even better one. Over the years, Gillette has brought us the Blue Blade, the Platinum Plus, the Trac II, the Atra, the Sensor, then the SensorExcel.

---

[29]Joseph Pereira, "Guffaws Aside, New Scooter Makers Zip Ahead," *The Wall Street Journal,* August 20, 1998, p. B-1.

[30]This case is based on Mark Maremont, "How Gillette Brought Its MACH3 To Market," *The Wall Street Journal,* April 15, 1998, p. B-1.

In April 1998, Gillette announced the next generation of razor: a three-bladed pivoting cartridge system called the MACH3.

The idea of a three-bladed system was being investigated by Gillette engineers as early as 1970, without much success: they irritated the skin, yet didn't produce a closer shave. During the 1970s and 1980s, they launched the twin-bladed Atra, and the Sensor, which had its blades mounted on tiny springs, meanwhile continuing the design work on the three-bladed system.

By the early 1990s, the design problems that had stalled the three-bladed system had been overcome. A prototype three-bladed razor (code-named the Manx) was developed, and shown to outperform the Sensor in internal tests. A key element of the Manx's design was the positioning of the three blades: each blade was a little closer to the face than the previous one. This patented design reduced the irritation caused by the third blade. In addition, the pivot point was moved to the bottom of the cartridge (those familiar with Sensor know that its pivot point is in the middle of the cartridge). The new pivot point made shaving feel a little like using a paintbrush, added to the cartridge's stability, and ensured that the bottom edge of the cartridge always touched the face first (ensuring that hairs were lifted properly). Other design features were also built into the Manx. To the white lubricating strip found on the Sensor, a blue indicator was added that gradually faded, indicating when the blade needed to be changed. And engineers were working on better blades, perfecting a way to make them thinner and harder, thanks to new metal technology borrowed from the manufacture of semiconductors. Furthermore, consumer studies found an interesting problem incurred by Sensor users that suggested a potential product improvement: 18 percent of men put the cartridge on the razor upside down! A new snap-in mechanism was developed that would only work in the right direction.

Unfortunately, the new design was going to be costly to manufacture. There was internal resistance within the ranks of Gillette, with some managers believing that the company should go with a less-revolutionary, three-bladed SensorExcel rather than a costly and risky introduction of a totally new product. Alfred N. Zeien, Gillette's CEO and an engineer by training, favored the new design, believing that the best chance for a sure winner was to go with the most technologically-advanced design. Michael T. Cowhig, director of manufacturing for the North Atlantic group, felt that the new metal technology, excellent for making computer chips, would not be ready to make blades, especially in the numbers Gillette expected to sell annually. He said, "I knew we could make one blade; I didn't know if we could make 3.6 billion." His assessment was that the MACH3 blade would cost about 50 percent more to manufacture than SensorExcel, the premium Gillette blade at the time.

Nevertheless, the new design (now called by the code name 225) was locked in during the month of April 1995. The next three years were spent in designing and producing the equipment needed to manufacture the new cartridges—most of the machinery had to be specially designed for the task. Meanwhile, product use tests with consumers were showing that the MACH3 was outperforming the SensorExcel 2 to 1, and doing even better against competitive brands. The consumer tests were also suggesting that users were fairly insensitive to price—the MACH3 tested well even at a 45 percent price premium over SensorExcel.

Gillette geared up for an April 1998 launch. All told, the MACH3 development took six years and $750 million, about four times what the Sensor cost. Further, $300 million was allocated for marketing in the first year ($100 million in the United States and $200 million elsewhere), so the up-front costs broke the billion dollar barrier. The rollout began in the United States, Canada, and Israel in July 1998, then Western Europe and part of

Eastern Europe in September. The plan was to have the MACH3 available in about 100 countries by the end of 1999. By comparison, the Sensor (largely regarded as a global marketing success) needed five years to reach that level of distribution. To accommodate the rollout, production ramp-up was targeted to 1.2 billion cartridges per year by the end of 1998. The price point was set high (about 35 percent above the SensorExcel's price of $1 per blade; sticker shock was reduced by putting fewer blades in each pack. At the time, at least one industry expert, Pankaj Ghemawat of Harvard, was saying that even SensorExcel's price was "outrageous," though Zeien and other top Gillette executives believed that the MACH3 was so good, it would sell itself.

Based on what you see in this case, what strategic role did design play at Gillette? What are the risks involved in the decision to go with the really new MACH3 design, versus making incremental design improvements to the older SensorExcel technology? Play the role of both Mr. Zeien and Mr. Cowhig. And what about that aggressive marketing and rollout plan? Would you recommend they take it slower? What are the pros and cons?

CHAPTER 14

Development Team Management

Setting

In Chapter 14, we focus our attention on the **team,** a form of management now a given in less routine new product processes. The subject of team management is a difficult one. Team structure and management fills the business literature.[1] We know so much, yet we seem to know so little. There is a growing conviction that most team management is the same as individual management; good business common sense seems to prevent most big problems.[2]

What Is a Team?

Describing, building, and managing teams is treacherous, because there are teams, and teams, and teams. Drucker focused on the dilemma when he talked about sports teams:[3]

- *Baseball teams:* They are like assembly line "teams." Their work fits together, and all the players are needed, but they generally work as

[1]Two excellent examples are: Shona L. Brown and Kathleen M. Eisenhardt, "Product Development: Past Research, Present Findings, and Future Directions," *Academy of Management Review,* no. 2, 1995, pp. 343–78; and Ann Donnellon, "Crossfunctional Teams in Product Development: Accommodating the Structure to the Process," *Journal of Product Innovation Management,* November 1993, pp. 377–92.

[2]An example of the newer viewpoint is Brian Dumaine, "The Trouble with Teams," *Fortune,* September 5, 1994, pp. 86–92.

[3]Peter F. Drucker, "There's More Than One Kind of Team," *The Wall Street Journal,* February 11, 1992, p. A16.

individuals, in their own ways. The double-play combo is a clear exception. Work is generally in a series.

- *Football teams:* These have fixed positions, but they play as a team. Japanese car teams are of this type. Work is parallel, not series. But one player does not come to the aid of another.
- *Tennis doubles teams:* The players work with and support each other. The result is important only as the team scores a point or wins a match. Partners are dedicated. Volleyball teams are another example, as is the jazz combo.

Baseball and football managers are quite strong, but there are no tennis doubles managers. Some training people feel that volleyball is the best analogy for today's teams; there are more players, they develop skills at all positions, and the very unique role for the manager is comparable to that of the new product team manager.

The new products team is so far from the traditional and comfortable hierarchical world that there is great learning required, a shortage of people who currently know how to play the game, and performance appraisal is tough because only the team's overall performance matters. It offers the greatest risk to upper level managements. Since the team members all have different backgrounds and play different roles, there is no one to "score" them against.

Structuring the Team

The new products organization can be structured in many ways. One useful listing of **organizational structure options** is shown in Figure 14–1. The options shown in this figure can be thought of as five segments of a continuum: the farther across the figure, the greater is the commitment of company personnel to the new product project.[4]

The first option, **functional,** means the work is done by the various departments, with very little project focus. There usually is a new products committee or a product planning committee. The work is usually low risk and probably involves the present line of products—improvements, new sizes, and so on. The ongoing departmental people know the market and the business;

[4]New product organizational options have been expressed in scores of ways. But only one listing came from empirical research on the form and on the success or failure of actual new product projects. It was originally stated in David H. Gobeli and Eric W. Larson, "Matrix Management: More than a Fad," *Engineering Management International,* 1986, pp. 71–76. The only change is that what the authors called project team is here called venture to reflect recent preferences. The same authors also later published a much larger empirical study on the same subject: Erik W. Larson and David H. Gobeli, "Organizing for Product Development Projects," *Journal of Product Innovation Management,* September 1988, pp. 180–90.

FIGURE 14–1

Options in new products organization

Options				
Functional With or without committee	*Functional matrix*	*Balanced matrix*	*Project matrix*	*Venture* Inside Outside

0% ________ 20% ____________ 40% ____________ 60% ____________ 80% ________ 100%

Degree of projectization*

*Defined as the extent to which participants in the process see themselves as independent from the project or committed to it. Thus, members of a new product committee are almost totally oriented (loyal) to their functions or departments; spinout (outside) venture members are almost totally committed to the project.

they can get together and make the necessary decisions easily and effectively. Literally, the functional people working on a project are a group, but they are not a team.

Of course, not much innovation occurs that way. So we have the other four options—and all of these are teams of one type or another. Three of them (in the middle of Figure 14–1) are matrix variations. If the people on the optical scanner project in Figure 14–2 get together to make some decisions, they may be 50/50, or the power may lean toward the head of the functional department, or it may lean toward the project manager. Leaning toward the project is called **projectization,** as defined in Figure 14–1.

The **functional matrix** option has a specific team, with people from the various departments (such as manufacturing, R&D, marketing, and finance), but the project is still close to the current business. It requires more focus than routine product improvements, but the departments call the shots. Team members think like functional specialists, and their bosses back in the departments win most of the face-offs.

The **balanced matrix** option is for situations where both functional and project views are critical—neither ongoing business nor the new product should be the driver. This traditional matrix was for a long time held in disfavor for new products because either the new product required push or it didn't. Using 50/50 thinking would just make for indecision and delay. Texas Instruments used balanced matrix for many years in its product innovation—and then discarded it for just this reason.[5] But today's managers have apparently found ways to make it work. See Figure 14–3 for recent data.

[5]"An About-Face in TI's Culture," *BusinessWeek,* July 5, 1982, p. 77, and Bro Uttal, "Texas Instruments Regroups," *Fortune,* August 9, 1982, pp. 40–45.

FIGURE 14–2

The matrix concept of business organization

Program/Project Leader	*Marketing*	*R&D*	*Manufacturing*	*Finance*	*Others*
Boltron project Gary Shilling	Ron Thomas	Fred Mansfield	Jim Swaston	Christi Statler	—
Gates project Beth Politi	Ron Thomas	Dennis Hilger	Mary Morrison	Hartmut Richert	—
Optics program Barb Mertz	Kirk Weirich	Dennis Hilger	Ken Fedor	Heather Dumont	—
Tenson project Andy Anderson	Gideon Feldkamp	Lucy Mazrui	Jim Swaston	Heather Dumont	
Bell-tron project K. C. Gupta	Loretta Berigan	Sabine Klein	Ken Fedor	Coyne Grady	—
Others	—	—	—	—	—

Explanation: For the Boltron project, Gary Shilling is the leader, also called manager, coordinator, and so on. Ron Thomas is on the team representing marketing, Fred Mansfield for R&D, Jim Swanson for manufacturing, and Christi Statler for finance. Functional people often represent their departments on more than one team—see Dennis Hilger and Heather Dumont. If a project uses a functional format or a venture (see Figure 14–1), there really is no matrix. Otherwise, all people in the functional columns are like Loretta Berigan, who reports to K. C. Gupta for the Bell-tron project and to her department head for the function. When their wishes intersect, she must work her way through the differences to avoid a timely or costly conflict.

FIGURE 14–3

Performance success of the five organizational options

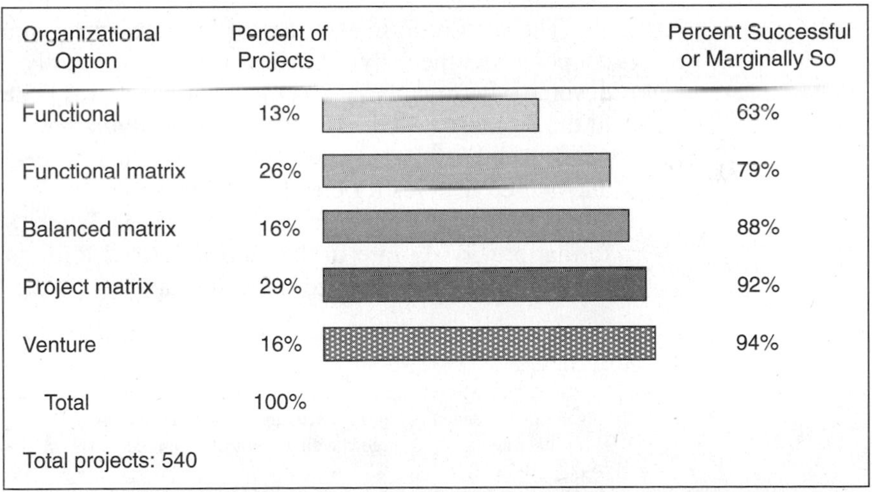

Source: Erik W. Larson and David H. Gobeli, "Organizing for Product Development Projects," *Journal of Product Innovation Management,* September 1988, pp. 180–90.

The **project matrix** option recognizes the occasional need for stronger project push. Here projectization is high. Team people are project people first and functional people second. A packaging team member will be "carrying the message" to the packaging director. Department heads complain that their people have sold out to the project and are trying to drive the project even against the departments' best interests. And they are.[6] For example, when IBM was trying to learn how to compete in the personal computer business, it set up a separate company called IBM PC Co. One of the early steps of that division's leadership was to take its executive group to Tokyo in September 1990; there would be no going home until they came up with a plan to break down functional boundaries. The plan was completed December 18![7] Later, the team manufacturing member argued for having outside manufacturers make most of the key pieces in the system. The new product had to be made fast, and the team didn't think IBM's manufacturing department could do it fast enough. They won.

The **venture** option extends projectization to its ultimate. Team members are pulled out of their departments and put to work full time on the project. A *think-tank* environment, designed to identify new ideas or solutions to new product-related problems, is one type of venture. The venture may be kept in the regular organization, or it may be spun outside the current division or company—a **spinout venture.** How far out it goes depends on how critical it is that there be no influence on the team from current departments, policies, and so on. Ford sent its new Mustang team to a converted furniture warehouse in Allen Park, Michigan, a few miles south of Dearborn.[8] IBM sent its PC team from Armonk, New York, to Boca Raton, Florida. Other firms have sent venture teams to another part of the city or to another part of the firm's building complex.

The venture form also merges into the joint venture (where another *firm* cooperates in the activity). Allied Chemical recently began using spinouts to develop what it called orphan technologies—R&D developments that didn't fit the business when they appeared and sat around on shelves, sometimes for years. Another spinout was Metaglas Products' work to develop lightweight alloys used in cores for electrical transformers.

Ford used a venture team for its classic Taurus/Sable project, a venture format previously rare in the auto industry.[9] Reports overflowed with such phrases as "stealing a page from the Japanese," "the first step was to throw

---

[6]Steven C. Wheelwright and Kim B. Clark, "Organizing and Leading 'Heavyweight' Development Teams," *California Management Review,* Spring 1992, pp. 9–28.

[7]Catherine Arnst, "A Freewheeling Youngster Named IBM," *Information Processing,* May 3, 1993, pp. 134–38.

[8]Joseph B. White and Oscar Suris, "How a Skunk Works Kept Mustang Alive—on a Tight Budget," *The Wall Street Journal,* September 21, 1993, p. A1.

[9]For example, see "How Ford Hit the Bull's Eye with Taurus," *BusinessWeek,* June 30, 1986, pp. 69–70.

out Ford's traditional organizational structure," "normally the five-year process is sequential," "Team Taurus took a program management approach," "worked together as a group," and "the team took final responsibility for the vehicle."

Ventures are not for everyone, partly because the firm may not be able to do what ventures require. For example, one study of ventures found that all but 1 of the 11 successes in the sample sold to established customers, used experienced market research personnel from the parent organization, obtained market-experienced personnel from outside, and based the new product on market need, not technological capability. The 17 losers in the study almost uniformly did not.[10] Exxon created a series of ventures in the office products area, and they all failed to achieve their objectives. A study of them showed they lacked congruencies between each new venture and its market. New products organization may involve many other terms and approaches. A couple of them are common enough that we should show their relationships to the above classification.

Product Manager. This common term is applied to people who manage ongoing products. A *new* products manager handles new products and may or may not also be handling ongoing ones.

Task Force and Project Team. These terms apply to new product teams, and their use is so varied that they are virtually useless. The five terms used for the options (above) are much more descriptive and should replace these older terms.

Another Look at Projectization

Any time two or more people from different departments (functions) of an organization gather to work on a project, issues of priorities are raised. Should they put first priority on the project or on the function they represent? Legislators face this problem daily (well-being of the total society versus well-being of the voters back home). So do student homecoming committees, civic development groups, and many others. When a sales manager, for example, goes to a new products *committee* meeting, there is little doubt about priorities because committee members are engineers or marketers first and committee members second. The sales manager is "functionalized," not projectized. Committee members want the company to make a profit; they are not disloyal. But they have independent opinions about how any particular new product may contribute to a profit. The sales manager may see a new package size as meeting customer demands and adding sales; the engineer may believe

[10] Eric von Hippel, "Successful and Failing Internal Corporate Ventures: An Empirical Analysis," *Industrial Marketing Management*, 1977, pp. 163–74.

FIGURE 14–4

Operating characteristics of the options

	Spectrum of Options				
Operating Characteristics	*Functional*	*Functional Matrix*	*Balanced Matrix*	*Project Matrix*	*Venture*
Decision power of leader	Very little				Almost total
Independence of group from depts.	None				Total
Percent of time spent on one project by member	Very low				Total
Importance of project(s)	Low				Critical
Degree of risk of project(s) to firm	Low				High
Disruptiveness of project(s)	Low				High
Degree of uncertainty in most decisions	Low				Very high
Ability of team to violate company policies	None				Almost total

Interpretation: This array shows how the various options of Figure 14–1 differ on each of several operating characteristics. The three matrix forms are at points between the extremes of functional and venture.

production costs will go up more than the sales volume; accounting objects to another line item that may split customers' current purchases and add to cost; R&D says work on the new package size will pull a key person off a far more important project needed next year.

These are not idle concerns. They are the reality of new product life, and they are legitimate (ignoring the political problems that also arise). Projectization is the way we handle them. If a project is important and faces lots of opposition of the types just mentioned, then we increase the projectization. We go to functional matrix, balanced matrix, or project matrix. If the opposition is very high (for instance, imagine the problems when steel firms first started making plastics products), then we move to the venture.[11]

Choosing an Organizational Option

Figure 14–4 summarizes how the five organizational options differ on various dimensions. We choose among them much the same way we buy a refrigerator. We begin with what we want the organization to do and then buy as much organizational power as needed to do the job. The more the power of the team, the more the "cost" to the firm in terms of personnel, disruption, and so on.

[11]For a recent look at Toyota's organizational structure for new product development, see Durward K. Sobek, II, Jeffrey K. Liker, and Allen C. Ward, "Another Look at How Toyota Integrates Product Development," *Harvard Business Review,* July–August 1998, pp. 36–49.

FIGURE 14–5

Decision rules for choosing among the options

To aid in the decision as to which of the five basic organizational options (Figure 14–1) to use on a particular project, score the situation on each of the following factors on a scale of 1 to 5. The more the factor exists (e.g., the more difficult), the more points this project gets.

Score	*Factor*
________	1. How critical is it, at this time, to have new product revenues?
________	2. In general, how difficult is it to get to new products through this firm?
________	3. How important is it that we beat competition to the market on this project?
________	4. How much personal risk is there for persons working on projects like this?
________	5. Will the products require new procedures (e.g., methods, or materials) in their manufacture?
________	6. Will the products require new procedures (e.g., stakeholder sales calls) in their marketing?
________	7. How high is the dollar contribution expected from products that come from this project?
________	8. Are there unusual politics surrounding this project?
________	9. How difficult will it be to acquire needed skills from elsewhere in the firm?
________	10. Will the products from this project be free of connections with other products in your line?
________	11. Are you, as a firm, experienced in using the more highly projectized forms of organization?
________	12. How difficult will technical accomplishment be on this project?

Interpretation: If the total score given to the proposed project is below 30, the functional or functional matrix modes would probably work. From 30 to 40 the project probably requires a balanced matrix. Beyond that the situation probably calls for project matrix or even a venture.

We determine how much team power is needed by study of the situation. The form in Figure 14–5 can be used, and the factors can even be weighted as is done on scoring models (Chapter 10). Special factors, fitting the situation, can be added.

Building a Team

Most managers and almost all researchers have concluded that new product teams must be created to fit their situations. There is no right method or correct paradigm, just as there is no right method of concept testing, or spelling out a product innovation charter. Nor are there right people; most team members and team leaders tell of their own personal growth during such assignments. Sales managers and scientists, alike, must become something else, something appropriate to a group task.

The Importance of Culture

Few people disagree with the importance of culture in business. There is even the saying that "Every firm should have a culture, even a bad one." For product improvements and near line extensions, the new products people must take the culture of the ongoing organization. At Heinz, for example, the Big Red brand team (tomato catsup, etc.) will dominate its new products work. But as the task becomes tougher, the culture must be more supportive.

Culture is a very soft term, but for new products a good culture brings us:

- *Freedom.* The freedom to roam around the firm, freedom to have extensive interaction across functional lines, freedom to differ with bosses, freedom from punishment for an honest mistake made in the quest for a new method, freedom to participate in a task assignment.
- *Egalitarianism.* As humans, people are essentially equal. Each deserves respect and courtesy.
- *A constructive environment,* in which people are happy, upbeat, positive, encouraged, challenged, rewarded, networked.
- *Absence of hidden agenda,* open statement of goals and objectives, forthright appraisals.

It is said that styles of management create cultures. But cultures evolve slowly; management can change suddenly. Culture may be overemphasized; it only *permits* action and accomplishment. It does not itself produce any output from the new products system. Still, the team working with no clear culture in place is at risk. So, too, is a team operating with almost exactly the wrong culture, as happened at Lexmark in 1992. The firm, a leveraged buyout by IBM executives, was steeped in IBM culture, yet went outside to get away from the very culture they brought with them.[12]

The Team Assignment and Ownership

A clear understanding by everyone involved as to what the team is for, its mission, and its strategy, is critical. One manufacturer of reasonably technical medical care products wanted only the moderate risks of *innovative imitation,* so R&D was made responsive to the directions of marketing. New projects originated only in marketing, key product attributes were determined before R&D began, and a marketing manager ran each project. Another firm in an allied industry wanted to implement an *aggressive technical innovation* strategy, but two qualified R&D directors came and went before management realized the short-term focus of a dominant marketing department was totally misleading the teams. Funny things happen when new product teams lack strategy because they pick up whatever strategy they think is correct, and technical people may feel that team success is measured by technical performance. The customer has a different opinion.

Also critical is "buy-in" on the part of everyone on the team—this is sometimes called taking **ownership** of the project. With ownership comes

---

[12]Paul B. Carroll, "Culture Shock: Story of an IBM Unit That Split Off Shows Difficulties of Change," *The Wall Street Journal,* June 23, 1992, p. A1.

enthusiasm, commitment, energy and pride. Ownership is *not* entrepreneurship—white knights do not ride around a firm waving a sword and conjuring up new products. *Groups of skilled specialists* create new products, not individual leaders. Some firms use the term *product champion* to describe those who have taken ownership, but want all members of the team to join in the ownership.

Ownership requires training, empowerment, and motivation. *Training* helps assure that no one will take ownership without the skills and knowledge required by the task. **Empowerment** means that a person has been cut loose. It is far more than delegation (which usually has strings attached—budgets, policy, procedures, etc.) It could be stated this way: "You know the nature of this project, you have a statement of mission such as a PIC, you know the firm's general standards, you are smart and trained, and you know how to use corporate staff (legal, etc.) Given all those, we are ready to trust your judgment."[13] *Motivated* means the person has been encouraged to want to succeed; we will talk about that in more detail later.

Functional people will sometimes not want to take ownership. Power yes, but not ownership. And they often can't because the conditions above haven't been met. A Citicorp manager once said the bank had to move innovation of retail products to a corporate new products group because the line departments just weren't doing the job. They refused to take ownership (including the responsibility for failure.)

A new car owner recently called his dealer about several minor items. The telephone service attendant gave one set of instructions, the check-in manager gave a different set, the body shop corrected them both, and finally the parts manager had yet a different view of what should be done. One customer, but four "dealers." None had taken ownership. They used to say that bad new products were developed by committees. They were right.

Selecting the Leader

Given the overall strategy and the decision on how much team the firm needs for the job at hand, it is time to select a leader. Sometimes, this process is simple—for example, when the firm uses a product manager system and the new product concerns an addition to a particular person's product line. Or when, as in the case of 3M, the project originates from a particular person's technology.

Leaders must be *general managers.* They must be able to spot the need for change, and convince others of this need. They also need to get potential team members to accept the idea of being on a team, and to feel comfortable

[13]Tony Eccles, "The Deceptive Allure of Empowerment," *Long Range Planning,* December 1993, pp. 13–21; and Josef Frischer, "Empowering Management in New Product Development Units," *Journal of Product Innovation Management,* November 1993, pp. 393–401. The latter is an empirical study of European firms. Also, a firm has to work at empowerment—top management support is a must. See Lawrence R. Rothstein, "The Empowerment Effort That Came Undone," *Harvard Business Review,* January–February 1995, pp. 20–31.

FIGURE 14–6
Factors associated with project leadership

1. General management skills.
2. Green thumbs: make little seeds grow into big things.
3. Blank-page vision: lead without a map.
4. One-man band: play all the instruments (at least to some extent).
5. "Miss-a-meal" pains: be hungry, impatient.
6. Christopher Columbus syndrome: explorers who can't sit in port.
7. Night sight: vision improves while others grope in the dark.
8. Lead from the middle: able to work in the trenches and cause change in the whole organization.
9. Velvet hammer: hit without inflicting lasting damage.
10. Stamina: physical and mental.
11. White liar: trick people into doing what they later will be proud they did.
12. Veterinarian: hear the clues, even when the situation is not speaking.
13. Ideaphile: love ideas—anybody's, anytime—store them, talk about them.
14. Biblical: "Let my people go," leave them alone, encourage them, praise little victories.
15. Audacious: think big and bold.
16. Tinker, tailor, try: be able to try, try again.
17. Execution overkill: relentless, meticulous execution, with the job done right.
18. Manners matter: "thank you" and "please," 50 times a day.

Source: Larry Wizenberg, *The New Products Handbook* (Homewood, IL: Irwin Professional Publishing, 1986), pp. 212–15.

working with people from other functional areas.[14] They lead without direct authority, and so must win personal support. Various studies show that team leaders must have strong self-confidence (based on knowledge and experience, not just ego), have empathy (be able to look at things from another person's point of view), have a good self-awareness of how others see them, and be expert in personal communication. An even more interesting list of factors is shown in Figure 14–6.

But the irony is that leaders probably have to be strong in one set of directions and strong in the opposite too. Tom Peters said a team leader must have a total ego *yet* no ego, be an autocrat *and* a delegator, be a leader *and* a manager, tolerate ambiguity *yet* pursue perfection, be good at oral communication *and* at the written form as well, acknowledge complexity *yet* be a KISS (keep it short and simple) fanatic, think big *and* small, and be an action-fanatic *while* building for the future.[15] It has been said that a new products project really needs two leaders: a creative, inspiring type for early on, and a tough disciplinarian for the later stages. Rare is the person that can be both.[16]

---

[14]Michael F. Wolff, "Creating High-Performance Teams," *Research-Technology Management,* November–December 1993, pp. 10–12.

[15]"Mastering These Dilemmas Can Give Project Managers the Leading Edge," *Chicago Tribune,* April 29, 1991, section 4, p. 7.

[16]Göran Ekvall, "Creativity in Project Work: A Longitudinal Study of a Product Development Project," *Creativity and Innovation Management,* March 1993, pp. 17–26.

Sometimes people wonder whether the leader should be chosen first or selected by the team members themselves. The latter is an attractive idea, and is used occasionally, including once in a well-publicized program at Signode Corporation. But most managements prefer to pick the leader and then let that leader identify the team players. This increases the likelihood of good team chemistry and commitment, but also assures that a capable leader is leading. Many companies recognize the difficulties in locating talented leaders, and highly prize those that they find. Toyota and Honda, for example, have them stay on as managers of their cars after launch, through three major upgradings, and then back onto the start of another new car project. They keep them on new product projects, and off of the general track to top executive positions (with their concurrence).[17]

Selecting the Team Members

When selecting the members of a new product team, it is important to remember that each one of them is on the team as the representative of a group of others "back home" in their department. The R&D team member can't do all the technical work, and may do none, but does stimulate, direct, and encourage others in R&D to do it. This is usually in the face of competition from other R&D representatives on other teams, who are also trying to win time for *their* projects. The same goes for team members from the other functions. Chrysler wants team members to be change agents. Bausch and Lomb (B&L) wants members to have real functional influence and a broad-business view. B&L believes so strongly in teams that a conference speaker from the firm brought along (and introduced) five core members of his team.

So we seek people who are knowledgeable in their respective areas, have the respect of their departments, and want to be on the team. If they have to be talked into the job, they will probably not do it well.

Most people in a business are of three types regarding their interrelationships outside their departments. Teams need the *integrators,* who love to relate to people from other departments or other firms. They naturally give, and get, respect. *Receptors* respect others and welcome information from them but do not desire personal relationships. They are good contacts but not particularly good team members. *Isolates* prefer to be left alone. They are deep specialists in their field and really want nothing to do with people from other functions. They are rarely able to play a role in new product team operations.[18]

---

[17]Alex Taylor III, "Why Toyota Keeps Getting Better and Better and Better," *Fortune,* November 1990, pp. 66–79.

[18]Another listing focuses on personal skills of people (problem finders versus problem solvers): Mosongo Moukwa, "A Structure to Foster Creativity: An Industrial Experience," *Journal of Creative Behavior,* First Quarter 1995, pp. 54–63.

A good way to think about this is that team members should naturally be **collaborative** not just **cooperative.** The difference is vital.[19]

How many members should a team have? First, let's distinguish between core team, ad hoc team, and extended team. The *core team* includes those people who are involved in *managing* functional clusters. Thus, one marketing person may represent, speak for, and guide 10 to 12 others in the sales and marketing areas. The core team members are active throughout, and are supported by an *ad hoc group.* Ad hoc members are those from important departments (e.g., packaging, legal, logistics) whose importance is brief in time and thus not needed on the core team. *Extended* team members are less critical, and may almost seem incidental. They may be in some other division of the firm, work at corporate staff, or with another firm. Many experienced managers know that too-large teams (or empowered individuals) can become bureaucratic, so they keep their teams relatively small.[20]

Roles and Participants

People working on new products are sometimes not just functional representatives; they may assume other roles, some well-known and necessary. Figure 14–7 shows the full set, and what they do. Although these roles are not always present (for example, an *inventor* may not be needed), they usually are. Sometimes, who plays which role isn't clear, and people may actually compete for the role they want.

The most well known role is that of **product champion** (also called *process champion* or just champion). Projects get hung up at times by movements outside the team, in the supporting infrastructure. People lose interest; political conflicts arise; volume and cost projections turn sour; technical breakthroughs aren't achieved. The champion within the corporation plays a role similar to that of the entrepreneur starting up a new business. His or her role is to push past the **roadblocks:** bypass corporate hierarchy and persuade other people in the firm (from several functional areas) to support the innovation.[21] Champions can't win every time, but their task is to see that no project dies without a fight.

In most cases, the *project manager* plays the champion role. Other times the champion is self-appointed, often a technical person associated with the discovery that started the project. Today, many firms see the *core team* as the champion, since all should have strong concept commitment. Some firms are beginning to think that the champion idea has outlived its usefulness, since

[19]See Suzy Wetlaufer, "The Team that Wasn't," *Harvard Business Review,* November–December 1994, pp. 22–38.

[20]Charles Heckscher, "The Failure of Participatory Management," *Across the Board,* December 1995, pp. 16–21.

[21]Scott A. Shane, "Are Champions Different from Non-Champions?", *Journal of Business Venturing,* September 1994, pp. 397–421.

FIGURE 14–7

Roles/participants in the new products management process

*Participant**	*Activity*	*Participant**	*Activity*
1. Project manager	Leader Integrator Translator Mediator Judge Arbitrator Coordinator	4. Strategist	Longer range Managerial Entire program
2. Product champion	Supporter Spokesperson Pusher Won't concede	5. Inventor	Creative scientist Basement inventor Idea source
3. Sponsor	Senior manager Supporter Endorses Assuring hearing Mentor	6. Rationalist	Objectivity Reality Reason Financial
		7. Facilitator	Boost productivity Increase output

*The participant's role may be either formal or informal.

political obstacles should be addressed by the firm, not by an individual fighting what in many cases takes on a David/Goliath character.[22]

Generally (and ideally) the champion is expected to be vigorous and enthusiastic but play within the rules. Rarely, champions run roughshod over the rules. For example, a champion in a firm that made infant vitamin products surreptitiously charged a market research survey against the budget of a marketing research director who opposed a project the champion wanted. The survey proved the champion correct, and the product was successful!

The second most important role in Figure 14–7 is that of **sponsor.** This person does not drive anything but is higher up in the firm, is supportive, and lends encouragement and endorsement to the champion. Teams are wise to develop sponsors, whom some call godfathers or mentors. Figure 14–8 tells the story of a product champion, but note that the story was told by a sponsor. Another role is **facilitator:** this is the person on the team (or assigned to the team) whose task is to enhance the team's productivity and output. With

[22]See Albert L. Page, "Assessing New Product Development Practices and Performance: Establishing Crucial Norms," *Journal of Product Innovation Management,* September 1993, pp. 273–90. There is, however, recent evidence that project champions are important in at least one industry; see Gloria Barczak, "New Product Strategy, Structure, Process, and Performance in the Telecommunications Industry, *Journal of Product Innovation Management* 12, no. 3 (1995), pp. 224–34.

FIGURE 14–8

The saga of Donald Gorman: champion

An abbreviated version of a story told by L. J. Thomas, senior vice president, Eastman Kodak Company, in May 1980.

"I will focus attention on a particular Kodak inventor, now retired, who was responsible for available light movies, Donald Gorman—an inventor and researcher of the first order. . . . He was uncompromising. He had absolutely no regard for anything short of total victory. . . .He is always looking for a better way. . . . It was in Gorman's allegiance to the customer, in his quest for picture quality, that the available light movie program began.

"He needed a camera with a rapid pulldown [after the program was well underway]. There was such a camera—the Wittnauer Cine-Twin. Gorman learned that the Kodak patent museum had a Wittnauer in its collection, and he asked that it be sent to the Research Labs. It was sent to him and without the museum's knowledge Gorman dismantled it to look at the shutter. He quickly saw that the mechanism was ideal for his experiments.

"Gorman had really begun to interact with other members of the organization, many of whom were trying to discourage him because he had what they thought was a crazy idea. . . . At this point in his work, Gorman was badly in need of support from the top. Enter Dr. Chapman, Kodak's chairman of the board and chief executive officer at that time. . . . On one particular Tuesday morning, Gorman was projecting something from another projector for him on the screen. After that demonstration Chapman said, 'Mr. Gorman, come out from behind that projector and tell me what you are up to these days.' Gorman said, 'Dr. Chapman, I am glad you asked.'

"Of course Gorman hadn't gone through the proper channels because he had gone right to the top. All of us know that this is not always the best way to proceed. One moral here, never underestimate the power of a quiet lunch with the right people.

"Good decisions were Dr. Chapman's great contribution, just as innovation and invention in research were Don Gorman's. The two work together—and both are essential."

P.S. This story also highlights the role of the sponsor.

Source: L. J. Thomas, "Available Light Movies—An Inventor Made It Happen," in *Living Case Histories of Industrial Innovation* (New York: Industrial Research Institute, 1981), pp. 5–9.

today's reduced reliance on hierarchies, facilitators are increasingly playing an important role.

The other roles in Figure 14–7 are indicated by the activities listed for them.

Network Building

So far our people focus has been on the team leader and the team members. But sometimes there is no team. In fact, since most new products are improvements or close line extensions, most new products are developed in the functional mode, within the ongoing organization, entirely without a special team. In addition, the extended team includes people well outside the core and ad hoc team. In all of these cases, the participants who actually do the new product work comprise a network, and a simplified version of one is shown in Figure 14–9.

A **network** consists of nodes, links, and operating relationships. *Nodes* are people important to the project in some way. *Links* are how they are reached and what important ties they have to others in the network. *Operating relationships* are how these people are contacted and motivated to cooperate in the project.

FIGURE 14–9

Product innovation network, abbreviated version

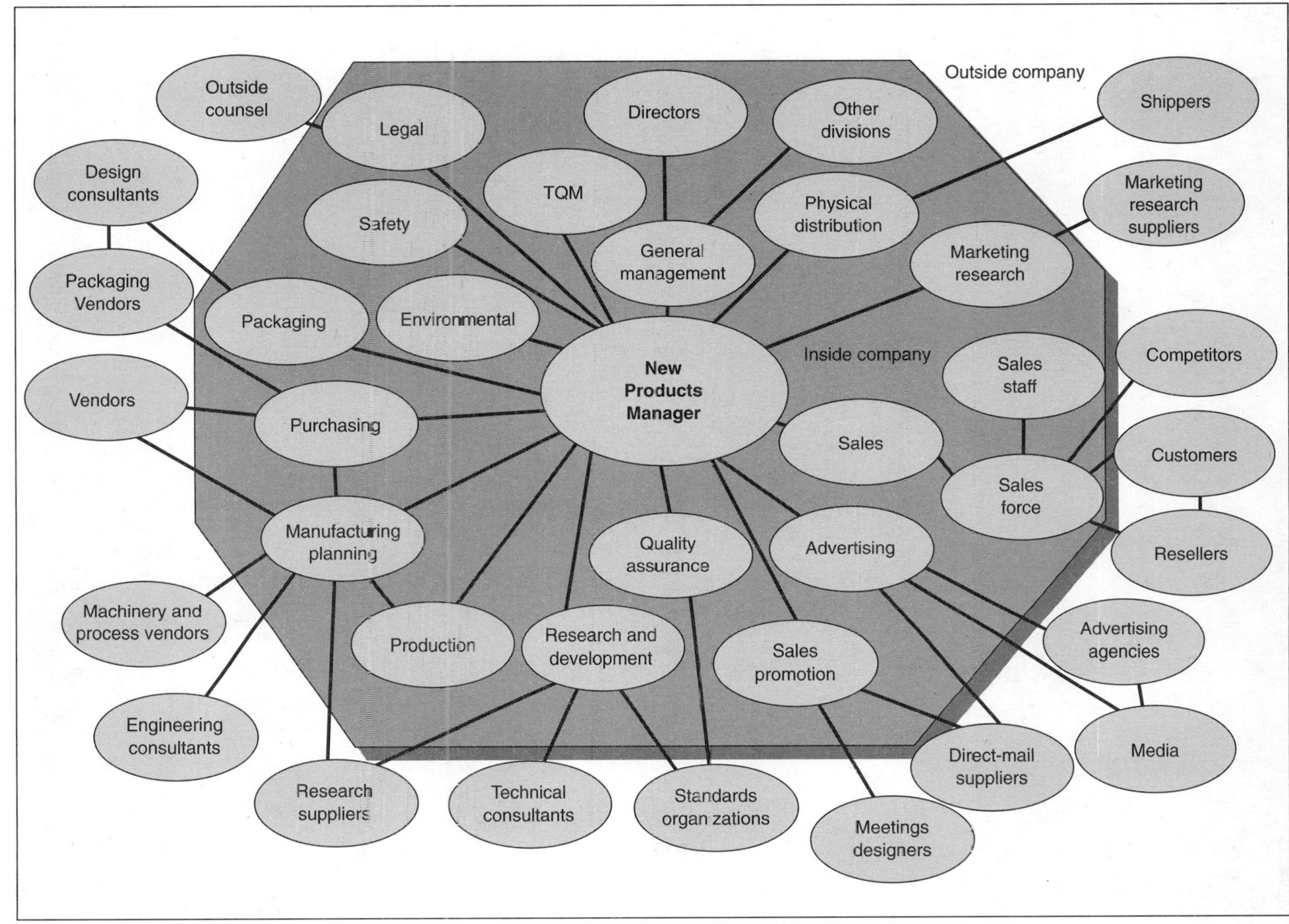

Who are the nodes? This is the toughest part. Any given project may enlist the support of hundreds (or even thousands) of people. Only judgment can decide how many of them should be put into a formal network and managed.

Networks drawn up on paper or computer are not meant to substitute for intensive, walk-around management styles. And they are fluid—changing from time to time in the life of the project, and from project to project as the importance of various functions ebb and flow. For example, the purchasing department was for a long time omitted from networks or placed way out on the edge. But today's focus on speed, quality, cost, and value has moved purchasing to a front row seat.

Network makers admit it's a lot easier to draw nodes and linkage lines than it is to work them.[23] But there is no choice, and networks are an aid, even if quite informal or even just mental pictures. Perhaps their greatest danger is that they can easily become bureaucracies. One manager, when asked during a training program, refused to draw up the network for a project he was then managing. He said he didn't want to see it all on one sheet and risk being overpowered by its complexity. And he didn't want his boss to see it, and thus get a better idea of the massive indirect costs involved in the activity.

Training the Teams

An appointed team is not yet ready to operate. There must be **top management support** (discussed later), and, hopefully, a good image of the team around the firm. Other managers sometimes come to doubt or fear a team, and they can isolate or ostracize it.

But the real need at this time is training. It would be nice to say we have a large cadre of experienced new product team members and leaders. We do not. Generally, firms start a team off with an intensive two- or three-day training session for the team members. At Digital Equipment, this pretraining is so critical that teams spend up to a month on it. But training sessions cannot bring team members up to the needed skill levels unless there is considerable skill to begin with.

An experienced team builder says he finds these mistakes commonly made:[24]

- *Confusing "getting to know one another" with skill building.* Barbecues are great, but they are no substitute for skill training.

---

[23]An excellent source for network training is Jessica Lipnack and Jeffery Stamps, *The Networking Book: People Connecting with People* (New York City: Methuen, 1986).

[24]William C. Byham, "Lessons from the Little Leagues," *Across the Board,* March 1992, pp. 52–53. Byham is the author of a clever explanation of today's team and network management methods: *ZAPP! The Lightning of Empowerment* (Pittsburgh: Development Dimensions International Press, 1989).

- *Offering sensitivity training instead of behavioral skills training.* Focusing on interpersonal issues may cause stress and loss of self-esteem. Talk about winning the game, and what that takes.
- *Confusing the acquisition of knowledge with the acquisition of skills.* One doesn't learn how to bat a baseball by reading a book, and neither does one learn how to be a good team player that way.
- *Trying to get training done fast.* Considering the leverage of skills over the life of a new product project, squeezing the training schedule is penny-wise and pound-foolish.
- *Doing the wrong things at the wrong time.* The team will operate over many months, through various project phases; the team members don't need to be trained at the start in all the skills they will ultimately need.

Team members need to have the skills of interpersonal and interfunctional relationships (for the latter, see Chapter 15.) They need to understand all of the players—customers, vendors, resellers, and more. Most people have served on *committees,* and thus have a warped view of what will be expected of them.

Managing the Team

Managing a team of the type developed for more important projects in the new products field is extremely difficult. The task embodies all of the ideas from the first three chapters of Part IV of the text. A few special thoughts follow.[25]

Ongoing Management of the Team

The most pressing problem on new product teams probably involves keeping the group enthusiastic. As work goes on, as creative needs are not met, as efforts fail, and as people tense up, it is imperative to give pep talks. Burn-out is a genuine, and not uncommon, problem, and the innovation-derailing patterns of behavior that new products face are almost unbelievable. Practitioners have discovered that team and nonteam participants have an unending supply of new ways of resisting change. Here is just one:

[25]For a discussion of the performance appraisal, pay, promotion, organizational culture, team leader, member selection, empowerment, and related topics, see Patricia J. Holahan and Stephen K. Markham, "Factors Affecting Multifunctional Team Effectiveness," in M. Rosenau, A. Griffin, G. Castellion, and N. Anscheutz, *The PDMA Handbook of New Product Development* (New York: Wiley, 1996).

The ambassador syndrome: On coming to the conclusion that more entrepreneurship is needed, management creates a team that will force its way past department blockades. But the departments all appoint ambassadors to the team, not individuals free to, or interested in, bypassing department power.

New products people live with these problems, but they grow weary. So some team leaders set up defenses against the well-intentioned suggestions they know will come up—a product variation, a technology that just appeared, or a new advertising approach. Such suggestions are terribly distracting if not kept away from the team.

Another aspect of the team management problem may appear trivial—the ability to run *effective meetings.* New product people seem to meet continuously. Some product innovators have caught on to this need and are now studying their own team meetings for ways to speed them up and improve the decisions. (See the Europa International Case at the end of Chapter 15 for another possible solution.)

Changes in team membership over the duration of the project can also cause problems. Losing key people from the team might cause important information to get lost. There is also a *job security* issue. In many firms, the ladders within departments or functional areas are a more secure road to promotion than is team membership.[26]

Team Compensation and Motivation

A delicate issue in team management is the matter of compensation. Team leaders and team members are usually paid a straight salary or salary plus bonus. Bonuses are equally split between company performance, individual performance, and project accomplishment. It is rare to have compensation ride on the new product's performance.[27] The reasons for this are strong: Employees should be treated equally (fairly), team members do not have the financial risks of an entrepreneur, and it is easier to transfer managers into and out of teams if compensation plans are equal. Still, all agree that finding good people willing to risk career-bypass by serving on a new products team and motivating them to give the necessary high level of effort and stress is a legitimate problem.[28] Firms that use equity awards (such as stock shares and product profits-sharing) tend to be smaller ones in Silicon Valley.

Many firms use a combination of monetary and nonmonetary rewards (such as prizes, plaques, recognition at a dinner, or even permission to work on pet projects on company time) to motivate their teams. Using only monetary rewards can lead to problems. Some may feel that the satisfaction of being on a successful team is reward enough, and the money isn't necessary.

---

[26]Tom Kiely, "Innovation Congregations," *Technology Review,* April 1994, pp. 56–60.

[27]See Albert Page, "Assessing New Product Practices," p. 278.

[28]Hollister B. Sykes, "The Anatomy of a Corporate Venturing Program: Factors Influencing Success," *Journal of Business Venturing,* 1992, pp. 253–65.

Others may complain that all team members get rewarded (even the lazy ones!)—a problem that is compounded if the same dollar figure is awarded to everyone on the team. Some may be resentful if their multimillion-dollar idea was rewarded with only a $1000 bonus![29]

TRW's Cleveland automotive group has instituted Project ELITE (Earnings Leadership in Tomorrow's Environment) to motivate and compensate its teams. In this endeavor, specific goals are set for each team project and also for each individual, and 10 to 25 percent of pay is tied to the accomplishment of these individual and team goals. DuPont uses a 360-degree review process in which team members are evaluated by peers, subordinates, and supervisors. Motorola is one of many firms that rewards team behavior rather than team results. Motorola recognizes that teams often need to take risks to make progress, and rewarding only results might make them risk-averse. It also makes sense to have one person in charge of the nonmonetary recognition programs, modifying them occasionally to make sure they are always worthwhile rewards.[30]

Of course, there are team leaders who very much want the challenge and risks of entrepreneurship. Procter & Gamble, the company that created the brand management system so long ago, changed in 1987 from strong *brand* managers to strong *category* managers with a true team structure. But they at least partially changed back in 1992, and a reason may have shown up when a former P&G brand manager complained that management could no longer see how good a person really is. He wanted the opportunity to build his own pedestal.

A classic team in the annals of new products development was that on the Eagle, a new minicomputer at Data General. Its exploits were chronicled in the best-seller, *The Soul of a New Machine,* and followed up five years later.[31] The team was so motivated in its entrepreneurial form that it decided to develop a *breakthrough* machine on a project that nonteam people had been led to believe was a *me-too* machine. But loyalty to the *team* was so great that the players could not resume a strong loyalty to the *firm* when the project ended. Nine of the 14 engineers in the book left Data General. The team leader and the three managers who reported to him had also left. Teams, depending on their management, can be extremely powerful, but also extremely dangerous. Of course, they may have returned later, as John Sculley thinks such departures did at Apple. Though a third typically were burned out and left, most returned in a few months to begin work on another new project.

---

[29]Perry Pascarella, "Compensating Teams," *Across the Board,* February 1997, pp. 16–22.

[30]These examples and suggestions are from Perry Pascarella, "Compensating Teams," and J. Gregory Kunkel, "Rewarding Product Development Success," *Research-Technology Management,* September–October 1997, pp. 29–31. See also Tom Kiely, "Innovation Congregations."

[31]Tracy Kidder, *The Soul of a New Machine,* (New York: Avon, 1981). The follow-up analysis was done by William Bulkeley in "Computer Engineers Memorialized in Book Seek New Challenges," *The Wall Street Journal,* September 20, 1985, p. 1.

Closing the Team Down

Strong differences of opinion arise regarding when a new product team should be closed down and the product turned over to the regular organization. Some firms *close out early,* well before the item is marketed; they bring in operating people bit by bit.[32] A second practice lets the team prepare for the marketing (for example, write the plan or train the people), but at the last minute, the *regular people launch it.* When this is done, the key team people are usually kept close to the action to help solve problems. A third, and rarer, practice lets the team actually *market the item* and either become the nucleus of its standing management as a new division or turn it over to the regular organization after it has been successfully established. As seen before, Toyota and Honda keep team leaders as ongoing managers of their new products for several major design upgrades, and then reassign them to a new development program.

No matter when the on-going staff takes over, they should be brought into the action in a way that lets them link into the new product organization. As one manager put it, "Treat this as a whirling gear being meshed with an idle gear; send a few people into the on-going organization early, to get the idle gear up to a speed where it can accept the rest of the new operation."

Summary

This chapter covered issues surrounding the team: what a team is, the various organization options, the methods for setting up a team and managing it through to completion—selecting the leader, selecting the team members, training them, and so forth.

As a closing thought, two new types of new product teams are emerging on the scene. One is a higher-level, multifunctional group (often heads of the key functions) whose task is to *manage the project teams.* As teams proliferate, they need a reporting home of some type. The other emerging team is a group of experienced new products people whose task is to *assist project teams in developing appropriate processes to follow.* The latter may just be a person with the title New Products Process Manager. Process is critical, and a firm needs some place to house the **organization learning** constantly taking place.

Chapter 15 addresses the matter of speed to market, and then points out several problems that arise in managing the way Chapters 13 and 14 have urged.

---

[32]Charles Heckscher, "The Failure of Participatory Management." Heckscher notes that permanent or "semi-permanent" teams tend to build walls around themselves, and recommends that teams get abandoned as soon as possible.

Applications

More questions from that interview with the company president.

1. "You explained earlier how the new product team leader's job is a lot like the conductor's job. I understand it's also a lot like the job of a professional quarterback, or at least that's what the head of our sporting goods division recently said. What do you think he had in mind? Surely he didn't think the quarterback is a manager! He must not know those pro football coaches very well. Next thing you know, he'll be telling us college and high school quarterbacks have that type of job too!"
2. "Actually, I'm not convinced that any particular organization formats are better than others. I've run into too many exceptions. For example, that great portable tape player, Walkman by Sony, was conceived and pushed through by Akio Morita, Sony's chairman of the board. He got the idea from seeing a past chairman wearing a headset in the office, and he personally directed the project through its technical phases, even over the opposition of his people in manufacturing and sales. Even gave himself the title of project manager. I'll bet that approach doesn't fit any of your academic formats. And, I'll bet you wouldn't discourage it."
3. "You mentioned culture! Now there's a human relations cult if I ever heard of one. Human resource and organization design people are great, and out of their work has come some of the most valuable new business methods of the past 15 years. But culture isn't one of them. It's vague, never defined, full of soft terms like *happy, egalitarian,* and *forthright.* Life just doesn't work this way. Don't misunderstand me, managers must respect their people, and we can't let strong opinions get in the way of our increasing productivity. But good people want honest motivations, not games or manipulations. Yeah, I said manipulation, because that's what the culture thing is. Tell me, what kind of a culture do you like best in the classroom where you use this book? Is that culture consistent with the general ideas of management we have had for years?"
4. "Several of our divisions say they get tremendous help from their vendors when it comes to new product development. But, to tell you the truth, I think they're just lazy. They've got good talent in those divisions, or darn well should have, and all they're doing is letting vendors get a bigger piece of our innovation profits. Most vendors don't pull their share in these funny partnerships. Besides, the initiative should be theirs, not ours; they stand to gain more from so-called integrated operations and alliances than we do."

CASE: MARKO PRODUCTS

As a major and very profitable division of a large conglomerate for the past seven years, Marko Products was one of those acquisitions that worked out well. They specialized in medical supply products (items bought by physicians for use in their offices, not medical products for the patient).

Marko's president, Bill Wong, was an aggressive executive who tried to keep his firm poised for maximum market impact. He had installed the product manager system three years ago and was pleased that it seemed to be working well. The product managers were in the marketing department, and although they did not have the almost unlimited informal authority of their packaged goods counterparts, they were respected around the firm.

Marko had two manufacturing divisions: one for consumer supplies (e.g., bandages, rubber gloves) located in a different state and another for equipment (examining tables, cabinets, ophthalmoscopes, etc.) located at headquarters. All R&D was physically centralized, but the VP for that function had divided her staff into six parts, each dedicated to a particular technology such as rubber, laminated materials, electronics, and so forth.

One sales force sold the entire line, but in the more populated regions the firm used separate salespeople for supplies and for equipment.

Top-management staff included a long-range planning group, an international marketing division organized by areas of the world, a governmental/public relations department, finance, human resources, and legal. Packaging and quality control were part of the manufacturing staff.

Marko Products' management chased tough goals in profit and market dominance. They planned to hold the number one or two spots in each major market or else would pull back promotional and R&D support.

They recently held a two-day planning retreat, which produced new product innovation charters for each of their businesses. It had been a productive session but not without controversy because most of the managers thought Marko should concentrate on what they did best: manufacture top-quality examining room furniture. They argued that furniture earned most of the profits and that supply was a commodity business Marko entered only because it came with the cabinetry business of Mainline Medical (a firm Marko acquired six years ago). Bill Wong was pleased that he had persuaded them to become more aggressive and to set their sights on bigger and better things.

Following are two of the charters:

> **Medical Office Equipment, Nonscientific:** Marko will actively develop any and all new products in which might be called the "furniture" category, for use in doctors' and hospitals' examining and consultation rooms. The items will typically (and desirably) utilize our skills in "metal bending" and our knowledge of examining room procedures. The goals of this activity are (1) to add $70 million profit contribution over the next four years and (2) to assure that we dominate (actual or close) in each major market we enter.
>
> To do all this we will rely primarily upon our marketing department for input on market needs, supported by input from knowledgeable technical staff who maintain market contacts. Each new product will be unique in at least one critical dimension, and we hope it will make a contribution to examining room procedure. We intend to continue our reputation as the leading light in this industry, and all new items will be of the highest quality ["absolutely no schlock," as Wong put it]. Our major

contribution will be in designing products that can be manufactured to the traditionally high standards of our operations group.

Disposables: In recent years the medical community has turned to disposables to solve many of their operating problems, and Marko wants to take advantage of this trend. Our two small lines of disposable gloves and disposable aprons will be the springboard for this activity. The key to dominance here is predicting what new methodologies the medical personnel will agree to convert to disposability next. We want to develop products that extend disposability and are thus unique. Finding these product concepts will be difficult and will require a combination of office procedure knowledge, attitude study, and technical capability.

Profit goals are not clear for this operation, but we do want the program to get us into at least 10 new lines over the next five years, to dominate at least 8 of those lines (plus gloves and aprons), and to be the firm contacted by persons in medicine who see an opportunity for disposability. Minimum ROAs will be developed as the projects come along.

Some new disposable products will be reasonably nondifferentiated add-ons to capitalize on our position in a given market.

Wong now wondered which of the five organizational structures in Figure 14–1 would be appropriate for each of the two PIC groups.

In addition, Wong knew that putting a structure into place was not enough—the people in any structure had to work effectively as a group. So please take whatever organization option you choose for the nonscientific medical office equipment and then go through the following topics, commenting on how each topic would relate specifically to the equipment group management: (1) culture, (2) team ownership, (3) selecting the leader, (4) need for product champions, (5) compensating the team.

CHAPTER

15 Special Issues in Development

Setting

Chapter 13 looked at the new role played by designers in the new product process. Chapter 14 talked about building and managing teams, and offered a set of options for organizational structure. In this chapter, we turn our attention to one of the most desired consequences of teamwork: accelerated speed to market. We also explore several other goings-on at the development phase, including managing the interface between functional areas, the role of top management, and global considerations. We also include a look at how marketing's role in the new product process accelerates during development, as marketing gears up for the impending launch.

Speed to Market

Behind many of the things we talked about in Chapter 14 is one of today's most discussed management goals—*speed,* or **accelerated product development** (APD). When we let the development process lag, when things take too long to get to market, we lose the competitive race. The firm that gets to market first has a major short-term advantage, and may sustain that advantage for many years if its follow-up development practices are sharp.[1]

There is plenty of evidence in many different industry settings that cross-functional teams contribute greatly to increasing speed to market. Software

[1]An interesting, but challenging, piece of evidence on this comes from the science of Darwinian evolution. Chris Farrell, "Survival of the Fittest Technologies," *New Scientist,* February 1993, pp. 35–39.

development is often marked by intensive "crunch time" periods due to approaching deadlines, and many firms in this industry rely on small, cohesive core development teams to meet time goals while at the same time not sacrificing quality.[2]

But virtually every action that accelerates development and marketing takes something from the process, something that may just be a bureaucratic waste or that may be critical to a successful project. Slashing time right and left, cutting budgets across the board, and demanding everyone double efforts and finish faster is poor management. Far better is to use such devices as *benchmarking,* where a firm studies other firms who have been successful in speeding up their operations. Kodak used the consulting firm of Arthur D. Little to lead them in this type of study for speeding up their design, engineering, and product development work.

Note that the *cycle time metric,* that is, the way management measures speed to market (or, frequently, *time to market*), is often "getting the idea to the shipping dock faster." This assumes that there has already been technical accomplishment—the R of R&D has been concluded successfully. Basic research does not respond well to the clock or the calendar. Second, ideation and pretechnical evaluation are already complete. Third, note that getting the item manufactured (on the shipping dock) is the end of the measurement, but *not the purpose for the project.* The PIC probably has some specific profit, sales, or market share goals. These are not achieved on the shipping dock, so the better metric would be *from idea to market success.*[3] Figure 15–1 illustrates this concept. From the point of view of technical development, speed to market success means not just time to the shipping dock, but also *post-shipping technical speed;* for example, are corporate services (such as legal and environmental) in place? Figure 15–1 also shows that if one uses the metric of time to success rather than time to the shipping dock, marketing has a much bigger role to play in accelerating cycle time. Marketing can strive to accelerate *premarket speed* (i.e., pretesting the marketing plan more quickly or getting up to speed on field coverage through alliance formation) and also *postannouncement* speed (i.e., speeding up coupon redemption or getting sales reps into the field more quickly).

The emphasis on speed over the past 5 to 10 years has prepared us to know what our options are in accelerating cycle time. Figure 15–2 summarizes these options. Actually, many firms have found most of their speed from

[2]B. J. Zirger and Janet L. Hartley, "The Effect of Acceleration Techniques on Product Development Time," *IEEE Transactions on Engineering Management,* May 1996, pp. 143–52, looks at cross-functional teams in electronics firms, and Alfredo M. Choperena, "Fast Cycle Time: Driver of Innovation and Quality," *Research-Technology Management,* May–June 1996, pp. 36–40, examines the development of an immunoassay diagnostic system. Both found evidence that teams drive speed to market without sacrificing quality. See also Erran Carmel, "Cycle Time in Packaged Software Firms," *Journal of Product Innovation Management* 12, no. 2 (1995), pp. 110–23.

[3]See Bengt Barius, "Simultaneous Marketing: A Holistic Marketing Approach to Shorter Time to Market," *Industrial Marketing Management,* 1994, pp. 145–54.

FIGURE 15–1

Speed to market and the role of marketing (when the goal is success, not just launch)

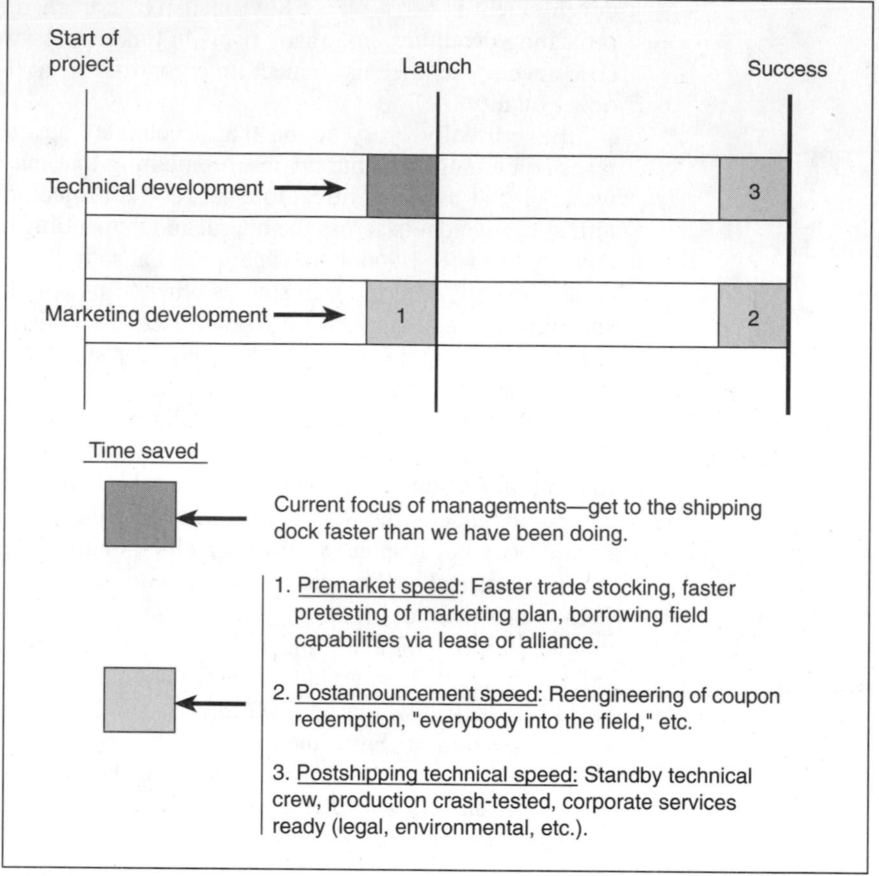

a direct attack on lackadaisical attitudes and practices. It is very possible that most actions are perfectly obvious to managers who become convinced their top bosses are serious about speed.[4]

Overall Principles and Guidelines

- *Do the job right the first time.* A small amount of time in the early phases can save many times that later, in rework alone.
- *Seek lots of platinum BBs rather than one silver bullet.* This means look at every step, every action, every meeting; small savings add up.

[4]A handy metric is one that measures current cycle times. See Abbie Griffin, "Metrics for Measuring Product Development Cycle Time," *Journal of Product Innovation Management,* March 1993, pp. 112–25.

FIGURE 15–2

Set of techniques for attaining speed in a new product project

Organization Phase

1. Use projectization—project matrix and venture teams.
2. Use small groups and other techniques to thwart bureaucracy.
3. Empower a team, motivate it (incentives and rewards), and protect it.
4. Destroy turf and territory.
5. Make sure the supporting departments are ready when called on.
6. Clear the tracks in shared departments.

Intensify Resource Commitments

1. Integrate vendors; reduce numbers as necessary.
2. Integrate other technology resources.
3. Integrate resellers; reduce numbers as necessary.
4. Integrate customers; reduce numbers, get them some product fast, even rough.
5. Use simultaneous/parallel/concurrent engineering.

Design for Speed

1. Computer-aided design and other forms of rapid prototyping.
2. Design-aided manufacturing: reduce number of parts, set tolerances with eye on the manufacturing process, design modules, one-way assembly.
3. Use common components across families.
4. Make the product easy to test.
5. Design-in the qualities that make for a fast trial—relative advantage, etc.

Prepare for Rapid Manufacturing

1. Simplify documentation.
2. Use standardized process plans.
3. Use computer-aided manufacturing.
4. Go to just-in-time delivery of materials and components (flexible manufacturing).
5. Integrate product use testing, and start it early.

Prepare for Rapid Marketing

1. Use rollouts, not test markets.
2. Seed the firm's reputation ahead of marketing.
3. Spend what it takes to get immediate market awareness.
4. Make trial purchasing as easy as possible.
5. Get customer service capability in place ahead of need, and test it.

Source: The above is a composite of techniques from many sources, but particularly useful for further study of this subject were: Rene Cordero, "Managing for Speed to Avoid Product Obsolescence: A Survey of Techniques," *Journal of Product Innovation Management,* December 1991, pp. 283–94; Murray R. Millson, S. P. Ray, and David Wilemon, "A Survey of Major Approaches for Accelerating New Product Development," *Journal of Product Innovation Management,* March 1992, pp. 53–69; Edward F. McDonough III and Gloria Barczak, "Speeding Up New Product Development: The Effects of Leadership Style and Source of Technology," *Journal of Product Innovation Management,* September 1991, pp. 203–11; Ed J. Nijssen, Arthur R. L. Arbouw, and Harry R. Commandeur, "Accelerating NPD: A Preliminary Empirical Test of a Hierarchy of Implementation," *Journal of Product Innovation Management,* March 1995, pp. 99–109.

- *Training of every one involved.* People who don't know their jobs, who are assigned work without proper skill-building, won't know how to speed things up.
- *Communication.* Huge amounts of delay can be traced to someone, somewhere, waiting for a piece of information. A 1.5 week production time for an electronic part was actually performed in nineteen minutes. E-mail and the Internet have made collaboration much easier and quicker, and have greatly improved speed of communication in many firms.
- *Flexibility.* Look for machines that can do many jobs, people who can switch from one job to another, stand-by vendors, and more. Attitudes are important too: Mattel's Top Speed toy cars depended on an open-mind designer, so they brought in a new person.[5]
- *Fast decisions.* Managers know that people sometimes get blamed more for things they *do* than for things they *don't do.* Retraining them to make decisions as soon as they reasonably can, *and* managing them in such a way that we don't destroy that willingness, is a key step to a fast program.
- *Cutting things wisely.* There is a common bureaucratic practice of meeting a budget cut of 10 percent by cutting all of its components 10 percent. A better method is to take perhaps a 50 percent cut in noncritical steps, and 0 percent in the key ones. It's all risky, but why not take the risk on things that are more forgiving?

Specific Actions in the Various Parts of a Program

We cannot go through all of the actions in Figure 15–2. Many are obvious anyway. But there are a few that deserve comment.

Several of the actions embody *resource readiness.* A PIC helps assure it by directing us to skills and markets we are good at, and small groups do the same. But integration of our resources with those of others (for example, by strategic research alliances) is especially helpful, and firms are integrating each and every way—upstream to vendors, downstream to resellers and customers, and sideways to competitors and other sources of technical and marketing assistance. Apple, for example, turned to Sony for assistance in speeding up the development of the PowerBook notebook.[6]

---

[5]Eric Schine, "Mattel's Wild Race to Market," *BusinessWeek,* February 21, 1994, pp. 62–63.

[6]For alliances, see J. G. Wissema and L. Euser, *Long Range Planning,* December 1991, pp. 33–39. A good list of do's and don'ts can be found in Judith C. Giordan, "Forging Sound Strategic Alliances," *Research Technology Management,* March–April 1995, pp. 11–12. For the Apple example, see Douglas W. LaBahn, Abdul Ali, and Robert Krapfel, "New Product Development Cycle Time: The Influence of Project and Process Functions in Small Manufacturing Companies," *Journal of Business Research,* June 1996, pp. 179–88.

Another technique is to avoid over-engineering. Development time can be wasted by making a simple concept overly complex without getting guidance from customers as to what they actually want. A rough prototype may not make developers happy, but perhaps customers can examine and test it in their own minds and facilities. "Clean and neat" doesn't sell anymore; "clean enough for the task at hand" does. In fact, customers can be brought in as early as concept generation to provide input to both marketing personnel and the R&D department.[7]

While speed as a management strategy originated in the early technical phases, marketing people now get involved much earlier in the new products process, and can play a major role in accelerating time to market. A month saved on the way to a market-share goal is a month saved, whether in a design coup or in quicker product trial. The tendency of potential customers to postpone trial is legendary; we all do it. Yet we now know a lot about how to speed up trial, and we will look at the methods in Chapter 17. Secondly, we now work with resellers (distributors, retailers, and the like) to get their input and cooperation early, teaming up with them to do a job we will both benefit from.

All members of the team (including the marketing people) should consider the diffusion of a technological innovation. Without diffusion, there is apt to be no success. Many people know how long it took the microwave oven to become popular, but even the popular xerographic process (and the famous 914 Xerox copier) was delayed by being "ahead of its time." The marketing technique of leasing helped stimulate diffusion, but the market's lack of understanding of the item's full usage potential and lack of digital technology for color copying added at least 10 years to the time-to-market-success figure.[8]

Lastly, note the role of the computer in speeding products to market: for CAD and CAM, for design integrated manufacturing, for simulations of all types (including sales forecasting), for communication via e-mail, for the Internet and local intranets, for just-in-time systems, and more. But, JIT systems have to be watched because they tend to bring rigidity too—fixed models, fixed recording systems, efficient manufacturing layouts, and so forth.[9]

Caution: Although there is no question that most firms will benefit as they speed up their development processes, there will also be problems. There

---

[7]Simon J. Towner, "Four Ways to Accelerate New Product Development," *Long Range Planning,* April 1994, pp. 57–65.

[8]Joseph Morr, "Xerography: A Study in Innovation and Economic Competitiveness," *Physics Today,* April 1994, pp. 32–37.

[9]Ulli Arnold and Kenneth N. Barnard, "Just-In-Time: Some Marketing Issues Raised by a Popular Concept in Production and Distribution," *Technovation,* August 1989, pp. 401–31.

are lots of costs involved in speed, costs that are not evident and which can sometimes be disastrous.[10] For example, flexibility today is king of concern in Japanese manufacturing—being able to make scores of new products, usually on the same line. Honda tells of marketing over a hundred new motorcycles in one year. In the meantime, Dell Computers used line simplification, adapting production lines to handle just a *few* configurations, improving product quality and delivery times, and achieving great sales and profit growth on superior customer satisfaction. Massive lines or simple lines? Both can succeed. Another caution is that speed systems operate best in firms that apply the ideas across the board. Trying to have speed on just an occasional project doesn't seem to work, as IBM found out.[11]

The firm must also consider its situation and environment when making speed-to-market decisions. Greater competitive intensity, more rapid technological change, and faster changing market demographics all increase the need for speed—and perhaps the temptation to cut critical steps in the new product process in order to get cycle time down. It is critical for the firm to resist this temptation! A better way to cope when facing a high-turbulence environment is to keep product development as flexible as possible: Do not freeze the product concept until the last possible moment, but allow later stages in the new product process to run concurrently with concept development.[12]

Lastly, managers all hope they don't speed to the point where they have to "solve" problems like the Ford Mustang team did: A wiggle/shimmy in the new model's prototypes was temporarily solved by redesigning the rear view mirror so it wouldn't wiggle in response and thus tip off the driver to what was happening.

The Role of Marketing during Development

The role of the marketing personnel changes and accelerates as the product nears the end of the development phase and moves closer to launch.

---

[10]For the cautionary side, see C. Merle Crawford, "The Hidden Costs of Accelerated Product Development," *Journal of Product Innovation Management,* September 1992, pp. 188–99; and Abdul Ali, Robert Krapfel, Jr., and Douglas LaBahn, "Product Innovativeness and Entry Strategy: Impact on Cycle Time and Break-even Time," *Journal of Product Innovation Management,* January 1995, pp. 54–69.

[11]Paul B. Carroll, "IBM Bends Its Rules to Make a Laptop," *The Wall Street Journal,* April 15, 1991, p. B5.

[12]Marco Iansiti, "Shooting the Rapids: Managing Product Development in Turbulent Environments," *California Management Review,* Fall 1995, pp. 37–58. Roger J. Calantone, Jeffrey B. Schmidt and C. Anthony Di Benedetto, "New Product Activities and Performance: The Moderating Role of Environmental Hostility," *Journal of Product Innovation Management* 14, no. 3 (May 1997), pp. 179–89, looked specifically at high-hostility environments.

Marketing Is Involved from the Beginning of the Process

Years ago, when firms were still predominantly practicing the "selling concept" (i.e., "we sell what we make"), the role of marketing was simple: to sell the products that the firm makes. Marketing didn't really need to get involved in product development until technical personnel had done their job. With all this discussion of teams and speed to market, it is clear most firms aren't following this concept any more—or can't, if they want to stay competitive. Marketing people are now involved from the very beginning of the new product process, and have a very important role. Throughout the process, they advise the new product team how the product development underway fits in with the firm's marketing capabilities (such as sales and sales training, service availability, distribution strengths, etc.) and the market's needs. By early involvement, they can help the product succeed, as they represent the issues and concerns having to do with the marketing of the product.

It is too easy to say that marketing's role is to gather information from the marketplace. Too often, that means that marketing plays a gatekeeper role, funneling information from the marketplace to the new product team that it thinks is important, and possibly missing out on other, more critical information in doing so. The whole team needs to focus on the marketplace, not just marketing. All team members, whether technical personnel, design engineers, or marketing, can gather information. Indeed, the whole idea behind lead user analysis, discussed earlier, is that key customers are part of the team itself and provide information directly. It is better to think of marketing's task not as information *gathering,* but as information *coordination*—deciding what information the various sources have (customers, lead users, distributors, etc.) and what information the members of the new product team need.

A good illustration is provided by DuPont's development in the 1960s of an unusual ethylene polymer named Surlyn.[13] It was originally a totally technology-driven product with apparently interesting properties: It was strong, resilient, clear, and bouncy. It was envisioned, among other things, as a coating for golf balls—and, after much initial resistance from the golf ball manufacturers, was eventually adopted as the replacement for rubber-based ballata golf ball covers. Marketing eventually found out that there was a bigger market out there that was very interested in Surlyn—but not for the attributes originally thought to be most important. Surlyn, as it turned out, had exceptional oil and grease resistance, properties that made it an excellent sealer for the meat packing industry. Further applications were found over the years: as an adhesive for juice boxes, and an extrusion coating for paper. As more market information was gathered, the scientists were able to modify the process and develop related polymers for other applications, such as bowling pins and

[13]Parry M. Norling and Robert J. Statz, "How Discontinuous Innovation Really Happens," *Research-Technology Management,* May–June 1998, pp. 41–44.

ski boots. Clearly, the original technology-push innovation had done an about-face, and market needs were now driving further technical development.

Manufacturing's role has similarly evolved over the years. They also are involved in the new product process from the beginning, advising the team on the manufacturability of the product under consideration. Like marketing, manufacturing understands the need to be involved early, and resents being left out of the early stages of the process. The Hewlett-Packard DeskJet printer, for example, represented a new direction for HP: new products, markets, and customers, and a new product development process. Manufacturing got involved in the process at the very beginning; in fact, manufacturing engineers were moved to the R&D site and used as a resource by the design engineers throughout. The process went so well, designers lobbied to get even more manufacturing engineers! As a result of this project, manufacturing engineers increased in status within HP.[14]

Marketing Ramp-Up, or the "I Think We've Got It" Phase

While they make contributions to the process throughout, the roles of both marketing and manufacturing change as the process moves along. Often, an important turning point occurs when early prototypes are made and are passing performance tests. A new pharmaceutical to combat hypertension, for example, may show promising results in early animal testing. We might call this point the "I think we've got it" phase, and it is here that the team's whole attitude toward the project changes. Up to this point, the technical people on the team played the predominant role, with marketing and manufacturing acting more in an advisory capacity. Now, however, marketing's role increases as marketing people "rev up" their operations. They begin planning field sales and service availability for the product, investigate packaging and branding options, bring in the advertising agency representatives, and so on. In short, the "I think we've got it" phase is where marketing's work for launch begins.[15]

It's also where manufacturing's responsibilities pick up. In new product development, we often hear of "manufacturing ramp-up"—the stage at which manufacturing personnel plan the full-scale production of the product (which up till now has been manufactured in small quantities, sufficient for prototype evaluation). Just like manufacturing ramp-ups from prototypes to full

[14]Dorothy Leonard-Batron, H. Kent Bowen, Kim B. Clark, Charles A. Holloway, and Steven C. Wheelwright, "How to Integrate Work and Deepen Expertise," *Harvard Business Review,* September–October 1994, pp. 121–30.

[15]See discussion of the relative workloads of the marketing and technical personnel as the product moves from development to launch in Behnam Tabrizi and Rick Walleigh, "Defining Next-Generation Products: An Inside Look," *Harvard Business Review,* November–December 1997, pp. 116–24.

production, marketing can be said to ramp up for product launch—and marketing ramp-up begins here.

The Role of Top Management during Development

A common lament of product innovators is about top management—the CEO of a nondivisionalized firm or the general manager of an SBU. New products people claim that only top managements have the power to make decisions essential to their projects. But, in all fairness, top management support is needed for the overall new products *program*—they don't have time to champion *individual projects* except for rare, crucial ones. New products managers must make their own way through the daily jungle of functional conflicts.

Specifically, how can top management help? They should be smart, experienced general managers, for starters. They should know how to make timely decisions and realize the unique and extraordinary need of the new products staff for strategic direction, clear objectives and goals, and a responsiveness to policy and organizational troubles as they arise. They should spot the key checkpoints to watch, and they should know the subtle difference between *taking an interest* and *interference on details.*

Top managers should support (in fact, demand) a product innovation charter. They should supply a sponsor if one does not arise, and they should very clearly and emphatically make it known that functional interface friction (see below) is a sign of managerial failure. Add, too, a longer-term financial view and a managerial style that supports risk-taking and good communication.

Unfortunately, some top managements suddenly get interested in a new product when its introductory expenses begin showing up on the quarterly financial plan; inquiry after inquiry leads to change after change, and by the time the item finally gets to market it is indeed a poor product. Conversely, financial crunch time sometimes leads to top management over-support, stemming from a desire to get the promised revenues into the books as soon as possible, or to take some personal glory from the team's accomplishment.

Top management's interest and support should be clearly *signaled,* by open statements of confidence, by appointments of people who clearly are "comers" in a firm, by a stream of little things like dropping in at the laboratory or a focus group once in a while. Lip service from top management (such as "If I can help you in any way, let me know," or "Find some new products I will like") is not enough.

New products people in some firms worry that a functional head (e.g., VP marketing, VP R&D, or some powerful corporate staffer) may become negative and fail to support people from that function who work on a new products team. Functional heads are often career competitive, and the risk of new products can be damaging. Furthermore, top managements depend on strong functional heads for success in the *ongoing* operation. A president cannot just order a VP of engineering to move the best engineers onto a particular new product project, not if that VP claims the best people are needed to support an ailing multimillion dollar product which supplies the profits that pay for the new product work! A consultant who works a lot with top managements says the "barons" of the functions may hold more power than the CEO, especially when they ask directly: "What is more important—the current budget and forecast or that new product?" Weak or inexperienced top managements may be reluctant to deal with this kind of question.[16] Quantum Corporation is said to have addressed this problem by stating clearly that the path to the CEO's office leads through management in the new product area.

Functional Interface Management

As we have seen, product innovation involves people from many different functional areas and backgrounds: sales and marketing, R&D, design, engineering, manufacturing, operations, and so on. Part of the challenge in new products is managing the **interfaces** across the functional areas, as the key functions *must* cooperate often and effectively.[17] Most of the time, people on these interfaces get along pretty well, some very well. But, as Figure 15–3 reveals, frictions between functional areas can exist, threatening the project. It is up to all participants—including top management—to recognize these frictions, and to deal with them to minimize any possible negative effects.

Why the Friction?

Scores of differences across functional areas have been identified by research studies over the years.[18] Some go deep into the psyche of stereotypes, and most new products people can identify with this complaint: "Those marketers can't get through the day without a two-hour lunch at the most expensive restaurant in town." And this one: "Ever try to get a scientist to say clearly yes or no?" Or, "Why don't manufacturing people ever admit they goofed up?" But these are wildly unfair generalizations. In fact, cross-functional problems

---

[16]The source for the baron quote must remain confidential, but an article by another consultant speaking directly to the CEO/baron problem is Homer Hagedorn, "High Performance in Product Development: An Agenda for Senior Management," *Prism,* First Quarter, 1992, pp. 47–57.

[17]See Kenneth B. Kahn, "Interdepartmental Integration: A Definition with Implications for Product Development Performance," *Journal of Product Innovation Management* 13, no. 2 (1996), pp. 137–51.

[18]See Richard D. Hise, Larry O'Neal, A. Parasuraman, and James U. McNeal, "Marketing/ R&D Interaction in New Product Development: Implications for New Product Success Rates," *Journal of Product Innovation Management,* June 1990, pp. 142–55. For a recent global example, see X. Michael Song and Mark E. Parry, "Teamwork Barriers in Japanese High-Technology Firms: The Sociocultural Differences Between R&D and Marketing Managers," *Journal of Product Innovation Management* 14, no. 5 (1997), pp. 356–67.

FIGURE 15–3

Incidence and consequence of interface problems

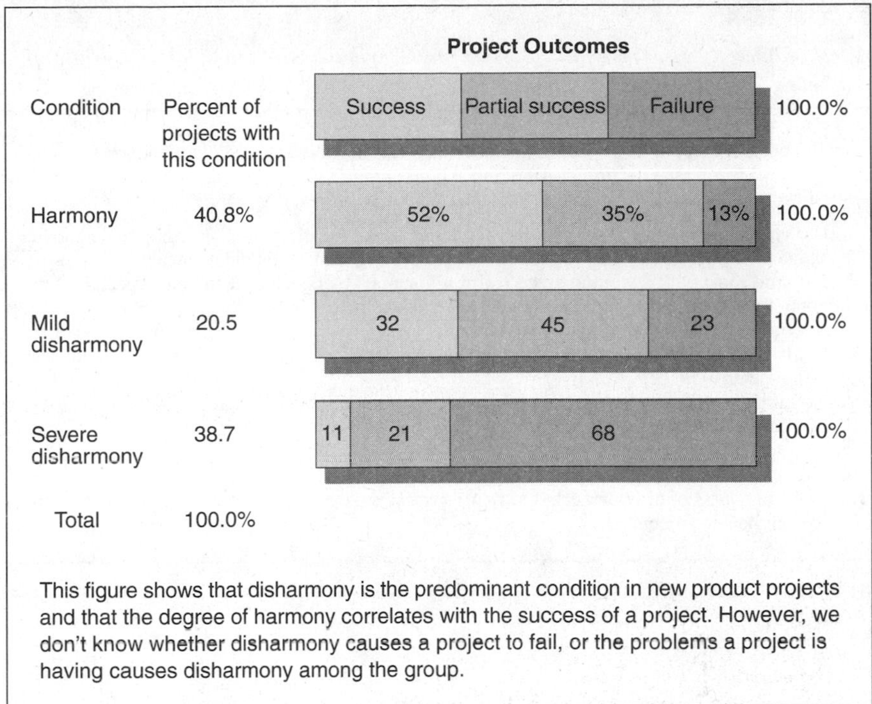

This figure shows that disharmony is the predominant condition in new product projects and that the degree of harmony correlates with the success of a project. However, we don't know whether disharmony causes a project to fail, or the problems a project is having causes disharmony among the group.

Source: William E. Souder, *Managing New Product Innovations* (Lexington, MA: Lexington Books, 1987), pp. 168–70.

are often much less combative than they are sometimes depicted.[19] But people do differ on their general time frame for one thing, and on their measure of success for another.

Sometimes interface problems are caused by ineptness in upper management. The head of R&D in one firm gave such a lashing to a staff scientist for telling marketing some bad news about a product test that the individual wouldn't talk to marketing for over a year. Neither did the other scientists. Their stock answer was "Call the boss and ask him."

A manufacturing manager recently tried an amusing challenge to show marketers how they overlook their own functional myopia. He listed 10 of the

[19]Jean-Philippe Deschamps, "Managing the Marketing-R&D Interface," *Prism,* Fourth Quarter, 1995, pp. 5–19. For some evidence suggesting that there is general agreement across functional areas, see Roger J. Calantone, C. Anthony Di Benedetto, and Ted Haggblom, "Principles of New Product Management: Exploring the Beliefs of Product Practitioners," *Journal of Product Innovation Management* 12, no. 3 (1995), pp. 235–47; and X. Michael Song, Mitzi M. Montoya-Weiss, and Jeffrey B. Schmidt, "Antecedents and Consequences of Cross-Functional Cooperation: A Comparison of R&D, Manufacturing, and Marketing Perspectives," *Journal of Product Innovation Management* 14, no. 1 (January 1997), pp. 35–47.

FIGURE 15–4

A test of interface sensitivity: the pressure on the manufacturing function today, as applied to the function of marketing

This is a chance for persons professionally interested in marketing to sense their reaction to urgings (demands) if put on them by people working in manufacturing. All of the actions are felt to be appropriate (even badly needed) in the area of manufacturing, but they have not been demanded of marketing until now. Are they appropriate?

1. **Use computer-integrated marketing.** Customer sales, logistics, costs—all into one computer system, accessible.
2. **Wage a war on waste.** Throw out bad coupons, wrong media, and old campaigns.
3. **Demand top-quality, standardized training for marketers.** All of them, but especially sales reps.
4. **Form more marketing partnerships.** Up and down the channel, with any group that influences our customers.
5. **Reevaluate accounts and prune those that are not profitable.** Use much more selective marketing.
6. **Put better marketing teamwork into place.** Arrange marketing people into teams, with customer focus, not geographical assignments as now.
7. **Adopt gain-sharing systems.** Let teams share bonuses, based on customer satisfaction surveys.
8. **Lower your unit costs.** Make a real attack on inefficiency, based on tight measurements of productivity and using innovative technologies.
9. **Focus your marketing programs.** Have fewer but better promotional campaigns, at the world-class level.
10. **Achieve a total quality orientation.** Develop new measures for all marketing actions that impact service quality, with full commitments to them.

Source: Allan J. Magrath, "What Marketing Can Learn from Manufacturing," *Across the Board,* April 1990, pp. 37–42.

general pressures put onto the manufacturing function in business—to gain flexibility, cut costs, increase quality, and so forth. He then applied them instead to marketing, as shown in Figure 15–4. If you lean toward marketing, is your reaction to these demands at all influenced by that interest?

Managing the Interfaces

Most interface management is straightforward, and experienced managers often know just what to do. Much research has focused on managing the friction between functional areas. The highlights of the research findings are shown in Figure 15–5. The essence lies in three statements:

- Top managers get the interfaces they deserve because they can eliminate most of the problems anytime they choose to do so.
- Interface management primarily takes time, not skills. One new product manager said he solved his team's problems by giving at least 40 percent of his time to seeing that all key players spent a lot of time with each other, on and off the job.
- Participants who continue to be a problem should be taken out of new product team situations; they get some perverse satisfaction out of reactions to their behavior.

At the most innovative firms, one sees real relationships across functions, and not just structured work assignments. 3M, for example, encourages early, informal communication among marketing, technical, and manufacturing

FIGURE 15–5

Clues to good policy in interface management

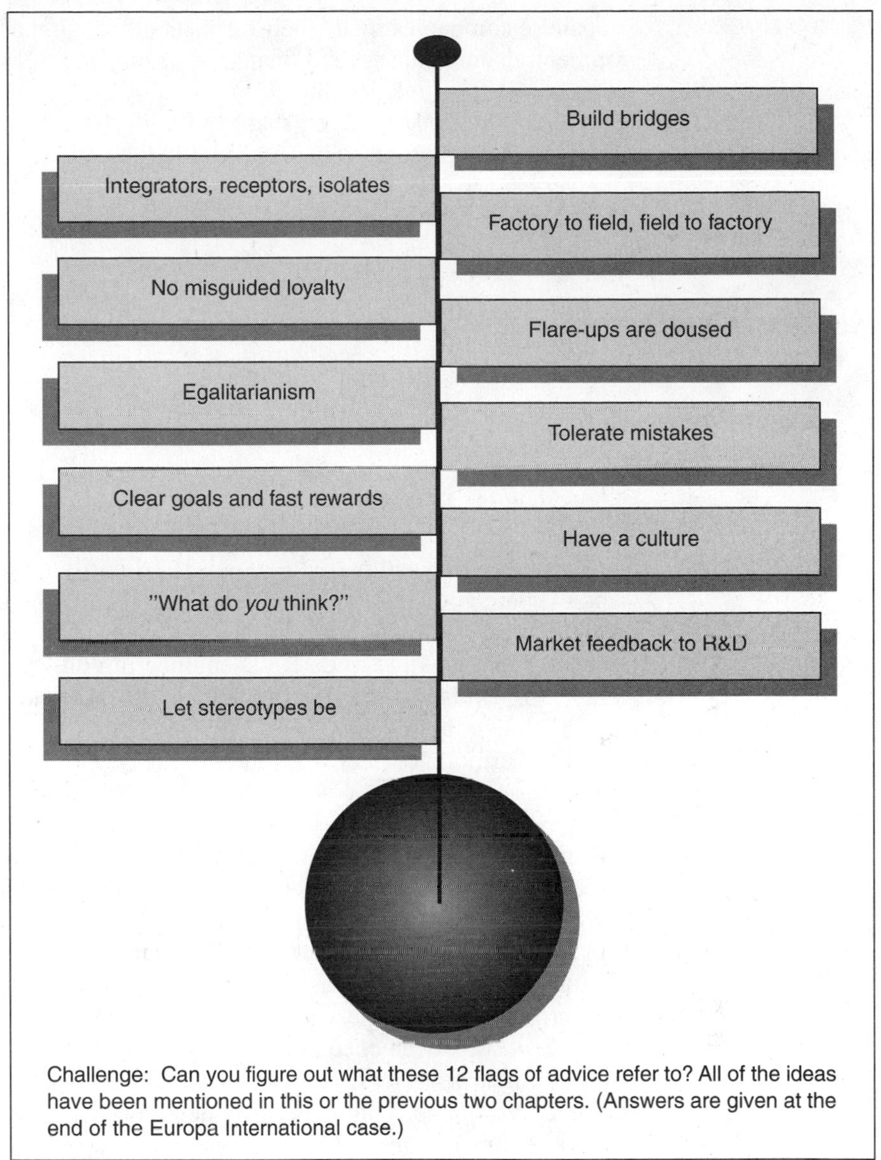

Challenge: Can you figure out what these 12 flags of advice refer to? All of the ideas have been mentioned in this or the previous two chapters. (Answers are given at the end of the Europa International case.)

staff (3M employees refer to this as the "three-legged stool"). Team members bounce ideas off one other and provide resources and information informally to each other. At the new Hoffman-LaRoche research and marketing facility, coffee bars are set up on each floor to encourage "shop talk."[20] Sony and other

---

[20]Eric M. Olson, Rachel Cooper, and Stanley F. Slater, "Design Strategy and Competitive Advantage," *Business Horizons* 41, no. 2 (March–April 1998), pp. 55–61.

Japanese companies rotate their managers through marketing, product development, manufacturing, and finance, thus developing well-rounded managers with a variety of relationships.[21]

Keep in mind, however, that even with these new approaches to teams, conflicts can still arise, so it is essential (to new product development and even the very survival of the firm!) that the people involved in cross-functional interaction cooperate with each other.

New Service Development

Before we leave the topic of managing during development, let's take a look at a group of products that might not seem to have a technical component to their development—**services.** Service firms do not have the customary R&D departments, engineering design, product design, manufacturing engineering, and so on. Or do they?

Services and goods are often arrayed on a scale of (1) pure service, (2) primarily service and partly a good, (3) primarily a good and partly service, and (4) pure good. Examples, in order, are consulting, insurance policy, automobile, and candy bar. Only in the first category does the product provider have nothing tangible to do R&D/engineering on, and there are very few of them. (You might argue that the consultant was the result of technical accomplishment by finishing a college degree!)

Furthermore, even on pure and primarily pure service products, there are tangible support items (such as ads, warranties, policies, and instructions). They need design, and they need production. The fact that this task may be given to an advertising agency doesn't avoid the point because design and production of electronic brake controls can be contracted out too.

Because of these facts, the systems that create service products tend to mirror the systems that create goods. The tools all fit (e.g., the product innovation charter, problem-based ideation, trade-off analysis, screening, protocol, prototype). Their purpose in each case is virtually identical, and services have frequently been cited as examples in this book. Indeed, a recent study of successful new services found that these tended to come from companies that used a systematic, comprehensive new service development process with clearly-defined stages and regular evaluations and reviews—that is, a process that is basically identical to the basic new product process we have presented in this book![22]

The ideas behind these tools also fit: organizational structure options, empowerment, speed, the role for top management, culture, and interface

[21]Karen Anne Zien and Sheldon A. Buckler, "From Experience: Dreams to Market: Crafting a Culture of Innovation," *Journal of Product Innovation Management* 14, no. 4 (1997), pp. 274–87.

[22]Scott Edgett, "The Traits of Successful New Service Development," *Journal of Services Marketing* 8, no. 3 (1994), pp. 40–49.

relations. The San Diego Zoo, for example, did a complete reorganization in which functional departments were made invisible to displays such as Tiger River. Each display area is run by "a team . . . led by a keeper . . . isn't hooked up to the zoo's mainframe . . . members are jointly responsible for the display . . . hard to tell who comes from which department . . . ."[23] Sound like the teams we have been talking about?

Of course, these concepts must be applied creatively, but still the parallels are there. Services firms, for instance, seem to have little in the way of R&D, but someone must design new systems for the performance of services. This function is apt to lie almost anywhere in the firm; rarely is there a services design department. Perhaps there should be.

Iterations are less expensive in the development of services (no tangible good to change), so they are more frequent; most development runs rather fast to prototype because there is less cost to do so. Functional interface frictions are about the same, only the players are often different. For example, bank marketers don't have manufacturing engineers to disagree with, but they do have very strong branches, where many of the services are produced. Marketers probably play a greater role in product innovation on services, but service firms seem less likely to have strong strategies for this work; consequently, marketers' influence is mainly on product modifications, not new-to-the-world products.[24]

One difference between services and goods is often claimed: There is no inventory of services, since they are produced at the point of consumption. Technically yes, but new products people see a connection—in the service business we inventory service *capability*. Take the example of McDonalds—they sell parking convenience as a service, but that convenience was actually created when the parking lot was built.

Even the consultant mentioned above as an example of a pure service, knows enough to drive the right make of car (expensive or cheap) when calling on a client, carry the right business case, and display the right clothing. All have an impact on how well the intangible service recommendations will be accepted and used. And such supportive goods are clearly a part of the new product creation task.

In a rare study of industrial new service development,[25] it was found that new services tended to be successful if they were delivered by trained expert personnel, if they were new to the market and fit well with market needs, or if the service experience to the customer was improved—in short, if a unique,

---

[23]Thomas A. Stewart, "The Search for the Organization of Tomorrow," *Fortune,* May 18, 1990, pp. 92–98.

[24]Axel Johne, Tim Howard, and Robert Davies, *Product Development Practices in British Based Insurance Companies,* Working Paper No. 119, May 1991, City University Business School, London.

[25]Ulrike de Brentani, "New Industrial Service Development: Scenarios for Success and Failure," *Journal of Business Research,* 1995, pp. 93–103.

superior service (as perceived by the customer) was offered. Failed new services tended to be quick and dirty line additions with little customer value, or me-too services offering no new benefits to customers.

Increasing speed to market is just as important to financial service providers as it is to manufactured goods producers. Although speed to market does not lead to increased market share or profits, since innovations are easier to copy and there are few protected markets, speed leads to enhanced reputations and images, and increased customer loyalty.

Solomon Brothers implemented many of the techniques we discussed in Chapter 14: teams, flat organizational structure, empowerment, new reward systems, relocation, and work-flow analyses, reducing development times by up to 80 percent. Other firms (such as Continental Illinois Bank) have accelerated speed to market by outsourcing information technology to specialists, or developing new software for credit card processing. Hiring the needed skills, developing strategic plans for innovation, and making a clear commitment to innovation and to the marketplace are all ways financial services firms can overcome the bureaucracy slowing down speed to market.[26]

Global Considerations

Very few product innovators today think nationally. In almost every case, they see foreign markets as viable options and organize accordingly. Structurally, global product innovation can be handled in several ways:

1. Make no special arrangements. Export what is developed for the home market. On the one hand this is called the *export* approach, yet when market conditions around the world are substantially the same, this approach of one product for all countries is called *global strategy.*
2. Keep structure the same, but develop versions of the new item to meet the needs of viable foreign markets. For example, if Philips comes up with a new razor for the European market, smaller, heavier, or safer versions may be developed for sale in Africa, the Pacific Rim, and other markets. This approach is usually thought of as a variation of the export approach or called *international* strategy.
3. Use the facilities of the home firm, but have separate projects directed by managers in each viable foreign area. These foreign managers learn of available technologies in the home firm, study their local markets to see how each might apply, and then set up

[26]Stephen A. W. Drew, "Accelerating Innovation in Financial Services," *Long Range Planning,* August 1995, pp. 11–21.

projects to develop what is needed there. This is often called a *multinational* strategy. Nestlé prefers this method, and calls it on-the-ground development, but the degree of on-the-ground varies from country to country.[27]

4. Assign the basic responsibility for product innovation to each foreign business large enough to have the resources for it. This usually means some local R&D, local manufacturing, and almost totally local marketing. The manager of each foreign business is a general manager and develops strategies and organizations according to technology and market opportunities. The people working in, say, Spain are free to "buy" service from the headquarters firm in Switzerland if they wish to do so. Operational cultures and policies will vary greatly from country to country. This strategy has no common name, but *local drive* would fit.
5. The last alternative is a mix of the above, variously called *matrix, country of excellence,* and other names. Essentially, the firm wants to be a major player in all viable markets of the world, but wants to develop strategies appropriate to each of those markets. It is often done by world region, continent, or other larger geographical division. NEC, Philips, P&G, L.M. Ericsson, Matsushita, ITT, and Lever use such strategy. Exporting may be used for one product line, an international approach on another line where central technical facilities are necessary to innovation, and multinational on yet another line or division. On another line, a system may be used where for each region the firm selects a country that has had success on the line and gives them the responsibility to extend that success to other countries in their area.

Within each of these strategies the actual new products practices do not vary much, nor should they.[28] There are problems in making adjustments to meet the varying level of resources in different countries (e.g., industrial design resources in Continental Europe and the U.S. are much greater than in the U.K.); and keeping some degree of control over such powerful programs when scattered all over the globe. The operation may involve technical creation in Germany, production in Brazil, financing from London, and marketing in Canada, all the while being directed from an electronic management center in Chicago. The consequence of all this is the demise of what used to be called national designs.[29]

---

[27]Carla Rapoport, "Nestlé's Brand Building Machine," *Fortune,* September 1994, pp. 147–56.

[28]See F. Axel Johne and Patricia A. Snelson, "Product Development Approaches in Established Firms," *Industrial Marketing Management,* 1989, pp. 113–24. See also the perspective of Timothy M. Devinney of the University of New South Wales, in "Significant Issues for the Future of Product Innovation," *Journal of Product Innovation Management,* January 1995, pp. 71–75.

[29]Marilyn Stern, "Is National Design Dead?" *Across the Board,* September 1993, pp. 32–37.

PepsiCo Inc. unveiled a plan in 1996 to improve their global market shares. Coca-Cola has long dominated global soft-drink markets, while Pepsi's global efforts have been less successful: Pepsi billboards were sometimes over 20 years old, they had problems with local bottlers in key markets such as Brazil, and there was no consistency in either taste or image from country to country. The new plan, named "Project Blue," calls for an electric-blue label to be used on all cans and bottles as well as on trucks, new freshness and quality standards, greater marketing spending throughout the worldwide distribution channel, and exciting promotions geared to each national market (such as painting the blue logo on Thai "tuk-tuk" passenger cycles and on the Concorde).[30]

In addition to the above strategies for bringing products to foreign markets, many firms such as McDonald's, Coca-Cola, and movie production houses are routinely searching foreign markets for new ideas to bring back to the domestic market. The Buenos Aires Häagen-Dazs ice cream shop, for example, developed a new caramel-like flavor called *dulce de leche,* which has since been picked up by the parent company and launched successfully throughout the United States and Europe. Nike has similarly brought several shoe ideas (including a soccer boot designed by Brazilian star Ronaldo) into the United States, and Levi's is experimenting with "hard jeans," made of a dark, stiff denim, that are already popular in Japan.[31]

Global search for new product ideas is not a novel idea, nor is it restricted to consumer-goods manufacturers. U.S. pharmaceutical companies had people based in Europe and the Far East scouting for ideas for the U.S. market at least 40 years ago!

Summary

In the overall sequence followed in this book, we have now completed enough technical work (or systems design for services) to have some kind of prototype. It is not ready to market until the end-users who asked for it tell us we have something useful. This they will (hopefully) do in some form of product use testing. For example, a firm may simply ask customers to look at an item and guess whether it would do the job for them. Or proxy opinions may be collected from resellers or end-user's consultants. Or a tough, full-scale test

[30]Robert Frank, Seeing Red Abroad, Pepsi Rolls Out a New Blue Can," *The Wall Street Journal,* April 2, 1996, pp. B1, B6; and Robert Frank and Jonathan Friedland, "How Pepsi's Charge Into Brazil Fell Short Of Its Ambitious Goals," *The Wall Street Journal,* July 30, 1996, pp. A1, A6.

[31]David Leonhardt, "It Was a Hit In Buenos Aires—So Why Not Boise?", *BusinessWeek,* September 7, 1998, pp. 56–58.

of the item in use may be conducted. The entire matter of customer reactions will be taken up in Chapter 16.

Applications

More questions from that interview with the company president.

1. "Angela Lopez is head of our division that sells consulting service to smaller colleges of various types, not the big, state universities. You probably don't even know such consulting exists, but it does, and it is very profitable for us. But at lunch Tuesday, Angela hit me with two tough questions. Seems she has been reading about this emphasis on speed in developing new products and wondered if it applied to her operation. They develop new consulting services regularly. One right now is designed to help smaller colleges teach retired people living in the college's area how they can earn money to supplement their pensions. She asked, 'How do I decide whether speed is *desirable* in my new product operation at this time?' And, 'Is it *feasible* for services?' "
2. "A minute ago you showed me a figure that had a bunch of phrases like *bridges* and *egalitarianism* on it. I know they are supposed to help reduce interface friction, but it seems to me they apply mainly to manufactured goods. Confidentially, one of our divisions is about to begin work on a private electronic communications system for use between parts of large firms—it would replace much of a firm's commercial telephone service, current fax systems, and more. Don't know what it would look like, but it will be a beauty if we can pull it off. Question, can you take that list and give me an example of each of those points, applied to the people working on this new service?"
3. "We have a Gap-type clothing operation that is now large enough to make its first attack on worldwide markets, and for now is committed to what it calls product line extension and adaptation from the United States to selected other countries. But there is some question about how to organize this activity. Management plans to make the decisions on adaptation in their St. Louis headquarters, and at least for now they will sell through importers or agents in other countries (occasionally through the marketing department of one of our other clothing divisions). What thoughts would you have about assigning this responsibility? That is, should it be given to the design department in the United States division, to the product managers in the marketing department, or to a separate group set up just to handle this global-to-be operation?"

4. "I had to laugh when you mentioned the importance of top management. I've been president of two different divisions and now president of the corporation for several years. I've heard that line—just give us your support and we can get that new item to market quickly. Sure they can, and fall flat on their faces, too. They do bad enough without our help; can you imagine what disasters would happen if I started telling people, 'I sure do like Joe Higgins; I'll support him all the way!' Listen, right now our Mountain States banking division has a team of people working on debit cards—they think there is a way to sell these cards and make a profit, even if they wipe out half of our credit card interest income. What would you have that division president do if he were asked to give top-management support to that project? I think the idea is that debit cards would be tied to long-term borrowing contracts and home mortgages, or something like that."

CASE: EUROPA INTERNATIONAL[32]

Gunter Schmidt, director of new businesses for the Europa International hotel chain (headquartered in Frankfort, and similar to several other large chains such as Marriott and Hilton) had just finished reading an interesting report from *Fortune* magazine about a new type of software called groupware.[33] It was then available from four American firms: Ventana, IBM, Lotus, and Collaborative Technologies. The fee for licensing varied from $25,000 to $50,000. Created originally for meetings, it was now getting wider application as a tool for almost any problem analysis and solution. On the marketing side, it could replace focus groups for people with keyboard competence.

The essence was that 5 to 15 people could be gathered on a network, either in one room, or in rooms scattered around the country or world (users didn't care whether the other end of the network was in Boston or Bangkok), and then proceed to discuss an issue by using their keyboards only. There was no open discussion in the room, anyone could write at any time without interrupting others, and any statements could be read by all. Questions could be asked and answered; ideas could be pooled and then systematically evaluated by some scoring system. A common arrangement was for people to sit in a U-shape around the table. Some of the systems were so complex that they required a facilitator to be present; others were not.

The article told how some firms were citing productivity increases from using the software. IBM had cut meeting times by 56 percent, and Boeing saved $6,700 per meeting. Boeing also cut 90 percent of the time it usually took to develop a standardized control system for use on machine tools. These were the first pieces of solid evidence of productivity gains from using computers, historically void of actual dollar and time savings. IBM's success led it to acquire marketing rights to a modified version of the Ventana groupware.

---

[32]The technology of this case is real; the case setting is realistic but hypothetical.

[33]The article mentioned was David Kirkpatrick, "Here Comes the Payoff from PCs," *Fortune,* March 22, 1992, pp. 93–102.

Other advantages were that the impersonal mode brought forth many ideas and comments that otherwise would have been repressed (politics), people can read faster than they can listen, ideas on the screen got credibility regardless of their source (this "democratization of data" was a great benefit for women and minorities), and the customary bazooka effect of "You've got to be kidding" was eliminated.

Groupware was very consistent with the early 90s' rush to team operations. Several of the firms using the systems talked about cutting out levels of management. And people leaving a groupware meeting seemed to have bought in better: They personally participated in the decisions reached. There was clearly more loyalty to the meeting results.

It was not all rosy, of course. Beyond the expense of the system and its operation, there was little gain for meetings that were informational—either from one speaker or for periodic status reports. Attentions wandered some if the participants were at isolated sites, and users noted that managements could submarine the whole thing. For example, experience showed that higher level managers tended to visit the meeting room and walk around, looking at the individual screens. They also sometimes spoke out in an obvious request for support on actions they were urging. They also had later access to every comment through the electronic files. And some executives resented the ability of individuals on the system to reach connections with others of their views, not previously known. Hierarchy was clearly being threatened.

Overall, the reactions to date had been so enthusiastic that Schmidt thought he had better give it some consideration. He particularly noted that users included service organizations (a hotel, an accounting firm, a bank and a power company) and that several of them had mentioned their global operations. Among the applications mentioned, he was especially interested in the ones involving product planning meetings, developing marketing strategies, overall strategic planning and even the selection of a name for a new service.

How could Europa International use groupware? Where would it seem to fit in the overall new products process, and where not? The chain had recently been putting new projects on a team basis, and had been trying to install new (empowerment-type) cultures in operations around the world. Yet their operations were widely scattered, they had language differences, each hotel was permitted considerable flexibility in its strategy and operations, many of their middle and upper-middle managers were not frequent computer users, and he thought some cultures would resist a manager actually sitting at a computer like a clerk. He also knew that several of the firms in the article were frequent experimenters with new technologies and what he called fads, so he discounted most of the results they claimed. Further, he wondered whether Europa International was already at the "I think we've got it" phase, where marketing needed to tune up its rollout plan, or whether the risks were just too high at this moment and he had better sit it out for a while.

Answers to Figure 15–5:

1. Build human and operational bridges between sides of key interfaces.
2. Put integrators and receptors into team work. Leave isolates alone.
3. Use job rotation between functions, especially between marketing and technical.

4. Watch for subordinates who think you *want* them to fight for your function.
5. Move quickly to resolve disputes; don't let anything fester.
6. Treat others (and expect to be treated) as equals. Ranks rankle.
7. Understand that functions you secretly resent will make honest mistakes too.
8. Avoid vague rules. Let everyone know how the game will be played, in advance.
9. Study up on culture, and structure the right one for your situation. Hold to it.
10. Ask for opinions across the functional interfaces. Respect capabilities of all.
11. See that technical people have a chance to know well what the customer needs/wants.
12. People *are* different. Let them be, and learn to be comfortable with the differences.

CHAPTER

16

PRODUCT USE TESTING

Setting

The first output of technical development is a prototype, which is checked against the protocol statement that guided its development and perhaps sent to the marketplace for a confirmatory concept test. The methodology for that is essentially the same as the original concept test except now we have a more tangible expression of the idea. Usually the end-user is not satisfied that the prototype would work on an extended basis, so more development work is done. The cycle continues until the firm has a good approximation of what will be the eventual product—a prototype that stakeholders like.

At this time, most firms like to make up a quantity of prototypes, whether "on the bench" or in some pilot production setup. And for the first time they can give the end-user a product concept that is in a *form for extended use.* No more guessing about whether it *would* or *might* satisfy the needs, based on internal laboratory, or bench, testing. Our task now is to devise a method for testing the end-users' experience with the new item. We call the activity **product use testing (PUT),** or *field testing,* or *user testing.* Sometimes it is called **market acceptance testing,** though this term may also mean *market* testing, as in Chapters 19 and 20. Product use testing is the topic of this chapter.

The importance of product use testing is clear, as it shows up in several of the key concepts driving the whole new product process—the *unique superior product,* the *repeat buying percentage* in the A-T-A-R paradigm, and the *requirements in the protocol.* A product that does not meet end-user needs fails on one of the three key causes of failure.

One other reminder: this chapter applies equally to services and to goods. An article in *The Wall Street Journal* lamented the confusion in airports. A key cause is poor signage, which never gets pretesting for clarity.[1]

What Is Product Use Testing?

Use testing means use under normal operating conditions. Consumers put a tire on a car and drive it, technicians put notebook computers in the hands of warehouse personnel, a bank installs a new check cashing service at three branch points, and so on. The product will probably not be perfect at this time, for more reasons than poor design. An example of *manufacturing* difficulties came from Weyerhaeuser. Their new UltraSofts disposable diapers worked well, very well, and sold at a discount price. But the pilot plant was a poor predictor of full-scale production. There were production line fires and other breakdowns, and suppliers refused to sign long-term contracts on the key diaper liner.[2]

Testing should continue until the team is satisfied that the new product does indeed solve the problem or fill the need that was expressed in the original protocol. Sometimes this can take quite a while, as shown in a Gillette deodorant. (See Figure 16–1.)

Is Product Use Testing *Really* Necessary?

Here is a composite statement of what we commonly hear at product use testing time:

We've been working on this thing for months (or years), and we've spent a ton of money on it. Experts were called as needed. Market research showed that end-users would want a product like this. Why dally around any longer? Top management is leaning on us for the revenues we promised, and we continue to hear that a key competitor is working on something similar. Look, we're now in an up mode; stopping to test suggests to management that we don't have faith in what we've been doing. Besides, customers can't just take the new item and try it fairly; they have to learn how to use it, then work it into their system, listen to our ads (or reps) advising them what to do and how good the results are. Worst of all, a competitor can get his hands on our creation and beat us to the market! No, it's just not worth the time and money to do extended use testing.

[1]Bridget O'Brian, "Signs and Blunders: Airport Travelers Share Graphic Tales," *The Wall Street Journal,* March 28, 1995, p. A1. She feels that confusion seems to be the intended result of signs not being tested.

[2]Alecia Swasy, "Diaper's Failure Shows How Poor Plans, Unexpected Woes Can Kill New Products," *The Wall Street Journal,* October 9, 1990, p. B1.

FIGURE 16–1

The product testing system used for Gillette's Dry Idea deodorant

1. Technical lab work in 1975 suggested available technologies to achieve a drier deodorant.
2. A 2,000-person concept study (cost: $175,000) determined that "Yes, roll-ons are good, but they go on wet and make you wait to get dressed." A concept was at hand.
3. Laboratory project assigned to scientist: find a replacement for water as the medium for the aluminum-zirconium salts that did the work.
4. A prototype using silicone was developed, and it wasn't wet or sticky. But it did dissolve the ball of the applicator (In-house lab test.)
5. Next prototype was tested by volunteers from the local South Boston area. It was oily. (Outside research firm employed to test college students in the area. Gillette often used in-house tests of employees too.)
6. By late 1976, a later prototype tested well on women recruited to sweat for hours in a 100-degree "hot room." (Test of market users in the Boston area who served on a regular panel.) Unfortunately, though it worked well, it eventually turned into a rock-hard gel.
7. By early 1977, another prototype had passed the "hot room" tests and was then sent to company-owned medical evaluation laboratories in Rockville, Maryland. (In-house test on rabbits and rats.) It passed the test.
8. Packaging was developed and tested by in-house package design engineers. Early packages leaked.
9. However, the package dispensed a product that test subjects felt was too dry going on! (Test of market users.)
10. They then returned to a conventional roll-on bottle, added a special leak-proof gasket, and enlarged the ball so the antiperspirant could be applied in quantities large enough to be felt. Another test of market users confirmed that people did indeed feel drier. This conclusion, when put with the earlier data that the product did have a good antiperspirant effect, was enough to go to market.

Note: This procedure used several different types of tests, with different objectives and formats, and with reiterations. The product was cycled until successful.

Source: Neil Ulman, "Sweating It Out," *The Wall Street Journal,* November 17, 1978, p. 1; and "For Some Concerns the Smell of Success Isn't Exactly Sweet," *The Wall Street Journal,* December 28, 1977, p. 1.

Now, sometimes that statement is a fact, not an argument. For example, the first fax machine probably could not be use tested by end-users—there was no network of others with whom to communicate. Same for the picture-telephone. Same for the first color TV when there were no programs being broadcast in color. How could one use test Internet? Hopefully it won't be as bad a situation as that in a well-known cartoon, where one lab scientist holds up a flask and says to another scientist, "It may well bring about immortality, but it will take forever to test it."

Are These Arguments Correct?

These arguments are persuasive, especially when put forth by the person on the top floor who has funded the work to date. But, except for very rare cases such as with the fax machine, they are incorrect. What we have is an unknown, with lots yet to be learned. The user whose problem started the project still hasn't told us that our product *solves* that problem.

Even more, the risks and costs of use testing are usually small compared to the loss of the earnings flow from a successful product (see Figure 16–2). About the only argument that really carries weight is the competitive one, and

FIGURE 16–2

Variable gains and losses from program of product use testing

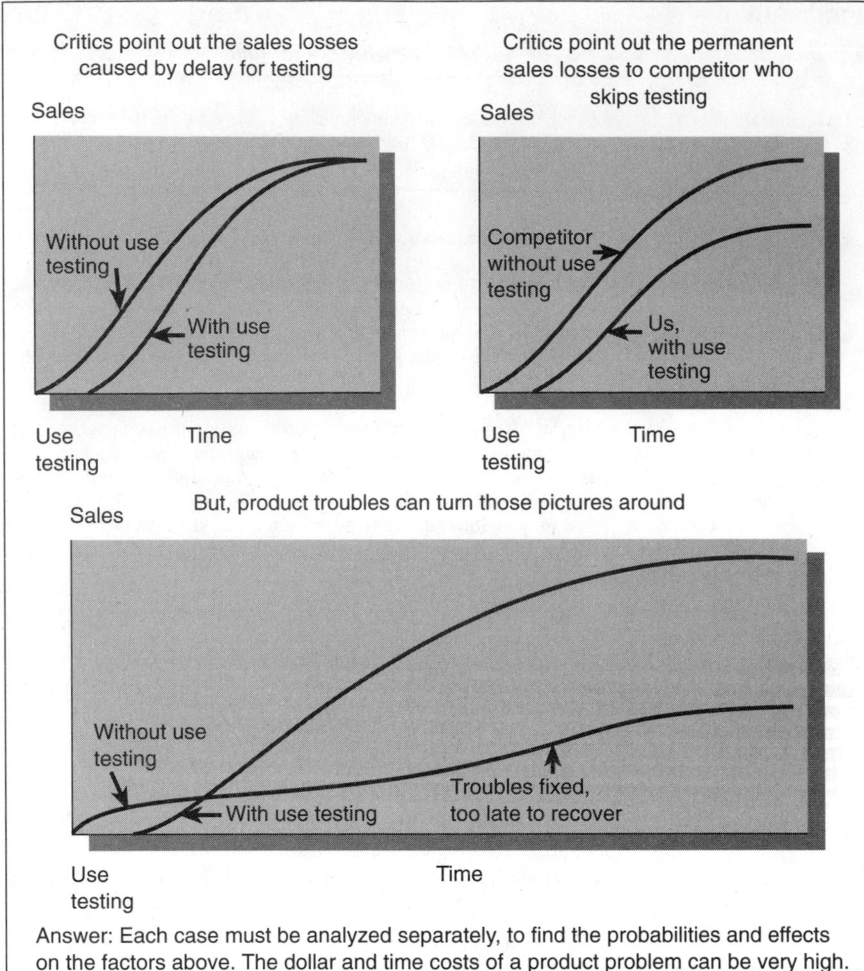

then only when our new product can be copied and marketed, fast. Many food products are like this, as are other items where no technical accomplishment is involved. If use testing clearly makes us second (or even third) into the market, most firms will opt for immediate marketing—without use testing. And, of course, they expect to fail often. Food products suffer an 80 to 90 percent failure rate, based on the minor improvements they offer, the small retail availability such products can get, and the fickleness of consumers who apparently cannot predict their behavior in a concept test.

But, even in those industries, there should be more serious consideration of the counter arguments *for* use testing. Here they are.

Regarding Competitors' Reaction. A firm developing new items is well advised to build its innovation on a technology base where it has some insulation from competitive copying (see the strategy discussions in Chapter 3). Second, competitors today are finding that copying someone else has small gains—others will copy *them,* price competition will take the profits away, the imitator usually copies the innovator's mistakes too, and the competitors we must worry about most are themselves involved in technology-based developments that cannot be thrown over on short notice.

Let's look at the case of Amdahl and IBM. In 1982, Amdahl was an established and successful maker of mainframe computers—big ones. But that year it rolled out a new line and "offered a convincing demonstration of how to do everything wrong . . . When [the machines] did arrive, they were infested with so many bugs that Amdahl field engineers had to scurry about doing retrofits . . . Predictably, the results were devastating . . . Share slumped to around 12 percent, from 17 percent."

Three years later, Amdahl announced its next generation of computers. It took the time to "do the job right," even though IBM got the jump on it. "By insisting on exhaustive, pre-rollout testing, President Lewis made sure the machines worked." The result was spectacular, with sales of 250 machines costing between $3 million and $9 million apiece. The following year, share was back up to 15 percent and climbing.[3]

In 1987, two years later, IBM itself marketed the AS/400 minicomputer (called the most successful product launch in IBM history). By the introduction date, potential buyers had field-use-tested 1,700 of the computers! A year later, they had bought 25,000 of them.[4] Maybe these two firms know something about competitive advantage and copying.

Customer Needs Are Complex Sets. In almost every industry, there is no one, simple, end-user need. Any new item foists onto the end-user a learning curve, there are trade-offs, and there is "baggage"—things that came with the new item that often surprise even the developer. For example, consider the case of GTE Airfone, the firm that developed and marketed a technology to permit telephone calls to go from ground to seated individuals on airborne planes. What seemed like a natural, is going very slowly—turns out that many fliers don't want to be disturbed during their rare "quiet" times. And nearby passengers don't think much of the idea either. Apple, for another example, was in a hurry to market the original Newton. When intended users heard about the new communicator, they raved, and many bought. But then they found that using it was not quite as simple as they had thought, habits had to be broken, frustrations abounded. Apple has spent years changing and improving the product, still without the success it originally intended. All

[3]Marc Beauchamp, "Learning from Disaster," *Forbes,* October 19, 1987, p. 96.

[4]Joel Dreyfuss, "Reinventing IBM," *Fortune,* August 14, 1989, p. 35.

because they didn't want to stop for a full use-test of the product the first time. End-use is indeed complex, and there is no way it can be simulated in laboratories, where use is isolated from user mistakes, competitive trashing of the concept, and objections by those in the user firm or family whose work or life is disrupted by the change.

End-users also often have trouble communicating their wants and their satisfactions, short of having the finished item. For example, two firms (Mars and Hershey) marketed food items with new synthetic fats (from NutraSweet and Procter & Gamble respectively). Both cases faltered on a surprise difficulty: just what do consumers really want in a dessert or a candy bar? Is sweetness an index of enjoyment, does the term fat substitute destroy expectations of pleasant taste, and so on. One firm went national and the other into an expensive test market before these obstacles became clear.[5]

It can take several product use tests for a company to get it right, especially in the case of a really new product. What is important is that the company learns from its errors. For example, the new product process followed by General Electric in the development of the CT scanner was unusually convoluted. It developed, in turn, a head scanner, a breast scanner, and a full-body scanner, none of which worked satisfactorily, according to the customers (physicians) who tried them. For their fourth effort, GE launched the 8800 full-body scanner that was vastly superior to competing products. GE ultimately captured over two-thirds of this market, leapfrogging EMI that previously was the top CT scanner manufacturer.[6]

Can We Deliver a Total Quality Product? Recall the idea of the augmented product—where there is a core benefit, then a formal product, and then the many augmentations of service, warranty, image, financing, and so on. The new product process tends to focus on the core benefit and the formal product, and even that may have implementation problems (see Weyerhaeuser, above). But firms often just *assume* they will be able to deliver the outer ring of augmented product quality—the sales force will be able to explain the new item well, early product breakdowns will not chase other potential buyers away, the finance division will approve generous financing arrangements, the advertising effectively answers competitors' claims, and warehouse personnel won't make a simple mistake and destroy half the product. These things happen, and often. Horror stories abound:

Black & Decker once pulled thousands of flashlights off store shelves and stopped shipment on a new line of smoke detectors that carried the

---

[5]For Mars: Gabriella Stern, "Attempt To Cut Candy Calories Sours for P&G," *The Wall Street Journal,* August 25, 1993, p. A1. For Hershey: No author, "Simple Pleasures," *Across the Board,* May, 1994, p. 39.

[6]Gary S. Lynn, Mario Mazzuca, Joseph G. Morone, and Albert S. Paulson, "Learning Is the Critical Success Factor in Developing Truly New Products," *Research-Technology Management,* May–June 1998, pp. 45–51.

Ultralife battery after Kodak discovered that an unexpected buildup of material affected its shelf life. The discovery was made during marketing, not during use testing.

General Electric took a $450 million pretax charge for a new refrigerator compressor, which was never field tested because the firm was sure it would work. The impossible happened.[7]

P&G was well into test markets with two new Party Cakes, before finding that pans used to bake the character cakes either charred or smoked while in the oven. The products had to be pulled from the shelves, and customers given refunds.

Wolverine World Wide marketed a new running shoe, only to find that "20% of runners stressed a seam in the gel pouch inside the heel, rupturing it over time. The cost: a one-year delay and $5 million."[8]

Coca-Cola marketed a new soda machine called Breakmate, a microwave-oven-size soda fountain for the home, the office, and on picnics. (Their haste was partly based on belief that PepsiCo would soon market its own soda fountain; but PepsiCo did a use test as part of a test market, and dropped the idea.) Coca-Cola ended up unable to build the proper distributor service capability, the product when used in the South attracted ants and roaches "from a hundred miles away," and some of the drip trays grew so much mold they looked "like a science project." It was a very expensive failure, even in executive pride and reputation.[9]

To bypass product use testing is a gamble that should be considered only when there is just cause. The burden of proof is on whoever argues for skipping it. Intel seemed to have a very good reason to cut short testing of their highly-publicized Pentium chip, and perhaps they did—the problems that appeared occurred only rarely (one needed 9th decimal calculation for one glitch to appear). But some managers' arguments are weaker. Like this one: "We don't like to do in-home use testing of our (paper) products, so we take care to make them right the first time!"

Knowledge Gained from Product Use Testing

As seen in the above examples, there is ample opportunity for the firm to learn from product use testing, and to use the knowledge gained to make the product more suitable to the desired market. Figure 16–3 shows the key pieces of knowledge that use tests provide.

---

[7]For the full story on this disappointment, see Thomas F. O'Boyle, "GE Refrigerator Woes Illustrate Hazards in Changing a Product," *The Wall Street Journal,* May 7, 1990, p. 1.

[8]Rita Koselka, "The Dog that Survived." *Forbes,* November 9, 1992, pp. 82–83.

[9]See John R. Emshwiller and Michael J. McCarthy, "Coke's Soda Fountain for Offices Fizzles, Dashing High Hopes," *The Wall Street Journal,* June 14, 1993, p. A1. The full story seems almost impossible, but even in good firms we find mistakes.

FIGURE 16–3

Set of new knowledge from product use tests

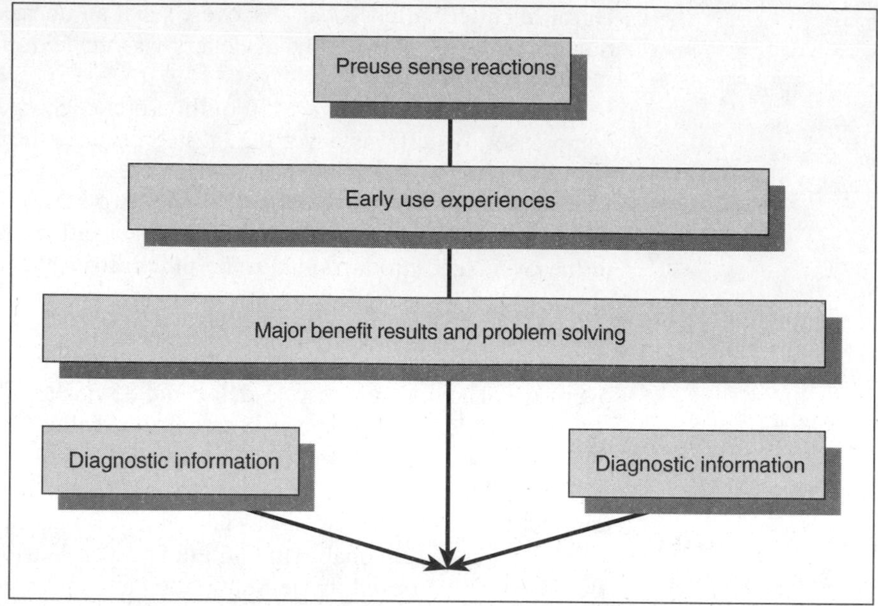

Preuse Sense Reactions. Almost every product gives the user a chance to react to immediate sensations of color, speed, durability, mechanical suitability, and so on. Initial reactions are important, especially on service products. For example, managers at Saturn feel the most important single reaction of a potential new car buyer is the impression upon first entering a dealership. In the marketing of the first Saturn managers designed dealerships for a good impression and measured to see they got it.

Early Use Experiences. This is "does it work" knowledge. Key specifics are such things as ease of use, surface variables, can they manage it, are there still bugs, and is there any evidence of what the item will eventually do.

Beta Tests. The ultimate use test of the protocol is to try it out at customer sites, to evaluate whether the product solves whatever problems led to development of the product in the first place. In some industries this latter point is a special problem. Computer hardware and software firms, for example, are under great competitive pressure and prefer to run what they call **beta tests.** These are short-term use tests, at selected customer sites (external customers or, sometimes, employees serving as internal customers). They are designed to tell the manufacturers one thing: does this product work, free of bugs? In fact, some have their people competing to see who can find the most bugs in a new item—better now than later.[10] They are not designed to tell them about

---

[10]Douglas W. Clark, "Bugs are Good: A Problem-Oriented Approach to the Management of Design Engineering," *Research Technology Management,* May–June 1990, pp. 23–27.

meeting customer needs and solving problems—such testing takes longer than the few weeks usually allowed on computer products.

Firms in the computer industry seem to be the champions at beta testing. Netscape launched Navigator Release 2.0 in January 1996, and had an early beta version of Release 3.0 up on its internal website by February. After getting early feedback from hundreds of employees, a second internal beta was made available two weeks later. A third beta version, this one available to the public, was released by early March. This procedure continued through several more beta versions until Release 3.0 was launched in August. Throughout this period, Microsoft was developing its competitive Explorer product, beta testing internally (with 18,000 employees) and also externally. Netscape was also monitoring the beta versions of Explorer product over this time.[11]

Unfortunately, beta tests are conducted under such time pressures that managers tend to ignore danger signals. What might become a classic was NCR's development of its Warehouse Manager computer package. In hurrying this product to market, the firm committed several mistakes:

- Concluded the beta tests before there was time for key bugs to show up. The program actually sabotaged customers' accounting and cost systems.
- Neglected to test thoroughly a part of their package that they licensed from another firm—Taylor Management.
- Continued selling and installing the $180,000 program after hearing of horrendous problems with it. Several big installations were made even after NCR ordered a halt to further sales.
- Promised "single source solution" to technical problems when in fact they depended on Taylor to handle problems on their part of the package.
- Took the stance with individual customers that the product worked well so the problems must be caused by the customer.

Note that inadequate use testing can lead to far more problems than product adjustments. NCR's court hassles multiplied the cost of adequate product testing many times.[12]

There are other concerns regarding beta test implementation. If done too late in the new product process, design may already be essentially fixed—or if design changes are required, they may delay the launch. But if a beta version of a new computer program is released before major bugs are worked out, the lukewarm results may get picked up in the popular computer press, damaging the product's reputation. (This was one reason why Microsoft chose to release only two or three beta versions of Explorer, rather than the six

---

[11]Marco Iansiti and Alan MacCormack, "Developing Products on Internet Time," *Harvard Business Review,* September–October 1997, pp. 108–117.

[12]Mile Geyelin, "How an NCR System for Inventory Turned into a Virtual Saboteur," *The Wall Street Journal,* August 8, 1994, p. A1.

FIGURE 16–4

Common pitfalls of beta testing

- Beta test site firm has no internal capacity to test the performance of the product at the required level and lacks the funding to hire an outside firm to do the test.
- Developer puts in a wishy-washy performance requirement like "user-friendly" which is meaningless unless a measurable specification is defined.
- Testing is done too late in the new product process, which almost ensures that development time will be extended and production delays will occur. Doing testing in increments throughout the process is a way to avoid this pitfall.
- Developers attempt to beta-test their own products. By definition they are too close to the product to critically test it and find problems.
- Developers ignore early negative results, hoping that the product will improve by itself during the new product process. All beta test results, whether positive or negative, need to be honestly evaluated.

Source: Robert Stoy, "Assembled Product Development," in M. D. Rosenau, A. Griffin, G. Castellion and N. Anscheutz, eds., *The PDMA Handbook of New Product Development* (New York: Wiley, 1996), pp. 271–86.

or seven versions of Navigator 3.0 released by Netscape.) Further, the firm testing the new product may need to obtain information from the beta test site customer (such as economic value) which might strain the supplier-customer relationship. Figure 16–4 summarizes the more common pitfalls of beta testing.[13]

Gamma Testing. Beta testing may not meet all of the developer's needs. In a beta test, users may not have had time to judge whether the new product met their needs or was cost-effective for them. Apple Computer's Powerbook notebook had faulty disk drives that were not discovered until after marketing, even though Apple did "field testing." As a result, a third term is becoming popular, **gamma testing** (gamma being the third Greek letter after alpha and beta). It designates the ideal product use test, where the item is put through its paces and thoroughly evaluated by the end user. To pass this test, the new item must solve whatever problem the customer had, no matter how long it takes. Gamma testing is so critical on new medicines and medical equipment that the United States demands it; such testing can take up to 10 years.

Even though gamma testing is the ideal test (and is urged here), firms anxious to save time and money, or to leapfrog competitors, nevertheless opt to go with beta testing. Some virtually have to—carmakers, for example. The very successful Saturn was beta-tested by market users who drove them on a prepared track, dealers who drove them at the Arizona proving grounds, and

[13]Beta testing is a large and complex subject. One very helpful study is Robert J. Dolan and John M. Matthews, "Maximizing the Utility of Consumer Product Testing: Beta Test Design and Management," *Journal of Product Innovation Management,* September 1993, pp. 318–30. For a full discussion of the benefits and risks of beta testing, see Robert Dolan, *Managing the New Product Development Process* (Reading, MA: Addison-Wesley, 1993), pp. 221–32.

automotive magazine writers and test drivers. But there was no testing over a time needed to really judge whether the new car actually met family needs.

Diagnostic Information. New products managers look for how items are used, and what mistakes are made. Use tests often suggest ways to improve performance or to reduce cost. General Foods carried to the very last test the issue of the relative proportions of instant coffee and roasted grains for Mello Roast; it needed the best trade-off between the lower cost of the grains and the effect on flavor. New product developers also seek specific pieces of information needed to back up their claims. Marketers want confirmation of target markets and product positionings. Product integrity is also on trial during a use test, since only the users' perceptions tell us whether the parts tie together into a meaningful whole, and whether product fits application.[14] Lastly, developers watch for any other red flag, a signal that users had some problems understanding the new item, or were slow to accept the results they got, and so on.

Apple and other software manufacturers may use *case-based research* as a very comprehensive form of product use testing that runs parallel to the software's development process, from early concept to finished product. The first stage is *investigation:* the developer interviews users to learn their expectations and how they will likely use the product. In the *development* stage, users are encouraged to try early prototypes of the new software and explore its menus and features. As an interesting twist, they speak out loud during product use, describing any problems they encounter. This stage is followed by the **alpha test** with end-users in real work environment. Product use problems are identified at this stage, and solutions to all of these will be provided in the software instruction manual. This is all followed by a standard beta test.[15]

Decisions in Product Use Testing

Any product use test, whether one of several or alone, whether industrial or consumer, whether for Egypt or Alabama, should be crafted carefully, and several key decisions must be made. First and foremost, managers should decide what it is they *need to learn* from the product use test. Though what we need to learn is totally situation specific, the objectives should still be clear and should include the requirements spelled out in the protocol. (See Chapter 12.) Some managers like to do what is often called a Potential Problem

[14]For more on this subject, see Kim B. Clark and Takahiro Fujimoto, "The Power of Product Integrity," *Harvard Business Review,* November–December 1990, pp. 107–18.

[15]Matthew Holloway, "A Better Way to Test Interface Design," *Innovation,* Summer 1994, pp. 25–27.

Analysis at this point. The remainder of this section examines other key questions faced in product use testing.

Who Should Be in the User Group?

Some use testing is done with *lab personnel* at the plants where the products are first produced. Alexander Graham Bell became the first telephone user when he called his assistant.

Experts are the second testing group (for example, the cooking staff in a test kitchen). Car companies have styling professionals; wine companies have tasters. Experts will give more careful consideration than will typical users and probably will express more accurate reactions. They will not be interested in the same things that interest customers, however.

The third test group option, *employees,* is widely utilized though often criticized. Company loyalties and pressures and employees' lifestyles and customs may distort opinions and attitudes. Obvious problems of possible bias can be overcome to some extent by concealing product identities and by carefully training and motivating the employee panel.

Stakeholders are the next choice, and the set includes customers and noncustomers, users and nonusers, resellers, end-user advisers (such as architects), users of competitive products, repair organizations, and technical support specialists whose reactions to new products have been sought.

Market researchers doing the use-testing are very careful to pick the right number of stakeholders. Sample size may vary from 3 to 6 for experts, 30 or more for employees, and from 20 to several thousand for end-users. A joint operation between Whittle Communications and Philips Electronics bet $70 million on a use test for a medical news service via TV; it involved 6,000 physicians.[16] As we have seen earlier, Netscape's Navigator and Microsoft's Explorer were tested at thousands of internal and external sites.

As usual, sample size is primarily a function of what is being tested. Any sample should be representative of the entire population for which the product is targeted and the results should be accurate (have *validity*) and reproducible (have *reliability*). A hair products firm marketed a new hair tonic for men, after use testing, and it flopped primarily because it was tested in humid areas of the country. In drier areas, the product evaporated too quickly to do the user any good.

How Should We Reach the User Group?

There are several options here. First we must decide on mode of contact: *mail* and *personal* are the most common. The mail method is more limited than personal contact in type of product and depth of questioning, but it is more

[16]Patrick M. Reilly, "Whittle, Philips Plan Interactive M.D. TV," *The Wall Street Journal,* June 26, 1992, p. B1.

flexible, faster, and cheaper. Burlington Industries used the telephone to ask people to serve on special one-time mail panels that evaluated new fabrics. Business-to-business firms often insist on personal contact, since they need a closeness far beyond that of most consumer products.

Second, there is a choice between *individual* contact and *group* contact. Most firms prefer individual contact, especially at this critical point in the development cycle, but it may be cheaper to deal with groups. (The traditional focus group is not a place for *use* testing.)

Third, the individual mode of contact brings up the question of *location.* Should the test be conducted at the *point of use* (home, office, or factory), or should it be conducted at a *central location* (test kitchen, shopping center, theater, or van)? The point-of-use location is more realistic and permits more variables to operate. But it offers poor experimental control and permits easy misuse. In contrast, the central location offers very complete facilities (such as kitchens, two-way mirrors, eating areas, pseudo stores), good experimental control, speed, and lower cost. The central location approach is winning out, but industrial firms will almost certainly stay with on-site studies. Sometimes one can be creative—TV networks test new pilot programs in Las Vegas, not at all representative, but oddly, a place where a wide range of people have time and desire to look at pilots, between runs at the machines and tables.

Should We Disclose Our Identity?

A key issue, **identity disclosure,** concerns how much the user should be told about the brand or maker identity of the product. Some testers prefer open disclosure, while others (the majority) prefer to keep it secret. It may be that the brand cannot be hidden—as with many cars, some shoes, and many business products. Persons have perceptions about various firms and brands. Knowing a new item's brand introduces halo-image effects, maybe distorting user reactions. One must keep in mind what is being tested. Developers may need a competitive comparison (only **blind tests** can determine this). Or they may want to know if users *perceive* the new item to be better (honest perception requires brands).

A good compromise is to do both, first a blind test, followed by a branded test. This covers most of the issues. Service products can rarely be tested blind.

How Much Explanation Should We Provide?

Some people conduct use tests with virtually *no comment* other than the obvious "Try this." But such tests run the risk of missing some of the specific testing needs. A second degree of explanation, called *commercial,* includes just the information the customer will get when actually buying the product later. The third level is *full explanation.* It may be necessary to include a great deal of information just to ensure the product gets used properly. Rolm gave Nissan's employees 90 days of training in the use test for its CallPath system.

Some people do one round of testing with full explanation, followed by a brief round at the commercial level.

How Much Control over Product Use Should There Be?

Most new medicines can be tested legally only under the control of physicians. This *total control* is essential when accurate data are required and when patient safety is a concern. Many industrial products also require total control to avoid dangerous misuse.

But most testers want users to experiment, to be free to make some mistakes, and to engage in behavior representative of what will happen later when the product is marketed. For example, a new blend of coffee may be tested under conditions of perfect water, perfect measuring, and perfect perking, but it should also be tested in the kitchen the way the average person will do it—right or wrong.[17] By providing this kind of freedom, the company can see how the product is likely to be misused. If Heublein had extensively product-use-tested its 1970s-era Wine & Dine meals (pasta, sauce mix, and a bottle of salted cooking wine in a box), they would have identified a problem that hit them in the marketplace instead. Many customers just drank the salted wine, gagged, and vowed never to buy the product again![18]

So two modes of looser control—*supervised* and *unsupervised*—have developed. If a conveyor belt manufacturer wants to test a new type of belting material, company technical and sales personnel (maybe even their vendor's people) will be at the user's plant when the material is installed (supervised mode). After early runs indicate there are no mistakes, the belting people go back home, and the material is left to run in an unsupervised mode for the full testing period (though developer personnel are never very far away).

Services are almost always under some supervision because they cannot be taken home to use. Olga restaurants test new menus in a few locations (supervised mode) and then roll them out if everything works well.

How Should the Test Be Conducted?

The product may be tested in many combinations, but three ways are standard (see Figure 16–5):

- In a **monadic** test, where the respondent tests a single product for a period of time. Services usually must be monadic, though there are exceptions.

---

[17]It has been said that one of the best ways to mislead product planners is to establish exacting controls in product use test that won't be duplicated in the real world. See Robert J. Lavidge, "Nine Tested Ways to Mislead Product Planners," *Journal of Product Innovation Management,* 2, (1984), pp. 101–5.

[18]Robert M. McMath and Thom Forbes, *What Were They Thinking?* (New York: Times Business, 1996).

FIGURE 16–5

Types of product use tests, as applied to a new toothbrush

Type	*Products*	*Instructions*
Monadic	The new product alone.	Try this new toothbrush, and tell me how you like it.
Paired comparison*	The new product and another toothbrush—(1) the market leader or (2) one known to be the best or (3) the leader in the segment selected for the new product or (4) the one currently used by the testee.	Try these, and tell me how you like them, which you prefer, etc.
Triangular*	The new product and two of the others. A variation is to use two variants of the new product and one of the others.	Same as on paired comparison.

*These multiple-product techniques can employ either of two product use approaches:

Side-by-side: Please brush your teeth with this toothbrush, and then brush again with the other one. Then give me your reactions.

Staggered (often called a sequential monadic): Please use this toothbrush for a week, and then switch to the other for a week. Then give me your reactions.

- In a **paired comparison** where use of the test product is interspersed with that of a competitive product. Either a side-by-side or staggered approach may be used (see Figure 16–5).
- In a **triangular** approach, in which the new product and two others are tested.

More sophisticated experimental designs exist, but they are only used in special situations.[19] The monadic test is the simplest; it represents normal usage of products. But it is less sensitive in results. The usual *side-by-side* or simultaneous form of paired comparison is the most unrealistic test, but it is by far the most sensitive. A *sequential monadic* is probably the ideal combination, though it takes longer. In the staggered format, a user may try out a toothbrush for one week then change to another for the second week, then go back to the first one.

Even monadic tests usually involve a silent competitor—the product being used before the new one appeared. When an established category (such as photocopiers) is involved, then it is almost a must to test a new product against the category leader. But in the absence of an established category, as was the case with the first fax machine, what does the developer do? The first fax should have been tested against photocopying, overnight delivery, and/or

[19]For added information on such matters as experimental designs, sequencing of stimuli, and sample design, see Howard R. Moscowitz, *Product Testing and Sensory Evaluation of Foods* (Westport, CT: Food and Nutrition Press, 1983). Another advancement (going to multivariate formations) can be found in Moshe Givon, "Taste Tests: Changing the Rules to Improve the Game," *Marketing Science,* Summer 1989, pp. 281–90.

the messenger service. If there is no direct predecessor, product developers usually just run a monadic test and then ask the user to compare the new product to whatever procedure was being followed before.

Over What Time Period Should the Test Be Conducted?

Some use tests require a *single* product experience (this may be all that is needed for a taste test); some require use over *short periods* of up to a week; and some require use over *extended periods* of up to six months. The longer period is needed if substantial learning is required (a shift in a paradigm) or if initial bias must be overcome. A longer period is also needed if the product faces a full range of variations in use (for example, entertaining in the home, carelessness in the office, or high-pressure overtime in the plant). Again, researchers opt more often to use several modes. The initial, quick test predicts the early reactions of those people we call "innovators." Failure here, even if perceptions are unjustified, will often doom a good product. On the other hand, favorable initial impressions must be sustained well past the novelty stage. Many products have flared briefly before sputtering to an early death.

Tests over a month long are rare on consumer products and difficult to defend to management. But if a new piece of business equipment will be positioned on its cost-cutting advantage, the use test had better run long enough for the user to see a significant cost reduction. Incidentally, those long tests of paint panels in the fields along highways are lab tests, not use tests. There is no testing of user carelessness in application, thick vs thin paint coatings, and the many other variations one gets in a true home use test. Apple gets closer when they test PowerBooks with common indignities such as spilled soda, and simulated bouncing in a car trunk. But again, this is not true use testing, where customers are far more inventive of destructive ways.

What Should Be the Source of the Product Being Tested?

Generally speaking, three different sources of the product are employed in a use test—*batch, pilot plant,* and *final production.* If the firm will employ just one type of use testing, then the final production material is far and away the best. Batch product should be used alone only if the production process is prohibitively expensive.

As with many other phases of product development, the decision on source of product is a trade-off between the cost and value of information. Being penny-wise at this point has proven over and over to be pound-foolish.

Often overlooked is the product left in the hands of users at the end of the test. In most cases, the product should be collected and examined for clues about user problems and actions during the test. If a patent application will follow soon, it is very important to pick up *all* of the product; otherwise, developers risk losing the originality requirement of the patenting process.

What Should Be the Form of the Product Being Tested?

One view favors testing the *best single product* the organization has developed. The opposing view favors building *variants* into the test situation—colors, speeds, sizes, and so on. The latter approach is more educational but also much more costly. Services are almost always tested in multiple variations, given that it is usually easy to make the changes.

The decision rests on several factors, the first being how likely the lead variant is to fail. No one wants to elaborately test one form of the product and then have that form fail.

Further, what effect will added variants have on users' understanding of the test? The more they test, the more they understand, and the more they can tell us. For example, a maker of aseptic packaging for fruit juices realized the juice and the package were both new to consumers, so the firm tested orange juice in the new package first and subsequently tested the new apple and cranberry juices. (Incidentally, the firm shipped the orange juice to its European factory for packaging so that it would spend the same time in the box as did the apple and cranberry juices.)[20]

How Should We Record Respondents' Reactions?

Essentially, three options are available, as demonstrated by Figure 16–6. First, a five- or seven-point verbal rating scale is generally used to record basic *like/dislike* data. Second, the respondent is asked to compare the new product with another product, say, the leader or the one currently being used, or both; this is a *preference score,* which can be obtained several ways. Third, for diagnostic reasons, testers usually want *descriptive information* about the product that covers any and all important attributes. Examples include taste, color, disposability, and speed. A semantic differential scale is the most common here. This is where we gather all of the other information called for in the objectives.

A research firm involved in studying opportunities for a new sausage had previously asked consumers to rate the sausage products then available on a variety of attributes, including greasiness and saltiness. The results showed strong aversions to both of those attributes, which were associated with low overall scores for product quality.[21]

The researchers presumed from this that the ideal sausage would have low levels of greasiness and saltiness, and several test products were developed accordingly. Needless to say, use testing proved just the opposite—the two top sausages in the test ranked first and second in saltiness, and they were

[20]Regardless what the form is, the test product should be representative of the product that will actually be launched—not of significantly higher or lower quality (yes this happens!). This is another of Lavidge's ways to mislead product planners. See Robert Lavidge, "Nine Tested Ways."

[21]Howard R. Moscowitz and Barry E. Jacobs, "Combine Sensory Acceptance, Needs/Values Measures When Researching Food Products," *Marketing News,* January 22, 1982, sec. 2, p. 6.

FIGURE 16–6

Data formats for product use tests (samples selected from the many available)

Like/Dislike

	1	2	3	4	5
Product A:	Dislike strongly	Dislike some	Neutral	Like some	Like very much

Test product: (frowning face) (neutral face) (smiling face)

Which of these words best describes your overall satisfaction with the test product? (circle one)

Happy Contented So-so Unhappy Angry

Preference

What was your preference between the two products?

- ☐ Much prefer C
- ☐ Somewhat prefer C
- ☐ Don't care either way
- ☐ Somewhat prefer M
- ☐ Much prefer M

Descriptive/Diagnostic

For each attribute below, please check your feelings about the test product:

Tastes great |—|—|—|—|—|—|—| Tastes awful

On which of the following applications would you want to use the new material?

- ☐ Floors
- ☐ Ceilings
- ☐ Walls
- ☐ Roofs
- ☐ Inside cabinets
- ☐ Other–please specify: ______________________

____

What changes would you like to see made in the test product?

____

____

among the greasiest. Some of the least greasy test products had some of the lowest overall scores. We have come to expect the unexpected, and plan for it.

Marketing research has spawned a large group of exotic research methodologies found to be useful occasionally in new product testing. For example, brain wave measurements help disclose users' inner thoughts, especially if they have a strong emotional reaction to the product being tested. Voice pitch analysis has been used to overcome product testers' efforts to be helpful and avoid hurting the tester's feelings. Galvanic skin response has been tried too.

One additional piece of information is very important at this point—intent to purchase. Recall that near the end of the concept test, we asked respondents how likely they thought they would be to try the product if it became available on the market (the top-two-boxes question). We have now asked them how well they liked the product and whether it was preferred to their currently used product. So again, we ask the buying intention question, this time as a measure of use test results, still not a predictor of actual trial rates.

In many *business* product use tests the market research flavor of this section is missing. They want all relevant information, and get it by close personal investigations and observations. Users may find applications the developers didn't even think of. There are few formal questionnaires in evidence.[22]

How Should We Interpret the Figures We Get?

Testers have long realized that they want *comparative* figures, not just *absolutes.* That is, if 65 percent of the users liked a product, how does that percentage compare with previous tests of somewhat similar items? If previous winners all scored over 70 percent on the "like" question, then our 65 percent isn't very impressive.

The 70 percent figure is a *norm.* Where we get norms and how we use them is often a serious question. The major source is obvious—the library of past experiences, thoroughly studied and averaged. The files of marketing research supplier firms are also helpful, but norms pulled from the air at committee meetings are virtually worthless.

Who Should Do the Product Use Test?

The first choice here is between personnel *within* the company and personnel *outside* the company. The firm may or may not have the necessary personnel skilled in information technology analytical capability.

Second, the *functions* (marketing, technical) historically have jockeyed for control. But today we have the development team responsible—the same team that handled the prototype concept testing. If vendor personnel are members of such teams, then they too participate.

---

[22]A review of some practice along these lines is Aimee L. Stern, "Testing Goes Industrial," *Sales and Marketing Management,* March 1991, pp. 30–38.

Special Problems

Some special ideas holding the attention of veteran new products people run through all product use testing situations.

Don't Change the Data Just Because They Came Out Wrong. One firm discovered a user problem in a use test but the president said, "They're just going to have to live with it." Unfortunately, the use test did not ask whether users were *willing* to live with it. They weren't, and the product failed. In many tests technical and marketing people warn of user problems only to be told that they are being negative—a case of "kill the messenger."

Be Alert to Strange Conditions. One industrial firm noticed that several electrical measuring instruments showed signs of tampering after a field test. On examination, they found users were making a particular change to aid the product's function; after a few telephone calls, they had an improved product design ready to go out for more testing.

What If We Have to Go Ahead without Good Use Testing? Try to work some use testing into the early marketing stages (e.g., in the rollout method discussed in Chapter 20) and try to have some alternatives ready to switch to as a hedge against negative outcomes.

There are also surrogate tests available if time or money limitations prevent a full product use test. Quick results are possible, for example, through *constructive evaluation* (the respondent uses the item, describing activities and explaining problems encountered) or *retrospective testing* (the user reviews videos of conventional product use testing previously done).[23]

Summary

Chapter 16 has dealt with the issues of whether a product solves customer problems, how it compares to other products in this regard, and what else can be learned about it at this stage. Getting this type of information would seem critical, but strong pressures are exerted to skip product use testing. We talked about the arguments for skipping and showed why they should be followed only when overpowering.

That paved the way for discussion of 12 decisions of product use tests, ranging from "What we want to learn from the test" to "Who should conduct it?" Each decision has several options, and selecting from among them usually follows an analysis of the situation.

[23]Stephen B. Wilcox, ed., "High-Octane Fuel for ID's Idealism: Usability Testing," *Innovation,* Spring 1994, pp. 14–32.

At the end of the testing, the product may have to be routed back into technical work to resolve problems, or it may be dropped. Otherwise, we now proceed to commercialization and the preparation of finished product, which, of course, is just a later version of the concept going into the greatest use test of all: marketing. Marketing is discussed in Part V.

Applications

More questions from that interview with the company president.

1. "That story in your book about NCR and the inventory management system is awesome. It seems to say that NCR was never interested in finding out whether their new product actually met customer needs or not! Guess they were under terrible pressure—maybe on cash flow, competitors, or something. Looking through your list of 12 decisions, where did they actually fall down—was it just on duration?"
2. "I think some research suppliers oversell a bit—they want us to do too much market research. For example, one of the biggest published data on a 'blind' versus 'identified' product test. Here are the results:

Branded		*Unbranded*	
Prefer A	55.5%	Prefer A	45.6%
Prefer B	44.5	Prefer B	54.4
Prefer A	68.0	Prefer A	60.7
Prefer C	32.0	Prefer C	39.3
		Prefer B	64.4
		Prefer C	35.6

I'm told the differences were highly significant statistically. The research firm concluded that there was no choice *between* blind and identified but that both should be used in just about every case where there was any reason to even suspect an effect of branding. Do you agree?"
3. "Colgate's marketing people apparently had some trouble a while back with a new detergent laced with a dye that turned laundry blue during introductory marketing. Another product of theirs, a dishwasher detergent packaged in waxy cartons like those used for orange juice, was rejected by test market parents who were afraid their children might think the cartons contained juice. Seems to me those errors were inexcusable. Shouldn't they have been discovered earlier, in product use testing? How would you have made sure of that?"

4. "Our pharmaceutical division, of course, develops new pharmaceutical products for use by doctors and hospitals. The technical research department does all the testing (they have different names for the various tests). The last phase is clinical testing, where the drugs are given to humans in a manner that will substantiate claims to the Food and Drug Administration. The clinical tests are conducted by M.D.s in the clinical research section, which is in our R&D department along with all the other technical people. Now it seems to me those clinical tests are designed to satisfy more people than just the FDA—physicians, pharmacists, nurses, and so on. But M.D.s in clinical testing are not too high on marketing research-type thinking, so it dawned on me that I should see that at least one thoroughly trained marketing research person was assigned to clinical research—to help me make sure the clinicals have maximum impact later in marketing. Do you agree?"

Case: Mountain Dew Sport[24]

In 1989, PepsiCo was about ready to enter the isotonic beverage market. Product had been decided upon, financing was approved, marketing strategy was decided, and the firm planned to market test its new product in Eau Claire, Wisconsin, a BehaviorScan market of Information Resources Inc. The brand chosen was Mountain Dew Sport. At issue now was whether the product was indeed right for this market. Decisions had to be made on how to conduct product use tests. To date, employees using the company fitness center had been given samples of Mountain Dew Sport to drink and had given their opinions. But the firm also wanted reactions from their intended market users, so a full product testing plan needed to be decided.

The isotonic market came into being in 1965 when Dr. Robert Cade, a nephrologist for the University of Florida football team invented a beverage he used for optimal fluid replacement to provide energy for the football players and to stabilize their blood sugar levels. He took the name Gatorade from the team's nickname.

Years later he sold his product to Stokely-Van Camp, which was then acquired by Quaker Oats Company. Quaker added national distribution and aggressive marketing effort; the result was a $500 million business, indicating sustained consumer demand for the product and a tremendous opportunity for other beverage firms.

PepsiCo had developed an internal strategy that called for creation of new products in beverage categories outside of its traditional carbonated soft drink business. It was stipulated that any such product should utilize the firm's existing bottling and distribution network.

The development of the product had been largely a matter of formulation and brand development, since the Gatorade business had been established many years before. For formulation, PepsiCo studied Gatorade and then made certain modifications to yield a

[24]This case is prepared from many public information sources.

product they thought would be more appealing. The new item would come in both bottles and cans, the glass bottle had a larger opening (for quicker drinking), and there were slightly different levels of carbonation, sweetness, sodium, and mineral nutrient contents.

The firm apparently felt that the strength of the market made concept testing unnecessary, so the only prescreening was done with Pepsi-Cola marketing managers and senior executives. Emphasis was put on branding, packaging, and labeling issues, more than product formula.

Meanwhile, in the marketplace, there had been double-digit growth in Gatorade, and usage was spreading from teams to individuals, many of whom were working out alone. Distribution was primarily through the grocery trade, but PepsiCo would bring distribution also to convenience stores, petroleum stores, and the thousands of vending machines scattered at public parks, school athletic fields, and so on.

There were a few small competitors—Snapple Natural Beverage Company, Sports Beverage Inc., and PowerBurst Corporation—but Quaker controlled 90 percent of the market. Quaker was large, of course, with revenue of $5 billion, but PepsiCo was a $15 billion company. The typical buyer of Gatorade was an 18–34 year-old athletic male, concerned with replenishing his body fluids and minerals after a strenuous workout. Users were in all income and demographic categories. Drinks were generally bought and consumed on a single bottle basis, not six-packs.

Information about Mountain Dew Sport indicated that it would replenish fluids and key nutrients; have a formulation of carbonation, sodium, and sweetness that would interact well with body chemistry; be appealing in color and taste; packaged to speed up individual usage; priced at competitive levels; and use packaging that was recyclable.

The strategy called for hitting a slightly different user segment than that of Gatorade. In an effort to broaden the market for its product, PepsiCo expanded the targeting of isotonics to include all "sweaty" occasions. This included tennis and golf players, persons mowing the lawn, construction workers, and anyone else working up a sweat on the job.

Mountain Dew Sport seemed positioned as a quick, thirst-quenching beverage for all sweaty occasions, designed to replace lost fluids and nutrients through a sweeter, better-tasting formula, with just a touch of carbonation (which Gatorade did not have).

Given the highly competitive nature of the market, it was important that the new drink be marketed quickly. Plans were made to roll out from the BehaviorScan market test as soon as things looked OK there.

But, at the moment, the issue of use testing was on the table.

FIGURE V–1

Launch

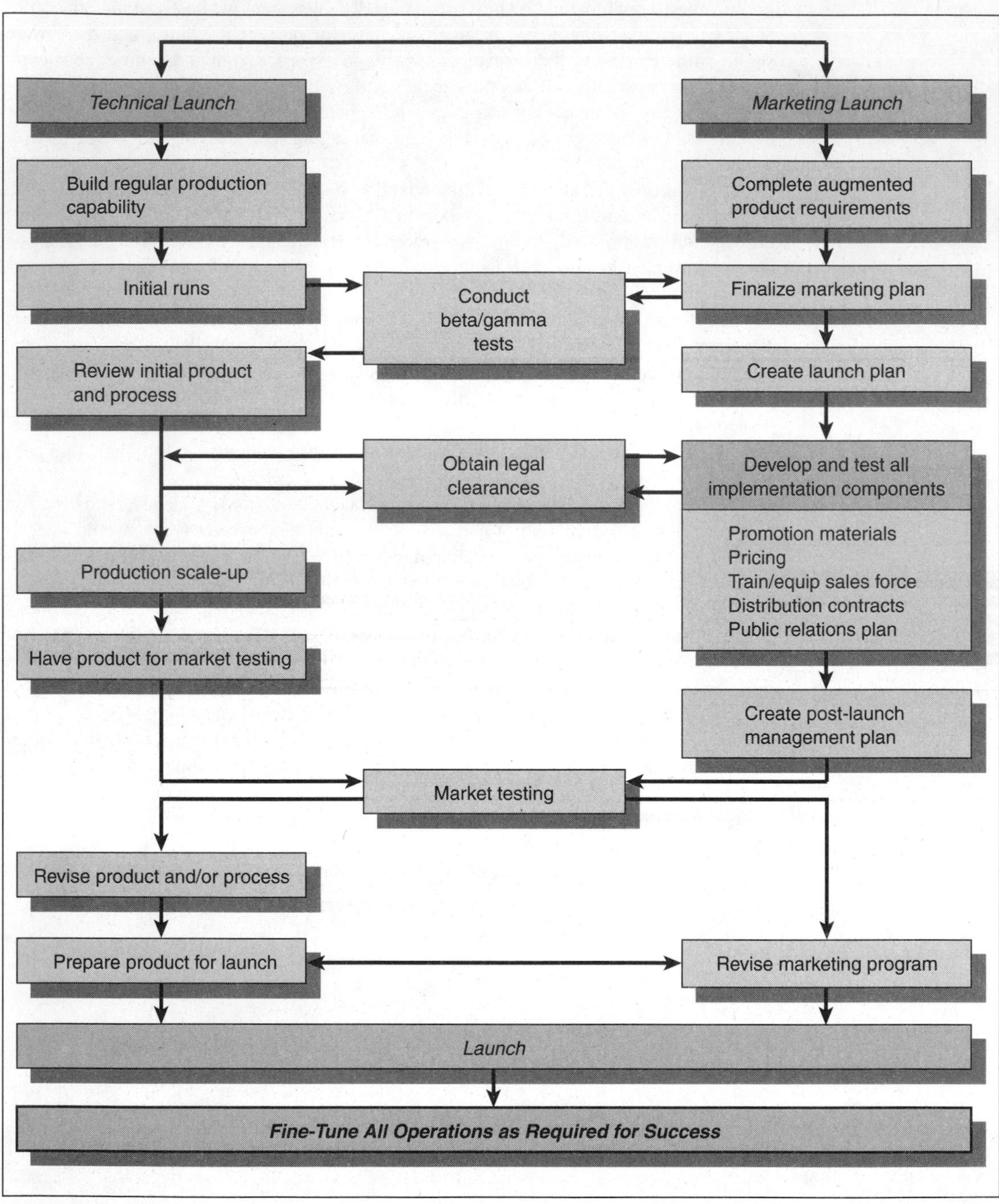

PART

V

LAUNCH

We saw in Part IV that both marketing and technical activity takes place throughout the development process. The intensity of activity on the so-called business or marketing side of the firm may be relatively low, especially early on in development, and there may be long periods of almost total inactivity as technical work gets hung up somewhere. But, as we have seen in Chapter 15, a point is reached in the development process where the balance of activity shifts toward marketing. We depicted the parallel marketing and technical activity during the development stage in Figure IV–1. Similarly, these twin streams of activity carry on through the launch stage, as is shown in Figure V–1.

Somewhere in the process, management becomes convinced that the new product should be marketed. This starts what we will call the launch stage, though sometimes you will encounter the term "commercialization." All of the functions (engineering, production, marketing, etc.) work before and after the launch decision. The shift in focus to marketing is often triggered by a commitment to produce the new item, and to risk the high costs of building a plant. At the end of development and throughout launch, marketing activity picks up intensity.

But remember that marketing actually begins near the start of the project. The product innovation charter calls for a market focus—usually a particular use or user that will eventually become our target market. After concept generation, concept testing uses a concept statement that soon will turn into our product positioning statement. But marketing activities after that cool for a while, until technical can come up with a prototype that seems to show it meets the protocol statement of requirements (see Chapter 12). Of course, this brief description does not match most service products—on them, there is far less technical development work, and the whole process telescopes dramatically. And, as Figure V–1 shows, a lot happens on the technical side of the launch, including making the initial production runs, scaling up to full production, getting sufficient product prepared for market testing, and making last-minute revisions to product and process.

The next four chapters deal with the activities during launch. Launch planning decisions use all of the previous activity, and a great deal of new thinking and testing, to build eventually toward launch capability. As will be shown in upcoming chapters, launch planning can be thought of in several phases. In strategic launch planning, the strategic decisions of marketing (such as targeting and positioning) are made; in tactical launch planning, tactics are developed to implement the strategic plan. In a later phase, the strategic and tactical decisions are tested in the marketplace. All of these phases comprise Chapters 18 through 21. One could also add the phase of launch management, or managing the new product to success. Chapter 21 examines launch management, because its planning is done at the same time and it concerns the post-announcement period.

A final launch plan is built from *five sets of decisions,* made somewhat in sequence. (See Figure V–2.) They are as follows. First, any new products team must accept some givens. That is, the firm has an established operation—one or more sales forces, a financial situation, and so on. Teams can skirt some of these limitations, but not all of them. So the first several "decisions" are not really decisions in the voluntary sense; they are called **strategic givens.**

FIGURE V–2

The five decision sets that lead to a marketing plan

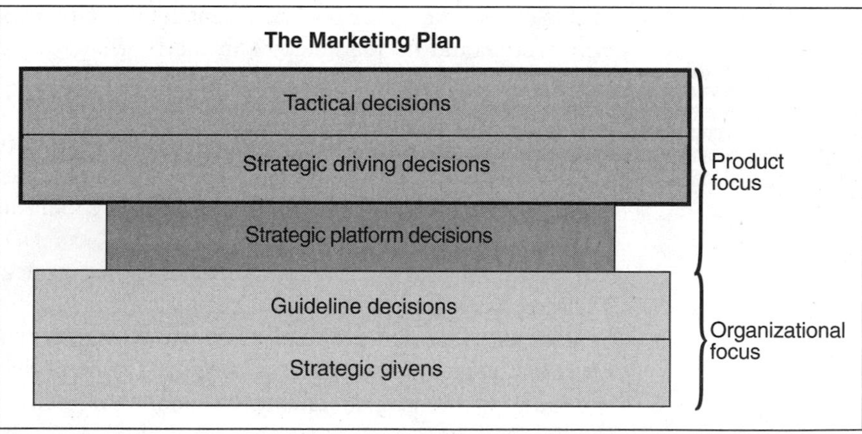

Second, there is another set of conditions that *are* decisions, but they have been put into place early on and won't be changed (without a fight) when launch planning starts. Specifically, the PIC probably called for a form of leadership (first-to-market, follower, etc.) and that has been achieved. For another, the firm may have a strong commitment to speed, in which case leisurely test markets are probably out of the question. Because they often appear in the PIC, they are called **guideline decisions.**

Third, the marketing planners will make a set of **strategic decisions** on matters where there are options; these are difficult and often critical. Some comprise a set called **platform strategies** because they set the stage for action, and others comprise a set of **driving strategies;** the latter drive the tactics.

Fourth, many **tactical decisions** must be made, though in this book we will only be able to include the most important of these.

Chapter 17 deals with the strategic givens and the strategic decisions, and Chapter 18 looks at the tactics. Be warned, of course, terms in the new products field are flexible, and one person's tactic is another person's strategy and still another person's given.

During launch, people actually *buy* machinery (rather than just estimating its cost), finalize sales call schedules, register brands, lock in R&D specifications, and spend money. More and more people are involved, with coordination meetings, massive information accumulation, greatly elevated risks and tempers, euphoria and disappointments, security problems, politics, and a far-too-attentive top management. Costs run higher than anticipated, market test results are unclear, competitors begin to hear of the development and do unexpected things, and some packaging machinery is a couple months late, making premature the announcement of the firm's ability to make delivery to customers. Near panic has set in, and will not cease for some time.

Closing out Part V is a chapter on public policy issues. They are with us throughout the process but come to the fore at time of launch and thereafter.

One caution is appropriate: Chapters 17 and 18 cover an activity that many people do not understand. They *think* they do, and some of them are actually in marketing departments. Our problem is not that people draw a blank—blanks are easy to fill in. Instead, we suffer from the existence of many myths—conditions *people think exist but do not.* Figure V–3 lists 11 of these myths. We encourage you to keep these in mind, and perhaps refer to them from time to time. As you read the next two chapters, see if you can find what makes each one of them a myth. Check your answers with those at the end of the Chapter 18 case.

FIGURE V–3

Some common myths about marketing planning for new products

Here are some statements that we often hear around people who have not done much new product marketing. All are myths, as explained at different places in Chapters 17–18. See if you can figure out the reasons on your own, and then check your answers with those at the end of Chapter 18.

1. *Marketing people make the decisions that constitute a marketing plan.*
2. *The technical work is essentially complete when the new item hits the shipping dock. Marketing people take over.*
3. *It's important that marketing people be required to use strategy-tactics paradigms. Clear thinking helps rein in their excess exuberance and excitement.*
4. *The marketer's task is to persuade the end user to use our new product.*
5. *The more sales potential there is in a market segment, the better that segment is as a target candidate.*
6. *The PIC guides the development stage and the marketing plan guides the launch stage.*
7. *The pioneer wins control of a new market.*
8. *A new product's goals are of two general types: sales (dollars or shares) and profits (dollars or ROIs).*
9. *People generally are pretty smart buyers—they will not be influenced by meaningless package designs.*
10. *A launch is no game—when we say go, that's it, sink or swim, and it had better be swim.*
11. *As with Broadway shows, opening night is the culmination of everything we have been working for.*

CHAPTER

17 STRATEGIC LAUNCH PLANNING

Setting

At this point in the NPD process, the team is ready to build the actual marketing plan. The task should be easy if the new item is an improvement to items already in the line. In such cases there is actually little to decide, as little has changed. If the product is really new (to the world, or to the firm), the firm faces a more substantial challenge. Firms often do not place enough emphasis on up-front strategic planning for product commercialization (such as defining strategic purpose or competitive positioning), especially in the case of really new products.[1] Weak strategic planning then shows up when the product reaches the market, and tactical errors (such as inefficient resource allocation) can compound the problem.

Whether the product is really new or not, the firm should think of product commercialization in three sets of decisions. Strategic *platform* decisions set overall tones and directions, strategic *action* decisions define who we are going to sell to and how, and *tactical* decisions define how we implement the strategic action decisions. For example, one platform decision that gets overlooked a lot is the level of aggressiveness. If the firm decides to be very aggressive (a platform decision), the target market (an action decision) must be rather broad, and the introductory advertising plan (a tactical decision) will probably call for mass media and a strong attention-getting campaign. The strategic platform and action decisions are covered here in Chapter 17; the tactical decisions come in Chapter 18.

[1]X. Michael Song and Mitzi M. Montoya-Weiss, "Critical Development Activities for Really New Versus Incremental Products," *Journal of Product Innovation Management* 15, no. 2, March 1998, pp. 124–35.

It is important to distinguish between strategic and tactical launch decisions. The former are usually made well before building the marketing plan and possibly even before product development begins, and are frequently difficult or costly to change once made. They do, however, determine the strategic context for the marketing plan and thus influence the tactical decisions made at this stage.[2]

Product commercialization often turns out to be the most expensive and risky part of the new product process, as well as the most poorly-managed.[3] To improve practice at this stage, it is important to have heavy marketing input, primarily because marketing will guide the implementation of the plan. The launch plan itself may be called a business plan, but more commonly it is the marketing plan or marketing program. In today's business, the marketing plan is recognized as a plan for the full business activity of launch; that's why full function teams are essential. But this is not the place to discuss plans. Instead, Appendix D contains an outline of a marketing plan and a discussion of some aspects of it.

The Strategic Givens

We begin by assessing the **strategic givens,** seen first in the introduction to Part V. (See Figure V–2 for clarification on how strategic givens relate to the other decisions needed in the launch planning activity.) These are decisions that are already made for us, so to speak; they come with the territory when a project is undertaken. Often we tend to forget them and their importance. They cover the full range of the organization's operations, and are often set in concrete without our knowing it. They comprise that awful resistance to change which new products people frequently lament about. In fact, strategic givens are such a problem that top managements often set up venture groups or skunkworks, organizational forms supposedly immune from whatever restrictions are endemic to the firm.

Some of the most common examples of problems we have with these givens can be indicated by an example. Sybron Corporation had a division in the dental furniture business; the division desperately needed new cash flow, and they had a new (and unique, superior) chair ready to go. But the corporation had a mandatory 50 percent gross margin requirement that the division product planners were sure would be waived when management saw the new

[2]Erik Jan Hultink, Abbie Griffin, Susan Hart, and Henry S. J. Robben, "Industrial New Product Launch Strategies and Product Development Performance," *Journal of Product Innovation Management* 14, no. 4 (July 1997), pp. 243–57.

[3]Roger Calantone and Mitzi M. Montoya-Weiss, "Product Launch and Follow-On," in William E. Souder and J. D. Sherman, eds., *Managing New Technology Development* (New York: McGraw-Hill, 1994), pp. 217–48.

chair. It wasn't, even when the gross margin came in at 47 percent. The division collapsed.

Sometimes the given is an individual—a strong member of upper management whose personal druthers become corporate law. A firm in the ethical drug products field had a sales manager totally committed to an indirect channel of drug outlet distribution. Ostensibly this practice fit the firm and the industry, but a new products team came up with a nutritional product that also showed potential in the grocery products channel. The team was hoping for dual-channel distribution, but had to sacrifice several millions of dollars in their product plan in the name of the thirty millions protected by the wholesaler-only channel policy. Only after two years of frustration was the policy waived—the new product produced more revenue than the rest of the firm combined!

Other examples of these operational understandings show up in relations with regulatory authorities, in ethical postures, in advertising policies, in centralized (or decentralized) manufacturing facilities, in geographical preferences, in pricing policies, and in almost every phase of the entire operation. One understanding often forgotten is the firm's posture toward brand names. Many firms today recognize that brand equity is among the biggest assets they have. If this is how the firm sees brand names, much more effort must be put into handling line extensions and new brands that compete with present brands.

If these restrictions are really important and recognized in advance, they are put into the PIC guidelines. But some items here called givens are far more subtle, perhaps not even recognized as firm, perhaps being held to for reasons that new products people don't even know about. Many are pure and simple habit, convenient and comfortable routines.

The point is, they need to be identified and studied. If the launch team wants to challenge such restrictions, fine, but they should do so early, and should be prepared to lose. Ultimately, as company organizations change, most of these restrictions will yield. They are silo or chimney holdings, and the horizontal management philosophy of today is designed to bypass just such restrictions.

Revisiting the Strategic Goals

Early in the new product process, when the product innovation charter (PIC) was being developed, a basic set of strategic goals (both dollar and nondollar) was outlined, and these goals have led the new products team up to this point. That original set may still be complete. But usually much has been learned in the new product process, competitive conditions may have changed, and customer or management needs may have changed. Therefore, at this early stage in the launch-planning process, the goals should be revisited and updated.

Unfortunately, business firms use a complex set of measures as goals, and research to date has not been able to find a recommended set.[4] The most used set of measures for individual products is as follows (from lists numbering in the hundreds):

Customer Acceptance Measures	**Product Level Performance**
Customer acceptance (use)	Product cost
Customer satisfaction	Time to launch
Revenue (dollar sales)	Product performance
Market share	Quality guidelines
Unit volume	
Financial Performance	**Other**
Time to break even	Nonfinancial measures peculiar to the new product being launched.
Margins	Example: competitive effect, image change, morale change.
Profitability (IRR, ROI)	

Regardless of how measures are expressed, there should be absolutely no doubt in the minds of any launch planners about what the launch is to produce or achieve.

Strategic Platform Decisions

Each launch planning team will want to make up its own list of platform decisions because they vary much from industry to industry, goods to services, industrial to packaged goods. But some of the more common ones are the following.

Permanence

On *permanence,* there are three options. The first is the usual one—we are *in to stay,* and no thought is given to getting out. The second is *in to stay if we meet our goals.* This cautions against alliances that would make escape difficult; it is especially useful when a firm is using the new product to enter another sphere of activity. Such a market development project can be tentative—probe an area, try hard to make it a winner, but pull out if competitive capability is inadequate.

The third option is *temporary.* This may sound strange—spending months or years developing a new item only to limit its life to a few months or at most a couple years. But this temporary option is used a lot. Baskin-Robbins, for example, has a basic cadre of flavors but runs others in

[4]Abbie Griffin and Albert L. Page, "An Interim Report on Measuring Product Development Success and Failure," *Journal of Product Innovation Management,* September 1993, pp. 291–308.

and out to give variety. Snack companies also have short-term products. Sometimes temporary products catch on and become permanent. Many tactical decisions change if the plan is temporary—using contract manufacturing rather than building a new plant, and borrowing a sales force from agents or other manufacturers.

Aggressiveness

Aggressiveness refers to an attitude as much as to dollars. An *aggressive entry* seeks lots of attention early on, so most of the promotional dollars are spent early, and most of the resources go to getting early trial. In contrast, some firms will slink into the market with a *cautious entry.* They are uncertain about something important—maybe product performance, maybe competitive reaction, maybe sales force capability to deal with a new type of market. This is not a negative posture, but one where being aggressive has a risk the firm wants to avoid. For example, some firms like to enter a new market cautiously so as not to alarm the leaders in that market.

Third, aggressiveness can be *balanced.* This simply means the firm is not trying to be pugnacious or slinking. The average of all new product introductions in a given industry would be balanced, but this does not mean normal; for some firms, aggressive is normal.

Sometimes this is a good place to raise the issue of marketing costs as *an investment.* Much of the marketing budget for a new product will pay off over many years; it is not an expense in the sense of an annual advertising budget. If the spending strategy is too stingy, try getting it thought of as an investment.

Type of Demand Sought

This may have been settled earlier, but if not the decision should be made now. Does the firm want to capture **selective demand** by taking market share from competition, or does it want to expand the total market by building **primary demand** for the category. The difference is critical to most of the strategic actions, including the market segment being targeted. Fortunately, selective versus primary tends to come up at the very start, when selecting end-users' problems.

Competitive Advantage

Another decision that tends to come up early concerns the basic offer we make to the marketplace: Will our product lower end-user costs by virtue of its *price,* or will our product offer new benefits by virtue of its *differentiation?* Today we often hear that a firm is committed to the triad of quality, cost, and speed (see Chapter 1). Its managers fully expect to have new products that offer benefits by virtue of differentiation, *and* that can be sold at a price below leading competition. So there is a middle choice on this option too: *both.*

Product Line Replacement

Most new products relate to existing products in the company's **product line;** they do not enter markets new to the firm. Naturally, the issue arises: How should we manage the replacement of the existing by the new? Some firms, perhaps without realizing it, follow the strategy of *let nature handle the switch.* Market the new and live with whatever rate of replacement occurs.

However, research shows that the marketer has several clearly different strategic options.[5] Several of them are as follows:

- **Butt-on:** The existing one is simply dropped when the new one is announced. Example: Ford's marketing of Mondero and dropping of Sierra.
- **Low-season switch:** Using butt-on, but arranging the switch at a low point between seasons. Tour companies use this switch when they develop their new catalogs.
- **High-season switch:** Using butt-on, but arranging the new item at the top of a season. Example: Polaroid used this strategy often, putting new replacement items out during the Christmas season.
- **Roll-in, roll-out:** This is another butt-on, but arranging it by a sequence of market segments. Mercedes introduced its C series country by country.
- **Down-grading:** Keeping the earlier product along side the new, but with decreased support. Example: The 386 chip stayed along side the 486.
- **Splitting channels:** Putting the new item in a different channel or diverting the existing product into another channel. Example: Old electronic products often end up in discounter channels.

Needless to say, the inventiveness of managers has produced many other variations. Casio has so many calculators that they are continuously renewing older ones, shifting the emphasis as they go along. The important point is, have *some* strategy decision and a plan. And have them early enough in launch planning that the total market offer (including augmentation such as service, warranty, and brand image) can be built to suit the strategy.

Competitive Relationship

Occasionally a product innovation charter will have a statement something like this: "The product(s) that will come from this program will not be aimed at XYZ Company, nor threaten a piece of business that is important to that firm." Colgate once had such a statement relative to Procter & Gamble, but

---

[5]John Saunders and David Jobber, "Product Replacement: Strategies for Simultaneous Product Deletion and Launch," *Journal of Product Innovation Management* 11, no. 5 (November 1994), pp. 433–50.

abandoned it in the 1980s. Other firms do just the opposite, shooting their new item directly at a specific competitor.

The practices lead to a three-option set: *make no reference to specific competitors, aim directly at a specific competitor,* and *avoid a specific competitor.* Unintentionally trying to do two or three of those mires the tactical managers in a frustrating set of conflicts.

Scope of Market Entry

This issue relates to a firm's desire to do market testing. Some introduce their new items into part of a market, watch what happens, and then roll them on out to the entire market as they overcome any problems. The difference in these approaches will be discussed more in Chapter 20.

Even in a **rollout,** there is still the option of trying to *roll out very rapidly* (barely holding up long enough to find crisis problems) or *roll out deliberately, as performance warrants.* And, of course, it appears most firms *go to the total market at the beginning.*

Image

The issue here is: Will the new product need *an entirely new image, a major change in an existing image, a tweaking of an existing image,* or *no change whatsoever in an image.* For example, the butt-on strategy of market replacement can destroy the prior brand if necessary to properly position the new. But the side-by-side strategy needs a continuing positive image in the item being upgraded. Images can be terribly resilient and long-lasting, so changing them should be undertaken lightly. Yet, an image can also be distorted by an almost trivial mistake in an ad or a label. And setting out to establish a new image can be frightfully expensive.

In the above analyses leading to *givens, guideline decisions,* and *strategic platform decisions,* one could conclude that we must be about finished. Most of the thinking in those sets is unpleasant because we are deliberately focusing effort or attention on single options from sets. Do this, rather than that and that.

The flip side is that once these higher-order decisions are made, the rest are easier. So we now turn our attention to what you may think of as the *real* marketing planning decisions: target market, product positioning statement, and creating unique value for the chosen target.

The Target Market Decision

Competition today forces the overwhelming majority of companies to market new items to specific target groups. Markets are so complex that one product cannot come close to meeting all needs and desires.

Alternative Ways to Segment a Market

What ways do new product marketers use to target a specific market segment? Thousands of them. Yet each target can be classified into one of several categories.

End-Use. Athletic shoes are specific for various types of athletic activity. Plastics are sold for hundreds of different applications. CD buyers have different time frames in mind. To test your own end-use orientation, try listing the many different shirts/blouses/pants/slacks/suits/dresses you have had in your possession—say, starting with designer blouse, dress blouse, and so on. Men, start with T-shirt, golf shirt, dress shirt, and so on. Notice how often the type of garment is defined by the activity it is worn for. Clothing manufacturers design for use, though not only for use.

Geographic and Demographic. Convertibles are not marketed aggressively in Norway, and Golden's fried pork skins are made for the Southern United States. Bran cereals are often targeted to the mature segment, Grey Poupon for the upscale, and Right Guard for males (originally). Fitness equipment manufacturers such as Precor have been designing simpler-to-use gear with large-display consoles, as the senior market's interest in fitness increases.[6]

Behavioral and Psychographic. Markets can be segmented according to psychographic variables: values, activities, and lifestyles. Lotus Notes was developed for people who needed to communicate in groups across great distances, and Kevlar bullet-proof jackets are for people exposed to guns. Products are targeted to lifestyles—tax shelters, clothing, cars, and so on. SRI Consulting follows trends in these variables, as well as in key demographics, using its well-known VALS (Values, Activities, and Lifestyles) questionnaire.

Benefit Segmentation. As we saw earlier in our discussion of joint space mapping, benefit segments are of great interest in new product development. Through surveys of customers and potential customers, we can identify segments based on benefits sought, and develop products to satisfy the needs of one or more of these segments. Recall that we had identified three benefit segments in our maps of the swimsuit market (see Figures 9–3 and 9–4). Of course, benefit segment information in combination with brand perceptions can be very helpful in developing a positioning strategy, a topic to which we return later in this chapter.

The PIC usually makes quite clear what market group the new project will focus on, and the target market may be clear from the *original concept*

---

[6]Terence B. Foley, "Muscle Machines: Makers of Fitness Gear Are Tailoring Their Products to an Older Market," *Wall Street Journal,* September 4, 1998, p. R-15.

generation. For instance, a sales rep notifies management that offices with southern exposure have problems with the new personal computer screens, and a new monitor evolves.

Second, the firm's *method of operation* may constrain the choice. If a firm's sales force calls on hospital accounting departments, its new line of tabular records will probably be so targeted.

Third, a focus may come from *concept testing or product use testing.* An early target market may reject a concept in an early trade-off analysis, or when they actually try out a prototype. Thus many firms use **parallel development,** keeping two or three target alternatives in development.

Micromarketing and Mass Customization

A current twist in target market selection is the trend toward smallness. Retail scanners and sales information systems yield the databases that display very small targets (neighborhoods or industrial subsets) with unique purchase patterns. These clusters have been labeled **micromarkets.** David Olson, new product researcher at the Leo Burnett advertising agency, uses scanner data to cluster food buyers into six groups:

Loyalists, who buy one brand at all times, like it, and don't use deals.

Rotators, who have a 2- or 3-product set, move around in that set, and don't use deals.

Deal-selectives, rotators whose movement is determined by presence of deals.

Price-driven, who buy all major brands, always on deals.

Store brand buyers, who do as their name implies.

Light users, who buy too little for a pattern to show. Light users comprise the biggest group in most categories.

Direct marketers have always used tighter segments than have mass media marketers, stemming from their databases. They talk about *database marketing* and *database product innovation,* and speculate that it will soon dominate.[7]

The ultimate smallness, and the ultimate in building in customer value, is **mass customization** (tailoring a good or service to the unique specifications of individual customers). Great advances in information technology and changes in work processes make mass customization feasible for many

[7]See "Database Marketing," *Business Week,* September 5, 1994, pp. 56–62. An example: Blockbuster keeps records on 36 million households; it can recommend movies based on past rentals, and modify other aspects of its service for tiny clusters of buying families.

FIGURE 17–1

Types of mass customization

- *Collaborative customizers* work with the customer in arriving at the optimal product. Japanese eyewear retailer Paris Miki inputs customer frame style preferences and facial features into a design system that makes frame and lens recommendations, which are further refined by customer and optician working together.
- *Adaptive customizers* let the customers do the customizing themselves according to their performance needs. Lutron Electronics markets a lighting system that allows customers to adjust lighting in several rooms simultaneously to obtain a desired ambience.
- *Cosmetic customizers* sell the same basic product to different segments, but adapt the product's presentation (such as its promotion or packaging) depending on segment needs. For example, Wal-Mart likes larger sizes of Planter's Nuts than does 7-Eleven. Planter's now offers a wide range of package sizes and adjusts its production order-by-order according to the wishes of the retailers.
- *Transparent customizers* do not inform their customers that they are customizing the product for them. ChemStation formulates industrial soap specifically to its customers' needs but packages everything it sells in the same kind of tanks. In this case, the customer cares about whether the product works and is delivered on time, not necessarily whether it is customized.

Obviously, any of these strategies has pitfalls that need to be avoided. It would be cost inefficient for Planter's, for example, to offer too wide a range of package sizes.

Source: James H. Gilmore and B. Joseph Pine II, "The Four Faces of Mass Customization," *Harvard Business Review,* January–February 1997, pp. 91–101.

products; the challenge is for managers to decide how best to proceed.[8] Firms can practice mass customization in a variety of ways, as seen in Figure 17–1.

As we approach the marketing date, intense pressure builds up in the organization to add just a few more buyer types, a few more store types, a few more uses or applications, because "The product is good for them too, isn't it?" We call this the *broaden the market* fallacy. The new item cannot be good for lots of different groups, unless it is so general it doesn't have any zing for any of them. And targeting to diverse groups can cause dissonance in the promotion. Does a fourth grader want a peanut butter sandwich like the one shown being eaten by a senior citizen? Further, changing the target can be disaster if promotional and trade-show materials and dates are all prepared, packaging, pricing and branding are fixed, and the concept and product use tests were conducted only with the original target group.

Lastly, keep in mind that whatever we do, the end users may disagree. A few years ago, sports utility vehicles (SUVs) were adopted by boomers for regular use. They were tired of minivans, and it didn't matter what the car companies *told* us these vehicles were for (or that the government said they were trucks). Some firms capitalize on this end user penchant by just launching the product and following up to see who the buyers are, then focus their

[8]Robert C. Blattberg, Rashi Glazer, and John D. C. Little, eds., *The Marketing Revolution* (Boston, MA: Harvard Business School Press, 1994).

promotions accordingly. This is strictly a wildcat operation—no charter, no concept or use testing, and so forth.

Targeting May Also Use Diffusion of Innovation

New products are innovations, and we call the spreading of their usage the *diffusion of innovation.* The original adoption and diffusion of the microwave oven was very slow, but it has been quite rapid for the cellular phone. For a cancer cure, it would be almost instantaneous.

When we used the Bass diffusion model in sales forecasting (Chapter 11), our forecasts rested on two key values: the rates of innovation and imitation. Taken together, these values define the speed of an innovation's adoption. Let's look closer now at the factors that affect this speed of the **product adoption process:** the characteristics of the innovative product, and the extent to which early users encourage others to follow.

Product Characteristics. There are at least five factors that measure how soon a new product will receive trial.[9]

1. The *relative advantage* of the new product. How superior is the innovation to the product or other problem-solving methods it was designed to compete against?
2. *Compatibility.* Does it fit with current product usage and end-user activity? We say it is a *continuous* innovation if little change is required, a *discontinuous* innovation if much is. Incompatibility produces learning requirements, and these must be overcome.
3. *Complexity.* Will frustration or confusion arise in understanding the innovation's basic idea?
4. *Divisibility* (also called *trialability*). How easily can trial portions of the product be purchased and used? Foods and beverages are quite divisible, but new homes and word processing systems are much less so.
5. *Communicability* (also called *observability*). How likely is the product to appear in public places where it is easily seen and studied by potential users? It is high on new cars, low on items of personal hygiene.

An innovation can be scored on these five factors, using primarily personal judgment plus the findings from market testing during earlier phases of the development. Launch plans can then be laid accordingly.

Next is the degree to which early users actively or passively encourage others to adopt a new product; if they do, its spread will be rapid. So interest has focused on the **innovators** (the first 5 to 10 percent of those who adopt

[9]The classic source on this subject is Everett M. Rogers, *Diffusion of Innovations* (New York: The Free Press, 1962). Many researchers have contributed to this list of factors.

the product) and on the **early adopters** (the next 10 to 15 percent of adopters). The theory of innovation diffusion states that if we could just market our new product to those innovators and early adopters, we could then sit back and let them spread the word to the others. Other categories of adopters include the **early majority** (perhaps the next 30 percent), the **late majority** (perhaps another 30 percent), and the **laggards** (the remaining 20 percent).[10]

The obvious question is, "Who will be the innovators and early adopters?" Can we identify them in advance, so as to focus our early marketing on them? Not always, but the following five traits have often emerged from the studies. They apply to business firms as well as to individuals.[11]

1. *Venturesomeness*—the willingness and desire to be daring in trying the new and different; "sticks his neck out"; "deviates from the group social norms."
2. *Social integration*—frequent and extensive contact with others in one's "area" whether work, neighborhood, or social life; a strong industrial counterpart.
3. *Cosmopolitanism*—point of view extending beyond the immediate neighborhood or community; interest in world affairs, travel, reading.
4. *Social mobility*—upward movement on the social scale; successful young executive or professional types.
5. *Privilegedness*—usually defined as being better off financially than others in the group. Thus the privileged person has less to lose if the innovation fails and costs money. This trait tends to reflect *attitude* toward money as much as possession of money.

Early users do come typically from the innovator group, but it is difficult to predict which ones. In the industrial setting, it's thought that early *business* adopters tend to be the largest firms in the industry, those who stand to make the greatest profit from the innovation, spend more on R&D, and have presidents who are younger and better educated. Business adoptions tend to follow consumer lines if the percentage of ownership is concentrated in one person, if there are many users for the product concerned, and if the innovation is quite essential. In general, the business adoption process goes slower, and the counterparts of opinion leaders are harder to find.[12]

---

[10]Note that these are percentages of those who end up *adopting* the item. They are not percentages of the target market. Late majorities and laggards would seem to be slow, but if a product fails they may simply be the last of those daring to try the item! The last group of users who wait 90 days to try a cancer cure are quite a different group from the last of the microwave oven adopters who waited for five years.

[11]For example, see Stéphane Gauvin and Rajiv K. Sinha, "Innovativeness in Industrial Organizations: A Two-Stage Model of Adoption," *International Journal of Research in Marketing* 10, 1993, pp. 165–83.

[12]Ralph L. Day and Paul A. Herbig, "How the Diffusion of Industrial Innovations Is Different from New Retail Products," *Industrial Marketing Management,* August 1990, pp. 261–66.

Launch planners have some flexibility here—they don't have to select just one market segment to target to. That means they can start first with innovators, then roll off to early adopters shortly after launch, then gradually add the early majority and so on through the set.

However it comes about, the target market decision essentially measures (1) how much *potential* is in each target market option, (2) how well our new product *meets the needs* of people in each of those markets, and (3) how prepared we are to compete in each—that is, our *capacity to compete* there.

Product Positioning

A **product positioning statement** is created by completing this sentence: Buyers in the target market should buy our product rather than others being offered and used because: ____________. Positioning originated as a concept in advertising, but is now seen as an ingredient of *total* strategy, not just an advertising ploy. Product, brand, price, promotion, and distribution must all be consistent with the product positioning statement.

New products managers have a big advantage on positioning—*the end-user's memory slate is clean;* potential buyers have no previous positioning in mind for a new item. Now is the best chance ever to effect a particular positioning for their item.

Positioning alternatives fall into two broad categories. The first is to position to an **attribute** (a feature, a function, or a benefit). Attributes are the traditional positioning devices and are most popular. Thus, a dog food may be positioned by a **feature** as "the one with as much protein as 10 pounds of sirloin." **Function** is more difficult and rarely used, but an example is the shampoo that "coats your hair with a thin layer of protein." (You are not told how this is done or what the benefit is.) The **benefits** used in positioning can be *direct* (such as "saves you money") or *follow-on* (such as "improves your sex life," an indirect result of the cleaner teeth or cleaner breath given by this toothpaste).

Feature-function-benefit work as a triad, and they are sometimes used that way. For example, a new Drano product was headlined with just three words: THICKER, STRONGER, FASTER. These in fact are feature, function, benefit. But trying to use all three can be confusing, and target buyers won't spend much time on clarification.

The second alternative in positioning is to use **surrogates** (or metaphors). For example, "Use our dietary product *because it was created by a leading health expert.*" This says the product differs because of its designer. Specific reasons *why* the product is better are not given; the listener or viewer has to provide those. If the surrogate is good, the listener will bring favorable attributes to the product. See Figure 17–2 for the various surrogate positioning alternatives, their definition, and examples of each, from a diverse collection of goods and services, as well as business and consumer products.

FIGURE 17–2

Surrogate positioning—definition of alternatives, with examples

Listed below are the type of surrogates currently being used. No doubt there are many others awaiting discovery. For each, the definition is given, followed by one or more examples. The surrogates are listed in order of popularity in use. The claim in each case would be that "Our product is better than, or different than, the others because. . . ."

Nonpareil: . . . because the product has no equal; it is the best (the Jaguar car and Nissan's 300ZX, the "convertible of convertibles").

Parentage: . . . because of where it comes from, who makes it, who sells it, who performs it, and so on. The three ways of parenting positioning are *brand* (Le Temps Chanel timepieces), *company* ("Everything we know about peanut butter is now available in jars" for Reese's peanut butter, "No one potpourries like Glade" for the new Peachpourri, and new "Adventures in Wonderland" TV show that has no features in its advertising but clearly comes from Disney), and *person* (the RL 2000 chair, designed by Ralph Lauren, *Dazzle,* a new book by Judith Krantz).

Manufacture: . . . because of how the product was made. This includes *process* (Hunt's tomatoes are left longer on the vine), *ingredients* (Fruit of the Loom panties of pure cotton), and *design* (Audi's engineering).

Target: . . . because the product was made especially for people or firms like you. Four ways are *end use* (Vector tire designed especially for use on wet roads), *demographic* (several airlines have service specially designed for the business traveler), *psychographic* (Michelob Light for "the people who want it all"), and *behavioral* (Hagar's Gallery line for men who work out a lot, "fit for the fit").

Rank: . . . because it is the best-selling product (Hertz and Blue Cross/Blue Shield); not very useful on a new item unless also positioned under parent brand.

Endorsement: . . . because people you respect say it is good. May be *expert* (the many doctors who prescribed DuoFilm wart remover when it was prescription-only) or a person to be *emulated* (NEC cellular phone keys were designed for Mickey Spillane).

Experience: . . . because its long or frequent use attests to its desirable attributes. Modes are *other market* (Nuprin's extensive use in the prescription market), *bandwagon* (Stuart Hall's Executive line of business accessories are "the tools business professionals rely on"), and *time* (Bell's Yellow Pages). The latter two of these are also of limited use on new products.

Competitor: . . . because it is just (or almost) like another product that you know and like (U.S. Postal Service Express Mail, just like the leading competitor except cheaper).

Predecessor: . . . because it is comparable (in some way) to an earlier product you liked (Hershey's Solitaires addition to the Golden line).

If there is no longer an open feature-function-benefit positioning that users want, developers can try to *build* preference for some unique attribute their product has, or they can turn to surrogates. This is where the art begins. Studying the list of alternatives in Figure 17–2 should reveal some good possibilities. These can then be copy tested with the target market to see if they communicate ideas we want the buyers to have. For example, in the early 90s the Skil Corporation, makers of the very successful circular hand saw, developed a line of benchtop tools such as a table saw. The new tools' features and benefits were not particularly unique, so the announcement headline said, "Besides evaluating its features, one should also consider its *ancestry.*" And, "Over *six decades ago* Skil introduced the world's first circular saw . . . Today we are continuing the Skilsaw *tradition* . . . lives up to its *namesake* . . . member of our new *family* . . . long-standing *reputation* for quality." This is surrogate positioning.

The market research techniques we encountered early on can be profitably put to use in developing a positioning strategy. Consider the joint space map of Figure 9–4 once again. It indicates not only the positions of the ideal brands of each benefit segment, but also the perceptions of the existing brands. We can use this map to hunt for worthwhile market gaps. We can, for example, select a position for our new brand such that it is near an ideal brand that is not served very well by existing brands. Segment 2 may be relatively large, but if there is heavy brand loyalty to the Aqualine and Islands brands, it may be difficult to get many sales there, and Segment 3 may be a better option. As a simple example, the Taylor Wine Company once identified a small group of heavy wine users and asked them what brands of wine they preferred. Surprisingly, none of the wines the heavy users bought was positioned on its great taste. Taylor positioned a wine of theirs as such, and succeeded immediately.

Creating Unique Value for the Chosen Target

Once a market segment has been targeted and a positioning statement created for it, we have a chance to cycle back to the product itself and see if we can enhance its value to the chosen market. After all, the role of a new product is usually to build gross margin dollars, dollars that come primarily from the values it has over its price.

Figure 17–3 shows how the buyer actually receives a bundle of things a product consists of. Here we view it as a package, bought and taken home, but the augmentation idea is the same as the bull's-eye shown in Figure 12–1. The core benefit of the product may receive the greatest attention during the development phase. But from the buyer's point of view, the bundle that he or she receives and takes home can comprise much more. During later stages of the new product process, we try to add extra benefits to the core product through branding, packaging, warranty, presale service, and so on—such that we increase the value of the augmented product to the customer.

Most firms now try to "freeze specs" late in development, and schedule others for soon after launch, to sustain value in the product. As the first product is coming down the pike, the first couple of line extensions should be in development. Then, after launch, when competitors are casting around for ways to come out with catch-up versions, we market them first.[13]

In the remainder of this section, we will focus our attention on two of the ways in which we can increase unique value to the targeted customer—**branding** and **packaging.**

[13]C. Merle Crawford, "How Product Innovators Can Foreclose the Options of Adaptive Followers," *Journal of Consumer Marketing,* Fall 1988, pp. 17–24.

FIGURE 17–3

Purchase configuration —what the buyer actually buys

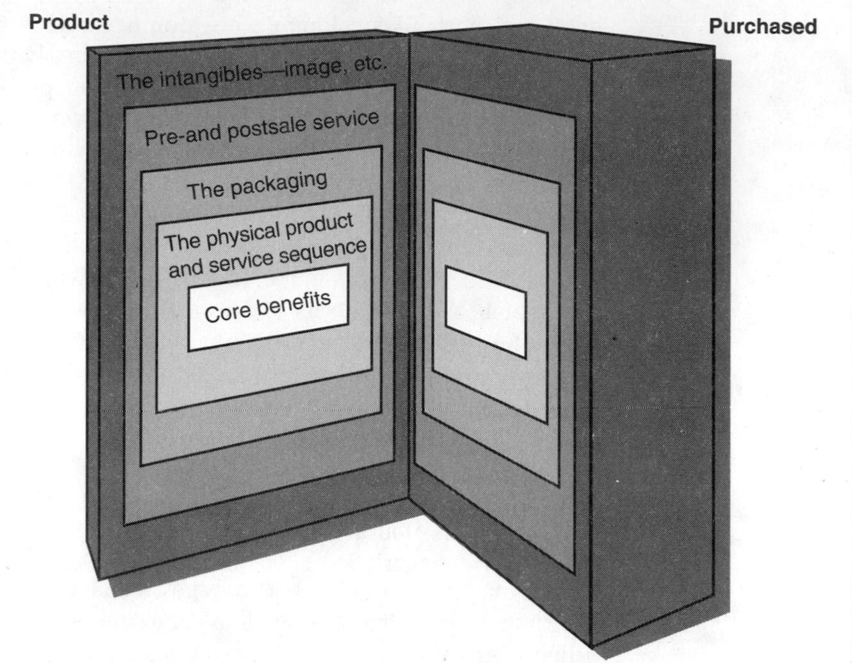

Explanation: One or more core benefits are wanted by the buyer; but to get them, the buyer must also take delivery on the physical product or service sequence, its packaging, its attendant service, and all intangibles that go with the brand and firm making/selling it. These other purchase "layers" may enhance the total value or detract from it, but they each offer opportunity for differentiation or for the core benefit to be destroyed or overpowered if not handled correctly by the new product manager.

Branding and Brand Management

Trademarks and Registration[14]

Every new product must be identified, and the accurate term for what identifies products is **trademark.** Under U.S. federal law, a trademark is usually a word or a symbol. That symbol may be a number (how many of the following products can you identify? 6, 21, 45, 57, 66, 76, 380, and 5000)[15] or a

[14]There are many sources for information on this topic, but the best thing a new product manager can do is make contact with the employer's in-house (or local area) trademark attorney. Most such departments have brochures for employees to study, but experts we should not try to be!

[15]If you want to guess their identities, they are, in order, a car, a restaurant, an ale, a line of condiments, a gasoline, another gasoline, a car, and a car. In 1991 Intel lost the rights to "386" as a registered name for its 80386 computer chip. But numbers and letters make for even more confusion, and should be used with study: Teresa M. Pavia and Janeen Arnold Costa, "The Winning Number: Consumer Perceptions of Alpha-Numeric Brand Names," *Journal of Marketing,* July 1993, pp. 85–98.

design (for example, the stylized lettering in GE, the golden arches of McDonald's, or the paint firm's Dutch boy). The law doesn't care how unusual the trademark is and just requires it to identify and differentiate the item using it.

Most businesspeople and their customers use the term *brand* instead of *trademark.* This book uses *brand* when talking about marketing strategy and *trademark* when talking about the legal aspects. Technically speaking, services have *service* marks, not trademarks, and businesses have **trade names,** not trademarks.[16]

Another definition is very important: **registration.** Historically, and still today in most countries, the *first user* of a trademark had exclusive rights. But in the United States you can ask that your trademark be registered. If you can get it registered, you can keep that trademark forever, even if another firm later displays proof of prior use. See Figure 17–4 for the process.

What happens if, shortly after launch, other manufacturers begin encroaching on our mark? We move aggressively to stop them. Aladdin began putting on its labels "Aladdin thermos bottle." Do you know what thermos bottles are? If you do, as most people do, then the term no longer just describes one maker's brand of vacuum bottles. Aladdin was sued by the firm that owned the thermos mark, and won; the original owner did not protect it. *Thermos* became a generic. Any company can use it. Over the years, so did aspirin, cellophane, brassiere, dry ice, shredded wheat, trampoline, yo-yo, linoleum, corn flakes, kerosene, high octane, raisin bran, lanolin, nylon, mimeograph, and scores more. Billions of dollars in value lost. But today, makers of in-line skates know that Rollerblades is aggressively protected, as is Mattel's Frisbee. Some Xerox Corp. advertising reminds customers that the word "Xerox" is a trademark and therefore a proper adjective. It should always be followed by a descriptive noun (as in "Xerox copier") and never used as a verb (as in "xerox this for me").[17] Incidentally, don't forget to seek protection for the new brand in all countries where it might be marketed.

Companies can also seek **trade dress** protection. Trade dress refers to a wide range of product identifiers: in addition to brand name, it can include packaging, product color (Brillo is the pink soap pad, SOS is blue), or décor (the distinctive look inside a certain fast-food chain, for example). The extent of protection a company has is not always clear-cut, but if a firm has data that show customers identify a given trade dress with a particular brand, protection is often allowed by the courts using the concept of *secondary meaning.* That is, the color, décor, or packaging takes on a secondary meaning, which

[16]Services get special treatment in Leonard L. Berry, Edwin E. Lefkowith, and Terry Clark, "In Services, What's in a Name?" *Harvard Business Review,* September–October 1988, pp. 28–30. Even lawyers chuckled when two trademark searching firms hit the headlines. Jonathan M. Moses, "Trademark-Research Firms Head Into Legal Tussle Over Copyright," *The Wall Street Journal,* October 29, 1991, p. 10.

[17]Maxine S. Lans, "On Your Mark: Get Set or It May Go," *Marketing News,* September 26, 1994, p. 12.

FIGURE 17–4

Registration of trademarks by the United States Patent and Trademark Office

Here are three conditions set forth by the U.S. Patent and Trademark Office for the giving of REGISTRATION. There are a couple of others, but these are the ones that concern new products managers.

First, the trademark cannot be *too descriptive* of a product type.

A court once found the brand Light too descriptive when used as the brand of a cigarette. The judges felt that Light identified all cigarettes with the lighter taste of a low-tar cigarette, not just the one firm's brand. Similarly, Overnight Delivery Service would not be acceptable as a competitor to Federal Express.

Second, the proposed trademark should not be *confusingly similar* to the marks of the other products.

This is the toughest requirement, given the huge number of goods and services on the market today, and the 127,000 U.S. trademark applications in 1991 alone. Here is an example of the problem. Quality Inns International, a nationwide motel chain, decided to develop a new economy hotel chain. Quality Inns wanted to name the new chain McSleep, capitalizing on the Scottish fame for wise spending. Reaction was prompt—McDonald's lawyer said its use of the mark would not be tolerated. McDonald's felt that the "Mc" (called a *formative*) would lead people to believe the motel chain was part of the McDonald's Corporation—using its good name and reputation to help Quality Inns. As a further confusion, McDonald's was at that time building a chain of truckstop-style operations called McStop, which offered gasoline, fast food, and lodging at one site.

A federal district judge ruled for McDonald's, and Quality Inns switched the new chain's name to Sleep Inns. The judge punned that his ruling was a McPinion. McDonald's also blocked a New York store from using McBagel.

Not funny to Mead Data Central was a court decision to allow Toyota to market a Lexus car against Mead Data's mark of Lexis for its legal-information network. The data firm then launched a sweepstakes in which the prize was an Infiniti (a Lexus competitor)!

Third, the trademark should not be *immoral or misleading.*

It should not disparge people or institutions, and it probably should not be the name of a person.

is the name of the brand. Private brands often use trade dress to establish themselves as competitors of well-known brands—the drug-store brand of aspirin may be in a package that resembles the Bayer Aspirin package. Typically, courts deny the private brand absolute rights to copy the well-known brand's trade dress.[18]

What Is a Good Brand Name?

Getting a good brand is not easy because most good combinations of letters have already been taken. But, if Xerox can work out OK, and Clabber Girl too, then there is hope for all. Experts have given us criteria to follow. Let's look at them.

---

[18]Paul F. Kilmer, "Trade Dress Protection 1995: A U.S. Perspective," *Journal of Brand Management,* October 1995, pp. 95–103.

What Is the Brand's Role or Purpose? If a brand is purely for identification, then an arbitrary combination of letters will work well. This combination is called a *neologism,* and examples include Kodak, Exxon, and Nerf. But the brand may have some special purpose. For example, if the brand is to help position the product (useful when the seller lacks advertising dollars), then we want to use letters that already have meaning, such as CareFree, DieHard, and Holiday Inn.

Will This Product Be a Bridgehead to a Line of Products? If so, the name should not limit the firm, as Liquid Plumr tended to do. Can you accept *Liquid* Plumr *crystals?* What started as Western Hotels had to change to Western International and, finally, to Westin.

Do You Expect a Long-Term Position in the Market? If so, a more general and less dramatic name is preferable; but if you're only going to be around temporarily, something like Screaming Yellow Zonkers snacks can (and did) work.

Have You Remembered the Physical and Sensory Qualities of the Brand? Specifically, the brand name should be easy to pronounce, easy to spell, and easy to remember. Some believe Honda was careless when it chose Acura; phonetically, the spelling should have been *Accura,* and Americans would have had little trouble, but Acura works much better on an international scale. And, before we get too critical about pronunciation, we should remember Grey Poupon and Häagen-Dazs!

Is the Message Clear and Relevant? Product characteristics should come forth clearly. For example, the meaning of *Isovis* motor oil to the engineers who named it probably was "equal or constant viscosity," but to the average consumer, it was just a mix of letters. New products people are too close to their developments; their brand proposals should get careful buyer testing. A real misfire was La Choy's Fresh and Lite line of low-fat frozen Chinese entrées—critics thought it might a feminine hygiene product, or perhaps a beer.[19]

Does the Brand Insult or Irritate Any Particular Market Group? For example, women told Bic that Fannyhose was objectionable, so the firm switched to Pantyhose. And several foreign firms would have difficulty using their brand names in English-speaking markets, as indicated in Figure 17–5. New products managers are having to learn entirely new paradigms of brand development.[20]

---

[19]"Flops," *BusinessWeek,* August 16, 1993, p. 76.

[20]For evidence on this point, see Gael M. McDonald and C. J. Roberts, "The Brand-Naming Enigma in the Asia Pacific Context." *European Journal of Marketing,* no. 8 (1990), pp. 6–19.

FIGURE 17–5

Bad brand names

Sometimes it seems that foreign companies choose brand names that would seriously limit their sales potential in English-speaking markets.

Crapsy Fruit	French cereal
Fduhy Sesane	China Airlines snack food
Mukk	Italian yogurt
Pschitt	French lemonade
Atum Bom	Portuguese tuna
Happy End	German toilet paper
Pocari Sweat	Japanese sport drink
Zit	German lemonade
Creap	Japanese coffee creamer
I'm Dripper	Japanese instant coffee
Polio	Czech laundry detergent

Of course it works in both directions. Two famous examples are the Rolls Royce Silver Mist ("Mist" means "manure" in German), and Colgate Cue toothpaste ("Cue" is the name of a French porno magazine). Clairol also experienced problems launching its Mist Stick curling iron in Germany. The lesson is that we need to be careful when introducing brands into foreign markets.

Sources: Anonymous, "But Will It Sell in Tulsa?", *Newsweek,* March 17, 1997, p. 8; Ross and Kathryn Petras, *The 776 Even Stupider Things Ever Said* (New York: Harper-Perennial, 1994); and others.

Beyond these general principles, there is no end to the specific advice given by branding experts. See Figure 17–6 for some of their suggestions. The branding decision is often very important; it can be botched or brilliant. This is made clear in what will probably become a classic case—the Saturn brand General Motors created for a new smaller car. They worked from early in the life of the project to build a brand along with the new car, and succeeded.[21] As a final word, be sure the budget is sufficient for adequately creating customer awareness and understanding. If you don't have the funds to put meaning into a meaningless combination of letters, avoid that type of brand.

Given an overall marketing strategy and the role that brand will play, it is useful to have some discussions with intended users (to learn how they talk about things in this area of use)—and also with phonetic experts, who know a great deal about such things as word structures. Then brainstorm or use computers to generate large numbers of possible combinations. Computer software (such as NamePro developed by The Namestormers, and IdeaFisher by IdeaFisher Inc.) is available to assist in brand name selection and development.

---

[21]David A. Aaker, "Building a Brand: The Saturn Story," *California Management Review,* Winter 1994, pp. 114–33. Lest we think that branding is mainly a tool of consumer product marketers, see David Shipley and Paul Howard, "Brand-Naming Industrial Products," *Industrial Marketing Management,* 1993, pp. 59–66.

FIGURE 17–6

Collection of practitioners' suggestions about branding

1. Use digitals for modernity.
2. Family brands are quick, cheap, and void of surprises.
3. Use "stop" letters (called *plosives*): B, C, D, G, K, P, and T.
4. Use geographical connotations: Rebel Yell, and Evening in Paris.
5. Do something ridiculous: P. Lorillard had Whatchamacallits cigarettes.
6. Embellish an ordinary word: the vine leaf intertwined in "o" of Taylor Wines.
7. Put one odd letter in the name: Citibank, Toys "R" Us.
8. Borrow clout: General Mills' Lancia pizza mix picked up the sports car image.
9. Use the word *The* in the brand for dignity: The Glenlivit.
10. Use personalities: Reggie Jackson candy bars.
11. Use an attention grabber: My Sin cologne.
12. Reinforce a low-price strategy with a name like Klassy Kut Klothes.
13. Play with letters: *Serutan* is *Natures* spelled backward.
14. Add a symbol to reinforce the brand: Travelers' red umbrella, the rock of Prudential.

Conduct interviews with users to screen the list down. Ask what the brands on your list mean. This is the stage where P&G caught Dreck (Yiddish and German definitions included garbage and body waste), so it was changed to Dreft. When down to less than 10 candidates, get a legal check on their availability, and negotiate over the remaining 2 or 3. For line extensions, the logical brand may be obvious. Or a product characteristic may dominate. It's good, however, to keep two or three brands alive and approved, just in case an unexpected problem pops up.[22]

Managing Brand Equity

There is more to brand management, of course, than brand name selection. The best brand names—Coca Cola, Levi's, Campbell, AT&T, and so on—are important assets that provide value to both the firm and its customers, as shown in Figure 17–7. This value is known as **brand equity,** and the firms that benefit the most from brand equity have invested in protecting this equity to maintain the value of their brand names.[23] A brand with high equity encourages loyalty among customers, making advertising and other forms of promotion more efficient. High equity also means high brand awareness, which makes it easier for the firm to create other associations (for example, McDonald's is associated with children, clean restaurants, Ronald McDonald and his pals, etc.). Brand equity can also be associated with higher perceived

---

[22]A useful guide in brand name development is Chiranjeev Kohli and Douglas W. LaBahn, "Creating Effective Brand Names: A Study of the Naming Process," *Journal of Advertising Research,* January–February 1997, pp. 67–75.

[23]The authoritative books on brand equity are David A. Aaker, *Managing Brand Equity* (New York: Free Press, 1991), and David A. Aaker, *Building Strong Brands* (New York: Free Press, 1996).

FIGURE 17–7
How brand equity provides value

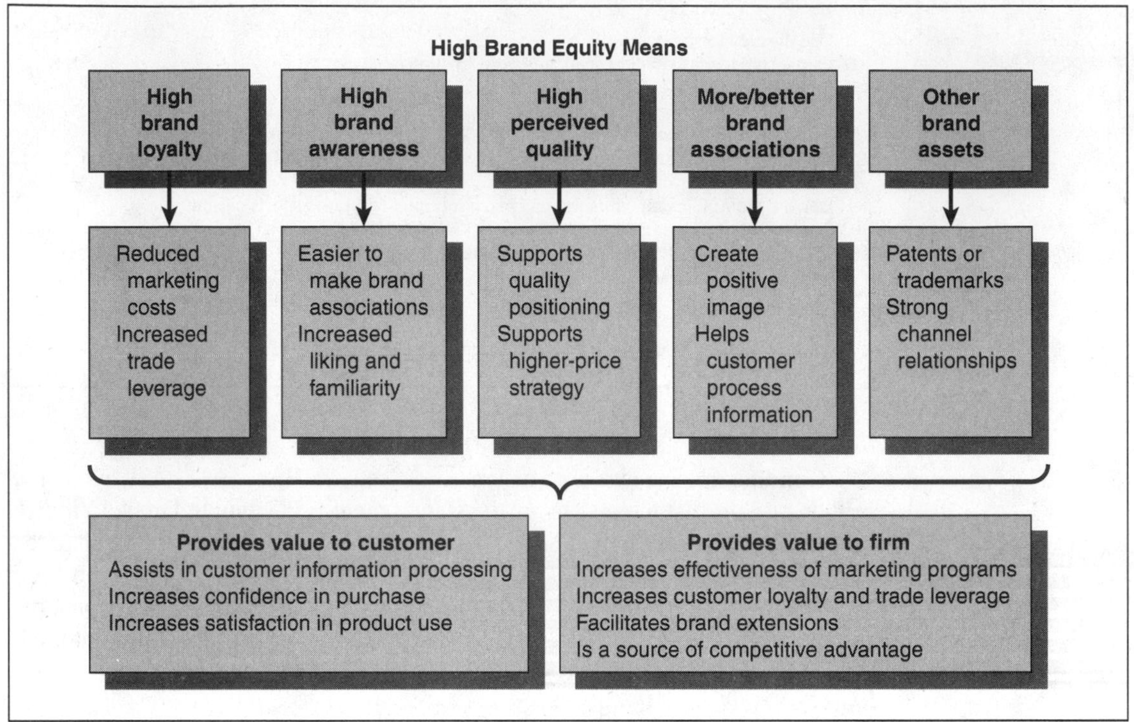

Source: Adapted from David A. Aaker, *Managing Brand Equity* (New York: Free Press, 1991), p. 17 and inside front cover.

quality, and thus support a premium positioning for a brand. Due to its high familiarity and positive associations, a high-equity brand can more easily be used as a bridgehead for launching **brand extensions.** In short, brand equity can provide sustainable competitive advantage.

Brand extensions must be managed carefully, as an unsuccessful extension, or too many extensions, can lead to brand equity erosion. Some companies have tried extending a well-known brand name into an inappropriate product category, with disastrous results. The Frito-Lay brand has been successfully extended to many snack foods, but Frito-Lay Lemonade didn't sell. Neither did Ben-Gay aspirin (what would that taste like?), Smucker's ketchup, nor Fruit of the Loom Laundry Detergent.[24] On the other hand, Nike recognized in 1998 that it was getting harder to make technological innovations to running shoes that were distinctive to consumers. To preserve its

[24]Robert M. McMath and Thom Forbes, *What Were They Thinking?* (New York: Times Business, 1996).

brand equity, the firm launched a new program in which athletes such as Tiger Woods would wear Nike "from head to toe," including watch and sunglasses, to take advantage of the Nike "halo."[25]

Although there is no one right way to extend a brand name, there are some guidelines to follow to avoid mistakes like these. For instance, emphasizing the product's name or benefits might create a safe "distance" from the brand being extended. When the Audi 500 automobile was allegedly experiencing problems with sudden acceleration, Audi 400 sales were hurt, but not Audi Quattro sales. Another consideration is whether the brand being extended has a functional or a prestige image. Gillette could probably launch a downscale extension of the Sensor razor easily, while Mercedes risks tarnishing its reputation if it launches a low-end Mercedes car. Master brands, those that are almost synonymous with the product category (such as Hallmark Cards or Planter's Peanuts), should be very carefully extended, and then probably only to brands of similar or better quality to avoid risking consumer confidence. Of course, concept testing a potential extension can identify any possible negative associations.[26]

Packaging

To many firms, packaging is less important, either because the goods require little packaging or because the shelf persuasiveness of packaging is not a priority. In these firms, packaging is for the most part assigned to packaging design departments. Of course, most services require no packaging. But in many other firms, packaging is of great importance, especially when the new item will be distributed through self-service environments, when the product category is already established so the new item will have to force its way in, and when many strongly entrenched competitors sit next to one another on store shelves. In such firms, packaging decisions are often made at the highest levels. In fact, more money is spent on packaging food and beverage products than on advertising them.

What Is Packaging?

Three "containers" are usually included in the term packaging, and some variations exist on those. *Primary packaging* is the material that first envelops the product and holds it, perhaps a bottle for pills or a polyethylene bag for a computer CPU. *Secondary packaging* is outside of a primary package. It may

---

[25]Bill Richards, "Tripped Up by Too Many Shoes, Nike Regroups," *The Wall Street Journal,* February 3, 1998, pp. B1, B12.

[26]Dennis A. Pitts and Lea Prevel Katsanis, "Understanding Brand Equity for Successful Brand Extensions," *Journal of Consumer Marketing,* no. 4 (1995), pp. 51–64; see also Sieu Meng Long, Swee Hoon Ang, and Janet Liau, "Dominance and Dilution: The Effects of Extending Master Brands," *Journal of Consumer Marketing,* no. 5 (1997), pp. 280–88.

gather a group of primary packages and holds them for transportation or display, or it may be a cardboard box that holds the pill bottle. *Tertiary packaging* is the bulk packaging that holds secondary packages for shipment—the large cardboard box or the pallet, for example.

The Various Roles of Packaging

These are easy to see. The major ones are *containment* (hold for transporting), *protection* (from the elements and the careless), *safety* (from causing injury), *display* (to attract attention), and to *inform* and *persuade.* All are important to a new products manager, sometimes enough so that there are legal problems; packaging design is a part of logo and trademark, where rights can be valuable.

But there are other roles. For example, assisting the user in some way—with instructions (pharmaceuticals or food) and with a use function (beer cans and deodorant dispensers). Other times packages are designed to permit reusability, meet ecological demands on biodegradability, carry warnings, and meet other legal requirements. They may also aid in disposability.

The Packaging Decision

Packaging is part of the new product manager's network. But it is so multifunctional it tends to have its own subnetwork (see Figure 17–8). It centers on a person most often called the director of packaging. The packaging decision may take months; it is a key target in most accelerated development programs.

Each company tends to develop a somewhat unique approach to packaging, but there are common steps. First, a packaging person is put on a new products team. Field trips are mandatory, as is access to the various market studies that have been made. A unique packaging approach for Pfeiffer's salad dressing was found when a packaging staffer visited supermarkets and noted that salad dressings were displayed by type rather than by brand; most competitive bottles were shaped like whisk brooms with flat iron heads.

The process for package development resembles that for the product itself. Tests include dummy packages, in-store displays, color tests, visual tests, psychographic tests, physical tests, distribution tests, warehouse legibility, and even some in-store selling tests. One of the strategies sometimes used in package design is **family packaging,** that is, using a key design, or some other packaging element, to integrate the packaging of several individual items. A package for a new Häagen-Dazs or Ben & Jerry's ice cream flavor, for example, is immediately recognizable. Coca-Cola and Pepsi are red and blue, respectively. In each case, the packages clearly belong to one set, but there are usually some individualizations, such as brand name.

Packaging can be a very powerful competitive tool. Between 1994 and 1997, the U.S. cereal sales declined by about 15 percent, and leading brands such as Kellogg's have suffered profit declines. The number-four cereal producer (Quaker) and a smaller competitor (Malt-O-Meal) managed to increase

FIGURE 17–8
Packaging network

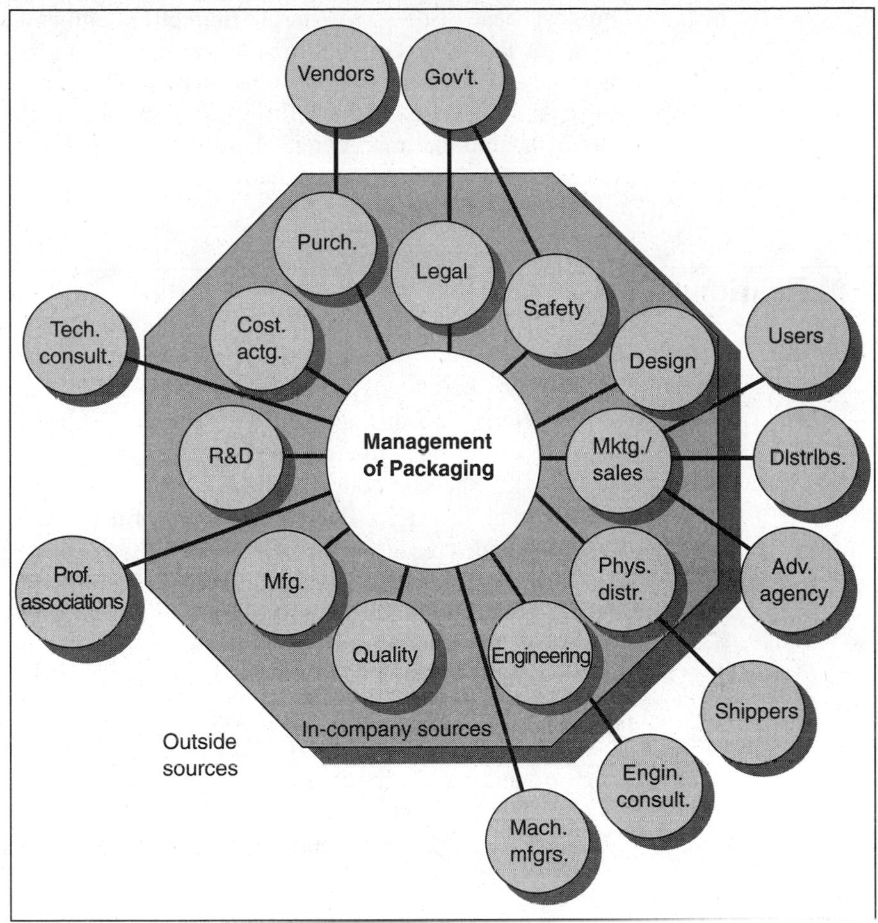

their market shares over this period by packaging their cereals in bags instead of boxes, and passing on the cost saving (about a dollar a box) to the retail customer.[27]

Summary

In Chapter 17, we have extended our look at the launch planning process by going into the platform decisions and the driving decisions. Both sets have a strong effect on the strategies chosen. The chapter also looked at three of the

[27]David Leonhardt, "Cereal-Box Killers Are On the Loose," *BusinessWeek,* October 12, 1998, p. 72.

biggest areas of decision—target market or segment, positioning of the new item for that segment, and creating unique value for that segment. We can now turn to those many things that make up the tactics portion of the marketing plan. But there is far too little space for an in-depth study in the many areas of operational marketing. Therefore, we will look at those issues which give new products managers the most difficulty.

Applications

More questions from that interview with the company president.

1. "My daughter is a newly appointed assistant professor at a school in North Carolina, and she recently was joking about how similar the development of courses is to the development of new products. In fact, she said courses have to be planned for and their marketing has to be just right. Even to the point of using positioning as a concept. I wonder if you could take a new college course, say, one on the application of new computer and telecommunication technologies to the operation of a retail store, and show me how you could position that course, using each of the various methods for positioning a new product."
2. "I like the way you keep referring to yourself as a new products person, not a marketer. Our marketers sometimes have trouble winning the confidence of other managers. I am thinking particularly of the troubles they have getting support of financial people and legal people for their new product programs. It seems to me sometimes they focus too much on their sales plans, their advertising, and their trade shows. Finance and legal aren't shown what *they* can do to help a launch. Oh, I know about general job lists, and how a budget is due at a given time, and how legal approval of advertising is scheduled. But I mean really help, play a positive role, be a member of the team, and so on. What could you suggest?"
3. "We're in the furniture business, and I'll bet you have used some of our stuff if you spent any time in your college dorms. But, I'll tell you something, there's not much profit in that business—too many competitors, too much standardization in products. You know, buying on bids, from purchasing department product spec sheets. I was aware of what you said a while ago about core benefits, and creating product value *around* that core, like in service, image, warranty, and so forth. But I'm not sure we could use that approach. Given that, physically, our desks and beds have to meet specs, how might we create value around that, to help us defend slightly higher prices?"

4. "Packaging must be terribly important today on lots of products. We spend a fortune on it. I read recently about a detergent packaging gimmick—an 'overcap.' It goes onto a bottle, over the regular cap. It can be torn away and sent in for a refund. Less likely to be cheated on than a coupon. Now that's creative. Are you creative? Could you come up with some ideas like that? We think there is a big packaging opportunity to differentiate our nonalcoholic beer. New products people on that line would sure appreciate some packaging ideas they have never heard of. Good ones, that is, not just a bunch of foolishness."

CASE: BARSTOW CHEMICAL COMPANY[28]

It had been evident for some time that any firm heavily committed to chemicals was going to have to do something to escape the brutal price competition so prevalent on commodity-type chemicals. So Frieda Fletcher, general manager of Barstow Chemical Company's Specialty Chemicals Division, asked her staff to suggest ways their resources could be used to come up with new product concepts that they could develop and with some modest help to market.

Barstow's home office was in Stamford, Connecticut, but Fletcher's group had been moved to Pittsburgh to "get away from the heavy chemicals mentality," as the chairman had put it. The move seemed to work because the Specialty Chemicals group now had four major projects under way: two in chemicals that could be sold to the automotive industry for undercar finishing, a fabric strengthener they weren't sure of a use for yet, and a shampoo.

The shampoo had been an accidental spin-off of the undercar treatment project. A chemist was working on chemicals that resisted cleansers of the type used in car washes and by car owners. He tried to find the strongest cleansers he could and even made up some new ones just to be sure the protectants really worked.

The surprise came when he tried a relatively simple concoction that cleaned everything he had been testing yet seemed very soft on the materials and on the hands of workers. (The firm would not comment on the chemicals used in the new concoction.)

By early 1996, Specialty Chemicals had a prototype product and had tested it with all ages, sexes, and social classes of people. It worked about the same with all of them: not better than present shampoos, unfortunately, because all of the shampoos tested were about the same (except for smell, thickness, and so on), but certainly as well. It was also safe and had passed several government tests. So far, it had no added conditioners.

The problem, of course, was how to sell it. The firm considered (and rejected) selling the formula to another firm already in the shampoo business; they wanted to market it themselves, as part of the overall corporate strategy to diversity, as described above. General Manager Fletcher was well aware that they were inexperienced in consumer marketing. So she wanted to put down some ideas that would serve to help guide the sales and marketing people as they put together a marketing plan for the shampoo. They all knew

---

[28]The situation of this case has been camouflaged, including the name, time frame, and location.

about target markets and product positioning statements (ideas that they used on industrial chemicals as well). But before getting into those matters she thought perhaps some of those strategic platform decisions mentioned in Chapter 17 would need to be looked at.

The company actually didn't know too much about the shampoo market and would be undertaking market research soon; but in the meantime, Fletcher had some information. One of her new products managers (Juan Jimenez) had formerly worked in a shampoo company, so she asked him to use his personal experience in the shampoo market to come up with decisions on each one of the strategic platform decisions. The new shampoo, as stated, worked about the same as the current market leaders, but it did have two noteworthy features. One, the formula was usually in a very thick gel and, in fact, could be as thick as Vaseline. Two, its natural aroma was quite pleasant and fresh, much like almonds. Fletcher said it would take some effort to get the chemical firm's management to approve specific targets and positionings (without wanting to play a role in deciding them), so she wanted to get them thinking along more strategic lines soon. The new products would be something they had never done before, but with the one experienced marketer on board and the firm's general experience in marketing, she felt sure they would understand the issues and could react understandably to whatever decisions they made on them at this time. Then, later, they could move on through the specifics of target, positioning, branding, and matters like that.

Fletcher felt that to break into the shampoo business might require some "off the beaten track" marketing, and hoped her staff was up to the task. She asked you to help Juan on his assignment.

Case: AT&T Magicphone Phone-Fax-Copier (C)[29]

Refer back to the AT&T Magicphone cases (A) and (B) at the end of Chapters 6 and 9. Suppose now that AT&T's competitive intelligence indicates that Executone is planning a launch of a phone-fax-copier within six months—far sooner than expected—at a price of only $1,050. Furthermore, all indications are that the Executone product will be more convenient to use than the Magicphone, but less productive (lower copier speed and fax transmission time). Using their best judgment, AT&T management rated the impending Executone product at 4.30 and 2.75 respectively on the attributes of convenience and productivity.

How serious is this competitive attack? What, if anything, should AT&T do now to minimize the threat posed by Executone? Or is it better for AT&T to wait until the Executone product is launched, and then react?

[29]This case is based on "AT&T Magicphone PFC," a case in Roger J. Calantone and C. Anthony Di Benedetto, *The Product Manager's Toolbox,* New York: McGraw-Hill, 1993. Used with permission. The material on product features and competitive information presented in this case was compiled from numerous published sources, and the name of the product is disguised. The competitive threat presented is fictitious and used for illustrative purposes only.

CHAPTER

18 IMPLEMENTATION OF THE STRATEGIC PLAN

Setting

Chapter 17 set up the strategic platform decisions and the strategic actions decisions. It then went into the building blocks of marketing by talking about the target market and the product positioning statement. That led to actions for building value into the product for the chosen target and positioning. And into the matters of branding and packaging—part of the product and part of the promotion. Now, we can move into the tactics area—how managements actually communicate all of these things to the end-user. The strategic implementation often calls for considerable creativity, and gets it.

The Launch Cycle

First, let's correct an impression many people have about the launch of a new product. They see the launch as a matter of announcing to the world the good news about our great new product. If it could be that simple!

What actually takes place is a **launch cycle.** The launch cycle is an expansion of the familiar introductory stage of the **product life cycle (PLC)** into substages; see Figure 18–1. It picks up the preparations during the **prelaunch** period, the announcement, the beachhead phase, and then the early growth stage that links the launch cycle back to the PLC.

Preparation occurs when we build our capability to compete. This means the training of sales and other promotional people, building service capability, putting out *preannouncements* if they are in order, and arranging for stocking of the product at the reseller level.

FIGURE 18–1
The launch cycle

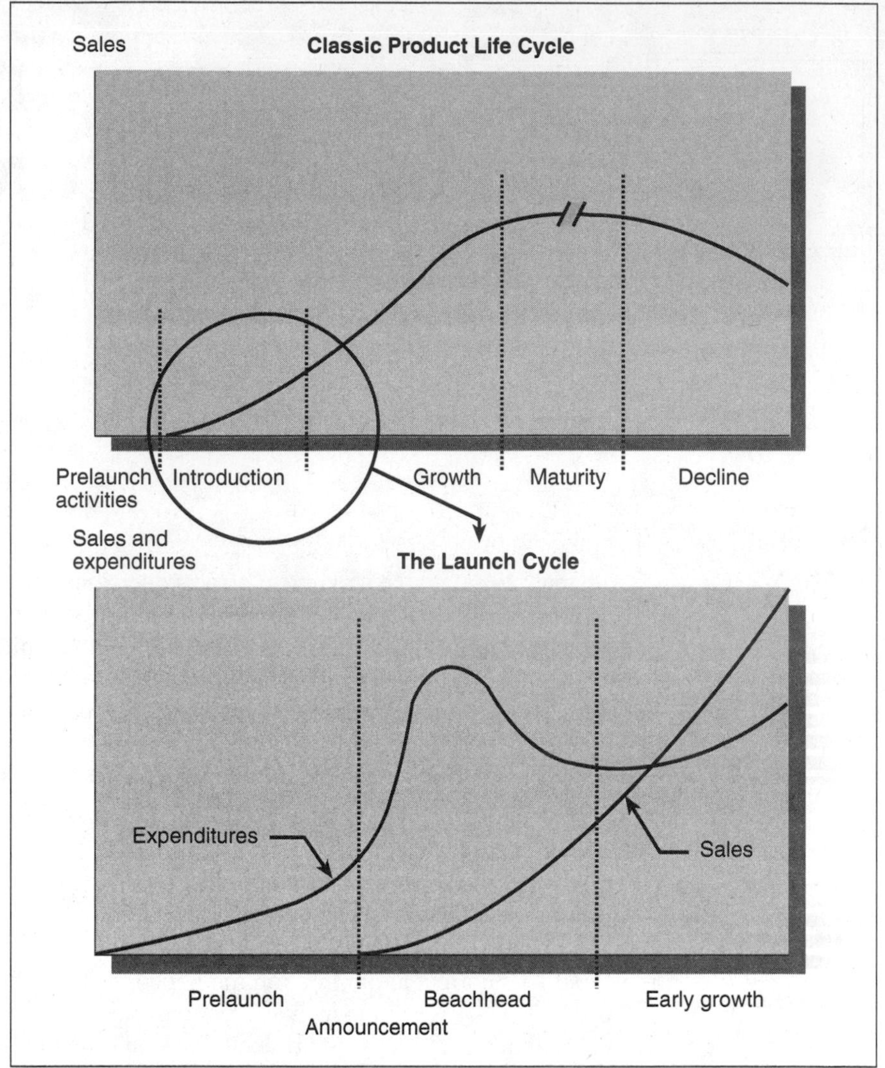

The new products novice almost invariably focuses on announcement as the culmination of the entire new product development process, which it clearly is not. In fact, only on very rare dramatic occasions is there one day when the announcement takes place. The car companies once keyed their announcements (with appropriate on-camera unveilings) to a date in the fall. But such drama does not play well today. In the first place, it is almost impossible to keep a secret, especially as the firm's formal announcement day approaches.

Instead, we see a planned sequence of announcements, often geared to keeping competitors guessing and to keeping competitors' customers from stocking up just prior to our product being available. One sequence of periods goes like this: (1) nondisclosures; (2) product testing, beta testers sign confidentiality forms; (3) anticipation—position releases telling about the problem being solved; (4) influentials—press kits for editors, industry researchers, and some customers; (5) broadcast PR—full press releases, product for reviews; (6) promo pieces—the start of advertising. Stages 3 and 4 are used for preannouncements, usually subtle *signaling,* sometimes orchestrated through planned leaks by selected individuals and sometimes just allowed to happen. The intent is to hype interest in the upcoming product and to motivate buyers to hold up long-term competitive orders until the new item is revealed. Of course, in many markets, there is almost no attempt to keep secrets. For example, the whole world knew Microsoft Corporation was announcing their new Windows 95 on August 24, 1995. It had been in beta tests with over 2,000 firms, some for more than a year. Its full details were known to every computer editor in the world.

Signals can be given by use of any of the marketing tools. Price was mentioned above. Others are advertising, trade shows, comments by sales people, a speech by a CEO at a security analysts' luncheon in New York City, London, or Tokyo, tips from vendors of packaging or production machinery, stocking calls made on distributors or retailers, appointment of new sales representatives with certain industry experience, and on and on. Some are so subtle they are missed. But in the main, they can be very effective, so much so that they constitute a field of unfair advertising law.[1]

The flip side of preannouncements is the preavailability competitive ploy. When it became known that Ford was introducing the new Windstar minivan, Chrysler put into operation an aggressive price promotion. This brought them many buyers who otherwise might have awaited Windstar, but it also tweaked interest in Chrysler's own new minivan scheduled for the following year.[2] It is somewhat dangerous to cut the price of an item being replaced because this can result in current buyers deciding to await the new; this makes it tough to clear out trade stocks of the old item. An early, successful British computer maker went bankrupt when this happened. However, Philips found out (on its digital compact cassette machine) that if the price cut is too much, customers will clean out retail inventories *before the new product arrives.*[3] The president

[1]Oliver P. Heil and Arlen W. Langvardt, "The Interface Between Competitive Market Signaling and Antitrust Law," *Journal of Marketing,* July 1994, pp. 81–96. A broader view of the tool is in Oliver P. Heil and Rockney G. Walters, "Explaining Competitive Reactions to New Products: An Empirical Signaling Study," *Journal of Product Innovation Management* 10, no. 1 (January 1993), pp. 53–65.

[2]Jerry Flint, "A Van for All Seasons," *Forbes,* December 20, 1993, pp. 43–44.

[3]Kyle Pope, "Philips Tries, Tries Again With Its DCC," *The Wall Street Journal,* October 3, 1994, p. B1.

of Compaq recently remarked at an international conference that there really is no "announcement" any more—new items are just developed and moved into the market, usually on a limited market area basis. (This will be called a market rollout in Chapter 20.)

Occasionally a firm can use *preannouncement signaling* to keep the finance markets happy, but there is a danger of not being able to fulfill the signal. In the software field this has resulted in what is called *vaporware*—signaled but not delivered until much later, if ever. A recent preannouncement gone awry was made by Pacific Scientific Corporation, makers of the Solium dimmable fluorescent light bulb. In 1994, the company hired a PR firm to announce the pending launch and the signing of a contract with a big-name industry partner to handle marketing. Annual revenues were projected in the $100-million range. Meanwhile, there were delays in product development and technology bugs were beginning to emerge. Stockholders began suing the company. By first quarter 1997, Pacific Scientific took a $12 million loss disposing of the Solium technology and watched its stock value plummet.[4]

A recent study showed that firms with smaller shares are more likely to preannounce, large firms will avoid preannouncing if they fear government criticism of monopoly, there will be less preannouncing in industries that are very competitive, and there will be more preannouncing where switching costs are high.[5]

The third stage of the launch cycle—**beachhead**—gets its name from a military landing on enemy soil, a good metaphor for many launches. Other expressions are: priming the pump, getting a fire started, getting the ball rolling, getting off the ground. In each situation, a standstill is followed by movement in a manner similar to that of a kite pulled into the wind, a descending bobsled, or a military invasion force expanding from a small strip of shoreline. In a product launch setting, beachhead refers to the heavy expenditures necessary to overcome sales inertia—Figure 18–1 illustrates this with a steeply rising expenditures curve up to the point where sales increase at an increasing rate.

Announcement kicks off the beachhead phase, and the conditions at the time are hardly conducive to good management. Communication systems fail, unexpected problems arise, supplies become scarce, and general confusion may reign. As the months go by, a subtle change in emphasis occurs as initial announcement gives way to "reason why" and then to the rationale of trial and the reinforcement of successful experience.

The key decision in the beachhead phase is to end it—inertia has been overcome, the product has started to move. This decision triggers a series of actions. Improvements and flankers will now be brought along as

---

[4]Stacy Kravetz, "Light Bulb Couldn't Match the Glow of Its Own Press," *The Wall Street Journal,* May 28, 1997, p. B1.

[5]Jehoshua Eliasberg and Thomas S. Robertson, "New Product Preannouncing Behavior: A Market Signaling Study," *Journal of Marketing Research,* August 1988, pp. 282–92.

scheduled; new budgets will be approved and released; temporary marketing arrangements will be made permanent (such as a temporary sales force, an advertising agency, or a direct-mail arrangement.)

One new products manager said he knew this decision had been made when the firm's president stopped calling him every couple of days for the latest news.

Communicating the Story to Prospective Buyers

Now let's go back to the launch planning effort, where it is now time to prepare the advertising, train sales people, and so on. For this we need to review the prevailing marketing mix. Look at Figure 18–2. It shows that the manufacturer (or creator of a service) can allocate its limited funds in five different ways—from spending to improve the product or add line extensions to it (that will make the item more attractive to buyers) to having a retailer put on a big in-store promotion around the new item.

FIGURE 18–2

The basic marketing mix

Demand for a new product comes about because of a combination of five stimulants put on top of a standing relationship (image, feeling, franchise) between the firm introducing it and the firms or individuals they are hoping will buy it. See the left-hand column for the key. See below for new product descriptions.

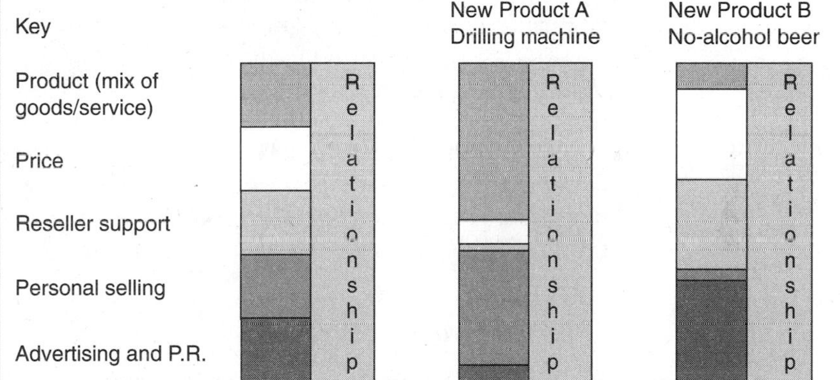

Laser drilling machine: High-tech, breakthrough, sold direct to heavy industry, from leading maker.
No-alcohol beer: Me-too product, hitting the price buyer, sold through restaurants and stores, from Miller's.

What would the two columns look like if Product A was a low-cost import, me-too, sold by distributors, for an unknown maker, and the no-alcohol beer was a technical breakthrough?

Developers have been following a mix from the very beginning—where decisions were made on R&D budgets. Pharmaceutical firms put the bulk of their money into technical research, White Consolidated (white goods) puts it into manufacturing process development, and Avon and Mary Kay into personal selling.

The Communications Plan

Communications is the term most widely used to cover all of the information and attitude effort we put into changing how the end-user sees our situation. It involves everything from technical products data to strong persuasion. The communications *requirements* are the specifics that must be communicated in our plan. They have been with us almost since the beginning of this project—for example, when we focused in on skiers because we were sure our new plastics technology could deal more effectively with the need for skis to both slide and hold. A communications requirement would be to remind skiers about their problems with sticking skis, tell them we have a solution, what it is, how they can get it, and so on. This comes from the PIC, from concept testing, and especially from the product protocol statement (where marketing requirements were listed alongside technical requirements.) It can be quite short or long, but is a powerful tool in all that follows. It should be based on a solid understanding of the end-user's attitudes and behavior.

The communications task is performed with a **communications mix.** There can be as many as four mixes: one for communications to the reseller by us, a second for communications to the end-user by the reseller, a third for communications to the end-user by us, and a fourth for the total communication effort by our team to the end-user. Service firms, and direct-selling manufacturers, appreciate a simplification of this task because there is usually no reseller. Direct-selling manufacturers also benefit this way. The job here is to make the best choices—a mix from each set, imaginatively implemented. New products people, in particular, have wide freedom—a clean sheet of paper. There are some restrictions (from the givens in ongoing company operation) but still there is always room for creativity.

The Copy Strategy Statement

Given the requirements that communications tools are to deliver, let's look at a device designed to communicate these requirements to those who, for example, create advertising. Its name varies a lot in practice, but **copy strategy statement** is a common one. It can be used to convey to every advertising and promotion creative person the following items (among many others):

The market segment being targeted

The product positioning statement

The communications mix, and the pieces covered by this statement.

The major copy points to be communicated. These are usually product attributes, including features, functions, and benefits as well as uses, but they can be almost anything important to that end-user making a favorable decision. For example:

The provider of this insurance policy is the largest in the world.

Black Pearls perfume was designed by Elizabeth Taylor personally.

This cellular phone has no geographical limitation.

Dockers are available at JCPenney.

Future neurosurgeons benefit from the hand-and-eye skills of computer games like this one.

There is no limit. But there must be focus on any one list. Communication capabilities today are under great pressure—humans are exposed to millions of messages and thousands of firms. It's fully OK to list lots of points in a selling piece or an ad, but only a few of them should be on the requirements list. Only a few *must* be accomplished at this time. And the copy strategy statement should be written by the team, not by the person who will create the pieces for it.

Personal Selling

The sales person is the workhorse of most new product introductions. Even on packaged goods **personal selling** is clearly essential—not very often today can we pull a product into good retail availability just by virtue of ads on the product story. So few things in business are changing as fast as the sales department. One observer commented recently:

> We don't need people saying "Nothing happens until somebody sells something." This notion was born when Willie Lomans ruled the day. The idea of getting the troops hyped, fired, and revved up, won't do the job today. The change has nothing to do with selling; it has everything to do with buying. Today, successful selling strategies must be built around strong relationships, trust, confidence, and—most important—the salesperson's expertise.[6]

This means the new products manager probably has to work harder than ever meeting the needs of these new professional sales operations. But being professional, they know what will sell, and are anxious to have new products if they are based on meeting customer needs. Because we are competing with other marketing managers for the limited pool of selling time with customers, getting sales support means internal marketing.

---

[6] John R. Graham, "What We Don't Need Can't Help Us Anyway," *Marketing News,* June 22, 1992, p. 4. An early description of how James River's Towel and Tissue Group converted its sales management focus into a business management focus was given in "Nurturing Grass Roots Responsibility for Planning and Sales," *The Conference Board's Marketing Briefing,* August/September 1989, pp. 1–2.

One issue that is sometimes difficult to decide is, how early should we involve sales people? An industrial firm developing new metal-grinding machinery will have downstream customer coupling, and by the time the project is ready for marketing, the sales department has been involved for a long time. Advertising people have not been. For consumer packaged goods, advertising people (including advertising agency personnel) are involved early on, but the sales department usually is not. For services, the new product developer is apt to *be* in the sales department.

Some managers want to keep salespeople away from product development ("no need for them to know," "we must continue selling today's products today"). Some firms find the answer in having sales *managers* involved. A common tactic is to have small groups of district or regional sales managers rotating on advisory teams.

A much more difficult question comes up when the new product needs a new sales force—that is, one reaching markets the current one doesn't cover. Hopefully less-disruptive adjustments can be made. Sometimes it is possible to add *some* of the uncovered customers, or hire a small group of specialists to hit the major pockets of new customers.

How to Motivate Sales People. A new product is an intrusion. It takes time. It disrupts schedules. It involves change and risk. Sales people are known for wanting new items to sell, but there are still negatives. Salespeople are not usually given reduced territories when asked to sell a new product. So it is important to (1) *investigate* in advance any possible reasons why salespeople might object to the new product, (2) give them all the *training and materials* they need to be effective, and (3) make sure the product is *available* in their territories, when they start seeking orders.

The key is to do our job such that they can do their job. That means to have a product that customers will understand and want to try, and to train the sales force to understand and communicate these things. This training should use the latest technology. SmithKline Beecham, when introducing a new feline vaccine, prepared an interesting game show for its sales meeting. It was loaded with 'neato' video graphics, computer animation, music, and sound effects. At the end of the meeting, there was a round of written questions on product knowledge, the winners of which got to compete for cash prizes. The competition involved regional teams of six members, and all audience members bet on which team they thought would win. Questions were very difficult and the contestants spent a lot of time preparing.[7]

The Client-Building Team. Over the last few years, under the prodding of very large buyers, business firms are reluctantly turning to a new mode of

---

[7]Cyndee Miller, "Training Pays Off—In Cash," *Marketing News,* July 22, 1991, p. 23.

customer contact. Rather than have product-line-based sales forces, they are going to customer-based sales forces. Each rep sells a longer line, but brings to the customer a team of company people who can address customer problems. The new approach makes customers happy (Wal-Mart had to force the system upon its suppliers, but is now P&G's biggest single customer). A customer-based sales organization requires less of the hard-sell pushing that product-based sales forces can provide.[8]

Alliances

Technical departments have, in recent years, come to realize that they needn't have every possible technical capability required on a new product project. Instead, they form **strategic alliances** with universities, government units, private research centers, and even competitors, to access what they need. Marketing people have been doing this for many years, and still do. In fact, the trade channel itself is a strategic alliance. Independent firms sign a franchise agreement wherein each side promises to do certain things, the result of which is to accomplish a task. Manufacturers don't *have* to use retailers—Avon dropped theirs many years ago.

Advertising is another area for alliances—long-standing agreements are signed with advertising agencies. Service organizations are often brought into a franchise situation. Ditto for warehousing companies, for competitors (to gain sales forces that can reach markets where it is more profitable to use an established organization than to do the whole thing themselves), and exhibit firms (for trade shows).

It has been said that, today, one can form an alliance with someone, somewhere, for every task that needs to be done.

A-T-A-R Requirements

In Chapter 8, you met the A-T-A-R model. It displayed the four key steps that an end-user must move through if there is to be satisfied adoption of a new product—Awareness, Trial, Availability, and Repeat Use. It is the task of the marketing organization to accomplish these, in a sufficiently large set of users to achieve the financial and other goals. They make a good framework for deciding just what marketing activities will be undertaken.

---

[8]For more on this swing in sales force thinking, see Patricia Sellers, "How To Remake Your Sales Force," *Fortune,* May 4, 1992, pp. 96–103; and Joseph Conlin, "Teaming Up," *Sales & Marketing Management,* October 1993, pp. 98–104.

Awareness

Awareness is the necessary first step toward adoption (though there are rare cases where a product can be consumed in ignorance or in a hurry, with awareness following that trial). Awareness means different things on different products, and is sought aggressively by almost all new product marketers.

Measuring Awareness. Let's look at three quite different situations. First is a new candy bar. To a lover of candy bars, the mere mention of a new bar is enough to trigger interest and probably trial purchase. Second is a new word processing software package being considered by a leading author of novels. Mere mention is not enough; there must be considerable information because of the inconvenience of trial and the cost of the package. Third is a new method of cleaning up black water in municipal water-treatment systems, and the target is civil engineers specializing in recommending municipal water treatment systems. There is so much at stake in their first trial recommendation that they may compile information over several years before making it.

All three people "heard of" their new items on a single day, and in a single message. They may even have heard the positioning and understood it. But one is minutes away from trial and the others months or years away.

Given that we want trial to follow awareness, what constitutes awareness differs greatly. There is no accepted definition, though consumer packaged goods usage tends to become standardized. For example, "Have you heard of a new candy bar made from burnt raisins and ground barley?" Some element of the positioning must be present.

Some business marketers measure it by whether people send in an inquiry for more information. Philips once apparently didn't think about awareness of *what*—it used some very unique MTV-style three-minute commercials about DCC, but forgot to tell what the acronym stood for.[9]

Methods for Getting Awareness. People working in every industry have a good understanding of how to get awareness of a new product in their industry. The ideal probably is a mix: an announcement ad or sales call, then favorable mention by a friend, then seeing the item in use, then a reminder of some type, then getting some professional endorsement in a news account or column, then a reminder of some sort, and then an opportunity to buy it (which stimulates consideration of all the information previously gathered.)

Providing all these stimuli is apt to be expensive; the less the product has going for it the more we have to spend on it. And there is never enough money to "do the job right."

---

[9]Digital Compact Cassette machine. Kyle Pope, "Philips Tries, Tries Again with Its DCC."

Fortunately, the marketplace can help us on awareness and trial if we are following the process of this book. That's because we made sure there was a problem and then worked until we had a good *solution.* If the activity (bowling, eating, machining, surgery, whatever) is important to the customer, so much the better. An interested, dissatisfied customer, for whom we have good news, needs little more than announcement to get awareness. It helps even more if the situation is newsworthy (sports, politics, financial markets, health, etc.) and if the product is one that customers see in use frequently (car, TV set, clothing, and the like).

Stocking and Availability

Services are usually sold direct, and so are many goods. But most goods use resellers, such as distributors and retail dealers. They help us push the product down the channel, but only rarely does a new product offer them really new business without any major troubles. For example, Abbott's of New England nearly went broke trying to get its new chowder products into supermarkets. So it persuaded some of the stores' deli counters to offer single portions of hot chowder. The products were soon in 20 percent of U.S. supermarkets.

Most resellers do a large volume of business in a rather standardized way, with a small margin. Many have constraints on what they can and cannot do—franchise agreements, long-time personal relationships with sales representatives, channel leadership roles, and selling and service systems of their own. They are not at all anxious to make changes in their systems.

Therefore, their thinking should be represented in the product development process. If a distributor is large and powerful, it is a candidate for including well up the development line—when product attributes are still being worked on, when packaging is being designed, and so on. Otherwise, it is usually sufficient to have the resellers' views represented by experienced sales people—sales managers and what are sometimes called trade relations directors.

We start with a statement of what the reseller's role will be. This role normally includes, for stocking distributors, (1) prestocking activities such as training and installation of equipment, (2) stocking of the new item, (3) preparation for promotion, including training salespeople and service people, and (4) actually doing the promotion, whether just listing the item in a catalog, adding the item to selling schedules, or working with individual buyers to determine their needs and convert interest into sales.

Somewhere along the line we have to know that resellers *can* do what we want and need, and that they *will* do it. Assuming they "can do," the "will do" is a matter of motivation, and for this we arrange a program of encouragement, based on items from the list in Figure 18–3. Without any question,

FIGURE 18–3

Alternative tools and devices for motivating distributors

A. Increase the distributor's unit volume.
1. Have an outstanding product.
2. Use pull techniques—advertising, trade and consumer shows, public relations, missionary selling.
3. Give the distributor a type of monopoly—exclusivity or selectivity.
4. Run "where available" ads.
5. Offer merchandising assistance—dollars, training, displays, points of purchase, co-op advertising, in-store demonstrations, store "events," and repair and service clinics.

B. Increase the distributor's unit margin.
1. Raise the basic percentage margin.
2. Offer special discounts—e.g., for promotion or service.
3. Offer allowances and special payments.
4. Offer to prepay allowances to save interest.

C. Reduce the distributor's costs of doing business.
1. Provide managerial training.
2. Provide dollars for training.
3. Improve the returned-goods policy.
4. Improve the service policy.
5. Drop-ship delivery to distributor's customers.
6. Preprice the merchandise.
7. Tray pack the merchandise or otherwise aid in repackaging it.

D. Change the distributor's attitude toward the line.
1. By encouragement—management negotiation, sales calls, direct mail, advertising.
2. By discouragement—threats to cut back some of the above benefits or legal action.
3. Rap sessions—talk groups, focus groups, councils.
4. Better product instruction sessions—better visuals, better instructions.

proof that the new item will sell is the best motivation.[10] But channel firms can be tough if they feel mistreated. Elizabeth Arden Division of Unilever had to cancel a planned introduction of a new Elizabeth Taylor fragrance called Black Pearls because the firm slashed monies for department store sales people. The stores refused to stock it, forcing Arden to plan distribution through mass merchandisers, but the whole deal was ultimately canceled, even though Black Pearls advertising had started running. The division looked to lose millions of dollars, and its president resigned by mutual consent. Moral: Don't deal carelessly with a necessary team player.

---

[10]Two articles that help immensely in understanding the way to work with distributors are: A case application to the heating, ventilating and air conditioning industry by Elizabeth J. Wilson and Arch G. Woodside, "Marketing New Products with Distributors," *Industrial Marketing Management,* February 1992, pp. 15–21; and the strategy of Pall Corporation, makers of industrial filters, by its senior vice president Nicholas Nickolaus, "Marketing New Products With Industrial Distributors," *Industrial Marketing Management,* 1990, pp. 289–299. A 3M division tells how they choose the best channel for a new industrial product in V. Katsuri Rangan, Melvyn A. J. Menezes and E. P. Maier, "Channel Selection for New Industrial Products: A Framework, Method, and Application," *Journal of Marketing,* July 1992, pp. 69–82.

Central Computer Products, Filmore, California, knew it might have problems of awareness and channel stocking, so it offered a $69.95 accounting software package for just a $6.95 shipping and handling charge. The maneuver created favorable word-of-mouth, and the firm leapfrogged over a retail trade already crowded with such packages. Over a million orders came in.[11] In several nonfood product categories, the practice of *stocklifting* is spreading. As an example, Midwest Quality Gloves purchased from Lowe's Home Improvement Warehouse 225,000 pairs of garden gloves made by its competitor, Wells Lamont, thus clearing the shelves to fill them with its own product. The competitor's product is then sold off to industrial customers as commodity goods, or sold to firms that dispose of stocklifted goods by reselling them to close-out stores or foreign distributors.[12]

One trade channel where the players seem to have run out of creativity is that of food products. Large retailers now often "sell" their scarce space, charging manufacturers sizeable *slotting allowances*—so much per store for minimum shelf positions. Large firms can buy their way in, but smaller firms are pretty much shut out. Again, however, a really new item for which there is consumer demand will face a softer resistance.

Trial

Getting product awareness is often difficult, but usually possible. The same goes for availability and some reseller promotion. Trial is another matter. This is the stumbling point for most products that fail, and it is the cause of winning products not winning a great deal more.

Trial of a new product is *limited usage,* hopefully under normal usage conditions, that will permit the customer to verify claims and learn the advantages and disadvantages of the good or service. Trial is on a scale from a taste test of a new cheese in a supermarket to a three-year experiment by a major company on a new telecommunications system. A firm can spend a fortune on free samples to generate trial, as Pepsi did with its launch of Pepsi One. An estimated 5.5 million cans were given away to Pizza Hut customers who ordered a pizza to go, and countless more were handed out to Wal-Mart shoppers by greeters at the front door.[13] There must be learning, relative to the adoption decision; thus the cheese taste may be a full trial if taste by the tester is the only issue. But if the rest of the family has a say, or if the package may or may not keep the cheese fresh, or if the product tends to turn gray while sitting on a table or in a sandwich, then the taste test was not a trial.

---

[11]"Business Bulletin," *The Wall Street Journal,* August 19, 1993, p. A1.

[12]Yumiko Ono, "Where Are the Gloves? They Were Stocklifted By a Rival Producer," *The Wall Street Journal,* May 15, 1998, p. A1.

[13]Nikhil Deogun, "Pepsi Takes Aim at Coke with New One-Calorie Drink," *The Wall Street Journal,* October 28, 1998.

Trial may be *personal, vicarious,* or *virtual.* With elevators, plant location services, and burial services, satisfactory personal trial conditions are difficult, though visiting the site of a previous buyer simulates trial. So buyers gather the trial experience of others, in a vicarious experience. Virtual trial can be achieved by various electronic setups, even a pseudo-virtual experience via video.[14]

A key requirement is that a trial must have some cost associated with it. The more important the trial, the more the cost, or there is not enough motivation for the necessary learning to take place. The cheese taste test, just mentioned, had very little cost (a few seconds of time, possible embarrassment in the store if the taste is awful), so the customer would consider little more than the taste, and perhaps color, aroma, and texture.

That is usually not enough for the next step in the process—the acceptance of the item, its adoption into a usage system, or its repeat purchase. The cheese taster probably would want to buy a small package and take it home for the *real* trial.

Barriers to Trial. Resistance to trial takes the form of barriers. Barriers to trial cause customers to delay or even permanently postpone trial. They must be anticipated and overcome. Here are what we consider to be the major barriers to trial:[15]

Lack of Interest in the Claim. They don't see the advantages to them, they don't have the problem, they are too busy for this minor issue, and so forth. Body deodorants were shunned by men for years because they "didn't need them." Later, the market delayed adoption of the microwave oven (an item that for several years was called the "most expensive coffee-warmer in town"). Another base for lack of interest is a strong negative belief, such as on the topless swimsuit for women, the birth control pill, and porno videos.

Lack of Belief in the Claim. It may be that the positioning statement doesn't offer enough proof, or that the customer simply doesn't feel the product can do what the claim says. No-suds detergents are a classic example here—without suds, how could the detergent clean?

Rejection of Something Negative about the Product. Every product has disadvantages; one of them may be strong enough to be a significant retardant to trial. The absolute extreme on this point would perhaps be cancer chemotherapy; patients know what it may be able to do, but the dreadful downside

---

[14]In 1992 Nissan was advertising the availability of a videotape that simulated a drive in its new *Quest* minivan. This technique may or may not have been used during development as a means of getting simulated user reactions.

[15]Some of these came from S. Ram and Jagdish N. Sheth, "Consumer Resistance to Innovations: The Marketing Problem and Its Solutions," *Journal of Consumer Marketing,* Spring 1989, pp. 5–14.

effects delay trial excessively. Another negative on new products is a change in role, as has been the case with computer conferencing, because many professional participants refuse to sit at a keyboard.

Complacency. Regardless of what the product has and doesn't have to offer, there will be many people who just don't get around to trying it. Most potential customers have busy lives and lots to think about other than trying a new item.

Competitive Ties. Most potential customers now buy something that we are hoping to replace. Makers of those other products have been busy building strong relationships with their customers, perhaps even tying them into long-term service contracts, warehouse-loading discounts, and just strong personal friendships. The loyalists mentioned as a market segment in Chapter 17 are very slow on trial. On the other hand, other segments of people (innovators and early adopters) routinely try anything that comes out, especially if there is an introductory deal on it.

Doubts That Trial Will Tell Them What They Really Would Like to Know. For example, how will flower show judges score the metallic shine on a new strain of roses?

Lack of a Usage Opportunity. Not every product is used daily or even weekly. Lots of potential triers may be waiting for an opportunity, delayed sometimes by poor weather conditions or a blip in the economy.

Cost of Purchase and Use. Prospective users may lack the funds to ever try the product, or they may lack the funds to try it now. Either way, for any but low-priced items, cost can be a major deterrent.

Routines, Automatic Buying and Consuming Systems. A producer of word processing software recently offered to accept any *competitive* package for the low upgrade price on its latest version. Many of the products we buy (and especially those that business buys) are tied up in usage routines that people don't like to break. Some people have even admitted they try to avoid *hearing* of new items in routine categories.

Risk of Rejection, Failure. Lots of people (those in business, too) don't relish the personal risk of an unsuccessful trial of a new item, especially if that usage had to be sold to a supervisor or spouse. Not any more perhaps, but for years it was known that purchasing agents could buy a new IBM product with no fear of criticism if it didn't work out; not so the other brands.

How to Overcome Those Barriers. Fortunately, development of the marketing program begins well ahead of launch, because that's when most of the

FIGURE 18–4

Methods for overcoming the barriers to trial

Here are methods suggested for overcoming the major cases of barriers to trial.

Lack of interest in the claim—education in promotion materials, forced vicarious trials.

Lack of belief in the claim—evidence, compiled and clearly presented, plus free goods to reduce the cost of learning for themselves, plus endorsements.

Rejection of something negative about the product—same as with lack of interest, plus development effort to overcome the negative, plus careful targeting to avoid these people, plus a direct attack on the objection using humorous self-kidding promotions that make the objection less serious.

Complacency—couponing and other action-stimulating devices, plus free goods if necessary, plus endorsements of urgency.

Competitive ties—a "signing" bonus to cover the costs of changing suppliers, plus strong arguments directed specifically against the competitor's product, plus prearrangements to defer premature commitments to competitors.

Doubts that trial will tell them what they really would like to know—offer endorsement or names of their acquaintances who made the trial and got the right information, plus defer payment for the trial period.

Lack of a usage opportunity—create a usage situation, usually by paying for it. If user just bought a year's supply, offer to refund the costs of one year's storage. Preannouncements will perhaps make them defer a rare usage opportunity (keeping the "window" open for a short while).

Cost—using penetration pricing strategy will help, though that approach is expensive. Temporary pricing reductions such as from discounts and rebates, plus try to cut the customer's total outlay that includes use of the product, servicing the product, and replacing the product, plus reduce up-front cost, plus take whatever dollars you think you may have to give them in discounts and see if you can buy something with that money they would like better (e.g., training of their personnel, insuring against rejects, cooperative advertising).

Routines—send in a service team to help work out the arrangements, plus stress one big advantage that would make some inconvenience worthwhile, plus provide simple nonroutine-busting usage opportunities, such as with demo disks for software, plus restress the benefits of our routine over the one they are now using, plus offer special inducements to persons who are "routine gatekeepers."

Risk of rejection—use endorsements to put the user in with a fine group of others who tried the product, plus use a brand name that gives rationale for trial, plus offer them a specific cash payment if the trial doesn't work out well for them.

barrier problems should be addressed, not at time of launch. And most of them come to developers' attention during concept testing and product use testing, as well as from experience in the industry. And most of the barriers respond to more than one solution. Figure 18–4 shows techniques that are used.

Note how many ways the barrier solution uses price—free goods, couponing, a signing bonus, deferred payment, refunding cost of competitor's stocks, entering with a penetration (low) price, discounts, rebates, free service, free replacement offer, cooperative advertising, direct cash payment for trying, and others. In most cases, the buyer is deferring trial because of anticipating loss of something—loss of time, loss of money, loss of prestige, and so forth. The most obvious answer is to pay the buyer for such loss.

This emphasis on price has led sellers to adopt complex discount schedules (it's easier later to drop a discount than to raise the list price). Using discounts also fits with the most popular of the new product price strategies:[16]

[16]For an actual case, with data and a "solution" as between skim, meet, and penetrate, see Arch G. Woodside, "Pricing an Industrial Technological Innovation: A Case Study," *Industrial Marketing Management,* 1995, pp. 145–50.

Premium—a very high price, intended to stay that way, with clear product differentiation.

Skim—a price clearly above the market, but appropriate to a differentiated product, nonthreatening to competition, and with room for some price manipulations.

Meet the market—though there may be no *one* market price, this strategy says pick a price that takes price out of the play as much as possible. Is a waste for a clearly superior product unless the marketer has no market acceptance.

Penetration—the price that is clearly low and designed to buy one's way into the market. Will be met perhaps, but in the meantime share is gained. Dangers: little room to discount, tough to raise later after share is achieved, and if met immediately, just wastes the opportunity and at a lower price.

Skim seems to achieve the benefit both ways—brings some of the product's value to our bottom line and gives marketers freedom to meet special opportunities, yet doesn't price ourselves out of the market. Of course, if the differentiation is worth a great deal, a true obsoleting of the earlier item, then premium pricing is defensible.

Repeat Purchase

If our target market buyers do a serious trial on our new item, and if we had previously been assured from the product use test that people would like it, repeat buying is virtually assured. There are competitive actions to repel and counter. There is the continuing problem of complacency especially in markets where our item's benefits are not crucial to anything. There is the careless new product manager who fails to keep a ready supply available for the buyer who wants to repeat. And, as always, we need to be sure customers are satisfied with their total relationships with our firm, well beyond the product itself.

Usually we have actions in the marketing program to encourage further usage (e.g., long-term discounts, new uses for the item, ready availability of additional product as well as of continued service).

And we will see in Chapter 21 how a measure of repeat purchase is a key part of the post-launch management program, in which we prepare to deal with at least some of the problems that may come up. If there is any evidence of product failure (which may be expected to happen if the product use test had to be skipped), it will be investigated promptly, and corrections negotiated through technical members of the team.

Summary

Chapter 18 was the second of a two-chapter set on the subject of marketing planning. It dealt with what some call the tactical portion of the planning task. So we looked at the launch cycle, the communication program, and the requirements of success: Awareness, Trial, Availability, and Repeat purchase (A-T-A-R). Each is very difficult to attain, given the on-going nature of life and business in the market and the actions of other players such as competitors. Since a marketing launch entails hundreds or even thousands of actions, we focused on those that seem most critical and most difficult in practice.

Once the full marketing launch plan has been worked out, many firms like to devise some way to hold a dress rehearsal—just to see if there are any glitches. After all, millions of dollars may be spent in the next few months. So, in Chapters 19 and 20, we will look at what is called market testing. It is the third of a testing triad—with concept testing (Chapter 9) and product use testing (Chapter 16).

Applications

More questions from that interview with the company president.

1. "You frighten me when you mention alliances in the marketing launch. Hardly a week goes by without some scientist saying we simply must join an alliance. Don't scientists ever work alone any more? Anyway, even though we need alliances on the technical side, that's no reason for them on the marketing side. I don't think I recall hearing about alliances over there—you mention ad agencies? And resellers? No, those are just contracts for service, and in almost every case those are pseudo contracts—they can be broken if it's important. Why does your text call them alliances?"
2. "I am a member of a committee of our Booksellers Association. We have a medium sized chain in that business—not a Barnes & Noble or a Borders, but we do pretty well. Our committee has worked up a new service to "sell" to our franchised retail outlets—they don't have to take every new service the trade association works up, but we have a good one—it relates to helping them avoid getting caught by one of these professors who writes a book and then goes around the country buying large quantities from several stores (at massive discounts), just to win a spot on the New York Times Best Seller List. Most of those books end up back on the market, again at great discounts, taking good customers from us. We are getting a group of industry experts to report any suspicious activity they spot, or even hear about. We will evaluate and verify, and then will fax each outlet the particulars. Question: We've picked an ad agency to prepare mailings to the stores, asking them to join up. Cost is only $50 per

month per store. Can you do what you talked about, that is, write out a Copy Strategy Statement for me to give the agency?"

3. "Incidentally, some of the folks in the software division have come up with an idea for a new service. Seems as though they found that computer people around the world have real trouble learning about new software—not about its existence and its general claims (that's in all the magazines and direct mail they get, in their own languages even.) No, what we're going to sell is reports of all favorable and unfavorable comments that appear in the press, anywhere in the world, about all new software. The customer can access this information, on-line, with reports classified by type and by brand of software, and in six languages. They think software users, particularly those out of the mainstream of personal business contacts, will like it. But, and this is a problem they worry about, the whole field of software is so full of announcements, news, people yelling. How in the world can they break through all that noise to get prospects informed (I guess you'd say made aware) of this new service to where they can *make a decision to try it.* (They have a trial package, by the way: five-day, 20 inquiries, for a very small fee.)"
4. "Sampling is another tool we like—you know, like that trial package I just mentioned. Samples are really effective in getting trial among the people who are somewhat inclined toward a new product in the first place. But several of our divisions can't use samples per se because of the nature of their products. Could you tell me what might be a substitute for samples in the marketing of a new type of each of the following?
   a. Heavy industrial elevators.
   b. Coffins.
   c. Milling machines.
   d. Diamond rings.
   e. Replacement tires."

CASE: SPIRALLOY, INC.[17]

Spiralloy, Inc. is a small firm located in a college town in northern California that is involved in the development of a new kind of metallurgy process. Though the technology is currently available only to the space program, Spiralloy is expecting that this new process will be available commercially within the next year or so, and they have identified an interesting application for it: making low-cost, functional furniture for selected markets. When available, the metal will permit making chairs, beds, desks, and wardrobes (portable closets) in a spiral-expanding process.

[17]This is a substantially revised version of the Spiralurgy Furniture Inc. case that appeared in the fifth edition of this book.

Extrusions are usually straight or flexible, but this metal has a molecular, built-in desire to spiral, and that spiraling can be controlled. It can be tiny, for a table leg, larger for a chair leg, and larger still for a desktop. It can be pressed while at very high temperatures during the extrusion process to make sheets of material that would be used for seats and assembled as sides and bottoms of the storage unit. Some degrees of flexibility can be introduced by addition of several chemicals, so they visualize flexible chairs, lamp fixtures, and more. The material is one of the toughest materials ever seen—even saws won't cut it unless equipped with a diamond edge (and that edge doesn't last very long). Assembly is easy, using the natural (though taut) spiraling effect of the material.

The advantages are several. Though utilitarian, the metal itself is a rather attractive off-white color, and unless pressed, the surfaces are attractive rounded spirals of different diameters. The material sets in such a way that it is virtually indestructible, even in student housing (a target the developers are currently working, given their location and positions as professors in the engineering school of the local college). Of course, it is peculiar, too. Some people will absolutely hate it because the metal has a tendency to spring back against any attempt to bend it. In development work at a laboratory in Sacramento, one of the developers lost part of an ear while trying to bend a leg to fit under a computer storage drawer. Landlords may object to buying it because roomers may not like that feature, or other features that may appear later in the development. Retailers will find it easy to sell, but the low price will make margins (in dollars) well below those in current furniture, even the synthetic oak at mass outlets.

Lots is yet unknown about the material—for example, its ability to hold paint and what types of paint, and whether the material tends to return to a more natural state over time (it hasn't so far, in four years of use). Though immune from damages by liquids normal in a residence, there are certain acids that will etch the surface.

If the developers do get an expected venture capital investment by a large manufacturer of lower-cost office furniture, they plan to market a line of furniture for school markets (college at first, and K–12 a few years later).

Consider the A-T-A-R model. What problems can you see Spiralloy having on awareness, trial, availability, and repeat? Which of the four components of this model is likely to cause the greatest difficulty, in your opinion, given the case information and what you know about the market? How might you overcome these difficulties? Assume for now that the furniture does perform well. How should the firm plan on getting the attention of students and renters? How can you bring them to where they might be willing to try the product? How might you achieve availability in your area? What are the natural outlets for products like these, and how might we approach them? How could the developers be sure they can get a good rate of repurchase (this is an issue, since many of the market's largest buyers will be buying for multiple students)?

Answers to the issues in Figure V–3:

1. *Teams* make these decisions, not one functional group.
2. Marketing people have been in all along. And there should be no "taking over" because technical people should stay.
3. These paradigms *aid thinking*. Exuberance and excitement we have, but they don't replace thinking.

4. Not *marketing's*—the *entire firm's.* Every part of the firm has contributed to what we offer the end user. Hopefully, the end user has a problem and will welcome the product.
5. A good target market has several dimensions, not just sales potential. A large piece of a favorable segment may be much more profitable.
6. The PIC guides *all* stages—it is a strategic plan for the entire operation through to whatever its goals call for.
7. Data don't support this. Quite often, a follower comes up with the winning design.
8. Goals may be expressed in customer satisfaction terms too, but there are usually other goals unique to the situation—e.g., build a bridge to new market dominance.
9. Perhaps if really meaningless, but they should be meaning*ful,* helpful in telling the product story.
10. The launch is *managed*—if we start to sink, let's hope there is a large dipper handy. (See Chapter 21.)
11. Opening night is the first salvo in a drive to achieve the project goals—success. A successful opening night brings little profit, but a long run brings a big one.

CHAPTER

19

Market Testing

Pseudo Sale Methods

Setting

At this time, glance back at Figure V–1 in the introduction to Part V. It shows the basic new product process, and where we are at this time. We have a physical product or the complete specifications for a new service. Early concept testing showed a need, and the use test indicated the emerging product met that need, without serious drawbacks. And we have a marketing plan.

Now what do we do? Market the item, quickly, before competition finds out what we are up to? Or find a way to check out what we have done, to see if it really looks like we will be successful, before spending what usually is a lot of money on the launch? The option open to us is called **market testing.** Chapter 19 gives the overall picture for market testing and introduces the first of the three methods—pseudo sale. Chapter 20 discusses the other two general methods of market testing.

Where We Are Today

Over the years, one *type* of market testing has been the most common one and the one people talk about—test marketing. Many people mistakenly think *market testing* means *test marketing,* but actually, there are several other methods. Test marketing is now a minor player, having suffered a major loss of ground to newer, faster, and cheaper techniques.

The basic idea of market testing is to test the combined package of product *and* its marketing plan. So what better method than that of science—finding a representative piece of the market and trying it out there? One could implement the entire plan in a couple cities or metropolitan areas, keep a couple other identical areas as a control, and then project the test results to the total market. People called what they did **test marketing.**

Of course, the market place made a poor test tube. As we will see later, the test market approach, using those matched cities, always had drawbacks. By 1970, managers didn't want to wait around the 3–12 months test marketing took. Competitive pressures piled up, managers were no longer so sure whether a test market was really successful, newer options become available, and managers grew smarter—they now had a better feel for just the one or two things they needed to know.

Fortunately, technologies came along that helped fuel the development of other market testing methods—mathematical models for forecasting sales with much less than complete market data, store-loading systems where it was no longer necessary to go to the trouble of "selling in" the inventory, scanner systems of retail store check-outs that compiled product data not even dreamed of in the good old days of test marketing, and communications systems that permitted a form of trial marketing over areas far greater than test market cities and from which one could quickly roll on into the total market as soon as assurances appeared.

The consequence is a variety of market research methods that used alone and in various combinations will meet the needs of any new products manager. But before getting into those methods, let's take a good look at the manager's situation.

We Are in a Very Competitive World. Several times in this book we have faced the effects of management's desire for speed—faster cycle time. Sometimes it appears we simply must get the new product to the market in a timely manner or it will no longer be competitive. This means we take risks, the biggest one being the management style of concurrent development or parallel processing. We skip steps not absolutely essential and start the next step before the earlier one is completely done.

The Engineers Have Developed Ways to Test the Components of a Product at the Time They Are Made. In the building of an automobile there was once a time (again more apocryphal than true to life) where the firm rushed to make the component parts (frames, engines, etc.), pulled them together at an assembly operation, assembled them, and then had a worker with a large rubber mallet standing at the end of the line to pound out any misfits. Today, the very principle of quality is that we *build quality in.* Testing for quality is essentially unnecessary as we go "upstream" in the process, build each piece properly and make sure it is right. *Then* we assemble them.

On the marketing side we now do the same thing. An ad is a component, so is a selling visual, a service contract, a trained sales rep, a price, a package, and so on. There are literally hundreds of things that marketing requires. These things we call *marketing plan components,* and we are encouraged to test them upstream too, not at the end, all together.

They only need further testing if their purchase and use by the customer puts demands on them in *synergy* with other components or with variables in the marketplace. Synergies we test at market testing time, not components.

Market Testing Is Not Solely in the Province of the Market Research Department. Market researchers play the lead role in market testing, just as design engineers do in the design of parts. But we have been knocking down the functional silos. (See Chapters 13–15.) We have teams leading projects, and sometimes they can get the information they need using methods you might not even recognize as market research. For instance, let's imagine that a new product manager meets with the manufacturing member of a team and an engineer from the one and only customer likely to be interested in a product now under development (say a big original equipment manufacturer, like Whirlpool). The question is, given a price that has been decided, how many of the new items would the customer want for a first run (the item has been previously tested in a product use test with that customer). A figure is worked out, and our people plan our production accordingly.

Was that a market test? Yes. With that customer, everything was in place—our product was ready to sell, and our marketing program (including price) was ready. A solid demand estimate was arrived it. Launch followed.

At the other extreme of complexity, on a consumer packaged good being rolled out in the mid-Atlantic region for a month or so before being rolled on into New York and New England, the entire firm is involved. Market research people gather some of the information; other managers gather other information—for example, product cost, incidence of product complaints, competitors' reactions, legal hits, ability of vendors to meet their time and quality requirements, ability of shipping to get product to distributors in the required condition, and so on. Reacting to all that information is a *team* problem—facts are not handled in isolation. The leader of a new products team is a manager. The market test of a highly advertised food product or shampoo is a huge responsibility, and puts heavy pressure on market research people. Still, it is the *firm's new products team* doing the testing.

The Market Testing Decision

The full set of market testing technique options will come later. First, we need to get a feeling for the decision to test or not to test.

When Is the Decision Made?

The decision of whether and how to test can be made at many different times. Figure 19–1 shows the trade-offs. On the one hand the longer we wait, the more we will know about our product and its marketing program; that makes testing more useful and more reliable. But the longer we wait to do the test,

FIGURE 19–1
Decision matrix on when to market test

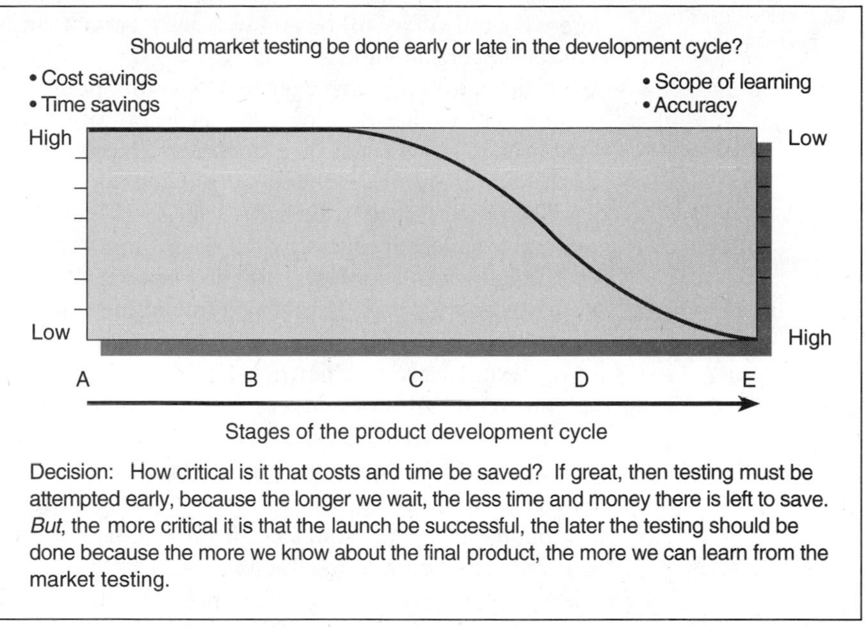

the higher the costs, the later the entry, the more damage competitors can do, and so on. The solution, of course, is to begin the testing as soon as a technique can be found that will tell us *what we need to know.* Some consumer products market testing actually begins before the product is even firmed up—it works with a concept statement! Other market testing, such as that with the appliance manufacturer above, cannot be done until we have everything in place ready to go.

Is This an Easy Decision to Make?

The really tough thing about market testing is that management leans heavily toward doing none of it. They doubt the fancy statistics, they don't like the costs, the team is already behind schedule, and they certainly dislike tipping their hand to competition. They would prefer a secret development, hitting the market as a complete surprise to competitors. Who wouldn't?

Internal decision makers, however, often have doubts—nagging, frustrating, dangerous doubts. Any time we make something new, we cannot really be sure about *anything.* Stop to think about this—with a few rare exceptions, everything we think we know about the new product and its marketing is *not a fact*—it is an opinion, a guess, a judgment, a hope, a dream, an order (from above). The full scenario of the new item's marketing will be played out on a playing field where all too many people still have to react to something. Even they cannot be sure of their reaction, especially when we aren't completely sure what our offer will be and we surely cannot anticipate what competition will tell buyers about it.

It takes a strong manager to say at this point, "I know we have spent a fortune, and we are running late, but I am not convinced we have made the right decisions. I want to take a couple of months (or more) to be sure." What kind of confidence does that inspire in the typical top management?

The fact seems to be this: if a firm (or an industry) believes in market testing, and practices it regularly, the decision *not* to do it in any particular case has the burden of proof. Asking for a market test is not a confession of failure on the team's part. This is also true in the sciences and many other fields. Major parts of the entertainment field market test almost every time (staging a trial performance of a new musical in Boston, for example).

The basic *value* of market testing is unquestionable. But we have a warehouse of examples where firms skipped it and were successful. Unfortunately, we have another warehouse full of failures that probably could have been avoided with a market test. IBM marketed the original PC without a market test; but the PC came from a crash 12-month program that had immense risks in it from the start, and billions of dollars were at stake in market shares. These were good reasons for skipping a test. Unfortunately, IBM did not have those good reasons for the IBM Jr., nor did RCA when it marketed the first SelectaVision videodisc player, nor did literally scores of others.

One of these others was a General Electric division, Fleet Services. Fleet Services developed a service called Car-Pro, a call-in service where a car owner with problems could talk with professional mechanics and get an objective view to offset suggestions received locally. When the service was marketed, it failed, primarily because people wouldn't pay the $49 fee. Although the firm said they had "test marketed" the service prior to launch, apparently whatever testing they did missed the price issue.[1] A market test tests the *entire* marketing plan, including price. It's altogether too easy for people to say they like an idea, because they probably do, but that answer is unreliable without a price dimension on the concept.

Figure 19–2 shows how market testing relates to other testing—the three major tests covering the three major causes for new product failure—concept testing for "lack of need," product use testing for "product does not meet need," and market testing for "marketed poorly." Many times a firm is in a hurry at all three of those stages, so it first skips the concept test, then it skips the field use testing, and then, if it also skips the market testing, it will be flying blind.

Interestingly, what we are saying about market testing (as with almost everything in this book) applies equally well to the public sector. Recently, a professor/consultant in California argued that the state had rejected "school choice" on the basis of claimed disadvantages, whereas it should have market-tested the proposal to see just what the benefits and disadvan-

---

[1]"Car-Pro," *Across the Board,* March 1994, p. 37.

FIGURE 19–2

How market testing relates to the other testing steps

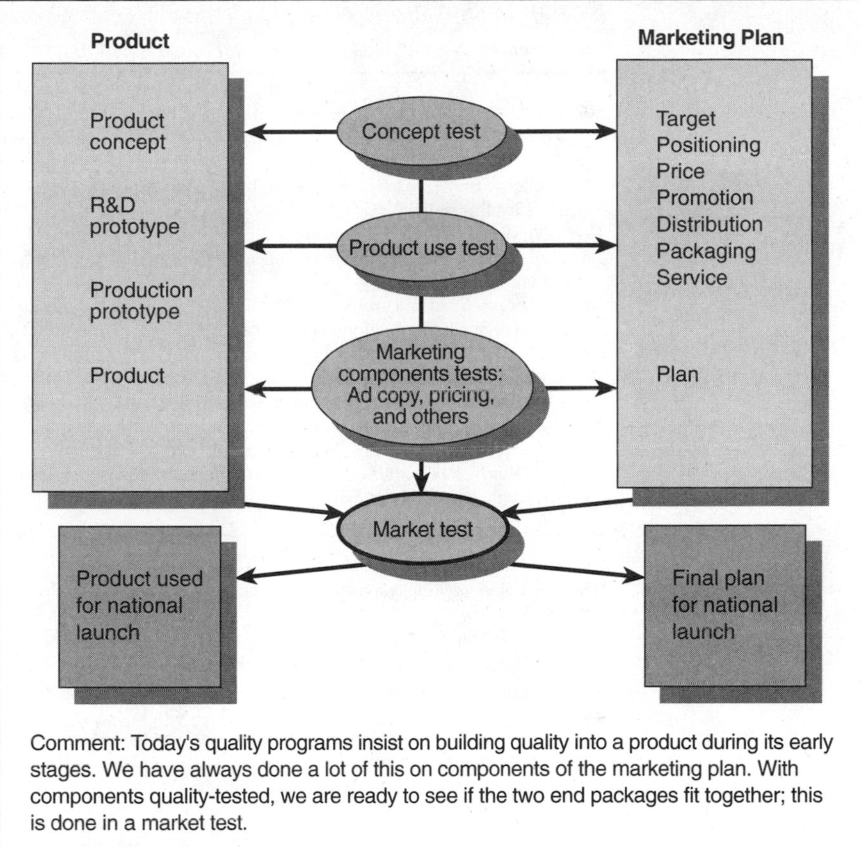

tages really are.[2] Actually, the federal government is a big user of market testing.

See Figure 19–3 for some classic examples, and we will talk about others as we work our way through Chapters 19 and 20.[3]

The Two Key Values We Get from Market Testing

First, planners need *solid forecasts of dollar and unit sales volume*—not the general market figures or ranges of possible shares that guided earlier planning decisions. Second, planners need *diagnostic information* to help them revise and refine anything about the launch that seems to require it—product, marketing

[2]"Big Unknowns Defeated School Choice," Robert A. Grayson, in Letters to the Editor, *The Wall Street Journal,* November 29, 1993, p. A11.

[3]A version of the decision process managers go through was given as a case study in Steven H. Star and Glen L. Urban, "The Case of the Test Market Toss-Up," *Harvard Business Review,* September–October, 1988, pp. 10–16.

FIGURE 19–3

Classic cases of firms that wish they had not skipped market testing

New Coke: The Coca-Cola Company had perhaps the most famous example of a thoroughly tested product marketed without a market test. Allegedly, some 200,000 people overwhelmingly preferred the New Coke. But when offered the chance to buy it, in the total milieu of a market full of publicity, they refused. Coke had to bring back the old formula, branded Coke Classic, and it is still the leading seller.*

TV-Cable Week: Staffers who developed Time Inc.'s competitor to TV Guide "repeatedly called for a small-scale market test and were repeatedly turned down." The $100 million investment lasted six months.†

Treesweet Low-Calorie Orange Juice: "Clinton E. Owens thought he had all the fixins for success in the juice business . . . industry veteran . . . innovative product . . . jazzy package . . . eye-catching ads . . ." A year later, after "betting the farm" without market testing, the product had failed, the juice lines were on the block, and Chapter 11 "was a possibility."‡

Toppels: In a 1986 article about companies getting on the fast track, "Frito-Lay skipped test marketing for its new Toppels cheese snack so competitors wouldn't have time to study the ingredients and copy them.§ 'We felt very strongly we had a winner and didn't want to tip our hand.'" But in 1989, after noting several failures in new snack products, "The debacle convinced Frito-Lay that true market testing is a necessity, even for a market leader."||

Sources:

*The New Coke story is told in many places, one good summary being "Coca-Cola's Big Fizzle," *Time,* July 22, 1985, pp. 48–52.

†Time Inc.'s $47 Million Belly Flop," *BusinessWeek,* February 17, 1986, pp. 14–15.

‡"A Juice Maker Squeezes Itself Dry," *BusinessWeek,* August 10, 1987, p. 42.

§Ronald Alsop, "Companies Get on Fast Trick to Roll Out Hot New Brands," *The Wall Street Journal,* July 10, 1986, p. 23.

||"Marketers Blunder their Way through the 'Herb Decade,'" *Advertising Age,* February 13, 1989, p. 3.

effort, you name it. There are usually controversies within the team that must be resolved. Examples of diagnostic information abound. Here are a few:

1. Cadbury tested a new fresh cream dessert in a tetra package. Retailers claimed that the package wouldn't stack, so it had to be changed.
2. A camouflage cosmetic worked well at concealing scars, as planned, but a much greater market opened up when women decided to use it for concealing minor blemishes.
3. An industrial firm developed a very complex new technology, gave it thorough technical testing, and went into a regional market test. Only then did the firm discover that the new system could be blocked by a group of consulting engineers who had not been included in the marketing plan.

The Decision Factors for Deciding Whether to Market Test

Each new product project has a unique situation, but here are the most common important factors considered in the market test decision.

Any Special Twists on the Launch. Did the original charter dictate a tight time schedule? There may be special considerations such as the need for new volume to help sell off an operation or the need to assist a new CEO get off to a quick start. Does the charter limit the funds for the project such that it *must* be rolled out, growing to each new stage as profits come in from earlier stages? Is this launch part of a far bigger launch program, for example, where the firm is trying to gain new industry experience in one world market to permit a critical expansion into another world market?

What Information Is Needed. We look first to see if this is one of those situations where huge sums of money have been spent and careers staked yet where no one knows what will really happen out there when the item becomes available. Conditions permitting, there is a strong argument for thorough market testing. This is partly to avoid a huge loss from market rejection, but also to protect against being surprised by too *much* volume. Nabisco launched Ritz Bitz directly to the national market, and immediately found demand outstripping their bakeries' output capacity. As a consequence, they now try to use the rollout market testing process discussed in Chapter 20.[4] Still, when the firm knew (from consumer reactions) that they had a big winner with SnackWells, they went national and were many months working their way out of backorders.

One experienced Procter & Gamble market researcher said he considers skipping the market test if the following conditions exist:

1. Capital investments are small, and forecasts are conservative.
2. The use tests went well, and consumer interest is high.
3. The company knows the business well, and has been successful there.
4. Advertising is ready and successfully tested; sales promotion plan does not depend on perfect execution.[5]

The second type of information need is more *operational.* It is for learning, learning *how* to do something that the launch requires. Remember, a launch involves the whole ball of wax, all functions, manufacturing, selling, servicing, financing, dealing with vendors and resellers, and so forth. Specifically, the more common needs are:

Manufacturing—besides the volume estimates, we also need the experience of running the system at a low level before turning it to full speed. New product annals are full of sad stories along this line, a

---

[4]Patricia Sellers, "How to Remake Your Sales Force," *Fortune,* May 4, 1992, pp. 97–103. Puns Nabisco Biscuit President and CEO Ellen Marram: We roll out gradually, "so that once appetites are whetted, customers are not left chomping at the bit."

[5]Robert E. Davis, "The Role of Market Research in the Development of New Consumer Products," *Journal of Product Innovation Management* 10, no. 4 (September 1993), pp. 309–17.

recent one being the case of Weyerhaeuser marketing a new concept in disposable diapers (UltraSofts). The manufacturing process called for spraying a liquid onto material, and when they set up a line to serve a market test in western New York state, the liquid got hot and caught on fire. The process was essentially defective, and although the firm regretted the failure of the item (it took off very well) they were glad they were only at test production levels. Earlier, pilot production for prototype material had worked perfectly.

Vendors—can they actually do what they have promised? In the diaper case just mentioned, a key vendor was unable to solve a problem that might have permitted the product to continue.

Resellers—again, can they do what there is reason to think they should be able to? Will there be special demands that we don't now know about?

Servicing infrastructure—partly ours, and partly that of others in the general market picture. To say one can service a product is, unfortunately, sometimes far from a guarantee.

Customers—will they buy, stock, and use the item as expected? Does acceptance of this item require a significant change in purchasing habits or product usage? And is there reason to think we might not be able to bring such a change about? Will there be special service requirements, special return privileges, unexpected demands for training personnel, and so on.

Skipped component testing—did we have to accept, say, an ad campaign or a new free-goods program because of time pressures? Did we skip the product use test? If so, one can be built into the first few weeks or months of a market test.

Cannibalization—most new products threaten to take at least part of their volume from other products the firm has on the market. This is a very difficult forecast to make; many new items have been marketed, sold well, and then discovered to contribute nothing but costs to the firm's treasury.

Conditions that reduce the need for information—the above factors argue *for* information, but today's managers anticipate this problem by building in customer involvement. Firms that involve customers from the very beginning (even to having customer engineers work on their new product teams) get early answers to lots of questions. Some firms approach this level of involvement by having customers pay for the material used in product use testing—for example, Owens-Corning wanted highway maintenance departments to take a new crack filling product seriously, so they charged for what was used in the use test. Far better learning took place. Additionally, some firms have programs in **total quality management** that force some of the learning needed for items earlier in this list.

We must remember that the people making the final "market testing versus full launch" decision are not working in the dark. In most cases they have done this many times before and usually have years of experience in the particular business at hand. When the operations manager at Bell Atlantic decides to offer licensed repair services a contract on a new cellular phone installation, this decision is not a guess.

Costs. Market test costs are of three types: (1) direct costs of the test—fees to market research firms, (2) costs of the launch itself—for production, selling, and so forth, and (3) lost revenue that a national launch would have brought. Sometimes the costs of launching are so great that firms don't even consider market testing. For example, in the automobile industry their big cost is getting finished product; once they have cars, there is little inclination to market them in a limited geographical area, or so they have felt. Lately some Japanese firms have begun rolling some new cars through the West Coast first, as a market test.

Nature of the Marketplace. If competitors can take retaliatory action that will hurt us, chances are testing will be quick if at all. Most new products have some protection, just by being first in the customers' minds, but few have the ability to keep a market for themselves.

Another marketplace characteristic is that customers may literally demand the new item. New pharmaceuticals, for example, are rarely market tested upon getting Food & Drug Administration permission for marketing. One can only imagine the public outrage if a confirmed remedy for AIDS was put into a six-month test market in Phoenix and Des Moines.

The marketplace may not be good for market testing. For example, most markets outside the United States and Europe are still very weak on scanner technology and other capabilities for testing. And many products (almost all consumer items not sold through food stores and drug stores) lack sales audits at the retail level even in the United States. Scanners will soon change this.

Capability of the Various Testing Methodologies. The trick is to find a method that fits management needs or that can be modified to do so. As you read through the following discussions on the methods available, keep in mind the requirements from the above discussion. Be a shopper, touring a store of market testing methods. The methods are all good and are proven in practice, often over many years. But do they fit the situation at hand?

Methods of Market Testing

The ingenuity of marketers is legendary. They have developed a seemingly endless array of market testing methods for new products. One firm uses a very large company cafeteria. Another uses small foreign divisions. Still

FIGURE 19–4

Methods of market testing, and where used

	Product Categories Where Useful				
	Industrial		Consumer		
	Goods	Services	Packaged	Durables	Services
Pseudo sale					
Speculative sale	■	■		■	■
Simulated test marketing			■	■	■
Controlled sale					
Informal selling	■	■		■	■
Direct marketing	■			■	
Minimarketing	■	■	■	■	■
Full sale					
Test marketing	■	■	■	■	■
Rollout					
By application	■	■			
By influence	■	■			■
By geography	■	■	■	■	■
By trade channel	■		■	■	

another uses the facilities of a chain of radio stations owned by a sister subsidiary. But the methods tend to fall into one of the following three general categories (see Figure 19–4).[6]

[6]At the time of this writing, the market research industry serving consumer packaged goods firms is continuing its history of rapid technology change and corporate ownership change. Language is changing too, so authors must chase new definitions. People are experimenting with Internet, virtual realities, and more. For example, one firm tried offering a computer disk method of having consumers shop at a dummy store. We cannot forecast where they will end up. Your professor may have more up-to-date information when you read this, but we suspect the uncertainty in packaged goods will remain for a long time.

Pseudo Sale

This approach asks potential buyers to do something (such as say they would buy *if* the product were actually available, or pick the item off the shelf of a *make-believe store*). The action is distinct and identifiable, and much of the marketing strategy is utilized in the presentation; but the key factor here is little pain for the buyer—no spending, no major risk. It is, as the name says, a **pseudo sale.** It can be done early on.

Controlled Sale

Here the buyer must make a purchase. The sale may be quite formal or informal, but it is conducted under *controlled conditions.* The method is still research because the product has not been released for regular sale. Some key variable (often distribution) is not opened up but is contrived. **Controlled sale** is more vigorous than the pseudo sale, however, and much more revealing.

Full Sale

In a **full sale,** the firm has decided to fully market the product (not so in the above methods). But it wants to do so on a limited basis first, to see if everything is working right. Barring some catastrophe, the product will go to full national launch.

Pseudo Sale Methods

Product innovators use two approaches to get potential users to make some expression or commitment resembling a sale without actually laying out money. The **speculative sale** method asks them if they would buy it, and the **simulated test market** (STM) method creates a false buying situation and observes what they do.

Speculative Sale

This is a technique used primarily by firms in business-to-business markets and consumer durables. It sounds very similar to the technique used in concept and product use tests, differing as follows:

> In the *concept test* we give the new item's positioning claim, and perhaps something about its form or manufacture. Then we ask, "How likely would you be to buy a product like this, if we made it?"

In *product use testing,* we give customers some of the product, have them use it in some normal way, and then ask the same question, "How likely would you be to buy a product like this, if we made it?"

In the *pseudo sale method called "speculative,"* we go to the customer, give them the full pitch on the product in a version close to ultimate marketing, answer questions, negotiate prices, and lead up to the closing question, "If we make this product available as I have described it, would you buy it?"

This testing is typically done by regular sales people, using selling materials that are developed and ready to go. They make pseudo sales calls—presenting the new product as though it were available for purchase. The difference this time is that the product is real, as are the price (with a full array of appropriate discounts), delivery schedules, selling presentation, and so on. The target customer is real, and the positioning is clear. The buyer has little to do except make a decision. That decision may be just to ask for some samples to try, but that's OK. Trial is industry's way of making the first purchase and is really what we are trying to measure at this time.

Although the tool is typically used for industrial products (because sale of most industrial products fits the method so well), it can also be used for certain consumer products. Rubbermaid is an example. Rubbermaid sells its products essentially by a push strategy, with some image advertising to consumers, but product presentation is confined to store counters. This setting can be duplicated easily, so Rubbermaid uses the speculative method in a setting that looks much like a focus group concept test (except using finished product with information on usage, pricing, and so on). The consumer faces a situation much like that in a store and can easily speculate on whether a purchase would be made.

Situations where the speculative method fits include:

1. Where industrial firms have very close downstream relationships with key buyers.
2. Where new product work is technical, entrenched within a firm's expertise, and only little reaction is needed from the marketplace.
3. Where the adventure has very little risk, and thus a costlier method is not defendable.
4. Where the item is new (say, a new material or a completely new product type) and key diagnostics are needed. For example, what set of alternatives does the potential buyer see, or what possible applications come to mind first.

There is no advertising in a speculative sale market test, and the ways of using it are many. For example, some people reject the idea of making a presentation to a buyer and then admitting there is actually no product available to buy. In such cases, they simply tell buyers that "we are getting ready to market a new product, and I want to know if you might be interested."

Simulated Test Market

Packaged goods firms do a great deal of product development, yet the speculative sale method, above, wouldn't work for them. They too wanted a method that was cheaper, more confidential, and faster than the controlled sale and full sale methods that follow. They found it in the A-T-A-R model discussed in Chapter 8. The method was a spin-out from concept testing and comes very early in the development process. For being early, it is sometimes called *premarket testing*—testing that is done prior to getting ready to market—but *simulated test marketing* is the more common term today. Most usage is well ahead of the time other market testing can be used.[7] The name simulated test market came to be used because mathematical formulas are used to simulate the market place, and at the time we were still calling all market testing test markets.

The central idea is to get estimates of *trial purchasing* and *repeat purchasing. Awareness* comes from the advertising agency's component testing, and the firm's managers supply the other factors of *market units, availability, prices,* and *costs* that are required to turn A-T-A-R into a sales forecast.

Basic Procedure. Here is the basic procedure used in a simulated test market, with modifications from one market research supplier to another:

1. Respondents are usually gathered in a *mall intercept*—they are approached as they walk through the mall and invited to participate in a marketing study. At least one major supplier selects and invites respondents by telephone. Respondents are qualified both by observation before interviewing (estimates of age, sex, income, family status, and so on) and by questioning (such as product category usage) during a brief interview in the mall corridor. It is important at this point to eliminate persons for whom security would be a problem (for example, employees of other manufacturers). If the respondent qualifies (fits the criteria for sample selection), he or she is invited to step into a nearby research facility (usually one of the empty mall store areas, though occasionally a permanent facility built in one of those areas).

2. In the facility, the procedure varies depending on the client and what is being tested, but generally the respondent will be given a self-administered questionnaire asking for their attitudes and practices in one or more product categories. Then comes either individual or small-group exposure to advertising stimuli. The advertisements are sometimes couched in a television presentation (for example, a TV pilot program that is itself being tested) or just any TV show that hides the key stimulus. The ads may be presented without pretense of a television show, or they may be in what appears to be a

[7]Don't confuse these STM models with other models, such as TRACKER, that are used for interpreting early results in test marketing cities. Marketing scientists have models to cover almost every step in the new product development and marketing process, but here we can cover only the usage leaders.

magazine or on separate tear sheets. Several ads are presented so the respondent isn't sure what is being tested. One of the ads, of course, is for the new product being market tested. It gives the full story, including claims and price.

3. The respondent is then taken into another room, usually what appears to be a very small convenience store with shelves of products. The test manager gives the respondent some play money (one supplier uses cash), not usually enough to make a purchase but enough to make such a purchase less painful. A respondent so inclined can walk right out without making a purchase, even with actual cash.

4. Hopefully, the respondent entering the "store" will now purchase the new product advertised in the first room—this yields the key variable trial. The leading seller of STM services does not use a pseudo store. Instead, it asks respondents the standard buying intention question we used in Chapter 16 on product use testing and then simply gives trial product to those who express buying interest.

5. Most of the participants are then free to go. Perhaps 10 percent are taken into another room where a focus group of 8 to 10 is held. Another 10 percent may be asked to fill out another self-administered questionnaire covering postexposure attitudes, planned product usage, and the like. If our product was purchased, we will be contacting the respondent later; but if it was not, we want to find out why. Nonbuyers are often given trial (forcing) packages of the product as they leave.

6. Some time later (time varies with the product category involved), the respondent is contacted by telephone. The call may be identified with the mall experience or it may be camouflaged. Information is sought about such things as product usage, reactions, and future intentions. Many diagnostics are obtained at this time, such as who in the family used the product, how it was used, and products it was used with.

7. At the end of the call, the respondent may be offered a chance to "buy" more of the product. This is the first step in a *sales wave.* Product is delivered to the respondent's home by mail or another delivery system, and the call is later repeated, new information gathered, and another sale opportunity offered. Note that we have used the sales wave to give us the second key variable in the A-T-A-R model—*repeat.*

These pretests usually involve 300 to 600 people, require 8 to 14 weeks, and cost from $50,000 to $300,000, depending on the number of sales waves. The service is offered in various forms and is being improved continuously. BASES, now part of A. C. Nielsen, stops people as they *enter supermarkets,* gives them the pitch, asks them questions, gives them a coupon, and then follows up with the store later to see how many actually bought the item which was then available. There are many STM services offered for sale, and the leading ones (with their suppliers) are:

* BASES, by A. C. Nielsen BASES.
* MACRO ASSESSOR, by The M/A/R/C Group, in Irving, Texas.

* ESP, by NPD Group, Port Washington, New York.
* LITMUS, by Shulman, Ronca, and Bucuvalas, New York City.[8]

Output. Consumers give their opinions on the product, they buy or ask for some, they react to it, and so on. But the key purpose is to estimate how well the product will sell, so the various services offer trial rate, repeat rate, market share estimates, and volume estimates. The latter comes when they combine trial-and-repeat rates with the client's assumptions on awareness, retail availability, competitive actions, and the like.

A key aspect of the method is its mathematical simulation. If the client doesn't like the sales forecast from a study, variations are easily tested. For example, the model can be asked what amount of trial would be necessary to get to the desired market share. In turn, the cost of getting that trial (for example, by doubling the number of coupons currently planned for the introductory period or by lowering the price for a while) can be evaluated.

There are two variations on the above procedure, and the difference comes in how the data are analyzed. The current leading provider of the service (BASES) takes a fairly simple approach, relying on heuristics (rules of thumb derived from trial-and-error experience with previous, comparable situations). They gather the raw trial and repeat data from the test, and calibrate them using their vast data set of thousands of comparable product introductions from the past to come out with adjusted trial and repeat measures. They then put these adjusted data through their version of the A-T-A-R model to project sales and market share.

Other leading suppliers use mathematical models, not heuristics, to derive their forecasts. This approach demands that more information be supplied by the client, but is more useful in running simulations. One of the more prominent models is ASSESSOR, which is distinguished by its ability to make two forecasts (one using an A-T-A-R model and one using a preference model), and comparing the two to come up with market share predictions.[9]

ASSESSOR's A-T-A-R model projects market share for a new product based on estimates of awareness, trial and repeat purchases. Based on the

---

[8]An excellent contrast and evaluation of these modeling operations can be found in Allan D. Shocker and William G. Hall, "Pretest Market Models: A Critical Evaluation," *Journal of Product Innovation Management,* September 1986, pp. 86–107. Unfortunately, these operations, their methods, and their supplier firms change often, so such listings as these will always be out of date. Example: when Chicago-based Information Resources Inc. (IRI) sold its popular ASSESSOR STM to Texas-based M/A/R/C Inc., the latter sued IRI because soon after selling the models it teamed up with the largest STM supplier and seemed to violate its "no competition" clause in the original sale contract. See Howard Schlossberg, "Potential Legal Snag Clouds Test-Marketing Pact," *Marketing News,* October 29, 1990, p. 8.

[9]The ASSESSOR model is described in A. J. Silk and G. L. Urban, "Pre-Test-Market Evaluation of New Packaged Goods: A Model and Measurement Methodology," *Journal of Marketing Research* 15 (May 1978), pp. 171–91; also see G. L. Urban and G. M. Katz, "Pre-Test-Market Models: Validation and Managerial Implications," *Journal of Marketing Research* 20 (August 1983), pp. 221–34.

marketing mix variables of advertising (affecting awareness), distribution (affecting availability), and sales promotion (affecting number of samples received), estimates of long-run or steady-state trial and repeat are obtained. Multiplying steady-state trial and repeat rates gives the projected long-run market share.

Participants in an ASSESSOR study are asked to list all brands they know in the product category, and to indicate their preferences among these brands. They may then be shown advertising for the test product and also for other brands. In the next stage, the participant is taken to a simulated store environment where the test product and other brands are available for sale. A small amount of money is given to each participant to spend in the store. Some participants will buy the test product on the basis of the advertising. Those who do not are given a sample of it to take home (to estimate the effectiveness of distributing samples). After a few weeks have passed (sufficient time to use the new product), participants are contacted by phone and asked about their intentions to purchase in the future. Thus, likely repurchase rates can be estimated. Participants may also be sent another package of the test product by mail and asked to redo their preference assessments, this time including the test product.

ASSESSOR allows the product manager to do "what-if" analysis, that is, to evaluate the effects of changes in marketing mix variables on market share and profit.

New Advances in STMs. We had discussed information acceleration (IA), a virtual concept testing technique, back in Chapter 9. Virtual testing techniques have been combined with traditional simulated test market procedures as well. One such development is called the *visionary shopper* (VS). Here, the respondent is brought into a virtual retail store environment and encouraged to shop around, "take products off the shelf" (by touching the image on the screen) and read the label, and make purchases. Recent work suggests that VS can be built into a shopping model as part of a STM, and advanced development of this technique is underway in the UK.[10]

Criticism. The STM technique has its critics. All major packaged goods firms use one or more of the methods, but we don't know how often or with what confidence. Mathematical complexity is a problem. Simulated market testing has a sense of magic, a mumbo-jumbo sometimes encouraged by the sellers of the services. Second, everything in the system is slightly false: the mall intercept creates false conditions at the start, then the stimuli are

---

[10]For a discussion of the use of virtual stores in sales forecasting, see Raymond R. Burke, "Virtual Shopping: Breakthrough in Marketing Research," *Harvard Business Review,* March-April 1996, pp. 120–31. This technique is also presented in Phillip J. Rosenberger III and Leslie de Chernatony, "Virtual Reality Techniques in NPD Research," *Journal of the Market Research Society,* October 1995, pp. 345–55.

unrealistically administered, the "store" is obviously fake, and much attention is focused on the behavior of the consumers being tested. Third, the calculations require a set of givens from the client before the formulas can be run (on the percent of stores that will stock the item, for example, or on the advertising budget, on how good the advertising will be, and on competitive reaction). Most of these numbers are assumptions.

Complexity, unreality, and assumptions comprise quite a charge and explain much distrust. Further, the method is not felt to be applicable to products that are totally new to the market (the first TV dinner, for example, because no category data exist in the data bank), highly seasonal (test it and then wait a year?), are sold by personal selling or point-of-purchase promotion (rather than mass advertising), or require significant presale service.

The firms supplying the service simply ask, however, "What other method comes close at such an early date?" Besides, their sales forecasts are often accurate, although it is felt that perhaps as much as a half of all such tested products that go on into some later form of market testing are unsuccessful there.[11] So usage and controversy continue.[12]

Leading packaged goods firms have often leapt from the results of a STM directly into national launch. They get to the market fast without the costs of a controlled sale test or a full sale test. We will come back to this issue near the end of the next chapter.

Summary

Chapter 19 was the first half of a two-chapter set on market testing. First we saw where and how market testing sits in the overall new products process. Then we looked at the market testing decision itself, when it is made and how one goes about making it.

That provided the platform for us to look at the various market testing methods that have been invented. After looking at the three basic types, we took up the first of these—the pseudo sale—which comes in the two formats: the speculative sale and simulated test marketing. Chapter 20 will take up the other two methods. Keep in mind that we primarily want good forecasts of sales volumes and good ideas on how to fine-tune the overall launch plan.

---

[11]Bruce D. Weinberg, *Roles for Research and Models in Improving New Product Development,* Cambridge, Mass.: Marketing Science Institute, 1990, p. 8.

[12]BASES recently repeated a long-time claim, "We get within 20% of actual sales 80% of the time," in Power, "Will It Sell," p. 47. But, in most cases these percentages are after the fact. After a tested product is marketed, the many assumptions about stocking and advertising effectiveness are replaced by actual data, and then the original forecast is recalculated. This helps a great deal, but providers of the service say it would be even more unfair to compare market shares calculated early with what eventually happens under totally different circumstances. Keep in mind that STMs are run early, sometimes even before technical work, if prototypes can be used or if verbal statements about the product can communicate its claims.

Applications

More questions from that interview with the company president.

1. "You know, we recently had a soft drink product (an exotic berry seltzer line) go through one of those simulated test markets, and it was a disaster. The new products people forgot completely about the possibility that the customers who bought the product in the shopping center pseudo stores might not actually get around to trying it. But it happened. Based on in-store purchases, everything was OK, but a good percentage of the purchasers changed their minds later; and if they used the product at all, it was limited trial by just one person. Solution, of course: A sales wave test added to the end of the store test. But that increases the cost considerably. Could you tell me when we should use the added sales wave and when we shouldn't?"
2. "I really was confused by something a corporate market researcher said in a seminar we held last week. It concerned our industrial tubing division, which sells extruded aluminum tubing of various smaller sizes for encasing wiring in commercial buildings. She was recommending that they market test their new items by going out to the customers and making what she called fakes—pretending to sell something they wouldn't have yet. This was so silly. Surely you don't agree with her, do you? Besides, it sounds dishonest to deceive potential buyers that way."
3. "One of our better divisions is in the publishing business. Among their products is a line of posters sold through college campus outlets. I was chatting with them recently about market testing, and they said they don't do any of it on posters! Would you like to guess what they said were the reasons for this policy?"
4. "That same division also handles small furniture and other equipment for children. One of their items at the moment is in the shape of a child's car seat—typical format, full support all around, straps, the works. But the catch is that this car seat is made of reinforced nylon and is inflatable. It deflates slowly, for storage and carrying. Pumping is powered by the cigarette lighter. So far the reactions have been enthusiastic, but the developers know they're going to have troubles with the legal and regulatory people. Does this matter of market testing relate to the inflatable car seat situation at all?"

CASE: SIMTEST DIVISION, ELECTRONIC MEASUREMENTS, INC.[13]

Bill Bergen, executive vice president and chief operating officer of Electronic Measurements, Inc., was on his way back from lunch in the cafeteria when he almost bumped into Ann Toliver. Ann, head of the SimTest Division's new customer department, seemed preoccupied. She invited Bill to stop for a chat, and he found out why. A member of Ann's staff (Chez Tronwath) was preparing for a presentation to the marketing group at a client—Midwest Condiments—and Ann had been helping him.

Midwest was a small- to medium-sized regional producer of a line of catsups, mustards, and other condiments. It had begun in 1974 with a tasty pickle relish and had added other items over the years since then. The company had been advertising from the beginning and held good share in its markets. But early this year, it had been acquired by a big food company—MasterFoods—and was now getting ready to move out nationally. Midwest had been told to sharpen its market research practice and to adopt better ways of market testing its new products. Two MasterFoods brand managers were made available for advice on how to plan better market research, and word had gone out to Electronic Measurements and some other firms that Midwest would be interested in learning what they had to offer.

As it happens, they had a lot to offer, and Ann Toliver was preparing a proposal for a simulated test market. Ann and Chez had been out to see Midwest the day before and had learned that a new line of sandwich spices was on its way to market. Apparently the new line would be marketed in special shakers, so when making a sandwich the consumer could sprinkle one or more types of spices onto its filling. Ann and Chez couldn't learn the content of the spice bottles, but apparently the combinations were unique and original.

The issue was, should Midwest use Electronic's simulated test market service in market testing the new spice line? The product had passed concept tests and had done well in a limited home placement use test involving employees. The testers didn't think the product was the best they had ever heard of, but it did make sandwiches more interesting, was easy to use, and had created lots of talk in the households where used. The price was reasonable. The spice line would be targeted to busy people who ate lots of sandwiches but were bored with them. Positioning was straight to the fun and excitement of more interesting sandwiches.

So far, no one had actually been asked to buy the product. The advertising agency had developed copy for local TV and in-store display use, tasting samples would be made available in most stores, price would be a bit upscale (Grey Poupon?), and the bottles and labels were clearly of upscale design.

Midwest was concerned about two things: (1) Would people take the product seriously enough to actually buy some and try it? and (2) Would they continue using it after the novelty had worn off? (The product use tests had lasted two months, but each bottle lasted longer than that, so users had not run out during the test.)

Ann and Chez had just finished putting together their presentation to Midwest, and Ann asked Bill if he would like to see it. Bill said he would, and a time was set for the following morning.

And then an odd thing happened. On his way on down the hall, he passed the office of CEO Edie Hopkins. Edie had developed the SimTest Division and done so well at it she

[13]This hypothetical case is based on realistic business circumstances.

got the nod to replace Electronic's founder when he took early retirement. She said she had made a visit to MasterFoods earlier in the week and was amazed to find that the MF sales force had absorbed the Midwest Condiment sales force. The condiment line would be sold along with the rest of the MasterFoods items. This surprised her because she had heard stories about the Midwest sales vice president, now just a regional sales manager for MasterFoods. Apparently, he had fantastic rapport with regional food chain buyers, built on his uncanny ability to predict winners and losers in the food business. People said he had never stocked the trade with a loser, either at Midwest or at another food company where he began his career. Edie knew no sales manager had product authority at MasterFoods (except for local, so-called micromarketing promotions). She wondered how he would handle the sell-in of new items he didn't think would be successful.

The SimTest division of Electronic Measurements offered a market modeling service based on consumer reactions to advertising and product display in one of the firm's four mall test centers. The test centers were much like several other research firms' centers. Consumers were found by mall intercepts or solicited by phone and invited to the center, screened for market fit, interviewed about product awareness and usage, invited to screen a proposed new TV sitcom, exposed to several TV ads (including the test product), invited to shop the firm's pseudo stores, given the test product if they didn't buy it in the "store," and followed up later to see if they had used it and whether they wanted more.

Electronic had been at this for about nine years, so it had a solid data base and had fine-tuned its sales forecasting models to make accurate forecasts of new product sales and market shares. The models did require some assumptions, and Bill was worried that Midwest might not be sophisticated enough to make them. For example, SimTest needed to know what percent of stores would stock the product, what type of awareness the planned advertising and in-store displays would generate, and what were viewed as competitive products, if any.

Bill saw a chance for he and Edie to sharpen their client presentations and, at the same time, learn a few things about their staffs. He proposed that he and Edie role play Midwest management the following day, and the SimTest group (Ann and Chez) would make a presentation *to them.* The presentation would aggressively argue that the new spice line should be market tested via the SimTest service.

All the players (including Chez, who would actually make the presentation) knew this was no easy sell. MasterFoods brand people had been using simulated test marketing for several years and were generally satisfied with it. But Midwest had never used it. Word was that if Midwest did anything at all, it merely put out a new item in a limited area near the plant and watched what happened. Losers were quickly "deep-sixed," as a Midwest product manager put it.

The SimTest Ann and Chez were thinking of would cost about $195,000 and take three months.

CHAPTER

20

Market Testing Continued

Controlled Sale and Full Sale

Controlled Sale Methods

The two pseudo sale methods of market testing discussed in Chapter 19 are unrealistic. They are useful as an early test and occasionally reliable as a final measure when the only issues involve how the customers react to the concept in a commercial setting. Users can argue, for example, that the STM fits well with how we actually buy food products—we see a commercial and then later meet the item on a store shelf. We buy or we don't buy. (See Figure 20–1 for information about all three categories of market test methods.)

Historically, however, we have relied on other market testing methods that introduce the matter of cash—real purchasing under some competitive environment. Marketers have sought market testing methods with a strong dose of reality but which also "control" away one or more dimensions of the situation. Launching new products usually requires *distribution,* or *sell-in.* Marketers have always wished for a market testing method that *assumes* distribution, or gets it automatically, without having to spend time and money to get it. This wishing has resulted in the **controlled sale** market testing methods.

Informal Selling

Much industrial selling is based on clearly identifiable product features. Product developers want potential buyers to see the product and hear the story, to make a trial purchase (or accept the offer of free trial supply), and to actually use the product. Repeat sales should follow unless product use testing was poorly done. Personal selling is the primary promotional tool, and there is little need to assess advertising.

FIGURE 20–1

A-T-A-R and the market testing methods

Information Needed by the A-T-A-R Profit Forecasting Method	Sources of This Information		
	Pseudo sale methods	Controlled sale methods	Full sale methods
Number of market units	*Market research* studies	*Market research* studies	*Yes*
Awareness of the new product positioning claim (A)	*Ad agency* provides it	*Ad agency* provides it	*Yes*
Decides to try the item (T)	*Yes*	*Yes*	*Yes*
Is able to get a trial supply (A)	Distribution estimates provided by *sales dept.*	Distribution estimates provided by *sales dept.*	*Yes*
Likes it and wants more (R)	*Yes—in sales wave*	*Team* estimates	*Yes*
Units used per year	*Yes—est.*	*Yes—est.*	*Yes*
Profit per unit (price-cost)	Price plan plus estimates from *accounting* on costs	Price plan plus estimates from *accounting* on costs	*Yes*
Additional diagnostic info.	*Yes—a little*	*Yes—more*	*Yes—tons*

So the obvious approach is to train a few salespeople, give them the product and the selling materials, and have them begin making calls. This informal selling method can even be handled at trade shows, either at the regular booths or in special facilities nearby. An example came from a 3M division that was in a crash program to market a new optical fiber splice; for market testing the item, the team manager found a trade show running just three months prior to launch date, where almost every potential buyer of the item would be present. As a footnote on this successful test, the night before the show opened it was necessary for the team to find why some fibers were slipping out of the splices; for this, they used a toy microscope purchased at a nearby mall.[1] New product marketers have to be quick on their feet.

The presentations in the informal selling method are for real, and cash sales take place. Often, enough time remains between the order and the expected date of shipment that production can be arranged after sufficient orders are obtained.

Informal selling differs from the speculative sale method discussed in Chapter 19. There we asked people if they *would* buy; here we ask them to buy. And just as Rubbermaid was mentioned as a consumer products firm using speculative selling, we find consumer firms using informal selling. All products sold primarily by salespeople directly to end-users can use it (most controlled sale methods avoid the retailer/distributor stocking problem). So can services of most types.

Direct Marketing

Another simple method of controlled sale is by **direct marketing.** Though usage of the term *direct marketing* varies, here it includes the sale of a (primarily) consumer product by the maker directly to the consuming unit by means of the mail, telephone, TV, fax, or computer network. As examples, L.L. Bean and Lands' End are large direct marketers. They can easily test a new service of some type, or a new product or product line, simply by listing it in *some* of their catalogs and counting the orders. The advantages are several:

- More secrecy than by any other controlled sale method.
- The feedback is almost instant.
- Positioning and image development are easier because more information can be sent and more variations can be tested easily.
- It is cheaper than the other techniques.
- The technique matches today's growing technologies of credit card financing, telephone ordering, and database compilation.

Minimarkets

Whereas the informal selling and direct marketing methods essentially avoid distributors and retailers/dealers, a third method involves outlets on a very limited basis. The new products manager first selects one or several outlets where sale of the new product would be desirable. In no way a representative sample, these are more likely to be bigger outlets where cooperation can be

---

[1]Steve Blount, "It's Just a Matter of Time," *Sales & Marketing Management,* March 1992, pp. 32–43.

obtained. Instead of using whole cities (as in test marketing), we use each store as a minicity or **minimarket,** thus the name.

Black & Decker, for example, could contact a couple "big barn" outlets and make arrangements to display and sell a new version of its Snake Light. It could not use local TV or newspaper advertising because the item is available in only one or two outlets, but the stores could list the item in *their* advertising, there could be shelf display and product demonstrations, and sales clerks could offer typical service. Some method (such as offering a rebate or a mail-in premium) could get the names of purchasers for follow-up contact by market research people.

The minimarket situation is more realistic: actual buying situations are created, great flexibility is allowed in changing price and other variables, somewhat more confidentiality is possible than with test marketing, and it is cheaper. Of course, it is still somewhat contrived, in that the ability to get distribution is not tested—minimarket testing is still controlled sale. Too, store personnel may "overattend" the product, that is, pay too much attention to it and give it assistance the item will not get when fully marketed. And, of course, sales cannot be projected to any national figure.

Several market research firms offer this service to manufacturers, using stores with which they have previously set up relationships and also using their fleet of vans to rapidly get product out to more than just a few stores. At least one of the firms has special new product racks in supermarkets, where the new items are displayed.

Note this method is not very scientific; it is used to catch the first flavor of actual sale and/or to work on special problems the developers are having (such as brand confusion, price, package instructions, product misuse, or different positionings). It tells us the trial, and gives some feeling about repeat.

One variation on minimarkets has gotten lots of attention in the consumer packaged goods field, though its method has not been applied to other consumer goods and services or business products. Called BehaviorScan, it was developed by IRI, the same firm previously active in simulated test marketing. The technology came about when retail store checkout scanners became available. IRI uses eight cities of around 100,000 people, for example, Marion, Indiana, and Visalia, California. In each city, it contacts all of the retail outlets for grocery store products, and asks them to install scanner systems if they don't already have them, at IRI expense. In return the retailers agree to share the scanner data with IRI, and to cooperate in a few other activities. Acceptance of this offer has been outstanding. Next IRI sets up two panels of 1,000 families each in each city. Participants agree to (1) have electronic technology installed on cable-based television sets, (2) report their exposure to print media, (3) make all of their purchases of grocery store products in the BehaviorScan stores, and (4) use a special plastic card identifying their family. The families get various incentives (such as lottery participation) to get their initial and sustained cooperation.

The key parts of this system are (1) cable TV interrupt privileges, (2) a full record of what other media (such as magazines) go into each household, (3) family-by-family purchasing, and (4) a complete record of 95 percent of all store sales of tested items from the check-out scanners. Immediate stocking/distribution in almost every store is assured by the research firm (this too is a controlled sale method). IRI knows almost every stimulus that hits each individual family, and it knows almost every change that takes place in each family's purchase habits.

For example, assume Kraft wants to market test a new version of cheddar cheese, called Cajun. It contracts with IRI to buy the cheese category in one or more of the eight cities. It then places Cajun in a city and starts local promotion. Another of the cities can be used temporarily as a control. Kraft gets the right to put its commercials (via cable interrupt) into whichever of the homes (for example, younger families) it chooses. Kraft knows whether the families watched TV at the times of the commercials, whether they bought any of the Cajun, whether they bought it again, and so on.

The two panels in each city allow Kraft to use two different positionings in its TV advertising, one positioning for each of the panels. And so on, and so on. The variations and controls stretch the imagination. Kraft can find out how many of the upscale homes who watched the initial commercial bought some of the product within the next two days. And what they bought on their prior purchase, what they paid, what else they bought at the time, and the like.

Scanner Market Testing

There are many variations on minimarket testing, all designed to meet special situations and needs. One of them, **scanner market testing,** came out of the same firm that developed the BehaviorScan minimarket service.

Once BehaviorScan was established, clients began asking the firm for more scanner data (fast and detailed in contrast to traditional market audit data that were slow and with less detail). They wanted to keep the BehaviorScan laboratories, but they also wanted data on large areas, preferably the entire country. So IRI developed what became known as InfoScan, a system of auditing sales out of outlets selling grocery store products. These audits were done in stores with scanner systems, and the data were reported for major metropolitan markets—first a few, and now over a hundred. In fact, the coverage is so good that the InfoScan total market service is bought now as a national system. Or it can be bought for single markets.

IRI has such good contacts with the stores it uses that, for a price, they can assure stocking of a new product. Without this assurance, the sell-in is left to whatever the firm can do. So InfoScan data can be used in a *minimarket test*—say buying market stocking in Indianapolis and Denver and measuring sales of the new item there. Most minimarket test methods (see above) are in a small subset of stores and thus do not allow advertising in the areas leading media—all local media are available in an InfoScan market. Or InfoScan data can be used in a test market where they introduce the new item by *natural sell-in,* regular calls on retailers and wholesalers in, say, Nashville and Albuquerque. If they want to, they can buy store data for two other cities, say Rochester and Kansas City where they do *not* sell the new product, for comparison with the two where it is being sold. The city pairs are not as carefully selected and matched as they are in traditional test marketing. Or, third, InfoScan data can be used where a firm starts selling a new product in major markets of the west, moves it out to nearby markets in the mountain states, and so on across the country. In a moment, we will see that this is a *rollout* market test.

InfoScan thus is a *method of market test design and data gathering.* By itself, it is not a method of market testing, but supports most of them. To help in this, IRI has also developed household panels in all of their markets, so clients can follow individual family purchases, taking on some aspects of their own BehaviorScan laboratory system. Some consumer firms' managers call InfoScan a *live* test market, to distinguish it from the simulated test marketing models, and others call it an *in-market* test to distinguish it from the smaller city "laboratories" of the BehaviorScan electronic testing service.[2] In the meantime, the great majority of business firms (all of those outside packaged goods) have no such system available.

The excitement of the InfoScan service lies in its flexibility to do many different things in many different markets, with allied coordinated services, and most of all, in rich details in days, not months. The A. C. Nielsen Company responded by altering its traditional every-60-days store audit system to take on more of the InfoScan character, but as of this writing, IRI has passed Nielsen in market share.

Full-Sale Methods

In full-sale market testing *all* variables are *go,* including competition and the trade. They test the realities of national introduction. First will come test marketing and then the fastest growing method of all, rollout.

Test Marketing

Test marketing refers to that type of market testing in which a presumably representative piece of the total market is chosen for a dress rehearsal. Typically, these market pieces have been cities, or more properly, the metropolitan markets built around cities. They are what we bring to mind

[2]IRI goes much further in designing variations on the basic service. For example, besides the controlled *market* testing just described, they also offer controlled *store* testing where activities in one chain are studied.

when we hear that a new product is "being tested" in Evansville, Atlanta, Boise, or Portland.

What typically happens is that a firm first picks, say, two cities to sell the new product into, and two cities very similar to the first where the product is not sold. All four are watched closely, stocking of the new product is audited, sales are audited—either by the InfoScan system we were just talking about or one of the traditional methods of collecting store purchase data and store inventories from which sales can be calculated. What they had, plus what they bought, less what they have left over on the auditor's next call, equals what they must have sold (ignoring what walked out).

This auditing service can be bought from the traditional leader, A. C. Nielsen, or from one of many regional and local market research firms who offer auditing capability.

The *purpose* of most test marketing today has changed. Whereas the early purpose was to predict profits and thus help decide *whether* to go national, firms today use it more to fine-tune their plans and learn *how best* to do so. Test marketing is too expensive to be used as a final exam.

This is a critical distinction, as shown by the market testing traditionally used for Broadway plays and musicals. Some of them *have* to play Detroit or Boston to prove their worth, but these are small, shoestring operations destined for an off-Broadway location. Big-time shows spend the real money getting *to* Detroit, where they fine-tune the operation, confirm volume and cost forecasts, and so on. A major production that fails in Detroit is a rarity.

An illustrative example of how a firm fine-tuned a marketing plan is given by Searle, in their development of NutraSweet (aspartame) artificial sweetener. When NutraSweet was first developed, Searle originally thought the natural target market would be artificial sweetener users who disliked saccharin's aftertaste. In regional test markets, they found that the real target market was quite different, and actually much larger and more lucrative: dissatisfied sugar users. It turned out that many saccharin users actually preferred saccharin's taste.[3]

Pros and Cons. In contrast to other test methods, test marketing is intended to offer typical market conditions, thereby allowing the best sales forecast and the best evaluation of alternative marketing strategies. It reduces the risk of a total or major flop.

The test market offers the most abundant *supply of information* (such as sales, usage, prices, reseller reactions and support, publicity, and competitive reactions) and many less important but occasionally valuable by-products. For example, a smaller firm can use successful test market results to help *convince national distributors* to chance stocking the item.

[3]Gary S. Lynn, Mario Mazzuca, Joseph G. Morone, and Albert S. Paulson, "Learning Is the Critical Success Factor in Developing Truly New Products," *Research-Technology Management,* May–June 1998, pp. 45–51.

The test market also permits *verifying production.* ITT Continental Baking had to withdraw its Continental Kitchens line of prepared entrees from a test market because suppliers of the retort pouch couldn't maintain deliveries. Nabisco had trouble with Legendary Pastries when a seemingly harmless ingredient in the canned topping mix caused the product to explode on kitchen shelves. Both firms saved great sums of money by opting for a test market.

Other firms have been surprised by the effects of *humidity* or *temperature, abuse* by distribution personnel, *ingenious undesirable uses* of the product, and *general misunderstanding* by company or distributive personnel.

Of course, the method is *expensive:* direct costs easily run $300,000 to $500,000 per city; many indirect costs (for preparing product, special training, and so on) must be considered as well.

These costs are often acceptable if the data are accurate, thus allowing the test markets to be projected to a national sales figure. But researchers have known for a long time that *test market results are not really projectable.* We cannot control all *environmental factors,* company people tend to *overwork* a test program, dealers may *overattend or underattend,* and the constant temptation exists to *sweeten the trade package* unrealistically in fear that inadequate distribution will kill the entire test.

In addition, there is the question of *time.* A good test may take a year or more, which gives competition full view of the test firm's strategy, time to prepare a reaction, and even the chance to leapfrog directly to national marketing on a similar item. Kellogg watched the early results of General Foods' Toast-Ems in test market and then went national ahead of General Foods to grab the major market share with Pop Tarts. Procter & Gamble, "once the archetypal cautious player [has] become a much speedier player."[4] Several years ago their Duncan Hines frosting was leapfrogged by General Mills Betty Crocker brand. General Mills vice-chairman Arthur Schulze once said that if someone else gets there first, you just have another me-too product.

Also, *competitors can mess up a test market city,* with a flood of coupons and other devices to falsely decrease the test product's sales. Not that long ago, the general manager of General Foods' beverage division told of test market "informants who live in the town and pay off the supermarket managers to be allowed to hang around. You see these mysterious characters watching how fast the Mighty Dog is moving and in what sizes." Other test market participants tell of bulk new product purchases by competitive salespeople to falsely increase sales reports.[5] Quaker used heavy coupons and ads

[4]Christopher Power, "Will It Sell in Podunk? Hard to Say," *BusinessWeek,* August 10, 1992, p. 46.

[5]This technique is still being used, this time in the book industry, where some authors have made purchases in those stores whose sales are being audited for inclusion in national best-seller lists. Most firms have urged sales people to recruit neighbors to make purchases and spur stocking by stores.

FIGURE 20–2

A risk of test marketing: showing your hand to the competitor

- Kellogg tracked the sale of General Foods' Toast-Ems while they were in test market. Noting they were becoming popular, they went national quickly with Pop-Tarts before the General Foods' test market was over.
- After having invented freeze-dried coffee, General Foods was test-marketing its own Maxim brand when Nestle bypassed them with Taster's Choice, which went on to be the leading brand.
- While Procter & Gamble were busy test-marketing their soft chocolate chip cookies, both Nabisco and Keebler rolled out similar cookies nationwide.
- The same thing happened with P&G's Brigade toilet-bowl cleaner. It was in test marketing for three years, during which time both Vanish and Ty-D-Bol became established in the market.
- While Campbell was test-marketing Prego spaghetti sauce, Ragú increased advertising and promotion (to skew the results of the Prego test), and also developed and rolled out new Ragú Homestyle sauce.
- General Foods' test market results for a new frozen baby food were very encouraging, until it was learned that most of the purchases were being made by competitors Gerber, Libby, and Heinz.

Sources: J. P. Guiltinan and G. W. Paul, *Marketing Management: Strategies and Programs,* 4th ed. (New York: McGraw-Hill, 1991); G. L. Urban and S. H. Star, *Advanced Marketing Strategy* (Englewood Cliffs, NJ: Prentice-Hall, 1991); E. E. Scheuing, *New Product Management* (Columbus, OH: Bell & Howell, 1989); Robert M. McMath and Thom Forbes, *What Were They Thinking?* (New York: Times Business, 1998); G. A. Churchill, *Basic Marketing Research* (Fort Worth, TX, Dryden, 1998); and others.

to thwart Pepsi when it test marketed Mountain Dew Sport drink in Minneapolis.

Finally, there is an inevitable temptation to *rationalize away a test market difficulty* by citing what the now-known trouble was and how the firm "can take care of it on national launch."

Figure 20–2 provides some pragmatic guidelines on when a full sale market test is or is not advised. Because of the risks involved, many firms now take products that do well in simulated test markets directly to national launch, bypassing full sale market testing. This happened in the cases of General Foods International Coffees, Sara Lee meat-filled croissants, Quaker Chewy Granola Bars, and Pillsbury Milk Break Bars. Procter & Gamble, which used to test market most new products extensively, now goes directly from a successful STM to national launch with many products, though in some cases where higher risks or uncertainties were present (such as Cinch dishwasher detergent), a full sale test market of as long as three years may still be employed.

The Test Parameters. A large body of test market literature is available, and most of the leading market research consulting firms stand ready to design tests appropriate to any situation, so no depth of detail is needed here. The most common questions are "Where should we test?" and "How long should the test run?"

Picking Test Markets. Each experienced test marketer has an ideal structure of cities or areas. Ad agencies keep lists. Picking two or three to use is not simple, but the most common factors are:

1. *Demographics*—population, income, employment, and so on.
2. *Distribution*—the structure of retail and wholesale firms, including any difficulties of getting in.
3. *Competition*—you need enough, but not too much.
4. *Media*—newspapers, radio, and TV covering just that market, not a huge surrounding area.
5. *Category activity*—no strong regional, ethnic, or economic peculiarities in product consumption.

Test areas need to be stand-alone, not be where there will be a lot of sales leakage into other areas, and yet representative of the nation or a big piece of it.

Duration of Test. There is no one answer to the question of how long a test market should last, as made clear by one marketing vice president who said he needed 24–36 months for a new plant care item but only 6–9 months for a candy snack. See Figure 20–3 for some data on purchase cycles; the wide variations are just one factor in the duration decision.

The Rollout

Test marketing is not dead, but marketers now prefer a market testing method called **rollout.** It gives the dress rehearsal value of a test market but avoids many of its problems. It is sometimes called tiered marketing or limited marketing.

Assume a major insurance company develops a new policy giving better protection, at lower rates, for people who exercise regularly. Management decides to market test the new service by first putting it out for sale in California, an area presumably prime for such a policy. Its independent agents do their job, the policy sells well, so the company offers it to the rest of its West Coast agents. Again, it sells well, and the *geographical* extension continues. One 3M division markets items in Argentina before rolling them out to the countries in Europe. Colgate follows a "lead country" strategy, and recently marketed Palmolive Optims shampoo in the Philippines, Australia, Mexico, and Hong Kong before rolling into Europe, Asia, and other world markets.[6]

The starting areas are *not representative areas* but, rather, areas where the company thinks it has the right people, and perhaps the right markets, to get the thing going. Some firms want the area to be difficult, not easy. For example, Miles Laboratories was marketing diabetes self-testing glaucometers, and realized that two of its sales divisions would have to cooperate; the Diagnostic

[6]U.S. multinationals have been urged to use Russia as a geographical rollout area. It offers a large market, with much less world-class competition, allowing the test company to gain experience and volume. Russian leaders have adopted policies on reexporting, etc., to aid such tests. James L. Hecht, "Let Russia Be Your Product Testing Lab," *The Wall Street Journal,* August 24, 1992, p. A8.

FIGURE 20–3

Purchase cycles on selected product categories

	Average Purchase Frequency (weeks)	*Average Four-Week Penetration (percent)*		*Average Purchase Frequency (weeks)*	*Average Four-Week Penetration (percent)*
Air fresheners	6	12.3%	Fruit drinks	4	27.8%
Baking supplies:			Presweetened powdered drinks	8	13.2
Brown sugar	17	13.6	Laundry care:		
Cake mixes	10	29.6	Heavy-duty detergents	5	50.4
Chewable vitamins	26	0.8	Soil and stain removers	25	4.7
Cleaners:			Liquid bleach	6	18.3
All-purpose cleaners	35	3.4	Margarine	3	71.7
Window cleaners	27	7.1	Milk additives	9	11.8
Rug cleaners	52	2.4	Mouthwash	13	9.7
Bathroom cleaners	25	4.2	Pet food:		
Coffee	3	53.1	Cat (total)	2	14.1
Frozen foods:			Dog (dry)	4	23.2
Frozen entrees	6	19.5	Dog (total)	2	41.8
Frozen pizza	8	21.1	Raisins	18	8.3
Furniture polish	27	7.0	Salad dressings	6	32.9
Hair care:			Salad toppings	8	1.2
Hair color	12	4.7	Snacks	3	17.7
Shampoo	8	23.4	Steak sauce	23	5.4
Juices/drinks:			Toothpaste	9	33.1
Fruit juices	3	33.6			

Note: The first column is the average time between purchases of the category cited, by the households in the ADTEL panel. The second column is the percentage of panel households that make at least one purchase in a four-week period. Both figures contribute to the decision on test market duration.

Souce: ADTEL, Inc.

sales people knew the technology, and the Consumer Healthcare sales people knew the retail druggists. They picked New York City, saying, "Because of the complexity of the market, if we could be successful in New York City, we could roll it out to other parts of the country with reasonable assurance of success."[7]

Second, there was no doubt about what the company was doing: *it was launching the new product.* So was General Mills when it launched Multi-Grain Cheerios in 25 percent of the country and rolled out over the next year. See Figure 20–4 for the decision on when to rollout and how far to increase the rollout before switching to a full national launch.

Kodak recently attempted a nationwide launch for its Advanced Photo System (APS), also known as Advantix, which in retrospect maybe should

[7]Leslie Brennan, "Meeting the Test," *Sales and Marketing Management,* March 1990, p. 60.

FIGURE 20–4

The patterns of information gained at various stages of a rollout

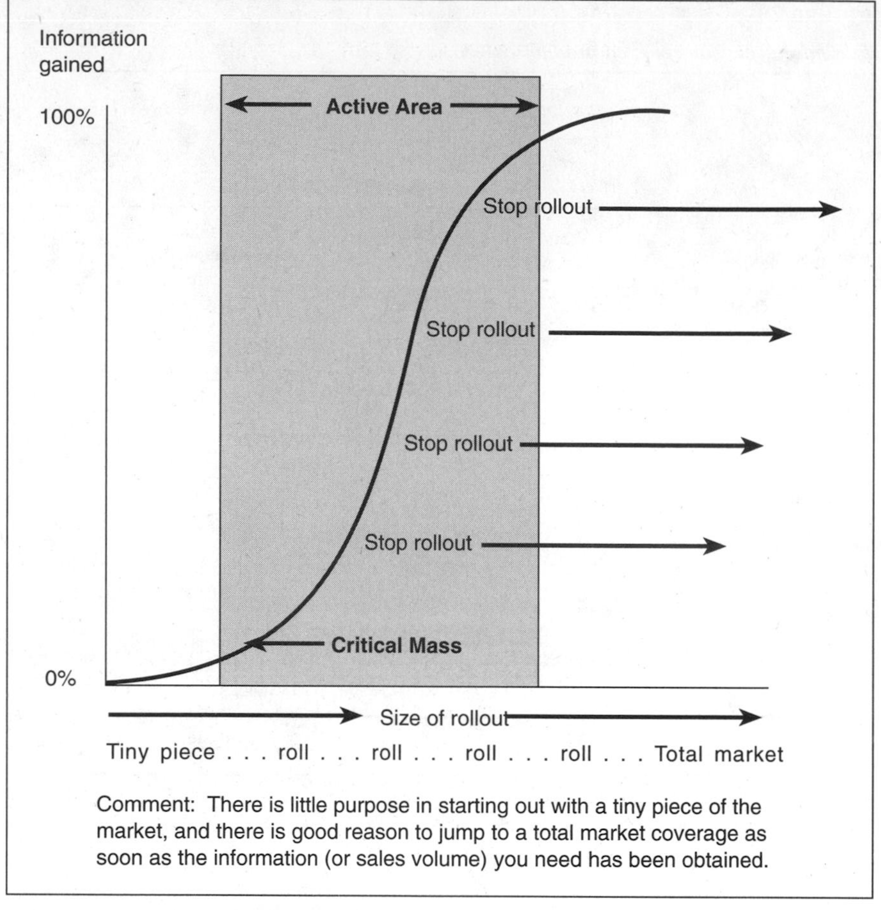

have been a rollout. The plan was to launch in early 1996, backed with a $100 million advertising campaign, catalogues, and other promotional items. The problem here was that demand far exceeded expectations. The trade press had given the APS system lukewarm reviews, possibly because product developers at Kodak did not give them complete information about the system's benefits. As a result, sales projections and production plans were tempered. The heavy advertising resulted in the unexpectedly high demand, and Kodak had to scramble to ramp production up to the new higher levels. Chains such as Wal-Mart and Phar-Mor had APS cameras and film in only some of their stores, if any, as late as August (when the peak summer picture-taking season was winding down). By this time, advertising support and in-store promotions had slowed considerably. Industry insiders felt that if Kodak insisted on a nationwide launch, they probably ought to have waited until at least June, if not the fall. A roll-out might have helped Kodak calibrate the level of sales in a small market and adjust full-scale production and advertising support upwards as the product went national.[8]

Let's take another example. Assume an industrial adhesives firm develops a new adhesive that works on many *applications,* including fastening bricks to steel plates, fastening insulation siding to the two-by-four studs in a house, and fastening shingles onto plywood roofing sheets. It has been field tested in all three applications and has been tested in informal selling to roofing firms in one use (shingles), where it received a good response. Should the firm offer it for all three applications at once? Arguments against this include (1) the adhesive has not been market tested in the first two applications, (2) such action would strain resources, (3) multiple uses might confuse customers, all of whom are in the construction field and will hear of all three selling efforts, and (4) the new products manager wants to have some successful experience to talk about when entering the brick and siding fields because they are highly competitive.

Answer: Market the new adhesive in the shingles business first, gain experience, build up some cash flow, and establish credibility. Then gradually begin selling it to the siding firms and make whatever changes are indicated. Still later, roll it on into the brick field.

A third example of rollout would be the same adhesives firm if there were only one major application and the product (1) was only marginally better and (2) required lots of training for the distributors' reps. The adhesives firm could choose to begin selling the adhesive through one of its best (and friendliest) distributors, a firm willing to go along on the new item. When that went well, it could gradually roll it out to other distributors with whom it had increasingly less *influence,* using prior successes to persuade them.

A fourth example can be found in the magazine publishing field, where new magazines are often offered first through the newsstand *channel,* and then, if they sell well, they are offered in direct mail promotion for mail subscribers.[9]

Other Forms That Rollout Takes. Those examples catch the four leading forms taken by roll-outs—geography, application, influence, and trade channel. Here are some other rollout situations:

- Sega wanted to get a jump on Nintendo and Sony for shelf space ahead of fall and Christmas. So it used selected stores of Toys "R"

[8]Wendy Bounds, "Camera System Is Developed but Not Delivered," *The Wall Street Journal,* August 7, 1996, p. B1, B6.

[9]Patrick M. Reilly, "Publishers Turn Page on Hype, Taking Subdued Approach to Magazine Rollouts," *The Wall Street Journal,* January 8, 1991, p. B1.

Us, Babbage's, Software City, and Electronic Boutique to sell some new items into, in April.[10]

- P&G responded to Kimberly-Clark's move of their Pull-Up diapers into Europe by introducing Pampers Trainers into Ireland and Holland. They also rolled the new Trainers into Canada, but refused to state when the rollout would continue throughout Europe or from Canada into the U.S.
- Prodigy was first rolled into San Diego, and Discover card into Atlanta, both examples of using a rollout when the nature of the service was still being worked out.
- Tom's of Maine uses rollouts to enter markets one at a time, without the costs of advertising and slotting allowances. They use radio with a localized personal approach. Strategy is "model for growth."
- Even large firms must do this if they are entering a market where they have little clout. United launched its shuttle service by targeting frequent flyers—most likely to be interested and reachable at lower costs via billboards near airports. With volume here, they too moved into other "markets."
- A popular game, Magic: The Gathering, could easily be copied, so the firm developing it wanted to sneak in without too much attention or too much evidence of success. They rolled out for almost a year, leading up to the industry's big trade show when they went national.
- Sometimes a firm has a product whose acceptance requires a change in market thinking—concept tests are not reliable. In 1995 PepsiCo introduced Pepsi XL, a 70-calorie version, in five major Florida markets (with InfoScan major-market data service). The rollout had to first demonstrate that a mid-diet segment actually exists.[11]
- We will long remember one of the most ballyhooed introductions of all time—that of Windows 95, in August of 1995. But, Microsoft had been running beta-site tests for over two years, adding new applications and users every month, to a total of over 2000. This was a rollout, and August 1995 was not a single, total-market introduction.

Contrasts with Test Marketing. A rollout has many advantages. The biggest are that it gives management most of the knowledge learned from a test market, it has an escape clause without losing the full budget if things bomb, and yet we are well on our way to national availability as early rollout

---

[10]Jim Carlton, "Sega Leaps Ahead by Shipping New Player Early," *The Wall Street Journal,* May 11, 1995, p. B1.

[11]Laurie Grossman, "Pepsi Plans a Test of 70-Calorie Cola For Young Adults," *The Wall Street Journal,* March 29, 1995, p. B4.

results start coming in. This is important in the competitive battle because test marketing gives the competition time to launch their products while we are still in test market or getting geared up to go national.

Does this sound like the best of all worlds? What's the catch? In many situations, there isn't any catch, and the technique is justifiably growing rapidly. Other firms may find roll-outs to be just as big a risk as full launch. Here is why:

1. Their biggest investment may be in a new production facility, and to roll out requires the full plant at the start.
2. They may be in an industry where competitors can move very fast (for example, because no patent or new facilities are required), so a slow marketing gives them as much chance to leap-frog as would test marketing.
3. Available distributors are powerful, and none are willing to trust them.
4. They need the free national publicity that only a full national launch can get them; rollouts tend not to be newsworthy.

What does a firm do? The answer is to go through the same decision process given in Chapter 19. Many of the answers depend on conditions at the moment—maybe a firm doesn't want any unfavorable publicity, maybe it wants fast cash in an acquisitions battle, maybe top management is new and wants a couple of successes before the first loss, and so on. There are no recipes here.

Wrap-Up on Market Testing Methodologies

Each of the 10 methods in the three categories of Figure 19–4 can be used alone, and many firms use the one they think is best in terms of cost and what they can learn. But some firms want a system of two or more techniques.

Such firms usually begin with a pseudo sale method—the speculative format, if they are industrial or in a business where personal selling is the major marketing thrust, or a form of STM, if they are in consumer packaged goods. Pseudo sale is cheap and quick. Learning is limited, but it is a good leg up on the problem. It often doesn't hold up the process.

The firm then turns to one of the controlled sale methods, especially informal selling for industrial firms or minimarkets for consumer firms. If the second test will be the last, firms tend to slide directly into a full sale method. Thus, an industrial firm might use a speculative sale followed by an applications roll-out. A packaged goods firm might start with an STM followed by a geographical roll-out, or an STM followed by a minimarket and then full launch.

FIGURE 20–5
The past and future for market testing methods

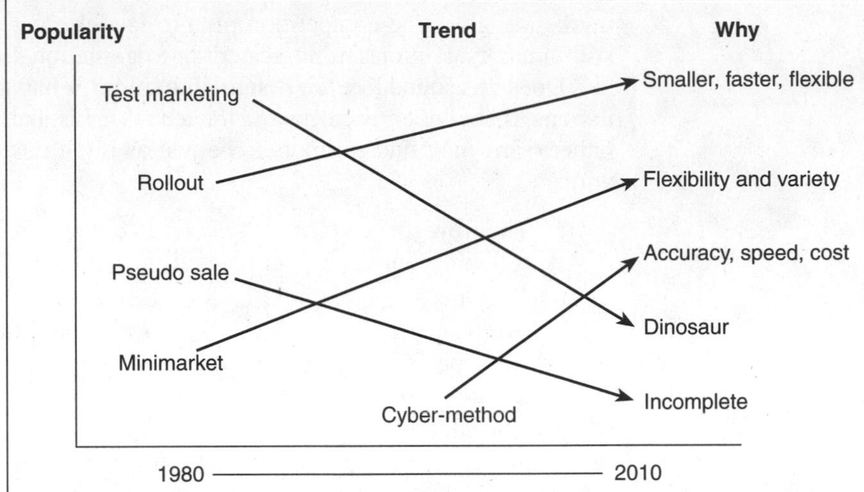

Comment: Given that we could never agree on how to measure a technique's popularity (whether by number of users, dollars spent, value to user, etc.) and lacking valid research reports, this figure is meant to be a representation of change. Our needs have changed, and will change more. There will be new technologies too, especially something here called Cyber-method. Built on electronic networks, data are fed from InfoScan-type store setups. Measurements will be built to answer just the one or two key questions an organization has, with exquisite degree of detail, and (maybe later) a virtual market that models reality down to households and individual business firms.

Figure 20–5 gives some opinions on the popularity of the various methods and some thinking about what may happen in the future.

Summary

Chapters 19 and 20 have covered the market testing phase of the overall evaluation task that involves putting product together with marketing plan. The techniques of market testing vary from the simplistic (and quite unreliable) one of making a sales presentation about the new product to potential buyers and then asking them if they would buy it if available, to a rollout.

The appropriate market testing methodology for any particular new product cannot be stipulated here. Some new product innovation is of such low risk that no market testing can be defended. The toughest issue of all is probably that of technology-based firms that develop what they feel the customer needs and *will* want; but customers don't *know* they want these new items until they have had a long chance to see them and think about them. Examples are many, ranging from the bath tub to the microwave oven. As a result, technical innovators sometimes distrust any kind of intermediate testing.

The bottom line seems to be that we now have a set of methods to meet the needs of almost any developer, and total use is growing. The biggest addition has been the rollout, where the product is marketed; there is no "interruption just to test some more." Many firms will deny using market testing, but be active users of rollout.

At the time of entering any controlled sale or full sale market test, and at the national launch, many firms have adopted some of the thinking of space launches—using a launch control system to prepare them for unexpected, but possible, traumatic events. This is the topic of Chapter 21.

Applications

More questions from that interview with the company president.

1. "I am personally familiar with the United Airlines shuttle situation you mentioned, but I didn't know they rolled it out first to us frequent flyer types. That was very clever. Yet what happens when they grab a foothold with the frequent flyers and want to move to another group of flyers—do they have to change their advertising copy, all of their posters and signs in the shuttle area, and so forth? They all point clearly to frequent flyers."
2. "I get a kick out of how scientific market researchers can become, with their careful samples, balanced quotas, etc. But at a conference in California recently, a speaker was telling how Honda market-tested over 250 models of motorcycles in one Japanese city, in one year! Says they do it all the time. And there's a city in Japan where all the electronics firms test their TVs, compact disk players, etc. They introduce hundreds of models too. The electronic stores there look like supermarkets, with over a thousand items to choose from. How in the world could you defend that?"
3. "Several of our divisions have lately been using this so-called minimarket testing method. We had some shaving products use BehaviorScan, and a new upscale bandage line used a somewhat similar service from A. C. Nielsen. But I am increasingly concerned about the panel members in those test cities. My concern is not that the people become accustomed to the testing or that they overreact to stimuli. These are valid concerns, but there's not much I can do about them. I am concerned, however, that our people do not *know the effect* of these things on the data we get. How would the results of our tests be affected if people like the testing too much? Or if they tend to become professional test participants and begin thinking like judges?"

4. "About 10 years ago I was in the food specialties business, and I can recall a New Cookery line marketed by Nestle; it was greatly talked about at the time. Well, the line didn't work out in test market quite as well as expected. In fact, it was soon withdrawn with no plans announced for the future. Seems as though retailers complained the products in the new line were often priced higher than competitive products. Some said the items lacked a clear-cut reason for being because although advertised as low-calorie, the catsup product for example was only marginally lower in calories than Heinz and Del Monte catsups. Other comments were 'People here aren't thinking much about diet and health when they're shopping' and 'The concept was too esoteric and incomprehensible to the ordinary consumer.' Now, maybe the line was just a few years ahead of its time, but it came from a fine firm, and the advertising was by one of the biggest and most successful advertising agencies. Just how could such a disappointment have come about?"

Case: Square D Remote Lamp Dimmer[12]

In the late 1980s, the Consumer Products Division of the Square D Company had completed technical development of a new product designed for the home: a remote dimmer to use on table lamps. It used a fairly new technology for its time, but of course would now be well out of date. The product would soon join other consumer division products (particularly door chimes, weatherproof wiring devices, circuit breakers, and smoke detectors) for sale to the retail market.

The idea for the product had come originally from Ron Rogers, national sales manager of the division, and was based on his previous experience with motor speed controls and his having read a report on dimmer technology. The development had taken 14 months and cost less than $20,000. The product used a radio frequency that did not interfere with radios, TVs, or other household items. Its signal could penetrate house walls, with a 30-foot range. The remote unit had an on/off control as well as brightness-level control over lamp wattage. At the time of launch the unit would work only on upright lamps, but eventually they thought they could make the dimmer technology work for wall lamps and even ceiling lighting.

Ron decided that the U.S. market (the product's major potential at this time) consisted of 75 million households with an average of eight table lamps in each. That would indicate a potential sales volume of 75 to 600 million units. There was no direct competitor to the new dimmer, although wall-switch dimmers had been available for many years. It was not known whether there would be any patent protection, but the likelihood was not strong.

The product was primarily designed for use by a person returning home after dark. After entering the garage, a click on the Square-D Dimmer would turn on one or more lamps inside the house or apartment, so that the person never had to enter a totally dark

[12]This case was compiled from information provided by the firm.

area. It would also appeal to handicapped persons, who would use it from bed and going from room to room. As a third use, parents could use it to turn off or on a lamp in a child's room without disturbing sleep. And there were many more possible uses, such as to turn on a lamp in the basement or on an outdoor porch if a strange sound occurred.

The unit would come with four possible channels, A to D. Thus the user might buy one unit with the A channel to turn on a lamp in the kitchen or entry hallway, and a B channel unit for use inside the house to turn on lamps in some other room.

The lamp dimmer retail package consisted of two pieces heat-sealed inside a display hanger. The first piece was a small space-capsule-shaped control that screwed into the lamp; the bulb was then screwed into the unit so that the control piece was between the bulb and the lamp socket. The second product piece was the remote control, which was much like a small TV remote control unit. The product was priced to retail for $33.50, with better than average trade margins because retailers would be doing most of the promotion.

Square D was a large and prosperous firm in the industrial equipment arena, although the Consumer Products Division was much younger. The lamp dimmer product had not been use-tested in the home, although some engineers and company managers had used it in their homes. The principal market study to date was a survey of manufacturers' reps who endorsed the concept. This division sold through a national force of reps who called on such retail organizations as hardware stores, mass merchandisers, and department stores. Most marketing strategy was push oriented with a minimum of consumer advertising. They thought retailers would be willing to stock the item, put up in-store displays that encouraged potential buyers to pick up a unit and use it on a small lamp incorporated into the displays. They also hoped some retailers would give it some space in their weekly advertising if they allocated them an additional $2 promotional discount per unit bought. Granted, the technology was not exciting, and there were many more advanced electrical adjustment products on the market. But none of them did what this product would do, and none of them could offer something similar at the low price.

The issue for you is, how would you have recommended to Mr. Rogers that the product be market tested? Or would you have recommended no market testing? Please state your recommendation with supporting logic.

CHAPTER

21

Launch Management

Setting

Once the new product is ready to market, the long trek through the development process may appear to be ended. The people involved in the program are happy, satisfied, and anxious for a well-earned rest.

But the group was charged with launching a *winning* product. Just as managerial control over the *development process* was needed (checking actual progress against the plan and making adjustments where it appeared there would be trouble meeting the schedule), control over the *marketing of the new product* is needed. Launch management lasts until the new product has finished its assault on given objectives, which may take as long as six months to a year for an industrial good and commercial services or as little as a few weeks for some consumer packaged goods.

What We Mean by Launch Management

Comparing a NASA space capsule to a youngster's slingshot will explain the subject of this chapter. After firing at a crow in the upper branches of a tree, the youngster quickly panics and runs if the rock sails well over the crow and heads directly for the kitchen window of the neighbor's house. That's when the youngster would rather be in the NASA control headquarters in Houston, Texas, because NASA scientists launch *guided* space capsules, not *unguided* slingshot rocks. NASA would have anticipated that an in-flight directional problem *might* occur and thus would simply make an in-flight correction allowing the space capsule to continue its *controlled* flight. Not having in-flight corrective powers, the youngster simply runs.

This analogy isn't as farfetched as it may sound. It offers the new products manager a choice—NASA or a run for cover. Good tracking systems make successful launching of new products more likely. The manager who has to run for cover simply isn't a manager.[1]

Unfortunately, only a minority of firms systematically use new product launch management. Historically, the day of launch was thought to seal the fate of a new product. Prior to launch, management could pour overtime dollars into a project that was behind schedule, but there was no counterpart of overtime on the launch side.

That view is being rejected. If troubles are anticipated properly, and if contingency plans are thought out at least informally, then there is indeed time and opportunity to correct marketing troubles early—perhaps early enough to achieve original goals.

Apparently, most managements today are at least receptive to the concept of a guided launch; a few use such a system, some are experimenting with parts of systems, and the rest are watching what the others are doing.

The Launch Management System

A launch management system contains the following steps.

1. Spot potential problems. The first step in getting ready to play NASA on a new product launch is to identify all potential weak spots or potential troubles. These problems occur either in the firm's actions (such as poor advertising or poor manufacturing) or in the outside environment (such as competitive retaliation). As one manager said, "I look for things that will really hurt us if they happen, or don't happen."

2. Select those to control. Each potential problem is analyzed to determine its expected impact. Expected impact means we multiply the damage the event would cause by the likelihood of the event happening. The impact is used to rank the problems and to select those that will be controlled and those that won't.

3. Develop contingency plans for the control problems. Contingency plans are what, if anything, will be done if the difficulties actually occur. The degree of completeness in this planning varies, but the best contingency plans are ready for *immediate* action. For example, "We will up commission on the new item from 7 percent to 10 percent, by fax to all sales reps" is a contingency plan. It's ready to be put to work immediately. "We will undertake the development of a new sales compensation plan" is no contingency plan.

---

[1]People marketing new products are not the only ones using NASA-type systems today. Manufacturing quality control managers have the same difficulties in anticipating problems that might endanger product quality, watching to see if these problems are coming up, and being ready to do something if they do.

FIGURE 21–1

Graphic application of the general tracking concept (with remedial action)

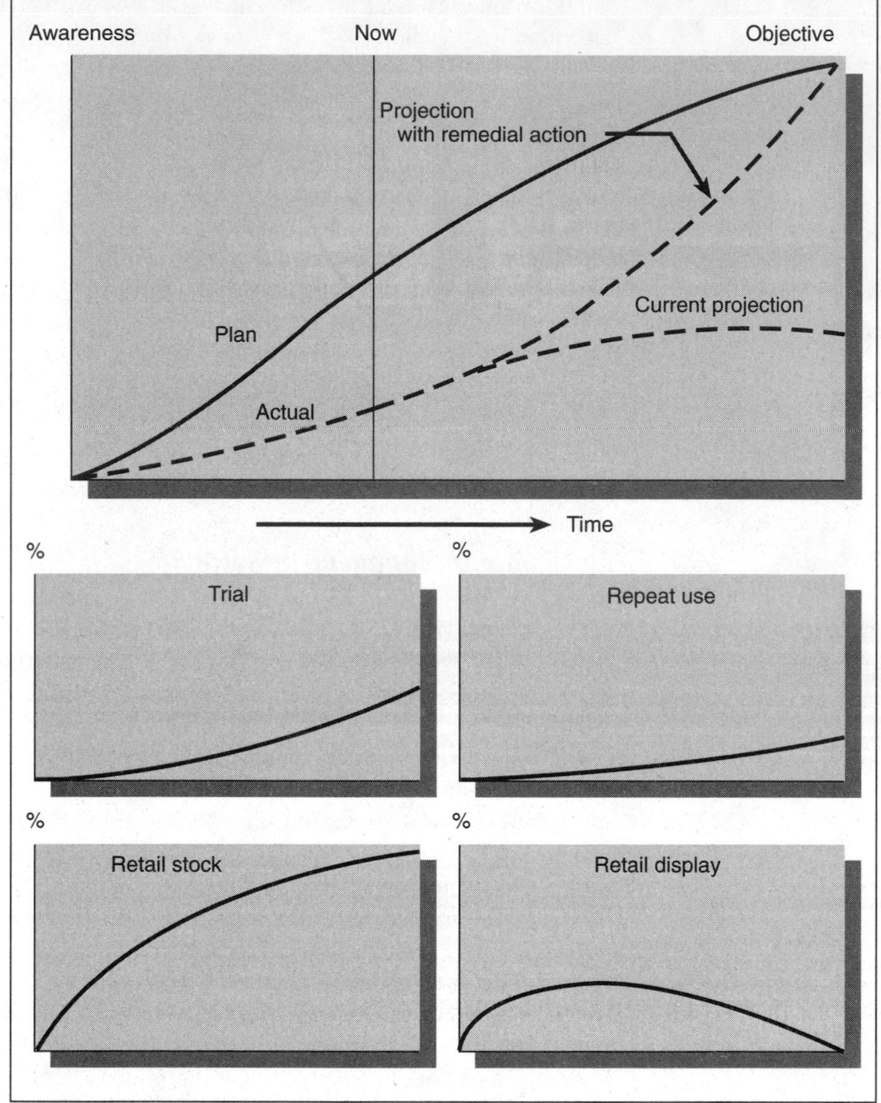

4. *Design the tracking system.* As with NASA, the *tracking system* must send back usable data fast. We must have some experience so we can evaluate the data. (Is our slow-down in technical service typical on big electronic devices like ours, or do we have a problem building?) There should be *trigger points* (for example, trial by 15 percent of our customers called on, by the end of the first month). These points (if not met) trigger the contingency plan. Without them, we just end up arguing. Remember, money to execute a contingency plan has to come from somewhere (someone else's budget), and

thus every plan faces opposition from people who want to delay implementing it.

If a problem cannot be tracked, no matter how important its impact may be, then we don't have it under control. For example, a competitor's decision to cut price by 35 percent is an act; it cannot be tracked like dealer stocking percentages can be. But we *can* have a contingency plan ready if it happens. This situation is not ideal because managerial control tries to anticipate a problem before it gets here; then we implement the remedial action in time to soften the negative effects. (See Figure 21–1.)

On the following pages, we will look in depth at each of these four steps in a launch management system.

Step One: Spot Potential Problems

Four techniques are used to develop the list of potential problems. First is the *situation analysis* made for the marketing planning step. For example, government lawyers may recently have criticized an ingredient used in the product. Or buyers may have indicated a high level of satisfaction with present products on the market, suggesting trouble in getting them to try our new one. The *problems* section in the marketing plan will have summarized most of the potential troubles from the situation analysis.

A second technique is to *role-play what competitors will do* after they have heard of the new product. Vigorous devil's advocate sessions can turn up scary options that competitors may exercise—they usually have more options than we think of at first glance.[2]

Third, we *look back over all of the data* accumulated in the new product's file. Start with the original concept test reports, then the screening forms, the early alpha testing, the rest of the use tests (especially the longer-term ones with potential customers), and records of all internal discussions. These sources contain lots of potential troubles, some of which we had to ignore in our efforts to move the item along.

For example, a food product had done well in all studies to date, except when the project leader ran a simulated test market (see Chapter 19). The sales forecast from the research firm came out very low. Study of the data indicated that consumers interviewed by the research firm had given a "trial" forecast of 5 percent, whereas the agency and the developer had been anticipating a trial of 15 percent. The difference was highly significant because success depended on which estimate was right. The developers believed *they* were right, so they stopped the STM tests and introduced the product. But they made trial the top-priority item on the problem list. Shortly after introduction, surveys showed that 15 percent was the better estimate, and the

---

[2]Some ways of anticipating competitive actions are given in Carolyn M. Vella and John J. McGonagle, Jr., "Shadowing Markets: A New Competitive Intelligence Technique," *Planning Review,* September–October 1987, pp. 36–38.

FIGURE 21–2

A-T-A-R launch control patterns (actual) for three pharmaceutical/nutritional products

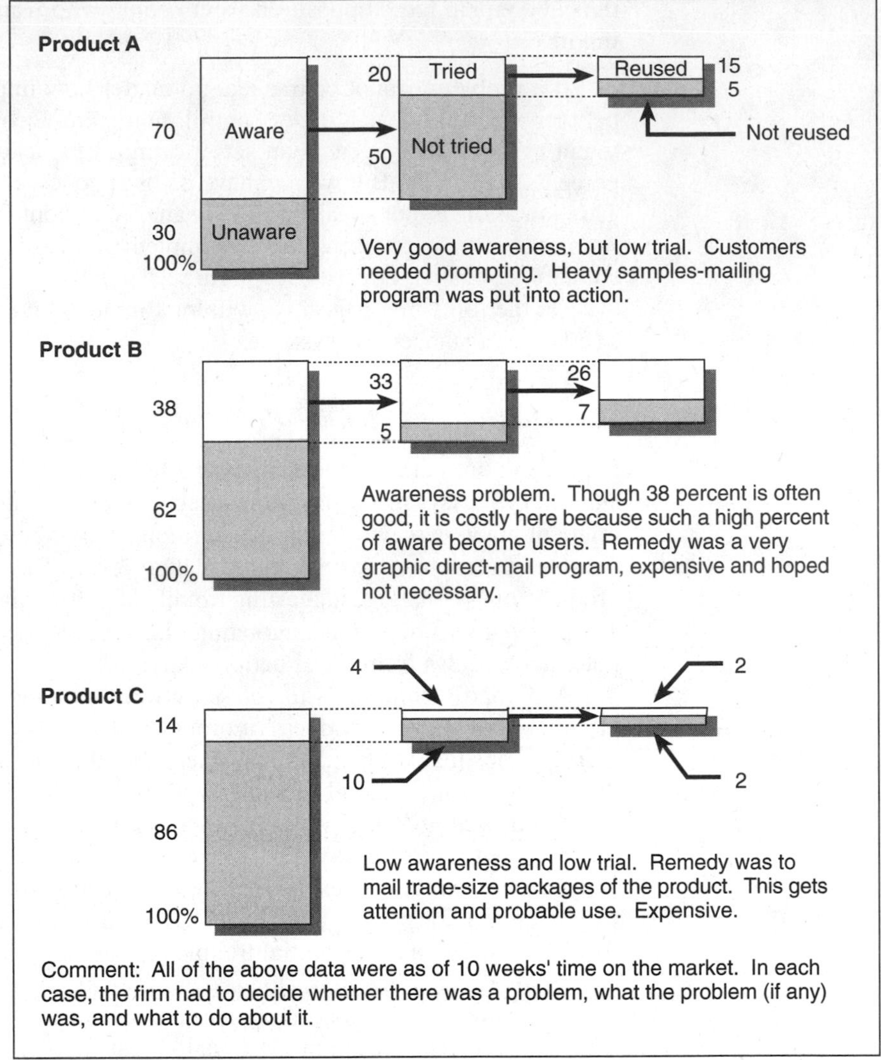

contingency plan was happily discarded. But they were ready if action had been warranted.[3]

Fourth, it is helpful to start with a satisfied customer or industrial user and work back from that satisfaction to determine the *hierarchy of effects* necessary to produce it. On consumer packaged goods, this hierarchy is the same one used earlier in the A-T-A-R model. Figure 21–2 shows that model when applied to the marketing of three ethical pharmaceutical and nutritional

[3]From the files of David W. Olson, Vice President of New Product Research at Chicago advertising agency Leo Burnett.

specialty items. Note each product had a different problem and required different remedial action (contingency plan). All three items were marketed by one firm in one year.[4]

But the hierarchy of effects will vary in other situations. Thus, for example, the satisfaction point for an industrial drill may be "known, provable, substantially lower output cost." But reaching that point requires the customer to measure actual costs. It also requires the customer to have data on what the drills cost previously. These are like rungs on a ladder—the customer cannot get to the top (satisfaction) without having stepped on the rungs of "know previous costs" and "know actual costs of the new drill." Both are potential problems, given that most firms do not have such sophisticated cost systems.

Later in this chapter (in Figure 21–7) you will see a sample launch management plan for a new industrial multimeter. There the five key potential problems were: salespeople will fail to call as requested, salespeople will fail to understand the product, potential customers do not order a trial instrument, buyers do not place quantity orders after the trial, and a competitor markets a similar item. All were potential "killers," and one of them did strike.

For another contrast, let's look at a new service. Peapod is an online grocery shopping service, used via computer, from the home. Introduced into the Chicago area in 1990, Peapod was concerned about the common claim that consumers would not pay extra for the convenience of shopping online. In their case, conventional wisdom was wrong, and in fact, consumers were willing to pay a $29.95 start-up fee, $4.95 monthly service fee, plus $6.95 and 5 percent of their grocery total per order! But the firm was ready.[5]

Another example concerned a consumer durable product—this time a combination of the sturdy mountain bike and the thin-framed nimbler racing bike. But Huffy, the maker, failed to anticipate one potential problem that became a $5 million mistake. Huffy chose to distribute the new bike through their regular channels (mass merchandisers and chain specialty shops like Toys "R" Us.) Unfortunately, the special hybrid bikes needed individual sales attention at the point of sale; such knowledgeable salespeople only work at bike specialty shops. A launch management system might have discovered this soon enough to permit necessary changes.[6]

Yet another example concerns the product you have met twice before in this book—the digital compact cassette machine (DCC) marketed by Philips Electronics. Their original launch of this product met with the following problems, all of which could have been anticipated and managed:

---

[4]Even in established markets (such as consumer packaged goods), the common measures vary. For example, a study in the United Kingdom cited three measures: number of first-time triers, their rates of repeat buying, and how their buying related to other brands in the market. See Dee M. Wellan and A. S. C. Ehrenberg, "A Successful New Brand: Shield," *Journal of the Market Research Society,* January 1988, pp. 35–44.

[5]Susan Chandler, The Grocery Cart in Your PC," *BusinessWeek,* September 11, 1995, pp. 63–64.

[6]"Flops," *BusinessWeek,* August 16, 1993, pp. 76–82.

- *Advertising:* Missed on the matter of product understanding—example: the ads used the acronym DCC without defining it.
- *Resellers:* Sent it out to all dealers, but in the relaunch marketed only to those dealers who supported the concept and were willing to invest their money in the educational effort it required.
- *Price:* Early models didn't sell, so they cut the price to move them out of the stores before the replacements arrived. Not being sure how much of a cut this would require, they cut too much—shelves were bare before the new ones came in, and dealers started sending back their stock of tapes.
- *Consumer attitudes:* Consumers love CD-ROMs, but they do not believe that tape can be as good. True or not, this belief was a potential disaster, and it worked against them.[7]

All of this is not to say the companies were wrong—all new products are a gamble, and we never have enough time and money to do the job "right." But the problems represent what we are looking for when we do our launch management—knowing what problem might happen, we can at least be on the lookout for it, and hopefully have something in place ready to go if it does happen.

Oddly, one problem usually overlooked is the possibility of being too successful. It's kind of a happy hurt, but it can be expensive and should be anticipated if there is any particular reason to think it might happen.[8]

Before leaving the matter of potential killer problems, don't forget that the firm has yet to prove it can do what it proposes to do—that is, produce and distribute a product that does what we claim it will. So launch management plans also contain problem items such as:

- Vendors fail to deliver the new fillibrator parts in the volume promised.
- The new conveyor lines will be stretched to their limit. The stress limits provided by suppliers may be in error, and/or our manufacturing workforce may misuse the technology.
- Samples of the new product are critical in this introduction, yet we have not proven our ability to package the small units needed.

These too are potential problems. Any one of them can cause the new item to fail, so we must manage our way through them too. Incidentally, this reinforces a key issue in new products management today: the development does not end when the item arrives at the shipping dock. It ends when enough, good quality product has performed satisfactorily in the hands of the end-user. The full team manages the launch management operation.

---

[7]Kyle Pope, "Philips Tries, Tries Again with Its DCC," *The Wall Street Journal,* October 3, 1994, p. B1.

[8]Joshua Hyatt gives examples of this problem, including one successful firm that barely avoided bankruptcy from a too successful launch, in "Too Hot to Handle," *Inc.,* March 1987, pp. 52–58.

Last, note that one item has not been mentioned—actual sales. We do not control sales and do not have tracking lines and contingency plans for low sales. It might seem we should, and most launch management plans put together by novices include sales. But stop to think. If the sales line is falling short of the forecast, what contingency plan should be ordered into action? Unless you know what is *causing* poor sales, you don't know what solution to use.

Instead, we use the above efforts to list the main reasons why sales may be low and then track *those reasons.* If we have anticipated properly, tracked properly, and instituted remedies properly, then sales will follow. Otherwise, when sales lag, we have to stop, undertake research to find out what is happening, plan a remedial action, prepare for it, and then implement it. By then, it's far too late. Contingency planning is a hedge bet; it is a gamble, like insurance. Most contingency planning is a waste, and we hope it all will be.

Step Two: Select the Control Events

No one can managerially control the scores of potential problems that come from the analysis in step one. So the planner's judgment must cut the list down to a number the firm can handle. (See Figure 21–3 for a graphic

FIGURE 21–3

Decision model for building launch control plan

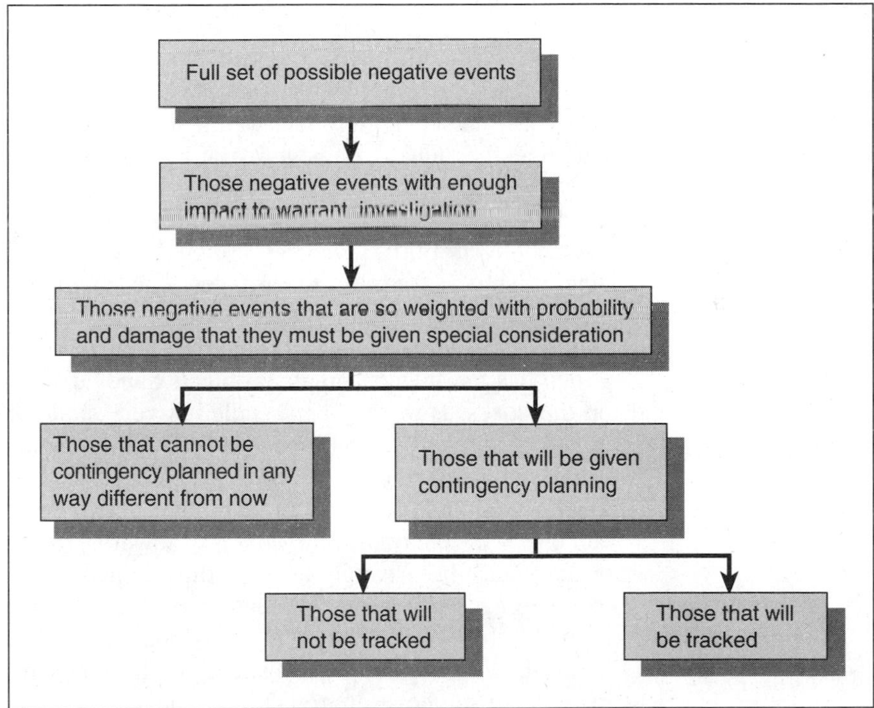

FIGURE 21–4

Expected effects matrix for selection of control events

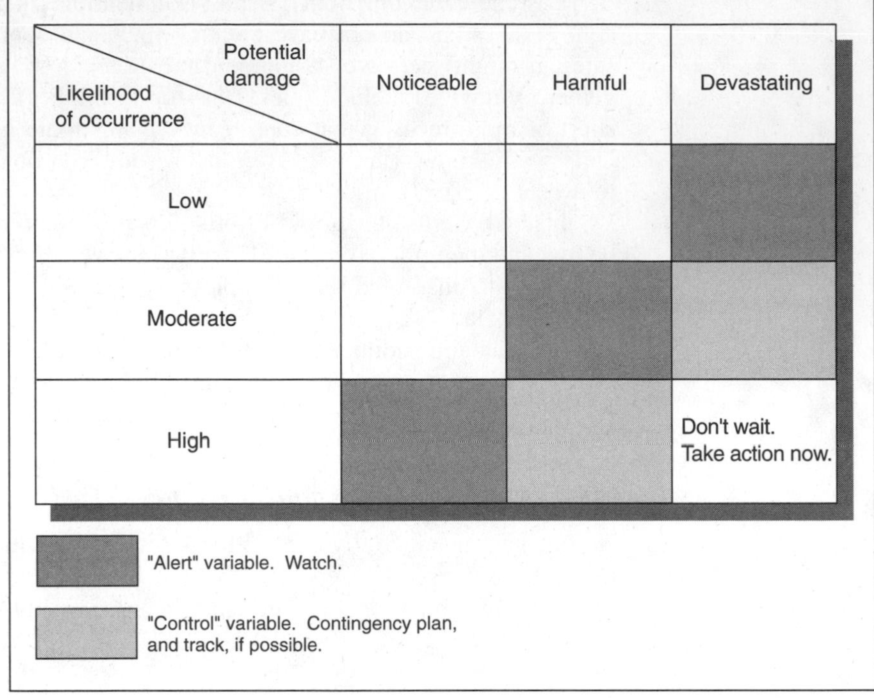

representation of what follows.) Some people say never more than six, but a new televised shaving product would surely warrant more contingency planning than the launch of a new line of jigsaw blades.

The judgment used to reduce the list of problems is usually based on the potential damage and the likelihood of occurrence. Figure 21–4 shows an **expected effects matrix,** indicating how the two factors combine to produce nine different categories of four types. Those with little harm and little probability can safely be ignored. Others farther down the diagram cannot be. At the bottom/right are problems that should be taken care of now; they shouldn't have gotten this far. In between are problems handled as suggested by the patterns on the boxes. How they are handled is very situational, depending on time pressure, money for contingencies, the firm's maturity in launch management, and the managers' personal preferences.

For example, most new product managers have been burned on previous launches and so have developed biases toward certain events. They may have been criticized so severely for forgetting something on a previous launch that they never forget it again. One new products manager recommended that the problems be sorted into two piles—potholes and sinkholes. Potholes are harmful, but sinkholes are disaster. Potholes rarely hurt us because we anticipate them; sinkholes are tough to anticipate.

Step Three: Develop Contingency Plans

Once we've reduced the problem list to a size the firm can handle, we have to ask: "If any of those events actually comes about, is there anything we can do?" For example, although competitive price cuts and competitive product imitation are on many lists, there is usually little the firm can do. The competitor will try to hold most of its share, and the developer is usually better off to ignore those actions and sell on the uniqueness of the new item.

For the other events, our planned reaction depends on the event. Let's take two different types: a company failure and a negative buyer action (consumer failure). The most common company failure is inadequate distribution, particularly at the retail or dealer level. Correcting the problem usually depends on how high a price the company is willing to pay.

Retailers sell the one thing they have—shelf space exposure to store traffic. Shelf space goes to the highest bidder, so if a new product comes up short, the remedy is to raise the bid—special promotions, more pull advertising, a better margin, and so on (see Chapter 18). These were rejected options when the marketing program was put together, so contingency planners usually have lots of alternatives from which to choose.

A consumer failure is handled the same way. To get awareness, the marketers' program called for particular actions (sales calls, advertising, and so on). If it turns out that awareness is low, we usually do more of the same action—increase sales calls or whatever. If people are not actually trying the new item, we have ways of encouraging trial (such as mailing samples or trade packages as in Figure 21–2, or giving out coupons).

Many product developers have marveled at how easy good contingency thinking is while preparing to launch, compared to doing it under the panic conditions of a beachhead disaster.

Step Four: Design the Tracking System

We now have a set of negative outcomes, for most of which we have standby contingency plans ready to go. The next step is developing a system that will tell us when to implement any of those contingency plans. The answer lies in the concept of tracking.

Tracking. The tracking concept in marketing has been around for a long time but probably got its greatest boost when Russia launched the Sputnik satellite. This launch led to the absorption of the rocketry lexicon into all leading languages. Though we had guided missiles for some time before that, they lacked the drama of a launch into outer space, especially with the spectacle of television.

The concept of tracking as applied to projectiles launched into space fits the new product launch well. There is a blast-off, a breakout of the projectile into an orbit or trajectory of its own, possible modification on that trajectory during flight, and so on. The launch controller is responsible for tracking the projectile against its planned trajectory and for making whatever corrections are necessary to ensure that it goes where it is supposed to go.

Applying this tracking concept to new products was as natural as could be. Earlier, Figure 21–1 showed the graphic application of the basic concept to a new product.

Three essentials are involved: first is the ability to lay the *planned trajectory.* What is the expected path? What is reasonable, given the competitive situation, the product's features, and the planned marketing efforts? Although it is easy to conjecture about such matters, setting useful trajectory paths requires a base of research that many firms do not have when they launch a new product.

The new product research department at Leo Burnett Company, a large advertising agency, studied all of the new product launches that the agency had participated in and plotted the actual awareness tracks and trial tracks.[9] From these scatter diagrams, the director of research computed generalized paths that could be applied to future new product situations (see Figure 21–5). A firm that lacks experience can sometimes acquire the data it needs from such outside sources as advertising agencies, marketing research firms, trade media, or industry pools.[10] Such ready-made options are important in these days of global marketing; fortunately, there is an increase of market research data and service organizations with international operations.

Second, there must be an *inflow of actual data* indicating progress against the plan. This means quick and continuing marketing research geared to measure the variables being tracked. As an illustrative example, a short list of the kinds of questions used by Leo Burnett Company when tracking a new product is provided in Figure 21–6.

Third, we have to *project the probable outcome* against the plan. Unless the outcome can be forecasted, we have little basis for triggering remedial action until the outcome is at hand. The key is speed—learning fast that a problem is coming about, early enough to do something that prevents it or solves it.

Selecting the Actual Tracking Variables. Now we hit perhaps the toughest part of launch management. How will we actually measure whether one of our key problems is coming about?

---

[9]David W. Olson, "Anticipating New Product Problems—A Planning Discipline," unpublished working paper. See also David W. Olson, "Postlaunch Evaluation for Consumer Goods," in M. Rosenau, A. Griffin, G. Castellion, and N. Anscheutz, eds., *The PDMA Handbook of New Product Development* (New York: Wiley, 1996), pp. 395–411.

[10]A source that may help some readers is Christopher J. Easingwood, "Early Product Life-Cycle Forms for Infrequently Purchased Major Products," *International Journal of Research in Marketing,* no. 1 (1987), pp. 3–9.

FIGURE 21–5

Advertising weight versus awareness created for selected products

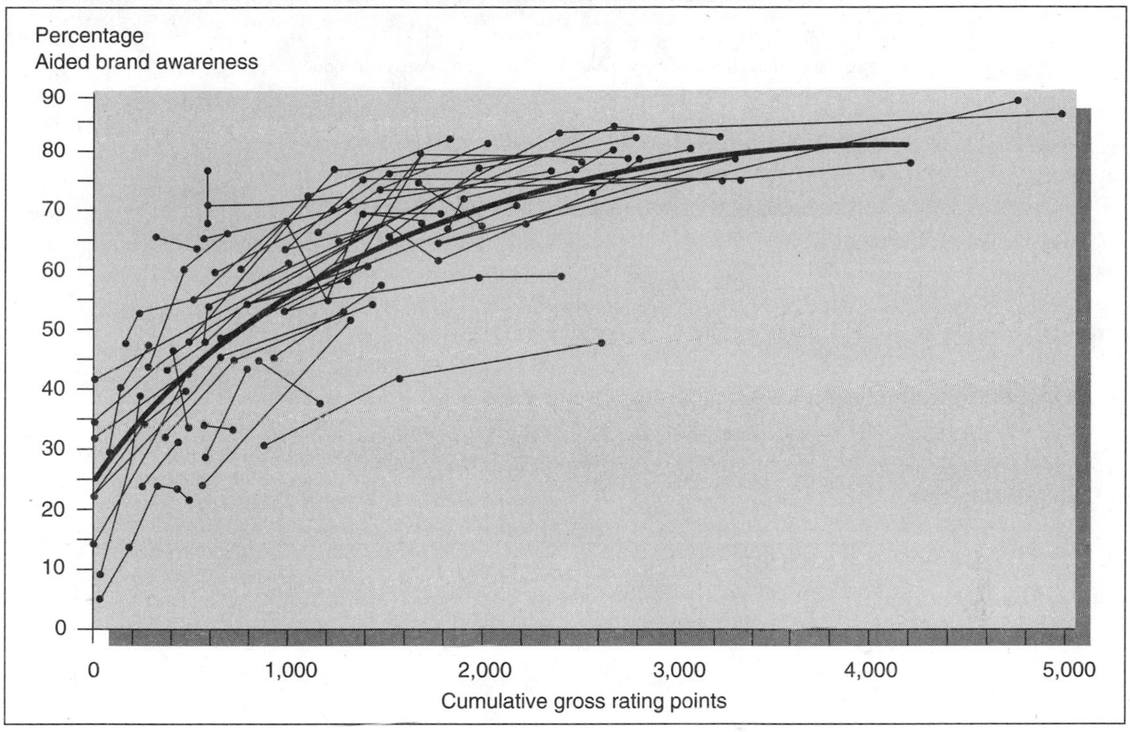

Source: David Olson, unpublished working paper, Leo Burnett Company.

If the problem is some specific step of action or mind, like awareness, then the answer is clear—find out how many people are aware of the new item. Trial is easy; repeat purchase is easy. What about trade support? Many new product marketers fear they will not get the push they need. But does trade support mean stocking the product? Displaying the product? Advertising the product locally? Giving presale service? Gearing up to give post-sale service? The launch planner has to decide.

We need relevant, measurable, and predictable tracking variables. A variable is *relevant* if it identifies the problem, *measurable* if we can get a statistic showing it is or isn't, and *predictable* if we know the path that the statistic should follow across the page.

Look back to Figure 21–1. The top graph displays awareness: "Have you heard of . . .?" It is a percentage of all people in the target market. The track line, labeled *plan,* shows what we *expect* to happen. The broken line shows what we find *is* happening, and what we fear *will* happen if we do nothing. The tracking variable is relevant, measurable, predictable.

Figure 21–6

Questions from a new product tracking study

Category Usage Questions
In the past six months, how many times have you bought (product category)?
What brands of (product category) have you ever heard of?
Have you ever heard of (brand)? (Ask for four to six brands)
Have you ever bought (brand)? (Ask for four to six brands)
About how many times have you bought (brand) in the past six months?

Advertising Awareness Questions
Do you recall seeing any advertising for (brand)? (Ask all brands respondent is aware of.)
Describe the advertising for (brand).
Where did you see the advertising for (brand)?

Purchase Questions
Have you ever bought (brand)?

If "Yes":
How many times have you bought (brand)?
How likely are you to buy (brand) again?
What did you like/dislike about (brand)?
What do you think of the price of (brand)?

If "No":
Did you look for (brand) in the store?
Why didn't you try (brand)?
How likely are you to try (brand) in the future?

Each response is interpreted by Leo Burnett Company according to standard guidelines or norms. For example, the repurchase likelihood is measured on a five-point scale, and a modified "top-two-boxes" score is used: 100% of the "Definitely's" + 50% of the "Probably's". For the price question, the norm is no more than 30% should say "fair" or "poor" value.

Source: Adapted from David W. Olson, "Postlaunch Evaluation for Consumer Goods," in M. Rosenau, A. Griffin, G. Castellion, and N. Anscheutz, eds., *The PDMA Handbook of New Product Development* (New York: Wiley, 1996), pp. 395–411.

But let's look at dealer support. At the bottom of Figure 21–1 is a track of retail stocking, the percentage of target dealers who have stocked the item so far. This too is relevant, measurable, and predictable (based on our past experience). But what about shelf space? The height of the stocking, the number of facings, and the department in which it occurs are all aspects of shelf space. They differ in relevance, they are all tough to measure without actually calling on stores and looking at the shelves, and we are apt to lack the experience we need to predict them. Figure 21–1 also shows retail display, but such a track is mainly a guess.

In addition, watch out for situations where even a fairly obvious variable may be tricky to define. Take awareness (perhaps the most common variable tracked), for example. In Chapter 18 we talked about the marketing program to achieve awareness, and how it can be the ability to recognize the brand name, knowledge of the product's positioning, or ability to recall the brand. Awareness is a state that leads to trial, and that varies across product classes.

There is no way to settle this argument, so most firms just arbitrarily pick a reasonably good definition that they can measure and use it every time.

Many developers shun launch management because of problems in finding good tracking variables. If they can't easily measure the emergence of a problem early on, the whole idea of controlling the way to success makes a lot less sense.

Selecting the Trigger Points. Given that we have found useful variables for warning that a problem is coming about, the last step is deciding in advance how bad it has to be before turning the contingency plan loose. Say, for example, we have a low budget situation and are worried that customers may not hear of our new item—low awareness. If our objective for three months out is 40 percent of customers aware, and tracking shows we actually have only 35 percent, should we release the standby direct-mail program?

This is not an easy decision to make under beachhead conditions, for political reasons as well as for time constraints. Throwing the switch for direct mail admits that the original advertising has failed. This admission is not popular, and arguments will be made that the advertising is working as planned and the awareness will soon increase.

To avoid these no-win situations, agree in advance what level will be the trigger and put the triggering decision in the hands of a person with no vested interest. With this, the tracking plan is complete. With diligent implementation, the launch will probably be controlled to success.

Nontrackable Problems. What do we do when we have a problem that worries us but cannot be tracked because we can't find a variable for it, or because we don't have a track that the variable should follow, or because there is nothing we can do if the problem is found to be coming about? The answer is, very little.

Typically, management watches sales, and if they are falling below the forecast, someone is asked to find out why. This means interviewing salespeople, customers, distributors, and so on. It's a difficult inquiry because things are changing so fast and because most participants have vested interests—they may not reveal the true problem even if they know it.

When the cause is found, a remedy is devised. If it's not a fast-moving market, time may be available to get the new product back into a good sales pattern. If it's too late, the new item is dumped or milked for a while. The loss may be very little if the costs of launch were low, as they often are for small firms, for line extensions, and for products that were never expected to amount to much.

A Sample Launch Management Plan

Figure 21–7 shows a sample launch management plan. In it are samples of real-life problems, specific variables that were selected to track them, trigger points, and the standby contingency plans ready to go into effect. Note

FIGURE 21–7

Sample launch management plan

Setting: This launch control plan is for a small or medium-sized industrial firm that is marketing a unique electrical measuring instrument. The device must be sold to the general-purpose (i.e., factory) market, whereas past company products have been sold primarily to the scientific R&D market. The firm has about 60 salespeople, but its resources are not large. No syndicated (e.g., audit firm) services are available in this market.

Only a few parts of the marketing plan are presented here, but the control plan does contain the total set of control problems, a plan to measure those that could be measured, and what the firm planned to do if each problem actually occurred.

Potential Problem	*Tracking*	*Contingency Plan*
1. Salespeople fail to contact general-purpose market at prescribed rate.	Track weekly call reports. The plan calls for at least 10 general-purpose calls per week per rep.	If activity falls below this level for three weeks running, a remedial program of one-day district sales meetings will be held.
2. Salespeople may fail to understand how the new feature of the product relates to product usage in the general-purpose market.	Tracking will be done by having sales manager call one rep each day. Entire sales force will be covered in two months.	Clarification will be given to individual reps on the spot, but if first 10 calls suggest a widespread problem, special teleconference calls will be arranged to repeat the story to the whole sales force.
3. Potential customers are not making trial purchases of the product.	Tracking by instituting a series of 10 follow-up telephone calls a week to prospects who have received sales presentations. There must be 25 percent agreement on product's main feature and trial orders from 30 percent of those prospects who agree on the feature.	Remedial plan provides for special follow-up telephone sales calls to all prospects by reps, offering a 50 percent discount on all first-time purchases.
4. Buyers make trial purchase but do not place quantity reorders.	Track another series of telephone survey calls, this time to those who placed an initial order. Sales forecast based on 50 percent of trial buyers reordering at least 10 more units within six months.	No remedial plan for now. If customer does not rebuy, there is some problem in product use. Since product is clearly better, we must know the nature of the misuse. Field calls on key accounts will be used to determine that problem, and appropriate action will follow.
5. Chief competitor may have the same new feature (for which we have no patent) ready to go and markets it.	This situation is essentially untrackable. Inquiry among our suppliers and media will help us learn quicker.	Remedial plan is to pull out all stops on promotion for 60 days. A make-or-break program. Full field selling on new item only, plus a 50 percent first-order discount and two special mailings. The other trackings listed above will be monitored even more closely.

particularly that this was not a large firm, it had no market research department, and it was not then sophisticated in how to launch new products. Still, the plan covers the main bases, puts launch management into the hands of available managers, and provides effective action if any of the possible problems come about.

Larger firms with big budgets will have more sophisticated plans, but in principle they will be exactly the same—problem, tracking variable, trigger point, and remedial plan ready to go. Very small firms may have the energy to deal with only a couple of problems; the manager may use what we call eyeball control to move around the market and find if they are coming about, and then have in mind what will be done if they are.

But whether in the mind, in the format of Figure 21–7, or in a sophisticated formal plan, the essentials are the same.

Objections to Launch Management

Every manager has heard of contingency planning and uses a lot of it. But on new products? Here they often draw the line. Some say it takes too much time and costs too much because of the market research and the unused contingency marketing materials. Life insurance is wasteful too, if you don't die!

But their occasional concern that "We can't forecast what all of our troubles may be" is a stronger issue. New products are risky, and we are trying to change buyers' behavior. Competitors are never idle. Proponents readily admit these things, but they answer that it is also costly to turn on a dime, crisis management can be frightful, and we should strive harder to do our jobs right the first time. A crisis seldom offers the time required to develop sound plans.

A trickier objection is that contingency planning can destroy morale, having people stop right in the midst of launch planning to talk about what can go wrong. This relates to management style, and is strictly a personal preference. Same thing when they don't want new product managers doing "escape clause" thinking. Or having to lay out plans for cutting budgets in case of sales disappointments. This can actually upset a team that has been working cohesively for some time because the cutbacks will not fall evenly.

No Launch Management on Temporary Products

Some products unintentionally live short lives. Occasionally, however, products are marketed that the managers know from the start will be on the market only a short time. Such products include fad products, temporary fillers of a hole in a product line, products keyed to a market participant's special needs, and occasional products. One producer of *occasional* products is Baskin-Robbins, which has a standing set of flavors always available and another stable of flavors that move into and out of the line.

Temporary products have much less need for launch management, mainly because there is nothing that can be done—everything is committed. Advertising and personal selling monies are needed to load up distributor/retailers (no out-of-stocks can be allowed because they represent permanently lost sales) and to build immediate sales. Sales promotion works only on awareness and trial. There are no follow-on products scheduled, production is contracted out if possible, inventories are moved out, and production runs are matched to the reorder rate. No long-term service facilities are built, prices are held steady (or at the most, reduced), and most effort after announcement is put into market intelligence needed to know when sales are leveling and heading down. By the time any launch problems are identified, the time to solve them is past.

Product Failure

Despite everyone's best efforts, products do sometimes fail or appear to be failing. As Figure 21–8 shows, this can occur for a number of reasons, not all of which are controllable by the firm. When the product appears to be in decline, the firm first thinks of how additional money can best be spent, and

FIGURE 21–8

Reasons for product discontinuation

Reason	*Examples*
Technology advances lead to product obsolescence.	386 chip replaced by 486; 486 chip by Pentium
New generation product cannibalizes demand for current product.	Windows 3.1 replaced by Windows 95; Windows 95 by Windows 98
Users prefer or demand alternative solutions.	Slide rule, 8-track tape player
Profit margins shrink due to greater competition or operational cost increases.	New car sales
Product category does not fit the firm's strategic focus.	Sears spun off Allstate; Coca-Cola spun off Columbia Pictures
Product category does not fit other company product categories or groups.	Kraft Foods sold Entenmann's Bakeries; General Mills sold Olive Garden
Key components are no longer available through suppliers.	Raw paper and lumber supplies
Product is too difficult to support, due to unique or complex technologies involved.	AT&T withdrew from PC business
Increased global competition.	Airlines, microwaves, televisions
Product presents a toxic or hazardous situation.	Ford Pinto, breast implants
Funds are reallocated to other new product opportunities.	New Coke, consolidation of new car models by Jaguar Motor Cars

Source: Patricia A. Katzfey, "Product Discontinuation," in M. Rosenau, A. Griffin, G. Castellion, and N. Anscheutz, eds., *The PDMA Handbook of New Product Development* (New York: Wiley, 1996), pp. 413–25.

strategy is reviewed. Of course, time permitting, the product can be changed or stand-by add-ons can be sent to market while longer-term changes are made. If the market situation is particularly difficult and solutions lie only in longer-time product changes, it may be necessary to pull the product temporarily, or, at best, stop all promotion and hold the market in a freeze until the problem solution has been found. If things in the development area don't move along successfully fast, it is usually necessary to abandon the product; that is, to abandon the market opportunity. Most firms have many new product options and like to get their losers out of sight and out of mind. The politics are bad, people are scurrying to escape the sinking ship, critics are reminding everyone how they predicted this trouble, and so on. Of course, if new plants were built, if major promotional programs were undertaken, or in any other way major financial commitments were made, then there will be efforts to hold on—at least until there has been time to put through a relaunch.

If a product or product line is discontinued, it may still hold revenue opportunities. It can be sold to another firm outright. Alternatively, the firm can sell the rights to the product or its brand name, its formulation or blueprints, its manufacturing process, its distribution channel, its technology or core subassemblies, or the whole business unit.[11] These opportunities should be explored if feasible.

If **abandonment** is necessary, the manager's job is not finished. A lot of people need to be notified (including customers, governments, distributors, and trade groups). If persons or firms have become dependent on the product, it may be necessary to have a gradual stock-reduction program, a stockpiling of parts, and to offer a period of repair service. The cost, and required time duration, of this after-the-fact support needs to be estimated.

Summary

This chapter brings us to the point where we introduce the product. We have the product, we have the marketing program for it, and we are prepared to control its way to success.

The requirements of launch management are a plan, measurement of progress in the market, analysis of events to determine if prearranged contingency actions should be put into play, and continuing study to ensure that any problem becomes known as soon as possible so action can be taken to avert or at least ameliorate it.

Launch management and tracking are especially tough because most of the activity is out in the marketplace, variables will change, and measurements

[11]Patricia A. Katzfey, "Product Discontinuation," in M. Rosenau, A. Griffin, G. Castellion, and N. Anscheutz, eds., *The PDMA Handbook of New Product Development* (New York: Wiley, 1996), pp. 413–25.

are difficult and expensive (not like walking through the factory in the eyeball control method). But the methodology is available, and when the situation warrants this effort, a new products manager can certainly gain from it.

We can now turn our attention to a topic ever-present in new product work. Are there public policy issues involved in the new product's manufacture, distribution, use, or disposal? Are there ethical issues involved? What the developer thinks is, of course, not the point. But what does the public think? What do government people think? This issue is the subject of Chapter 22.

Applications

More questions from that interview with the company president.

1. "Thanks for telling me about that launch management idea you were studying. But look, I'm a bit mixed up on one thing. You mentioned (1) critical events, (2) control events, and (3) tracking variables. You say you have to list all three things? Isn't one event likely to be on all three lists? For example, take awareness of the new product's key determinant attribute. Not getting it is a critical event, selecting it for control makes it a control event, and tracking it makes it a tracking variable. Right? Help!"
2. "I've had occasion several times over the past year to see a new product land in trouble—great expectations and terrible sales. And the saddest part is that so many people try so hard to deny the inevitable—the product has bombed, and the quicker one gets away from it the better. Otherwise, it's just sending good money after bad. In fact, I'm going to make a speech to that effect at our next general executive meeting, and you could do me a favor. Would you please develop a list of all possible reasons why someone might want to string a loser along? That would help me be sure I've answered all of the objections before I give the speech."
3. "Don't get me wrong—I believe in contingency planning and in what you call launch management. If you have anticipated a problem and have an action planned in case it comes up, I'll buy going ahead, at least for now. But a lot of companies don't necessarily agree with me. I recall one time when one of the big electronics firms was in quite a dispute with its dealers over whether a new device they had launched would catch on. It might have been RCA and that Selectravision compact disk they developed. Anyhow, the dealers said no way. The company insisted it just takes longer on innovations like theirs. They wouldn't have had that argument if they had done their contingency planning, right? They would have had standby plans ready to go. Tell me, if a new product team neglects to do contingency planning and then hits trouble, what can they do then

to get a handle on the problem as soon as possible? (Preferably before someone like me tells them to pull the plug.)"

4. "If I remember right, the whole idea of launch management depends partially on having a track or plan that each variable should follow if everything is going OK. I believe you showed me some figures with those plan lines on them. But it seems to me those plan lines are just pure conjecture, at least in the case of really new products. For example, one time I was reading about Arco Solar Inc. (a division of Atlantic Richfield). It had a solar-powered plate that could be set on a car's dashboard and feed power to the car's battery. That power was to make up for the natural self-discharge of a battery, the drain from electric clocks, and so on. Now, how in the world would they know what the normal path of awareness or trial would be? Are they unable to use launch management? Lots of our divisions are developing really new things like that."

Case: Interfoods, Inc.: Valley Butter[12]

Interfoods, Inc., was a large international food company headquartered in Paris whose Colombian subsidiary was about to introduce a new butter product called Valley Butter. There were doubts about this introduction, so the product manager, Carlos Minago, wanted to be sure the launch went well.

Interfoods began its Colombian operation by acquiring a Bogota firm that had, among other products, a line of nonbutter products. These included a nonrefrigerated margarine called Planet, which sold nationally with around 80 percent of that market, and a refrigerated margarine called Dairy Planet, which was distributed only in the major cities (because of the need for refrigeration) and had a 90 percent market share. Planet made little money and was no longer being actively promoted. Dairy Planet was very profitable. The total spread market was about $4 million at the factory and at this time was divided 50 percent to butter, 30 percent to refrigerated margarine, and 20 percent to nonrefrigerated.

Moreover, that 50 percent share for butter had been achieved within the past three years, and almost all went to the Ahoy brand. Butter had previously been a very expensive import, but the Ahoy firm produced it locally and was rapidly gaining sales from Dairy Planet. Its price was now only about 30 cents against Dairy Planet's price of 19 cents.

The Valley Butter project had been under way for about a year and a half, although corporate management in Paris wasn't enthusiastic about it. They wanted the market to stay with margarines, where Interfoods dominated, and they didn't really think the Colombian Interfoods people knew much about butter.

General knowledge was that taste was the big thing in butter and that taste had been winning Dairy Planet customers to Ahoy. So Valley Butter was supposed to taste better than Ahoy—and it did (though it took six versions; the previous five had flopped when tasted by employees). The most recent in-home, blind, paired-comparison use test showed

[12]The situation of this case has been disguised.

Valley was preferred by a statistically significant 55 percent to 45 percent. To get this preference, the cost was unfortunately increased to the point that Valley would not be as profitable as new brands were supposed to be.

No test market would be undertaken because the butter market was essentially the three cities of Bogota, Medellin, and Cali. Colombia as yet had no research firms offering simulated test markets or scanner market testing. The strategy was to use fairly heavy advertising backed by four consumer promotions (two pricepacks deals and two premium offers printed on the wrappers) to force trial. The advertising would be a three-month saturation drive on TV stations and in movie houses, plus radio and newspapers. The total budget for Valley advertising would be more than Ahoy had been spending but less than the firm would normally spend because of the higher product cost and the firm's basic desire for the market to stay with margarines.

The sales forecast called for a 10 percent market share after one year, but management made it plain they expected much more than that soon thereafter or it wasn't worth the effort. The target consumers were the top economic class—about 10 percent of all people in the leading cities.

The product was positioned as the "better-tasting butter," and the copy strategy was simply to communicate the positioning. Valley was chosen as the name because it connoted delicious-tasting butter and an image of quality. It came from a list prepared by the ad agency and was selected by consumers as easily remembered and pronounced and connoting a high-quality butter. The packaging would also be expensive (foil wrapper versus Ahoy's plastic wrap). A consumer packaging test confirmed that the package communicated a quality image. The price was to be the same as Ahoy's. Colombian Interfoods had a national sales force of about 55 people, but Valley would be handled only by the special 10-person sales force created just to sell Dairy Planet in the major cities. The sell-in by this smaller group would begin about two weeks ahead of advertising break.

It was company policy to have launch management plans, so Carlos now had the job of preparing a list of potential problems, narrowing them down to the ones he had to do something about, and then planning how he would track them and what he would do if any of them occurred.

CHAPTER

22

PUBLIC POLICY ISSUES

Setting

Throughout the past 21 chapters, we have dealt with the various problems of developing and launching a new product. To simplify matters, we have deferred until now some major questions of public policy. They concern the relationship between the firm (people, product, whatever) and the citizenry. In every country on earth, there are ways in which the new product function is limited or directed. Usually for very good reason. So managers need to understand the rules, and they need to understand the edges of the law where issues are usually under movement or unclear.

Chapter 22 gives the life cycle of a public concern, the attitudes of business regarding product innovation and public policy, and deals with the most critical of the concerns—product liability. It then goes into the other concerns, such as environment and some related managerial issues

Bigger Picture: A Cycle of Concerns

All public pressure situations go through a life cycle of the following phases (see Figure 22–1).

Phase I: Stirring

Individuals begin to sound off long before enough people have been injured or irritated to cause a general reaction. Letters to company presidents, complaints in newspaper articles, letters to political representatives, and tentative expressions of concern by knowledgeable authorities are typical of phase I.

FIGURE 22–1
Life cycle of a public concern

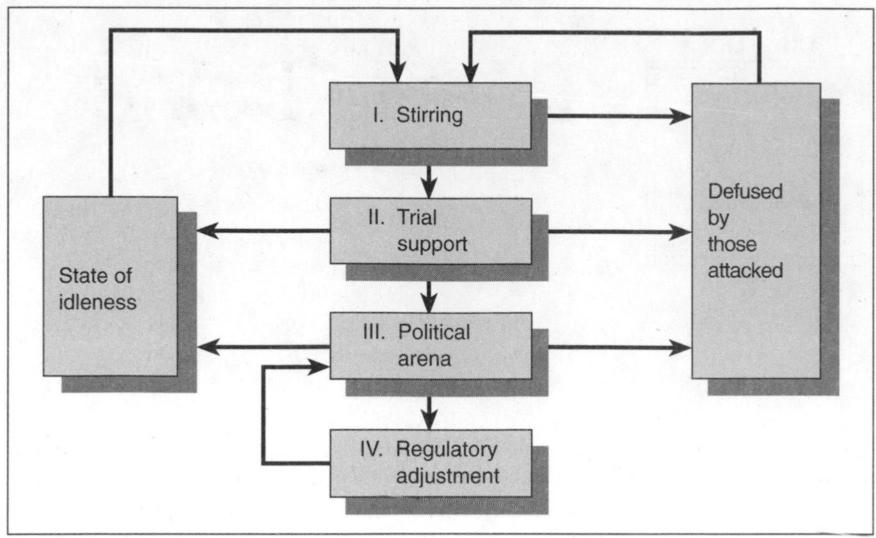

Most people ignore these periods, but they are easy to identify, looking back. Consequently, the stirring phase may last a long time—decades, in fact.

The problem for new products managers is that they don't know what will happen. Will the stirring flare up, or die away?

Phase II: Trial Support

As the stirrings over an issue increase, a champion may decide to take it on as a cause. Such champions used to be individuals, and were often unknown, as Ralph Nader was when he tackled auto safety. Today, cause support tends to come from organizations, whose leaders attempt to marry the basic unrest in a situation with a desire for contribution and publicity. As an example, makers of wood preservatives (some of which are very toxic) need to watch the stirrings of the National Coalition Against the Misuse of Pesticides, which is calling for the end of wooden utility poles, one of the biggest applications for wood preservative products.[1] The key question to these organizations often is "How widespread is the unpublicized unrest?" Or, "How dramatic can the headlines be made?" This may sound crass, but remember there are scores of budding issues at any time, and an organization may lose its power if it squanders its scarce resources on issues that die out.

In phase II, a complex set of loosely affiliated parties may emerge over time. In July 1996, *USA Today* reported the danger of seating children under 13 directly in front of a car air bag. At the time, automakers, regulators,

[1]Anonymous, "Utility Poles Cited as Chemical Danger," *The New York Times,* February 5, 1997, Page A-15.

insurers, and consumer advocacy groups (who had pushed for air bags) all shared responsibility for the fact parents were not warned of this danger. By 1998, however, parents who had lost children through such accidents were teaming with the consumer advocacy groups to take the automakers to court—something the advocacy groups have much experience in.[2]

In any event, phase II is a period when the would-be leader and the muted cause are on the stump, seeking a political base. If achieved, the action moves to phase III unless the industry under attack can defuse the situation or the cause fails to capture broad support.

Phase III: The Political Arena

By the time an issue has acquired a political base among the voting public, the opportunity for defusing has usually passed. Now, companies must gird up for political battle in state and/or federal legislatures or in the various regulatory arenas. The issue is the content of new laws or regulations, and companies usually recognize the widespread consumer demands and are only trying to achieve the least costly and least restrictive mode of meeting them. Occasionally, companies fight vigorously against settlement. The cereal industry did, and won on several dimensions. However, the political base is usually all the cause leader needs to force some modification in a practice, one severe enough to require legislation or a court ruling.

Phase IV: Regulatory Adjustment

New regulatory legislation is rarely precise, and this imprecision leads to a period of jockeying by the adversaries over its interpretation. The Consumer Product Safety Act, for example, directed the **Consumer Product Safety Commission** to order the seizure of any "imminently hazardous consumer products," four terms each impossible to define. Imprecision may well be a necessary, or even wise, approach in regulation. The phase often lasts for years, and sometimes general shifts in a country's political thinking cause various issues to move into or out of the idle state, a point dramatically underscored by the sharp decline in product-related political controversies in the Reagan and Bush administrations.

Business Attitudes toward Product Issues

Business firms deal with public policy issues on a much broader base than just new products. So they have reached a structure of beliefs on this matter of interface between business and society. Most of those beliefs support product innovation, and society agrees. Granted, there are some issues that we

[2]Jayne O'Donnell, "Child-Death Cases Say Automakers Failed to Act," *USA Today,* July 13, 1998, p. 3B.

haven't yet figured out. For example, how do we pay the costs of product misuse where the consumer was unable to read and understand labels? What is the responsibility of a food company whose customers want great taste but whose government wants quality nutrition? In general, most of the headlines today are for problems that came up years ago, and our concerns are "at the margin," that is, dealing in areas of temporary uncertainty and change.

For example, at the turn of the millennium, people are honestly confused on how we address the problem of pornography on Internet. Ten years from now we will have decided.

The new product that causes unexpected concern on the public policy front is probably the result of careless management. Note, *unexpected.* A lot of our problems we expect, and in most cases have methods to avoid them or hedge bets, or prepare to deal with them. Of course, no manager can walk through the minefield shown in Figure 22–2 without occasionally tripping up.

Current Problem Areas

New products managers face many specific problem areas as they attempt to deal with social and legal pressures—product liability is the most complex, and at the moment the most frustrating, partly because of the seriousness of the potential suits and the costs of error.

These issues are worldwide, though our discussion will mainly use American examples. Members of the European Union are still wrestling with the product liability question because of their 1985 commitment to strict liability. Although going slower than it was supposed to, the directive will apparently be implemented. Germany is a world leader in environment. China has only recently instituted a product liability law, while many other nations in the world have yet to face even this issue.

Product Liability

The scenario here is simple: You buy a product and are injured. The injury may have come when you carried the product home, when you opened it, when you stored it, when you used it, when you tried to repair it, or when you disposed of it. If you were injured and if you think the maker or the reseller of the product did (or didn't do) something that caused the injury, then you have a product liability claim. If guilty, the accused party is liable for the cost and the pain of the injury, plus punitive (punishing) damages as well.

Historically, **product liability** applied to goods, not services, and there have been many lost attempts to extend the law to cover services. Yet services are products (both in fact and as we use the terms in this book); they are sold and bought in good faith, injuries do occur, and some redress should be possible. For example, an engineering consulting firm gave an opinion that a building was in good shape; the buyer later found this untrue when an injury took place. Negligence on services can produce a product liability case.

FIGURE 22–2

The "battle" as viewed by a new products manager

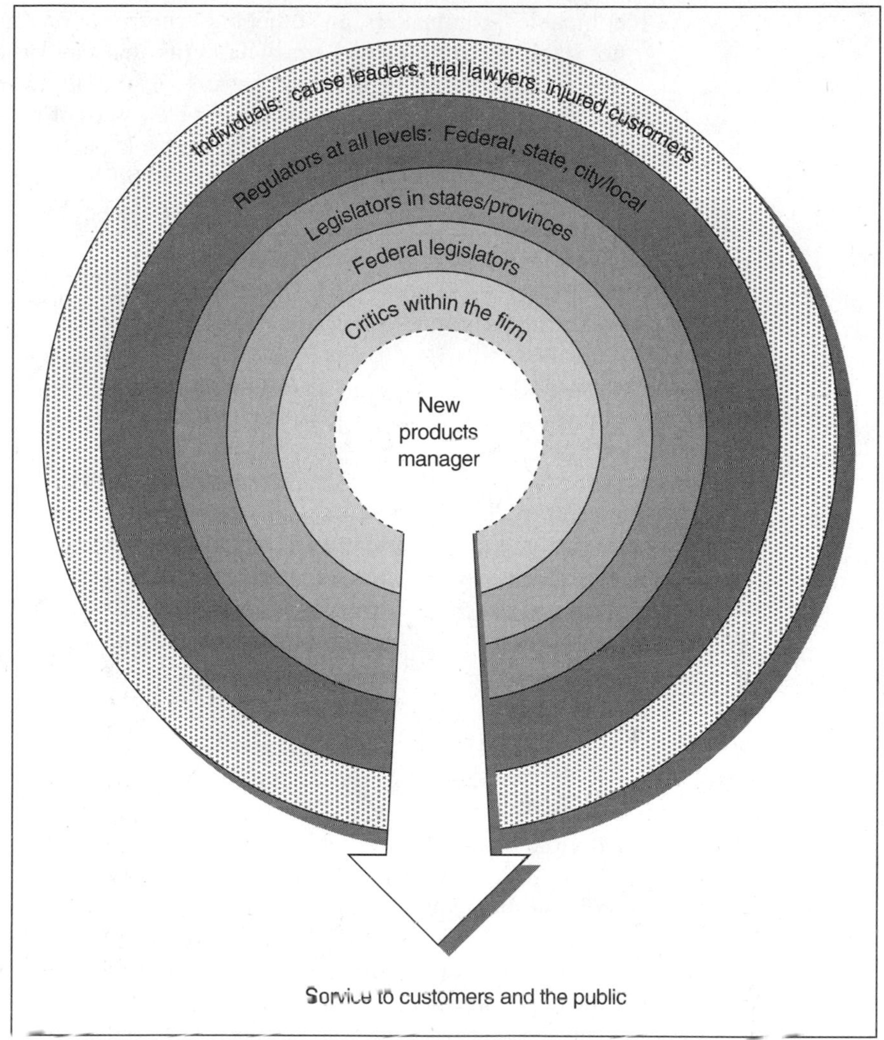

How important is product liability? Most suits are settled out of court so we don't have good dollar data. Many billions of dollars are at stake (though suits are not as common as the press on asbestos, breast implants, and cars make it appear), and as a result, it can get complicated.[3] For years, chemical

[3]Two authors who have tried to straighten out the misunderstandings are Gregory B. Rogers, "Factors Contributing to Compensatory Damage Awards in Product Liability Cases Involving Personal Injury," *Journal of Products Liability,* 1991, pp. 19–29; and Frances E. Zollers, "Labels, Tables, and Fables: A User's Guide to Product Liability Studies," *Journal of Products Liability,* 1991, pp. 1–17.

companies, automakers, and other big firms have sought federal laws on product liability, to limit the size of lawsuits that can be brought for allegedly defective products. In 1998, supporters of the bill felt the need to slim down certain parts of it, in order to increase the chances of its passing by the Clinton administration. The parts that were stripped out included caps on punitive damages and an end to "joint and several liability," which often results in multiple defendants winning huge judgments against big companies. As a result, many of the biggest firms began lobbying against the very legislation they had been pushing for (ironically siding in with trial lawyers and consumer groups in the process), while at the same time smaller firms were still supportive of it.[4]

Typology of Injury Sources

Here is a list of the ways we get into trouble, and most of them are double trouble on *new* products.

1. Many products have *inherent risks.* For example, blood transfusion carries the risk of hepatitis infection, and dynamite will explode. Because the risk cannot be avoided, we get more understanding in the courts.

2. *Design defects* can cause the manufacture of an unsafe product in three different ways. First, the design may create a *dangerous condition,* say a steam vaporizer whose center of gravity is so high that the unit is likely to spill. Second, an essential *safety device* may be absent. For example, a hair dryer may lack an overheat cutoff switch. Third, the design may call for *inadequate materials,* which perform their function at first but may eventually deteriorate and become dangerous.

3. *Defects in manufacture* have perhaps always been a new products problem. Inadequate quality techniques may result in defective units even if the product is well designed. Poorly welded ladders are an example.

4. The manufacturer may produce an acceptable product but *fail to provide adequate instructions for use or warnings against particular uses.* If used improperly, the power mower is a potentially dangerous device. The instructions should tell the user how to use it *and* how not to use it. But courts are much more interested in how strong the warnings are against misuse (even unforeseeable misuse). Thus, Sears and several other suppliers had to pay $4.8 million to a Corpus Christi, Texas, man who was burned when fumes from a barbecue grill being used *indoors,* exploded. A half-dozen warnings were in the literature, but the plaintiff's attorney charged that the warnings should have been written in larger letters.[5]

---

[4]Richard B. Schmitt, "Some Big Firms Are Trying to Kill Legislation on Product Liability," *The Wall Street Journal,* July 7, 1998, p. B10.

[5]Leo Smith, "Trial Lawyers Face a New Charge," *Fortune,* August 26, 1991, pp. 85–89.

With the high risk of lawsuits, firms often go to what seem to be absurd lengths to ensure they have adequately warned customers against possible misuse of their products. A manufacturer of cardboard windshield sunscreens instructs users to remove it before driving the vehicle. A hair dryer is labeled with a warning not to use while sleeping. An iron has a label reading "Do not iron clothes while being worn." And a plastic inflatable sled is marked, "Not to be eaten or burned."[6]

What constitutes adequate warning will never be known for sure, but here is what courts have used in recent years. The warning should be placed conspicuously on the product, it should be where the user most likely can be expected to see it, it should communicate the level of danger, it should instruct the user in how to avoid the potential hazard, sellers should not engage in marketing activities that vitiate an otherwise adequate warning, and it should not be accompanied by statements that the product is safe. The user should be told what may happen if the warning is ignored. Makers must also be prepared to prove that the user *got* the warning, not just that the maker *posted* it.[7]

5. Finally, dangers sometimes appear *after use,* and the manufacturer's liability may continue into this period. For example, manufacturers of spray cans have to urge that the discards not be burned in fireplaces.

Caution

We must approach the product liability matter cautiously because of the tendency of the press to distort problems. For example, it was widely publicized recently that an overweight physician with a heart condition had bought a Sears mower, suffered a heart attack while starting the mower, and was awarded $1.8 million. In fact, court records showed that the mower mechanism *was defective* and required an *abnormally large number of pulls.* The doctor, incidentally, *did not have a heart condition.*

A U.S. Representative, in the House, railed over the number of boxes of cookies the Girl Scouts must sell just to pay their liability premiums. The Girl Scouts of U.S.A. denied they even have a problem let alone frivolous lawsuits.[8]

Casual readers of the press rarely have enough information to reach a good judgment, though they do form opinions.

The Four Legal Bases for Product Liability

The four main routes to liability for a product manufacturer are shown in Figure 22–3. All cases require a basis for the claim, and the manufacturer has

---

[6] *20/20* report, ABC Television, October 28, 1998.

[7] For the thoughts of a lawyer talking to marketing people, see Howard J. Newman, "Warnings About Product Dangers," *Marketing Management,* no. 4 (1993), pp. 62–64.

[8] Richard B. Schmitt, "Truth Is First Casualty of Tort-Reform Debate," *The Wall Street Journal,* March 7, 1995, p. B1.

FIGURE 22–3

Forms and sources of product liability

A manufacturer or reseller may be found guilty of product liability via these four routes:

	Negligence	*Warranty*	*Strict Liability*	*Misrepresentation*
Source	Common law, 1800s; Once required privity, but dropped in 1960.	Uniform Commercial Code; Enhanced by Magnuson/Moss Act.	Court decisions, 1960s.	Common law.
Conditions	Defective product by design or manufacture, and with failure to warn.	Defective product: Implied warranty of merchantability or of fitness for particular purpose. Express warranty: Untrue claim.	Defective product: No requirement for negligence or privity, and no disclaimer is allowed. Reasonably foreseeable.	Untrue claim or misrepresentation that led to injury. User relied on it. No need for defective product.
Defense	Not negligence; product not defective	Not implied by common usage; Not actually stated; Normal puffery.	Buyer knew, so assumed risk. Unforeseeable misuse. Product not defective.	Was truthful. Normal puffery. Buyer should have known better.

to have done something—at the very minimum, make, sell, or lease the product to someone.[9]

Negligence. In the 1980s, under common law, injury claimants had to prove that (1) the manufacturer was *negligent* in operations, let the product become defective and thus injurious, and (2) there was direct sale from the manufacturer to the injured user (*privity*). Perhaps a wagon maker was careless and failed to attach a wheel securely to the axle. The wheel came off, the driver was injured, and **negligence** was easy to establish. The wagon maker failed to exercise "ordinary" care (the care that a reasonable person would use). The mistake could be made by salespeople, advertising, labeling, retailers and wholesalers because one aspect of negligence is *failure to warn.*

In 1916 a court ruled that a defectively manufactured product was "inherently dangerous"; it didn't have to be sold direct. By 1966, every state had accepted this line of reasoning, and lack of privity as a defense against negligence was useless.

[9]A good general source on the following issues is George D. Cameron, *Business Law: Legal Environment, Transactions, and Regulation* (Plano, Texas: Business Publications, 1989).

Warranty. It was still difficult to prove negligence. Thus warranty, a development of the first half of this century, is relevant. **Warranty** is a promise, and if a promise can be proved and is not fulfilled, the seller can be charged with breach of warranty, whether negligent or not. A careful manufacturer of a new product may still be found guilty of causing injury.

Warranty is express or implied. An *express warranty* is any statement of fact made by the manufacturer about a product, whether made by salespeople, retailers, or others. The major issue with express warranty is the degree of puffing a court will allow. *Implied warranty* arises when a maker offers a product for a given use. An implied *warranty of fitness for a particular purpose* is part of the sales contract and means the product is of average quality and can be used for the purposes for which such products are customarily used. The buyer is justified to depend on the seller being right—an expert who knows how people customarily use the item.

But there was constant court bickering over who said what to whom and whether the distributor could have known as much as the maker. Our society is too complex for law that confuses more than clarifies, so we next saw the development of the strict liability concept.

Strict Liability. Under the concept of **strict liability,** the seller of an item has the responsibility for *not putting a defective product on the market.* If the product is defective, the manufacturer can be sued by any injured party even if that party was only a bystander. *There need be no negligence; there need be no direct sale; no statement by the seller will relieve the liability.*

However, the manufacturer may be able to use three key defenses. The first is *assumption of risk.* If the user of the product learns of the defect and continues to use it regardless of the danger, a suit may not be sustained. Second, the manufacturer has the defense of *unforeseeable misuse,* meaning the injury occurred because the user misused the product in a way that the seller could not reasonably have anticipated. Managers of new products may lack the expected experience, yet courts expect them to be completely market-wise. Third, the defense may be that the product, though causing injury, is not defective. For example, a man hit his eye on the pointed top of a small ventilation window on the side of his car. Though he leaned over and accidentally bumped the window, the jury held that this injury did not mean the window was defective. Presumably, the plaintiff should have been more careful.

Misrepresentation. Actually, a product itself doesn't have to be defective (as it does in the three other situations above) so long as an injury took place when the product was used on **misrepresentation** (intentional or not) by the seller. These cases are rare, but an example was the helmet manufacturer who made a helmet for motorcyclists and showed a motorcyclist wearing one in a picture on the carton. An experienced police officer bought one for use while riding on duty, but the helmet was not made to be used as a safety helmet. The court ruled there had been misrepresentation.

Other Legislation

Many industries have had unique problems leading to specialized legislation. The Food and Drug Administration, for example, was created in 1906. There are restrictions on alcoholic beverages, automobiles, scientific instruments, metals, and scores more. Attention frequently goes to the Consumer Product Safety Act and its Consumer Product Safety Commission (CPSC). Although the commission's direct impact has been much less than anticipated, the indirect impact has been substantial. It has power to set standards for products, order the recall of products, issue public warnings about possible problem products, stop the marketing of new products, ban present or proposed products, and levy substantial civil and criminal penalties. Manufacturers have made many changes to avoid trouble with the law.

Attempts at Standardization and Clarification

Manufacturers have had special troubles dealing with the varying laws of 50 states, and object to cases where a user changes safety equipment on a machine and then sues when injured, or when a machine was built before better technology was discovered, yet they are responsible by today's standards. Their biggest complaint concerns the discouragement of innovation. High-technology firms are reluctant to develop new products if there are major risks of trouble. Pharmaceutical companies call it "drug lag." New medical devices have almost ceased to come out. Evidence is piling up on this point.[10]

Many in government agree with these concerns, and attempts have been made to pass federal legislation to settle them. Opposition by consumer and trial lawyer groups have beaten these proposals back every year. There is some progress in particular product areas, such as general aviation, where some of the above issues have been taken care of selectively.[11]

Other Areas of Public Policy Debate on New Products

This is a huge topic, and in a book like this we can only scan the issues, point out why they are important, and cite some sources for readers who would like to investigate one or another of them.

---

[10]Laura Jereski, "Block That Innovation," *Forbes,* January 18, 1993, p. 48. See Paul A. Herbig and James E. Golden, "Innovation and Product Liability," *Industrial Marketing Management,* 1994, pp. 245–55. Also, W. Kip Viscusi and Michael J. Moore, "Product Liability, Research and Development, and Innovation," *Journal of Political Economy,* 1993, pp. 161–84.

[11]"Snatching Defeat from the Jaws of Victory," *BusinessWeek,* August 1, 1994, pp. 76–77; and Howard Banks, "Cleared for Takeoff," *Forbes,* September 12, 1994, pp. 116–22.

Environmental Needs

People sensitive to loss of our environment are striving for change and are getting it. Business sometimes leads the way, but twists and bends in the road often frustrate the task of developing new products.

A new product is said to hurt the environment if (1) its raw materials are scarce or hard to get to, (2) its design or manufacture causes pollution or excess power usage, (3) its use causes pollution, as on cars and insecticides, and (4) any disposal problem cannot be handled by recycling.

The Managerial Dilemma

The above concerns are justified. The dilemma seems to deal with the problems of reconciling tradeoffs between cost and efficiency in the firm and between price and environmental benefits to society. And there is much we do not know—even about the environmental effects of our new products. Social costs and social benefits are not easily measured. Even environmental firms have found the swamp here—such as when Greenpeace badly overstated the damage done by destruction of oil drilling platforms in the North Sea. Interestingly, we are finding we don't even know what happens in landfills—new anthropological studies show that material in dumps reacts differently than we thought.

Improvements are many, involving action on all of the needed areas. Honeywell asks buyers of its home smoke alarms to return them to the factory for disposal. Some firms have begun market testing in Germany and Scandinavian countries, to pass what is felt to be the world's toughest greenness test.[12] Rubbermaid, with its acclaimed Sidekick school lunch bucket, is developing new items aimed squarely at these needs. Toyota researchers are working on developing new, unique trees that can absorb car pollutants and may counteract global warming.[13] Cars pollute less, recycled paper appears in packaging, and on and on. Of course, there are occasional bloopers—P&G was congratulated for its ecology-friendly Ariel Ultra detergent in Europe, but was blindsided when critics found they had used animal testing in its development. And, more recently, both Honda and Ford agreed to pay millions of dollars of civil fines levied by the Justice Department and the

[12]Though maybe not a precursor for the rest of the world, the situation in Germany is worthy of study. New laws implemented in the middle 1990s sharply changed the new products picture. For example, much product packaging (including foam packing and aspirin boxes) must either be returned by retailers to the manufacturers who used it, or returned by consumers to retailers who will shunt it to recyclers who will then bill manufacturers for the costs. Philip White, "Waste Not," *International Design,* May–June 1992, pp. 67–69.

[13]See Zachary Schiller, "At Rubbermaid, Little Things Mean a Lot," *BusinessWeek,* November 11, 1991, pp. 27–30; and Emily Thornton, "Only God and Toyota Can Make a Tree," *BusinessWeek,* March 30, 1998, p. 58.

FIGURE 22–4
Public policy problems and the new product process

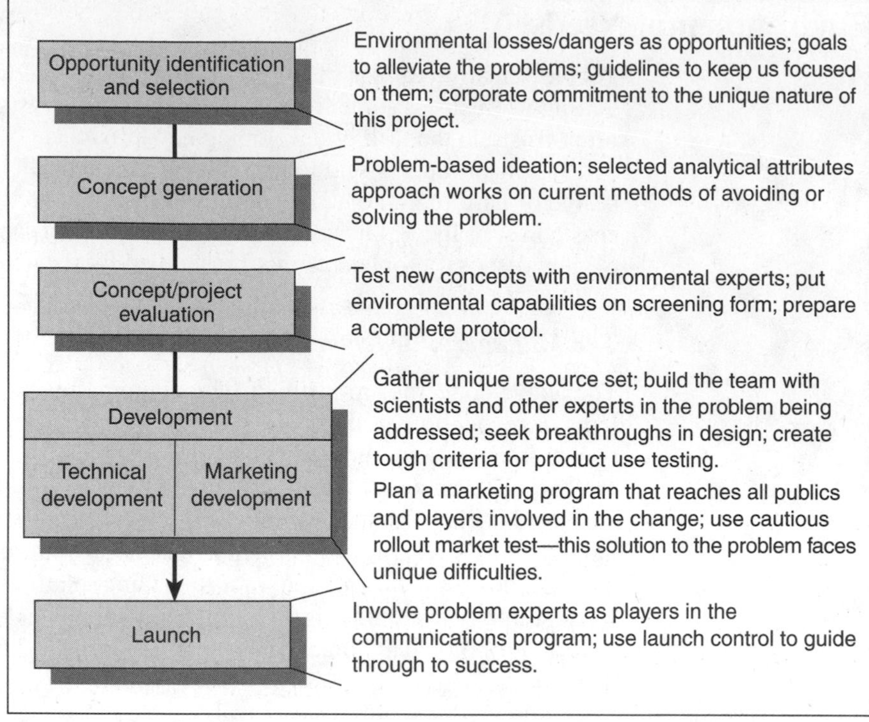

Environmental Protection Agency, for selling cars that passed emission tests but actually emitted too-high levels of pollutants, thus violating the Clean Air Act.[14]

There are many times, even today, when the cost-benefit analyses come out wrong, but a strong need for environmental protection is here to stay. This focuses us on protocol (to get the real needs), design (to solve problems creatively), and testing (to learn the effects of our creations).[15] We are even learning better ways to do "green" marketing. During the early 1990s, many firms noted that making environmentally friendly claims and catering to green concerns was becoming a hot marketing strategy—which resulted in exaggerated claims of environmental benefits on packaging and in advertising, and

---

[14]Matthew L. Wald, "Honda and Ford are Fined Millions," *The New York Times,* June 9, 1998, page A-1.

[15]It is no longer enough to slap green colors on packages, with pictures of ferns and waterfalls. See Michael Evamy, "Eco-Friendly, But Fern-Free," *Design,* November 1990, pp. 30–32; and Vasanthakumar N. Bhat, "Green Marketing Begins with Green Design," *Journal of Business and Industrial Marketing,* no. 4 (1993), pp. 26–31.

ultimately, increased customer skepticism.[16] See Figure 22–4 for how the overall new product system contributes to public policy problems just as it does to other problems.

Worthy Products

The makers of Folgers, Maxwell House, and Nescafe were under strong pressure from a consumer group in 1991 to stop buying coffee beans from El Salvador. P&G decided to offer a new blend of coffee, under the Maryland Club label, without such beans, though Folgers would continue to contain them. Other manufacturers have been asked to create special exercising equipment for handicapped individuals, better foods for people who need to diet, modified products for the elderly (e.g., with bigger printing on washer dials), and products keyed to the special interests of smaller ethnic groups. The Orphan Drug Act provides federal aid for the development and marketing of drugs that otherwise may not be commercially feasible because of the relatively small number of potential users. An example resulting from this law is a new drug for treating narcolepsy, which is the tendency to suddenly fall asleep regardless of place or action if the person happens to laugh or enjoy even a small bit of elation. Until this drug was available, 40,000 sufferers had to remain completely emotionless.[17]

Morality

It used to be satellite receiver makers who were criticized for bringing pornography into our living rooms. Today it is the Internet, and by the time you read this it may be some other mode of communication. Here, morality concerns whether society should be denied certain new products for its own good. We have new alcoholic beverages, new gambling devices, and new sex

---

[16]Joel J. Davis, "Federal and State Regulation of Environmental Marketing: A Manager's Guide," *SAM Advanced Management Journal,* Summer 1994, pp. 36–44; and Maxine S. Lans, "New Laws on Green Marketing Are Popping Up All the Time," *Marketing News,* February 15, 1993, pp. 22–24. Also see Héctor R. Lozada and Alma T. Mintu-Wimsatt, "Green-Based Innovation: Sustainable Development in Product Management," in *Environmental Marketing: Strategies, Practice, Theory, and Research,* Michael Jay Polonsky and Alma T. Mintu-Wimsatt, eds, Binghamton, New York: Haworth Press, 1995, pp. 179–98.

[17]An odd case arose in 1987 when Genentech complained to the FDA that profits from its human growth hormone orphan drug were being threatened by an Eli Lilly product. A supposedly unprofitable orphan drug was so profitable that the company sought protection against Lilly. "Genentech's Custody over an Orphan Drug," *BusinessWeek,* March 23, 1987, p. 39. By 1989 the issue involved several products and led to an article entitled "These `Orphans' Don't Need Nurturing Any More," by John Carey and Joan O. Hamilton, *BusinessWeek,* July 2, 1990, p. 38.

devices. Radar-detectors get better and better. Anheuser-Busch was forced to withdraw a product from test market when the public complained that the level of alcohol in what was a "kid's drink" would "train" youngsters to like alcoholic beverages. R. J. Reynolds marketed Dakota cigarettes, targeted to 18- to 24-year-old women with a high school education or less. Dual-drive VCRs permit (encourage?) illegal taping from rental videotapes. Caller ID permits us to learn who is calling us before we pick up the phone.

Product innovators know what is going on, and carefully position their products as they wish. Society stops them when they are wrong. They rarely walk into a surprise, and no one expects a weakening on this point. But it is difficult to predict the outcome of any particular controversy, something product developers must try to do, in advance.

Monopoly

The charge of monopoly is occasionally applied to new products. Some economists believe market dominance constitutes monopoly, and outstanding new products can lead to (or protect already achieved) market dominance.

Apart from fringe exceptions, free market forces have almost always prevailed. Bell and Howell once claimed that Kodak secretly developed some film products and introduced them before Bell and Howell had a chance to retool its own cameras and projectors to use the film. Bell and Howell lost, as did others. But recently, in the United States matters have turned, and right now we cannot predict where they will go.

In 1993 Xerox was found guilty of antitrust by refusing to sell some copier parts to independent operators selling and servicing high-volume copiers and printers. They paid a $225 million settlement. In 1994, a vigorous Justice Department challenged a patent licensing agreement of a type that had been approved for years. Bayer had to license an insecticide licensed from a European firm for exclusive sale in the United States. On the other hand, Steelcase (the office furniture maker) was recently ordered to pay competitor Haworth over $211 million for a patent infringement on prewired office panels. A Haworth spokesperson said that while copying was frequent in that industry years ago, there are more patents filed now and firms have to be much more careful.[18] Amgen, IBM, Hewlett-Packard and Digital Equipment are among the many firms now involved with suits over alliances or consortiums.[19]

---

[18]The Xerox, Bayer, and Steelcase examples are from, respectively: Milo Geyelin, "Xerox Agrees to Vouchers in Settlement," *The Wall Street Journal,* December 8, 1993, p. B8; Brigid McMenamin, "Eroding Patent Rights," *Forbes,* October 24, 1994, p. 92; Rebecca Blumenstein, "Steelcase Must Pay Big Sum Over Patent," *The Wall Street Journal,* December 31, 1996, p. A10.

[19]Andrew Pollack, "Antitrust Actions on the Rise," *The New York Times,* Sunday, November 10, 1991, Section 3, p. 12.

Personal Ethics

Some criticisms are difficult to fit into the above categories. People who react to them more often call them matters of personal ethics, not economics or business management. They are issues where people pretty much reach individual decisions, rather than seek court decisions. Here is a set of them—not complete, but in sufficient variety to let you see the problem product innovators deal with. As with all personal ethics situations, they are not just in the marketplace—they are in the labs, factories, and offices too. As Pogo said, we have met the enemy and they are us.

To get the full effect of this problem, try to find a person who will make an individual set of answers for comparison with your answers—both having been made privately first. Would you, or would you not, support continuing each of the 15 practices? How you would handle them if they came up in *your* new products organization? That is, what would you do *managerially,* not individually? Note that personal ethics situations exclude the clearly illegal—e.g., scientists have been known to steal company secrets and sell them to competitors, but such cases are not issues in ethics.

1. Ideation or concept generation often leads us to explore the minds of customers, to find something they want or will want when they hear about it. Your firm uses *intrusive techniques,* such as unannounced observation and psychological projective techniques. A customer recently said it is unethical to trick people into telling you what they want.
2. One of your divisions has a *purely imitative product innovation charter.* Is it ethical to help a firm market something that is not new in any way?
3. Your market research director uses focus groups for concept testing, and lets company people *secretly sit behind the mirrors* as your customers react to the new concepts. They often joke about customers' product usage practices.
4. You introduce a temporary product that will be replaced when a better one in development is ready a year from now. You are told *not to let distributors or your sales force know* it is only temporary.
5. You work for a management training firm and are about to market a new seminar service for banks. Your firm, for a fee, will run seminars during which you will train bank personnel in investment counseling. But there is no product use test on the seminar, and *you don't know that the bank people will really learn how to counsel.*
6. You work for a detergents company and recently learned that over the years thousands of rodents have been force-fed each new product, including versions in development. The *force-feeding goes on until half of the rodents die* (the so-called LD50 test).
7. You are currently working on a patented item that schools will use for map displays. It is so good that virtually every K–12 school will buy several of them. You come across the cost figures and calculate that the *gross margin*

will run about 80 percent. A co-worker comments that the price could be cut in half and the company margin would still be a healthy 60 percent.

8. You work for a leading software firm that introduces new versions of its word processing system with many *unannounced features.* That is, there are things the system can do but users are not told about them. The firm then markets a line of instructional books that include these features; competitive instruction firms, not knowing of the features, thus have books that are much less helpful to the users. (Of course, there is the other side of the coin—perhaps it is not ethical for an independent author to profit from an instruction book to be used by purchasers of Word Perfect. Should only Word Perfect get that market?)

9. You work for a database service that recently began collecting patient records from physicians and now offers a new service of *information for pharmaceutical firms.* The records sometimes contain names, and often include age, sex, and so forth, of the patients. Information includes nature of illnesses and treatments.

10. The Food and Drug Administration has charged that your new Freshland spaghetti sauce is processed and sold nonrefrigerated; it therefore *cannot be called "fresh"* as it is, in its brand name. Your firm counters that it is fresher than the leading competitor, and besides, lots of products are advertised as being fresh when they technically aren't, by the arbitrary FDA definition.

11. A set of "educational" game cards, made by your firm and not really very educational, are known to be bought by less intelligent parents for their children. There are several far better sets of such cards on the market.

12. Your strategy is to stir up the waters—marketing a long line of similar products to confuse customers and keep them from being able to buy intelligently.

13. You have a line of party products that seem to be in sync with many younger people, but are sexually oriented. You market them through mass outlets, not adult stores, and although some retailers won't stock the items, many will. Sales have been outstanding.

14. You work as a sales rep for a pharmaceutical company. Food and Drug Administration rules prohibit "off-label promotion," that is, marketing a drug for uses other than those approved by the FDA. Your company funds thousands of medical-education programs yearly, at which doctors and other health professionals make presentations about the use of certain drugs, some of which are not yet approved by the FDA (but written up in the medical journals as effective). They say they are doing nothing wrong, but you see this as a clear violation of off-label promotion rules. For you, the last straw is when you attend a sales meeting at which you are instructed to recruit medical speakers to talk about approved *and unapproved* uses of a new blood clot drug.[20]

---

[20]This example is real. See Elyse Tanouye, "Staffers of Drug Maker Say It Pushed Product for Unapproved Uses," *The Wall Street Journal,* September 15, 1997, p. A1, A7.

15. You work for a brewing company that has just launched a fad product—beer containing hemp seeds. The hemp is completely legal (it is imported into the U.S. only after being sterilized and cleared by the Drug Enforcement Agency and cannot be cultivated). The ad campaign, however, flaunts obvious drug imagery: psychedelic patterns and colors, and tag lines like "undetectable to police dogs." Even the label has a marijuana leaf on it.[21]

The Underlying Residual Issues

A few really tough issues thread their way through the above confusions. They are such that we will never be free of problems working in the public policy area. One of them is: *What are reasonable goals for action here?* A risk-free existence is totally unreasonable. Zero-defect quality control is a goal in many firms. But with the complexity in most of today's consumer products, nothing short of government decree would stop consumers from making errors—and then only because they would not be making any decisions at all.

Besides, even if we could hope to reach a 99.99 percent level of risk reduction, that would still leave 27,500 people on the wrong side of the statistic in the United States alone. Worldwide, the number would certainly be much higher.[22]

Another one is the *trade-off problem.* Even when a particular situation seems to have a clear-cut guiding principle, we often find a contrary principle of equal merit. Which of two worthy options should be accepted? The discoverer of DDT won a Nobel prize because the material would markedly enhance world crop productivity and thus reduce world hunger. Yet the discovery was ultimately banned in large areas because it produced undesirable effects.

A third is, *Where should the costs fall?* In many of the controversies that affect new products, the argument is not so much *what should be done as who should pay for it.* Assuming (1) no production system can ever make products perfectly and (2) no consumer group will ever use products with perfect wisdom, there will always be injuries and waste. Who should pay? Governments are already under pressure for tax reduction. Insurance companies know the negative reactions to inflated rates. So the no-fault approach is becoming popular—or, as the manufacturer says, the *total*-fault approach. The manufacturer assumes all responsibility and is expected to pass along the costs somehow.

[21]Another real case, this one involving Lexington Brewing Co's Kentucky Hemp Beer. See Sally Beatty, "This Hemp Beer Is Legal, but Its Ads Hint Otherwise," *The Wall Street Journal,* July 15, 1998, p. B1, B6.

[22]Many areas of controversy are discussed in Warren T. Brookes, "The Wasteful Pursuit of Zero Risk," *Forbes,* April 30, 1990, pp. 161–72.

What Are New Products Managers Doing about All This?

At the start of this chapter, it was stated that managements today generally have the public policy problem in hand. They have learned how to run the new product process to minimize the problems. The previous sections showed many ways in which actions are being taken. Here are a few, more general, ones.

Strategy and Policy

More top managers are personally involved today. They want safe and useful products because they sell better. For example, at a firm making v-style accordion gates for children, the CEO rejected a proposal, said the team could do better—they came out with something better *and* less expensive. Second, product innovation charters set the standards in guidelines, and also point out opportunities where there is new product opportunity in regulations.

Control Systems

Managements today demand tough standards, rigorous auditing at all points, good record-keeping, and training of new product employees. Disaster plans help. When Campbell's routine checking program disclosed a can containing botulin, the company immediately stopped shipments from the plant involved, canvassed 102,000 food outlets in a 16-state area, and inspected 65 million cans. A new manufacturing process was abandoned, two dozen spoiled cans were discarded, and the firm was back on top of the situation. Pfizer found a potentially flawed heart valve and had to contact 55,000 people with the implant. They had the records to do so.

Product Testing

Firms learn how customers will use products, and if that use looks like it will cause problems, then action is taken now, not after injuries mount. Then they add stress testing, to catch misuse and overuse. They use common sense: anybody could have seen that the all-terrain vehicles would be problems, and they were.

Marketing

They prepare adequate warnings. The Manville Corporation defended against asbestos-death lawsuits as early as 1929. The firm's chief physician allegedly urged caution labels in 1953, but they didn't go on until 1964 and even then apparently did not indicate the gravity of the risk. Bankruptcy was ultimately necessary to survive. Firms today manage the marketing and distribution process with the same vigor they manage design and manufacturing. If a product is unsafe in lay people's hands and must go through professional channels, it is plainly labeled with an explanation of why.[23]

Market Testing

Market tests, combining product and promotion, can spot miscommunications. Distributors may not understand promotions, discounts, instructions, or service. People who shouldn't buy an item may be doing so.

Education

Managements now consider themselves in the education business, first with *company personnel* (through ombudsmen, consumer affairs officers, scientific advisory panels, etc.) and second with the *consumer* (through labels, warranties, how-to sheets, and more instructional advertising.)

External Affairs

Most industries now aggressively greet every legislative thrust on new products, and vigorous public affairs programs are standard fare. They work together more, and even include consumer units on their task forces. Going almost unnoticed are routine announcements such as this newswire release on July 19, 1991 by P&G:

> The Procter & Gamble Company is voluntarily withdrawing Duncan Hines Pantastic Party Cakes . . . from a limited test area. . . . Five consumers have reported charring or smoking of the baking pan included in the party cake kit. Peter Morris, Vice President–Product Research, said, "Based on extensive product testing, we have found no safety problems. But rather than run any risk, we think it's in the best interest of our consumers to voluntarily withdraw this product from its limited test area until we can further investigate these few incidents."

Summary

This concludes our trip through a troublesome dimension of the new products process. The pressures are very real, and the difficulties are at times almost overwhelming. Some unresolved issues have no answers, and new variations in the general problem areas will continue to unfold.

[23]Another good general source of preventative actions to take is Marisa Manley, "Product Liability: You're More Exposed Than You Think," *Harvard Business Review,* September–October 1987, pp. 28–41. This article cites the case of a hair bleach product from Curtis that was so marketed and labeled. When an injured customer sued, the court ruled she was responsible by buying at a beauty shop, mixing two products, and ignoring the labels.

New products managers, however, find they can manage under these circumstances if they do their homework well. Avoiding needless troubles requires that they understand the process, stay close to their legal departments, get management's support at critical times, and follow up marketing with more aggressive launch management than ever before used in American industry. All temptations are to do just the opposite because time can be the Achilles' heel of new products management, as we have seen more than once.

Although we have covered the major areas of product policy concerns in the new products field, you should know that there are far more problems and issues buried in the labs, plants, and offices of today's new products manager. Every industry has scores of them. As a final example, think of the problems scientists in the pharmaceutical industry face when they field test an experimental drug known to be dangerous. With whom must they work, whose approvals are necessary, what controls should they use on the actions and record keeping of physicians and hospital personnel, and how far and hard should they search for side effects—to the third generation? Does it matter if the medicine tested came from a rare frog on the endangered species list? Does it matter if the drug (assuming it is successful) will cost over $4,000 a month for 10 months of treatment, and have a lifetime dosage level of $1,000 a month?[24]

The point here is this: Thousands of people deal with these troublesome issues every day—they know the problems, and they have worked out balance between need to know and need to move ahead. They manage, risks and all.

Applications

More questions from that interview with the company president.

1. "The worst thing about product liability is what they call strict liability. Now, I know it's hard to prove negligence against a typical large corporation of today, but that's no reason to go to the other extreme and say a company is guilty when there is no evidence it did anything wrong. We market thousands of products involving thousands of people. Strange things are going to happen. Employees are not robots—they make human errors. You've probably already made a mistake or two today; yet if you were in a business, you

[24]For an interesting summary of the problems, see George Anders, "Testing a New Drug Entails Daunting Costs and Clashing Interests," *The Wall Street Journal,* January 7, 1994, p. A1.

could be sued, found guilty, and then hit with a punitive damages ruling like a common criminal. That's just not fair."

2. "We're currently about to market a new type of hair dryer. It's not a blower in the usual sense—there are no wires that get hot. Instead, we have combined two chemicals that tend to heat up if they are charged with an electrical current. The air is directed through the wire mesh container in which these chemicals are kept (they're solids, not liquids), and whenever there is electricity, there is heated air. If you feel you understand the moral and legal issues of product liability, would you please tell me what you think we should have done, and what we should do in the future, to conform with what the public generally expects of us and with what the law requires of us? We still have several months before we market the new dryer, but the product specifications are frozen and the item is currently about to be started through production."
3. "Two other firms I know about were less fortunate. Morton-Norwich Products introduced Encare, a vaginal suppository contraceptive, and American Home Products came out with a similar product called Semicid at about the same time. Both advertised that the products were safer than IUDs and that, unlike the Pill, they had no hormonal side effects. They called the items a safe, medically tested, positive method of birth control, which they are. But the Federal Trade Commission has ruled that the firms cannot claim a comparative advantage over other methods unless they also state that the new product is not as effective as the others. The FTC says the only novel aspect of the new products is the suppository form, and that has very little advantage to the consumer. Both firms now have to distribute a new pamphlet telling the advantages and disadvantages of all forms of birth control. All of this may be well and good—I don't know—but the aspect that bothers me is that the two firms were ruled responsible for telling consumers the *good* things about their competitors, not just the bad. Why do you suppose the FTC ruled the way it did, and is this a forecast of what we are all going to face? Since when am I responsible for helping potential customers choose a competitor's product?"
4. "When you first told me about those, what do you call them, public policy issues, I was thinking about our health industry group. It is rapidly developing a line of health maintenance organizations (HMOs) by acquisition, primarily, and several by invitation of leading hospitals. They will all be in the service business and not-for-profit operations (they have other advantages for us), so it is pleasing to think that at least this part of our corporate family won't raise public policy issue problems. That's right, isn't it?"

CASE: ONLINE SERVICE PROVIDERS TASK FORCE[25]

The online service firm, by 1996, had become an established part of the life in the computer age. Firms such as America Online offered the leading sources of access to the Internet as well as access to a wide range of services within their own systems. Offerings included stock broker services, business information, electronic encyclopedia, travel reservations and tickets, news, classified ads, magazine subscriptions, merchandise, trip routing, service listings (restaurants, for example), and much more. For many subscribers (who paid a monthly charge and/or a per-hour charge) the leading value of the service was the chance to send messages to their friends also on the service. This e-mail activity was very inexpensive and trained subscribers in the skills they would soon need when on the Internet.

From a central menu, the user selected categories and then went into subcategories, detailed information, action options (buying), and so on. The systems were user friendly from the beginning and used simple English commands. Originally, users had substantial costs for a new PC and for a modem, but these had pretty much become commonplace.

There were various ways to reach the Internet, and aggressive access providers existed in every area of the United States and around the world. Before 1993, there had been virtually no mention of public policy issues on these services. There was no stirring. There were no suits for injurious service or for damaging the environment or for providing unworthy products, and so forth. No politician had adopted a videotex service as a crusade cause. Occasionally there were brushes with legal aspects—a New York state court had already ruled that Prodigy could be held liable for slanderous and libelous comments made on the Internet through its connection, and CompuServe occasionally censored users' e-mail.

However, as more people used online services Internet cyberspace became contaminated. The Internet was a network that was open to people anywhere in the world who had the necessary software for connecting into it. Once in, they had access to an unbelievably large set of information on what they called the World Wide Web. Anybody could (at a fairly high cost) set up his or her own website on the Internet. There was also messaging, bulletin boards, merchandise being sold, even advertising being displayed to users of the Internet. Services and information offered for sale used passwords.

What happened, however, could probably have been anticipated—pornography entered—in pictures, stories, e-mail messages, chat groups, the works. And what precipitated the problem in this case were the child porn arrests in September of 1995. A large group of people had been using Internet to transmit photos that constituted child pornography. They were arrested and charged. There was apparently no question they were acting illegally.

But for the managers of the online services, there were two problems. First, what could or should they do to prevent illegal activities? American Online was directly concerned as the access provider in the porn cases, but the other two leaders knew they could be next. Second, for the longer term, what other types of trouble might they get into? Not the illegal types (they would have to be handled some way or another) but rather the ethical or social responsibility type.

---

[25]This case was developed from a large variety of public sources, a leading one of which was David Kirkpatrick, "Online Services," *Fortune,* May 1, 1995, pp. 86–96.

Although online was a service, not a good, and product liability had traditionally applied to goods, the providers knew they were just a court decision away from being involved. Already legal people were referring to the "permanent *injury* to young minds from the pornography." And already, people concerned about the pornography problem were blaming the access providers. The First Amendment (free speech) was seen as in need of compromise with other freedoms.

In addition, industry wondered if their new position of power might start people thinking about new definitions for environmental pollution, worthy products, personal ethics—the full set.

So, as they had done in 1995 to deal with the criminal case, they formed a task force of managers from the three firms to deal with the broader social responsibility question. Other online services might or might not participate: General Electric's Genie, News Corp.'s Delphi Internet, Apple Computer's eWorld, and Microsoft's Network. So too might sellers of software for direct access to the Internet.

You work for one of these firms and have been asked to go to the first task force meeting with a statement—what problems might the industry face, what the rationale would be, what defense would you have, and for the most likely ones, what should you do to reduce your chances of ending up in court again?

Bibliography

This bibliography displays (1) general books on product innovation in recent years, both business- and college-oriented and (2) selected other publications frequently sought for their reference value or some unique contribution. Books and articles on specialized aspects of new products management are given as footnotes throughout the text.

Betts, Jim. *The Million-Dollar Idea.* Point Pleasant, NJ: Point Publishing, 1985. (A collection of some of the most helpful ideas from past issues of *The New Product Development Newsletter.*)

Boothroyd, Geoffrey; Peter Dewhurst; and Winston Knight. *Product Design for Manufacturing.* New York: Marcel Dekker, 1994. (By some of the pioneers in this field.)

Booz, Allen & Hamilton. *New Products Management for the 1980s.* Chicago: 1982. (A survey of industry practice, dated now but often referred to.)

Choffray, Jean-Marie, and Gary L. Lilien. *Market Planning for New Industrial Products.* New York: John Wiley & Sons, 1980. (Focuses principally on advanced techniques of management science as applied in the industrial field.)

Clark, Kim B., and Steven C. Wheelwright. *Managing New Product and Process Development.* New York: The Free Press, 1992. (A Harvard case book.)

Cooper, Robert G.: *Winning at New Products: Accelerating the Process from Idea to Launch.* 2nd ed. Reading, MA: Addison-Wesley, 1993. (A business-oriented book based on recent research findings.)

Cooper, Robert G.; Scott J. Edgett; and Elko J. Kleinschmidt. *Portfolio Management for New Products.* Hamilton, Ontario: McMaster University, 1997. (Product portfolio management and strategy, and maximizing portfolio value.)

Deschamps, Jean-Philippe, and P. Ranganath Nayak. *Product Juggernauts: How Companies Mobilize to Generate a Stream of Market Winners.* Boston: Harvard Business School Press, 1995. (Stories of successful companies.)

Dolan, Robert J. *Managing the New Product Development Process.* Reading, MA: Addison-Wesley, 1993. (A Harvard case book, emphasis on marketing science.)

Gruenwald, George. *New Product Development.* 2nd ed. Chicago: NTC Publishing Group, 1992. (A business-oriented book especially for consumer packaged goods.)

Guile, Bruce R., and James Brian Quinn. *Managing Innovation.* Washington, D.C.: National Academy Press, 1981. (Collection of seven stories of successful product innovation in eight industries, from a parts catalog to a bridge construction service.)

Hisrich, Robert D., and Michael P. Peters. *Marketing Decisions for New and Mature Products.* 2nd ed. New York: Macmillan, 1991. (A college text.)

Hooley, Graham J., and John Saunders. *Competitive Positioning: The Key to Marketing Strategy.* Englewood Cliffs, NJ: Prentice-Hall, 1993. (A business-oriented book.)

Hopkins, David S. *The Marketing Plan.* New York: The Conference Board, 1981. (Basic compilation of marketing plans in survey of members.)

Katzenbach, Jon R., and Douglas K. Smith. *The Wisdom of Teams: Creating the High-Performance Organization.* Boston: Harvard Business School Press, 1993. (A business-oriented book that presents the idea of teams in a construct of horizontal management.)

Kidder, Tracy. *The Soul of a New Machine.* New York: Avon Books, 1981. (A classic story of a new products team as they developed a new minicomputer for Data General.)

Kinnear, Thomas C., and James R. Taylor. *Marketing Research.* 4th ed. New York: McGraw-Hill, 1991. (A basic college text on the subject.)

Kotler, Philip. *Marketing Management: Analysis, Planning and Control.* 7th ed. Englewood Cliffs, N.J.: Prentice-Hall, 1991. (A general marketing management text.)

Kuczmarski, Thomas D. *Managing New Products.* 2nd ed. Englewood Cliffs, NJ: Prentice Hall, 1992. (A business-oriented book that emphasizes the management consultant's view of strategy and organization.)

Lilien, Gary L., and Arvind Rangaswamy. *Marketing Engineering: Computer-Assisted Marketing Analysis and Planning.* Reading, MA: Addison-Wesley, 1998. (A wide range of computer models that can support analysis for new product development.)

McGrath, Michael E. *Product Strategy for High-Technology Companies.* Burr Ridge, IL: Irwin Professional, 1995. (How to achieve growth, competitive advantage, and increased profits: a consultant's experienced view of the matter, primarily from the top management perspective.)

McMath, Robert M., and Thom Forbes, *What Were They Thinking?* New York: Random House, 1998. (Dozens of examples of failed new product launches, some of them quite humorous, each illustrating a basic marketing or new product development lesson.)

McQuarrie, Edward. *Customer Visits: Building a Better Market Focus.* Thousand Oaks, CA: Sage Publications, 1993. (A business-oriented book.)

Meltzer, Robert J. *Biomedical and Clinical Instrumentation.* Buffalo Grove, IL: Interpharm Press, 1993. (Fast tracking from concept through production in a regulated environment.)

Moore, William L., and Edgar A. Pessemier. *Product Planning and Management: Designing and Delivering Value.* New York: McGraw-Hill, 1993. (Broad scope with special attention to systems that use management science and especially computer modeling.)

Moskowitz, Howard R. *Food Concepts and Products: Just in Time Development.* Trumbell, CT: Food & Nutrition Press, Inc., 1994. (A business book.)

Nystrom, Harry. *Technological and Market Innovation.* Chichester, England: John Wiley & Sons, 1990. (A report of research conducted primarily on industrial firms in Sweden.)

Osborn, Alex F. *Applied Imagination.* 3rd ed. New York: Charles Scribner's Sons, 1963. (The basic brainstorming work.)

Pinchot, Gifford, III. *Intrapreneuring.* New York: Harper & Row, 1985. (By the creator of the intrapreneuring concept.)

Pine, B. Joseph. *Mass Customization: The New Frontier in Business Competition.* Boston: Harvard Business School Press, 1992. (The story as told by the person credited with creating the concept.)

Rosenau, Milton D., Jr. *Faster New Product Development.* New York: AMACOM, 1990. (A business-oriented book focused as indicated by its title.)

Rosenam, Milton D.: Abbie Griffin; George Castellion; and Ned Anschuetz, eds. *The PDMA Handbook of New Product Development.* New York: John Wiley & Sons,

1996. (Practical information on all stages in the new products process, written by both academics and practitioners.)

Rosenau, Milton D., Jr., and John J. Moran. *Managing the Development of New Products.* New York: Van Nostrand Reinhold, 1993. (A business-oriented presentation, stressing the technical phases known as development.)

Schnaars, Steve P. *Managing Imitation Strategies.* New York: The Free Press, 1994. (How later entrants seize markets from the pioneers; 28 case histories, plus patterns from them.)

Slade, Bernard N. *Compressing the Product Development Cycle Time: From Research to Market Place.* New York: AMACOM, 1993. (How to achieve a faster movement through the technical phases.)

Smith, P. G., and Donald G. Reinersten. *Developing Products in Half the Time.* New York: Van Nostrand Reinhold, 1991. (One of the original sources on this subject. A business book.)

Souder, William E. *Managing New Product Innovations.* Lexington, MA: Lexington Books, 1987. (Compilation of the author's research findings from 10 years of studies, mainly industrial.)

Souder, William E., and J. Daniel Sherman, eds. *Managing New Technology Management.* New York: McGraw-Hill, 1994. (A collection of articles on several topics in new product development: front-end decisions, implementation, and emerging issues. Extensive discussion of product launch.)

Thomas, Robert J. *New Product Development: Managing and Forecasting for Strategic Success.* New York: John Wiley, 1993. (For the business practitioner, with special emphasis on forecasting.)

Twiss, Brian C. *Managing Technological Innovation.* 3rd ed. New York: Longman, 1986. (A U.K. technical perspective.)

Ulrich, Karl Y., and Steven D. Eppinger. *Product Design and Development.* New York: McGraw-Hill, 1995. (A view of the new product process through the eyes of design—broader than some in this area.)

Urban, Glen, and John R. Hauser. *Design and Marketing of New Products.* 2nd ed. Englewood Cliffs, NJ: Prentice Hall, 1993. (An updated and expanded version of their original book that made heavy use of mathematical modeling for sales forecasting and other purposes.)

Utterback, James M. *Mastering the Dynamics of Innovation.* Boston: Harvard Business School Press, 1994. (How companies can seize opportunities in the face of technical change.)

Von Hippel, Eric. *The Source of Innovation.* New York: Oxford University Press, 1988. (The basic source of the lead user concept and its use.)

Walsh, Vivien; Robin Roy; Margaret Bruce; and Stephen Potter. *Winning by Design.* Oxford, United Kingdom, 1992. (The product creation story from the vantage point of designers.)

Wheelwright, Steven C. and Kim B. Clark. *Revolutionizing Product Development.* New York: The Free Press, 1992. (A business-oriented book.)

Wizenberg, Larry, ed. *The New Products Handbook.* Homewood, IL: Dow Jones-Irwin, 1987. (A business-oriented book.)

Zangwill, Willard I. *Lightening Strategies for Innovation: How the World's Best Firms Create New Products.* New York: Lexington Books, 1993. (A business-oriented presentation of the book's title.)

Appendix A
Sources of Ideas Already Generated

New product ideas come from many places, some of which are peculiar to particular firms or industries. Here are the more broadly used sources.

Employees

Many types of employees can be sources of new product concepts. Salespeople are an obvious group, but so are technical groups, manufacturing, customer service, and packaging employees, and, in the case of general consumer products, any employee who uses the products. Manufacturing and engineering personnel are frequently part-time inventors who should be encouraged to submit their ideas. These people need to know that their ideas are wanted, and special mechanisms (and even cultures) must usually be constructed to gather those ideas.

Employee suggestion systems are not dependable ways to turn up ideas, and special idea contests have an equally disappointing record. Toyota ran an Idea Olympics for some time and in one year produced 1,300 employee-inventor entries. The firm did not comment on the quality of the ideas.

The most helpful suggestions come from employees whose work brings them in contact with customer problems. For example, a drill manufacturer's service department found that many drills were burning out because customers were using them as electric screwdrivers. Adding a clutch mechanism to the drill created a new product. Complaint-handling departments also become familiar with consumers' use of products. Salespeople know when a large order is lost because the firm's product is not quite what the customer wanted.

Dun & Bradstreet had a fine new products track record and reported that most of its new product ideas came from field personnel. Eligible D&B employees could receive $5,000 for suggesting an idea that went national. Some firms have used an "idea miner"—an employee whose job is to scout around among other employees, encouraging and collecting their ideas.

Customers

The greatest source of new product ideas is the customer or user of the firm's products or services, although their ideas are usually only for product improvement or nearby line extensions. Some people believe the majority of all new products in certain industries originate with users. Because some specialized user groups are personally involved with devices, new product people occasionally delegate new product concept development to them. Similarly, most auto parts and components manufacturers look to their giant OEM buyers for new product initiatives. On the other hand, one firm solicited 2,800 ideas from customers and was not able to use a single one.

The most popular ways to gather consumer ideas are surveys, continuing panels, special focus groups, and the mail. Some firms get so many suggestions in the mail that they do not read them. Industrial firms usually take the more initiative approach of using personal contacts by salespeople or technical staffs, especially lead users.

Resellers

Brokers, manufacturers' reps, industrial distributors, large jobbers, and large retail firms may be quite worthwhile. In fact, some mass merchandisers have their own new products departments and invite manufacturers to bid on specifications. Many industrial representatives are skilled enough to be special advisers to their clients, and selling agents in the toy industry not only advise but actually take on the new products function if the manufacturer wishes.

One chemical distributor suggested using a low-cost polyethylene bag to line steel drums to prevent corrosion; and a millwork producer learned about a new competitive entry from a dealer and then suggested how the new item could be improved. Both suggestions were successfully implemented. Kroger once told manufacturers that its customers want more easy-to-cook, single-portion frozen dinners, and another chain suggested a low-calorie enchilada.

Suppliers/Vendors

Most manufacturers of plastic housewares are small and thus look to the large plastics firms for advice. Virtually all producers of steel, aluminum, chemicals, metals, paper, and glass have technical customer service departments. One of their functions is to suggest new products made of the firm's basic material.

Competitors

New product idea generators are interested in competitors' activities, and competitors' new products may be an indirect source for a leapfrog or add-on new product; but competitors (as with government-mandated cross-licensing of ideas) are rarely sources of new product ideas except in industries where benchmarking has been accepted as a strategy. The first firms bringing a new product to a particular market segment (such as the smaller city banks) do use their innovative competitors as sources, but this is effective only when market segments are insulated. At Ford Motor Company, once the engineers get their hands on a new competitive product, it is systematically torn down into its 30,000 parts. All are cataloged and then mounted on panels so others can examine them.

The Invention Industry

Every industrialized country has an "industry" consisting of a nucleus of inventors surrounded by firms and organizations that help them capitalize on their inventions. Though tending to lose out to corporate research centers, individual inventors still submit almost a fourth of all patent applications. The auxiliary or supportive group includes:

Venture capital firms	Banks
Inventors' schools	Inventors' councils
Attorneys	Small Business Administration
Trademark and patent offices	Technology expositions
Consultants on new business	Patent shows
Patent brokers and others	Inventor newsletters
Inventor assistance firms	State entrepreneurial aid programs
Individual investors	University innovation centers

Currently, both the inventor and the potential manufacturer are frustrated by the communications, legal, and funding problems existing in this supportive network. Fortunately, this highly fragmented new industry is in the process of shaking down and should soon settle on several dominant organizational formats with which manufacturers can deal.

One example of this emerging format was InstanTechEx, a service provided by Dr. Dvorkovitz & Associates. Dvorkovitz sponsored an annual international technology exchange exposition where hundreds of firms and scores of governments displayed technological advancements that they wanted to sell. The show was a supermarket of technology and an emerging format for standardizing the new invention industry.

Other new organizations are merging the financial, legal, and managerial consulting assistance that inventors usually require, either as venture firms that actually take over and develop the idea or as facilitator firms that reach out to established manufacturers. In the meantime, some firms have what they call "inventors' farm systems" to get both quantity and variety of invention input. NordicTrac makes inventors their primary source of new products and cultivates that group with almost as much marketing effort as used on their customers.

Miscellaneous

Among the many other sources of outside new product ideas are the following:

1. Consultants. Most management consulting firms do new products work, and some specialize in it—for example, McKinsey, A. D. Little, Mercer, and PRTM . Some consulting firms are devoted exclusively to new products work and include idea generation as one of their services. Unfortunately, the stigma of being outsiders is strong in the new products field, as exemplified by the not-invented-here syndrome. Companies report very favorable experiences but also many horror stories. One alternative is to bring industry experts to discussion sessions with company personnel. General Mills has used a newspaper food editor, a trade journal editor, an advertising copywriter, a restaurateur, a division manager of a food chain, and four company junior executives.

2. Advertising agencies. This source of new product ideas is badly underrated. Most agencies have the creative talent and the product/market experience to generate new product concepts. Some agencies have full-blown new products departments, and some take their concepts all the way to market, including premarket tests and rollouts. Consumer product agencies do more new products work than industrial agencies do, although the West Coast agencies specializing in the computer industry render a wide range of services because their clients are often small.

3. Marketing research firms. Normally, marketing research firms get involved in the idea-generating process by assisting a client with need assessment. They rarely stumble across an opportunity that they pass along to a client. Some of the bigger marketing research firms also serve as management consultants.

4. Retired product specialists. Industrial new products people, particularly those with technical strength, often retire from their firms and become part-time consultants to other firms. One company actually tracks the retirements of all qualified specialists in its industry. Conflict-of-interest problems may arise, and divulging competitive secrets is ethically questionable, but most arrangements work around these problems easily.

5. Industrial designers. Industrial design firms sometimes function as part of a team implementing a new product decision that has already been made. However, many industrial designers are extremely creative. Industrial design firms and individual industrial designers are increasingly capitalizing on their own new product strengths. Industrial design departments of universities are sometimes assigned by government and other service organizations to do original new products work.

6. Other manufacturers. Most firms have potentially worthwhile new product ideas that they do not want because these ideas conflict with the firm's strategy. These ideas are usually allowed to remain idle. One such firm, General Electric, established a Business Opportunities Program in the 1960s in which it offered its "spare" technologies for sale. Sometimes, the offering was just an idea, but other times, prototypes and even molds, dies, and finished goods inventories were offered, depending on how far GE had taken an idea before deciding not to develop it further. In later years, GE expanded this service by listing the technologies of others in its monthly editions of *Selected Business Ventures* and in annual compilations in its *New Product New Business Digest.*

7. Universities. Professors and students occasionally offer new product ideas, especially in schools of engineering, the sciences, and business. Dentists, physicians, and pharmacists are scientific groups that play a major role in new products work.

8. Research laboratories. Most of the world's leading countries now have at least one major research laboratory that will do new products work on contract from manufacturers and that occasionally comes up with interesting new product ideas. The Battelle Memorial Institute in Columbus, Ohio, received millions of dollars for its role in getting xerography off the ground. Other leading research laboratories are the Illinois Institute of Technology, the Stanford Research Institute, and Great Britain's National Engineering Laboratory.

9. Governments. The Patent Office of the United States government offers several services designed to help manufacturers find worthwhile new product ideas. The *Official Gazette* provides a weekly listing of (1) all new patents issued, (2) condensed descriptions of the patented items, and (3) which patents are for sale or license. Patent Office reports and services also make known what government patents and foreign patents are available.

The military services have a want list of products that they would like to buy; the Department of Agriculture will help manufacturers with new products; and state governments have programs to aid industries.

One by-product of today's regulation of business is increased assistance from regulators for solving such problems as unsafe products and unsafe working conditions. For example, the Occupational Safety and Health Act stimulated several companies to develop first-aid kits.

10. Printed sources. The hundreds of technical and scientific journals, trade journals, newsletters, and monographs are occasionally sources of ideas for new products. Most of the ideas indirectly result from accounts of new products activity. Some publications are more direct sources of new product ideas—for example, *Newsweek's* annual *New Products and Processes, New Technology* (London), the *Soviet Technology Bulletin,* and such compilations as *New Product News.* Though not new product ideas directly, there are now at least two online computer databases of actual new products marketed: *Thomas New Industrial Products* and *Predicasts, New Product Announcements.*

11. International. Minnetonka executives got the idea for pump toothpaste while browsing in a West German supermarket. Powdered Tide was developed by scientists in Cincinnati, but Liquid Tide used a formula for surfactants from Japan and a mineral salts antagonist from Belgium. Unfortunately, few firms have systematic programs to find ideas from other countries. Some establish foreign offices to monitor various technologies, others ask their advertising agencies' foreign offices to gather ideas, and still others subscribe to one or more reporting services.

12. Internet. At this time we can only guess what will happen, but some web sites already are getting into new product ideas, and various bulletin boards post suggestions for product change.

Managing These Idea Sources

These sources of ideas do not function without special effort. For example, salespeople must be trained how to find users with good ideas and how to coax the ideas from them. International markets must be covered on the spot by trained people. Studying the competition must be systematic to catch every change in competitors' products. Each special source is also a potential source for the competition, and the firm that utilizes these sources most appropriately will acquire the best ideas.

Appendix B
Other Techniques of Concept Generation

Chapters 4, 5, 6 and 7 presented the leading ideation techniques with the best track records and the greatest chance of producing valuable new product concepts. Perhaps hundreds of other techniques are available, some of which are proprietary (confidential to the consulting firm that originated each), and some of which are techniques given here but with different names.

Forty-five of the other techniques have been selected for brief review here. They are probably not necessary, but different individuals have found them useful. Perhaps you will too.

Techniques to Aid Problem Analysis

Composite Listing of Needs Fulfilled. By simply listing the many needs met by currently available products, there is a good chance some otherwise overlooked needs will come to mind. This mechanical process is successful only if the listing is pushed to one's mental limits.

Market Segmentation Analysis. By using one segmentation dimension on top of another, an analyst can develop a hierarchy of smaller and smaller market segments. For example, bar soap segmentation could use sex, age, body part cleaned, ethnic groups, and geographic location. All possible combinations of these would yield thousands of groups—for example, elderly Jewish women washing their faces in New York City. Each combination is potentially a group whose needs are peculiar and currently unmet. (Psychographic and behavioral segments are especially useful today.)

Dreams. This approach analyzes the dreams of people who have the problem(s) under study. Dreams offer a greater range of insights, equitably involve other persons in the problem situation, and offer paranormal aspects of the dream itself. Various famous people, one of whom was Robert Louis Stevenson, have attributed part of their creativity to dreams.

Techniques to Aid Scenario Analysis

There are many techniques for finding meaningful seed trends (trends that could be extended). Some are discussed in Chapter 5, and here are nine more.

Trend People. Many believe certain people have a predictive sense and should be watched. Women's Wear Daily is one publication that uses this method, and the people it watches are well known to regular readers.

Trend Areas. Major changes in American life and practice traditionally begin on the West Coast and gradually make their way east. Although television and other mass media have reduced the time lag, some firms station personnel in California just to be closer to the changes going on there.

Hot Products. The automobile, television, and the computer have had a dramatic effect on lifestyles in this century. Others that may do so include fiber optics, biogenetic engineering, condominiums, VCRs, the compact disk, and the Internet. One way to gather meaningful seed trends is to study such products and their effects. But watch out for false prophets, such as the CB radio of the 1970s.

Newspapers. Some persons like to read leading newspapers, particularly the *New York Times,* cover to cover and make note of every trend, activity, or idea around which significant scenario change might take place.

Hypothetical. A few persons believe one should use any seed trend to create arbitrary scenarios. The more hypothetical the better because the exercise is to stimulate creativity.

Technological Changeover. This approach predicts when one technology will substitute for another and seeks the implications of the substitution for all products and systems involving either the new or the old. Doing this involves time series analysis, graphic analysis, and forecasts by technical people.

Technical Innovation Follow-on. This procedure analyzes the implications for technical breakthroughs across a broad spectrum of technology, not just the immediate technology in which the breakthrough came. For example, a breakthrough in solar heating could be analyzed for effect in plumbing, clothing, furniture, or even entertainment.

Technological Monitoring. Some scientists keep journals of technological progress. Every meaningful event is carefully logged, and from time to time the journals are studied for meaningful trends. The technique helps guarantee the analysis of one event in the construct of other events.

Cross-impact Analysis. First, list all possible changes that may occur over the next 20 years in a given area of activity (say, transportation). Then apply these changes to other areas of activity, much as is done in technical innovation follow-on above. The difference is that this method is not restricted to forecastable breakthroughs.

Techniques to Enhance Group Creativity

Phillips 66 Groups. To increase participation, Dr. J. Donald Phillips broke Osborn's 12-person groups into subgroups of six members each, sending the subgroups to break-off rooms for six minutes each, rearranging the subgroups, sending the new subgroups off for another six minutes, and so on. Rearrangement was Phillips's key to eliminating the problem of dominant or conflicting personalities. The Phillips 66 groups are sometimes called buzz groups, free association groups, and discussion 66 groups.

Brainstorming Circle. This approach forces the conversational sequence around a circle, and each person expands or modifies the idea expressed by the prior person in the circle. The brainstorming circle is more orderly and forces all persons to participate equally.

Reverse Brainstorming. This approach concentrates on a product's weaknesses or problems rather than on solutions or improvements. The discussion attempts to ferret out every criticism of, say, a vacuum cleaner. Later, attempts are made to eliminate the weaknesses or solve the problems.

Tear-down. The rule of suspended judgment is reversed in this approach. Instead of avoiding criticism, tear-down requires it, and participants must find something wrong with the previous idea to get a talking turn.

And Also. In this approach, each speaking participant enlarges or extends the previous idea. No lateral moves are permitted unless the chain runs dry. The approach has been called idea building and modification.

Synectics. In its pure form, synectics does not differ much from brainstorming. Synectics provides more structure and direction by having the participants think along the lines of certain operational mechanisms—usually analogy and metaphors. The system has a forced sequence through these mechanisms and other steps—viewpoint, forced fit, and so on. However, in recent years the two individuals involved in creating this approach have led their respective creativity firms into use of many ideation techniques. Analogy prevails as a critical feature, but the term *synectics* has come to mean two businesses running creativity seminars.

Gordon Method. Prior to developing synectics, W. J. J. Gordon used groups that were not told what the problem was. In this method, if a discussion is to develop new ideas for recording musical performances, the group is encouraged to discuss opera. Eventually the leader turns the discussion toward the problem but still without divulging it.

Delphi. Although occasionally touted for ideation, Delphi is really a method of organizing a forecasting survey. Panels of experts are compiled, they are sent a questionnaire calling for forecasts within a given area of activity (e.g., hospitals or data processing), the questionnaires are tabulated and summarized, the results are returned to the panel for their reaction and alteration, new summaries are prepared, the results are sent out again, and so on. The iterations continue until conformity is reached or until impasse is obvious. The method is essentially a cop-out because the individuals still must use some method to make their own forecasts. But in certain situations, it has been deemed effective, and it can be used quite easily in modified format. It is especially desirable where the industry itself is new, and there are no historical data to aid forecasters.

Think Tanks. This too is more a matter of organizing people than a mechanism of stimulating creativity. Think tanks are centers of intensive scientific research. Xerox, for example, maintains a center in Palo Alto at which, among other things, scientists are working on artificial intelligence. What they are studying today may be meaningful 5 to 20 years from now. The key to success here is the environment, which is thought to stimulate creativity. If the people in a think tank are charged with converting their outlandish ideation into useful products for marketing, the term *skunk works* is often applied.

Techniques of the Analytical Attribute Approach

Benefit Analysis. All of the benefits that customers or users receive from the product under study are listed, in the hope of discovering an unrealized benefit or unexpectedly absent benefit.

Use Analysis. Listing the many ways buyers make use of a given product is also sometimes revealing. Some firms, 3M among others, have spent large sums of money asking consumers to tell them of new uses. Johnson Wax got into the car-polishing business when it found that its floor wax was being used on cars. One must contact users, however—not just list the uses already known to the company.

Function Analysis. In between feature and use is an activity called function. Thus, for shampoos, we know the chemicals and product features present, and we may know the full reasons for using shampoos. But it is also creative to list all possible ways that shampoos function—scraping, dissolving, depositing, evaporating, and so on.

Attribute Extension. Also called parameter analysis, this technique begins with any attribute that has changed recently and then extends that change. Thus, for example, bicycle seats have gotten smaller and smaller. Extending that idea, one might imagine a bicycle with no seat at all; what would such a bicycle look like, and what would it be used for?

Relative Brand Profile. Every brand name is flexible or elastic, meaning it can be stretched to cover different product types. People can understand a Minute Maid jelly or Minute Maid soup. But people also tell us that they cannot accept other "stretchings" —such as Minute Maid meats. Various market research techniques can be used to make these measurements, and any stretch that makes sense to the buyer is a potential new product. Incidentally, this thinking applies to goods and services, industrial as well as consumer.

Pseudo Product Test. By using what psychologists call a projective technique, one can ask consumers to evaluate what is presented to them as a proposed product but is actually an unidentified product currently on the market. They will typically find unique characteristics matching the needs they have. These attributes can then be the base for a new product.

Systems Analysis. This is a technique for studying complete systems of activity rather than products. Standard Brands once studied food preparation systems that involved margarine. It noted that virtually every one included an instruction to "melt the butter or margarine, stir in flour," and so on. From that came a stick-form sauce base called Smooth & Easy.

Unique Properties. This technique is primarily valuable in technological fields. The analyst seeks unique properties of any product or material currently on the market. To aid in this, one usually begins by listing all common properties because the unique ones quickly pop out.

Hierarchical Design. Here an organization chart design is formed, with product usage at the top and material types fanning out below. One such design began with deodorants, followed at the second level by roll-on, stick, and aerosol. The brands were listed under roll-ons. Under each brand could be package size or target market segment. Another design had light construction at the top, followed by wood, steel, and concrete. Wood was broken into metal roof, tar or shingle roof, and so on. The technique is mainly a way of forcing one to see all aspects of a situation, which is the essence of the analytical attribute approach.

Weaknesses. All weaknesses of a product or product line (the company's own and those of the competition) are identified. This primarily defensive technique identifies line extensions and flanker products. Every resolvable weakness offers a new product concept.

Achilles' Heel. Some analysts prefer to prune the list of weaknesses to one or two that are so serious a competitor might capitalize on them.

Theoretical Limits Test. Both opportunities and threats can be visualized by pushing a known apparatus or device to its theoretical limits. The technique works especially well on a reasonably new technology that appears to have exhausted its usefulness.

Techniques to Enhance Lateral Search

One school of thought holds that all nearby creativity produces only insignificant line extensions and modifications. These people have only disdain for matrixes, analogy, and attribute analysis. They insist the mind must be pushed beyond where it wants to go, in a lateral search. This approach was not mentioned in Chapter 5, or 7, but here are some techniques they recommend.

Free Association. This approach begins when the ideator writes down one aspect of the product situation being studied—a product attribute, a use, or a user. The trick then is to let the mind roam wildly while jotting down every idea that comes out. The process is repeated for other aspects of the product situation. The associations are usually quite direct in the early stages when creativity is being stimulated, but with time they become much less related and much more valuable as insights.

Stereotype Activity. Here one asks, "How would ________ do it?" The blank is filled in with a stereotype. Particular individuals can also be used, and the question can be reversed to ask what the stereotype would *not* do. Thus, a bicycle manufacturer might ask "What type of bicycle would a senator ride? Loudspeaker on it? Pedal both ways?"

Cross-field Compilation. As scientific disciplines have become increasingly blurred, a creative technique has been developed to bridge the between-field barriers. If a firm works primarily in the chemical area, its product developers may systematically scan developments in, say, physics or biology. Scientists in those fields may not know that some of their ideas have applications in chemistry.

Key-word Monitoring. Closely allied to the big-winner approach is the task of monitoring newspapers and magazines and tallying the number of times key words appear. One firm used this approach to spot increasing use of zodiac, and it promptly marketed a series of successful products featuring the zodiac symbols. Some take this approach with electronic databases and call it database tracking.

Use of the Ridiculous. Just to show that anything can be done, some ideators deliberately try to force themselves to use ridiculous approaches. In one session, participants were asked to write out the most preposterous methods of joining two wires together. One answer was, "Hold them with your teeth," and another was "Use chewing gum." Those present were astounded to realize they had just reinvented alligator clips, and they promptly gave serious consideration to the chewing gum. It turns out that some ingredients in chewing gum may sometime be marketed for use in wiring!

Study of Other People's Failures. Any product that has failed offers a chance for the next trier to spot its problem. Robert McNath runs a firm called Marketing Intelligence Service Ltd. in Naples, New York, where he displays over 10,000 actual failed products in a barnlike store. The failures apparently stimulate creativity.

Lateral Thinking—Avoidance. Some people have stressed the use of avoidance techniques to keep an idea from dominating thinking as it has in the past.

Keep asking, "Is there another way of looking at this?"

Keep asking, "Why?"

Deliberately rotate attention to a phase or aspect of the problem other than the logical one.

Find an entry point into the problem other than the one habitually used.

List all possible alternatives to every aspect of the analysis.

Deliberately seek out nonstandard concepts other than those inherent to the problem. Try "unconcepting" or "disconcepting," or try dropping a concept.

Fractionalize concepts and other aspects of the problem.

Bridge two or more concepts to form still other concepts.

Other people call the approach disparate thinking, zigzag, and divergent thinking. This method was claimed to have partially solved a long-standing problem of light bulb theft in the Boston subway—light bulbs were made to screw in counterclockwise.

Forced Relationships. The two-dimensional matrix and the morphological matrix are based on relevant product or market characteristics. Sometimes, however, interesting viewpoints are achieved by forcing relationships between normally unrelated (or even opposed) things. The forced relationships technique has spawned many preferences; the most quoted is the catalog method. In this method, a catalog, journal, or magazine is selected, and then a relationship is forced between everything in it and something else (perhaps a product or a consumer group). Some suggest using the table of contents in magazines or the Yellow Pages in telephone directories. Other names for the forced relationships approach are pick-a-noun and random walk.

Creative Stimuli. The idea subject is specified first—the problem, the product, and so on. Then the tangible goal is stipulated—the desired result or what the specified idea should accomplish. Last, a long list of words, names, and phrases is studied for ideas that accomplish the tangible goal. These are proven stimulants (why, we don't know). Some of them are:

Guest stars	Charity	Family	Photography
Alphabet	Education	Timeliness	Interview
Truth	His and hers	Videotape	Testimonials
Outer space	Style	World	Decorate
Chart	Nation	Birth	Showmanship

Gauge scale	Weather	Ethnic	Floor, wall
Zipper	Habit, fad	Push button	Participation
Fantasy	Transportation	Snob appeal	Music
Folklore	Symbolism	Romance	Direct mail
Subconscious	Calendar	Parody	Seasons
Hobbies	Rhinestones	Graphics	Strawberry
Holidays	Curiosity	Sketch	Telephone

For a complete set of the stimuli words and phrases, see Donald Cantin, *Turn Your Ideas into Money* (New York: Hawthorn Books, 1972). A much newer version that combines stimulating terms with variations on checklist is the product improvement checklist (PICL) by Arthur VanGundy. It is available from New Product Development Newsletter, P.O. Box 1309, Point Pleasant, NJ 08742.

Big Winner. Many successful firms, teams, or individuals in sports, politics, television, and so on are uniquely in tune with the thinking of society. Studying these big winners may lead to principles that can be generalized to new products. As of 1999, for example, something might be found by studying the Denver Broncos, *Star Wars: Episode One,* the Internet, Providence, swing dancing, Starbucks, sidewalk cafes, the new Beetle, and health cost reduction. One consulting firm compiled a list of the 20 all-time best-selling packaged goods; from this list, the firm generalized principles to transfer to clients' new products.

Competitive Analysis. Many firms claim that by studying the strategic plans and actions of competitors, they can detect new product approaches, especially defensive ones. For this purpose they watch competitive announcements, surveys, financial reports, trade show exhibits, detailed analyses of their products, and other such techniques. Life-cycle models help a firm estimate when competitors will take over any of its markets and thus stimulate new products to defensively cannibalize sales.

Technological Mapping. This is a form of relevance-tree forecasting in which the competitive capability of each competitor is predicted. It lays the groundwork for decisions to push or play down certain technologies in the home firm. Strategic analysis permits direct forecasting of probable future changes in competitors' technological commitments by studying mergers, acquisitions, sell-offs, patent applications, patent sales, and so on. A keen analyst can predict major market swings and thus suggest new product opportunities (or lack of opportunities) for the firm.

APPENDIX C
SMALL'S IDEATION STIMULATOR CHECKLIST

1. Can the dimensions be changed?

Larger	Economy-size packages, photo enlargements, puffed cereals
Smaller	U.S. paper money, hearing aids, tabloid newspaper, pocket flashlight, microfilm
Longer	King-size cigarettes, typewriter carriage for bookkeeping
Shorter	Men's shorts, women's panties
Thicker	Rug pads, heavy edge on drinking glasses, glass bricks
Thinner	Nylon hose, seersucker suits, wristwatches
Deeper	Deeper pockets in work clothes and army uniforms, grooved battery plates
Shallow	Wading pools, children's drinking fountain
Stand vertically	Skyscrapers (to increase floor space on expensive land), upright piano
Place horizontally	Ranch-style homes (to avoid stair climbing)
Make slanted or parallel	Reading stands, car mirror, eyeglasses frames
Stratify	Plywood, storage pallets, layer cake
Invert (reverse)	Reversible coats, soft shoes to be worn on either foot, inverted ink and glue stands
Crosswise (bias, counter)	Bias brassieres and slips, pinking shears
Coverage	Mechanical artificial hands, ice tongs
Encircle	Spring cake form, knitted coasters to slip on bottoms of highball glasses, Life-Savers
Intervene	Buffers used in drug products to temper a harsh active ingredient
Delineate	Contour lathe, Scotchlite reflective sheeting
Border	Mats for pictures, movable office partitions, room separators

2. Can the quantity be changed?

More	Extra-pants suits, three stockings—a pair with a spare
Less	Variety of 1-ounce boxes of cereals, ginger ale splits
Change proportions	Nested chairs or dishes, hot-cold water faucets
Fractionate	Separate packings of crackers inside single box, 16-mm movie film usable as two 8-mm films, faucet spray
Join something	Trailer, hose couplings
Add something to it	Cigarette filter tip
Combine with something else	Amphibious auto, outboard motors, roadable airplanes

---

Complete	Freezer unit added to refrigerator, Bendix washer and dryer single unit

3. Can the order be changed?

Arrangement	Car steering wheels left-handed in United States, right-handed in England; Dewey decimal system of filing
Precedence	Rear-drive automobiles
Beginning	Self-starter, red tab to open cigarette package, red string to open Band-Aids
Assembly or disassembly	Prefabricated articles, knockdown boat kits
Focus	Kellogg packages—name placed in left corner instead of center; Hathaway shirt ads—men with eye patch

4. Can the time element be changed?

Faster	Quick-drying ink, dictating machine, intercom system
Slower	High-tenacity yarns for longer-life tires, $33^1/3$-rpm long-playing records
Longer	Jiffy insulated bags for ice cream, wood preservative
Shorter	Pressure cooker, one minute X-ray machine
Chronological	Defrosting devices, radio clocks
Perpetuated	Photographs, metal plating, permanent magnets
Synchronized	Uniform vacation periods, group travel tours
Anticipated	Thermostat, freezer food-buying plan
Renewed	Self-charging battery, self-winding watches
Recurrence	Switch clocks for lights and electrical appliances
Alternated	Cam drive, electric current

5. Can the cause or effect be changed?

Stimulated	Generator
Energized	Magneto, power steering
Strengthened	AC-DC transformer, Simonize car coating
Louder	Volume control, acoustical aids
Softer	Sound insulator, rubber heels
Altered	Antifreeze chemicals, meat tenderizer
Destroyed	Tree spraying, breath and perspiration deodorants
Influenced	Legislation to permit sale of colored oleo, wetting agent catalyst
Counteracted	Circuit breaker, air-conditioning, filters

6. Can there be a change in character?

Stronger	Dirt-resistant paint
Weaker	Pepsi-Cola made less sweet, children's aspirin
Altered	Aged or blended whiskey, transit-mixed cement
Converted	Convertiplanes (for vertical or horizontal flights)
Substituted	Low-calorie salad dressing (made without oils)
Interchanged	Interchangeable parts, all-size socks
Stabilized	Sperry gyroscope, waterproof plastic bandage
Reversed	Two-way locomotives
Resilient	Form-rubber upholstery, cork floors

Uniformity	Standards in foods, drugs, fuels, liquor
Cheaper	Coach air travel, paper cups
More expensive	Cigarettes in cardboard or metal boxes, deluxe editions of books
Add color	Color television, colored plastics
Change color	Variously colored toothbrush handles, automobiles, electric light bulbs

7. Can the form be changed?

Animated	Moving staircases, package conveyors
Stilled	Air brakes
Speeded	Meat-slicing machine
Slowed	Shock absorbers, gravel driveway
Directed	Flowmeters
Deviated	Traffic islands
Attracted	Magnetic devices
Repelled	Electrically charged fencing
Admitted	Turnstiles
Barred	Gate, fence
Lifted	Forklift truck
Lowered	Ship locks
Rotated	Waring blender, boring machine
Oscillated	Electric fan
Agitated	Electric scalp stimulator

8. Can the state or condition be changed?

Hotter	Electric hot plate, washed coal
Colder	Freezer, thermos jug, water cooler
Harden	Bouillon cubes, cream shampoo (instead of liquid)
Soften	Krilium soil conditioner, water softeners
Open or closed	Visible record equipment, electronically operated doors
Performed	Prefabricared housing, prepared Tom Collins mixer
Disposable	Bottle caps, Chux disposable diapers, Kleenex tissues
Incorporated	Counting register on printing press, cash registers
Parted	Caterpillar tractors, split level highways
Solidified	Bakelite and other plastics, citrus concentrates
Liquefied	Chemical plant foods
Vaporized	Nasal medication vaporizers
Pulverized	Powdered eggs, lawn mower attachment to powder leaves, disposal garbage pulverizer
Abraded	Snow tires or chains
Lubricated	Self-lubricating equipment
Wetter	Hydraulic brakes
Drier	De-Moist for cellars, tobacco curing
Insulated	Fiberglas, Dr. Scholl's foot appliances (insulate feet against pressures)
Effervesced	Alka-Seltzer
Coagulated	Jell-O and Junket desserts
Elasticized	Latex girdles, bubble gum, belts
Resistant	Rubber footwear

Lighter	Aluminum luggage, automatic electric blanket
Heavier	Can opener with weighted stand

9. Can the use be adapted to a new market?

Men	Colognes, lotions
Women	Colored-tip cigarettes
Children	Junior-size tools, cowboy clothes
Old	Walking stick chairs
Handicapped	Chair lifts
Foreign	*Reader's Digest* foreign editions

APPENDIX D
THE MARKETING PLAN

Basic marketing management books have rather complete descriptions of the marketing planning process. This appendix will not duplicate that material, but will focus on the actual form of the marketing plan itself, that is, the *plan,* not so much the *planning* that is covered in Chapters 17–18.

No two firms use quite the same format of marketing plan, but Figure D–1 gives a marketing plan outline based on the best information we have. The plan generally follows these guidelines:[1]

Summarize the analysis done for this plan.

Give overall strategic thinking.

Give the tactical actions, including those for departments other than marketing.

Make sure everyone knows the financial situation and how the plan will be measured and evaluated.

The outline should communicate the plans to everyone involved, have built-in control mechanisms, and serve as a permanent record.

Contents

Certain sections of the marketing plan deserve additional comment. But remember: If the new product is a line extension, many of the early sections of the plan are unnecessary because the information is not new. You will recall that as part of the early evaluation process it is wise to thoroughly study (or restudy) the industry in which concepts are going to be generated. The list of information gathered for this is shown in Figure D–2.

Consumers/Users/Buyers. This section addresses the key element in the product's rationale. Data are given on the various buyer categories, the extent to which buying differs from using, the existence of influencers, and the specific process by which users acquire the merchandise. This includes buying motives, brands considered, information sought, product preferences, images, and unmet needs. It also covers how products are actually used and by whom.

This section will help anyone who reads the plan to understand the decisions described later—for example, on targeting, positioning, and push-pull strategy. It also summarizes the general equilibrium of the market and highlights any instabilities that can be capitalized.

Competition. All plan readers must be told about the competitive situation because many of them are not in a position to have regular contact with it. Specific company and brand names should be listed, and a detailed comparative description given for each. All of our differences should be clear. If the product manager doesn't know the determinant

[1]A still-excellent source of guidance for writing new-product marketing plans is David S. Hopkins, *The Marketing Plan,* Report no. 801 (New York: The Conference Board, 1981).

FIGURE D–1

Outline of marketing plan for a new product, to be adapted to fit individual firms

I. Introduction. This section briefly describes the product, tells who prepared the plan, and its timing.

II. Situation analysis.
   A. Market description.
      1. Consumers, users, and other market participants.
      2. Buying processes pertinent to this plan.
      3. Direct and indirect competitors.
      4. Current competitive strategies.
      5. Market shares on sales, profits, and budgets.
      6. Available distribution structure, plus attitudes and practices.
      7. Key environmental or exogenous factors.
   B. Full description of new product, including all pertinent test data and comparisons with competition.

III. Summary of opportunities and problems.
   A. Key exploitable market opportunities.
   B. Key problems that should be addressed by this plan.

IV. Strategy.
   A. Overall guiding statement, including key actions and their quantitative and qualitative objectives.
   B. Market targets/segments, with positioning for each.
   C. Overall marketing efforts.
      1. General role for product, including planned changes.
      2. General role for advertising, including copy platforms.
      3. General role for personal selling.
      4. General role for such other tools as sampling and trade shows. Copy platforms for any creative units.
      5. General role for distributors (wholesale, retail).
      6. Price policy, including discounts and planned changes.
      7. Any special roles for nonmarketing departments.

V. Economic summary.
   A. Sales forecasts in dollars and units.
   B. Expense budgets by category of activity.
   C. Contribution to profit, with pro forma income statement.
   D. Risk statement: major problems, with cash flows.
   E. Future capital expenditures, with cash flows.

VI. Tactical plans. This section is situational to the firm. It includes each tool, what will be done with it, objectives, people responsible, schedule, creative units needed, etc.

VII. Control.
   A. Key control objectives for reporting purposes.
   B. Key internal or external contingencies to watch.
   C. Information generation schedule.

VIII. Summary of major support activities needed, including data processing, warehousing, technical service, R&D, finance, personnel, public relations.

IX. Chronological schedule of activities.

attributes in this market or how the new product compares on those attributes with products already out there, the firm isn't ready to market the new item.

The competitors' overall business and marketing strategies are also needed, especially those which appear to be effective. This includes positioning, pricing, claims, and distribution.

FIGURE D–2

Basic market description

Market Size

Definition: By nature of product, by supplier, by user.
Sales: Dollars, units, by total and subgroups.
Trends: Growth total and rate by subgroups.
Key segments: demographic, attitude, behavior.
Special aspects where appropriate: Cyclicality, seasonality, erratic fluctuations.
International variations and trends.

Distribution Structure Available

Retailers: Types, shares, demands, activities, current margins and profits, trends and forecasts, attitudes.
Wholesalers: Distributors, jobbers, agents, types used, functions performed, policies, compensation, attitudes, trends, variances, by segments.
Bargaining power and channel control.
Degree of, and trends in, vertical integration. Variations by geographic area.
Use of multiple or dual channels.

Competition

Current brands.
Manufacturer source for each.
Sizes, forms, materials, etc. All variations, temporary and permanent. Quality levels.
Prices: Final discounts, special, changes.
Market shares: Dollars, units, by segments, using various definitions of *market.*
Changes: Trends of entries and exits, reaction times.
Profits being achieved: Sales, costs, ROIs, paybacks, trends.
Promotional practices: Types, dollars, effectiveness.
Manufacturing and procuring practices.
Financial strengths.
Special vulnerabilities, instabilities.
Possible new entrants, current R&D activities, skills, track records.
Full description of derived demand aspects.
Industry life cycle analyzed by segments.

Special Aspects

Government and regulatory restrictions, especially trends and expectations.
Third-party influences: Scientists, institutions, research centers, associations, standards, pressure groups.
Effects of inflation, labor rates, union activity.
Upstream participants: Supplier manufacturers, importers, technology control.
General social attitudes and trends.
Industry productivity and efficiency in use of personnel and other resources.
Trends in industry costs: Materials, labor, transportation.

Exogenous Factors and Change. Markets are not static, and everyone involved needs to be apprised of likely changes. No surprises should appear, and none will if the planner has been careful. Some often overlooked changes are government regulations, competitive product improvements, direct selling (skipping a distributive level), price breaks, new competition based on new technologies, and future changes in how this type of product is bought and/or used.

Product Description. In some cases, a product can be described in a few sentences; in others, readers of the plan almost need a seminar. Product complexity cannot be allowed to destroy understanding. The plan should guide other people in doing their parts in the overall marketing effort, so they need to know just how good this new product really is. The plan should summarize the key findings of concept testing and product use testing. It should include product strengths and weaknesses, perceptual problems, unusual uses of the product, physical characteristics, costs, and restrictions applied to any applications.

Objectives. A statement of what is expected from marketing this new product should be included near the start of the strategy section. But let's differentiate between objective and goal. A goal is a long-term direction of movement (sometimes not easily quantified) used for guidance, not internal control. For example, "It is our goal to become a leader in the snacks market." An objective is an intermediate point on the road toward attainment of a goal. For example, "It is our objective to capture a 15 percent share of the snacks market during our first year on the market." Objectives should be clearly and precisely stated in fairness to the new products manager. A narrative at this point in the plan will help clarify objectives.

Restraints. Every new product marketing effort has some built-in restraints that should be made clear. Here are some examples from previous marketing plans:

> The new product will be marketed in accordance with the division's customary reliance on its industrial distribution system.
>
> The sales force currently questions the ability of the new products department to come up with winners. Because the morale of the sales force is quite important to this division, actions will be taken to ensure the success of this particular product.
>
> The strategy will not introduce potential problems of interpretation by the Federal Trade Commission, nor will it conflict with outstanding consent decrees.

Such restraints as these can have obvious effects on a marketing plan; if they are not stated, readers may not understand why certain actions are taken.

Management of the Task

Putting together a marketing plan is a complex process, filled with grand strategic decisions interspersed with trivia. Experienced new product marketers never underestimate the contribution of the many nonmarketing departments in the firm, but novice new products people often do. For this reason, the new products team should do the marketing planning right along with the product development. As team members help construct the plan itself, they will have suggestions to make. Each function involved in the new product's marketing has ideas about what that function should do; they differ from what other people think that function should do. All are experienced people, and we have worked with them for some time. We would like to ask each of them what they want to do and then put their requests into a package and call it a marketing plan. Some plans are actually developed that way.

Such plans don't work very well, however, unless we have a new product that essentially sells itself, or unless the new item is a simple line extension, marketed totally as a new member in a line of products. The product line marketing plan captures the new item and tells what will be done.

In rare instances our new item doesn't have to be marketed at all, in the usual sense. For example, we may make it in response to a military order, where the sale was made at the time our bid was accepted. Or we may develop an item for a major producer of complex products (such as automobiles); in such a case, the producer essentially told us what to make, and all we have to do is deliver it and stand by to service it.

But these are exceptions; in most cases, the new item needs its own strategy, at least in concept. Otherwise, the various players will never come together to make up a team.

Let's distinguish between planning and a plan. *Planning yields a strategy; the plan states the strategy, adds the tactical details, and directs the implementation.* New products can use both, but the strategy is critical. Once the new products manager begins to concentrate on the plan, with its many budgets, dates, and other details, no strategy in the world can keep the players motivated, integrated, and effective.

Some new products managers orchestrate the team by dint of personal leadership. These people may miss dates and budgets but market a successful product. In some situations, a product marketed well over budget—but on time—makes more money than a product marketed within budget but three months late.

This line of thinking does not apply to established products, which need annual or quarterly marketing plans. They already have the infrastructure, the stature, the support base within the firm, and the experienced players that the new product lacks.

So as you go through the actual marketing planning process, keep in mind that we look at things that really make a difference. That's all that most new product managers have the time to seriously think about.

One other thought: Top-management approval is needed on marketing plans. "Whoever pays the fiddler calls the tune," so new products managers must deal with the frustrations caused by highly participative top managements.

The Strategic Components

Chapters 17–18 explain the components of marketing strategy for a new product and the general approach to how they are derived. This section of a marketing plan simply summarizes them and explains the background thinking on any issue known to be controversial in the firm. The target markets are explained first, followed by the product positioning statement (several of the items are being positioned differently for different target groups). After that the marketing plan becomes very situational, reflecting company practice and personal interests. Marketing mixes differ so in nature, complexity and implementation that it does little good to outline a method for telling people about them

It is typical that firms state their general mix strategy—what is the lead horse and how the other tools support that one. All people who will implement the plan should understand how product, price, promotion, and distribution work together, and what their individual roles are. If they work well together, it is like any other team situation—good synergy can double the power.

Details and Implementation

What follows the general statement about strategic components is the full listing of what each tool will do, when, managed by whom, and so forth. Media schedules, sales staffing and calling schedules, all of the printed materials needed, sales meetings, and (in some cases) the hundreds of things that must be done to implement the launch. This section of marketing plans tends to give marketing planning a bad name. To many people, the plan document (actually a very large book in many cases) is the purpose of planning, yet huge planning documents quickly become file documents under the relentless pressures of change. Better to have a smaller overall plan and a set of tool documents prepared and implemented by the various departments in the firm.

APPENDIX E
GUIDELINES FOR EVALUATING A NEW PRODUCTS PROGRAM

This is a rather unique checklist. It is made for use by anyone evaluating the new products program of some organization—an internal review, a consultant, whatever. It presumes the organization uses all of the recommended methods, and it would be nice if the world worked this way. But product innovation managers face many problems—people, resources, competition, and so forth. They make many compromises, so if you use this form to evaluate a program, think of the gaps as suggestions or possible considerations. Most people who have tried the form find that they have to say no (or a very qualified yes) to a third or more of the items. The form is especially good at covering important activities that are especially difficult or of recent development.

The terminology used in this checklist matches that used throughout this text, but occasionally a second statement has been added for clarity.

If the form is used within an organization, a good approach is for two or more people with experience in the firm's new products activity to go through the list separately, checking each item individually, as they know it. Then the scorings can be discussed in a joint session to bring out differences, which in turn can be discussed for clarification and possible remedial action.

Yes	*Maybe Some*	*No*	
____	____	____	1. The senior mangers of this firm or division (general manager plus top key functional heads) are committed to innovation in general. They want innovation in all phases of the operation, including that of product line.
____	____	____	2. This management attitude toward innovation has been clearly and unequivocally communicated throughout the organization.
____	____	____	3. Senior managements, both at corporate and at division, have gone through a planning exercise that established the overall goals for the product innovation function in each division.
____	____	____	4. Outside directors know the future role for product innovation and support actions to achieve it.
____	____	____	5. We have an innovation reward system. It includes insulation against punishment for failure, and there is evidence for all to see.
____	____	____	6. The firm's or division's top executive has assessed the ability and inclination of each senior functional manager to generate innovation, particularly product innovation. This assessment has included input from persons reporting to those senior managers.
____	____	____	7. General managers have learned the art of delegating full authority on new product projects while still sharing fully in the responsibility for them. (This managerial approach is unique to the product innovation function.)
____	____	____	8. New product project responsibility is nonfunctional. That is, project leaders report in such a way that they are free of functional constraints and biases. Specifically, responsibility for new products is no longer housed in R&D.
____	____	____	9. Senior management attempts to assess the productivity of the new products program. Standards of measurement have been established and communicated.
____	____	____	10. If senior management is dissatisfied with the overall product innovation program, specific causes have been determined and remedial plans put into place. Continuing dissatisfaction is not acceptable.

Yes	Maybe Some	No	
____	____	____	11. The firm's failure rate on marketed new products is somewhere between 10 percent and 20 percent. Less than that suggests no commitment to innovation, and more than that suggests an inadequately managed program.
____	____	____	12. Senior management has studied the industry's new product situation and has shared ideas with other industry leaders. Work is under way to find industrywide solutions to obstacles hindering product innovation in this industry.
____	____	____	13. Specific people in each division have been charged with opportunity identification—the creative assessment of technologies and markets available to the division.
____	____	____	14. Senior management is aware of the fundamental conflict between process innovation and product innovation. Efforts are taken to keep either from dominating the other and to see that decisions at the interface are made at general-management levels.
____	____	____	15. The firm has an overall process for developing new products, and its phases are known to participants.
____	____	____	16. Product innovators on each project know their group's focus (arena of operation or turf).
____	____	____	17. They also know the general goal and specific objectives of their project.
____	____	____	18. Each project group makes use of both market drive *and* technology drive. That is, they work to resolve one or more specific problems in a selected marketplace, and they bring to that solution one or more technologies at which the firm is very good.
____	____	____	19. There are no hidden agendas on our new product projects.
____	____	____	20. All people playing major roles in new product groups are rewarded in some way that reflects the *group's* accomplishment of assigned goals/objectives.
____	____	____	21. For every new products project, it is clear who is the one person heading up that project and responsible for its success.
____	____	____	22. Every project is assigned one of three projectization levels—functional matrix, balanced matrix, or project matrix. We try to avoid the purely functional approach, and we use a venture (spin-out) only when absolutely necessary. Players understand projectization.
____	____	____	23. We recognize the values of design. To the extent appropriate, we actively integrate both industrial (esthetic/functional) designers and engineering (technical/functional) designers, as key team players.
____	____	____	24. Our technical/marketing/manufacturing people are close together physically. Preferably, they are no farther than a five-minute walk apart.
____	____	____	25. We use the concept of the rugby scrum rather than that of the relay team's hand-off. All functions are represented at all phase points in the project including project specification and postlaunch.
____	____	____	26. Managers of new products projects understand that they are really nontitled general managers and that they should manage their team of people as a general manager would. They also understand what a network is and how one should be built and managed.
____	____	____	27. We actively use upstream and downstream coupling by building in roles for suppliers and other vendors as well as direct involvement of potential customer personnel. These people are almost like members of the team.
____	____	____	28. We have an overall concept evaluation system in place and use it to carve out a special system for each project.
____	____	____	29. A basic market or technology study is made of each strategic arena before ideation begins, and that study is updated as needed during the project's life.
____	____	____	30. We believe in building the marketing plan right alongside the building of the product. It is a twin-streams, or coincident, operation.

Yes	*Maybe Some*	*No*	
____	____	____	31. We accept the idea that new products come into existence only after they have been successfully established in the marketplace. Even after they go to market, they are still only concepts (being modified as necessary) until we meet the objectives set for them.
____	____	____	32. We have proactive concept generation. That is, we don't just wait for new ideas to come in from the field, the lab, and so forth.
____	____	____	33. Our technical people are familiar with what customers think about products currently on the market, what they use, and how.
____	____	____	34. To the extent possible, our new concepts begin their lives stemming directly from solutions to proven problems/needs of the intended customers.
____	____	____	35. We use a quantitative scoring model for screening concepts prior to any substantial development expenditures.
____	____	____	36. After screening, we make sure that technical people have a statement of the product requirements (product attributes in benefit format and any other deliverables). The marketing people also receive a statement of marketing requirements (what the marketing program is to accomplish —market penetration, speed, etc.) The product requirements speak to what the product should *do for the customer.* Both sets of requirements combine into a product protocol statement.
____	____	____	37. We do user-based product use testing on every item we develop, whether a good or a service. At least part of the testing is with typical potential users who are not our friends.
____	____	____	38. We believe product use testing should measure whether the product actually works as we had hoped, *and also* whether it solves the problem we started with and is satisfactory overall to the customer. That is, if we have been using beta testing, we want to do gamma testing too.
____	____	____	39. Our marketing program also is tested by exposure to the intended consumers of the new product. The testing method used is situational, but at the very least a rollout is employed.
____	____	____	40. Our marketing efforts recognize that getting trial use is the most critical (and difficult) of the several steps to sales success.
____	____	____	41. When marketing a new item, we have identified each potential problem that would be very damaging and that has a reasonable probability of coming about. We have agreed in advance what we would do about each, if it occurs.
____	____	____	42. We use postlaunch tracking systems for guiding the product to success. That is, we have set up measuring systems to track each critical problem and give us early warning. We have also agreed in advance about what will constitute evidence that each problem is actually coming about.
____	____	____	43. Marketing strategy is built around the accomplishments of awareness, trial, availability and repeat use (satisfaction). The plan clearly shows how each will be achieved.
____	____	____	44. Marketing plans for new products are distributed in draft form to all persons who are key to the launch process, certainly to the basic functions of technical, production, and finance.
____	____	____	45. Unless the new item is itself a line extension, we have at least the next two extensions to it already on their way down the pike. Each follow-- on item is intended to foreclose an option our adaptor competitors would find lucrative.
____	____	____	46. All financial evaluations are much more than net present value calculations. In fact, we try to use a sales or profit threshold test rather than a specific dollar test.
____	____	____	47. We try to anticipate ways in which customers will misuse a new product, we develop legally sufficient warnings for those misuses, and we keep records relevant to all aspects of product liability.
____	____	____	48. Attention is given to any potential conflicts between the ethics of an operation and the ethics of the people working on it. Attempts are made to resolve these.

INDEX